UNDERSTANDING EMOTIONS

To Natalie, Serafina, Simon,
Grant, and Hannah

UNDERSTANDING EMOTIONS

THIRD EDITION

Dacher Keltner

Keith Oatley

Jennifer M. Jenkins

WILEY

Vice President & Executive Publisher	Jay O'Callaghan
Executive Editor	Christopher Johnson
Assistant Editor	Brittany Cheetham
Marketing Manager	Magaret Barrett
Senior Content Manager	Lucille Buonocore
Senior Production Editor	Anna Melhorn
Design Director	Harry Nolan
Senior Designer	Maureen Eide
Production Management Services	Suzanne Ingrao/Ingrao Associates
Senior Photo Editor	Jennifer MacMillan
Cover Photo Credit	Smith Collection/Stone/Getty Images, Inc.

This book was set in 10/12pt Times-Roman by Thomson Digital and printed and bound by Edwards Brothers Malloy.

Founded in 1807, John Wiley & Sons, Inc. has been a valued source of knowledge and understanding for more than 200 years, helping people around the world meet their needs and fulfill their aspirations. Our company is built on a foundation of principles that include responsibility to the communities we serve and where we live and work. In 2008, we launched a Corporate Citizenship Initiative, a global effort to address the environmental, social, economic, and ethical challenges we face in our business. Among the issues we are addressing are carbon impact, paper specifications and procurement, ethical conduct within our business and among our vendors, and community and charitable support. For more information, please visit our website: www.wiley.com/go/citizenship.

Evaluation copies are provided to qualified academics and professionals for review purposes only, for use in their courses during the next academic year. These copies are licensed and may not be sold or transferred to a third party. Upon completion of the review period, please return the evaluation copy to Wiley. Return instructions and a free of charge return shipping label are available at www.wiley.com/go/returnlabel. Outside of the United States, please contact your local representative.

ISBN-13 978-1-1118-14743-6
ISBN-10 1118-14743-X

Printed in the United States of America

10 9 8 7 6 5 4 3

BRIEF CONTENTS

Contents

PART II ELEMENTS OF EMOTIONS 81

PART IV EMOTIONS AND THE INDIVIDUAL   261

13　MENTAL DISORDER AND WELL-BEING IN ADULTHOOD　326

FIGURES

TABLES

PREFACE

The strange thing about life is that though the nature of it must have been apparent to everyone for hundreds of years, no one has left any adequate account of it. The streets of London have their map; but our passions are uncharted.

Virginia Woolf, Jacob's Room

As we present the third edition of *Understanding Emotions*, we are aware and grateful that this has become the standard undergraduate textbook on emotions and are glad to be part of this growing scientific field. Dacher, Keith, and Jenny have continued to enjoy working together, and we thought it was Dacher's turn to take the lead.

According to written and oral traditions, people have been interested in emotions for thousands of years. In most societies emotions are at the center of people's understandings of themselves and others and their relationships, rituals, and public life. In the era of scientific research in psychology, we present here an approach to understanding that can enter ordinary conversation and that takes seriously the rapidly growing body of scientific evidence.

In psychology, emotions have now moved into their proper place, at the center of our understandings of the human mind and of relationships in the social world. Our book, and we would claim the whole topic of emotions, is not just psychology. It extends, too, across neuroscience, psychiatry, biology, anthropology, sociology, literature, and philosophy.

In this edition, we reflect the growing realization that although emotions occur in individuals' brains and bodies, they also mediate our relationships with each other, in both intimate and public ways. They provide a grammar of social life. In fact, in the third edition of this book, honoring developments in the field, we arrive at the organizing thesis that emotions are social to their core.

We hope you will like the third edition, which continues the traditions of the earlier editions, but with new features that we hope will make it easier and more pleasurable for both instructors and students to use. In this edition we have collaborated with some graduate students in particular chapters: Mark Wade in Chapter 8, Heather Prime in Chapter 11, Dillon Browne and Mark Wade in Chapter 12, and Hannah Oatley in Chapter 13. We are very grateful to these people; they have improved on what we would have been able to do on our own. We are also very grateful to colleagues who read and sent us feedback and suggestions on chapters: Gerald Cupchik, James Gross, June Gruber, Terry Maroney, Batja Mesquita, Randolph Nesse, Ira Roseman, David DeSteno, Emiliana Simon-Thomas, and Jessica Tracy.

Exciting advances continue to be made in the field of emotions, and we have done our best to reflect the new currents. We have also responded to colleagues' suggestions for updating this book. Changes in the third edition include the following:

- Updated references throughout, including recent research and data in psychology, psychiatry, the social sciences, and the humanities, as well as in neuroscience.
- Increased emphasis on the interpersonal and social functions of emotions, with stimulating discussions of how emotions work between people in different kinds of relationships.
- New discussions of contemporary research on evolution, and on genes in interaction with the environment, as well as on the neuroscience of empathy, pleasure, caregiving, and social rejection.
- New sections on: social and antisocial motivations, emotions and morality, law and emotions, consciousness, emotion regulation (including a discussion of free will), well-being, and the physiology of the stress response.
- Four kinds of boxes have been included, to depict *Significant Figures (in understanding emotions), Individual Emotions, Novels and Films,* and *Reflection and Cultivation.*
- End-of-chapter *Summaries* are now accompanied by *Suggestions to Think About and Discuss.*

Science and the humanities both depend on entering the tradition of earlier writers. Bernard of Chartres, a scholar of the 12th century, seems to have been the first to remark that if we can see further now, it is because we stand on the shoulders of giants, that is to say of those who have come before us. Our job as writers is to present some of what can be seen from this position, and to evaluate theories and evidence. You as a reader can then evaluate what we say in relation to what else you know, and can take part in the debate that is the social process of science and discussion, by means of which understanding is increased.

This book is intended for anyone with an interest in emotions, to show how far conceptualization and research have progressed toward understanding. Although some have argued that emotions are too heterogeneous for systematic study, we believe that the fact that we can write a textbook shows that, from a complex field, order has emerged.

Any discussion of human emotions without a point of view would be dull and largely incomprehensible. The quantity of publications—now numbering in the thousands—in the field makes it impossible to be exhaustive. We have therefore chosen studies that we believe are representative, hoping to convey an image for you to think productively about this vast field. As well as an overall narrative arc in the book, there is a story line for each chapter, including pivotal characters, foundational ideas, and intellectual controversies and tensions. Where there are debates we discuss them, so that you can look at the field from different points of view. But we have also worked to produce a coherent book. Although ours is not the only point of view, we think that by seeing that there is a coherent perspective in this area, you will be able to agree or disagree or modify it. Knowing that any piece of evidence is not conclusive on its own but that each is a step in exploring an idea, we hope that an integrated picture will take shape for you with concepts and ideas you can modify and apply to your own interests.

We have done our best to be fair-minded in our treatment of evidence, but our knowledge is necessarily incomplete and our views are necessarily biased toward our own interests and conceptualizations. Our interests are in thinking of emotions in cognitive, evolutionary, social, and developmental terms, in understanding their role in mediating everyday social interaction, and in comprehending what goes wrong in the states known as emotional disorders. We see emotions as based on biological processes, elaborated in our close relationships, and shaped by culture. Like the skilled action when you write your signature, an emotion has a biological basis of components and constraints. It also has a history of individual development. It is only fully understandable within an interpersonal and cultural context.

We write about emotions largely in the Western tradition. This does not imply universality of Euro-American assumptions; we present a lot of cross-cultural comparisons. At the same time, we imagine that most of our readers will be members of, or will be conversant with, the Western tradition. We believe that, by characterizing and identifying with this tradition, the ideas and findings about emotions that have substance within it can be seen clearly. We, and others, can then both form understandings based in that tradition and also better understand other culturally distinctive ways of thinking.

As well as a general introduction to the area, the book is designed for use as a textbook for a course on emotions for second- to fourth-year undergraduates, or for graduate students at the master's or PhD level. But it is a textbook of a particular kind. Most textbooks in psychology nowadays are compendia of many things to be remembered and a few to be conceptualized. By contrast, I. A. Richards (1925) said that a book is "a machine to think with" (p. 1). We have written our book to invite your thinking. Our conclusions make up our narrative thread. But by offering you sufficient detail of the evidence from which we draw our conclusions we hope to make it possible for you to draw your own conclusions.

The 14 chapters of this book can be covered in semester-long courses at the rate of one a week, perhaps with one or two chapters omitted according to the judgment of the instructor. For full-year courses, each chapter can be divided. Throughout, we keep in mind both the issue of prompting understandings of emotions and practical applications in clinical psychology, psychiatry, health care, education, and the issues of organizations. We envisage that many instructors who use the book will supplement it with other readings. At the end of each chapter we offer some suggestions for further reading, typically reviews and books.

We have tested our ideas and coverage by going to conferences, and attending to the currents of publications in the field, which has its own journals, its international society for research, its review volumes, and its handbooks. One of us (DK) continues to keep the material of this book in register with students in his undergraduate course of emotions at the University of California at Berkeley. All three of us use the material presented here in our courses and lectures.

An Instructor's Manual with lecture notes and teaching tips is available upon request.

ACKNOWLEDGMENTS

As with any book, we, the authors, are not the only ones who brought this object into being. This text is a reflection of the work of many people: researchers and thinkers, our teachers, our students, and our colleagues. We would like to thank once more those who assisted with the first and second editions of this text.

In addition to the colleagues whom we have thanked above, we are grateful to the following people at Wiley who have contributed to the third edition: Chris Johnson, the Executive Editor, and Brittany Cheetham, Maura Gilligan, Suzanne Ingrao, Jennifer MacMillan, and Anna Melhorn, who worked with us very helpfully in the production process.

The editor and publisher gratefully acknowledge the permission granted to reproduce the copyright material in this book:

M.D.S. Ainsworth & S. M. Bell, Fig. 2, "Frequency of crying in the 'Strange Situation' test," in "Attachment, exploration, and separation: Illustrated by the behavior of one-year-olds in a strange situation," p. 58 from *Child Development* 41(1). The Society for Research in Child Development, Inc., 1970. Copyright © 1983 by *Child Development*. Reprinted by permission of Blackwell Publishing Ltd.

Rita L. Atkinson, Richard C. Atkinson, Edward E. Smith, & Daryl M. Bem, Figs. 2.6–7, "Exploded view of human brain and human brain as if sliced in the midline," pp. 42–3 from *Introduction to Psychology,* 10th ed. Wadsworth, 1989. Copyright © 1989. Reprinted with permission of Wadsworth, a division of Thomson Learning: www.thomsonrights.com. Fax 800 730 2215.

R. A. Baron, Table 3, "Positive and negative items mentioned in interview by interviewers in happy or despondent mood" in "Interviewer's mood and reaction to job applicants," p. 920 from *Journal of Applied Social Psychology* 17. V. H. Winston & Son, Inc., 1987. Copyright © V. H. Winston & Son, Inc., 360 South Ocean Boulevard, Palm Beach, FL 33480. Adapted by permission of V. H. Winston & Son, Inc. All rights reserved.

L. Berkowitz, S. Cochran, & M. Embree, "Rewards and punishments," pp. 687–700 from *Journal of Personality and Social Psychology* 40, 1981. Copyright © 1981 by *Journal of Personality and Social Psychology*. Reprinted by permission of the American Psychological Association and the author.

G. H. Bower, Fig. 4, "Results of Bower's study of memories," p. 133 from *American Psychologist* 36. American Psychological Association, 1981. Copyright © 1981 by *American Psychologist*. Reprinted by permission of the American Psychological Association and the author.

Neil Carlson, Fig. 3.21, "The autonomic nervous system and the target organs and functions served by the sympathetic and parasympathetic branches," p. 90 from *Foundations of*

Physiological Psychology, 6th ed. Boston, MA: Allyn & Bacon, 2004. Copyright © 2004 by Pearson Education. Reprinted by permission of the publisher.

J. F. Cohn & E. Z. Tronick, Fig. 1, "State transition diagrams for infants where mothers were normal or depressed," in "Three-month-old infant's reaction to simulated maternal depression," p. 189 from *Child Development* 54. The Society for Research in Child Development, Inc., 1983. Copyright © 1983 by *Child Development*. Reprinted by permission of Blackwell Publishing Ltd.

R. J. Davidson, Fig. 6, "EEG activation," in "Anterior cerebral asymmetry and the nature of emotion," p. 145 from *Brain and Cognition* 20. Academic Press, Inc., 1992. Copyright © 1992 by *Brain and Cognition*. Reprinted by permission of Elsevier.

N. L. Etcoff & J. J. Magee, Fig. 1, "Series of faces in equal increments from happy to sad," in "Categorical perception of facial expressions," p. 231 from *Cognition* 44. Elsevier Science Publishers, 1992. Copyright © 1992 by *Cognition*. Reprinted by permission of Elsevier.

Julian Jaynes, Fig. 5.5, "Chimeric faces," p. 120 from *The Origin of Consciousness in the Breakdown of the Bicameral Mind.* London: Penguin Books Ltd. Copyright © 1976, 1990 by Julian Jaynes. Reprinted by permission of Houghton Mifflin Company and The Penguin Group UK. All rights reserved.

J. M. Jenkins & M. A. Smith, "Psychiatric symptoms in children whose parents had good or conflictual marriages," in "Factors protecting children living in disharmonious homes: Maternal reports," p. 64 from *Journal of the American Academy of Child and Adolescent Psychiatry* 29. Williams & Wilkins for figure. Copyright © 1990 by *Journal of the American Academy of Child and Adolescent Psychiatry.* Reprinted by permission of Lippincott, Williams & Wilkins.

D. M. Mackie & L. T. Worth, Fig. 11.1, "Attitude change in happy and neutral moods," in "Feeling good but not thinking straight: The impact of positive mood on persuasion," p. 206 from J. P. Forgas, *Emotion and Social Judgments*, 1991. Copyright © 1991 by Elsevier. Reprinted by permission of the publisher.

D. Morris, P. Collett, P. Marsh, & M. O'Shaughnessy, "Two coarse gestures of contempt," p. 107 in 1st ed. of *Understanding Emotions from Gestures: Their origin and distribution.* London: Cape, 1979. Copyright © 1979 by D. Morris, P. Collett, P. Marsh & M. O'Shaughnessy. Reprinted by permission of The Random House Group Ltd.

K. Oatley, Fig. 30.1, "The differentiation of normal emotions from depressive breakdowns," in "Life events, social cognition and depression," p. 552 from S. Fisher & J. Reason, *Handbook of Life Stress, Cognition and Health*, John Wiley & Sons, 1988. Copyright © 1988 by John Wiley & Sons Limited. Reprinted by permission of the publisher.

S. Scarr & P. Salapatek, Fig. 3.5, "Fear of visual cliff, dogs, noises, and jack-in-the-box," in "Patterns of fear development during infancy," pp. 64–5 from *Merrill Palmer Quarterly* 16. Wayne State University Press, 1970. Copyright © 1970 by *Merrill Palmer Quarterly*. Reprinted by permission of Wayne State University Press.

R. M. Seyfarth & D. L. Cheney, "Three different kinds of fearful response by vervet monkeys," in "Meaning and mind in monkeys," p. 124 from *Scientific American* 267 (Dec). Scientific American, Inc., 1992. Copyright © 1992 by Patricia J. Wynne. Reprinted by permission of the illustrator.

M. Sherif, "Hostility towards an outgroup," in "Experiments in group conflict," p. 58 from *Scientific American* 195. Scientific American, Inc., 1956. Copyright © 1956 by Sarah Love. C. E. Vaughn & J. P. Leff, Fig. 1, "Schizophrenic patients relapsing, as a function of high and low expressed emotion of families," in "The influence of family and social factors on the course of psychiatric illness: A comparison of schizophrenic and depressed patients," p. 132 from *British Journal of Psychiatry* 129. Royal College of Psychiatrists, 1976. Copyright © 1976 by *British Journal of Psychiatry*. Reprinted by permission of the journal.

Perspectives on Emotions

PART I

Approaches to Understanding Emotions

1

Photo Credit: *The Expression of the Emotions in Man and Animals by Charles Darwin, 1872*

FIGURE 1.0 Young girl in hat, from Darwin (1872).

Why is every critical moment in the fate of the adult or child so clearly colored by emotion?

(Vygotsky, 1987, p. 335)

CONTENTS

Introduction

Imagine you could flip a switch that would shut off your emotions. No more tongue-tied embarrassment around a romantic interest. No more saying something in anger that you will regret. No more anxiety that interferes with your ability to do as well as you can. Would you flip this switch?

If so, you are in good company. For over two thousand years, many thinkers have argued that our emotions are base and destructive, and that the more noble reaches of human nature are attained when we control our passions with our reason. Others have warned of the perils of particular emotions: for instance, it has often been thought that anger is destructive.

In this book, you will read about a different view, one that has emerged in the recent study of human emotions, the view that emotions serve important functions, especially in our social lives. This does not mean that emotions are always rational. It does mean that we can now make sense of most facets of our emotions. In this book you will find answers to long-lasting questions, because after a slow start, research on emotions has moved rapidly and has yielded many discoveries. Where do emotions come from in our evolutionary history? How are emotions different in different cultures? How are our brains and bodies involved in emotions? What happens when we express our emotions? How can we cultivate emotions in our relationships, and through the life course? When are emotions dysfunctional? What is happiness?

In this introductory chapter, we lay foundations for answering these questions. We first look at how the study of emotion emerged in psychology and social science. But first: What is an emotion?

What Is an Emotion? First Ideas

We have all experienced emotions, and in this sense we know what they are. But some psychologists have worried that they are difficult to define. In fact, such difficulties are rather usual. We all know what a tree is, even though we don't know its proper definition. It's one of the wonderful properties of language to be able to refer to things even when we don't know exactly what we mean (Putnam, 1975). To have a good definition, you need a good theory. With the help of this book, we hope you will formulate your own good theory of emotion.

But we need to make a start so that we can agree upon roughly what we are talking about. An emotion is a psychological state or process that mediates between our concerns (or goals) and events of our world. As Sylvan Tomkins (whose work we discuss later in this chapter) has said: at any one time an emotion gives priority to one concern over others. It gives that concern urgency. If we are crossing the road and nearly get run over, our concern for self-preservation takes priority and we are motivated by fear. The urge is to jump back onto the curb. If someone demeans us, we are angry and it becomes urgent to concentrate on the wrong that's been done to us. So, rather than thinking that emotions are irrational, psychologists now tend to think of emotions as being locally rational: their rationality doesn't range over all possible considerations. Instead, emotions are rational in that they help us deal adaptively with concerns specific to our current context. They are local to the concern that has achieved priority, and the emotion makes it urgent.

Emotions, too, are the source of our values (Solomon, 2007), including our deepest values: whom and what we love, what we dislike, what we despise.

Most importantly, emotions help us form and engage in our relationships. Whom do we choose to spend our lives with? How do we feel about members of our family? Who are our friends? Why do we worry when separated from someone with whom we're very close? Why do we find it difficult to be in the same room with someone we don't like? How do others see us? Although emotions do occur to us individually, most of our important emotions don't just occur to us individually. They mediate our relationships. Think of love, anger, fear of certain people, or sadness at the loss of a friend.

Psychological researchers tend to focus on trying to discover what is going on in the individual mind and brain. Until recently, research on emotions was based on, for instance, the individual's perception of facial expressions, the individual's physiological responses, and the individual's responses to questions about his or her experience. But now research is catching up with what we know: that as well as happening to us individually, most of our important emotions happen between us and others. In this book we emphasize this aspect because we believe not only that it's the way research is going, but that it's the way it ought to go.

What's the interpersonal equivalent of an emotion giving priority to a concern? It's that an emotion is a kind of commitment to another (Aubé, 2009). When we love someone, even if the love is brief, and even if it is not spoken about as love, we commit ourselves to that other, at least for a while. We make the other's concerns our own, be it in sex, or in childrearing, or in cooperating as soldiers or firefighters do in situations of danger. When we are angry with someone, we commit ourselves to seeing the matter through, to a resolution, or to a parting.

These thoughts derive from modern research, but we can also relate them to our personal knowledge and intuitions. How do these ideas seem to you? Do they make sense?

Nineteenth-Century Founders

Modern ideas about emotions can be thought of as deriving from Charles Darwin, William James, and Sigmund Freud; here's how their ideas have been influential.

Charles Darwin: The Evolutionary Approach

Our descent, then, is the origin of our evil passions!!—
The Devil under form of Baboon is our grandfather!
Charles Darwin, notebook, Gruber & Barrett, 1974, p. 289

In 1872, Charles Darwin, the central figure in modern biology, published the most important book on emotions yet written—*The Expression of the Emotions in Man and Animals* (1872). Earlier, in *The Origin of Species* (1859), he had described how all living things have evolved to be adapted to their environments. Knowing this, you might imagine that Darwin would have proposed that emotions had functions in our survival. Indeed, many psychologists and biologists assume that this is what he said. But he didn't. His argument was both closer to common sense, and more subtle than anything that we might commonsensically believe.

Darwin began writing notes on his observations of emotions in 1838. At that time, the accepted theory was that God had given humans special facial muscles that allowed them to express uniquely human sentiments. A central tenet of Darwin's theory, however, was that humans are descended from other species: we are not only closer to animals than had been

Table 1.1   Emotional expressions discussed by Darwin (1872), the bodily systems used, and the type of emotion that was expressed

Expression	Bodily system	Emotion example
Blushing	Blood vessels	Shame, modesty
Body contact	Somatic muscles	Affection
Clenching fists	Somatic muscles	Anger
Crying	Tear ducts	Sadness
Frowning	Facial muscles	Anger, frustration
Laughing	Breathing apparatus	Pleasure
Perspiration	Sweat glands	Pain
Hair standing on end	Dermal apparatus	Fear, anger
Screaming	Vocal apparatus	Pain
Shrugging	Somatic muscles	Resignation
Sneering	Facial muscles	Contempt
Trembling	Somatic muscles	Fear, anxiety

Source: Oatley (1992).

thought, but we ourselves are kinds of animals. Darwin gathered many observations that would have enduring effects on the contemporary study of emotion (Darwin 1872/1998).

In his book on emotions, Darwin asked two broad questions that still guide emotion researchers. First, how are emotions expressed in humans and other animals? Table 1.1 is a taxonomy of some of the expressions Darwin described.

The second question Darwin asked is: Where do our emotions come from? He proposed that emotional expressions derive largely from habits that in our evolutionary or individual past had once been useful. So, emotional expressions are based on reflex-like mechanisms, and some of them occur whether they are useful or not. They can be triggered involuntarily in circumstances analogous to those that had triggered the original habits. His book is full of examples of such actions: of tears that do not function to lubricate the eyes, of hair standing on end in fear and anger to no apparent purpose, and so on.

For Darwin, expressions showed the continuity of adult human emotions with those of lower animals and with those of infancy. Because these expressions occur in adults "though they may not . . . be of the least use," they had for Darwin a significance for evolutionary thinking rather like that of fossils that allow us to trace the evolutionary ancestry of species. More precisely, he thought emotional expressions were like the appendix, a small organ that is part of the gut but which seemingly has no function. Darwin proposed that this is evidence that we are descended from pre-human ancestors in whom this organ had a use. He argued that many emotional expressions have the same quality: for instance, that sneering, in which we partially uncover the teeth on one side, is a behavioral vestige of snarling and of preparing to bite. This preparation was functional in some distant ancestor, but is so no longer. Though we sometimes make mordant remarks, adult human beings do not now generally use the teeth to attack.

Darwin traced other expressions to infancy: crying, he argued, is the vestige of screaming in infancy, though in adulthood it is partly inhibited. He carefully described screaming in young

(a)   (b)

FIGURE 1.1   Two of Darwin's (1872) photographs, sneering and crying: (a) Plate IV No. 1; (b) Plate 1 No. 1.

babies, and gave an argument for the function of closing the eyes and the secretion of tears to help protect them when this occurred. When adults cry they still secrete tears, but adult tears no longer have a protective function. One of Darwin's most interesting suggestions is that patterns of adult affection, of taking those whom we love in our arms, are based on patterns of parents hugging young infants. (See Figure 1.1.)

For Darwin, our emotions link us to our past: to the past of our species and to our own infancy. He helped provide descriptions of facial expressions, and he argued for the universality of such expressions. It is a claim that has generated numerous studies, as we shall see in Chapter 4. He gave a perspective on the question of how beneficial emotions are that is reflected in the quotation at the head of this section. Might we be better off if we could rise above bestial passions, which emerged in a pre-human phase of our evolution? Indeed the bulk of his book is given over to examples in which emotional expressions occur whether or not they are of any use. Only toward the end of his book does he write:

> The movements of expression in the face and body, whatever their origin might have been, are in themselves of much importance for our welfare. They serve as the first means of communication between the mother and her infant; she smiles approval, and thus encourages her child on the right path, or frowns disapproval. We readily perceive sympathy in others by their expression. . . . The movements of expression give vividness and energy to our spoken words.
>
> (Darwin, 1872/1998, p. 359)

Despite his reservations, Darwin thought that emotions have useful functions; they help us navigate our social interactions. And that is a hypothesis we shall pursue in this book.

William James: The Physiological Approach

> . . . bodily changes follow directly the perception of the exciting fact . . . and feeling of the same changes as they occur, is the emotion.
>
> James, 1890, p. 449

Significant figure: Charles Darwin

Charles Darwin's mother died when he was eight. At the age of 16, Charles was sent by his father to Edinburgh University to study medicine, but he would skip classes to collect specimens along the shores of the Firth of Forth, developing his strong interest in natural history. In despair about the failure of his son's medical studies, his father next sent him to Cambridge to study theology. Again, young Darwin was not fully engaged with his courses: he was more interested in collecting beetles, and in hunting. He obtained an ordinary BA in 1831, and seemed headed for a life as a country parson with the hobby of natural history. He had not been idle at Cambridge, however. He had won the esteem of a number of scientists and, at the age of 22, he was appointed naturalist on the *Beagle,* a British Navy ship with a mission to chart coastlines in South America. Two years after his return from his five-year voyage, Darwin proposed to a cousin, Emma Wedgewood and, a few months later, they started a long and generally happy marriage. Darwin was a bit of a hypochondriac, and after he and his wife had settled in a house in a village outside London, he seldom went out, except to health spas to take cures.

The couple had ten children, two of whom died in infancy. Charles and Emma were devoted parents, and the death of their daughter Annie at age 10 was devastating for both of them. Although evolution is often seen as in conflict with religion, Charles did not see his discoveries and theory as incompatible with his Christian beliefs. But the death of Annie did make him doubt the existence of God.

From 1837, Charles's notebooks show him struggling to understand the change of one species into another. He proceeded slowly, and it wasn't until 1859 that his book, *On the Origin of Species*, appeared.

From 1838 onward, Charles's notebooks reflect a growing interest in emotional expressions in humans, as well as in nonhuman species, with many visits to the zoo. He enlisted others to make observations for him. He realized the importance of cross-cultural study. He was one of the first researchers to use questionnaires: he sent a set of printed questions to missionaries and others who could observe people all round the world, asking them to observe particular expressions. He received 36 replies. He was one of the first to use photographs for research. He used both naturalistic and posed expressions of emotion (such as the one at the head of this chapter) to make scientific arguments. Darwin's 1872 book on expression is the scientific study of emotions. His 1877 paper in the journal *Mind*, in which he describes observations of his infant son William's emotional and cognitive development, is one of the first contributions to developmental psychology. (Biographical information from Bowlby, 1991; Gruber & Barrett, 1974.)

In this well-known quotation from *The Principles of Psychology* (1890), William James argued against the commonsense idea that when we feel an emotion it impels us in a certain way, that if we were to meet a bear in the woods, we would feel frightened and run. Instead, James proposed that when we see the bear, "the exciting fact" as he put it, the emotion *is* the perception of changes of our body as we react to that fact. When we feel frightened, James thought, what we feel is our heart beating, our skin cold, our posture frozen, or our legs carrying us away as fast as possible. (In 1855, Carl Lange independently published the same idea, which thus is sometimes known as the James-Lange theory.)

James's idea is about the nature of emotional experience. He stressed the way in which emotions move us bodily. We may tremble or perspire, our heart may thump in our chest, our breathing may be taken over as we weep or laugh helplessly. The core of an emotion, James contended, is the pattern of such bodily responses. This vital point about the embodied nature of emotion is captured in this observation of James: "If we fancy some strong emotion and then try to abstract from our consciousness of it all the feelings of its bodily symptoms, we find we have nothing left behind" (James, 1890, p. 451). This proposal has guided study of emotion in two important ways.

First, James concentrated on experience, and argued that this experience is embodied. He proposed that our experience of many emotions, from fear to joy, involves changes of the autonomic nervous system (that part of the nervous system that concerns inner organs, including the heart, the blood vessels, the stomach, and the sweat glands) as well as changes from movements of muscles and joints. James prompted modern interest in the physiological reactions associated with the different emotions. We discuss this in Chapters 5 and 6.

Second, James proposed that emotions give "color and warmth" to experience. Without these effects, he said, everything would be pale. Colloquially we speak of "rose-colored glasses" or a "jaundiced view of life" to indicate how our emotions affect our perceptions. In different parts of this book we will look at how scientists have studied this question. In Chapter 10 we see that emotions guide our judgments, from what is right and wrong, to what is fair and just.

Sigmund Freud: The Psychotherapeutic Approach

"I came away from the window at once, and leant up against the wall and couldn't get my breath . . . "
(description given by Katharina, subject of one of Freud's early case histories).

Freud & Breuer, 1895

Sigmund Freud proposed that certain events can be so damaging that they leave emotional scars that can shape the rest of our lives. His principal exposition was in a series of case studies.

Freud was one of the first to argue that emotions are at the core of many mental illnesses. An early patient, Katharina—a quotation from whom is at the head of this section—described how she suffered from attacks in which she thought she would suffocate. Asked by Freud to give more details, she said: "I always see an awful face that looks at me in a dreadful way, so that I am frightened" (p. 192). She could not say whose face it was. Freud was clear that the attacks were of anxiety. Katharina would now be diagnosed as suffering from panic attacks (American Psychiatric Association, 2000).

Like Darwin, Freud thought that an emotion in the present could derive from one in the past, in the patient's early life. His aim in therapy for Katharina was to discover how her attacks had started, and who the feared person was. The method Freud developed was called psychoanalysis, and in Katharina's case we see elements of how this kind of therapy developed: the telling by a patient of her or his life story, which is found to have gaps (in this case the gap of having no idea whose was the awful face that appeared to her in her attacks), the filling of such gaps by "interpretations" of the therapist, and the insights of the person receiving the therapy, who realizes something of which he or she had been unconscious. Although in his original case history of 1895, Freud was able to elicit from Katherina parts of her story, which involved sexual molestation, he disguised his account. In a footnote to his case, which he added in 1924, he wrote: "I venture after the lapse of so many years to lift the veil of discretion and reveal the fact that Katharina . . . fell ill, therefore, as a result of sexual attempts on the part of her own father" (p. 210).

FIGURE 1.2   Group photograph from the conference to mark Freud's honorary degree at Clark University in 1909. In the front row Freud is fourth from the right, Jung third from the right, and William James third from the left.

Although psychoanalysis was one of the earliest and most influential psychological therapies, it is often energetically criticized, especially by therapists who prefer newer methods such as behavior therapy and cognitive-behavior therapy (these issues are discussed in Chapter 14).

Perhaps most importantly for our understanding of emotions, Freud's work suggests that the emotional life of adulthood derives from relationships we had in childhood with parents or other caregivers. This idea was the foundation of the work of John Bowlby, a psychoanalyst who, from 1951 onward, developed the theory of attachment—the love between an infant and its mother or other caregiver—and his idea that all later social development derives from this emotional base. Arguably, this was the most important new element in 20th-century psychological research on emotions. It was a huge step, and understanding of the emotional development of children would now be unthinkable without it. We discuss it in Chapter 11.

Freud's theories were also critical to the influential theorist Richard Lazarus (1991), who combined them with the Darwinian evolutionary idea of adaptation to propose that emotions derive from how we evaluate events in the environment in relation to our goals. We discuss this and related theories in Chapter 7.

Philosophical and Literary Approaches

Darwin, James, and Freud laid important foundations in the study of emotion, but they were not the first in the Western tradition to think about emotions. Philosophers have grappled with the nature of emotion, as have writers of fiction. In this section, we focus on three thinkers who influenced important currents in the understanding of emotions, and whose ideas are still alive.

Aristotle and the Ethics of Emotions

> *. . . there is nothing either good or bad but thinking makes it so.*
> Shakespeare, *Hamlet,* II, 2, 1. 249–250

Aristotle, who lived from 384 to 322 BCE, offered some of the first systematic analyses of emotions. His most fundamental insight was that whereas many assume that emotions happen to us outside of our control, really they depend on what we believe. In this way, we are responsible for our emotions because we are responsible for our beliefs.

In his book, *Rhetoric*, Aristotle discussed how different judgments give rise to different emotions. "Anger," he says, "may be defined as an impulse, accompanied by pain, to a conspicuous revenge for a conspicuous slight directed without justification towards what concerns oneself or towards what concerns one's friends" (1378b, 1.32). The emotion is defined cognitively in terms of our belief that a slight has occurred. To be slighted is to be treated with contempt, or thwarted, or shamed.

In Aristotle's discussion of the role of emotion in persuasion, we see the message echoed by Shakespeare's quotation from *Hamlet* at the head of this section: that our emotional experiences are shaped by our judgments and evaluations. Think of it like this. It's a warm summer evening and you are lightly dressed, waiting in line at a cinema. A light touch on your arm by the person you invited to the movie might trigger a surge of affection. The very same pattern of touch from a stranger might make you feel anxious, angry, or even repelled. Our experience depends on our judgment.

In *Poetics*, which is about narrative writing, mainly about tragedy, Aristotle concerned himself with further questions about emotion. Drama, said Aristotle, is about human action, and what can happen when human actions miscarry and have effects that were unforeseen. We are humans, not gods. We simply do not know enough to predict the consequences of everything we do. Nonetheless, and this is the root of human tragedy, we remain responsible for our actions.

Aristotle noticed two important effects of tragic drama. First, at the theater, people are moved emotionally. As the principal character grapples with consequences that were unforeseen and uninvited, we see the somber spectacle of a person who is good being tortured by circumstances to which he or she has contributed but cannot control. We are moved to feel sympathy (or pity) for this person—and to fear for ourselves, because in the universal appeal of these plays we know that the principal character is also ourself. (See Figure 1.3.)

Second, we can experience what Aristotle called *katharsis* of our emotions. This term is widely mistranslated as purgation or purification, as if one goes to the theater to rid oneself of toxic emotions, or to elevate them. But as philosopher Martha Nussbaum (1986) argues, for Aristotle *katharsis* meant neither purgation nor purification. It meant clarification—the clearing away of obstacles to understanding. By seeing predicaments of human action at the theater we may come to experience emotions of sympathy and fear, and understand consciously for ourselves their relation to the consequences of human action in a world that can be known only imperfectly.

Taking up this line of thought, that emotions are evaluations and depend on our beliefs, not long after Aristotle's death, two important schools of philosophy grew up. The first was Epicureanism, based on the teachings of Epicurus, who lived near Athens around 300 BCE in a community of like-minded friends. The second was Stoicism. It got its name from the *stoa*, where the philosophers of this school taught; the *stoa* was a colonnade, a bit like a cloister, that ran alongside the marketplace in Athens (see Figure 1.4).

Photo Credit: Noboru Komine/Photo Researchers

FIGURE 1.3 The theater in classical times was an important institution, constructed to portray dramatic action in the context of fellow citizens who sat in full view of each other.

Though dictionaries tell us that *epicurean* now means "devoted to the pursuit of pleasure," and *stoic* means "indifferent to pleasure or pain," these meanings are distant from their origins; but the fact that these words are in modern languages testifies to a continuing influence.

One could say the Epicureans and Stoics were the first emotion researchers in the West. The doctrines of these schools had important influence in the development of Western thought. The Epicureans developed ideas of natural human sociality that influenced both the American and French Revolutions. The idea that human beings have a right to the pursuit of happiness is distinctively Epicurean, as is the idea of living naturally, in harmony with an environment of which we are stewards. The ideas of the Stoics are thought to have influenced the acceptance of Christianity by the Romans following the conversion of the Emperor Constantine.

The Epicureans taught that one should live in a simple way and enjoy simple pleasures, like food and friendship, rather than chasing after things that make one anxious, like wealth, or are unnatural, like luxuries, or are ephemeral, like fame. To allow ourselves to have such goals can only lead to painful emotions: anger when someone frustrates one's will, greed at wanting more and more, or envy at someone having something we do not. The Epicureans recommended shifts in attention from such irrational desires to more worthwhile ones.

Photo Credit: ©akg-images/Helmut Kalle/The Image Works

FIGURE 1.4 A *stoa* (portico) that runs alongside the *agora* (marketplace) in Athens. It was in such a place that the Stoics taught the management of emotions. (The *stoa* in this picture is not the original but one constructed a century after the founding of Stoicism and rebuilt in the 1930s.)

The Stoics were more radical than the Epicureans. They thought that because emotions derive from desires, to free oneself from crippling and destructive emotions one should extirpate almost all desires. The only values that are outside the vagaries of chance or the control of others, and therefore are subject to one's own will, are one's own rationality and good character. The Stoic understanding was that most emotions, especially such emotions as anger, anxiety, and lust, are damaging to the self and to society, and so should be disciplined out of our daily experience. As Christianity began to spread, the bad desires and bad thoughts that the Stoics sought to extirpate became the Seven Deadly Sins (Sorabji, 2000).

Epicurean and Stoic philosophy is called *ethical* because the members of these schools did not only have the goal of understanding how emotions work, but also the goal of understanding how one could shape one's life for the better (Nussbaum, 1994). *Ethical* does not mean knowing what one should do. It is about all the considerations we might have as to how best to structure our own life in relation to others. It's been said that when one gets right down to it, there are only two real choices in life: epicureanism, living in a way that is pleasurable though moderate, and stoicism, living so that rationality is the highest virtue.

Just as medicine sought a cure for bodily ills, so the Epicureans and Stoics thought of philosophy as a cure for the soul, and focused on emotions as the chief sources of the soul's diseases. One may get lovely insights into Stoic thinking from the Roman writers Marcus Aurelius (c. 170) and Epictetus (c. 100), one an emperor and the other a former slave.

Two thousand years after the Epicureans and Stoics, people who think about emotions (including philosophers) and their contribution to our ethical behavior and pursuit of happiness tend to seek answers in psychology. Think of the introductory sections of this chapter: we've introduced emotions as being strongly biological, as driven by the unconscious, and as arising in the body. How—in the face of such forces—can we influence our emotions? How can we live a life that is satisfying and meaningful, and tip the balance toward enjoyable engagement in what we are doing rather than toward resentment or alienation? Despite the fact that our emotions are strongly affected by our genes and upbringing, how might it be possible to use whatever free will we have to live in a way that is right for us and those we love? How can we escape from disabling depression, anxiety, or addiction? How can we have worthwhile influence on society despite our selfish desires? These are questions we seek to offer answers to in Chapter 14. Skip ahead, if you like. This book can be read in any order. But it's good to start thinking about questions such as these as soon as possible, and to keep thinking about them with the growth of your own understanding of emotions.

René Descartes: Philosophically Speaking

The Passions of the Soul

Book title of Descartes

René Descartes is generally regarded as the founder of modern philosophy and of the scientific view of the world. Descartes wrote in 17th-century Holland, which had just blossomed from having been an obscure Spanish colony to a center of commercial and intellectual life, perhaps at that time one of the few places in Europe where bold thinkers could work and publish without persecution. Descartes focuses on the emotions in *The Passions of the Soul* (1649), which offers a detailed discussion of sensory and motor nerves, reflexes, and memory.

As for the emotions (which in those days were called the passions), Descartes opens his book as follows: "There is nothing in which the defective nature of the sciences which we have received from the ancients appears more clearly than in what they have written on the passions" (p. 331).

What new insights does Descartes offer? He claimed that six fundamental emotions—wonder, desire, joy, love, hatred, and sadness—occur in the thinking aspect of ourselves, which he called the soul. At the same time they are closely connected to our bodies, for example, to our heart beating rapidly, to blushing, or to tears. Descartes differentiated emotions from perceptions of events that happen in the outside world and perceptions that arise from events within the body, such as hunger and pain. Whereas perceptions tell us about the outer world, and bodily states like hunger and pain tell us about critical events in the body, emotions tell us what is important in our souls—as we might now say, in our real selves, in relation to our concerns and our identities.

Having identified the origins of the emotions in our souls, Descartes then describes how emotions cannot be entirely controlled by thinking, but they can be regulated by thoughts, especially thoughts that are true. So, he says:

> . . . in order to excite courage in oneself and remove fear, it is not sufficient to have the will to do so, but we must also apply ourselves to consider the reasons, the objects or

examples which persuade us that the peril is not great; that there is always more security in defense than flight; that . . . we could expect nothing but regret and shame for having fled, and so on.

(Descartes, 1649, p. 352)

Like Aristotle, Descartes suggests that the emotions depend on how we evaluate events. Descartes was also one of the first to argue that emotions serve important functions:

> . . . the utility of all the passions consists alone in their fortifying and perpetuating in the soul thoughts which it is good it should preserve, and which without that might easily be effaced from it. And again, all the harm which they can cause consists in the fact that they fortify and conserve those thoughts more than necessary, or that they fortify and conserve others on which it is not good to dwell.

(Ibid, p. 364)

We might reflect on how, when we love someone, our love perpetuates and extends our thoughts of this person; when we are overanxious or depressed we dwell on issues we cannot affect. Descartes's idea—a perceptive one—is that our emotions are usually functional but can sometimes be dysfunctional.

Descartes wrote at the end of the Renaissance. He was a contemporary of William Harvey, who discovered the circulation of the blood, which formerly had been thought to be one of the four humors. Ideas of these humors derived from Greek doctors such as Hippocrates and Galen, who thought that disease was caused by imbalance among the humors, with an increase of each humor giving rise to a distinct emotional state. Blood gives rise to hope and vigor, and from it comes the term *sanguine*; phlegm gives rise to placidity, and from it comes the term *phlegmatic*; yellow bile gives rise to anger, and from it comes the world *choleric*; black bile gives rise to despair, and from it comes the word *melancholy*. Before the mid-17th century it was thought that the very emanations of these humors were the experience of each kind of emotion, that we become melancholy (for instance) from an excess of black bile, which gives off the experience of sadness as a stagnant pool gives off a stench (Paster, Rowe, & Floyd-Wilson, 2004). Among those making new efforts of imagination was Descartes. In the new physiology to which he contributed, emotions arise in the mind, functionally enable our plans, and affect our bodies.

George Eliot: The World of the Arts

> *No life would have been possible to Dorothea which was not filled with emotion . . .*
> George Eliot, *Middlemarch*, p. 894

Many of the greatest insights into emotions come from novelists and poets—Virginia Woolf on the stream of consciousness, D.H. Lawrence on emotional dynamics between women and men, J.D. Salinger on the self-consciousness of adolescence. The writing of George Eliot (pen-name of Mary Ann Evans) offers some of the most impressive ideas regarding emotional experience and its place in intimate relationships.

In 1856, George Eliot wrote an essay for the *Westminster Review*, entitled "The natural history of German life" (Pinney, 1963). In it she reviewed two books by von Riehl, a pioneer anthropologist, who described the life of German peasants. Her essay was a kind of manifesto for her own novels. It includes the following:

> The greatest benefit we owe to the artist, whether painter, poet or novelist, is the extension of our sympathies. Appeals founded on generalizations and statistics require a sympathy ready-made, a moral sentiment already in activity; but a picture of human life such as a great artist can give, surprises even the trivial and the selfish into that attention to what is apart from themselves, which may be called the raw material of moral sentiment . . . Art is the nearest thing to life; it is a mode of amplifying experience and extending our contact with our fellow-men beyond the bounds of our personal lot.
>
> (George Eliot, *Essays*, 1883, p. 192–93.)

Although the word *emotion* isn't used here, this passage is about the importance of literary art for the emotions and, in a way that has influenced our approach in this book, emotions not just in individuals but between people. So, Eliot says, "sympathies"—emotions that connect us to each other—can be extended by novelists and other kinds of artists to people outside our usual circle of friends and acquaintances.

In the years 1871 to 1872, Eliot published *Middlemarch,* a novel about emotions, which portrays experience from inside the person's own consciousness. Each character has aspirations and plans, but each is affected by the unforeseeable accidents of life. Eliot's question is this: If we are unable to foresee the outcomes of all our actions, if there is no fate or divine force guiding us toward an inevitable destiny, how should we find our way in life? Her answer is that our emotion can act as a sort of compass. It's also the principal means by which we affect other people.

In the book, Eliot contrasts Dorothea, who longs to do some good in the world, with Edward Casaubon, an elderly scholar whom Dorothea admired and married in the hope of gaining entrance to the world of learning. Dorothea is responsive to the emotional currents of her own and others' lives, whereas, for all his erudition, Casaubon barely recognizes his emotions at all. About a third of the way through the book, Casaubon has a heart attack in suppressed anger following an argument with Dorothea. Lydgate, the town doctor, attends and counsels Dorothea to avoid all occasions that might agitate her husband.

Some days later, Lydgate makes another call and Casaubon asks him to be candid about his condition. Lydgate says that although prediction is difficult, he is at risk. Casaubon perceives that he might die, and sinks into bitterness. When Lydgate leaves, Dorothea goes into the garden with a sympathetic impulse to go at once to her husband.

> But she hesitated, fearing to offend him by obtruding herself; for her ardour, continually repulsed, served with her intense memory to heighten her dread, as thwarted energy subsides into a shudder, and she wandered slowly round the nearer clumps of trees until she saw him advancing. Then she went towards him, and might have represented a heaven-sent angel coming with a promise that the short hours remaining should yet be filled with that faithful love which clings the closer to a comprehended grief. His glance in reply to hers was so chill that she felt her timidity increased; yet turned and passed her hand through his arm.
>
> Mr Casaubon kept his hands behind him, and allowed her pliant arm to cling with difficulty against his rigid arm.

There was something horrible to Dorothea in the sensation which this unresponsive hardness inflicted on her. That is a strong word, but not too strong; it is in these acts called trivialities that the seeds of joy are for ever wasted.

(Eliot, 1883, p. 230–31)

In this passage we see many of Eliot's ideas about how emotions arise and are communicated. They are what relationships are made of. They have powerful effects upon how we perceive other people and situations in which we find ourselves. We come to understand that we experience our own emotions differently from how people see them. We readers are moved emotionally in ways that succeed in "extending our sympathies." Later George Eliot wrote in a letter:

. . . my writing is simply a set of experiments in life—an endeavour to see what our thought and emotion may be capable of—what stores of motive, actual or hinted as possible, give promise of a better after which we can strive.

(Haight, 1985, p. 466)

Brain Science, Psychology, Sociology

Thus far we have considered how founding figures grappled with the nature of emotion. How would the scientific study of emotion emerge? During the first half of the 20th century there was resistance to its study from behaviorism, which saw only overt behavior as worthy of psychological inquiry. Over the past 50 years, however, at first gradually and then with gathering momentum, the study of emotions has come into its own in the brain sciences, in psychology, and in the social sciences.

John Harlow, Tania Singer: New Brain Science

Even though empathy has been extensively discussed and investigated by philosophers and social scientists, only recently has it become a focus for neuroscience.

Tania Singer et al., 2004, p. 1157

One of the earliest and most striking pieces of evidence about how the brain is involved in emotions came from a horrific accident, written up by a country doctor, John Harlow.

The case about which Harlow wrote was that of Phineas Gage, a likeable foreman of a group of men working to construct a railroad in Vermont. On September 13, 1848, they were about to blast a rock, which had been drilled and the hole filled with gunpowder. Gage rammed the powder down with an iron rod, three and a half feet long, an inch and a quarter in diameter. It weighed 13 pounds. This tamping rod must have struck up a spark, for there was an explosion. The rod entered Gage's skull just beneath the left eyebrow, left via a hole in the top of his head, and landed 50 feet away. Gage bled terribly, suffered an infection of his wound, but recovered, in body though not in mind. (See Figure 1.5.)

Harlow, who attended Gage, wrote that the "balance, so to speak, between his intellectual faculties and his animal propensities seems to have been destroyed" (1868, p. 277). The effects were emotional. Although previously he was amiable, Gage was now impatient, irreverent, and easily

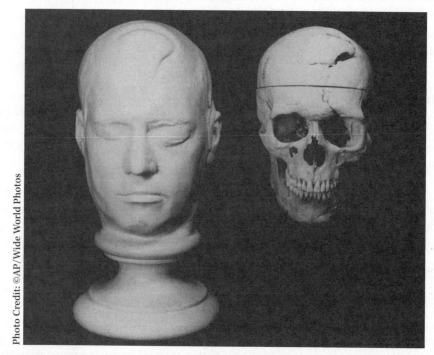

Photo Credit: ©AP/Wide World Photos

FIGURE 1.5   On the left a model of Phineas Gage's head, and on the right his skull showing the exit hole made by the iron tamping rod in the accident of 1848.

moved to anger. His employers, who had regarded him as their "most efficient and capable foreman," could not give him back his job.

Antonio Damasio started his 1994 book with this case, and then went on to describe more recent cases in which people—"modern Phineas Gages"—had suffered damage to the frontal lobes. The most striking aspect of their condition was the loss in their ability to conduct their relationships. Their spouses divorced them because they had become unreliable. They lost all their money to people who took advantage of them. Their social lives were in chaos because they no longer knew what was emotionally important to themselves or others. We discuss these matters further in Chapter 6.

Before the age of electronics, and the finding that the brain itself works by sending electrical signals, the main evidence about emotions and the human brain function came from accidental damage of the kind that happened to poor Phineas Gage.

Among the pioneers of more modern brain research as it affected emotions was Walter Cannon, who argued against his Harvard colleague, William James. He started a paper in 1927 by citing observations by commentators that James's theory is "so strongly fortified by truth and so repeatedly confirmed by experience" (p. 106) that he felt trepidation at venturing to criticize it. Cannon uses the term *trepidation* rhetorically. He probably felt no such thing. His 1927 paper was one in a line of criticisms he published of the James-Lange theory. His principal evidence was that if James were right, then when the viscera (from which bodily feelings were supposed by James to arise) were severed from the brain of laboratory animals, one would expect a reduction in their emotions. With this operation, however, no such reduction occurred.

Instead, as Cannon found, it was transection of neural pathways at a quite different level that had huge and striking effects on emotions. Cannon showed that when, in a laboratory cat, the cerebral cortex was severed from the lower parts (subcortical regions) of the brain, or removed altogether, the result was an animal that showed very intense emotions, for instance, strong anger with no provocation. The phenomenon contributed to the idea that higher regions of the brain—the cortex—act to inhibit the lower regions where emotions reside.

Though Cannon may have been right about many aspects of James's theory, one needs to be wary of the kind of inference that Cannon made, which even before his time was a pervasive idea in the burgeoning field of neurology, that a function of the so-called higher regions of the brain (the cortex) was to inhibit the lower (sub-cortical) regions. One might as well take a hammer and whack the back of one's television set and then remark that the function of the region one has destroyed is to inhibit the fuzzy flickering image now seen on the screen. Any useful account of a complex mechanism must be in terms of the properties of components and their interactions, not in terms of activation or inhibition of some aspect of the whole mechanism's outer behavior.

In modern times, research on emotions in the human brain has moved from the study of brain damage to tracking patterns of brain activation using methods of neuroimaging, particularly functional magnetic resonance imaging (fMRI), which picks up tiny changes of blood flow in regions of the brain when the neurons in those regions are active. Using imaging of this kind, Tania Singer and her collaborators (2004) assessed brain activity while volunteers experienced a painful electric shock and compared it to that elicited when they observed a signal indicating that their loved one—present in the same room—was receiving a similar shock. Although some areas of the brain (for instance, the somato-sensory cortex) were activated only when the participants experienced pain through their own senses, other regions, including the anterior insula and parts of the anterior cingulate cortex, were activated both when subjects received pain and when they were signaled that their loved one experienced pain. This emotional aspect of pain was shared; it was affected by the participants' own pain and imagination of pain in their loved one.

The brain regions involved, which included the anterior cingulate cortex (see Figure 1.6), mediate the important emotional quality of empathy. On the basis of studies of this kind, Frederique de Vignemont and Tania Singer (2006) defined empathy as:

a. having an emotion, which

b. is in some way similar to that of another person, which

c. is elicited by observation or imagination of the other's emotion, and that involves

d. knowing that the other is the source of one's own emotion.

One has to be careful with fMRI studies not to think in terms of a new phrenology, that is to say, to think that any part of the brain that is activated is the region solely responsible for a particular function. But with careful experiments, such as that of Singer et al., and with theoretical proposals, such as de Vignemont and Singer's, that derive from them, important new understandings have been achieved. It is probable that in our closer relationships we recognize other people's emotions not just by the expressions that Darwin studied, but empathetically, in a way that coordinates the other's emotions simultaneously with our own. Empathy has become a new growth point in the study of emotions.

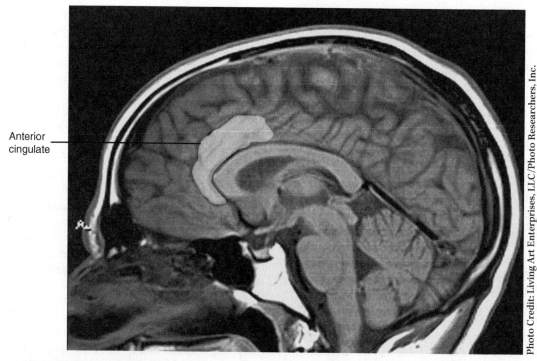

Anterior cingulate

FIGURE 1.6   Section through the human brain showing the anterior cingulate cortex (highlighted).

Novels and films: Avatar

James Cameron's (2009) film *Avatar* was a big hit, and it continues to be worth seeing. An avatar is a conceptual being that can represent us in a game. In this film the avatar is a being from another planet, into which the human mind of Jake Sully (played by Sam Worthington) is inserted. Sully has been a Marine. He was wounded in combat, and made paraplegic. Despite being confined to a wheelchair, he has special skills that qualify him to join a group of humans on a mission to Pandora, in the Alpha Centauri solar system, in the year 2154. The body that Jake's mind enters is that of a Na'vi, a species of nine-feet-tall, blue-skinned beings, who are lithe and elegant, who move gracefully through beautiful forests with which they live in harmony.

Humans have come to Pandora to obtain a valuable mineral, "unobtainium," needed to solve the energy crisis that threatens the Earth. The film's plot parallels the plunder of the Americas by Europeans, with contempt for indigenous peoples. At one level, *Avatar* is a conventional film in which a likeable hero first suffers, then overcomes seemingly insurmountable obstacles, and then gets the girl, the lovely Na'vi princess, Neytiri (played by Zoe Saldana), who inducts him into ways of living in the Pandoran forests.

But Cameron is a deeply psychological filmmaker (Oatley, 2010). Jake enters a series of empathetic identifications with people who first are like him, then progressively are more different from him. His first identification is with Colonel Quaritch, military commander of the human mission to Pandora. Having been in the military, Jake can easily identify with him. Next, Jake identifies with a second human, a woman: Dr. Grace Augustine, an anthropologist who wants to understand the Na'vi because she is in charge of the mission to cajole them into disrupting their living place and giving up their valuable mineral deposits. She arranges for Jake to be inserted mentally into the body of a Na'vi, to infiltrate this group that seems to be obstructing human purposes. Finally, Jake empathizes and identifies with a member of another species, Princess Neytiri, with whom he falls in love.

The most important psychological issue for Cameron concerns our human propensity to empathize with members of the group to which we feel we belong and our accompanying potential for contempt toward members of groups to which we feel we don't belong. Such groups can be defined by nationality, by political ideas, by gender, by skin color, or, indeed, by anything. You might see something of this in yourself in your preferences for an athlete or sports team.

In a review of empathy and its opposite—*schadenfreude* (taking pleasure in others' misfortunes)—Cikara, Bruneau, and Saxe (2011) argue that although our dispositions to care about and help each other are at the very foundation of human society, there are powerful motivations not to care about or help members of outgroups: sympathetic and empathic feelings toward such people are rare and fragile. Cikara et al. review studies in which empathy has been induced for members of outgroups. Arguably, films such as *Avatar* might contribute in this way.

Magda Arnold, Sylvan Tomkins: New Psychological Theories

> . . . *emotions involve a double reference, both to the object and to the self experiencing the object.*
> Magda Arnold and J. Gasson, 1954

> *It is my intention to reopen issues which have long remained in disrepute in American psychology.*
> Sylvan Tomkins, 1962

In the second half of the 20th century, faintly at first, voices were heard expressing concerns that emotions had been neglected in the academy. Among the voices were those of Magda Arnold and Sylvan Tomkins; in 1954 both published works that would guide to the present day the scientific study of emotion. Arnold (with J. Gasson) proposed that emotions are based on appraisals (evaluations) of events, and in the same year, at a meeting of the International Congress of Psychology, Tomkins offered a theory about the relation of emotion to facial expression.

Most researchers now assume that emotions derive from appraisals people make of events. The idea is similar to Aristotle's idea of emotions as evaluations (Nussbaum, 2001). If we know what appraisals (or evaluations) are made of an event, we can predict what emotion is likely to occur. Or, if we know what emotion is currently being experienced, we can infer what appraisals have probably been made.

Arnold and Gasson's idea of appraisal was that an emotion relates self to object. Unlike perception, which is about our knowledge of what is out there, or personality, which is about what each of us is like in ourselves, emotions are essentially relational. Arnold and Gasson put it like this: "An emotion . . . can be considered as the felt tendency toward an object judged suitable, or away from an object judged unsuitable" (1954, p. 294).

So appraisals involve at first attraction to, or repulsion from, some object, and they determine whether the emotion is positive or negative. Then come further distinctions, depending on whether the object of the emotion is present or not, and whether there are difficulties in acting. "Impulsive" emotions arise if there is no difficulty in attaining or avoiding an object. The "emotions of contention" arise when there are difficulties in acting. Particular emotions, Arnold and Gasson argue, arise according to these appraisals. If an object is judged suitable and if it is present, then the impulse emotion tends to be love; if an object is judged unsuitable and is not present, then the contending emotion is fear. These ideas would be widely influential, as we shall see in Chapter 7.

Like Magda Arnold, Sylvan Tomkins saw emotions as central to human life. Beginning in a series of books, the first of which was published in 1962, Tomkins' central claim was that affect is the primary motivational system. Emotions are amplifiers of drives. It had long been assumed that drives, such as hunger, thirst, and sex, are the primary determinants of behavior. Not so, argued Tomkins: "This is a radical error. The intensity, the urgency, the imperiousness, the 'umph' of drives is an illusion. The illusion is created by the misidentification of the drive 'signal' with its 'amplifier.' Its amplifier is its affective response" (Tomkins, 1970, p. 101). What Tomkins meant by "drive signal" was a neural message about some event, for instance, a signal of a potential sexual partner. What he meant by "drive amplifier" was the "umph," for instance, a strong attraction to this person.

In Tomkins's account, human action and thought reflect the interplay of motivational systems, each capable of fulfilling a certain function (such as eating, breathing, sex), each potentially capable of taking over the whole person. What prioritizes these systems? It is emotion. It does so by amplifying one particular drive signal, just as loudness of sound on an audio system is amplified by turning up a control to adjust its volume.

Here are two of Tomkins's illustrations. First: when, for any reason, there is some sudden obstruction to breathing, as when drowning or choking, it is not the shortness of oxygen that is obvious, it is a panicky fear that amplifies the drive signal making us struggle to breathe again. Those pilots in World War II who refused to wear oxygen masks suffered lack of oxygen, said Tomkins. But the effect occurred slowly. It was not unpleasant. The signal was not amplified, and some of these pilots died with smiles on their lips. Second: when we are sexually excited, it is not the sexual organs that become emotionally excited. It is the person who is excited, and moves toward the other person and to fulfillment. The bodily changes, for instance, in the sex organs, amplify the sexual drive, making it urgent and taking priority over other matters.

Tomkins offered arguments that would inspire the study of facial expression. He claimed that changes of facial expressions are the primary amplifiers of emotions in humans. Emotion-related changes in blood flow and muscle movements in the face direct attention to some particular need or goal. We return to these ideas about the face in Chapter 4.

Arnold, with her idea of appraisal, can be seen as focusing largely on inputs, on the perceptual side. Tomkins, with his idea of bodily feedback and priorities among drives focused on outputs, on the motor side. They had in common a concept of emotion as central to normal functioning, and it made possible a new era of research.

Alice Isen: New Experimentation

The warm glow of success

From the title of a paper by Alice Isen, 1970

For psychology, the period from the 1950s to the 1990s was a time of renewal and expansion, in large part because of advances in experimentation. In perception and learning, as well as in social psychology, the ideal was to find some participants (animals or people), and randomly assign

Table 1.2 Examples of effects found by Isen and her associates in which happiness was induced. In each study comparisons were made with effects of neutral and/or negative moods

Study	Method of induction	Effect of induction
Isen, 1970	Told of skill success	Larger donation to charity, and help stranger
Isen & Levin, 1972	Given cookies	More helpful, less annoying in library
Isen et al., 1978	Free gift	Better recall of positive memories
		Report fewer problems with consumer goods
Isen et al., 1985	Positive word association and two other methods	More unusual word associations
Carnevale & Isen, 1986	Cartoons and gift	Integrative bargaining, less contentiousness
Isen & Geva, 1987	Bag of candy	More cautious about loss when risk is high, less cautious about loss when risk is low
Isen et al., 1987	Comedy film or candy	Better creative problem solving
Kraiger, Billings, & Isen, 1989	Watching TV bloopers	More satisfaction in performing task
Isen, 1990	"Stickers" for children	More advanced developmental levels
Isen et al., 1991	Told of anagram success	Faster clinical diagnosis, extra interest in patients

them to experimental groups or control groups, to compare the effects of the experimental manipulation with that of the control condition.

Early influential experiments on emotion were conducted by Alice Isen, who investigated something we regularly experience—how happiness influences our perception of the world. In one experiment (1970) she gave a test of perceptual-motor skills. Some people, randomly selected, were told that they had succeeded in this test, and as a result were made mildly happy. As compared with other participants, who had taken the same perceptual motor test but who were not told they had succeeded, the happier participants were more likely to help a stranger (an associate of the experimenter) who dropped her books.

Later, Isen and her colleagues (1978) induced a mildly happy mood in people in a shopping mall by giving them a free gift. In an apparently unrelated consumer survey, these people said their cars and television sets performed better than those of control subjects who had received no gift. Emotions color how we perceive the world—a deep theme in the study of emotion and cognition (see Chapter 10). In subsequent research, Isen has shown that happiness has widespread effects on cognitive organization (Isen et al., 1978), which we summarize in Table 1.2. It can make people more creative in problem solving, and induce them to give more unusual associations to words.

Isen's work provided some of the first evidence on how emotions affect our perception and actions in the social world. The finding that an emotion or mood that arises in one situation can affect social behavior and judgment is now one of the most firmly established effects in experimental social psychology. In Chapter 10, we explain how this effect is strongest when the person concerned does not know the source of his or her original emotion or mood, and also how emotions influence cognition.

Erving Goffman, Arlie Russell Hochschild: Selves and Others

Create alarm

Slogan on an office wall of a debt-collecting agency

Erving Goffman proposed that when Shakespeare wrote, "All the world's a stage" (in *As You Like It*, 1623), this was not a metaphor: we literally give dramatic presentations of ourselves to each other and create the social reality in which we live. From such performances moral worlds are created. From them we derive our own selfhood, and from them others derive their sense of who we are.

Experimentation like that of Alice Isen is not the only way of doing science. Goffman, a sociologist, introduced into social science the method of careful observation through a theoretical lens. His lens was his idea that life is a kind of drama in which we take on roles. For understanding emotions, Goffman's most instructive work is perhaps the essay "Fun in games," published in his book, *Encounters* (1961). It is one of the most important analyses since Aristotle of the nature of happiness. It is also a reworking in social terms of Freud's *The Psychopathology of Everyday Life* (1901). It shows how emotions are constructed within specific roles, such as being with your family, or with your boss, or with a first date.

We can think of each kind of social interaction, at the mall, in the workplace, in the family, or out on a date, as being like a game, says Goffman. When we enter it, we pass through an invisible membrane into a little world with its own rules, its own traditions, its own history. We take on a role that is afforded in that kind of interaction—when out on a date we may be the one who charms and flirts; in a school or university our role may be that of student. Within the membrane, we give a certain performance to sustain our role, following the outline rules or scripts that are relevant within that world. So, out on a date we tell jokes and disclose vulnerabilities; as a student we try to learn. These performances are viewed by ourselves and others as good or bad of their kind, as correct, incorrect, or partially correct. They invite commentary from others—including suggested modifications, blame, and praise. The distinctive rules within each kind of membrane give rise to social and moral worlds that provide the subject for much of our conversation.

Now comes Goffman's insight into emotions: as well as giving a more or less good performance we can ask how strongly engaged we are in a role. Games are fun because they invite wholehearted engagement (we discuss this further in Chapter 9). By extension, we can see that happiness occurs more generally when we are engaged fully in what we are doing. But in much of life there can be inner conflict: we can follow the rules, enact the script, take part in the interaction, but not be engaged. We might prefer to be doing something else. Then occur some of the upsetting and unsatisfying aspects of our lives.

Arlie Hochschild, a sociologist, was influenced by Goffman. In her work she explored the tension that may occur when the person is in conflict about the role he or she plays, when there are questions about who one is in oneself and the performance one is giving.

Hochschild's parents were in the U.S. Foreign Service, and she describes how at the age of 12 she found herself passing around a dish of peanuts at a diplomatic party and wondering whether the smiles of those who accepted her offerings were real. Her parents often commented on gesture: the "tight smile of the Bulgarian emissary, the averted glance of the Chinese consul, and the prolonged handshake of the French economic officer" (Hochschild, 1983, p. ix). These gestures did not just convey meaning from one person to another—they were messages between governments. Had the 12-year-old just passed peanuts to actors playing prescribed diplomatic roles? Where did the person end and the job begin? How much of emotion is not involuntary, but a dramatic performance guided by strategy and rules and even deception?

As a graduate student, Hochschild sought answers to this problem: Do sales people sell the product, or their personalities? She developed a theory of "feeling rules." These rules can be private and unconscious, or socially engineered in occupations that require us to influence other people's emotions and judgments.

Hochschild observed the training of Delta Airlines cabin staff, which includes learning how to act in emergencies, how to serve food, and so on. But what Hochschild described was how in becoming a Delta stewardess one had to learn to give a particular kind of performance. The trainee had to play a role, much as if she were an actor. The main aim is to induce a particular emotional tone in passengers: "Trainees were exhorted: to 'Really work on your smiles . . . your smile is your biggest asset'" (Hochschild, 1983, p. 105). They "were asked to think of a passenger as if he were a 'personal guest in your living room.' The workers' emotional memories of offering personal hospitality were called up and put to use, as Stanislavski would recommend" (p. 105). Both practicing particular expressions and recalling memories to aid performances are parts of the training that Stanislavski (1965) proposed for professional actors; it is now generally referred to as method acting. It is easier to give a convincing performance when one fully enters into the part.

Work that involves constructing emotions in oneself in order to induce them in others is quite widespread: Hochschild calls it emotional labor. She calculated that in 1970, 38% of paid jobs in the United States needed substantial emotional labor. Within the job categories that called for such labor there were roughly twice as many women as men. The purposes served are social. The job of personal assistant requires amiability, cheerfulness, and helpfulness: its purpose includes providing pleasant emotional support for the boss. Many jobs that require emotional labor are at interfaces between companies and customers. As in the airline business, often their purpose is to sell more of the company's product.

Not all jobs requiring emotional labor are intended to induce pleasant emotions. Being a debt collector is something like the opposite of being an airline stewardess: "Create alarm" was the motto of one debt-collecting agency boss (Hochschild, 1983, p. 146).

Goffman and Hochschild offered a view in which culture-related roles, values, and social obligations determine our emotions. This will be a central theme in our treatment of culture and emotion in Chapter 3.

What Is an Emotion? Some Conceptions

Earlier in this chapter we began by asking, "What is an emotion?" Let's take this a step further, and concentrate on two questions: What is an emotion? And how do emotions differ from related phenomena, such as moods, emotional disorders, and personality traits, which you will learn about later in this book?

Researchers' Conceptions of Emotions

To consider what emotions are, let's do two things. First, pay attention to your own emotions. You might like to keep a diary of them (see box in Chapter 7) and reflect on their properties. Second, let's look at theorists' conceptions of emotion in Table 1.3.

Table 1.3 Leading theorists' conceptions of emotion

James, 1884	My thesis . . . is that the bodily changes follow directly the perception of the exciting fact, and that our feeling of the same changes as they occur is the emotion.
Arnold & Gasson, 1954	An emotion or an affect can be considered as the felt tendency towards an object judged suitable, or away from an object judged unsuitable, reinforced by specific bodily changes.
Lutz & White, 1986	Emotions are a primary idiom for defining and negotiating social relations of the self in a moral order.
Tooby & Cosmides, 1990	An emotion corresponds to a distinctive system of coordination among the mechanisms that regulate each controllable biological process. That is, each emotional state manifests design features "designed" to solve particular families of adaptive problems, whereby psychological mechanisms assume unique configuration.
Lazarus, 1991	Emotions are organized psychophysiological reactions to news about ongoing relationships with the environment.
Ekman, 1992	Emotions are viewed as having evolved through their adaptive value in dealing with fundamental life-tasks. Each emotion has unique features: signal, physiology, and antecedent events. Each emotion also has characteristics in common with other emotions: rapid onset, short duration, unbidden occurrence, automatic appraisal, and coherence among responses.
Frijda & Mesquita, 1994	Emotions . . . are, first and foremost, modes of relating to the environment: states of readiness for engaging, or not engaging, in interaction with that environment.
Izard, 2010	Function of emotion: 1. Interrupts/changes processing and focuses attention and direction of responses. 2. Motivates cognition and action and provides emotion information (including evolutionarily conserved communicative signals) to guide and coordinate the engagement of the individual in the physical and social environment for coping, adaptation, affiliation, and well-being.
Campos, Walle, Dahl, & Main (2011)	Working definition of emotion: 1. Registration that an event is important; 2. The attempt by the person to establish, maintain, change or terminate the relation between the self and the environment on those matters that are important to the person.

In Table 1.3, we have offered some conceptions of emotions that you might like to think about and discuss, to see whether they articulate your own experience and your own emerging understanding of emotions. These conceptions summarize large amounts of research. They can be thought of as definitions, but they are not really sets of necessary and sufficient conditions of the kind that are usually demanded of definitions. Moreover, there have been complaints that in the very wide usage of the term *emotion* the category is too heterogeneous to define (e.g., Griffiths, 1997). Izard (2010) draws attention to the many meanings of emotion, but also to the considerable agreement among researchers as to how emotions are elicited and what their functions are. The definition in Table 1.3 by Izard derives from responses of 34 emotion researchers to whom Izard wrote to ask about functions of emotions; for item #1 (in Izard's conception cited in Table 1.3) there was a mean rating of 8.87 out of 10 (where 10 meant completely agree) among the 34 emotion researchers, and for item 2, a rating of 8.23. In the same way Izard found the researchers gave a rating of 8.92 agreement to the idea of the structure of emotion as involving "Neural systems dedicated at least in part to 'emotion' processes" (p. 365). Izard concludes there was strong agreement among researchers on the structure and function of emotions, as well as on elicitation. His survey also showed, however, that there is no fully agreed definition of emotion, but this seems much less important than the degree of convergence on the issues of structure, function, and elicitation.

We agree with Frijda and Mesquita (Table 1.3) that "Emotions . . . are, first and foremost, modes of relating to the environment: states of readiness for engaging, or not engaging, in interaction with that environment," particularly—we would add—with the social environment. This same theme is taken up in the definition of Campos, Walle, Dahl, and Main (2011).

The approach we take in this book is that emotions are related to action; they are urges, or as the technical term has it, "action tendencies." In humans, most of the emotions we care about are social. They help us to form attachments to offspring, to form friendships and romantic bonds, and to negotiate social hierarchies. In Table 1.3, many of the "fundamental life tasks" to which Ekman refers are social, and as Lutz and White put it, they help negotiate "social relations of the self in a moral order." A "moral order" means that, in the social world, people act in relation to others, and all of us constantly make judgments of whether we and other people are doing the right thing.

Our summary of theorists' conceptions yields a further conclusion: emotions have at least three facets (Lang, Greenwald, Bradley, & Hamm, 1993; Levenson, 1999). The first facet is behavioral: we often express emotions in facial and vocal expressions, as well as in posture, gesture, touch, and other actions: this is the aspect that Darwin (1872) called "expression." A second facet is physiological: emotions involve activations in the brain, the autonomic nervous system, and other systems within the body. Bodily aspects are those on which James (1884) focused; they help to prepare us for actions of a particular kind, for instance, to approach or escape, and they help us make certain actions. Third is the experiential aspect: we often become conscious of our emotions so that we can represent our experience of emotions in language, for instance, when we discuss emotions we have experienced with other people (Rimé, 2009). Emotional experiences can also give rise to inspiring forms in fiction, poetry, music, visual art, and dance.

These different facets organize our chapters on communication, autonomic physiology, central nervous system physiology, and language, experience, and appraisal. These different facets of emotions serve different functions and together help us engage adaptively with the social environment.

Putting these insights together, one can propose, to start with, that emotions are multifaceted responses to events that we see as challenges or opportunities in our inner or outer world, events that are important to our goals—particularly our social goals.

Before the age of science, definitions used to be all-important for understanding. Now we know that it is more important to understand deeply how a particular process works. Think of it like this. Several hundred years ago the motions of planets were defined as circular. It was not until the understandings offered by Newton, that planetary motions depended on the forces of gravity and inertia acting at right angles to each other, that it was understood that planetary motions were better understood as ellipses. Understanding preceded definition. Writing a textbook relies on a good start having been made in a field of research, and we believe a good start has been made on understanding emotions. We may not have quite reached the equivalent of the Newtonian stage. That is why we have proposed that the conceptions of Table 1.3 are suggestions and starting points and not quite definitions, but not matters to be contentious about.

The Emotional Realm: Emotions, Moods, Dispositions

The English language has hundreds, even thousands, of words to describe how people feel. We might say that our roommate is angry, or irritated, or hostile. We might say that we ourselves are feeling sad, or blue, or depressed. Many scientists use the word *affect* to encompass phenomena that have anything to do with emotions, moods, dispositions, and preferences, though some people refer to this whole realm as that of the emotions. In Figure 1.7 we show this spectrum in terms of the duration of each kind of state.

Episodes of Emotion

The term *emotion,* or *emotion episode*, is generally used for states that last a limited amount of time. As indicated in Figure 1.7, facial expressions and most bodily responses generally last for seconds, and in the case of some bodily responses, minutes. When researchers record states of which people are conscious and can report, by asking them to keep structured diaries of these episodes or by getting people to remember episodes of emotions, people typically report experiences lasting between a few minutes and a few hours. Sometimes, however, the term *emotional* can have a wider reach, and mean the same as *affective.*

Moods

The term *mood* refers to a state that typically lasts for hours, days, or weeks, sometimes as a low-intensity background. When it starts or stops may be unclear. Whereas episodes of emotion typically have an object, moods are often objectless and free-floating (Frijda, 1993). We feel emotions about specific people and events. Philosophers call the focus of an emotional experience its "intentional object." When you are angry, you usually have a very clear sense of what you are angry about (e.g., your roommate's arrogance or your dad telling an embarrassing story about your first date). When you are in an irritable mood, in contrast, it may not be obvious why you feel as you do: the intentional object is less clear.

Emotional Disorders

Emotional disorders such as depression and clinical anxiety states last for weeks or months, some for years. Such disorders are now routinely assessed by research interviews, which relate them

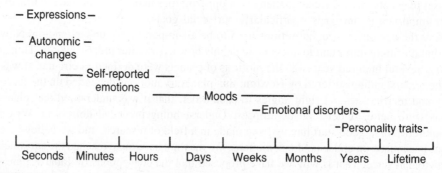

FIGURE 1.7 Spectrum of emotional phenomena in terms of the time course of each.

to categories in the most recent version of the *Diagnostic and Statistical Manual of Mental Disorders*, or *DSM-IV-TR* (American Psychiatric Association, 2000). Thus major depression is a mood disorder that includes depressed mood, or loss of interest or pleasure in most activities, and that lasts at least two weeks. It is a matter of considerable research interest to find what relation episodes of depression have to normal episodes of sadness. We will take up this issue further in Chapters 12 and 13.

Personality Traits

In a further step along the spectrum, there are terms used to describe emotional aspects of personality that can last a lifetime. We say that people are "warm" or "sarcastic." Shyness implies a tendency to feel anxiety in social settings; agreeableness involves a tendency to feel love and compassion for others. The term *trait* is used to designate any long-lasting aspect of personality. As we shall see in Chapter 11, many significant aspects of personality have emotions at their core, and these emotional tendencies can shape people's lives, sometimes in profound ways.

SUMMARY

The new sciences that contribute most to this book have venerable and influential roots. In this chapter we offer a sampling of insights into the nature of emotion. We began with Charles Darwin, who can be thought of as starting the scientific study of emotion. We then moved to William James, founder of American psychology, and Sigmund Freud, a founder of the psychological therapies. We then reviewed formative ideas of philosophers Aristotle and René Descartes. These founding figures identified some of the abiding questions of this book: What are emotions? How do we express them? Where do they come from? How do they shape our reasoning? What functions do they serve?

We then reviewed the approach of the novelist George Eliot. Her deep concern was the role of emotions in our relationships with others, an issue to which the modern psychology of emotions is heading, and which is a central feature of this book.

Early on, brain science drew on the study of accidents, and John Harlow's account of the effects of the damage to Phineas Gage's brain remains striking. More recently, brain imaging has become important, as in the studies of Tania Singer and her colleagues on empathy. We described the influential theories of approaches of Magda Arnold and Sylvan Tomkins, and the effects of inducing emotions by Alice Isen. We saw how Erving Goffman and Arlie Russell-Hochschild showed how emotions are constructed within the roles we adopt in our social life.

Finally, we offered conceptions of emotion as functional processes that relate outer events to our inner goals, and help us navigate our social world. This book is about the realm of the emotions. It will cover emotional episodes, which are briefer and more specific than moods. By the second half of the book we move to yet-longer-lasting states known as emotional disorders, and to traits of personality.

TO THINK ABOUT AND DISCUSS

1. Which of the approaches we've discussed in this chapter appeals to you the most in your own understanding of emotions? Why?

2. How can studies of the brain complement studies of a psychological kind in understanding emotions?

3. How can a piece of art such as a novel or film enable us to think about our own emotions?

FURTHER READING

Among the several good handbooks on emotions are:

David Sander & Klaus Scherer (Eds.) (2009). *Oxford companion to emotion and the affective sciences.* New York, NY: Oxford University Press.

Michael Lewis, Jeannette Haviland-Jones, & Lisa Feldman Barrett (Eds.) (2008). *Handbook of emotions, 3rd edition.* New York, NY: Guilford.

A useful book with distinguished contributors, the fourth volume in a series on Feelings and Emotions that started with the Wittenberg Symposium in 1927, is:

Antony Manstead, Nico Frijda, & Agneta Fischer (2004). *Feelings and emotions: The Amsterdam Symposium.* Cambridge, UK: Cambridge University Press.

These books by philosophers range thoughtfully across diverse approaches:

Martha Nussbaum (2001). *Upheavals of thought: The intelligence of emotions.* New York, NY: Cambridge University Press.

Robert Solomon (2007). *True to our feelings: What our emotions are really telling us.* New York, NY: Oxford University Press.

A history of emotions and how they have been thought about is found in:

Keith Oatley (2004). *Emotions: A brief history.* Oxford, UK: Blackwell.

Evolution of Emotions

2

Photo Credit: Harper & Row. Photo by Frans de Waal

FIGURE 2.0 About ten minutes before this photograph was taken these two male chimpanzees had a fight that ended in the trees. Now one extends a hand toward the other in reconciliation. Immediately after this, they embraced and climbed down to the ground together.

Like all primates, humans are an intensely social species. Indeed we probably owe our success as a species to our sociality.

Robin Dunbar (2001), p. 175

In 1860, on hearing that humans are descended from apes, the wife of the Bishop of Worcester is said to have remarked: "My dear, descended from the apes! Let us hope it is not true, but if it is, let us pray that it does not become generally known" (Leakey & Lewin, 1991, p. 16). Although we are not exactly descended from present-day apes we do share common ancestors with them. The line that led to modern humans diverged from that leading to modern chimpanzees about six million years ago. **Evolution**, the theory of how species developed, has become the central concept of biology. It also offers insights into the nature of emotions (Dawkins, 1986; Keltner, Haidt, & Shiota, 2006; Nesse & Ellsworth, 2009).

Among the evidence that Darwin advanced for his theory of evolution was the similarity of human **emotional expressions** to those of other animals. In his book on emotions, Darwin (1872) argued that "some expressions, such as the bristling of the hair under the influence of extreme terror, or the uncovering of the teeth under that of furious rage, can hardly be understood, except under the belief that man once existed in a much lower and animal-like condition" (1872, p. 12).

Darwin's analyses gave birth to the modern study of emotional expression, which we discuss in Chapter 4. His broader theory of evolution would change how we think about emotion. Understanding the evolutionary approach to emotion is the task of this chapter.

Elements of an Evolutionary Approach

In *On the Origin of Species*, Charles Darwin (1859) described evolution in terms of three processes. The first he called **superabundance**: animals and plants produce more offspring than are necessary merely to reproduce themselves. The second he called **variation**: each offspring is somewhat different than others, and differences are passed on by heredity. The third he called **selection**: those characteristics that allow better adaptation to the environment are selected because they enable survival, and hence are passed on. The influential philosopher Daniel Dennett (1995) has proposed that Darwin's idea about evolution is the single most important idea anyone has ever had.

As scientists have built upon Darwin's concept of evolution, they have identified three important concepts that shed light on the evolution of emotions, and these are the subjects of the next three subsections.

Selection Pressures

At the core of natural selection are **selection pressures**. For humans these are features of the physical and social environment in which humans evolved that determined whether individuals survived and reproduced. Some selection pressures involve threats or opportunities directly related to physical survival. To survive, individuals need to find food and water, to stay at the right temperature, and to avoid predation and disease. Many systems such as our preferences for sweet foods and aversion to bitter foods, our thermoregulatory systems, our fight and flight responses, developed in response to these kinds of selection pressures.

The elements that Darwin knew little or nothing of, but that we now know as genes, are passed during reproduction from one generation to the next. Two kinds of sexual selection pressures determine who reproduces. **Intersexual competition** refers to the process by which one sex selects specific kinds of traits in the other sex. For example, around the world, women and men prefer mates of good character (Buss, 1987), presumably because they will be generous, faithful partners. Through this selection process, traits related to good character will be selected for and are more likely to become part of the human design.

Intrasexual competition is competition for mates within a sex. In many species there is continual struggle of this kind, often among males. Stags lock horns and engage in battles that are at times violent, to find who is dominant and who therefore has access to mates. One could argue that the status dynamics of young men—the teasing, aggressive encounters and tests of strength—serve a similar function: to determine who rises in status, and who will be preferred by young women. Within intrasexual competition, those traits, whether they be strength, beauty, cunning, emotional intelligence, or humor, that allow some to prevail are more likely to be passed on to succeeding generations.

Evolutionary theorists have proposed that our capacity to enter cooperative social relationships has been very important. Nesse (2010) has argued that **fitness**—the likelihood of surviving and reproducing successfully—is increased for those who are preferred by others as social partners in the same way that fitness is increased for those preferred as sexual partners (see also Flinn & Alexander, 2007). We are an ultra-social species, one whose chances of survival rest upon evolutionarily influenced capacities to form strong relationships.

Adaptation

A second important concept is **adaptation**. Adaptations are genetically based traits that allow the organism to cope well with specific selection pressures, and to survive and reproduce. In Table 2.1 we list adaptations that have emerged in the course of human evolution.

Consider our dietary likes and dislikes. The typical human has 10,000 taste buds that allow us to experience sweet, sour, salty and bitter tastes. The preference for sweet tastes helps us identify foods of nutritional value. Plants also contain toxic compounds that deter animals from eating them. They are bitter-tasting and pungent-smelling. When you eat a turnip or cabbage, you are getting a sub-lethal dose of such toxins. Our distaste for bitter foods helps us avoid these toxins (Rozin & Kalat, 1971).

Now let's consider a central problem in evolution: reproducing with healthy mates who are likely to help produce and care for offspring makes these offspring more likely to be healthy, to survive, and to reproduce themselves. Here we see interesting insights into women's and men's romantic attractions. It is disadvantageous to devote resources to the pursuit of mates who might bear unhealthy offspring. As one solution to this problem, humans find symmetrical

Table 2.1   Examples of adaptations

Problem/Pressure	Adaptation
Avoid eating toxins	Distaste for bitterness
Find healthy mate	Perceive facial symmetry as beautiful
Share costs of raising offspring	Preference for male with status, resources
Find fertile mate	Preference for mate with youthful appearance
Protect offspring	Emotional response to baby-like cues

faces more attractive than asymmetrical faces. Exposure to parasites early in development is associated with facial asymmetry, and in more extreme cases, disfiguration. Our preference for facial symmetry, then, may guide us toward potential mates who have been resistant to parasites. Recent evidence suggests that the faces we find beautiful may also seem inherently good to us. Tsukiura and Cabeza (2011) used fMRI scans and found that activity in the medial orbitofrontal cortex, a region involved in the processing of rewards, was increased both by attractiveness and by ratings of goodness of an action, whereas activity in the insular cortex decreased with both attractiveness and ratings of the goodness. Our preferences for people who are physically attractive are bolstered by inferences that they are of good character—both tendencies leading us to attempt to reproduce with individuals with better genes.

The same sort of analysis reveals interesting differences in the triggers of romantic passion in women and men. Because women are the child-bearers, they have to devote more resources to raising children than do men. Women report attraction to men of higher status, who will have more resources (Buss, 1992; Fletcher et al., 2004). If you are a woman, it's probably better to choose a guy who is sweet and resourceful rather than one who is cool and aloof.

For men the problem is different. It is to pass on genes they carry by way of women who are physically healthy and of optimal child-bearing age. So—the argument goes—men are attracted to women with full lips, youthful skin, and an hourglass figure. The effect of having a slim waist in relation to the size of the hips has been confirmed as a signal of female attractiveness in diverse racial groups (Singh et al., 2010), although there are also large cultural differences. Men's experience of attraction also more readily seems to track their physiological responses to sexual images. Chivers et al. (2010) have found that heterosexual men's attraction to pictures of naked women and of heterosexual intercourse correlated strongly with measured blood flow in their genitals. Women were also aroused by such pictures, but they didn't always report they were aroused mentally when they were physiologically. The pressure for women to be choosy, to wait for mates with status and resources, may in part be reflected in this tendency to base less of their sense of attraction on their physiological response (Ogas & Gaddam, 2011).

As a final example of an adaptation, let's consider the human preference for baby-like cues found in the facial features of stuffed animals, anime figures, and other humans. An important determinant of whether one's genes are passed on is survival during infancy (Hrdy, 1999). Human babies are very vulnerable. They require tremendous care, devotion, and resources. Evolutionary theorists have argued that our responses to baby-like cues ensure that parents help their offspring reach the age of viability. The overwhelming love parents feel for their offspring, in response to baby-like features (large forehead, big eyes, small chin), their smiles, coos, and laughs, their smells, and the softness of their skin, overwhelms the many costs of raising children and increases the chances that genes will be passed from one generation to the next. The depth with which people often love their children is remarkable, and this is no doubt due to natural selection.

There are some qualifications to what we have just said. Not all human traits or behaviors are adaptations. Some human traits, from snoring to nervous leg jiggles, serve no apparent evolutionary function and are better thought of as by-products. Moreover, you should not conclude that all, or even most, human traits emerged to meet survival- and reproduction-related problems and opportunities. Evolution is a tinkerer, and often endows old anatomical and behavioral features with new functions. A trait that acquires a new function like this is called an *exaptation*. Andrew (1963, 1965) used this principle to propose how facial expressions in primates, including

Photo Credit: ©Exactostock/SuperStock

FIGURE 2.1 Woman raising her eyebrows in greeting.

humans, were developed from reflexes. Many animals have a reflex in which they flatten their ears when startled or when they approach another member of their species. Its original function was to protect the ears. But as well as being protective the pattern is easily recognized by others: if we think a dog looks friendly, part of this look may be due to the flattened ears. Humans are not able to retract their ears, but raising the eyebrows seems to derive from this same movement, and Eibl-Eibesfeldt (1970) has shown, by inconspicuous filming in many different cultures, that a brief raising of the eyebrows, lasting a fraction of a second, occurs when people approach one another during greeting, and in flirting (see Fig. 2.1). It is probably a human universal.

Natural Design for Gene Replication

So far we have seen that an evolutionary approach would suggest that emotions are adaptations that help humans meet particular selection pressures related to reproduction, survival, and social cooperation.

As you may know, in the nuclei of each of the 100 trillion cells that make up your body are chromosomes. From your parents, you inherited 23 pairs of chromosomes, which contain genes made up of DNA. Altogether, humans have about 25,000 genes, which are responsible for creating proteins in your cells, which in human development come to form the many structures—hands, fingers, facial muscles, circuits in the brain, branches of your peripheral nervous system, the eye, and so on—that make up you. As you will learn in this book, genes also help build the physiological and anatomical systems—neural networks, branches of the peripheral nervous system, muscle groups—that are engaged in emotion.

Here is one counterintuitive notion of evolutionary theory as it has combined with modern genetic theory. Are you ready for it? People tend to think that our genes are in our service, that we have received them from parents and that we pass them on to our children. No! That's completely the wrong way around. Modern evolutionary genetics has taught us that our genes pass themselves on to the next generation. That's their main property: they reproduce themselves. The genes are not ours. Our bodies are their means of passing themselves on.

Based on the DNA from which they are composed, genes replicate. They copy themselves, and the copies become the genetic code for making the structure of plants and animals they will inhabit in the next generation. There is no possibility of humans being immortal, but genes are potentially immortal. Though they combine and recombine, and occasionally mutate, they skip from generation to generation, ever the same. The problem for genes—if one may put it like that—is that they can't survive on their own. They need the body of a plant or animal to contain them and enable them to reproduce. Plants and animals, including ourselves, are the vehicles they use to pass themselves on.

Following from the work of Richard Dawkins (1976), Keith Stanovich (2004) has put this issue in a stark way. As the genes' vehicles, we humans are really robots, programmed by them to behave in certain ways, which by means of natural selection have increased the chances of our survival. The technologies of housing and medicine, which we have developed, have enhanced our abilities to be good robots. With such technologies we make it more likely that the genes will reproduce and leap into the next generation. Now there are seven billion of us genetically constructed to be of the human kind. We're not just doing the job our genes set for us; we're doing it better than might have been imagined. Dawkins is famous for the phrase he used as the title of his 1976 book, *The selfish gene*. But, as Nesse (2006) has pointed out, this phrase doesn't mean that we humans are selfish. Mostly, our socially based adaptation (which helps the genes survive) involves us being decent to each other, and even altruistic (see, for instance, Vaish & Warneken, 2011).

How do the genes program us? You've guessed. A principal way is by our emotions. We humans are very good vehicles. Equipped with the emotion of fear, we protect our bodies by avoiding dangers so the genes we carry will be safe. By being emotionally drawn to food that is nutritious, attracted to sweetness and repelled by bitter-tasting toxins that we reject in disgust, we build our bodies. By being interested in sex—in lust or in love—we enable our genes to pass themselves on to the next generation. By means of the emotion of love for our children, we are enabled to take good care of them. By being decent to each other we create societies in which our children can grow up.

Here is the issue. In some instances our genes program our emotions so closely that when certain events occur we respond in a reflex. In his book of 1872, Darwin described the following experiment upon himself:

> I put my face close to the thick glass-plate in front of a puff-adder in the Zoological Gardens, with the determination of not starting back if the snake struck at me; but, as soon as the blow was struck, my resolution went for nothing, and I jumped a yard or two backwards with astonishing rapidity. My will and reason were powerless against the imagination of a danger which had never been experienced.
>
> (Darwin, 1872/1965, p. 38)

In this reflex the programming of the genes was absolute. The avoidance of striking snakes has been so critical, it seems, that everyone who was our ancestor had it wired in, and so do we, whether or not we ever confront a snake.

Individual emotion: Disgust

On his voyage round the world on the ship *Beagle*, Charles Darwin took copious notes that would set the stage for his theory of evolution. One was about a native of Tierra del Fuego who, he wrote, touched some preserved meat that Darwin was about to eat. Finding the meat was soft, the man made a facial expression of disgust. This expression is now regarded as universal. It involves wrinkling the nose and retracting the upper lip. Darwin said that although the man's hands seemed clean, this quite put him off his lunch.

Disgust is an emotion of rejection, originally of something bitter. In this sense it can be seen as an evolved emotional reaction to potential toxins. But during the course of children's development, it can extend to anything that has been, or may have been, contaminated (Rozin, Haidt, & McCauley, 2008). Disgust, the argument goes, comes to signal to the person that something—a person, action, or idea—is impure and morally wrong.

A study using neuro-imaging by Wicker et al. (2003) showed that the same area of the brain—the anterior insula—is involved both in feeling and in recognizing disgust. The argument is that when we recognize disgust in others, we often do so by generating the experience of disgust in ourselves. Perhaps, for Darwin, it wasn't just the fact that someone he didn't know touched his food that put him off his lunch. It might have been his own feeling of disgust, which mirrored that of the man who touched his preserved meat.

Disgust at the sight of something one would refuse to eat has been found by Chapman et al. (2009) to be exactly the same reaction as that of moral disgust, rejection of an unacceptable or unjust action by another.

This kind of fear response, as shown in Darwin's jumping back from the striking snake, may be the best example of his principle that modern human emotions derive from ancestors who lived in different ways than we do. And in fact many of the simplest and most automatic elements of emotions might be thought of in the same fashion—the soothing touch of a parent in response to a child's distress calls, the wince of disgust in response to a putrid smell, and even the reflex-like arousing of the male sexual organs and felt desire of attraction towards potential sexual partners or even photographs or videos (Tinbergen, 1951).

Of course, these reflexive elements of emotional reactions are situated within complex social relationships and are shaped by a particular culture, as we shall see in the next chapter. Our human purposes can become more important than the purposes of our genes.

So the programming of our emotions and desires by our genes has a range. At one end is the peremptory—the reflex—as with Darwin's leap backward when the snake struck. At the other end are all those attractions and urges that our culture, or we ourselves, can modify. At the closely coupled end, the genes command us. In the middle are emotions like anger and some kinds of fear, which are sometimes compelling but which we can sometimes modify. At the loosely coupled end, genetically based emotions whisper suggestions. In Chapter 14 we discuss how we might deal with the emotions' commands and whispers. We consider how far we might, in the words of Stanovich, be able to take part in "the robots' rebellion," to enable human purposes—our own and those of our species—to become more important than the press of our genes' purposes which have been crafted by millions of years of mammalian evolution.

Perhaps the most striking conclusion from the realization that our genes can program us by way of our emotions is that these effects can occur unconsciously. Unconscious effects—outside our immediate will and occurring for reasons about which we find it difficult to reason—can affect us as emotional biases, impulses, and instinctual urges.

Three Social Motivations and One Antisocial Motivation

How should we understand our evolutionary heritage? The first and most important thing to say is that we humans are social. We come from a line of creatures called mammals, the defining characteristic of which is to be born live (not from eggs) so that during a period when we are unable to fend for ourselves we are given milk and nurtured by parents. In the most social of the mammals—primates (of which we are members)—this early sociality is amplified. Primates live in groups. We humans are not just social, we are hypersocial: we live in families, in societies that have developed cultures (ways of thinking and acting in social collectives).

Some motivations such as curiosity and self-preservation in the face of physical dangers need have no social component. Nevertheless, the key to most human emotions is that they involve others. They enable us to live social lives.

In Chapter 1, we discussed Aristotle's idea that emotions are evaluations of events in relation to goals (motivations). The next step is to say that most of our goals and concerns are social. What are they? This section offers an answer. We propose that there are three primary social motivations and one antisocial motivation.

The social motivations and the antisocial motivation can be thought of as adaptations, selected for during evolution. Understanding these core motivations offers bases for understanding our most important emotions. Our genes have committed us to our hypersocial life, from which there is no escape. Our intense sociality, language, and consciousness have also bequeathed to us possibilities of making meaning of our experience, of being able to express our genetic tendencies creatively in different ways, and of being able to choose among some of our emotions. To learn how to do this is important to being human.

Attachment

The psychological accompaniment of the physiological fact that as babies we are nurtured with milk is **attachment**. The idea of attachment was conceived by John Bowlby (1951), who joined his research on children separated from their parents with the theory of **imprinting**. Konrad Lorenz (1937) conceived the idea of imprinting to describe how, shortly after hatching from their eggs, goslings learn to recognize and follow the first largish, moving, sound-making object in their environment. Usually this is the mother goose, and that's what evolution has arranged: a biological mechanism that enables goslings to keep close to their mothers. But the recognition pattern is not closely specified: if no real mother appears, characteristics of the first crudely plausible moving object are learned instead. In Lorenz's studies, this object was sometimes himself. You may have seen pictures of Lorenz walking across a field followed by a gaggle of goslings who thought he was their mother. The effects are irreversible. Geese imprinted in this way didn't recognize other geese. They made social signals to Lorenz.

Attachment can be thought of as a human form of imprinting. Its function is to protect and care for the infant. The infant and caregiver cooperate to allow the infant to thrive. The human infant is so vulnerable that it would not survive without a caregiver, typically a mother, who is preoccupied with protecting it. For our evolutionary forbears, threats to the infant included predators. Nowadays, parents worry about germs, busy streets, and falling down stairs.

Even with parental protection, early childhood remains the most vulnerable period of life. Attachment keeps the mother close by, or ready to be summoned by crying. Bowlby also

Table 2.2 Ainsworth's (1967) list of attachment behaviors

1. Differential crying (i.e., with mother as compared with others)

2. Differential smiling

3. Differential vocalization

4. Crying when the mother leaves

5. Following the mother

6. Visual motor orientation toward the mother

7. Greeting through smiling, crowing, and general excitement

8. Lifting arms in greeting the mother

9. Clapping hands in greeting the mother

10. Scrambling over the mother

11. Burying the face in the mother's lap

12. Approach to the mother through locomotion

13. Embracing, hugging, kissing the mother (not seen in Ugandan infants but observed frequently in infants in Western societies)

14. Exploration away from the mother as a secure base

15. Flight to the mother as a haven of safety

16. Clinging to the mother

proposed the idea of the mother as a **secure base**. When the baby starts to move about, he or she can explore the features of the new environment when the mother is present: the baby can retreat to her if necessary, and she keeps a watchful eye open. The functioning of the mother as a secure base continues into adolescence (Allen et al., 2003). Trust, of the kind emphasized by attachment theorists as well as theorists of stages of emotional development (e.g., Erikson, 1950, 1959), includes confidence that one is, and can continue to be, safe.

Mary Ainsworth (1967) made naturalistic studies of babies and mothers in Uganda, where she discerned a set of behavior patterns that young children showed when they were with their mothers but did not show with anyone else. Her list of attachment behaviors is in Table 2.2.

When an infant's mother is present there is a sense of security, and a distinctive set of actions occurs. When the mother is absent, entirely different actions occur. Comparable attachment patterns can be seen in different societies. They serve the vital function of keeping close to the mother, and of keeping her nearby, ready to protect the infant from any and all threats (Bowlby, 1971).

Attachment does not stop here. Bowlby thought that love (by which he meant attachment) in the early years was as important for emotional development as proper nutrition is for physical development. Among his ideas was that the attachment relationship of infancy creates a template for all later intimate relationships, and he coined the term **affectional bonds**. Here's what he said:

> Affectional bonds and subjective states of strong emotion tend to go together, as every novelist and playwright knows. Thus, many of the most intense of all human emotions arise during the formation, the maintenance, the disruption, and the renewal of

affectional bonds—which, for that reason, are sometimes called emotional bonds. In terms of subjective experience, the formation of a bond is described as falling in love, maintaining a bond as loving someone, and losing a partner as grieving over someone.

(Bowlby, 1979, p. 69)

Try this little experiment on yourself. Think about the 16 attachment-related behaviors listed by Ainsworth in Table 2.2. Now, imagine that instead of being patterns of infants with their mothers, these are descriptions of interaction between two adult lovers. Do the patterns fit? Do lovers show differential smiling and vocalization with each other, do they follow each other, gaze at each other, do they show distress at separation? If so, might this support Bowlby's hypothesis that adult love is formed on a template of the infant attachment relationship? Intimations of the idea were put by Darwin (1872), who supposed that the infant pattern of holding and being held is elaborated in adult caressing. Adult romantic love and sexuality, according to this idea, is an elaboration upon universal, evolved, behavioral patterns of earlier life.

Assertion

Another kind of social motivation, the first in order of its emergence during evolution, is **assertion**, or **power**. We human beings live in status hierarchies. Such hierarchies have arisen in many parts of the animal world; for instance, male lobsters fight when they first encounter each other, and the one who wins becomes dominant. Subordinate lobsters recognize the dominants and grovel if they meet them again. Dominance hierarchies, among the lobsters and many other animals, are structures of competition that give preferential access to sexual partners, food, and other resources to those who are high in the hierarchy.

Hierarchies occur in much of what we humans do, in the academy, in sports, in politics, and in music. Each, it seems, must have its number-one, top person. Think of the word *loser*, oozing with contempt. If you are skeptical about the importance of hierarchy in human history, look at the monumental architecture in the world's civilizations: the pyramids in Egypt and the Mayan Empire, the ziggurats of Mesopotamia, and even the cathedrals of medieval Europe, all built to inspire awe and to let us know how great were those whose influence was spread from them.

Although status and power are important among humankind, in most societies power for most people is carefully regulated, for instance, by fear of revenge or the possibility of peril to one's personal reputation (Miller, 2006), and, in modern times, the law. Power often has responsibilities, for instance, of a parent to care for children. In this way it's an accompaniment of the social motivation of attachment. There is also the responsibility of a teacher to care for and teach students, the responsibility of an employer to pay and maintain benefits for employees, the responsibility of a superior to protect the rights of an inferior, and the responsibility of police to protect the public.

Assertion is the motivation to move upward in the social hierarchy, and to resist challenges from those who would move us downward. It is the motivation of competition and of conflict. Shame is the social emotion of having one's social status diminished. So important is maintaining one's status that Scheff (1997) calls shame the master emotion. But it's often taboo to talk about it. A good part of our emotional life, as we shall see in Chapter 9, seems to be devoted to maintaining our sense of ourselves, maintaining our status.

Affiliation

The third human social motivation is **affiliation**, which can also be called **affection**. In their discussion of functions of social motivations, Goldberg, Grusec, and Jenkins (1999) concluded that alongside the protective functions of attachment, which one can see from the earliest time in the relationships of parents and their babies, there is another function that is separable but equally important: the system of affiliation, warmth, and affection. Affiliation and warmth are fundamentally important in human development, but they involve different processes than those of protection (MacDonald, 1992). For example, Fox and Davidson (1987) found that babies seeing their mothers approaching with open arms showed joy and an activation of the left side of the frontal cortex. The system activated here is part of affiliation. By contrast, distress on separation from a caregiver involved not so much a reduction of such activation, but changes in a separate system, on the right side of the cortex. MacDonald (1992) also points out that although attachment occurs among all primates, only some species form affectional bonds based on warmth.

MacDonald (1992) and Goldberg et al. (1999) hypothesized that the separate systems of attachment and affiliative warmth can be differently prioritized in different cultures. The system of affiliation and warmth is built on positive reward, and it is closely associated with the system of touch. We touch and hug those to whom we feel affectionate. Clark and Finkel (2005) have written about affiliation in terms of what they call communal relating (caring) as opposed to relating in terms of exchange, such as "I'll do this for you if you do that for me," which has a more commercial quality. People express more emotions in relationships that are communal (i.e., caring relationships). Whereas assertion is the motivation to compete, affiliation is the motivation to cooperate.

You might think that sex would be among our strongest social motivations. In a sense it is. But whereas, as we'll discuss below, sexuality among our relatives the chimpanzees is usually a somewhat perfunctory business, among us humans it's very much bound up with love, and love is very much bound up, as we said earlier, with the motivation of attachment, and also, as we'll explain here, with the motivation of affiliation, warmth, and cooperativeness. As Djikic and Oatley (2004) explain, the evolved motivation of sexuality becomes, by combining with these other evolved motivations, a state in which sexual partners can bestow love on each other.

One way in which this works is that human sexual partners often cooperate to raise children. In evolutionary terms it is likely that the elaboration started with the joining of the affiliative-warmth system to the reproductive one, according to the **male provisioning hypothesis** (Lovejoy, 1981). Lovejoy argued that the critical evolutionary moves occurred when humans started to walk upright when, with the formation of specialized feet, infants could no longer cling to their mothers as ape babies do, so that mothers had to devote more resources to tending them. At the same time, males started to make a contribution to the rearing of specific infants. This was enabled by movement away from the promiscuity characteristic of apes, among whom it's not known who the fathers of any infants are because females copulate with many of the males in their group. In humans, long-lasting sexual relationships between specific human females and specific human males began: **pair-bonding**, which is rare among other primates. A pair-bonded male and female maintain a lasting sexual interest in each other. The effort a male puts into supporting a child is likely to benefit the genes he carries. In return for her exclusive sexual attention—so the idea goes—the female acquires from the male resources to contribute to child rearing. There'll be a good deal more discussion of human sexuality and love in Chapters 3 and 9.

Human infancy is so long and so demanding that it strains the resources of a single caregiver. The human family—a woman, her offspring, and, typically, a male partner—are bound together by emotions of affection. The demands of raising offspring, and group living more generally, often require cooperation with non-kin as well (Hrdy, 1999), and have given rise to forms of affection that are the bases of friendships.

Affection and cooperation in humans are not just related to sexuality. Cooperation of every kind, being able to do things together that we cannot do alone, friendship, teamwork, are all fundamental aspects of human life, all influenced by evolution (Nesse, 2010). Although inklings of these abilities occur in the apes, in humans they have come to represent central aspects of who we are.

Emotions in the Space of Three Social Motivations

We can think of social emotions as managing social goals and as moving us in a three-dimensional space of the three primary social motivations, as shown in Figure 2.2. In Chapter 9, we will see how these three social motivations exert powerful influences upon our emotions. Typical positive emotions associated with the presence of an attachment figure are trust, comfort, and reassurance, while loss of such a figure produces anxiety and distress. The typical emotion of assertion is anger, while loss of status is accompanied by shame or embarrassment and other emotions of deference. Typical positive emotions associated with affiliation are affection, warmth, and liking, whereas loss of someone for whom one felt

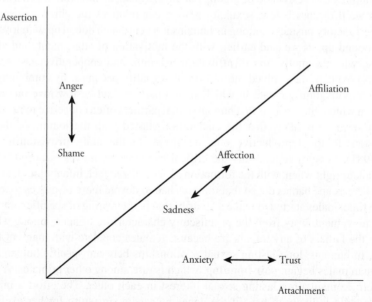

FIGURE 2.2 Jenkins's and Oatley's schema of three principal social motivations—attachment, assertion, and affiliation—as orthogonal dimensions, with emotions represented by lines with arrows as movements in this three-dimensional space.

affection produces sadness and grieving. The three social dimensions of attachment, assertion, and affiliation are depicted in Figure 2.2.

Antisocial Motivation

Attachment, assertion, and affiliation are not the only motivations of human social life. Evolution has also bequeathed us an antisocial motivation of **hostility**: to exclude, to denigrate, and sometimes even to destroy others in rivalries or in war. Among the emotions associated with this motivation are contempt and hatred. It seems to be an aspect of humankind's remarkable capacity for emotional bonding cooperatively within **in-groups** that people who are not in these groups, who are members of **out-groups**, can become targets of prejudice, cruelty, and even genocide (cf. Sober & Wilson, 1998).

The evolutionary origin of this kind of motivation can be glimpsed from studies of chimpanzees, for instance, by Goodall (1986). She records how among the chimpanzees she was studying in the wild, in Gombe, Tanzania (an area of rugged forest about the size and shape of Manhattan), a small contingent formed a separate community. It was with profound shock that, in 1974, researchers saw gangs of the larger northern community start to patrol, attack, and kill members of the southern group if they came across them either alone or in numerically weaker groups in the forest.

The smaller contingent, which had tended to range south of Goodall's camp, had six adult males. Though the two sub-communities met occasionally, for example, to get fruit at Goodall's camp, and though some inter-individual contacts were sometimes friendly, in general, the two groups were tense on meeting. They started to avoid each other. Finally, southern males stopped visiting the camp. Violent episodes began. Northern males, who would patrol their borders, started to make incursions into the southern range. On one occasion a group of six adult males, an adolescent male, and a female came across a southern male on his own. He tried to flee but was caught by the northern males. While one held him, the other males beat him with fists for about 10 minutes, and one bit him several times. When they left him he was severely wounded, and although his body was never found, he was presumed to have died from his injuries. One by one, all the other adult animals of the southern group, including a female, were killed in like manner. Adolescent females from the southern group joined the northern group. The attacks were clearly meant to kill: they lasted longer than fights within a community and included biting and tearing flesh of the kind seen when eating animals of other species. Attacks were not caused by victims being strangers. Some had previously been friends of some of the attackers.

Annihilating the southern community seemed not predominantly territorial. Hostilities seemed to have more to do with the southerners becoming an out-group: "them," no longer "us."

The emotional preference for "us" and hostility to "them" seems to be an inherited human universal. It can be seen, for instance, in Tajfel's studies (Tajfel & Turner, 1979), which consist of assigning people, such as schoolchildren, to groups randomly (that is to say, meaninglessly) and finding that people give preference to other members of the group of which they had been told they were members (the in-group). This occurred even when those asked to describe their preferences did not know who else was a member of the in-group or the out-group, and even when their actions and preferences had no effect on themselves.

The ancient Stoics thought that the most dangerous emotion, the one most important to subdue, was anger—in particular, rage. From our modern perspective, it's our antisocial motivation of hostility and related emotions like contempt and social disgust and hatred that are our biggest handicap as a social species. It's an evolutionarily bequeathed tendency to genocidal aggression and uncaring contempt for others whom we see as different from ourselves, even though we are fundamentally the same. These others can include people of different skin color, people of different religion, people who live in different places. Not only does this tendency erupt time and again in war and genocide, it operates in our inability to care much about others who are less well-off in our own society, or others among whom our own children and grandchildren will live, to whom we will bequeath environments that we have not looked after with care. As we think about building stronger, more cooperative societies, it is the emotions of hatred and its cognates on which we need most urgently to reflect, and with which we need to come into a thoughtful relationship.

Why Human Emotions Are As They Are

We have just considered four core motives that shape human emotional life. Let's now place these motivations within an evolutionary framework and begin to develop an evolutionary approach to the emotions, as adaptations that have helped us meet selection pressures during evolution (Tooby & Cosmides, 1990; Nesse, 1990; Nesse & Ellsworth, 2009). To give specific meaning to this analysis, evolutionary theorists situate emotions within the **environment of evolutionary adaptedness**, a description of the environment to which human emotions became adapted as our species evolved during the six million years since the human line branched off from the line that led to chimpanzees and bonobos. The primary thing to say is that this was a social environment of humans living in groups of the kind we now see as extended families. The idea that there was just one physical environment is, however, misleading. An important theory, due to Potts (1998), is that human adaptation is to varying physical environments due to severe climate changes that have occurred in the past six million years. Adaptation to variability has given a selective advantage to flexibility and versatility as human characteristics.

Evolutionary theorists have relied on several kinds of evidence to explain why human emotions are as they are. In the following three subsections we consider three: the social lives of our relatives the chimpanzees and bonobos; human ancestry; and contemporary human societies who live in ways that may be like those of early humans. These three kinds of evidence suggest a conclusion that is central to this book. The story of human emotions is the story of lives that are intensely social. With our social emotions we have developed families, technologies, and cultures based on cooperation and competition and on preferences for our own social groups. Our sociality is the key not just to the success of our species but to what we most value in life.

Social Lives of Chimpanzees

Evidence of our relatedness to other animals is now extensive. Anatomical and behavioral correspondences provide qualitative indications. With the new science of genomics, the genetic code of a chimpanzee has been worked out and compared with the genetic code of humans (Chimpanzee Sequencing and Analysis Consortium, 2005). The divergence of our DNA from that of chimpanzees is about 4%. One needs to be a bit careful with this kind of estimate; for instance, we share a good deal of our DNA with lettuce, which has many of the same mechanisms by which all living cells work.

Significant figure: Jane Goodall

Apart from Charles Darwin, no one has done more to explore the relatedness of humans to our primate relatives than Jane Goodall. Encouraged and mentored by palaeontologist Louis Leakey, Goodall studied chimpanzees in Gombe, in Tanzania. She did a PhD at Cambridge, based on her early observations—one of a tiny number of people who have been allowed to do so without first having a bachelor's degree.

Goodall's important work, published in her 1986 book, *The Chimpanzees of Gombe*, was to document the lives of chimpanzees as individuals with distinctive personalities, distinctive emotions, and distinctive relationships with each other. First, she realized that she had to gain their trust. This involved sitting for hours close to groups, until they became used to her and tolerated her presence. She realized that she had to learn to identify each one as an individual and give each a name. As well as following particular individuals for many days and recording their activities, she made observations on groups.

It was Goodall who first identified chimpanzees' abilities to hunt small monkeys and share and eat them. It was she who saw that chimpanzee emotions were very much like human emotions, including the antisocial emotions involved in killing members of groups of their own species who had separated themselves from the main group.

Today, Goodall is an advocate for chimpanzees as an endangered species, and an advocate, also, for looking after our Earth and its habitats.

What do we learn about the emotions of chimpanzees? Answers emerge from the work of people like Jane Goodall (1986) and her colleagues, who spent many years observing chimpanzees in Gombe, Tanzania. Goodall describes a family that includes Melissa, her daughter Gremlin, and Gremlin's infant Getty, who:

> dangles above his mother, twirling, kicking his legs, and grabbing at his toes. From time to time Gremlin reaches up, idly, tickling his groin. After a few minutes he climbs away . . . [then] suddenly drops down, plop, on her belly. With a soft laugh his grandmother holds him close.
>
> (Goodall, 1986, p. 594)

Goodall then describes how Getty goes to lie beside his mother, and suckles her. Then comes a noise of pant-hoots from the other side of the valley. It is Evered, probably in his nest. Another young member of Melissa's family, Gimble, holds her arm as he sits up and looks towards the sound. He starts an answering chorus, because Evered is one of his heroes.

With such observations, Goodall documented many chimpanzee emotions: apprehension at a stranger, fear at an aggressive interaction, distress when lost, annoyance at a bothersome juvenile, anger in a fight, and mourning following the death of a parent, which could lead to immobility and death. Goodall also catalogued emotional displays, including threats made with bared teeth, hair standing on end during excitement (sexual or aggressive), a pant-grunt indicating social apprehension, squeaking and screaming indicating fear, angry barks, distressed whimpers, laughter and panting that accompany the enjoyment of play and body contact, and pant-hoots and roars that accompany social excitement.

These expressions are bases of distinctive patterns of interaction. So, when they find a tree with a lot of fruit on it, chimpanzees pant-hoot. Others come to the spot and everyone eats together with infectious enjoyment. In maternal–infant interactions, in the play of juveniles, and in reconciliations there is affectionate body contact, touching, stroking, and hugging. If an animal is hurt, it screams a distinctive SOS call, which summons others to its aid. When patrolling their range, groups of males are tense and alert to sounds, and they become excited when they attack an animal from outside their community.

Attachment and the Mother–Infant Bond

As we described above, attachment is a process of protection, and it's seen strongly among chimpanzees. Hirata (2009) has reviewed the literature on ways in which, in addition, chimpanzee mothers share food with infants, sometimes offering them preferred food. Chimpanzee mothers have also been observed teaching their infants and helping them in other ways, all evidence of concern, or as we might say, love.

Assertion and Hierarchy

Chimpanzee social life is hierarchical. Hierarchies in mammals generally enable group members to decide quickly and relatively peacefully how to allocate resources. Along with rules associated with reciprocity, they provide heuristic solutions to problems of distributing resources, such as mating opportunities, food, and social attention, and the labor required of collective endeavors (De Waal, 2005; Fiske, 2010).

Among chimpanzees the **alpha male** is the individual to whom all others defer. He may win his position by defeating the previous holder, and reinforce his position with intimidation displays that might involve charging, pulling branches, throwing stones, and making a great din (Goodall, 1992). Occasionally, there are overt fights. But often the alpha may not be the largest male. He may be the one who is most skilled at making alliances with others, especially females. The alpha male usually holds his position for several years. Other males have a status in a rough hierarchy below him. Females, too, have a parallel hierarchy. Animals of both sexes defend their position, or challenge to ascend the hierarchy, usually by angry threats sometimes backed by overt fights, which often occur after two animals at about the same level in the hierarchy have not met for an interval.

Chimpanzees eat mainly fruit, but will hunt opportunistically for small animals such as cebus monkeys or piglets they may come across in the forest. When chimpanzees make a kill, high-ranking animals tend to get more of the food, even if they took no part in the catch (Nishida et al., 1992). High-status chimpanzees do not monopolize the food; they have sophisticated rules for sharing food (Boesch & Boesch, 1989; De Waal, 1996). In his observations of over 5,000 incidents of food sharing, De Waal found that chimps systematically shared with other chimps who had shared with them, as well as with other chimps who had groomed them earlier in the day. Chimpanzees trade and reciprocate. High-ranking individuals also spend a good part of their time breaking up the conflicts of lower-status chimps.

In reviewing the large ethological and cross-cultural literature on this topic, Eales (1992) concluded that gestures of appeasement and submission to those of higher status are inherited universals among higher primates, including humans. They include looking downward, hunching the body, averting or lowering the gaze, immobility, and facial expressions of fear.

Affiliation and Cooperation

Mother and infant chimpanzees spend a good amount of time in play; we mentioned earlier an instance recorded by Goodall (1986).

Young chimpanzees play with each other. Play is an activity in which mammals, but perhaps not other kinds of animals, take part. It is affiliative, affectionate, and cooperative. It involves laughter and humor. Panksepp (2005) has argued that play is subserved by a particular brain system, and that it facilitates the development of pro-social behavior.

De Waal (1996, 2008) has studied how chimpanzees reconcile following conflicts, how they share food, and how they come to the aid of other chimps in distress. And chimpanzees do things for others in their group, which don't confer any advantage on them individually. De Waal has catalogued remarkable acts of caregiving. Chimpanzees, baboons, and macaques become intensely distressed when they witness harm to other group members. Primates take care of vulnerable individuals. For example, monkeys, like humans, are sometimes born blind, which exposes the blind monkey to numerous dangers, ranging from falling out of trees to straying from the group. De Waal observes that other monkeys in the group will take on the burden of protecting the blind monkey and helping with such activities as feeding. Caregiving is a way of life in our primate relatives.

De Waal has also observed how pairs of chimpanzees or macaques behaved after angry conflicts. He compared those behaviors with how the same pairs behaved during calmer, less strife-ridden times. He discovered that previous antagonists were actually more likely to remain in physical proximity with one another, and they would reconcile with each other (see the photo at the head of this chapter). Sometimes the aggressor initiates reconciliation, sometimes it's the defeated animal. In the latter case, he or she would approach with trepidation and engage in submissive behaviors, like bare-teeth displays, head bowing and bobbing, and submissive grunts. This eventually would lead to affectionate grooming, physical contact, and even embraces that would repair the social bonds (De Waal, 2000).

Even though sexual encounters are pretty quick in chimpanzees, they involve cooperation. Once they are sexually mature at age 15, female chimpanzees advertise their sexual receptiveness by a large pink patch of sexual skin (the labia). During the period of receptiveness, typically lasting 10 days out of the 36-day menstrual cycle, a female may copulate several dozen times a day, with all or most of the adult males in her social group. Alternatively, she may go off with a single male consort, away from the rest of the community. Aggression and jockeying for access to female chimpanzees are common among male chimpanzees. Sexual harassment of females by males and even rape are not unknown, but usually females choose whom they mate with and when. Mothers raise infants more or less on their own. Males make contributions to the community, but not to individual offspring.

Bonobos are a kind of chimpanzee, now recognized as a separate species, possibly more closely related to humans than the species of common chimpanzee. They are less aggressive than common chimpanzees, and their social lives seem to revolve around sex (Kano, 1992; De Waal, 1995). Bonobo females are sexually active for about five years before they become fertile. They are receptive for more than half the time in each menstrual cycle. They copulate freely with many of the adult males in their social group. Female and male homosexual relations are also common. Younger males often engage in sexual activity with older females in what might be thought of as sexual initiation play. Sexual contact among bonobos is the basis of friendships, conflict reduction, and play.

Antisocial Acts among Chimpanzees

In an earlier section of this chapter we described Goodall's (1986) observations of how groups of chimpanzees sought and killed members of a neighboring group. Because of the criticism that distribution of fruit at Goodall's camp might have triggered this kind of behavior, which otherwise would not have occurred, it is significant that killing of adult chimpanzees has been observed elsewhere, in circumstances where this criticism cannot be made (Boesch, Head, Tagg, Arandjelovic, Vigilant et al., 2007). So, although chimpanzees can be, and often are, aggressive to their companions, it is an entirely different kind of motivation that leads chimpanzees to kill members of their own species.

Selfishness and Deception

So far we have described evolutionary bases of social life, but of course individual behavior and selfish behavior occur, too. Primatologists have indeed found that, like ourselves, chimpanzees spend a good deal of the time acting selfishly, for instance, in disputes over status. Among the most interesting aspects of selfish behavior are acts of deception, which involve understanding others, which we discuss in Chapter 8. Call and Tomasello (2008) concluded that chimpanzees don't really understand their fellow chimpanzees as having beliefs, wants, and feelings, but they do understand that others have certain perceptions and goals, and this enables them to deceive others.

Animal Emotions

Do chimpanzees really have emotions? Or could it be that real emotions are entirely human? The argument might be that, because we can't ask the animals, we will never know. But this is not the view of most biologists, starting with Darwin, who observed clear continuities between human emotions and those of other animals.

In an interview, De Waal (Wonderlance.com, 2011) has said:

> Animals probably have many of the same emotions that we have. This is assumed in many brain studies, in which rats or monkeys show expressions of fear or anger when parts of the brain are stimulated that also in humans are active when we feel fear or anger. So, neuroscientists generally have no trouble assuming similar emotions in humans and other mammals even though in the eyes of so-called behaviorists this is still very much taboo. . . . If a baboon female returns a week after the disappearance of her offspring to the spot where it happened to climb high up into a tree and scan the environment while uttering plaintive contact calls, repeating her agitation and calling for weeks every time her troop passes through this specific area, it is hard for the human observer not to assume a sense of loss or grieving.

Panksepp (2005) has argued that our emotions derive from the neurodynamics of brain systems that generate instinctual emotional behavior in other mammals. As we have proposed in Chapter 1, emotions are based on action tendencies, urges to act in this way or that, and Panksepp identifies a set of these that are sufficiently important for him to name with capital letters. They include: SEEKING, FEAR, RAGE, LUST, CARE, PANIC, and PLAY. These systems have been elaborated as mammals evolved, and have reached their most elaborate versions in the lives of social primates such as chimpanzees and ourselves.

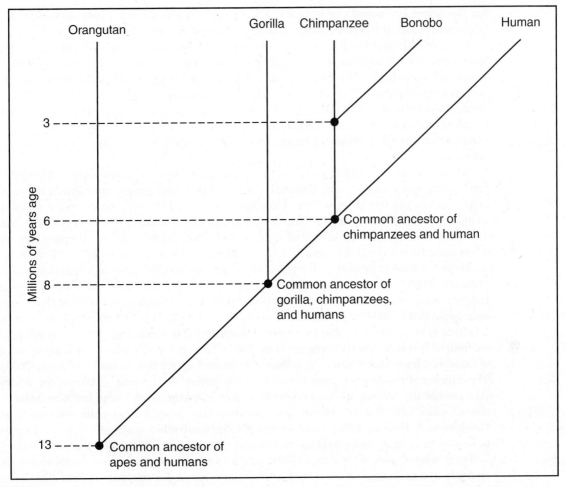

FIGURE 2.3 Human relatedness to the apes, showing how the line that led to humans split from that leading to orangutans about 13 million years ago, and split from the line leading to chimpanzees about six million years ago.

Human Ancestry

The way we live now with cars, cell-phones, and friends on Facebook is very different from the environments in which human emotions evolved. Wilson and Cann (1992) estimated that 200,000 years ago was the time when the common forbears of all living human beings—our ancestral Eves—lived in Africa. Processes that today are essential to life, such as deriving food from agriculture, began only some 10,000 to 12,000 years ago (Diamond, 1997). Shortly afterward, came the invention of cities as centers of trade (Leick, 2001). In such movements, the evolution of human cultures overtook the evolution of species. If we take the 10,000 years of civilizations, this is just 5% of the period since the ancestral Eves lived, and a quarter of a percent of the period since our separation from chimpanzees. In other words, the majority of our differentiation from ape-like beings into humans took place in a world that was very different from our world today. One constant over the period since human species began has been our intense sociality.

It seems likely that the family was important to our ancestors in their nomadic lives. The human family is a group that often includes both sexes and individuals of all ages, living with a female and her offspring. In the group there is usually at least one adult male, most often the woman's sexual partner. The extended family group typically includes other relatives, such as siblings, older offspring, and their sexual partners who have joined the family from other groups. (A taboo on incest, and social mechanisms for people to marry outside the family, are other human universals.) By contrast, a chimpanzee or bonobo family is a female and a small group of her offspring.

One human pattern is that of groups of 10 to 20 people living closely as an extended family, as scavenger-hunter-gatherers, and frequently meeting other such groups who shared the same range. Such people would know about 150 others (Dunbar, 1993, 2004), to some of whom they would be related as kin. Flint tools have been found from two-and-a-half million years ago, and they imply an emotional engagement of acquiring and exercising the skills to make them. The use of fire started about 700,000 years ago, and one can imagine it was used not just for warmth, but for preparing food to be shared. Language arose perhaps 200,000 years ago (Henshilwood & Dubreuil, 2009), and with it came the emotion-based arts of conversation, disputation, gossip, and the making of joint plans. A factory for making ochre, used for painting bodies or objects, has been found that is 100,000 years old (Henshilwood, D'Errico, Van Niekerk, Coquinot, Jacobs, Lauritzen et al., 2011). The oldest art objects, shells drilled to make beads for personal display, are from 82,000 years ago (Bouzouggar et al., 2007). The emotionally important communication of music is at least 43,000 years old as shown by the finding of a flute of that age (Huron, 2003). The evidence of ritual burials from around the same period (Bowler et al., 2003) implies that by then emotionally moving stories were being told of people who were dead but alive again on another plane. The earliest known cave paintings date from 31,000 years ago (Chauvet, Deschamps, & Hillaire, 1996). Attraction to paintings and other works of art is now thought to be subject to emotionally evolved preferences (Kawabata & Zeki, 2004; Dutton, 2009).

The making of tools, the making of fire to prepare food, the use of language, and the making of art are human universals (Brown, 1991). All are innovations that mark us off from other living primates. All are social. All have emotional aspects.

Among the concerns of early hominid groups were demands of raising offspring (Hrdy, 1999). A critically important evolutionary step was the emergence of monogamy (discussed above). It led to division of labor, which meant that men could scavenge and hunt and bring home meat.

Although the proportion of societies (like Western ones) where monogamy is official policy is only 16% among a total of 853 societies sampled (Van den Berghe, 1979), and although extramarital activities are not uncommon in most societies, in practice monogamy is a very common sexual pattern. Even in societies where one male can have several wives, this pattern is practiced only by a few men who have large resources. The emotional accompaniment of the adoption of monogamy is jealousy, which tends to occur when the pair-bond is threatened by an interloper (Dunbar, 2004).

Evolution of Language

Perhaps the most important species-typical characteristic of humans that distinguishes us from our nonhuman relatives is language. Robin Dunbar (1993, 2003, 2004) has observed that chimpanzees and other primates use grooming to maintain social bonds. Grooming makes up a fair amount of all social interaction, and chimpanzees spend about 20% of their waking time doing it. In this activity, they sit quietly and affectionately with another individual, taking turns picking through each other's hair. Dunbar's hypothesis is that laughter and conversation have replaced grooming as the glue that holds society together. Conversation is the verbal equivalent of grooming. As compared with manual grooming, which can be performed with only one other at a time, we can converse with more than one person and also while we are doing something else, like preparing food or walking. The huge increase in the size of the human neocortex in comparison with the neocortex of chimpanzees is thought to have occurred because in our highly social lives we build and maintain mental models of about 150 people whom we know, models that we elaborate in conversation. This compares with the much simpler models of up to 50 individuals in their social groups that chimpanzees have to maintain. We humans recognize others as like ourselves. We have a theory of mind: we can think about what others might be thinking and we can know some of what others know. In addition, we can share intentions. These are abilities beyond anything chimpanzees can manage (Tomasello, 1999, 2008).

Conversational language replaced grooming, argues Dunbar, because manual grooming of all the individuals with whom we need to maintain friendly relationships in a maximum group size of about 150 would vastly have exceeded the 20% of their time that chimpanzees devote to grooming, with their group size of 50. The far larger group size of 150 (of humans and human ancestors) could not have been achieved by manual grooming during evolution, because this kind of grooming in the larger group would have made too much of an incursion into the time required for the other activities necessary to sustain primate life.

Photo Credit: ©Frans Lanting/©Corbis

FIGURE 2.4 Two chimpanzees grooming. Dunbar's hypothesis is that in humans this emotionally intimate activity, which functions to maintain friendly relationships, has been replaced by conversation.

Human brains became enlarged in part due to the growth of regions of the cortex that allow us to have mental models of people in our social group, and in addition, conversational language allowed us to discuss what these others might know, how they feel, and how to do things together. Language does not replace communication by glance, facial expression, or gesture; it augments it. With language we can share aspects of emotions with others and understand their emotional minds in ways far beyond anything that occurs among our primate cousins. In the next chapter we will discuss how language and culture work to shape the raw materials of biologically based emotions.

Conflict between Groups

During the six million years since the human divergence from the chimpanzee line, some 20 different hominid species are known from the fossil record. Some may have been our forebears. The last hominid species to have become extinct was of the Neanderthals, who died out 28,000 years ago. Did competition and the superior technology of our ancestors drive the Neanderthals into extinction because our ancestors made war against the out-group?

Reviewing the paleontological evidence of contact between anatomically modern humans (our ancestors) and Neanderthals, Mellars (2004) concludes that there was:

> Direct competition for space and resources between the two populations, in which the demonstrably more complex technology and apparently more complex organization of the anatomically modern populations would have given them a strong competitive advantage over the Neanderthals. (p. 464)

Before their extinction, Neantherthals were the hominid inhabitants of Europe. Then there was an influx—should one say colonization?—by anatomically modern humans who, just before the extinction of Neanderthals, came to outnumber them by 10 to 1 (Mellars & French, 2011). Recent genetic evidence indicates that some Neanderthals interbred with humans, but the question remains as to whether the Neanderthals, in general, were driven to extinction by our ancestors.

Now that we are the sole surviving hominid species, we show ourselves all too ready to draw on our antisocial motivation and to turn our genocidal capacity on ourselves. We descendants of these early humans are willing to make war against out-groups, combining aggression with the latest technology. The prehistory of war is not a jockeying in hierarchies within our social group. It is based on emotions of in-groups, of contempt, cruelty, and hostility, directed at members of out-groups, who may differ from the in-groups in ways that are of no more importance than skin color.

Though we are used to thinking of war as politics by other means, the military historian, John Keegan (1994), is more blunt. He says that war is a very emotional matter. It's based on an urge to kill others whom we see as different from ourselves.

Modern Hunter-Gatherer Societies

We can get another glimpse of the origins of human emotions by asking what is known about existing cultures of **hunter-gatherers**. In Australia and in the savannas of southern Africa, some people have continued the hunter-gatherer way of life into modern times. This was the way of life of the San of the Kalahari, who include the !Kung and the G/wi. (Their languages include clicks: "!" designates a click made by drawing the tongue sharply away from the roof of the mouth, and / is made by drawing the tongue away from the front teeth, like the *tsk* of scolding.) Lorna Marshall and her family lived among them in the 1950s (Marshall, 1976; Thomas, 1989). In the 1960s and 1970s, Lee (1984) and other American anthropologists visited these peoples.

Until its recent erosion by Western influences, !Kung and G/wi peoples lived in a semi-desert land, and traveled over a range of several hundred square miles that they knew intimately. Thomas describes the G/wi as small and lithe, living in extended families. In their travels they met other families to whom they were related by blood or marriage. Around a fire, the G/wi scooped out shallow impressions in the ground to sleep in. The women especially were expert botanists: they gathered roots and other vegetable foods from the land, and obtained fluid from tsama melons. The men hunted and shot animals with bows and arrows tipped with poison made from a grub. They may have had to follow a shot antelope for a day before it died. It was brought back to camp, and there were complex rules about how it was divided. Nothing was wasted.

It is probable that for a long period since their descent from the ancestral Eves of 200,000 years ago, *Homo sapiens* lived in semi-nomadic hunter-gatherer groups of 10 to 30 people, in extended families, and meeting other groups from time to time, much like the G/wi and !Kung. Many of our emotions, then, may be adapted to living in this way—ranging over different environments, cooperating, though with division of labor, in obtaining, preparing, and sharing food, and in rearing and protecting children.

Photo Credit: ©John Warburton-Lee Photography/Alamy

FIGURE 2.5 Group of !Kung hunter-gatherers.

Emotions as Bases of Human Relationships

We have seen that genes use emotions to program the human vehicles that carry them. In some cases the programming is mandatory, as with Darwin finding himself unable to avoid springing backward at the zoo when a puff adder struck at him. As we move across the range, we find that some emotions can still affect us strongly even when they are not reflexes. Strong anxieties and strong angers are difficult to modulate. In the center of the range, the emotions of sexual attraction and sexual functioning, essential for genes' replication, are important for us humans, too, but for us they can be modulated both by culture and the individual. At the far end of the range, some genes whisper to us, to suggest preferences for a piece of music, or a piece of visual art, or a novel or film. In this we may have the most choice.

From our primate relatives, from the fossil records of human ancestry, and from studies of modern hunter-gatherers, we learn that emotions structure interactions in ways that enable people to live in social groups. The varying environments of evolutionary adaptedness were defined not primarily by physical factors, but by social characteristics: sexual attachments, caregiving for offspring, hierarchies that regulate allocation of resources, cooperation within groups, and hostility to certain members of other groups. As Oatley (2004c) put it, projecting backward from current emotional patterns, our environments of evolutionary adaptedness must have been ones:

> in which people were made happy by being with friends, close relatives, lovers. Just as now, our ancestors were concerned for their children, concerned that friends and loved ones liked them, upset if something, or someone, they valued was lost or taken. (pp. 28–29)

In Table 2.3 we summarize contributions to understanding how emotions arose in our forbears and continue today (Bowlby, 1971; Ekman, 1992; Frank, 1988; Izard, 1971, 1977; Keltner & Haidt, 1999, 2001; Nesse, 1990; Oatley, 1992, 2004; Plutchik, 1991; Tooby & Cosmides, 1990; Trivers, 1971). Nesse (1990) has argued that to understand the evolution of emotions we should concentrate not on particular emotions but on recurring situations. If we do so, we find that, although some emotions, like fear of a predator, may be distinctive, many emotions tend to overlap into particular situations.

Emotion provides the structure of human social life: outline patterns that enable people to relate to each other. In Table 2.3 you can see that emotions of attachment and affiliation help form and maintain cooperative bonds, the emotions of assertion (power) enable us to relate the hierarchies of our lives, and the antisocially motivated emotions of hatred and cruelty are aspects of relations between groups. In addition, of course, there are emotions that need have no immediate social component.

In the West we tend to think of ourselves as individuals, but it may be that primarily we are members of social groups. This starts with our first social group, of infant and caregiver; then (for most) comes the family. Later comes membership in other groups. Group memberships are highly emotional. In one way of thinking about them, Donald (1991) has proposed that a phase of human evolution has involved imitation, doing the same as others. We see it in dancing and music, in people's fondness for uniforms of both the formal kind and the informal kind (called fashions). If you think, one-by-one, of all the actions you do in a day, you may find that most of them have an aspect that is constrained by or performed in relation to a group. In another way,

Table 2.3   Motivations, relations, recurring situations, and emotions

Motivation	Relation	Recurring situation	Emotion
Attachment	Attachment	Maintain contact with parents	Love of parents
	Sexual contact	Reproductive possibility	Sexual desire, Love
	Maintaining pair-bond	Threat of interloper	Jealousy
	Interruption of attachment	Separation	Distress, Anxiety
	Resumption of attachment	Reunion	Relief (Maybe Anger)
	Loss of attachment	Parting, death	Sadness, Despair
Assertion	Reduce status of other	Unfair rise in other's status	Anger, Envy
	Other's successful assertion of power	Appeasement, giving signals of submission	Shame, Humiliation, Embarrassment
	Induce other to repair	Transgression	Anger
	Endow with power	Other seen as greater than self	Awe
Affiliation	Friendliness	Cooperation, caring	Affection, Warmth, Gratitude
	Sexuality	Flirting, intercourse	Desire, Affection
	Loss of relationship	Parting, death	Sadness
	Repair bond	Mistake	Guilt, Forgiveness
Antisocial goals	Hostility	Intergroup conflict	Hatred, Cruelty, Contempt
Non-social goals	Enacting plans	Progress: Failure:	Happiness, Energization Sadness, Frustration, Effortfulness
	Resources	Seeking, finding	Enthusiasm
	Explore environment	Novelty	Interest, Surprise
	Avoid danger	Threat	Fear
	Avoid contamination	Toxicity	Disgust
	Predation	Hunting	Excitement
	Being hunted	Fleeing	Fear

we derive our identity from groups (Tajfel & Turner, 1979). We can think of ourselves as members of a school, a place of work, perhaps a religious affiliation, perhaps fans of a particular person, or band, or team. Within a group, differences between individuals are minimized, and between-groups differences are emphasized. Such groupings include being male or female, being black or white, and being American or of some other nationality.

As well as growing into group allegiances we develop individuality, and we can be very selfish. Then, also, with more effort, we can start to see others in their own individuality, to see other people as individuals whom we can care about.

In the evolutionary approach to emotion, critical evidence concerns whether our emotions serve social or individual functions, the extent to which they are universal and have biological bases, and the extent to which they are culturally distinctive.

SUMMARY

Our genes use us as vehicles to enable them to reproduce. In this chapter we've discussed how they program us, partly by means of our emotions, to keep ourselves safe, and to enable sexual activity to occur. Some of this programming is mandatory. With some of it, we can choose among options, at least to some extent. The evolutionary success of the human species derives from living in groups, in which emotions derive from three social motivations: attachment, assertion (power), and affiliation (affection), together with the anti-social motivation of hostility between groups. Among the evidence for the sociality of our emotions are studies of chimpanzees and bonobos, the prehistory of the human species, and studies of modern societies living as hunter-gatherers.

TO THINK ABOUT AND DISCUSS

1. What are your reactions to the idea that we don't pass on our genes, but that genes use us as vehicles to pass themselves on?

2. Think of an emotion you have experienced that concerns another person you know, such as love, or anger, or jealousy, or envy. How has your reflection on this emotion affected how you think of yourself? How has it affected how you think of the person who was the object of this emotion?

3. How far do you think we humans will be able to modify the emotions of hostility to members of out-groups? You might start thinking about this from your knowledge of terrorism, of wars of the 20th and 21st centuries, and of the civil rights movement.

FURTHER READING

An introduction to evolutionary theory as it affects emotions is:

Dacher Keltner, Jonathan Haidt, & Michelle Shiota (2006). Social functionalism and the evolution of emotions. In M. Schaller, J. A. Simpson & D. T. Kenrick (Eds.), *Evolution and social psychology* (pp. 115–142). Madison, CT: Psychosocial Press.

The social and emotional lives of chimpanzees and ourselves:

Frans De Waal (2005). *Our inner ape: The best and worst of human nature*. London, UK: Granta.

For readable discussions of human evolution:

David Christian (2004). *Maps of time: An introduction to big history*. Berkeley, CA: University of California Press.

Robin Dunbar (2004). *The human story: A new history of mankind's evolution*. London, UK: Faber.

Cultural Understandings of Emotions

3

Photo Credit: ©Asian Art & Archaeology, Inc./Corbis

FIGURE 3.0 Two bronze figurines from the Han dynasty in China, made more than 2,000 years ago, probably representing people from alien northern tribes.

CONTENTS

Though we travel the world over to find the beautiful we must carry it with us or we find it not.

(Ralph Waldo Emerson, Essays, xii, Art)

For nine months the American anthropologist Catherine Lutz lived on a tiny island in the Pacific Ocean, Ifaluk, studying the emotional lives of the 430 people who lived there (Lutz, 1988). One day, sitting with another woman, Lutz watched a five-year-old girl dancing and making silly faces, showing happiness, *ker* as it was known in the island's language. Lutz responded warmly to the little girl, whom she thought was rather cute. "Don't smile at her," said her companion, "she'll think that you're not *song*," meaning justifiably angry (p. 167). The woman was indicating that the girl was approaching the age at which she should have social intelligence, the concern for others that is so valued on Ifaluk, and that she should not show inappropriate levels of happiness, which is disapproved of on Ifaluk as showing off.

In this exchange, Lutz saw how different the emotional lives of people on Ifaluk were from her own. On Ifaluk, the little girl should not have displayed *ker*, with its risk of misbehavior. She should have been sitting quietly, as good socially intelligent people do. One also sees differences in the nature of anger. On Ifaluk, *song*, or justifiable anger, occurs with a public breach of social rules. So *song* is not anger as we in the West tend to experience it, arising from violation of a right. It is people's social duty to express *song* if they notice anything that might disrupt social harmony. The proper response to *song* is *metagu*, which means anxious concern for others.

The Construction of Emotions in the West

At this point we should say what a culture is. It's a system of ideas and practices that are held in common in a particular society, or set of societies. A society is a group of people who live in a particular place at a particular time.

How might we characterize our implicit theory of emotions in the culture of the West? First, we might note a distrust of emotions. If you want to disparage another person's argument, just say that person is being "emotional," meaning "irrational." The idea goes back at least to Plato (375 BCE), who thought emotions arise from the lower part of the mind and pervert reason. The distrust was brought into the modern era by Darwin (1872), who implied that, in human adults, expressions of emotions are obsolete, vestiges of our evolution from our hominid predecessors and of our development from infancy.

We in the West are not, however, very consistent, because we also think emotions are the very guarantee of authenticity, our best guide to our true selves. As Robert Solomon, one of the influential voices in the philosophy of emotion, has put it: "Emotions are the life force of the soul, the source of most of our values" (1977, p. 14). As you shall learn later (Chapters 7 and 10), emotions signal how events in our environment correspond to our core concerns and interests.

These different stances toward emotion are constructions of Western culture. Appreciation of emotions became marked in Europe and America during the historical era of **Romanticism**. (The era must be distinguished from the term *romantic*, which is a synonym for "sexual" as in "romantic love."). In the Romantic era emotions came to be valued in personal life, in politics, in literature, and in philosophy.

Jean-Jacques Rousseau (1755) was responsible for one of the first articulations of the Romantic spirit. He published the idea that religious sensibility is based on how you feel rather than on authority, or on Scripture, or on arguments for the existence of God. He critiqued cultivated pursuits as artificial and corrupting, proposing instead that education should be natural, and that people's natural emotions indicate what is right—people have merely to be alive to the feelings of their conscience. His ringing phrase from the beginning of *The Social*

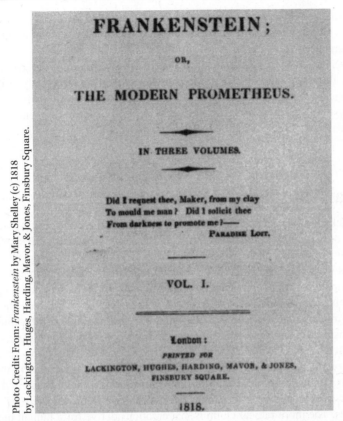

FIGURE 3.1 Title page of volume 1 of Frankenstein, written by Mary Shelley but published anonymously.

Contract (1762), "Man is born free, and is everywhere in chains," became a rallying call in the French Revolution, and such thoughts crossed the Atlantic to help fuel the American War of Independence.

If you'd like to get a sense of Romanticism, take a look at a novel of the Romantic era that became famous, *Frankenstein,* by Mary Shelley, daughter of the famous feminist, Mary Wollstonecraft, and the social reformer, William Godwin. At the age of 16, Mary Shelley eloped with the Romantic poet Percy Bysshe Shelley. When she was 18, Mary, her husband, her stepsister Claire, Lord Byron (another Romantic poet), and another friend were on holiday during an "ungenial" summer in the Alps. They read a great deal and had long conversations on literature, philosophy, and biology. One day, Byron suggested that each should write a ghost story. Retiring to bed, Mary Shelley could not sleep. Prompted by a conversation about experiments in which electricity was used to stimulate muscle movements in dead creatures, there rose to her mind an image of a scientist with a powerful engine beside him, kneeling over a hideous phantasm of a man that he had put together. Her story became *Frankenstein* (1818), one of the world's first science fiction stories.

We now think of *Frankenstein* as a horror story, but really it's about the emotional themes of Romanticism, about the artificial creature's initial natural emotions of kindness, as he works secretly to help a family who live in a humble cottage, and then a further set of natural emotions, of the creature's rage in reaction to how humans attack him for his unnatural ugliness. Then come the creature's emotions of dependency toward the scientist, his creator.

In *Frankenstein* are many of the themes of Romanticism: settings amid wild scenery, the emphasis on the natural, distrust of the artificial, apprehension of humans arrogantly overstepping their boundaries. There are thought-provoking, prescient ideas about our construction of clever but risky technological systems (Perrow, 1984). More generally, in the Romantic movement, we see core beliefs about emotions as primordial, authentic causes of behavior, beliefs that are alive today.

A Cultural Approach to Emotion

Our cultural background has many elements: our country of origin, the geographical region from which we hail; our ethnicity or race; and our social class, religion, and gender. We shall learn in this chapter how such forms of culture shape emotion. The values, concepts, and ideas about the self that are part of a cultural background, as expressed in art, in rituals, in social practices, and in institutions, shape how members of societies experience emotion in often strikingly different ways. Our beliefs about emotion in the West, that emotions are both irrational and also authentic aspects of the true self, are products of the culture of Europe and North America, which is different, for instance, from the belief systems of the people Catherine Lutz met on Ifaluk.

What does it mean to take a cultural approach to emotion? Most importantly, a cultural approach involves the assumption that emotions are constructed primarily by the processes of culture. Aspects ranging from how emotions are valued to how they are elicited are shaped by culture-specific beliefs and practices, which in turn have been affected by historical and economic forces. The more radical claim is that emotions derive from human meanings, which are necessarily cultural. They are like languages or works of art. They are radically different across cultures, so that the interest in emotions across cultures is an interest in their differences. Your experience of love, for example, might not be comparable to the experience of love of people from a different culture.

A second assumption of some cultural approaches is that emotions can be thought of as roles that people fulfill to play out culture-specific identities and relationships. You'll recall Arlie Hochschild's work in Chapter 1 on the emotional role that airline stewardesses perform. Averill (1985) argues that falling in love, like many emotions, acts as a temporary social role. It provides an outline script for the role of "lover" in which it is permissible for other social roles to be suspended, for instance, in relation to parents or to former loved ones. The emotion "falling in love" accomplishes a transition from one structure of social relationships to another.

Batja Mesquita (2001) contends that cultural approaches focus on the "practice" of emotion, in contrast to the "potential" for emotion. *Potential* means asking whether people of different cultures, if put in an appropriate experimental situation, would be capable of showing certain universal emotional responses in terms of experience, expression, and physiology (for relevant studies, see Tsai & Levenson, 1997; Tsai, Levenson, & Carstensen, 2000; Tsai et al., 2002). The answer is probably *yes*, and this is in keeping with the evolutionary approach we detailed in the previous chapter. In contrast, *practice* refers to what actually happens in people's emotional lives. The day-to-day emotional experiences of people from different cultures do differ, often dramatically. For instance, some cultures permit public expressions of anger (e.g., the Ilongot chronicled by Rosaldo, 1980), while others work hard to suppress all such expressions (e.g., the Utku Inuit people described by Briggs, 1970; see Chapter 9). In some cultures (such as the Western one), shame is seen as damaging and to be avoided; in more hierarchically structured societies shame seems more valued and positive, in particular when displayed by the lower-status person in an interaction (Abu-Lughod, 1986; Doi, 1973; Menon & Shweder, 1994). As Mesquita, Frijda, and Scherer (1997) observed: "People from different cultures appear to be similar in their emotion potential, especially when this potential is described at a higher level of meaning. Yet, despite the similarities in basic elements of emotional life, concrete emotional realities in different cultures may widely vary." In the following three sections we'll consider three specific cultural approaches to emotion (Peng, Ames, & Knowles, 2001).

Self-Construal: Independent and Interdependent Selves

First, consider the following quotations. The first is a famous passage from the Declaration of Independence of the United States:

> We hold these truths to be self-evident, that all men are created equal, that they are endowed by their Creator with certain inalienable rights, that among these are Life, Liberty, and the pursuit of Happiness.

Now consider this, from *The Analects*, a book by the great Chinese philosopher, Confucius:

> A person of humanity wishing to establish his own character, also establishes the character of others.

The American Declaration of Independence and the *Analects* of Confucius have shaped the lives of billions of people. The Declaration of Independence prioritized the rights and freedoms of the individual, and it protected the individual from having those rights and liberties infringed upon by others. Confucius emphasized the importance of knowing one's place in society, of honoring traditions and roles, and of thinking of others before the self. In Western societies, as we learned in our discussion of Romanticism, people are concerned about their individuality, about self-actualizing, about freedom, and about self-expression. "The squeaky wheel gets the grease." "If you've got it, flaunt it." In Asian cultures, homilies and folk wisdom encourage a markedly different self: "The empty wagon makes the most noise." "The nail that stands up is pounded down."

In an influential way of thinking, Hazel Markus, Shinobu Kitayama, Harry Triandis, and others have characterized two kinds of **self-construal** that affect emotions (Fiske et al., 1998; Hofstede, 1980; Markus & Kitayama, 1991, 1994; Triandis, 1989, 1994, 1995); see Table 3.1.

Independent self-construal is also referred to as individualism (Schimmack, Oishi, & Diener, 2005). The imperative is to assert one's distinctiveness and independence, and to define oneself according to unique traits and preferences, with a focus on internal causes, such as one's own dispositions or preferences, which are thought of as stable across time and social context.

For people with interdependent, or collectivist, self-construals, the self is fundamentally connected with other people. The imperative is to find one's status, identity, and roles within the community and other collectives such as families and organizations. The emphasis is on the social context and the situational influences on behavior. One thinks of oneself as embedded within social relationships, roles, and duties, with a self that is ever-changing and shifting, and shaped by different contexts, relationships, and roles.

Table 3.1 **Two different self-construals. This table outlines the contrasting elements of the independent, individualist self, widespread in much of Northern Europe and North America, with the interdependent self, prominent in much of Asia, Africa, and South America**

The independent self	The interdependent self
I am autonomous, separate	I am connected to others
I have unique traits and preferences	I fulfill roles and duties
My behavior is caused by internal causes	My behavior is the result of the social context
Who I am is stable across contexts	Who I am varies across contexts

Individual emotion: *Amae*

In Japan there is an emotion called *amae*, for which there is no simple translation in English (Ferrari & Koyama, 2002). *Amae* is an attachment emotion. It's an emotion of interdependence, experienced as a merged togetherness, and deriving from comfort in the other person's complete acceptance.

It is not that this emotion is unrecognizable in other cultures, or that it lacks universal significance. Rather, it has no fully approved place in Western adult life. The original Chinese ideogram of *amae* was of a breast on which the baby suckled. As Westerners imagine this emotion, they may think they should have grown out of it because it seems a bit regressed. In Japan this is not so. This can be an emotion of an accepting relationship within the family. Lebra (1983) has said that it can be the dependence a less powerful person feels in relation to a more powerful one, which allows the less powerful person to be passive, with the satisfying knowledge of being accepted. At the same time, *amae* can also be experienced as a mutual dependency between lovers.

Given the radically different ways of construing the self, one would expect large differences in the emotional lives of people from independent cultures, such as Northern Europe, Canada, or the United States, and interdependent cultures, such as much of Asia, Mediterranean Europe, Africa, and South America. For example, one way of thinking about emotions is according to the degree to which an emotion is socially engaging, that is, connects the individual to other people, or socially disengaging, or creating distance from other people. Kitayama, Mesquita, & Karasawa (2006) asked Japanese and American college students to report in a diary, over 14 days, their most intense emotional episode each day, and to say what emotions they felt during that episode. The interdependent Japanese students reported more intense experiences of positive, socially engaging emotions (e.g., respect, sympathy) and negative socially engaging emotions (shame and guilt, which recognize others' evaluations of the self and motivate behaviors that restore social relationships). The more independent-minded American students reported more intense experiences of positive, socially disengaging emotions (pride, high self-esteem) and negative, socially disengaging emotions (anger, frustration).

Studies guided by the self-construal perspective not only reveal how culture influences the kinds of emotions we experience, and which emotions we privilege and value, they also reveal culturally specific ways in which emotions evoke responses in others. For example, Japanese and American infants respond to the anger expressions of their parents in dramatically different ways. Miyake et al. (1986) showed interesting toys to American and Japanese infants of 11 months, pairing each toy with the mother's voice expressing joy, anger, or fear. American and Japanese infants were no different in how soon they moved after the sound of their mothers' joyful or fearful voices. Cultural differences were pronounced, however, after their mothers had spoken in an angry voice: American infants started moving toward the toy an average of 18 seconds later, but Japanese infants took significantly longer, an average of 48 seconds, to start moving. Within interdependent cultures, anger is infrequent and highly negative because it so readily disrupts social harmony. Japanese babies were probably more inhibited by their mother's angry expressions because such highly negative events were rare.

Finally, cultural differences in self-construal also influence how people find happiness. Look again at Table 3.1 and generate your own hypotheses. Where might you find cultural differences in the determinants of happiness? Mark Suh and his colleagues found that people from interdependent cultures find greater happiness in fulfilling duties and abiding by cultural norms, whereas people from independent cultures found greater happiness in their expression of positive emotion (Suh, Diener, Oishi, & Triandis, 1998).

Values

A second approach seeks to understand cultural differences in emotion in terms of differences in **values**, principles that govern our social behavior. Numerous values govern how we as members of a culture coexist in communities and accomplish tasks like allocating resources, folding into family structures, or punishing moral violations. For example, people from different cultures attach different priorities to values like freedom, individual rights, equality, expressing thoughts and feelings, respect for authority, sexual purity, or hierarchies (Haidt, Koller, & Dias, 1993; Rozin et al., 1999; Shweder et al., 1997; Tsai, Simenova, & Watanabe, 2004). As one illustration, the anthropologist, Benedict (1946), explained, in a book written in the last year of World War II and commissioned by the U.S. Government to help understand the Japanese, who were the adversaries, that to be sincere in America is to act in accord with one's innermost emotions. In Japan, the concept usually translated as sincerity, *makoto*, means something different: doing a social duty, not according to inner feelings, but doing it completely, with expertise, without inner conflict.

Members of cultures that differ in the importance of specific values should experience different **elicitors** of emotions related to that value. Consider one striking finding showing that elicitors of jealousy that seem obvious in one culture do not seem to evoke jealousy in another. In the West, jealousy tends to be felt when the sexual attention of a primary partner turns toward someone else (Buss et al., 1992; DeSteno & Salovey, 1996; Harris, 2003; Harris & Christenfeld, 1996; Salovey, 1991). As Hupka (1991) points out, in Western society monogamy, which leads to the two-parent family, is a cherished value and a key to establishing one's adult status, economic security, housing, rearing of children, adult companionship, and sex. A sexual interloper threatens this value and the accompanying social structure, so, in Western society such a person is jealously feared and hated.

In some other societies, however, the self is more interdependent, collective, and extended. Cooperative effort supports everyone, including the elderly; child-rearing is distributed among several people; adult companionship derives from many relatives; and monogamy is not so highly cherished. In some such societies, extramarital recreational sex is customary. At the beginning of this century, the Todas of India were visited by anthropologists and were found to live in a society of this kind (Hupka, 1991). They were not jealous when marriage partners had lovers from within their social group. Instead, Toda men did become jealous if their wives had intercourse with a non-Toda man, or if a second-born son got married before the first-born—an unlikely elicitor of jealousy in the West.

Drawing upon observations of this kind, cultural psychologists have made the argument that cultures vary as to which emotions are *focal,* or prominent in daily life, according to cultural differences in values (Markus & Kitayama, 1994; Mesquita, 2003; Mosquera Rodriquez et al., 2004). Members of a particular culture may be more or less prone to feel and express emotions like anger, compassion, gratitude, or awe. One would expect focal emotions to be more readily elicited and experienced more intensely, and signaled in more intense display behavior.

In some cultures the value of honor is focal; it involves paying respect to others in acts of politeness and deference. Rodrigues-Mosquera and her colleagues have documented that in cultures that prioritize concerns over honor, honor-protecting emotions such as shame or anger are more focal. Individuals from high-honor cultures (Spaniards) responded with greater shame and anger when insulted than individuals from other cultures, because these emotions protect honor and "face," and in the case of anger, restore the individual's social standing in the face of insults (Rodrigues, Fischer, & Manstead, 2000). In fact, not showing anger would mean that one is weak. In the U.S. South there is a more pronounced emphasis on honor, so that when people from the South were insulted (for instance, called an "asshole" by a confederate in an experiment), they showed more anger in their facial expressions than did students from the North (Cohen et al., 1996); they also showed higher levels of testosterone and cortisol, they shook another person's hand more firmly, and they refused to move out of the way of an imposing confederate walking toward them in a narrow hallway. Osterman and Brown (2011) have found that not only are certain kinds of interpersonal violence more widely tolerated in high-honor societies, but so is violence against the self: suicide is more frequent in high-honor American states than in states where honor is less important. In high-honor cultures, suicide may be a preferred choice when compared to living a life lacking the respect and esteem of others.

Cultural differences in specific values have also been found to influence spontaneous emotional response. For example, consider Iris Mauss and her colleagues' work on the influence of the value of emotional control in different cultures. Emotional control is more highly valued in East Asian cultures; the spontaneous expression of emotion is thought to risk disrupting social harmony, and is discouraged. By contrast, more spontaneous emotional expression is more highly valued in Western European cultures, steeped in the Romantic tradition, for it is a means by which individuals express their authentic selves. The experience of anger should be particularly influenced by these cultural differences in the value attached to emotional control, for, of all the emotions, anger might disrupt social relationships most. One might expect people from cultures that value emotional control, like many East Asian cultures, to inhibit their expression of anger.

To test this hypothesis, Mauss and colleagues had Asian American and European American college students do a highly stressful task—they counted backwards in specific units, say 7, from a large number such as 13,822 (Mauss et al., 2010). While they carried out this frustrating task, a rude experimenter interrupted the participant several times, and commented on the participant's mistakes and disappointing progress—no doubt a frustration to the participant. And in keeping with the argument laid out here, the European American participants reported more anger and expressed more intense anger in the face in response to the rude experimenter,

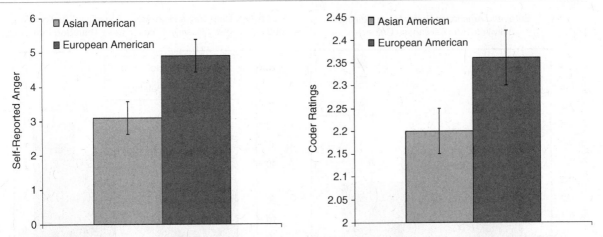

FIGURE 3.2 European Americans experience and express greater anger in response to a frustrating experimenter (adapted from Mauss et al., 2010).

although members of the two cultures did not differ in their physiological response to the frustrating event.

Finally, to the extent that emotions reinforce particular values of importance to a culture, those emotions should be highly valued. Jeanne Tsai's **affect evaluation theory** brings this thinking into focus (Tsai, 2007; Tsai, Knutson, & Fung, 2006). Tsai reasons that emotions that promote specific cultural values and ideals are valued more and as a result should play a more prominent role in the social lives of individuals. For example, Tsai and colleagues reason that in the United States excitement is greatly valued. Excitement enables individuals to pursue a cultural ideal of self-expression and achievement. In contrast, in many East Asian cultures greater value is attached to feelings of calmness and contentedness, because these positive emotions more readily enable the individual to fold into harmonious relationships and groups (Kitayama, Karasawa, & Mesquita, 2004; Kitayama, Markus, & Kurokawa, 2000; Kitayama, Mesquita, & Karasawa, 2005; see also Mesquita, 2001; Mesquita & Karasawa, 2002). These differences in which emotions are valued readily translate into striking cultural differences in emotional behavior. Americans, as compared to East Asians, are more likely to participate in risky recreational practices (for example, mountain biking), are more likely to advertise consumer products with intense smiles of excitement, are more likely to get addicted to excitement-enhancing drugs (cocaine), express preferences for upbeat, exciting music rather than soothing, slower pieces, and their children's books are more likely to feature highly excited protagonists (Tsai, 2007). These differences are observed in Figure 3.3 and in influential texts as well: in the Christian Gospels and popular books today about Christianity, high-arousal, positive emotions ("proud," "glory") are valued more, whereas in classical Buddhist texts and popular books about Buddhism, low-arousal, positive emotions ("serene," "peace") are valued more (Tsai et al., 2007). All of these differences in social practice, Tsai reasons, flow out of the value placed on excitement in America.

An important new movement in understanding how emotions are perceived and understood emphasizes not just specific emotions and their displays but the contexts in which the emotions occur (Barrett, Mesquita, & Gendron, 2011); we discuss this further in Chapter 7. How any emotion is expressed, how it is understood, and what its implications are depend critically on the

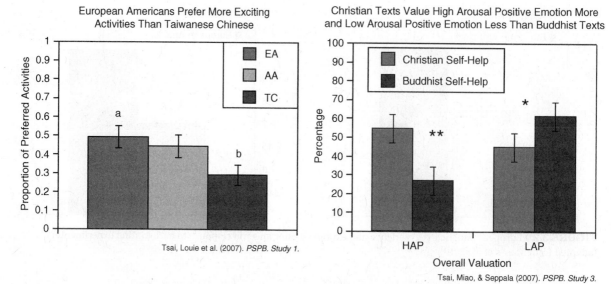

FIGURE 3.3 European Americans (EA) reveal a greater preference for exciting recreational activities than Asian Americans (AA) or Taiwanese Chinese (TC) participants (left panel adapted from Tsai, Louie et al., 2007); Christian texts place a greater emphasis on high arousal positive (HAP) emotions, whereas Buddhist texts place a greater emphasis on low arousal, calm, positive (LAP) emotions (right panel adapted from Tsai, Miao, & Seppala, 2007).

context, and this context differs depending on a range of factors that include the gender of the people involved, their power relationships, and most fundamentally the practices of the culture in which it occurs. The context of a joke made by a British person will enable it to be understood as a token of affection by another British person, but it may be met with incomprehension by an American and be seen as rude by a Japanese person.

Epistemology

Epistemologies are ways of knowing. They refer to knowledge structures and theories that guide thought, emotion, and behavior in domain-specific ways (Peng, Ames, & Knowles, 2001; Peng & Nisbett, 1999). Kaiping Peng and Richard Nisbett have characterized the epistemologies of East Asians and Western Europeans (Peng & Nisbett, 1999). East Asians are guided in their knowledge and thought by a holistic, dialectical system of thought that has its roots in the great intellectual traditions of East Asia, including Confucianism, Taoism, and Buddhism, from 2,500 years ago. This epistemology is based on five principles: (1) change, so that nothing is static; (2) contradiction, that opposites often are consistent and both true; (3) covariation, so that events are interrelated in complex fields or systems; (4) compromise, so that truth may lie in the synthesis of opposites; and (5) context, so that events occur not alone but in contexts.

In an imaginative demonstration, Peng and Nisbett (1999) tested the hypothesis that Asians should find greater meaning, and even pleasure, in contradictory ideas than do Americans. They first found that Chinese proverbs involved more contradiction (e.g., "Half humble is half proud") than American proverbs, which involved more one-sided, singular truths ("Half a loaf is better than no bread"). Then Chinese and American students were presented with a set of proverbs. Chinese students found contradictory, dialectical proverbs to be more comprehensible, likeable, and usable. U.S. students preferred the more linear proverbs.

In light of principle 2, the principle of contradiction, one would expect that as compared with Americans, East Asians might experience greater **emotional complexity**: the simultaneous experience of contradictory emotions, such as happiness and sadness, compassion and contempt, or anger and love (Miyamoto, Uchida, & Ellsworth, 2010). Perhaps East Asians would be more willing to endorse multiple, even contradictory, meanings for the complex social situations and, as a result, experience contradictory emotions. By contrast, Westerners might focus more on singular meanings of a situation and experience simpler emotions.

Recent findings are in keeping with this prediction, and speak to how culture-related epistemologies shape the complexity of emotional experience. Thus, in **experience sampling** studies, in which students were beeped electronically and reported on their current emotions, as well as in laboratory studies, Chinese, Japanese, and South Korean participants were more likely than Western European students to report feeling positive and negative emotion in the particular moment (Schimmack, Oishi, & Diener, 2002; see Kitayama, Markus, & Kurokawa, 2000, for similar results using a different methodology). Among Western Europeans, the more they reported of one kind of emotion, say happiness, the less they reported of its opposite, say sadness.

Michelle Shiota et al. (2010) have documented similar tendencies in the reports of contradictory emotion in European American and Asian American romantic partners. After talking about personal events, European Americans' experiences of love were negatively correlated with experiences of anger and contempt, but Asian American partners showed positive correlations between these contradictory emotions. More generally, it seems that Westerners strive to maximize positive emotion and minimize negative emotion, whereas Asians seek a balanced emotional state (Kitayama et al., 2000).

Finally, consider principle 5, the principle of context. There are striking differences within cultural epistemologies regarding the extent to which contexts figure in making sense of social situations. People in many parts of the world, in particular in East Asian cultures, tend to pay greater attention to the context in giving meaning to social situations, whereas people in Western European cultures tend to focus more on the individual (Peng & Morris, 1994). This contextual focus of East Asian epistemologies is evident even in their artistic traditions. In an analysis of several hundred paintings from East Asian and Western European museums, paintings from East Asian cultures devote greater space to the background than paintings from Western European cultures, which devote greater space to people's faces (Masuda et al., 2008). This focus on context should lead to large differences in the meaning of emotion across cultures.

For example, one might expect different events to elicit emotions in East Asian and Western European cultures. In this vein, we might expect East Asian individuals to experience gratitude or awe as the result of contextual casues—a favorable economy, being part of a collective gathering—and people from Northern European cultures to experience gratitude or awe as the result of actions of specific individuals. This same cultural difference in the focus on context should also influence the kind of emotions people experience. For example, people in East Asian cultures might be more likely to experience collective pride (e.g., in the successes of a group) and Western Europeans individual pride. And in Chapter 4 we shall see that East Asian individuals are more likely to factor information about the social context into their judgments of others' emotions.

Approaches to Studying Cultural Influences on Emotion

Cultural psychologists have made enormous progress in understanding cultural variations in emotion by simply comparing cultures that differ on a variable of interest (e.g., self-construals, the value of honor, epistemology). We have seen that this research has yielded compelling insights into how cultures construct emotions in different ways. Let's look at other cross-cultural comparisons of emotion, to get a fuller picture of how cultures vary in their emotional responses.

Cross-Cultural Comparisons

Emotions begin with elicitation. Do cultures differ with respect to elicitors of emotions? Researchers have given participants from different cultures emotion terms, like *anger* or *fear*, and asked them to describe situations that would produce each kind of emotion (e.g., Boucher & Brandt, 1981). Or they have provided situations and asked participants to report what emotions they might feel. Or they have given members of different cultures pictures of facial expressions of different emotions, and asked them to describe an event that would produce the emotion in the photo (Haidt & Keltner, 1999).

While there are universals in the elicitors of emotion, which we examine more closely in Chapter 7, cultures have been found to differ in their emotional responses according to whether the elicitors of emotion are socially "engaging" and involve other people, or "disengaging" so that they primarily involve the self. As you might have anticipated from findings we described earlier, members of interdependent cultures such as the Japanese, Surinamese, and Turkish tend to experience positive emotions (calm, elation) when they are in contexts that are socially engaging, for example, in informal exchanges with friends (Kitayama, Karasawa, & Mesquita, 2003; see also Mesquita & Leu, 2007). By contrast, Americans and Dutch people are more likely to experience positive emotions in contexts that are less about social engagement and more about the expression of personal preferences or individual achievement (see also Frijda & Mesquita, 1994).

Novels and films: *Welcome to the sticks*

A wonderfully funny film about cultural differences is *Welcome to the Sticks*. It was said to be the most popular film of all time in France. If you are French, you will know about it (*Bienvenue chez les Cht'is*); if you're not, then think of renting it and see how you like it.

The film is about a post-office manager, Philippe (Kad Merad). His wife, Julie (Zoé Félix), is grumpy and difficult. She wants Philippe to get a transfer to the French Riviera. To move to such a favorable spot is difficult, so, to help his chances, Philippe decides that he needs to be disabled. He buys a wheelchair. When an inspector arrives, his ruse is discovered and, perhaps as a punishment, the Post Office Human Relations Department transfers him, instead, to Bergues at the opposite end of France, which people who live in the south of France think is the North Pole. Philippe sets out for his new job in his car. He goes alone because Julie won't accompany him. He's so reluctant that he's stopped by the police for driving too slowly on the highway. He explains to the cop that he has been transferred to the North. "Be brave," says the cop, and lets him go without a fine.

The staff of the Bergues Post Office are so warm and kind to Philippe that he becomes happy in his new position but, as this occurs, almost unintentionally, in phone calls to his wife, he finds himself saying the place is even worse than he expected. Where Julie had been demanding, she now becomes understanding; where she had been cold, she now becomes affectionate. Every two weeks, Philippe goes south for the weekend, to see her. Just as his job is better than it's ever been, so, now, is his marriage—so much better that, after a few weeks, Julie decides to move to Bergues, too. Philippe confides to his post-office staff that he has told his wife that the people of Bergues are coarse and his situation is miserable. So, when Julie arrives, they put on a show of making everything seem far more awful than she could possibly have imagined.

Some differences between people tend to make us laugh at them. But this film isn't of that kind. Instead, cultural differences are transcended, and the film is based on a joining-in-together laughter, in which we in the audience take part.

The question of why we laugh was asked by Henri Bergson (1900/1911). First of all, Bergson thought laughter is solely human, and by that he meant social. We don't laugh at landscapes, and we laugh at animals only when they seem human. Bergson thought we find it funny to see humans behaving in a machine-like way because to be human is such a fragile state. Second, Bergson said, we need to be a bit detached to laugh. We don't laugh when we feel sympathy for a person. Third, and most important, Bergson said laughter needs a social echo. We laugh only when we are in touch with others. Laughter, then, says a lot about the culture in which it arises.

Among the best modern studies of laughter is a paper by Panksepp (2005); he, too, sees laughter as social. It begins in infancy and continues in children's play, says Panksepp. In chase games the child being chased laughs more than the one who is chasing. Panksepp has found that rats make chirping sounds when they play with each other: animal precursors of laughter. When humans tickle them so that they make these sounds, the rats become bonded to these particular humans.

Recently, David Matsumoto and his colleagues carried out one of the most ambitious cross-cultural comparisons in the field of emotion, to understand cultural differences in emotional suppression (Matsumoto et al., 2008). The study involved over 3,000 participants from 23 cultures. Participants reported on their tendency to suppress their emotion, that is, to inhibit it according to features of the social context. Matsumoto and colleagues also gathered data on the values of importance to the different cultures. In highly hierarchical cultures, individuals reported the more robust tendency to suppress their emotions. By contrast, participants from more egalitarian, individualistic cultures reported that they suppressed their expression of emotions less, which is in keeping with the idea that in more individualistic cultures individuals are free to express their emotions in the spirit of expressing a more authentic self. Later you will learn about the costs of emotional suppression, in particular for people from Western European cultures. Matsumoto and colleagues documented cross-cultural findings related to this theme: across the 23 cultures, the more individuals suppressed emotion, the less one observed problems of social adjustment, such as drug use and violence, but across cultures greater emotional suppression was associated with lower levels of happiness and well-being.

This research on emotional suppression was shaped by earlier studies of **display rules**, which are thought to influence how and to whom it is appropriate to express different emotions. We saw at the start of this chapter, for example, that on the Pacific island of Ifaluk it is not appropriate to express too much happiness. More generally, people can de-intensify their emotional expression, for example, suppressing the urge to laugh when someone is pompous at a public meeting. People can also intensify their expression, for example, smiling more appreciatively upon hearing a boss tell the same story for yet another time.

Across cultures, people vary in how they modulate their expression of emotion. For example, in many Asian cultures it is inappropriate to speak of personal accomplishments, and in these cultures individuals may de-intensify their expressions of pleasure or pride at personal success. Among the Chewong, a small group of aboriginal hunters and shifting cultivators in Malaysia, prohibitions exist against the expression of all emotions with the exception of fear and shyness (Howell, 1981). The Chewong have explicit behavioral rules about what to do and what not to do in different circumstances. Penalties of severe bodily ills are believed to occur if rules are broken. The result is that the Chewong are emotionally inexpressive with each other. "They rarely use gestures of any kind, and their faces register little change as they speak and listen" (pp. 134–135). This raises the interesting question of whether the Chewong actually experience the emotions they seem to avoid expressing.

The original demonstration of display rules is an experiment by Ekman and Friesen (Ekman, 1972; Friesen, 1972). Participants were 25 American and 25 Japanese males, each in his own country. In Phase 1 participants were alone and watched film clips of a canoe trip, a ritual circumcision, a suction-aided delivery of a baby, and nasal sinus surgery. In Phase 2, a graduate student from the participant's own society entered the room and interviewed the participant briefly about his experience while viewing the clips. In Phase 3, the interviewer remained, sitting with his back toward the screen and facing the subject, while the very unpleasant clip of nasal surgery was replayed, and the interviewer asked the participant: "Tell me how you feel right now as you look at the film." In each phase, participants' facial expressions were videotaped, although they did not know this.

When they were alone, in Phase 1, American and Japanese participants displayed similar facial expressions of fear and disgust at almost exactly the same times in the films. But in Phase 3, facing the interviewer and the screen, the Japanese participants smiled more and inhibited their negative expressions more than the Americans. When viewed in slow motion, the videotapes showed Japanese participants beginning to make a facial expression of fear or disgust, but then masking it with a polite smile.

In a more recent study, Safdar, Friedlmeier, Matsumoto, Yoo, Kwantes, et al. (2009) compared display rules of Canadian, U.S. American, and Japanese university students. They found that, as compared with North America, in Japan display rules tended to inhibit expression of powerful emotions such as anger, contempt, and disgust, but that Japanese people varied the displays of these powerful emotions more depending on who their interaction partners were—their emotional expression was shaped to a greater extent by the concerns of the social context. Japanese participants also thought they should express happiness and surprise significantly less than the Canadian sample.

Ethnographies

A further method by which we gain insights into the cultural influences upon emotion is the ethnographic approach, the method used by Lutz, with whose anecdote of the little girl who made silly faces we started this chapter. **Ethnographies** are in-depth descriptions of the social lives of members of a particular culture. They are typically written by anthropologists who have made intensive study of the history, language, practices, customs, and rituals of a people, and who have lived among them, often for several years.

Rather than focusing on fairly brief emotional responses within thin slices of time, ethnographers aim to offer what the influential anthropologist, Clifford Geertz (1973), has called "thick descriptions," which, in the case of emotions, concern not just what emotions occur but their settings and cultural significance. Ethnographies often focus on **discourse**—the means by which people use language in its many forms to make sense, socially, of emotional experience. Ethnographers study not just the single words people use to label their emotions, but more complex acts of communication: apologies, gossip, songs, poetry, and community meetings about disruptive people, for example (Abu-Lughod & Lutz, 1990; Lutz & White, 1986). Several influential ethnographies of the emotional lives of people of different cultures have profoundly shaped how emotion researchers think about emotion (e.g., Abu-Lughod, 1986; Briggs, 1970; Rosaldo, 1980). Let's consider Lutz's work in greater depth to give you a sense of a thick description.

Emotions on Ifaluk

Ifaluk, where Lutz did her work, is a tiny Pacific atoll about one-fifth the size of New York's Central Park. Lutz (1988) wanted to see "if and how it was possible for people to organize their

Photo Credit: University of Chicago Press. By permission of Catherine Lutz.

FIGURE 3.4 An Ifaluk woman smiles as she makes an impromptu headdress for her small son. This kind of socially responsive smiling is of a lower intensity and signals something different from *ker*, meaning "excited happiness."

lives in such a way as to avoid the problems that seemed to me to diminish American culture, in particular its pervasive inequality of both gender and class and its violence" (p. 17). Ifaluk is a highly interdependent society. People have come to rely on each other on this island, which has its highest point just a few yards above sea level and where typhoons sometimes sweep the huts away, destroy the taro gardens, and deplete fish in the lagoon.

During her first weeks on the island, Lutz asked some young women who came to visit her hut: "Do you (all) want to come with me to get drinking water?" (p. 88). Their faces fell. Lutz writes that it was not until later that she realized what she had done wrong. By addressing them as "you" she had implied a separation between them and her own decision-making independent self. She writes that a more correct form, indicating an interdependent self, would be something more like: "We'll go and get water now, okay?" implying that such decisions are collective.

There are noticeable differences between social meanings of emotion in the United States and Ifaluk. Take the Ifaluk *ker*. Lutz translates it as "happiness/excitement." In the United States, people believe that it is a self-evident truth that there is "a right . . . to the pursuit of happiness" (U.S. Constitution). On Ifaluk people do not think they have any right to the pursuit of *ker*. They think they should avoid it. *Ker* is not contentment or interpersonal pleasantness, which are common on Ifaluk. A person feeling *ker* is likely to be too pleased with him- or herself. It can lead to showing off, perhaps even to rowdiness, behavior of which the Ifalukians disapprove. In interdependent cultures, certain forms of happiness can separate people from each another. They are avoided because they can lead to people not thinking enough about others. For the Ifaluk, it is better to be "*maluwelu*, gentle, calm and quiet" (p. 112).

The differences between her own and Ifalukian culture caused Lutz to make many social mistakes. One night she was frightened by a man entering the doorless hut that she had negotiated for herself. Her scream awakened her adopted family, who came to see what was wrong. They were asleep a yard or two away in their communal hut, with each one's sleeping mat touching others so that no one would be lonely. The man had fled, and the family laughed hilariously when they heard Lutz had been alarmed by such an event. She said that she had been on the island long enough to know that men sometimes called on women at night for a sexual rendezvous. But she had imported the American idea that an uninvited visit from a man inevitably meant harm. On Ifaluk, Lutz says, although men may very occasionally seem frightening in public if drunk, so that others may fear that a disagreement might break out between them, interpersonal violence is virtually nonexistent, and rape unknown. Hence a night visitor means the very antithesis of fear. The incident became a topic of conversation. Although no one could understand why Lutz had been frightened, she sensed that her adopted mother showed some satisfaction in the story of the event because, although the anxiety that Lutz displayed was inappropriate, it was anxiety: her adopted mother thought that this meant that at last Lutz was capable of showing this valued emotion!

The most valued emotion on Ifaluk, Lutz discovered, is *fago*, translated as "compassion/love/sadness." It is the primary index of positive relationships, including those with children, relatives, and sexual partners. It is felt particularly when loved ones are in need in some way, including when they are absent, since in this absence they will be separated from those on whom they depend. It expresses the sadness that a needful state implies, and the compassion that has transmitted this sadness to the more resourceful person in the relationship.

By studying the emotional lives of the Ifaluk people, Lutz helped show that cultures can differ dramatically in the value they attach to particular emotions, and in the elicitors of emotion. She moved the emphasis, moreover, from thinking of emotions as brief responses toward thinking of them as complex, unfolding social roles and rituals that enable individuals to situate themselves within communities.

Historical Approaches

An enlightening, although infrequently used, cultural approach to emotion is the **historical method**. A hundred years from now scientists employing this method might study talk shows and soap operas, cell-phones, MTV, Facebook, video games, Internet chat rooms, and tweets to glean insights into the emotional lives of 21st-century Westerners. For different historical periods, other kinds of documents, such as religious texts (Menon & Shweder, 1994; Tsai et al., 2007), etiquette manuals (Elias, 1939), poems and love songs (Abu-Lughod, 1986), and popular music have been revealing of the emotional life of a culture at specific historical moments. Distinguished historians such as David Konstan (2006) and Barbara Rosenwein (2007) now conduct research on emotions, and see historical societies as based on cultures that can give us acute insights and contrasts with emotions of the modern world.

Consider what Stearns and Haggarty (1991) learned about the period 1850 to 1950 in their survey of 84 American advice manuals for parents and popular literature aimed at children. Before 1900, three features stood out: warnings to parents about dangers of arousing fear in their children, silence on the subject of childhood fears, and boys' stories aimed at inspiring courage and acting properly despite fear. Then a change occurred: "Twentieth-century parents were told not only to avoid frightening their children as a disciplinary device but also to master their own emotions lest they give disturbing signals" (Stearns & Haggarty, 1991, p. 75). Benjamin Spock (1945) in his influential manual described childhood fears as requiring careful management. Separations from toddlers arouse fears in them and are to be avoided. If fears occur, they should be met with patience and affection. As to boys' stories, by the 1940s the idea of acting well despite fear had disappeared and was replaced by adventures in which tough guys felt no fear at all. In U.S. society, the control of fear has been important, first because fear prevents one from being a good citizen, and latterly because it prevents one becoming an effective individual. As President Franklin Roosevelt famously put it in his 1933 inaugural address: "The only thing we have to fear is fear itself."

Consider another set of historical documents, related to the Western idea of falling in love. Here is a newspaper story from the early 1950s:

> On Monday Cpl. Floyd Johnson, 23, and the then Ellen Skinner, 19, total strangers, boarded a train at San Francisco and sat down across the aisle from each other. Johnson didn't cross the aisle until Wednesday, but his bride said, "I'd already made up my mind to say yes."
> (Cited in Burgess & Wallin, 1953)

Corporal Johnson later explained that they had done most of the talking with their eyes. On Thursday the couple got off the train in Omaha, Nebraska. By that time they had made plans to be married but, because in Nebraska they would have needed to obtain the consent of Ellen Skinner's parents, they crossed the river to Council Bluffs, Iowa.

More than 30 years after the events recounted in the newspaper, Averill (1985) showed the story to a sample of U.S. adults: 40% of them said they had had experiences conforming to the ideal embodied in the story. Another 40% said their experiences of love definitely did not conform to it, basing their responses on an unfavorable attitude to this ideal plus any single departure they had felt from it. In responding in this way, they, too, indicated that they were influenced by this ideal.

Averill argues that love of this kind has features that are distinctive to Western culture. Certainly, passionate sexual love occurs worldwide. It is experienced as joyful and energizing. It is enacted in courtship, and it includes a biological core, including increased levels of phenylalanine in the brain (Diamond, 2003; Liebowitz, 1983). To investigate its universality, Jankowiak and Fischer (1992) surveyed ethnographies of 166 societies, asking whether the writer, typically an anthropologist, made a distinction between love and lust and noted the presence of at least one of the following attributes of love occurring within the first two years of a couple meeting, irrespective of whether they married or not: (a) personal anguish or longing, (b) love songs and the like, (c) elopement due to mutual affection, (d) indigenous accounts of passionate love, or (e) the anthropologist's affirmation that love occurred. In 147 of the 166 cultures (88.5%) there was evidence of this kind of passionate, sexual love.

The point that Averill (1985) makes, however, is that the Western ideal of love, eagerly taken up by Hollywood, enacted 50 years ago by Floyd Johnson and Ellen Skinner, and still very much alive today, is not just the same old worldwide story. It has features that are distinctive to the West and that started their development in medieval Europe.

The germ of the idea was *courtly love*, created in Provence in the 11th century and elaborated in many medieval documents. The word *courtly* originally meant occurring at a royal court; the later meaning of *courtship* is derived from it. The idea was that a nobleman might fall in love with a lady and become her knight. Courtly love had to occur outside marriage. The lady was at first seen at a distance, and was unattainable. The knight had to offer his service, do whatever she might wish, however dangerous or however trifling, and worship her. Although the knight had to be a paragon of Christian virtue, the very idea of worshiping a lady gave the extra frisson of bordering on blasphemy.

For several hundred years courtly love was the subject of some of Europe's greatest poetry. Prototypical was the story of Lancelot and his love for Guinevere, the queen and wife of King Arthur at his court in Camelot, told by the French poet, Chrétien De Troyes, in *The Knight of the Cart* (Chrétien De Troyes, 1180).

Later came the *Romance of the Rose* (De Lorris & De Meun, 1237–1277). The first part, written by Guillaume De Lorris, is an extraordinary psychological allegory, in which the lovers are represented as a set of emotions and psychological characteristics, each of which is a distinct actor in the drama. The poem begins with the lover, a young man, falling asleep and dreaming. As interpreted by C.S. Lewis (1936), the reader experiences the story through the young man's eyes. He strolls by the river of life, then enters the beautiful garden of courtly love, and sees a lady there. As the wooing proceeds, his consciousness is represented by the appearance in turn of distinct characters, Hope, Sweet Thought, Reason, and so on. The lady also does not appear as a whole. She, too, is a cast of characters: Bielacoil (meaning "fair welcome" from the Provençal *belh aculhir*) is something like the lady's conversational self, pleasant and friendly, and it is, of course, via this aspect that the young man must first approach. Then there is Franchise (the lady's sense of aristocratic status), and Pity. But then there are others: Danger, Fear, Shame. When the young man sounds a false note, Bielacoil disappears for hours, and only Fear or one of these others is present. Then, in addition, there is Jealousy, and the god of Love, not permanent characteristics of either the young man or the lady but able, in a somewhat unpredictable way, to take over either of them. As the young man reaches toward the Rose in the center of the garden, it is the god of Love who fires arrows at him and makes him Love's servant.

One might argue that some elements in this pattern occur elsewhere. For instance, in the Bible, Jacob is devoted to Rachel for a long period before they can unite. Nonetheless, the Western idea

Photo Credit: ©Fine Art Images/SUPERSTOCK

FIGURE 3.5 The origin of the culturally distinctive version of romantic love that occurs in the West is traced from courtly love in medieval Europe. The most famous book depicting this was *Roman de la Rose*, for which this was an illuminated illustration from about 1500 depicting the garden of courtly love.

of being in love involves elements that do seem to be distinctive. Falling in love (in the Western way) happens suddenly, unexpectedly, involuntarily. In the full pattern, devotion becomes a kind of worship. It unfolds as a script (Schank & Abelson, 1977; see also Frijda, 1988). Some 400 years ago it was described rather exactly in another historical document: *Romeo and Juliet*, by William Shakespeare (1623). Here is the script, in Schank and Abelson's sense (Oatley, 2004b): Two people must be open to the experience. Each sees the other, a stranger, and is attracted. Looks pass between them, words are not necessary. Then there is an interval of separation during which fantasies build. Then there is a meeting at which there is confirmation that the fantasies are mutual. *Ping!* One is in love. The state includes devotion. Shakespeare has Romeo show this by touching Juliet and saying in his very first words to her:

> If I profane with my unworthiest hand
> This holy shrine, the gentle sin is this,
> My lips, two blushing pilgrims, ready stand
> To smooth that rough touch with a tender kiss.
> (Romeo and Juliet, *1, 5, 90–4*)

Here, Romeo speaks to Juliet as if she is a statue of a saint ("this holy shrine"), whom he comes to worship and whom he has just touched with his hand. The state of being in love includes the other within the circle of selfhood (Aron & Aron, 1997; Aron, Aron, & Allen, 1989; Aron et al.,

1991). It becomes a temporary role that enables people to overcome difficulties and to relinquish previous commitments and relationships. What made the story of Floyd Johnson and Ellen Skinner so newsworthy is that it fits this pattern so perfectly.

Averill (1985) argues that without such cultural elaboration, we would not experience love as we do today. La Rochefoucauld (1665) said: "Some people would never have fallen in love if they had never heard of love" (Maxim 136). Averill and Nunley (1992) go further: they doubt whether anyone would fall in love if they had not heard of it.

Integrating Evolutionary and Cultural Approaches to Emotion

In Chapter 1, we raised enduring questions about the nature of emotion. In exploring evolutionary and cultural approaches to emotion in this and the previous chapter, we have begun to answer some of those questions. While it is tempting to highlight differences between evolutionary and cultural approaches to emotion, it is just as important to recognize their convergences (Matsumoto & Hwang, 2012). Both approaches start from the assumption that emotions contribute solutions to basic problems of social living. Both assume that emotions help humans form attachments, take care of offspring, fold into hierarchies, and maintain long-term friendships. The central theme of this book is squarely at the heart of the two approaches.

Evolutionary and cultural approaches both assume that emotions serve important functions. The two approaches focus on different kinds of functions, with evolutionary approaches focusing on how emotions enable survival and gene replication and cultural approaches focusing on functions that are particular to the social life of a culture; but both assume emotions are functional and adaptive. Gone is the view that emotions are dysfunctional, maladaptive, and pernicious to social life.

There are numerous differences, however, as one sees in Table 3.2. A first concerns the simplest question: What is an emotion? For evolutionary theorists, emotions are universal affect programs that solve ancient, recurrent threats to survival and occurrences of opportunity (Ekman, 1992; Plutchik, 1980; Tomkins, 1984; Tooby & Cosmides, 1990). Emotions, from this perspective, are species-characteristic patterns of response and action, derived from natural selection. For cultural theorists, the core of an emotional experience is the social unfolding of an emotion within a slice of a culture's social life, often manifest in acts of communication, in words, in metaphors, and in concepts that permeate the conscious experience of emotions. Emotions are

Table 3.2   Comparison of evolutionary and cultural approaches

Question of interest	Evolutionary approach	Cultural approach
What is an emotion?	Biological processes	Interpretations, language, beliefs, roles
Are emotions universal?	Yes	Possibly not
What are the origins of emotions?	Environment of evolutionary adaptedness	Practices, institutions, values
Functions	Individual: Action readiness	Reify intentions and values
	Dyadic: Social coordination	Reify roles, identities, and ideologies

discourse processes, and they are roles that we fulfill within relationships. For these theorists, some elements of emotion may be universal, but what is most striking are pronounced cultural differences in emotion that are socially learned in the process of social discourse and social practices and rituals and relationships, according to culturally specific concerns about identity, morality, and social structure (Averill, 1985; Lutz & White, 1986; Mesquita, 2003; Shweder & Haidt, 2000).

Cultural theorists, in particular those who do ethnographies, often push cultural specificity one step further. They sometimes contend that the experience of different emotions is not really comparable across cultures. The argument is, for instance, that *fago* is distinctive to Ifaluk. It can be hinted at by describing how it arises, and indicated by a composite of English terms (compassion/love/sadness), but you cannot experience the Ifaluk emotion *fago* unless you are a member of that society. Similarly, as Averill (1985) argues, you could not experience falling in love, with its mixture of sexual attraction, devotion, the feeling of altruism, and the making of a lifelong commitment, unless you have been enculturated in the West.

On the question of where emotions come from, we hope you now have a sense of how the two approaches each answer this question. Evolutionary theorists locate the emergence of emotions in our phylogenetic history, identifying emotions in nonhuman primates, and see them as adaptations to problems or opportunities that are specific to the environment of evolutionary adaptedness. Cultural theorists locate the origins of emotions within the history of cultural developments. They trace the origins of emotions to the emergence of new institutions, values, technologies, cultural narratives, social practices, and the like.

So why do we have emotions? Evolutionary theorists tend to concentrate on how emotions serve functions for the species by way of species-characteristic mechanisms possessed by individuals. At the individual level of analysis, emotions prepare the individual for action in his or her best interest (e.g., Frijda et al., 1989; Levenson, 1999). At the dyadic level of analysis, the focus is on communication and coordination of emotion through facial, vocal, and postural channels (Keltner et al., 2003; Scherer, Johnstone, & Klasmeyer, 2003). At this level, emotions communicate information about current emotions, intentions, and dispositions, to help accomplish mutuality or conflict and coordinated responses to problems and opportunities in the environment.

Cultural approaches offer great insights at the individual and dyadic levels of analysis, revealing how emotions are part of the individual's sense of self and culturally specific relationships. At the same time, cultural theorists tend to focus on another level of analysis: on how emotions serve functions for groups and societies. They see emotions as helping define values and enabling group members to negotiate roles (e.g., Clark, 1990; Collins, 1990). The ritualized experience of shame, for example, signals the individual's place within group hierarchies and reinforces certain roles and values. At this cultural level of analysis, emotions help individuals achieve identities, and they help reify, or fortify, cultural ideologies and power structures, regarding gender roles, for example (e.g., Hochschild, 1990; Lutz, 1990). The emotions of a culture are also essential to defining that culture: so, for instance, people's emotions within a culture tend to be similar. De Leersnyder, Mesquita and Kim (2011) found that when people immigrated to another country, their emotions tended to become more similar to those of the host group, depending on their amount of exposure to, and engagement with, the host culture.

Let us conclude our integration of the evolutionary and cultural approaches to emotion by considering how researchers working within the two traditions would approach one emotion:

embarrassment. Researchers guided by an evolutionary approach would seek to document the biological bases of embarrassment—the blush and its characteristic nonverbal display, for example—and how these aspects of embarrassment are universal, and can even be seen in the rudimentary appeasement displays of nonhuman primates and other species (Keltner & Buswell, 1997). This approach would claim that embarrassment informs the individual of transgressions to avoid, that it signals to others a sense of remorse for the transgression, thus evoking forgiveness, and in these ways prompts reconciliation following conflict and social transgressions.

From a cultural approach, what's interesting about embarrassment is how it is represented in words, how it is valued, and how it is associated with important values such as deference, modesty, and submissiveness. Researchers working from a cultural approach would seek to document how the meaning, value, and elicitors of embarrassment vary dramatically across cultures, according to the cultures' self-construals, or values, or epistemologies. Cultural theorists would seek to identify the origins of a culture's specific version of embarrassment within that culture's social history. In ancient Japan, for instance, embarrassment was a focal and valued emotion. In *The Tale of Genji* (Shikibu, c. 1000), which is thought to be the world's first full-length novel, written 1,000 years ago by Murasaki Shikibu, a lady in the Emperor's court in what is now Kyoto, we see that embarrassment can occur by being in the presence of a higher ranking individual. (You might get a glimmer of this kind of emotion if you have ever felt shy in the presence of an important person.) Here are some glimpses from that distant culture. When the youthful Prince Genji visits the house of his former nurse, who is ill, the nurse speaks to Genji fondly and tearfully. Her children are "acutely embarrassed . . . before so unbecoming a show of emotion in Genji's presence" (p. 57). The children would not have been embarrassed if their mother had spoken to them in this way; it is Genji's rank that causes their embarrassment. Later in the same chapter Genji stays the night with a lover, Yugao, who is of lower social status than he. She wakes in the morning, in her humble house, to the sound of her uncouth neighbors calling out to each other. In the West one might be annoyed at such a din, or worried that it might wake the sleeping loved one. Not so for Yugao: she is "deeply embarrassed by this chatter and clatter all around them of people rising and preparing to go about their pitiful tasks" (p. 63). Had they awoken in a royal palace there would have been nothing pitiful. All would have been appropriate to Genji's high status. All these examples show the importance of context, and particularly cultural context, in theorizing about emotions. A cultural approach would suggest, for instance, that embarrassment serves important functions for particular groups in particular societies. It communicates the individual's position within a group, and conveys commitments to cultural mores and standards. We believe that to understand emotions fully in social life, we need the wisdom of both evolutionary and cultural perspectives.

SUMMARY

How do we explain cultural differences in emotion? To answer this question, we first considered how emotions in the West themselves are products of a particular culture known as Romanticism, which prioritized the emotions in social life. We then outlined the basic assumptions of a cultural approach to emotions: emotions are shaped by dynamic cultural processes, they can be thought of as roles, and insights into the cultural influences upon emotion are gleaned when we focus on emotional practice, that is, how emotions are experienced in day-to-day living. Having outlined the basic assumptions of cultural approaches to emotion, we considered three specific approaches to cultural variation in emotion. One approach traces culture-related differences in emotion back to differences in self-construal, a second to cultural differences in values, and a third back to differences in culture-specific epistemologies, or ways of knowing. We then reviewed how to study cultural influences on emotion. We looked at cross-cultural comparisons of emotions, rich descriptions of culture known as ethnographies, and historical approaches. As we reviewed these different conceptual and methodological approaches to culture, we saw that cultures vary in the value they attach to different emotions, in emotion display rules, in the elicitors and language of emotion, and in the complexity of emotional experience. We concluded our chapter by integrating evolutionary and cultural approaches to emotion.

TO THINK ABOUT AND DISCUSS

1. Think about how you have seen an individual from a different culture express emotion in a different way than you might. How would you explain this difference from a self-construal perspective, or a values perspective?

2. Think of a context in which there are clear display rules about how people should express their emotions. What context is that, and what are the display rules that guide people's emotional behavior?

3. Now that you have surveyed evolutionary and cultural approaches to emotion, how do you weave these two kinds of theorizing into your own understanding of emotion? In what ways do you think emotions are evolved and universal and in what ways do they vary across cultures?

FURTHER READING

The most famous European romantic novella of the 18th century is a semiautobiographical piece by Germany's most famous author: the scientist-novelist-playwright, Goethe. It's still a good read:

Johann von Goethe (1774). *The sorrows of young Werther* (translated by M. Hulse). Harmondsworth: Penguin (1989).

A book based on living for nine months on a tiny Pacific island. A classic of emotional life and customs:

Catherine Lutz (1988). *Unnatural emotions: Everyday sentiments on a Micronesian atoll and their challenge to Western theory.* Chicago, IL: University of Chicago Press.

Two excellent reviews are:

Batja Mesquita & Janxin Leu (2007). The cultural psychology of emotion. In S. Kitayama & D. Cohen (Eds.), *Handbook of cultural psychology* (pp. 734–759). New York, NY: Guilford.

Richard Shweder, Jonathan Haidt, Randall Horton, & Craig Joseph (2008). The cultural psychology of emotions: Ancient and renewed. In M. Lewis, J. Haviland Jones, & L. F. Barrett (Eds.), *Handbook of emotions, third edition.* New York, NY: Guilford.

Elements of Emotions

PART II

Communication of Emotions

4

CONTENTS

Photo Credit: Andersen Ross/Blend Images/Getty Images, Inc.

FIGURE 4.0 People communicate emotions in many ways, non-verbally by expressions, gestures, and touch, as well as verbally in what we say and how we say it.

. . . there is a kind of universal language, consisting of expressions of the face and eyes, gestures and tones of voice, which can show whether a person means to ask for something and get it, or refuse it and have nothing to do with it.

(Augustine, Confessions, 1–8)

Next time you leave a classroom, look at the students standing around and talking, perhaps hashing over an inspired lecture they just heard or planning the weekend. You're likely to see some people flirting. If you look closely, you may conclude that everyone is flirting, almost all of the time.

To document how people flirt, Givens (1983) and Perper (1985) spent hundreds of hours in singles bars, painstakingly writing down the patterns of nonverbal behaviors that predicted whether women and men would pursue a romantic encounter. They discovered a layered and varied language of nonverbal behavior by which women and men negotiate romantic inclinations. In the initial attention-getting phase, men roll their shoulders and raise their arms with exaggerated gestures to show off signs of their social status—their well-developed arms or flashy watches. At the same time, women smile coyly, they look askance, they flick their hair, and walk with arched back and swaying hips. In the recognition phase, women and men gaze intently at each other, they express interest with raised eyebrows, singsong voice, melodious laughter, and subtle lip puckers and extended eye contact. In the exploration phase, women and men touch each other with provocative brushes of the arm, pats on the shoulder, or not-so-accidental bumps against one another, looking for subtle signs of delight or disgust. Finally, in the keeping-time phase, the potential partners mirror each other's glances, laughs, gazes, and postures, to assess their interest in one another—the more they mimic, the more likely they are to take the next step in the romantic encounter.

In most social interactions, like flirting, people express emotions. The communication of emotion is a grammar of our social life; it is central to the playful wrestling of siblings, the grieving over a lost loved one, the arguing of romantic partners, the soothing of a young child, and people's negotiation of their status in groups. People express emotions with facial actions, with their voice, with touch, with posture, and with their gait (Montepare, Goldstein, & Clausen, 1987). The communication of emotion occurs in different channels, many of which were recognized by Darwin in his study of emotional expression, discussed in Chapter 1 (see Table 1.1).

Five Kinds of Nonverbal Behavior

Words such as *smile*, *laugh*, *gaze*, and *touch* seem simple enough, but they can refer to many classes of nonverbal behavior, with often contrasting emotional connotations. Take the word *smile*. There have been heated debates about what smiles mean, and the extent to which they necessarily accompany the experience of positive emotion (e.g., Fernandez-Dols & Ruiz-Belda, 1995, 1997; Frank, Ekman, & Friesen, 1993; Fridlund, 1992; Kraut & Johnston, 1979). The answer is that different smiles have different meanings. We smile to be polite, to hide feelings of disapproval, to express romantic attraction, to signal weakness, to pretend that we are following what another person is saying, and so on. Often single words like *smile* fail adequately to describe the language of **nonverbal communication**.

In their studies of emotional expression, Paul Ekman and Wallace Friesen (1969) organized nonverbal behavior into five categories. First are **emblems**: nonverbal gestures that directly translate to words. For English speakers these include the peace sign, and in the late 1960s, the raised, clenched fist to indicate Black Power. Researchers have analyzed over 800 emblems throughout the world. No doubt there are many more.

Emblems vary in their meaning across cultures. For instance, the gesture of extending the index finger and little finger of one hand toward someone (see Figure 4.2) indicates contempt in Italy and Spain, but it is largely unknown in Britain and Scandinavia. In Britain the equivalent gesture is raising the first and second fingers of one hand with the palm facing toward the sender,

Photo Credit: Alfredo Dagli Orti/The Art Archive at Art Resource, NY

FIGURE 4.1 "Flirtation," by the Hungarian painter Miklós Barabás, showing characteristic elements: the man shows direct interest with body and head oriented toward the woman; the woman shows classic coyness, with head and gaze cast away.

and it is largely unknown elsewhere. In America the equivalent gesture is raising the middle finger, and in Australia it is raising the thumb. All four gestures have comparable meanings as insults with a coarse sexual connotation, but except for being made with fingers they share few morphological features. They are like a word in four different languages.

A second category of nonverbal behaviors is the **illustrator**, a nonverbal gesture that accompanies our speech, to make it vivid, visual, or emphatic. We gesture with our hands often when we speak—spend a few minutes observing. McNeill (2005) has shown that these

Andrew Holt/Getty Images, Inc.

FIGURE 4.2   Coarse gesture of contempt, as seen in Britain but not in Southern Europe. Such gestures are based on learned conventions, like words.

gestures slightly precede the corresponding words we say. We also use facial gestures to illustrate and dramatize our speech. We raise our eyebrows when articulating the most important point in a phrase. We nod our heads to strengthen a point we are making with words.

Regulators are nonverbal behaviors that we use to coordinate conversation, behaviors such as head nods and eyebrow flashes and encouraging vocalizations of interest. People look and point at and orient their bodies toward people whom they want to start speaking. They look and turn their bodies away from those they wish would stop speaking. It is a remarkable feat of human social life that people can carry on collaborative conversations in groups without explicitly designating who is to speak and who is not. They often do so by using regulators.

A fourth kind of nonverbal behavior is the **self-adaptor**: nervous behaviors that lack seeming intentions, as if simply to release nervous energy. People touch their faces, tug at their hair, jiggle their legs, bite their lips, and scratch their chins. We are often unaware of self-adaptors that are part of our self-presentation, and they can cost us: when you are showing self-adaptors, people are more likely to believe that you are lying.

Finally, there are **displays of emotion**: signals in the face, voice, body, and touch that convey emotion.

Facial Expressions of Emotion

How can we differentiate emotional expressions from other kinds of nonverbal behavior? What distinguishes a smile of enjoyment from one that occurs when someone receives a painful injection? How does a sincere expression of anger at being slighted differ from a mock expression of anger, in which someone dramatically enacts the expression of anger in order to have an effect, but in actuality feels little emotion?

Markers of Emotional Expressions

Several characteristics differentiate emotional expressions from other nonverbal behaviors (Frank et al., 1993). Most of these criteria have been established in the study of facial expression, but are likely to apply to the voice and to touch. First, expressions of emotion tend to last just a few seconds (Bachorowski & Owren, 2001; Ekman, 1993). A smile accompanying enjoyment will typically start and stop within a span of 10 seconds. A polite smile that does not accompany the experience of emotion might be exceptionally brief, lasting a quarter of a second, or it might endure for some time, as when someone smiles politely through the entire course of an unpleasant dinner party.

Second, facial expressions of emotion involve involuntary muscle actions that people cannot deliberately produce and cannot suppress (Dimberg, Thunberg, & Grunedal, 2002; Kappas, Bherer, & Thériault, 2000). The facial expression of anger, for example, involves the action of the muscle that tightens around the mouth, which most people cannot produce voluntarily. Feigned expressions of anger, therefore, would lack the muscle tightening around the mouth. These involuntary actions that accompany emotional expressions have a different neuroanatomical basis than voluntary facial actions such as the furrowed brow or lip press (Rinn, 1984). We suspect you can think of many occasions when it really mattered to you whether a person's expression of emotion—for example, of love or sympathy or anger—was indeed sincere.

Third, as Darwin speculated, human emotional expressions often have parallels in displays of other species, a thesis that has guided numerous studies of embarrassment, laughter, love, and the human voice, as we shall see.

Studies of the Universality of Facial Expressions

As we discussed in Chapter 1, in making his case about the evolution of human emotion, Darwin (1872) drew on observations of animals at the zoo, of peoples from other societies that he encountered in his voyages, and of his own children. He derived three principles to explain emotional expressions (Hess & Thibault, 2009; Shariff & Tracy, 2011). First, according to the **principle of serviceable habits**, expressive behaviors that helped individuals respond adaptively to threats and opportunities in the evolutionary past will reoccur in the future. For example, the furrowed brow, which protects the eyes from blows, and exposed teeth, which in our ancestors signaled that they were about to attack, tend still to occur in modern humans when they are angry. Second, the **principle of antithesis** holds that opposing states will be associated with opposing expressions. For example, you will learn later that pride is signaled in dominant, size-expanding displays—chest expansion and tilting the head back— whereas shame is signaled in submissive behavior—drooping shoulders and downward movements of the head. Third, the **principle of nervous discharge** states that excess, undirected energy is released in random expressions, such as face touches, leg jiggles, and the like.

Darwin advanced the thesis that because facial expressions derived from our evolutionary heritage they are human universals. Sylvan Tomkins, Paul Ekman, and Carroll Izard carefully read Darwin's book, and distilled his observations into two hypotheses (Ekman, Sorenson, & Friesen, 1969; Izard, 1971; Tomkins, 1962, 1963). First the **encoding hypothesis**: the experience of different emotions should be associated with the same distinct expressions in every culture. Second, the **decoding hypothesis**: people of different cultures should interpret these expressions in the same ways.

Significant figures: Sylvan Tomkins, Carroll Izard, Paul Ekman

A seminal figure who shaped profoundly the resurgence of interest in emotion in the second half of the 20th century was Sylvan Tomkins, who proposed what he called *affect theory*. In this theory, emotions are thought to be hardwired, preprogrammed responses that are genetically transmitted to all humans. Based on specific physiological mechanisms, Tomkins argued, affect derives from a small set of nine basic emotions, each of which is displayed in a distinct facial expression. As in Darwin's theorizing, Tomkins proposed that these distinct facial expressions are universal. What he needed was strong empirical data in support of his theory.

Toward this end, Tomkins inspired two young scientists he was mentoring—Carroll Izard and Paul Ekman—to go in search of evidence of the universality of facial expressions of emotion. Both would conduct groundbreaking studies in remote cultures of the universality of facial expression. Carroll Izard worked, at first, principally with children and developed a coding system based on which features of facial expressions enabled distinct basic emotions to be most clearly differentiated from each other.

Recently, Izard's work has tended to focus on how understanding of emotions can be used to improve children's and adults' functioning and health. Paul Ekman also developed in collaboration with his longtime co-author, Wallace Friesen, a coding system for emotions of a kind that was different from Izard's. Ekman and Friesen's Facial Action Coding System is anatomically based, and allows researchers to identify specific emotions according to the contraction of specific facial muscles and muscle configurations. Ekman's work on facial expressions of emotion that are recognizable in different societies of the world has been a cornerstone, both for those who accept the proposal of a small number of basic emotions that these expressions imply, and for those who question it. Recognized by the American Psychological Association as being among the most influential psychologists of the 20th century, Ekman has also made his way into popular culture with his work on how micro-expressions can indicate lying, which, as well as having been taken up by U.S. border officials, has become the basis of a well-regarded television program, *Lie to me*.

As a first test of these hypotheses, Ekman and Friesen took over 3,000 photos of different people as they expressed six emotions—anger, disgust, fear, happiness, sadness, and surprise—according to Darwin's descriptions of the muscle configurations. Ekman, Sorenson, and Friesen (1969) then presented photos of the most easily identified examples of each emotion to participants in Japan, Brazil, Argentina, Chile, and the United States, who selected from six emotion terms the one that best matched the feeling the person was showing in each photo. Across the five cultures, participants achieved accuracy rates between 80 and 90% for the six. In these studies, chance guessing would produce accuracy rates of 16.6%. Critics, however, noted a problem: participants in Japan, Brazil, Argentina, and Chile had seen U.S. television and films, and might thereby have learned American labels for the facial expressions.

To respond to this critique, Ekman traveled to Papua, New Guinea, and for six months lived with a people of the Fore (pronounced "Foray") language group who had seen no movies or magazines, who did not speak English or pidgin (a combination of English and a native language), and who had had minimal exposure to Westerners.

In the study with the Fore, Ekman and Friesen (1971) devised a little story appropriate to each of the six emotions. For example, the sadness story was: "The person's child had died, and he felt sad." They then presented photos of three different expressions with a story that matched one of the expressions, and asked participants to match the story to one of the three expressions (chance guessing would yield identification rates of 33%). In another task, the researchers videotaped

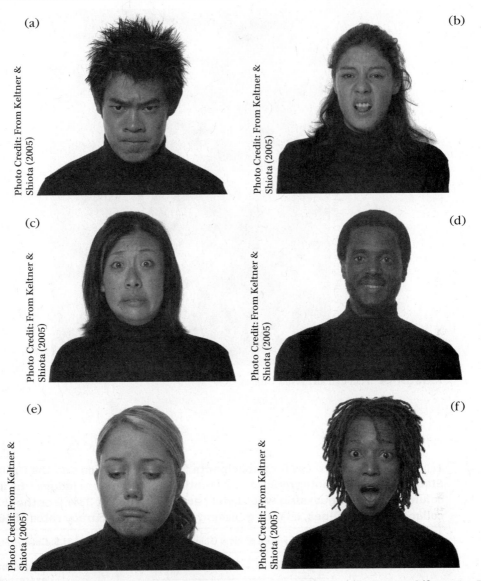

(a)   Photo Credit: From Keltner & Shiota (2005)

(b)   Photo Credit: From Keltner & Shiota (2005)

(c)   Photo Credit: From Keltner & Shiota (2005)

(d)   Photo Credit: From Keltner & Shiota (2005)

(e)   Photo Credit: From Keltner & Shiota (2005)

(f)   Photo Credit: From Keltner & Shiota (2005)

FIGURE 4.3 Six different emotions: (a) anger, (b) disgust, (c) fear, (d) happiness, (e) sadness, and (f) surprise. These photos are similar to those described by Darwin, to those used by Ekman and Friesen in their universality studies, and to those used in many other studies of facial expression.

Fore participants as they displayed facial expressions they would show in response to the emotion-specific story, and then presented unedited clips of these expressions to college students in the United States, who selected from six emotion terms the one that best matched the Fore's pose in each clip (chance guessing would yield identification rates of 16.6%).

The results from these two studies largely confirmed Darwin's thesis about the universality of emotional expression (see Table 4.1). The Fore participants achieved accuracy rates between

Photo Credit: Paul Ekman, Ph.D./Paul Ekman Group, LLC

FIGURE 4.4   Paul Ekman in New Guinea.

Table 4.1   **Accuracy rates for participants from New Guinea and the United States in judging photographs of six emotions. For the Fore judges (the first two columns), chance guessing would yield accuracy rates of 33%. For the U.S. college student judges, chance guessing would yield accuracy rates of 16.6%**

| | The Fore of New Guinea | | U.S. College Students |
| | Judging Ekman and Friesen's photos | | Judging emotional expressions posed by the Fore |
	Adults	**Children**	
Anger	84	90	51
Disgust	81	85	46
Fear	80	93	18
Happiness	92	92	73
Sadness	79	91	68
Surprise	68	98	27

Source: Adapted from Ekman (1972).

80% and 90% in identifying the six emotions portrayed in Ekman and Friesen's photos. This was even true of children, suggesting that the ability to judge emotions from facial expression occurs early in development, a thesis explored in depth in Chapter 8. The U.S. college students correctly interpreted the posed expressions of the Fore, with the exception of fear and surprise.

There have now been dozens of similar studies, and they have tended to find that people from cultures that differ in values, religion, political structure, economic development, and self-construals agree in how they label the photos that depict anger, disgust, fear, happiness, sadness, and surprise (Ekman, 1984, 1993; Elfenbein & Ambady, 2002, 2003; Izard, 1971, 1994). The recognition of the six facial expressions is a universal, evolved part of human nature (Brown, 1991).

Critiques of the Studies of Universal Facial Expressions

There have been several critiques of the universality evidence we just reviewed (e.g., Barrett, 2011; Fridlund, 1992; Russell, 1994). First is the *free response* critique. In Ekman and Friesen's study and most of those that followed it, participants were required to label the expressions using terms the researchers provided. Had participants been given the chance to freely label the facial expressions with their own words, might they have used much different emotion words than those provided by the experimenter? Might they have labeled a smile "gratitude" or "reverence" or "*amae*/pleasurable dependence" (see Chapter 3) rather than "happiness," or with some concept that does not map onto Western conceptions?

To address this critique, Haidt and Keltner (1999) asked participants in the United States and India to label photos of 14 different expressions, including the Ekman and Friesen expressions, in their own words. When coded, the freely produced labels revealed that participants from these strikingly different cultures used similar concepts in labeling facial expressions of anger, disgust, fear, happiness, sadness, surprise, and embarrassment (see also Izard, 1971). Haidt and Keltner concluded that among the 14 expressions they studied, "there is no neat distinction between cross-culturally recognisable and nonrecognisable expressions. Results are better described as a gradient of recognition" (p. 225).

A second critique is in terms of *ecological validity*: the expressions in Ekman's studies may not be those that people routinely produce or judge in their daily lives; they are highly stylized and exaggerated, often made by actors or others who are adept at moving their facial muscles. This raises the question of whether everyday expressions look like the expressions in the Ekman and Friesen photos, and whether more subtle expressions of emotion, perhaps more typical of everyday emotional expression, would be so reliably judged (Wagner, MacDonald, & Manstead, 1986). Most of the research on recognition of facial expressions has, for convenience, used static pictures. Ambadar, Schooler, and Cohn (2005) have shown that people are better at recognizing emotional expressions from dynamic displays, such as video clips, which come closer to real-life conditions.

More generally, Lisa Feldman Barrett (2011) has raised the question of the extent to which people express prototypical basic expressions during episodes of emotion (for one review, see Matsumoto et al., 2008). Among studies she cites is that of Roch-Levecq (2006), who found that expressions of 20 congenitally blind children asked to act out how they felt in response to verbally described events designed to elicit basic emotions were more difficult to recognize than those of 20 sighted children. Expressions of the blind children were not the full, basic prototypical expressions predicted by Ekman's kind of theory.

Extending this kind of argument, Barrett, Mesquita, and Gendron (2011) have proposed that the very same facial display can have different meanings dependent on the context. They say that visual scenes, voices, bodies, other faces, cultural orientation, and even words shape how emotion is perceived in a face. So, if we think of emotional communication as a kind of language, we might imagine that just as the word *bank* can mean one thing on an airplane, another in relation to one's savings, and yet another if we think about a river, so the same emotional expression can mean different things in different contexts. Barrett et al. say that incorporating context during emotion perception appears to be routine, efficient, and, to some degree, automatic.

Some responses to critiques of Ekman's line of research reveal that Darwin's hypothesis is still worth pursuing, but others point to alternative theories, for instance, of the kind that Russell, Barrett, and their colleagues propose. A debate is in progress. Certain expressions of emotion do seem to have some universal characteristics, although we may expect a new wave of research showing how context can affect the production and perception of displays. A different wave of research, to which we now turn, has looked for universal displays of emotions other than the basic set that Ekman studied.

Discovering New Facial Displays of Emotions

Evidence of the kind that Ekman collected suggested that anger, disgust, happiness, and sadness are associated with universal facial expressions, although evidence for expressions of fear and surprise was less strong. Have scientists discovered other universal expressions? The answer is yes. Contempt has been added to the list. It is expressed by an asymmetrical tightening of the lip corners or sneer, and conveys a moral disapproval of another (Matsumoto & Ekman, 2004).

What about still other emotions? Can you tell whether your romantic partner is or is not jealous by studying his or her face? Or a friend's guilt at having forgotten your birthday? How about love or gratitude, emotions crucial to romantic bonds and friendships?

To document such expressions, one needs to show that the experience of a specific emotion correlates with a unique pattern of facial actions (encoding evidence) and that observers in different cultures perceive that display as a sign of the target emotion (decoding evidence). For evolutionary claims it is also important to show that other species show similar expressive behaviors in contexts that resemble those of the emotion of interest. Recent studies guided by these principles suggest that there are distinct nonverbal displays for embarrassment, shame, pride, love, desire, and sympathy.

Self-Conscious Emotions: Embarrassment, Shame, and Pride

Darwin had many things to say about the self-conscious emotions, but he focused his analysis on the blush—a physiological response we will consider in the next chapter. The early universality studies of Ekman did not address whether the self-conscious emotions had distinct displays.

Two recent investigations, working within the Darwinian tradition, have established that embarrassment, shame, and pride have distinct nonverbal displays. Let's begin with embarrassment: how might one elicit it in the laboratory? Researchers have resorted to rather mischievous means. For instance, students have been asked to suck on a pacifier in front of friends or to model bathing suits. In perhaps the most mortifying test, participants had to sing Barry Manilow's song, "Feelings," using dramatic hand gestures, and then watch a videotape of their performance with a group of other students.

To characterize the embarrassment display, Keltner (1995) chose a task in which participants' heads would be relatively stationary, so that their facial actions could be coded in frame-by-frame analyses. So participants completed the following task. They followed muscle-by-muscle instructions, given by a rather stern experimenter, to achieve a difficult and odd-looking facial expression, while being videotaped. The instructions were:

Raise your eyebrows.

Close one eye. Pucker your lips.

Puff out your cheeks.

Typically, after a 15-second struggle, participants achieved the expression. They then were asked to hold the expression for 10 seconds, and then were told to rest. Performing this task resembles the effect of a common elicitor of embarrassment—loss of poise and composure in front of others (Miller, 1992; Miller & Tangney, 1994). For those participants who spontaneously reported experiencing embarrassment, Keltner coded the 10 seconds of behavior that occurred immediately after the participant was asked to rest.

Careful frame-by-frame analysis uncovered a fleeting but highly coordinated 2-to-3-second affective display (see also Edelmann & Hampson, 1979, 1981; Harris, 2001). First, the embarrassed individual's eyes went down, within .75 seconds. Then the individual turned his head to the side, typically leftward, and down within the next .5 second. As this head movement occurred, the individual smiled for about two seconds. At the onset and offset of this smile were other facial actions, such as lip sucks, lip presses, lip puckers. And while the person's head was down there were a few curious actions: the person looked up two or three times with furtive glances, and often touched his or her face. Like other expressions, the embarrassment display unfolded in a coordinated and reliable way within a period of 5 seconds. It had the fluid, gradual onset and offset times of an involuntary emotional expression.

Is there decoding evidence to show that observers can readily identify this display as embarrassment? In one study, participants were presented with 2-to-3-second-long video-clips of the embarrassment displays along with spontaneous displays of disgust, anger, shame, amusement, and fear (Keltner, 1995). Using a forced-choice method, they reliably judged the displays as communicating embarrassment. A second study turned to the issue of universality and whether participants can judge embarrassment from its static cues—the downward gaze and head movement, the controlled smile—in the absence of dynamic cues contained in the unfolding display of embarrassment represented in Figure 4.5. People from a small, Hindu temple town in India were presented with static photos of the embarrassment display and those of other emotions, and in their own words reliably interpreted the expression as embarrassment, and readily differentiated the display from that of shame, which is signaled in downward head movements and gaze aversion (Haidt & Keltner, 1999).

Do other species show similar, embarrassment-like behavior? Keltner and Buswell (1997) analyzed approximately three dozen studies of appeasement displays of other species to answer this question. In appeasement interactions, one individual, typically a subordinate, relies on certain signals to pacify and reduce the aggressive tendencies of another individual, often a dominant individual in the social hierarchy (de Waal, 1989). Human embarrassment displays do resemble the appeasement displays of other species. Let's take it behavior by behavior, in the Darwinian fashion, to understand the deeper significance of the elements of the embarrassment display.

First, there is gaze aversion. This is a classic behavior by which many species appease others. Many primates turn their heads away to interrupt escalating aggression. Extended eye contact signals the opposite: the intent to escalate. What about the head movements down? Various species, including pigs, rabbits, blue-footed boobies, pigeons, doves, and loons, use head movements down, head turns, and head bobs to appease. These head movements reduce the size of the body, signaling submissiveness. As for the embarrassed smile, it is more than a simple

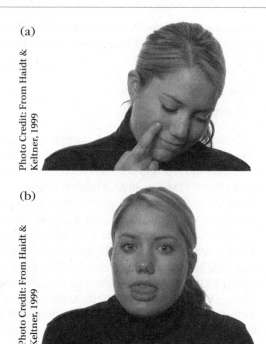

(a)

Photo Credit: From Haidt & Keltner, 1999

(b)

Photo Credit: From Haidt & Keltner, 1999

FIGURE 4.5   Universality and cultural variation in the meaning of the embarrassment display. People in the United States and India agree in their judgments of a prototypical embarrassment display, but only people in India recognize the ritualized tongue bite as a display of embarrassment. (Source: Haidt & Keltner, 1999. *Social psychology*, 2nd ed., WW Norton.)

smile; it has accompanying smile controls that include lip presses, no doubt a sign of inhibition, as well as lip puckers. This kind of controlled smile is a common signal of appeasement in certain nonhuman primates. The face touch may be the most mysterious element of embarrassment. Several primates cover their faces when appeasing, as do rabbits. The elements of embarrassment, then, are routinely seen in the appeasement displays of other species.

Jessica Tracy and Rick Robins (2004; 2007) have focused their efforts on pride, an emotion associated with gains in status through socially valued actions. Many nonhuman species, in particular primates, signal their rise in social status through expanded physical size—the classic chest pounding you might see apes engage in at the zoo. So, too, it would seem, do humans. In their research, Tracy and Robins first documented that displays of expansive posture, head movements up and back, and arm thrusts upward reliably signal pride to observers. Like Darwin and Ekman before them, they then took care to study a remote people, in their case in Burkina Faso, Africa; these individuals readily identified displays of pride as being of that emotion.

But do people in different cultures display pride in this fashion? In an imaginative use of naturalistic data, Tracy and Matsumoto (2008) analyzed the emotional expressions of sighted and blind Olympic athletes from 20 different countries just after they had either won or lost a judo competition, focusing their careful analysis upon several relevant behaviors, such as smiling, fists pumped in the air, chest expanded or contracted, and shoulder slouching. Darwin had suggested that the expressions of blind individuals are particularly germane to evolutionary claims of universality because they will not have been copied from seen behavior of others. Sure enough, as you can see in Figure 4.6, after victory, both sighted (on the top) and blind athletes

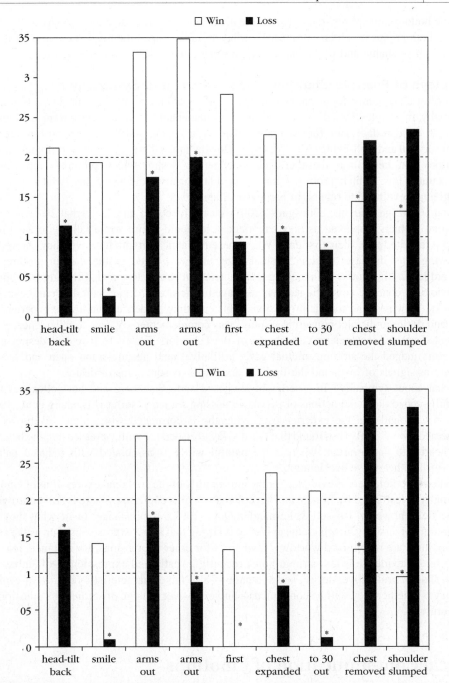

FIGURE 4.6 Sighted (top panel) and blind (bottom panel) Olympic athletes' nonverbal displays in response to winning and losing a competition. (From Tracy & Matsumoto, 2008.)

(on the bottom) alike threw their arms in the air with chest out as an expression of pride. After losing, both groups of athletes dropped their heads and slumped their shoulders in a display of shame. These shame and pride displays seem to be universal.

Displays of Positive Emotion: Love, Desire, and Sympathy

Let's offer a Darwinian focus on the displays of one final cluster of emotions: love, desire, and sympathy. In Chapter 2 we detailed how emotions that enable us to form long-term attachments in which we reproduce, care for vulnerable offspring, and form families and friendships are vital to our survival and well-being (Bowlby, 1969). Bowlby himself argued for three different positive emotions that help form these critical attachments: desire, which promotes reproductive interactions; love, which promotes long-term relationships; and sympathy, which motivates caregiving to vulnerable others, in particular offspring.

Gian Gonzaga and his colleagues (2001) carefully coded the nonverbal behaviors that romantic partners displayed as they experienced love and desire while talking to each other about a favorite topic, their first date. When these romantic partners felt love, they showed the following brief displays: smiling, mutual gaze, affiliative hand gestures, open posture, and forward leans. Many other primates signal an interest in being close and affiliating with similar behaviors. In contrast, romantic partners displayed their sexual desire with different behaviors: lip licks, lip wipes, and tongue protrusions. This encoding evidence relating the experience of love and desire to distinct nonverbal displays was complemented by decoding evidence. When presented with videotapes or still photos of the behaviors related to love and desire, naïve observers judged the smiling, mutual gaze, affiliative hand gestures, and open and forward posture as signals of love, and the lip licks and wipes as sure signs of desire.

What about sympathy? In a series of studies, Nancy Eisenberg and her colleagues have carefully coded the facial actions of people witnessing someone suffer (Eisenberg et al., 1989). They have found that the experience of sympathy is correlated with oblique eyebrows and concerned gaze. She also has found that this display is associated with increased helping behavior and heart rate deceleration, whereas the painful wince is associated with reduced helping behavior and heart rate acceleration.

Taken together, there is evidence for the universality of the six facial expressions of emotion originally investigated by Ekman and his colleagues, plus contempt. There is still controversy in the field, however. Russell & Fernandez Dols (1997), for instance, favor what they call minimum universality, in which the evidence is strong that some expressions such as the smile of happiness are recognized worldwide, whereas for other expressions, for instance, fear and surprise, the evidence is less strong. Some recently investigated expressions—of embarrassment, shame, pride, love, desire, and sympathy—also have characteristic features of evolved displays. Whether they will be confirmed as universal over a range of studies is a question for the future.

Vocal Communication of Emotions

The capacity to use the voice in language is an ability that sets humans apart from our closest primate relatives, and may contribute to the emergence of the enormous frontal lobes in the human brain (Dunbar, 2003). In this section, we will examine how humans communicate emotion in the voice.

Examples of Vocal Communication: Teasing and Laughter

As a testimony to the emotional richness of the voice, let's consider two commonplace social behaviors whose meaning is found in subtle changes in vocalization. Teasing occurs when one person playfully provokes another, typically commenting on some unusual and potentially undesirable act or attribute (Keltner et al., 2001). There are many forms of teasing, from the lifelong nickname to the tickle in the ribs. One kind is the sarcastic comment, in which the teaser states one thing, but in a tone of voice that implies the opposite. In commenting on a friend's out-of-key singing in the shower, a person might say "You're a regular Jason Mraz." Teasers rely on several acoustic markers to communicate that they don't mean what their words say: they utter words with unusual tempos (e.g., unusually slow or fast), clipped vowels, drawn-out syllables, and nasal-rich sarcastic tones, to communicate the opposite of what is said. Speech patterns transform the meaning of the spoken word.

Or consider laughter, which likely preceded language in its evolutionary emergence and has been part of the human communicative repertoire for several million years (Dunbar, 2004; Provine, 1992, 1993; Provine & Fischer, 1989). Facially, laughter involves the contraction of the muscle surrounding the eyes, and vocally, the making of distinct sounds. What emotion is being expressed? Perhaps it's "exhilaration" (Ruch, 1993), or perhaps "joy" (Panksepp, 2005). Panksepp has shown that laughter has an animal analogue and that it typically occurs in play.

Next time you're in a conversation with a group of friends, listen carefully to the varieties of laughter. There are laughs that reflect tension, anxiety, contempt, anger, sarcasm, embarrassment, and sexual desire. Many laughs seem to involve little emotion at all. People laugh to fill the empty gaps in conversations, to signal that they are tracking what the speaker is saying, or to encourage the speaker to continue.

Jo-Anne Bachorowski and her colleagues have mapped acoustic characteristics of different laughs (Bachorowski & Owren, 2001; Bachorowski, Smoski, & Owren, 2001; Smoski & Bachorowski, 2003). They have analyzed thousands of laughs gathered as participants responded to amusing film clips or engaged in amusing tasks together. There are cackles, hisses, breathy pants, snorts, and grunts, and voiced or songlike laughs, which include vowel-like sounds and pitch modulation thanks to the involvement of the vocal folds. Women more frequently produce voiced laughs, whereas men often laugh with snorts and grunts (Bachorowski & Owren, 2001). People find voiced laughs more attractive, because they have direct effects upon the listeners' emotions, and because they signal or remind the listener of positive experiences. Friends are likely to engage in antiphonal laughter, in which the two individuals overlap in their bouts of laughter. Laughter, then, is a sign of friendship, of play, and even intimacy (Smoski & Bachorowski, 2003). A common reason that women give for being with a long-term male sexual partner is: "He makes me laugh."

The Communication of Emotions with the Voice

Let us now think about how emotional states might alter vocalization patterns in discernible ways. Klaus Scherer has argued that several emotion-related physiological changes alter pitch, tempo, and loudness of speech (Scherer, 1986). For example, when in an anxious state, the muscles around the lungs are tense, thus restricting the air flow through the larynx. Our tense vocal chords will produce less variability in pitch. We are likely to have less saliva in the mouth,

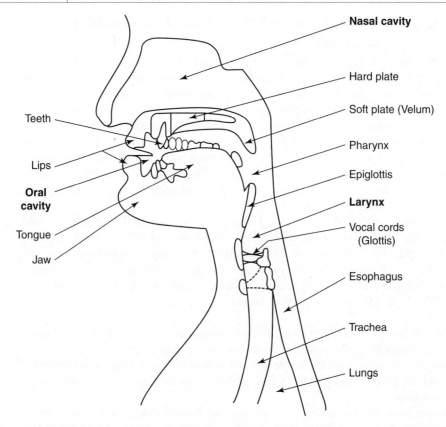

Nasal cavity

Hard plate

Soft plate (Velum)

Pharynx

Epiglottis

Larynx

Vocal cords (Glottis)

Esophagus

Trachea

Lungs

Teeth

Lips

Oral cavity

Tongue

Jaw

FIGURE 4.7   Anatomy of the vocal apparatus.

and the shape of our lips will tighten. All of these changes will influence speech patterning. Through these and other emotion-related changes in physiology, emotions should be signaled in distinct vocalizations.

To study whether people can communicate emotions with the voice, researchers have relied on two methods. In one, people, often trained actors, attempt to express different emotions in the voice while reading nonsense syllables or neutral passages of text (Banse & Scherer, 1996; Juslin & Laukka, 2003; Klasmeyer & Sendlmeier, 1999; Wallbott & Scherer, 1986). These vocal expressions are then presented to listeners, who select from a series of options to identify the term that best matches the emotion conveyed in the speech output. In one early study, Van Bezooijen, Van Otto, and Heenan (1983) had four male and four female native speakers of Dutch say the words *twee maanden zwanger* (meaning "two months' pregnant") in a neutral voice and in voices expressing nine emotions (disgust, surprise, shame, interest, joy, fear, contempt, sadness, and anger). Audio recordings of the phrases were then played to participants in Holland, Taiwan, and Japan. In a review of 60 studies of this kind, Juslin and Laukka (2003) concluded that hearers can judge five different emotions in the voice—anger, fear, happiness, sadness, and tenderness—with accuracy rates that approach 70% (see also Scherer, Johnstone, & Klasmeyer, 2003). Judgments are best when hearers listen to members of their own culture.

In a second kind of study, participants communicate emotions through **vocal bursts**, which are brief, non-word utterances that arise between speech incidents. Think how you might communicate fear or anger with a vocal burst. You're likely to shriek or growl. Or how about compassion or the feeling of savoring a delicious bite of ice-cream. Here we suspect you might say *aww* or *mmm*. In studies of vocal bursts, people are given a definition of an emotion (e.g., for example, the definition for awe would be "You are in the presence of something vast and that is not easy for you to immediately understand") and asked to communicate that emotion with a brief vocal burst, and to not use words (Sauter & Scott, 2007; Simon-Thomas et al., 2009). These sounds are then played to listeners, who attempt to label the sound with one of many emotion terms. This research is documenting that people are quite adept at communicating emotions with vocal bursts. For example, if you study the charts in Figure 4.8, which summarize findings from Simon-Thomas et al.'s study, you will see that people are quite able to communicate the well-studied emotions—anger, disgust, fear, sadness, and surprise—with vocal bursts as well as less studied emotions, such as admiration, awe, achievement, amusement, boredom, contempt, contentment, elation, pleasure, and relief (Simon-Thomas et al., 2009).

Are vocal bursts universal? To answer this question, Disa Sauter traveled to a remote part of Namibia to gather evidence from the Himba people, a group of 20,000 individuals living with no electricity or formal education, and with little history of contact with people from the outside (Sauter et al., 2010). Sauter presented vocal bursts of emotion of Western European individuals to the Himba, and found that they could reliably label vocal bursts of anger, disgust, amusement, fear, sadness, and surprise. She also gathered vocal bursts of the Himba, and found that Western Europeans could reliably judge those vocal bursts. Quite intriguingly, the Himba could not reliably label the Western vocal bursts of pleasure, relief, and admiration. It would appear that some vocal bursts are probably universal, while others have more readily identified meanings within a culture (Russell, 1994).

Is there evidence for continuity of human emotional vocalization with that of nonhuman species? Cheyney and Seyfarth (1990) describe how vervet monkeys have three main predators, and an avoidant action appropriate to each kind. When an eagle appears, a monkey hides in the undergrowth, when a leopard is seen the monkey climbs a tree, when there is a snake the monkey rears on its hind legs and looks downward. If any monkey sees a predator, he or she makes one of three species-characteristic alarm calls appropriate to the predator. The acoustic signal is heard by monkeys nearby, evokes the specific kind of fear in them, and induces them to take the appropriate evasive action.

Disa Sauter and Charles Snowdon have documented several nonhuman vocalizations that resemble those of humans (Sauter, 2010; Snowdon, 2003). Several species have high-pitched alarm calls with abrupt onset and offset times that resemble human fear vocalizations. Macaque infants will utter coos when separated from their mothers, sounds that resemble those that human infants make when separated from their mothers. Macaques also emit "girns," which are purr-like vocalizations that occur in the context of affiliation, and these may have parallels in humans expressing affection. Macaques in Sri Lanka utter a food call when they discover a source of ripe fruit, which may resemble vocal bursts of pleasure. Dominant primates often emit threat vocalizations that resemble angry vocalizations in humans. And chimpanzees emit calls when copulating—the male soft, short panting calls, the female long, loud screams—that have parallels in humans.

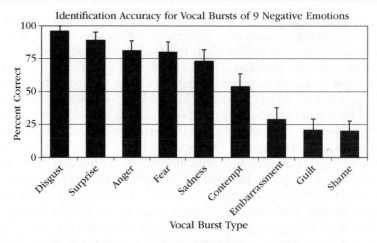

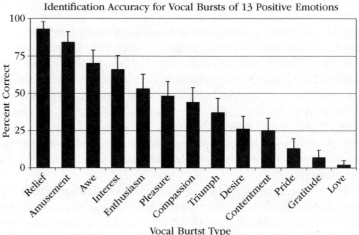

FIGURE 4.8 Observers are able to identify several emotions from vocal bursts (from Simon-Thomas et al., 2009).

Communication of Emotions by Touch

Touch is the most developed sensory modality at birth (Field, 2001; Hertenstein, 2002; Stack, 2001). Touch is a rich nonverbal language in which humans flirt, express power, soothe, play, and maintain proximity (Eibl-Eibesfeldt, 1989; Hertenstein et al., 2005).

Four Functions of Touch

Many nonhuman primate species spend significant portions of their day **grooming**, in which two individuals sit comfortably together, sorting through each other's fur (Dunbar, 1996). Chimpanzees, for example, can devote upwards of 20% of their waking hours to grooming, building affectionate relationships (De Waal, 1989). Studies of nonhuman primate grooming and human touch reveal four distinct functions of tactile contact.

FIGURE 4.9 Three different kinds of fearful response by vervet monkeys to three kinds of predator.

The first is that the right kind of touch soothes. For example, in one study, 30 human infants were observed during a procedure in which the infants' heels were cut by doctors (Gray, Watt, & Blass, 2000). In one condition, infants were held by their mothers in whole-body, skin-to-skin contact. In the other condition, infants received the procedure while being swaddled in a crib. The infants who were touched during the procedure cried 82% less than the comparison infants, they grimaced 65% less, and they had lower heart-rate during the procedure. In nonhuman primates, grooming reduces heart rate and displacement activities related to stress, such as striking others (Aureli, Preston, & De Waal, 1999). Rat pups who are handled extensively by their mothers show reduced activity of the hypothalamic, pituitary adrenal axis, which is involved in stress responses, and reduced corticosterone, a stress-related hormone, both immediately and when they are mature (Francis & Meaney, 1999; Levine & Stanton, 1984; Meaney, 2001).

A second function of touch is to signal safety. This insight emerged first within the attachment literature, where theorists observed that a primary need of infants is to know whether the environment is safe, and do so by gathering relevant information from their parent's touch (Main, 1990). In one illustrative study, Anisfeld and colleagues compared the attachment styles of infants who were carried in soft infant carriers that put them in close physical contact with their parents, with infants who were more often carried in harder infant seats (Anisfeld et al., 1990; Weiss et al., 2000). Infants who were carried next to their parents' bodies were more likely to be securely attached later, and confident when exploring the environment.

A third function of touch is to increase cooperation. Chimpanzees use touch as a reward and to encourage the trading of favors. For example, de Waal (1996) has found that chimps are more likely to share food with other chimps who groomed them earlier in the day. The same is true of humans: the act of touching produces cooperation. In one study, participants were asked to sign a petition in support of a particular issue of importance locally (Willis & Hamm, 1980). Those participants who were touched when asked to sign were much more likely to comply (81%) than participants who were not touched during the request (55%). In a recent study of touch among professional basketball players in the National Basketball Association, Michael Kraus and his colleagues coded all of the touch—the high-fives, fist bumps, head slaps, and bear hugs so common on the basketball court—each team showed during one game at the beginning of the 2008 season (Kraus, Huang, & Keltner, 2010). Even though each player on average touched his teammates about 2 seconds during the game, that touch proved critical to team functioning. The more players touched each other, the more the teams proved to be cooperative on the court (e.g., helping out in defending the other team, making good passes to each other), and the better the team played at the end of the season.

A final function of touch is to provide pleasure. The simple touch of the arm with a soft velvety cloth activates the region of the prefrontal cortex that is involved in the processing of pleasurable tastes and smells (Berridge, 2003; Rolls, 2000). Touch provides revealing information about the more and less rewarding times of a marriage. Couples who have been married longer tend to touch each other less than those in the early stages of the relationship (Willis & Briggs, 1992), and more happily married partners touch each other more than less happily married partners (Beier & Sternberg, 1977). Anticipating these functions of touch, William James (1890) observed that "Touch is the alpha and omega of affection."

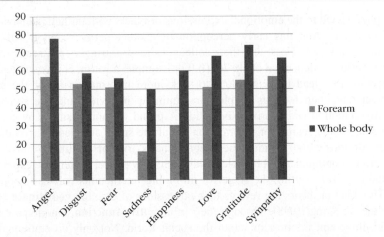

FIGURE 4.10 Accuracy with which individuals can communicate emotion by touching a stranger on the forearm (to left) or anywhere on the body (to right).

Communicating Emotions with Touch

The relational importance of touch and its several functions raises the question of whether touch can communicate different emotions. This question has motivated recent research by Matthew Hertenstein and his colleagues (Hertenstein, Keltner, App, Bulleit, & Jaskolka, 2006). In the first study in this research, an encoder (or toucher) and decoder (or touchee) sat at a table, separated by an opaque black curtain, which prevented communication other than touch. The encoder was given a list of emotions and asked to make contact with the decoder on the arm to communicate each emotion, using any form of touch. The decoder could not see any part of the touch because his or her arm was positioned on the encoder's side of the curtain. After each touch, the decoder selected from 13 response options the term that best described what the person was communicating. As you can see in Figure 4.10, participants could reliably communicate anger, disgust, and fear with a brief one- or two-second touch of another's forearm, as well as love, gratitude, and sympathy. In a second study, the decoder stood blindfolded in the laboratory, and the encoder was allowed to touch any part of the body to communicate each target emotion (Hertenstein et al., 2009). As you can see in the rightmost columns of Figure 4.10, participants proved to be more accurate in communicating emotion with touch when more free to touch other parts of the body than the forearm, and they could reliably communicate happiness and sadness.

Emotional Expression and the Coordination of Social Interaction

The central thesis of this book is how emotions are essential to how we engage in social relationships. Facial expressions, vocalizations, and patterns of touch bind people into patterns of behavior that make up important social interactions—the soothing of a distressed child, the flirtation between potential suitors, or status conflicts in groups. Within 500 milliseconds, people respond to the emotional expressions of others with mimetic behavior and physiological reactions. And this early perception of another person's emotional expression, Paula Niedenthal, Ursula Hess, and their colleagues reason, triggers a cascade of neural processes and reactions (Niedenthal et al., 2010). For example, a warm, enjoyment smile triggers neural processes that lead the individual to seek more information about the smile through eye contact, and then feelings of pleasure, mimetic behavior, and the somatic experience of positive emotion and approach behavior. A proud, dominant smile, by contrast, triggers the same automatic search for information about the smile and neural activation that leads to a sense of threat and avoidant behavior. What's true of smiling is most certainly true of emotional communication by voice and touch: they trigger systematic experiences and actions in the perceiver, setting the stage for unfolding interactions between people.

This kind of theorizing reveals that expressions of emotion **coordinate social interactions** (Keltner & Kring, 1998). Through their **informative function**, emotional expressions provide rapid, important information about the social world. Not only do emotional displays provide reliable information about the sender's current emotions, they also signal the sender's relationship with the target (Ekman, 1993; Fridlund, 1992). For example, anger clearly communicates strength and dominance vis-à-vis others (Knutson, 1996). When individuals express anger in the face or voice, they are perceived to have more power, and are more likely to get their way in negotiations (van Kleef et al., 2006). Emotional expressions carry information about the sincerity of the sender's intentions. For example, Eva Krumhuber and Tony Manstead and their colleagues have found that people trust interaction partners more, and will give more resources to those partners, who display authentic smiles (which have longer onset and offset times) than fake smiles, which have shorter onset and offset (Krumhuber et al., 2007). Finally, emotional expressions convey information about the environment, allowing individuals to coordinate their responses to outside opportunities or threats (e.g., Klinnert et al., 1986; Sorce et al., 1985). For example, parents use touch and voice to signal to their young children whether other people and objects in the environment are safe or dangerous (Hertenstein & Campos, 2004).

Emotional displays coordinate social interactions through their **evocative function**, to trigger specific responses in perceivers. For example, matching or mirroring the emotions of others is an important basis of empathy, which is important in social life. Sato and Yoshikawa (2007) unobtrusively video-recorded participants as they looked at static or dynamic displays of facial expressions of happiness or anger. Subjects' own facial expressions mirrored the expressions they saw. Oatley (2009) has proposed that, based on this kind of empathetic mirroring, emotions provide outline structures for specific kinds of relationship: when we see a smile, we feel happy and smile back, disposed to cooperate. We see tears, we feel sad, and are prompted to help. We see a frown, begin to feel angry, and become prepared for the possibility of conflict. When we hear someone's expression of alarm, we feel frightened ourselves. Each kind of empathetic emotion configures a particular kind of relationship. Think of it like this. On the stage, an actor learns a script, a set of words. The actor's job is to use the words and depict character-emotions that support certain relationships with other characters. In ordinary life, something like the inverse of this happens. Emotions provide us with scripts not of words, but of relating—in happy cooperation, in sad disengagement, in angry conflict, in shared fear, and so on—and we supply fitting words in our interactions with each other (p. 209).

As well as matched emotions, displays can elicit complementary emotions from relationship partners. For example, photographed facial displays of anger enhance fear conditioning in observers, even when the photographs are not consciously perceived (Esteves, Dimberg, & Öhman,

1994; Öhman & Dimberg, 1978). Expressions of distress can evoke sympathy in observers (e.g., Eisenberg et al., 1989).

Both matching and complementary emotions experienced by perceivers contribute to the experienced quality of social interactions. Lara Tiedens and Alison Fragale (2003) have found that when individuals complement one another in their postural behavior, responding with more expansive dominant posture to the constricted, submissive posture of an interaction partner (or vice-versa), they enjoy the interaction more.

Finally, emotional displays serve **incentive functions**, inviting desired social behavior. Warm smiles and touches are often used by parents to reward behaviors in children, thus increasing the probability of those behaviors in the future (e.g., Tronick, 1989). Laughter from interaction partners also rewards desirable social behavior in adults (Owren & Bachorowski, 2001). And through their informative, evocative, and incentive functions, emotional expressions give structure to our social interactions and relationships.

Cultural Variation in Emotional Expression

If you have traveled abroad, you may have been struck by how similar emotional expression is in different cultures. Stroll in a *zocolo* (square) in rural Mexico or a marketplace in Thailand or wait at a bus stop in Nigeria and you're likely to be impressed by the many similarities in emotional expression across cultures. You'll see children smiling and laughing as they play. Courting adolescents show coy expressions. People arguing furrow their brows or sneer in obvious disdain in recognizable ways. In this chapter we have seen a good deal of evidence that speaks to the universality of emotional expression.

At the same time, you will also see **cultural variation** in emotional expression. Early cultural researchers observed that cultures vary profoundly in how they express emotion. Briggs (1970) found that the Inuit who live in the Canadian Arctic (colloquially referred to as Eskimos) do not express anger. Seventeenth-century Japanese wives of Samurai soldiers were alleged to smile upon receipt of the news that their husbands had died nobly in battle. Along these lines, Birdwhistell (1970) concluded: "There are probably no universal symbols of emotional state. . . . We can expect them [emotional expressions] to be learned and patterned according to the particular structure of particular societies" (p. 126). So how do variations occur in different cultures?

Cultural Variation in Expressive Behavior

Researchers have identified three ways that members of different cultures vary in their emotional expression. First, cultures vary in the intensity of the expression of specific emotions. You learned in Chapter 3 that certain emotions are more focal in specific cultures, and thus can be expressed more intensely. In keeping with this, Tracy and Matsumoto (2008) found, in their study of the emotional expressions of Olympic athletes, that competitors from more collectivist cultures expressed more intense shame displays upon losing, which is consistent with the more pronounced emphasis on modesty and not standing out in collectivist cultures In a similar vein, Jeanne Tsai and Robert Levenson have found that in responding to various emotional stimuli, people from independent cultures are more likely to show intense smiles of excitement (Tsai & Levenson, 1997).

Second, cultures develop culture-specific **emotion accents**, which are stylized and culturally specific ways of expressing emotions (Elfenbein & Ambady, 2002). Recall that each emotional display has numerous actions involved in it. The anger expression, for example, involves the furrowed brow, the glare, the lip tighten, and the lip press. We saw that the embarrassment display involves gaze down, head turns and movements down, a controlled smile, and face touches. The idea with emotion accents is that cultures might take elements of an emotion display and elaborate upon it, dramatize it, and make it more stereotypical and exaggerated to express an emotion. Throughout much of Southeast Asia, the tongue bite and shoulder shrug combine to form an emotional accent that expresses embarrassment. It involves exaggerated versions of two elements of the embarrassment display: inhibitory muscle actions around the mouth (the tongue bite), and constricted, size-reducing posture (the shoulder shrug). To document cultural variation in the meaning of this emotion accent, Haidt and Keltner presented participants with two expressions of embarrassment, which are shown in Figure 4.5 (Haidt & Keltner, 1999). Members of both cultures interpreted the prototypical expression as embarrassment, but only the Indian participants readily perceived the tongue bite expression as a signal of embarrassment.

Finally, members of different cultures can vary in how they **regulate** their expressive behavior according to culture-specific display rules. Recall in Chapter 3 we learned that people are much more likely to suppress the expression of emotion in highly collectivist cultures like Japan. This is in keeping with the notion, more pronounced in collectivist cultures, that emotional expression makes the individual stand out, and potentially disrupts social harmony by imposing upon others.

Cultural Variation of Interpretation of Emotional Expressions

As investigators began to gather evidence about the universality of emotion recognition, they also began to document how members of different cultures vary in their **interpretation** of facial expressions of emotion. For example, members of different cultures appear to differ in the accuracy with which they identify emotions from display behavior (e.g., Matsumoto, 1990; Russell, 1991a). Matsumoto (1989) and Schimmack (1996) have both found that individuals from more individualistic, independent cultures are more accurate judges of facial expressions of emotion. Why might this be? One possibility is that greater emotional expression may be encouraged in individualistic cultures, and members of these cultures may therefore have greater practice in judging emotional expressions and as a result show greater accuracy when presented with photos of emotional expressions.

Second, individuals from different cultures differ in the emotional intensity that they attribute to facial expressions of emotion (Matsumoto & Ekman, 1989). For example, Japanese participants tend to attribute less intense emotion than Americans to all facial expressions of emotion (Biehl et al., 1997; Matsumoto et al., 1999, 2002). Why might these differences occur? Matsumoto et al. (1999) compared American and Japanese judgments of the intensity of the outward display and of the inner experience. Japanese people assumed that the display and inner experience of emotion were the same. Americans, in contrast, indicated that the external display of emotion was more intense than the inner experience, consistent with the emphasis in the United States on expressing feelings (see also Matusmoto et al., 2009, discussed in Chapter 3).

Reflection and cultivation: Improving your emotional intelligence

In this chapter you have learned about the rich languages in the face, in the voice, and in touch through which we communicate emotion. Throughout this book you will learn how central emotional communication is to healthy social adjustment. People who have pronounced abilities to communicate emotion and perceive emotion, who have high levels of emotional intelligence, fare well in all manner of relationships (see Chapter 9). People who struggle to read the emotions of others, like children with Aspergers Syndrome, have difficulties with social adjustment.

Given these findings, we suggest the following. Do you want to get a sense of how good you are at reading facial expression and vocalization? Go to http://greatergood.berkeley.edu/ei_quiz/, a free website in part created by one of this book's authors, and take the emotion test. See how well you do. Which emotions proved hard for you to judge, if any? Why? What did you learn about how emotion is communicated in the face and voice?

Finally, recent studies suggest that members of more collectivist cultures tend to rely on more contextual information in constructing the meaning of emotional expressions. In a telling experiment, Takahiko Masuda, Phoebe Ellsworth, and colleagues showed Japanese and American participants cartoon figures having various expressions on their faces (Masuda, Ellsworth, Mesquita, Leu, & van de Veerdonk, 2004). The central, target face was always surrounded by smaller, less salient faces, with expressions that were dissimilar to those of the target. For example, the target might appear to be happy, whereas most of the surrounding faces might appear to be sad. Japanese participants' judgments about the facial expression of the target were more influenced by the surrounding faces than were the judgments of the Americans. A happy face surrounded by sad faces was judged less happy by Japanese participants than by American participants, and a sad face surrounded by happy faces was judged less sad. This is the kind of evidence on which Barrett, Mesquita, and Gendron (2011) base their claim that emotional expressions should be recognized not in isolation, but in context.

Communication of Emotion in Art

In the experience of some of your emotions you may feel drawn to **artistic expression**. In a state of despair or longing, you might feel inclined to write a story, play the piano, or paint abstract patterns. When euphoric about a new loved one, you might write poetry or songs, or find cinematic images rising in your mind. Art is a kind of communication. Unlike a smile or a grumble, however, which are ephemeral, art persists in time and can travel beyond its place of inception (Oatley, 2003). Unlike saucepans and bicycles, which are made to be useful, works of art are often thought of as expressions of emotion that attain cultural significance. They are quintessentially cultural. Art differs widely from society to society, from the epics of ancient Babylon, to the bronzes of Benin, to the jazz of New Orleans. But art did evolve. It began to appear in the human archaeological record between about 80,000 and 30,000 years ago. Among recent discoveries has been that of Bouzouggar et al. (2007), who found in North Africa shells drilled to make beads for a necklace that dated to 82,000 years ago. As Mithen (1996, 2001) puts it, signs such as these indicate the uniquely human cognitive ability for metaphor. A metaphor often links something immediate and something imagined, so when Hamlet said, "Denmark's a prison," Denmark was present but the prison was that of his imagination. Unlike useful objects, which are what they are, objects of art both are what they are and are something else. A certain cave painting (the oldest known is 31,000 years old) is both a set of marks on a wall and is a mammoth. A shell is both a shell and a bead for a necklace. Human burial indicates that someone is both dead and alive in another place or another form about which stories may be told. Such artistic products have emotional significance.

Four Hypotheses from the Idea of Romanticism

It has long been believed in Western thought that in expressing our emotions in art, we come to understand them more deeply. This notion was the central theme of the intellectual and historical movement of Romanticism (Oatley, 2003), which we discussed in Chapter 1, and which we will use to organize our treatment of emotional expression in art. Artists themselves often understand their art as a mode of expressing and understanding emotions. The poet William Wordsworth said this about poetry:

> Poetry is the spontaneous overflow of powerful feelings: it takes its origin from emotion recollected in tranquility: the emotion is contemplated till by a species of reaction the tranquility disappears, and an emotion, kindred to that which was before the subject of contemplation, is gradually produced and does itself actually exist in the mind.
>
> (Wordsworth, 1802, p. 611)

The position was put succinctly by Martha Graham, the great dancer and choreographer: "The difference between the artist and the non-artist is not the greater capacity for feeling. The secret is that the artist can objectify, can make apparent the feelings we all have" (cit. Gardner, 1993, p. 298).

The Romantic idea translates into four hypotheses about the communication of emotion in art. The first is that sometimes we experience emotions that we do not consciously understand, and that prompts us to explore them by expressing them in art. Are our emotions sometimes unclear? Oatley and Duncan (1992) found that the proportion of everyday emotion incidents recorded in structured diaries that had some aspect that participants did not understand varied between 5 and 25% in different samples. Many emotional experiences have an inchoate quality (Oatley & Johnson-Laird, 1987). A principal aim of artistic expression is to explore such unarticulated emotions in the different languages of art, including the visual, the musical, and the linguistic.

A second claim of the Romantic idea is that this exploration involves creative expression. Emotions tend to occur when expectations are not met, or when plans meet vicissitudes, or when we have no ready answer to some pressing concern. Thus they often demand a creative response (Averill & Nunley, 1992). Art is a creative activity of expressing, and thereby understanding, such emotions, as revealed in the quotations of William Wordsworth and Martha Graham. Djkic, Oatley, and Peterson (2006) found that by comparing the words used in interviews by fiction writers and physicists, the writers were (probably unconsciously) preoccupied by emotions, particularly negative emotions, in ways that the physicists were not. To investigate further the relation of emotions to creativity, Csikszentmihalyi (1996) and his students interviewed 91 exceptionally creative people, including many artists. One of the themes that emerged is indeed that creative expression arises out of emotional experience. Here, for instance, is an excerpt from Hilde Domin, a leading German poet, in her seventies at the time of the interview. In her poetry, she says:

> [The emotion] gets fulfilled . . . it is a kind of catalyst . . . . You are freed for a time from the emotion. And the next reader will take the place of the author, isn't it so? If he identifies with the writing he will become, in his turn, the author.
>
> (Csikszentmihalyi, 1996, p. 245)

A third hypothesis that derives from the Romantic idea is that artistic expression often itself takes on themes and dynamic forms of emotions. For example, if you take to painting while enraged in the aftermath of a bitter breakup, your painting might have emotional tones of your rage and despair. Fiction that you write about a tragic childhood might center upon themes of loss and longing.

Further evidence of this third proposition, not so much in terms of themes as of dynamics, has been offered for music by Gabrielsson and Juslin (2001) and Juslin and Laukka (2003). They observe that the voice and music share many emotionally expressive properties, with acoustic features that the performer enacts, such as tempo, loudness, timbre, and pitch. This may account for how instruments such as the violin, cello, organ, the slide guitar, and saxophone can resemble the human voice. In the words of the famous composer, Richard Wagner, "The oldest, truest, most beautiful organ of music, the origin to which alone our music owes its being, is the human voice." The philosopher Susanne Langer arrived at a similar conclusion: "Because the forms of human feeling are much more congruent with musical forms than with forms of language, music can *reveal* the nature of feelings with a detail and truth that language cannot approach" (1957, p. 235).

In a recent analysis of the cues that people use to infer emotion from the voice and music, Juslin and Laukka (2003) found support for the claim that emotion is communicated in the voice and in music with similar acoustic parameters. They found that tempo, loudness, and pitch were used by listeners of vocal communication and music alike to infer that anger, sadness, happiness, and tenderness were being communicated.

A final hypothesis inspired by Romanticism is that readers or spectators of art should experience emotions that are communicated in art. Oatley's (2012) book, *The Passionate Muse: Exploring Emotion in Stories,* is about how fiction embodies themes both of characters' emotions and of the reader's own emotions. It is a hybrid book: a seven-part short story written especially for the book, together with psychological discussions of the emotions of each part.

People respond emotionally to the emotional content of art (e.g., Lipps, 1962). We experience the emotions of protagonists in novels or films based on human action (Tan, 1996). We soar toward the heavens in the vaulted space of a great cathedral. Kreitler and Kreitler (1972) have even found that 84% of the time visitors to museums will unwittingly imitate in their bodies the postures conveyed in sculptures.

How accurate are we in recognizing the emotion communicated in art? Within the domain of music, Gabrielsson and Juslin (2003) and Juslin and Laukka (2003) have reviewed studies in which a performer was asked to sing a brief melody with no words and attempt to communicate anger, fear, happiness, sadness, joy, and on occasion tenderness or love. The listener was then asked, in a forced-choice paradigm, to choose the word from a list of words that best matches the emotion conveyed in the performance. Across over a dozen studies of this kind, listeners on average achieved accuracy rates of about 70%, which is comparable to the accuracy with which we perceive emotion in the face and voice.

Aesthetic Emotions in the Natyasastra

Are there benefits to understanding and feeling the emotions expressed in art? As you will recall from Chapter 1, this question was at the center of Aristotle's analysis of *katharsis,* wherein he reasoned that drama expresses many of the universal predicaments and conditions of humanity. In drama, people suffer, they face mortal danger, they fall in love, they encounter infidelity, they strive for difficult goals. In viewing dramatic expressions of emotion, the spectator arrives at a clearer understanding of his or her own emotions. Freud arrived at a similar view, arguing that art allows us to express aspects of inner emotional conflicts in disguised forms that allow some satisfaction of expression while avoiding censure (1904/1985).

Juslin and his colleagues randomly beeped people on their cell phones during the day, and found that about 40% of the time young adults were listening to music, and most typically felt contentment, perhaps due to insights they gained into their own emotions (Juslin et al., 2008). Mar, Oatley, and Peterson (2009) found that the more fiction (but not nonfiction) people read, the greater was their empathy for others; the effect was not due to empathetic people being more likely to read fiction.

One of the most sophisticated treatments of the emotions and insights of art is found in a Hindu-Indian treatise, the *Natyasastra,* attributed to Bharata from around the second century BCE (Bharata Muni, 200 BCE). In this text, there are specific descriptions of how actors and dancers are to express emotions in performance. Hejmadi, Davidson, and Rozin (2000) presented participants in India and the United States with videotapes of Hejmadi's own renditions in dance of ten different emotions (she performed as a dancer in India for 20 years). The performances largely involved face and hand movements for ten different emotions: anger, disgust, fear, heroism, humor, love, peace, sadness, lajya (embarrassment/ shyness/modesty), and wonder. Each video-clip lasted between 4 and 10 seconds. Remark-ably, in both forced-choice and free-response exercises, observers were well above chance, achieving accuracy rates between 61 and 69%, in judging the ten emotions communicated with dance and gesture.

In the *Natyasastra,* Bharata also discusses the theory of **rasas**, which are distinct aesthetic emotions. They have recently been discussed in Western theories of emotions (Oatley, 2004c; Shweder & Haidt, 2000). Each *rasa* corresponds to an everyday emotion. But the idea of the ancient theorists was that in a *rasa* one would be able to experience and understand more clearly, without—as they put it—being blinded by our usual thick crust of egoism. In Indian texts on *rasas* the usual mapping is between everyday emotions and *rasas*.

Pursuing our interest in communication in this chapter, we have taken a slight liberty with this tradition in Table 4.2, in which we list emotions as enacted by an actor, the Sanskrit name of the corresponding *rasa*, and its approximate translation to indicate what would be experienced by the spectator. Seeing an actor suffering and sorrowful, for example, produces an aesthetic emotion of compassion, though because it is an aesthetic emotion it also includes the pleasure of understanding and insight. Seeing a performer persevere against all odds—a frequent theme in stories—inspires a heroic feeling in the spectator. A recent movement in Western theater has been to train actors in the theory of *rasas* (Schechner, 2001). You may also like to observe that each emotional theme in Table 4.2 corresponds to a particular genre (love story, comedy, tragedy, and so on).

Emotions, then, are communicated in everyday life, but these communications are usually ephemeral. So important are emotions to us, however, that artists have devised many and varied

Table 4.2 Emotions as performed by actors, *rasas*, and English translations of them as aesthetic emotions that spectators may experience

Performer's emotion	Rasa	Spectator's emotion
Sexual passion	srngara	Love
Amusement	hasya	Amusement
Sorrow	karuna	Compassion
Anger	raudra	Anger
Fear	bhayanaka	Terror
Perseverance	vira	Heroism
Disgust	bibhatsa	Loathing
Wonder	adbhuta santa	Awe

forms of expression that communicate emotions in longer-lasting ways that enable us to experience them in new ways, and to reflect on them.

SUMMARY

In this chapter we examined the communication of emotion by the face, voice, and touch, as well as in art. We began by breaking down the realm of nonverbal behavior into five categories: emblems, illustrators, regulators, adaptors, and emotion displays. We considered how emotion displays, such as smiles of enjoyment, differ from non-emotional expressions, like polite smiles, in terms of duration and incorporation of involuntary actions. We then considered the different ways that humans communicate emotion. We reviewed the studies of the universality of facial expression of emotion. We considered how vocal communication permeates communicative acts like teasing and laughter, and how people communicate emotion in the voice. We then turned to a less well-studied channel of emotional communication: touch. From the first moments of life, touch functions to soothe, to signal safety, to gain compliance,

and as a reward, and recent evidence suggests that humans can communicate several different emotions with brief touches to the arm, including love, gratitude, and sympathy. We next considered how emotional expression shapes social interactions and varies across cultures. Finally, we considered how emotion is communicated in art, exploring this question from the perspective of Romanticism. This perspective suggests four propositions: emotions that we don't fully understand motivate us to explore their meaning, this exploration is creative, artistic expression often takes on themes and qualities of expressive channels such as the voice, and observers experience emotions in engaging with art. We concluded this discussion by reviewing the ancient Indian *Natyasastra,* describing how emotion is expressed in dance and drama, and the nature of aesthetic emotion.

TO THINK ABOUT AND DISCUSS

1. Spend 10 minutes observing interactions in a group of friends, and take note of the different emblems, illustrators, regulators, and adaptors that you observe. What did you see?

2. Think about Darwin's principle of serviceable habits. How would you use this principle to explain why we express a particular emotion as we do? Try this for disgust, or embarrassment, or gratitude.

3. Consider a favorite piece of music. What insights has it given you into your emotions?

FURTHER READING

For Ekman's view of facial expression of emotion:

Paul Ekman (1993). Facial expression and emotion. *American Psychologist*, **48**, 384–392.

For a more recent evolutionary perspective on emotional expression:

A. F. Shariff & J. L. Tracy (2011). What are emotion expressions for? *Current Directions in Psychological Science*, **20**, 395–399.

For Barrett's view of expression:

Lisa Feldman Barrett (2011). Was Darwin wrong about emotional expressions? *Current Directions in Psychological Science*, **20**, 400–406.

For an extensive review of facial expression:

D. Matsumoto, D. Keltner, M. Shiota, M. O'Sullivan, & M. Frank (2008). Facial expressions of emotion. In M. Lewis, J. Haviland-Jones, & L. F. Barrett (Eds.), *Handbook of emotion* (pp. 211–234). New York: Guilford Press.

For a review of how emotions are communicated in musical performance:

P. N. Juslin (2010). Expression and communication of emotion in music performance. In P. N. Juslin & J. A. Sloboda (Eds.), *Handbook of music and emotion* (pp. 453–489). New York: Oxford University Press.

Bodily Changes and Emotions

5

Photo Credit: Alinari/Art Resource

FIGURE 5.0 Bernini: *St. Teresa.* Of this sculpture Gombrich (1972, p. 345) says that Bernini has "carried us to a pitch of emotion which artists had so far shunned."

A cold sweat covers me, and trembling seizes me all over.

Sappho (circa 580 BCE)

CONTENTS

Williams James is perhaps the most famous American psychologist. He corresponded regularly with his brother, Henry, who became equally famous as a novelist. Their letters are filled with references to their physical ills and bodily sensations—vivid and personal descriptions of back pains, upset stomachs, bodily fatigue. Were these experiences a clue to why William James proposed, in 1884, a radical idea that would turn the field of research on emotions on its head?

Most writers until that time had argued that the experience of an emotion is a response to an emotionally exciting event. Emotional experience in turn generates emotion-related bodily changes, including actions. James altered this sequence, and (as we described in Chapter 1) he located the origins of emotional experience in the body. For him the sequence was: (a) exciting event, (b) bodily responses to the event, (c) perception of these bodily responses as the experience of emotion. This would prove to be a controversial thesis, the repercussions of which continue today.

Poets have known for more than 2,500 years that bodily changes such as sweats, trembling, heart flutters, blushes and flushes, muscular tension, muscle movements, tears, and chills are involved in our experience of emotion. Yet James would take this idea further. He contended that every emotion, from anger to sympathy to the rapturous delight of hearing a favorite musician, involves a distinct "bodily reverberation" in the glands that make up the neuroendocrine system, in the autonomic nervous system, and in muscles by which action is produced. Emotion is the perception of such reverberation.

How did James arrive at this view? Largely through thought experiments. He asked his reader: What would be left of fear or love or embarrassment or any emotion if you took away the physiological sensations such as the heart palpitations, trembling, muscle tensions, sensations in the skin, and churning of the stomach? James argued that you would be left with a purely intellectual state. Emotion would be absent.

Significant figure: William James

William James was born in 1842, eldest of five talented children. William's father, a dreamer, a bit of a crank, a man of leisure with independent means, had inherited from his own Irish immigrant father a large house in New York, where William was born. William's mother Mary was the practical one of the family. His brother Henry, born in 1843, became one of the world's great novelists, while his only sister, Alice, as talented as her brothers, was not able to overcome the barriers to women in that period, and declined into chronic health ailments and invalidism. The family led an affectionate but chaotic life, with a potpourri of educational experiences for the children, including a procession of governesses and tutors, long stays in Europe, and periods in private experimental schools. At the age of 18, William studied art for a year, and then took up chemistry. Two years later he changed to

medicine, gaining an MD degree in 1869. He obtained an instructor's post in physiology at Harvard in 1872.

In 1878, a turning point occurred: he met Alice Gibbens, who introduced a degree of organization into his life, shared his interests, and helped him concentrate his energies. From then on his hypochondria, which had been disabling, decreased. In 1885, James became Professor of Philosophy. He was the founder of American psychology, and influenced the philosophical school of Pragmatism, whose adherents included John Dewey. James was an amiable, tolerant, widely read man, with a gift for thoughtful literary expression. His *Principles of Psychology* is still regarded as the best textbook that psychology has had.

Besides his *Principles of Psychology*, James's theory of emotions as end-points, as experiences of bodily changes that occur as a result of actions, is the work for which he is best known. It has continued to be influential, but not many Jamesians will tell you that James himself seemed to give up his own theory. In his only large-scale research project, which he published in 1902 as *Varieties* *of Religious Experience,* there is nothing of his theory of emotions as end-points. Instead, in this book, James found that in religious conversions emotions are causes. They are prime-movers by which people could change their identities and their lives (Oatley & Djikic, 2002).

James's analysis points to three questions that are at the heart of this chapter. The first is simple conceptually, but difficult empirically: Is there emotion-specific activation in bodily systems? A second is: To what extent is the experience of emotion based on activation of these bodily systems? And finally: To what extent do the bodily responses of emotion serve as guides to our social behavior?

These questions require an understanding of one bodily system in particular that has been the focus of scientific inquiry: the autonomic nervous system. To evaluate the plausibility of James's claims, let's look at this system to see how it might relate to emotion.

The Autonomic Nervous System

Neural signals from the cortex communicate with the limbic system and the hypothalamus (see next chapter), which send signals to clusters of neurons of the autonomic nervous system and target organs, glands, muscles, and blood vessels. These structures in turn send signals back via the autonomic nervous system to the hypothalamus, limbic system, and cortex.

The autonomic nervous system maintains the internal condition of the body to enable adaptive response to varying environmental events. The **parasympathetic** branch of the system helps with restorative processes, reducing heart rate and blood pressure and directing inner resources to digestive processes. The **sympathetic** branch increases heart rate, blood pressure, and cardiac output and shuts down digestive processes to help the individual to engage in physically demanding actions. These two branches control processes such as digestion, blood flow, and body temperature, as well as behaviors with direct relevance to emotion, including defensive behavior, sexual behavior, and aggression.

The autonomic nervous system's two branches originate in different parts of the spinal cord and are controlled by different neurotransmitters. A diagram of the system can be seen in Figure 5.1, with notes about it in Table 5.1. As you can see, the effects of the two branches of the system are far-reaching and related to several different functions.

Parasympathetic and Sympathetic Branches

The parasympathetic autonomic nervous system consists of nerves that originate in two different parts of the spinal cord. The vagus nerve arises near the top of the cord. The parasympathetic system decreases heart rate and blood pressure. It facilitates blood flow by dilating certain arteries. It increases blood flow to erectile tissue in the penis and clitoris, and thus is essential to the sexual response. It increases digestive processes by moving digested food through the gastrointestinal tract. The parasympathetic system also constricts the pupil and bronchioles.

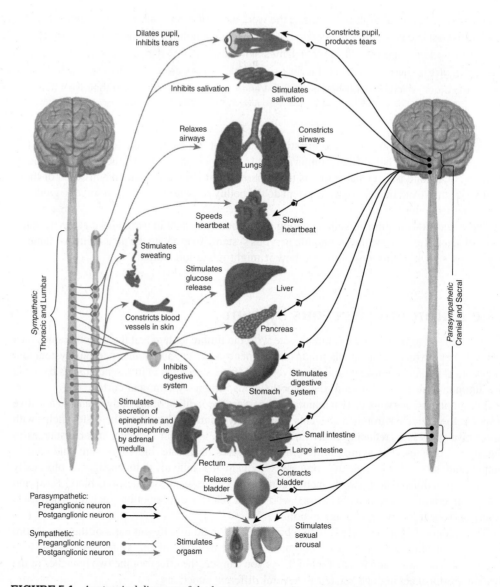

FIGURE 5.1   Anatomical diagram of the human autonomic nervous system.

It stimulates the secretion of various fluids throughout the body, including those in the digestive glands, salivation, and tears.

The sympathetic system is separate from the parasympathetic and involves over a dozen neural pathways originating at several sites on the spinal cord. Most typically the sympathetic system acts in the opposite way from the parasympathetic system. It increases heart rate, blood pressure, and cardiac output. It produces vasoconstriction in most veins and arteries. It shuts down digestive processes, which is why it can be hard to eat when experiencing great stress. It is

Table 5.1 Effects of the activation of the parasympathetic and sympathetic branches of the autonomic nervous system

Organ	Activation of parasympathetic nerves	Activation of sympathetic nerves
Heart muscle	decrease of heart rate	increase of heart rate
Blood vessels: arteries	decrease of contractility	increase of contractility
Trunk, limbs	0	vasoconstriction
Skin of face	vasodilation	vasoconstriction
Visceral domain	0	vasoconstriction
Skeletal muscle	0	vasoconstriction
Erectile tissue	vasodilation	vasoconstriction
Cranium	0	vasoconstriction
Blood vessels: veins	0	vasoconstriction
Gastrointestinal tract		
Circular muscle	increased motility	decreased motility
Sphincters	relaxation	contraction
Urinary bladder	contraction	relaxation
Reproductive organs		
Seminal vesicles	0	contraction
Vas deferens	0	contraction
Uterus	0	contraction
Pupil	constriction	dilation
Tracheo-bronchial muscles	contraction	relaxation
Piloerector muscles	0	contraction
Salivary glands	strong secretion	weak secretion
Lachrymal glands (tears)	secretion	0
Sweat glands	0	secretion
Digestive glands	secretion	decreased secretion
Metabolism		
Liver	0	glycogenolysis
Fat cells	0	free fatty acids in blood
Pancreas	secretion of insulin	decreased secretion of insulin
Adrenal medulla	0	secretion of adrenaline, noradrenaline
Lymphoid tissue	0	depression of activity (e.g., of natural killer cells)

Source: Adapted from Janig (2003).

associated with contractions in the reproductive organs that are part of orgasm. The sympathetic system leads to the contraction of the piloerector muscles that surround the hairs on the arms, neck, and back, which helps with thermoregulation and is involved in emotional responses that involve goosebumps. And it increases many processes that provide energy for the body, including glycogenolysis and the freeing of fatty acids in the bloodstream. At the same time the sympathetic system reduces activity of natural killer cells, which are involved in immune responses. This may account for chronic stress producing poor health outcomes. Given these effects, many have argued that the sympathetic system helps prepare the body for **fight-or-flight** responses.

Psychologists measure the activity of the autonomic nervous system in several ways. They measure heart rate. They assess the sweat response, which goes by the name of the *galvanic skin response*. They measure vasoconstriction in the arteries and veins. They measure blood flow to different parts of the body. They measure finger and facial temperature, which reflects changes in blood flow and vasodilation. To capture activation in the vagus nerve, they look at the relationship between the respiration and heart-rate cycles.

In Table 5.1, one finds two kinds of potential support for James's claims regarding **autonomic specificity** and emotion. A first is that there are over a dozen distinct autonomic pathways that activate different regions of the body, so different emotions could potentially be involved with distinct pathways in the autonomic nervous system (Janig, 2003). A second kind of support is that one can imagine many different ways in which components of the autonomic system could combine, including heart rate, blood flow to the skin (e.g., blushing), sweating, production of tears, stomach activity, and breathing. Such patterns could plausibly account for the diversity of emotional experience.

Post-Jamesian Theories

James's theory, although it was influential, did not sit entirely easily with early theories of emotional experience in the emerging scientific study of emotion. And so, ever since publication of the idea in 1884, theorists have tried to hold on to issues of bodily responses and the autonomic nervous system while they developed theories that they thought would improve on James's.

Cannon's Critique of Autonomic Specificity

Walter Cannon was first a student, then a colleague, of William James at Harvard University. He was unconvinced by James's arguments about emotion (Cannon, 1927, 1929). He proposed that bodily changes are produced by the brain, and that many different emotions involve exactly the same general activation of the sympathetic nervous system. This so-called **arousal response** includes release of the hormone adrenaline. The effects of this sympathetic-adrenal response amount to a shift of bodily resources to prepare for action, including what have been known as the three *F*s: fight, flight, and sexual behavior.

Cannon criticized James's autonomic specificity thesis by arguing, first, that the responses of the autonomic nervous system, the changes in heart rate, breathing, sweat responses, and so on, are too diffuse to account for the varieties of emotional experience. Heart rate, for example, can increase or decrease by small amounts in response to events. There might be slight increases or decreases in salivation or sweating. Changes of these kinds do not carry enough

FIGURE 5.2   In this setup in Robert Levenson's laboratory, two participants' autonomic physiology is recorded as they talk with one another. Receptors help gather measures of participants' activity, heart rate, pulse in the finger and ear, galvanic sweat response in the finger, skin temperature, and respiration (photo taken by Deepak Paul; courtesy of the Berkeley Psychophysiology Laboratory).

information to account for the many distinctions people make in their emotional experience, for instance, between gratitude, reverence, compassion, love, devotion, desire, and pride. The specificity and nuance of different emotions, Cannon contended, was to be found not in the body, but in the brain.

A second criticism was that autonomic responses are too slow to account for the rapidity with which we experience emotion or move from one emotion to another. The autonomic nervous system typically produces measurable responses within 15 to 30 seconds after the perceived stimulus (Janig, 2003). But people's emotional experiences can occur more quickly. The blush peaks at about 15 seconds after the embarrassing event (Shearn et al., 1990). Think back to the last time you felt acute embarrassment. You probably experienced feelings of embarrassment more rapidly than 15 to 30 seconds after the embarrassing event. Cannon contended that the experience of emotion arises more quickly than autonomic activity.

A third criticism was that the main actions of the autonomic nervous system, which James contended were specific to emotion, actually occur in a variety of other states, such as fevers, cold exposure, or asphyxia. Cannon argued that one might find that love and fevers have the same autonomic patterning. This is an intriguing possibility (and it might conform to your own view of love as a form of illness), but it does not support a strong version of James's hypothesis that each emotion is the perception of a distinct autonomic pattern.

Finally, Cannon questioned whether our sensitivity to change in the autonomic nervous system is refined enough to result in the many emotional states we experience. Cannon argued that for the most part we are insensitive to autonomic sensations that might arise, for example, from changes in blood flow, vasoconstriction, or digestion. Cannon noted, for example, that people actually feel little when their intestines are cut or burned. More recent studies have found that people are only moderately attuned to their heart-rate activity (Roberts & Pennebaker, 1995) or to other bodily responses (Katkin, 1985; Katkin, Blascovich, & Godband, 1981; Rimé, Philippot, & Cisamolo, 1990). Even if the autonomic nervous system generated emotion-specific responses, it is not clear that they would translate to distinct emotional experiences.

Two-Factor Theory of Emotion

In 1962, Stanley Schachter and Jerome Singer (1962) proposed a **two-factor theory** of emotion, based both on James's theory and on Cannon's critique of it, which became almost as influential as James's theory itself. Their theory suggested that emotional experiences arise as the product of two processes. The first is undifferentiated autonomic arousal, which gets the heart beating, the blood flowing, and the body ready for action. Arousal, however, has no specific emotional meaning without an interpretation placed on it. The second factor in Schachter and Singer's theory, then, is the construal or explanation the person arrives at for the undifferentiated arousal. In a well-known experiment that tested this formulation, Schachter and Singer produced general arousal in their participants by injecting them with adrenaline; some participants were uninformed of the injection's physiological effects, whereas others were given information of such effects. Then the experimenters put them in a social situation in which an experimenter's accomplice was either angry or euphoric. Those who were injected with adrenaline, who did not know its physiological effects, became happy if the experimenter's accomplice was euphoric, and angry if the experimenter's accomplice was angry at the rude questionnaire that both the participant and the accomplice had to complete.

Notwithstanding the fact that the experiment of Schachter and Singer (1962) has not been replicated in full (Manstead & Wagner, 1981; Reizensein, 1983), the theory has had two lasting influences upon the field of emotion. First, the theory added to the interest in **appraisal** of the kind that Arnold and Gasson (1954) had proposed (see Chapter 1).

The second influence was the finding that has been replicated, that when physiological arousal or an anxiety state does not have an obvious source, people tend to label and experience their arousal according to what is happening in the current situation. For example, in a state of anxiety you might arrive at the home of a first date where you are grilled by imposing parents who are rumored to have been involved with the CIA. In tension and anticipation, you fall madly in love as your date descends the stairs. In such examples, people can experience specific emotions—excitement or love—by attributing heightened arousal or anxiety to what is happening in their immediate social environment.

In more specific terms, Schachter and Singer introduced an interest in **misattribution** of arousal, which has been pursued in many experiments that explore how arousal from one source (for instance, difficulties at work) can be attributed to some other, salient source in the environment (tensions at home). Thus, people who have just engaged in physical exercise, which has aroused their body, find cartoons funnier and erotica more stimulating (Zillmann, 1978). The general finding, then, which has been replicated many times, is that arousal, sometimes purely physiological, and sometimes from certain emotions such as anxiety, can transfer to other situations and have effects on our emotional experience of the social world (see also Zillmann & Vorderer, 2000). We'll talk more of this effect of transfer of excitation in Chapter 10.

The Search for Physiological Specificity

Given the widespread acceptance of Schachter and Singer's two-factor theory, for several decades it was believed that there was little physiological specificity to emotion. The central claim of William James, that each emotion is defined by specific "bodily reverberations," enjoyed little supportive evidence. That would change in the early 1980s with an accidental discovery made by Paul Ekman and Wallace Friesen.

Directed Facial Action

In the 1970s, Paul Ekman and Wallace Friesen took several years to develop a coding system to identify facial muscles that were activated in emotional expressions (Ekman & Friesen, 1978, 1984; Ekman & Rosenberg, 1997), as we discussed in Chapter 4. To develop this system, Ekman and Friesen spent thousands of hours moving their facial muscles, taking careful notes about how these movements created new creases, wrinkles, dimples, bulges, and changes to the appearance of the face. In the course of this, Ekman noticed that moving his facial muscles changed how he felt. When he furrowed the brow his heart rate seemed to increase and his blood pressure to rise. When he wrinkled the nose and stuck out the tongue, as one does during disgust, his heart seemed to slow down. Might moving facial muscles into emotion configurations produce specific autonomic activity? This would be in keeping with William James's idea that specific bodily responses give rise to specific emotional experiences.

In a first line of research, directly building upon Ekman's observations, Robert Levenson and his colleagues (Ekman, Levenson, & Friesen, 1983; Levenson et al., 1990) employed a **directed facial action** task. They had participants follow muscle-by-muscle instructions to configure their faces into the six different expressions of the emotions that Ekman had studied in his cross-cultural judgment studies. For one expression participants were instructed to:

1. Wrinkle your nose.
2. Raise your upper lip.
3. Open your mouth and stick out your tongue.

In this case the emotion portrayed is disgust, but the participants did not know what emotion they were portraying. Once participants had made the pose in a fashion that conformed to the required specific emotional expression (which took some coaching), they held the expression for 10 seconds. As they did so, measures of autonomic activity were gathered and compared to a control condition. Table 5.2 presents results from one study using this task.

Table 5.2 Emotion-related changes in autonomic physiology observed in the directed facial action task

	Anger	Fear	Sad	Disgust	Smile	Surprise
Heart rate (BPM)	5.0	5.5	4.2	.70	2.4	.20
Finger temperature	.20	−.05	.07	.07	.01	.01
Galvanic skin response	.41	.58	.43	.52	.07	.07
Muscle activity	−.01	.01	−.01	.01	.01	.00

Source: Adapted from Levenson et al. (1990).

Let's put these results in the context of the claims about physiological specificity. At the time, there were two hypotheses inspired by Cannon about the nonspecificity of emotion-related changes in the autonomic nervous system (Levenson et al., 1990). The first was that all emotions involve elevated sympathetic response. The second was that negative emotions—anger, disgust, fear, and sadness in this study—all involve increased sympathetic arousal, whereas positive emotions involve reduced arousal. The results in Table 5.2 challenge two predictions of the kind that Cannon made: they reveal differences among negative emotions. As you can see from the table, large increases of heart rate occurred for fear, anger, and sadness, but almost none for disgust. Second, galvanic skin response (the measure of sweat activity) was greater for fear and disgust than for anger and sadness. Third, finger temperature was greater for anger than fear. One could make the case that this was because in anger blood flows freely to the hands (perhaps to aid in combat), whereas with fear blood remains near the chest to support flight-related locomotion. Thus, four negative emotions differed on certain measures of autonomic activity, suggesting that a one-arousal-fits-all model of autonomic activity is inadequate (although see Cacioppo et al., 1993 for critique). To the extent that these bodily responses are part of the evolved components of emotion, one would expect these differences in physiology to be observed in different cultures. Guided by this interest, Levenson and Ekman conducted a similar directed facial action study with the Minangkabau, a matrilineal people in West Sumatra, Indonesia (Levenson et al., 1992). For the most part, they observed similar emotion-specific physiological distinctions produced by the directed facial action task, suggesting that these distinctions may be universal. Subsequent studies have replicated these emotion-specific autonomic patterns in elderly adults, although interestingly, in general, elderly adults (aged 65 and above) showed attenuated autonomic responses (Levenson et al., 1991). A review of directed facial action studies has been written by Ekman (2007) in a collection of methods that have been used for eliciting emotions.

Other studies, of the blush, of stress, of shame, and of positive emotion, would build upon the results of the directed facial action task to lend further credence to James's thesis of physiological specificity.

The Blush

The blush involves the spontaneous reddening of the face, ears, neck, and upper chest produced by increases in blood volume in the subcutaneous capillaries in those regions (Cutlip & Leary, 1993). By contrast, the flush is a nonsocial response that often is associated with physical exertion, temperature changes, or alcohol consumption. The blush has long fascinated novelists (especially during the Victorian era), poets, adolescents (many of whom would give up all future earnings to blush less often), and people who are courting. The American satirist Mark Twain observed that "humans are the only species who blush, and the only one that needs to." As it turns out, Twain was not entirely correct: some nonhuman primates show reddening in the face, perhaps as an appeasement gesture (Hauser, 1996). But he was right in assuming that the blush serves a purpose related to mistakes and the seeking of reconciliation following them.

In his chapter on the blush in *The Expression of the Emotions in Man and Animals*, Darwin observed that the blush is associated with modesty, embarrassment, shyness, and shame. In essential ways, this thesis has been supported by findings we review below. In this analysis, though, Darwin offered a rather odd theoretical account: he posited that the blush is the product of self-focused attention. He reasoned that when we direct our attention to any part of the body, physiological activity is stimulated in that region so that when in shyness or embarrassment we think of our face as an object of attention, blood flows to that region. In one story passed on to Darwin by a doctor, as this man gradually opened the blouse of a female patient, button by button, incrementally baring her neck and upper chest, a blush extended to the newly exposed areas of her body.

More recently, Mark Leary and his colleagues have carefully analyzed situations that produce the blush. They have discerned specific elicitors of the blush and proposed a specific cause: negative self-focused attention (Leary et al., 1992). We don't blush when we receive desirable attention from others or when we think of what others think of us. Rather, we blush when we are the objects and recipients of **undesirable social attention**, that is, attention that is potentially damaging to our self-concept, in particular in the eyes of others.

So how is the blush related to emotion? People commonly report that they blush during embarrassment; some 21% of Spanish participants (Edelmann, 1990) reported blushing, as did 92% of American students (Miller & Tangney, 1994). Furthermore, the blush may be fairly specific to embarrassment: in one study people rarely reported blushing during shame or guilt (Miller & Tangney, 1994).

Is the blush distinct from the autonomic response of other emotions? One candidate with which one might make comparison is the autonomic response of fear. The experience of blushing often is associated with certain fears, most notably social anxiety. And we learned that fear is defined by elevated heart rate and other indicators of sympathetic response, such as vasoconstriction. In a study that compared the blush to anxiety-related physiology, participants' cheek blood flow and temperature, finger temperature, and galvanic skin response were recorded in two conditions. In an embarrassment condition, the participant and four confederates of the experimenter watched a videotape of the participant previously singing "The Star Spangled Banner." In a condition that elicited fear, the participant and confederates watched the frightening shower scene from Alfred

Individual emotion: Awe

Awe is the emotion that is felt when you are in the presence of something that is vast and transcends your understanding of the world (Keltner & Haidt, 2003). People experience awe in response to some of the most dramatic of life experiences—around spiritual and political leaders, in seeing great cultural artifacts like the Notre Dame cathedral in Paris or the Taj Mahal in India, when encountering vast natural objects like the great Redwoods or the Grand Canyon, or in response to music and art. It was a sense of awe and wonder, which Darwin experienced in his travels on the *Beagle*, that stirred him to develop his theory of evolution. In many ways, awe defines what is most meaningful to us and what binds us to other members of our group.

Is there an autonomic response associated with awe? One candidate would clearly be the chills, or goosebumps. The chills and goosebumps are referred in the scientific lexicon as piloerection and refer to the contraction of small muscles surrounding hair follicles, a sympathetic autonomic nervous system response. In nonhuman species, individuals show this piloerection response when they expand their size to signal strength. In humans, recent studies find, we have the response when feeling awestruck. Several recent studies have found that people report goosebumps (and not the shivers) when they are feeling awe but not other positive emotions like pride, love, or sympathy (Campos et al., in press) and that the goosebumps differ from the chills associated with feeling fearful or cold (Maruskin et al., in press). It will be for future theorists to theorize about the evolutionary origins of this emotion-related bodily response, a theoretical inquiry that could reveal the origins of such diverse things as our reverence for music and tendency to fold into social collectives.

Hitchcock's movie, *Psycho* (Shearn et al., 1990). Participants' cheek blood flow, cheek skin temperature, and finger skin conductance increased more while they and others watched themselves singing than while they watched the frightening film clip (see also Shearn et al., 1992).

Unlike many autonomic responses, the blush is highly visible, often to our chagrin. What social benefits might the blush serve? Here recent science has lent credence to Mark Twain's observation that we blush because we need to. Corine van Dijk, Peter De Jong et al. (2009) proposed that the blush is an involuntary, costly way in which people signal their awareness and regret for the mistake they have made. If this were so, observers should be more positively disposed to the individual who blushes in problematic social situations. In keeping with this hypothesis, van Dijk and colleagues found that social observers responded more positively to individuals who blushed after they made mistakes. The blush, so costly to the person blushing, can restore that individual's standing in the eyes of others.

The Hypothalamic-Pituitary-Adrenal Axis

William James's thesis that emotions are embodied in movements of the viscera refers to systems other than just the autonomic nervous system. For example, the neuroendocrine system involves a network of glands, such as the pituitary and reproductive glands, distributed throughout the body that releases hormones into the bloodstream, which in turn have effects upon different organs and muscle groups. One branch of the neuroendocrine system particularly relevant to emotion is the **hypothalamic-pituitary-adrenal (HPA) axis**, whose activation results in the release of the stress-related hormone *cortisol* into the bloodstream (see Figure 5.3). Fifty years of scientific study have found that stressful events activate the paraventricular nucleus of the hypothalamus, which sends electrochemical signals to the anterior pituitary, which produces adreno-cortico-tropic hormone (ACTH). ACTH stimulates the adrenal glands (which are on top of the kidneys) to release the stress hormone cortisol into the bloodstream.

Cortisol activates glucose production needed for metabolically demanding action. It increases heart rate and blood pressure, thus enabling the distribution of blood to appropriate muscle groups involved in fight-or-flight behavior. It suppresses our immune system.

In the short run, activation of the HPA axis and the accompanying increase in cortisol enabled our ancestors to respond to threats to physical survival—for example, an approaching predator or an enraged rival. Today, this same stress response helps us respond to immediate threats and problems: enabling us to study late into the night for an exam, to avoid danger, or to devote ourselves to taking care of a sick friend or child.

Specific emotions also appear to map onto activation in the HPA axis and the release of cortisol into the bloodstream. The science that pertains to this thesis has often employed the Trier Social Stress Task. In this nerve-wracking task, participants are required to deliver an impromptu speech to an audience of evaluators, who are instructed to look critical and frustrated. Needless to say, this task elicits elevated sympathetic autonomic nervous system activation as well as a cortisol response. In a review of relevant studies, Sally Dickerson and Margaret Kemeny (2004) have made the important point that the Trier Social Stress Task is most likely to trigger cortisol release when participants feel that their positive social identity is threatened. This suggests that our experiences of emotions that involve negative social evaluations—emotions like anxiety or fear or anger—are likely to involve cortisol response.

In more recent work examining how more specific emotions correlate with cortisol release, Moons, Eisenberger, and Taylor (2010) had participants complete the Trier Social Stress Task.

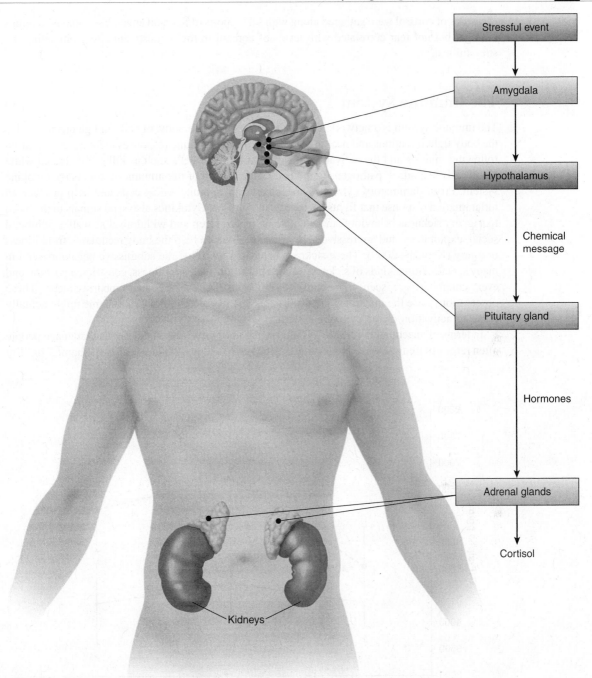

FIGURE 5.3 The hypothalamic-pituitary-adrenal (HPA) axis.

Measures of cortisol were gathered along with self-reports of fear and anger. Participants' feelings of anger but not fear correlated with levels of cortisol in the bloodstream after completing the stressful test.

The Immune System

The immune system is a network, distributed throughout the body, of cells and glands that helps the body fight infections and heal in response to injury. Immune responses include inflammation following injuries and the activation of different kinds of cells such as killer T-cells and white blood cells that attack pathogens in the body. One branch of the immune system is the cytokine system. Pro-inflammatory cytokines are released in immunological cells and help produce an inflammation response that fights bacterium and viruses. Cytokines also send signals to the brain to trigger "sickness behaviors" that include increased sleep and withdrawal as well as inhibited social, exploratory, and aggressive behaviors, all of which help the body recuperate from illness or injury (Kemeny, 2009). These sickness behaviors resemble the submissive behaviors seen in many species. Some kinds of sickness-related behavior, such as stillness, constricted posture, and even coughing, are seen in submissive emotions like shame and embarrassment. These observations raise the intriguing possibility that submissive emotions like shame might actually relate to activation of the cytokine system.

In terms of anecdotal evidence, it is interesting to observe that in the English language people often refer to submissive emotions with metaphors of disease—"I nearly died of shame," or "I'm

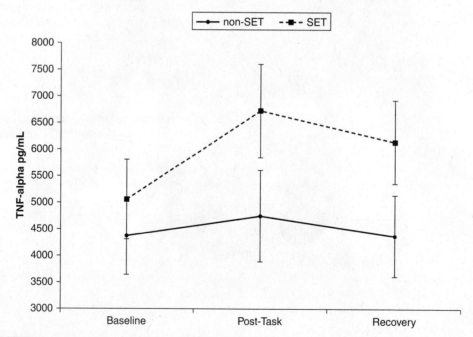

FIGURE 5.4 In situations of increased social evaluative threat, or SET (dotted line), one measure of cytokine release (TNF alpha) increases when participants must give a speech about why they would be a good candidate for a job (from Dickerson et al., 2009).

sick with envy." Perhaps these metaphors capture a relationship between submissive emotions and the activation in the cytokine system. Sally Dickerson and her colleagues have recently done research suggesting that the relationship between submissive emotion and activation of the cytokine system is more than just poetic metaphor (Dickerson et al., 2004). In one illustrative study, participants had to deliver a speech about why they would be the perfect applicant for a job in a condition of high social evaluative threat (SET in Figure 5.4). More specifically, in this condition two audience members looked on as the participant gave the speech, but reacted with common triggers of shame—critical, cold, rejecting facial expressions (Dickerson et al., 2004, 2009). As you can see in Figure 5.4, being judged in critical, rejecting fashion led to an increase in one marker of the cytokine system. And in the study previously reported, Moons et al. (2010) found that self-reports of fear correlated with cytokine levels after the Trier Social Stress Task. This again suggests that the cytokine system is involved in emotions related to a threatened, submissive self.

Parasympathetic Response and Positive Emotion

What about positive emotions? Here the story of autonomic specificity is less developed, but emerging studies are promising. Laughter is associated with exhalation and shifts in respiration and heart rate (Ruch, 1993). Smiling tends to reduce stress-related heart-rate acceleration, allowing the individual to return to a calmer state (Fredrickson & Levenson, 1998). Are there other ways that positive emotions activate specific autonomic responses?

One candidate emerges in the creative theorizing of Steven Porges (1995, 1998). Based on comparisons of the autonomic nervous systems of different species, Porges has made a case for three stages in the evolution of the autonomic nervous system. A first stage produced the **dorsal vagal complex**, which is present in all species. It regulates digestive processes, and it produces the immobilization response seen in many reptiles and fish when attacked by predators. Next to emerge in evolution was the sympathetic nervous system that controlled fight and flight behavior, and which appears to be engaged by emotions like anger, fear, and sadness. The last portion of the autonomic nervous system to evolve, and only in mammals, is the **ventral vagal complex**. It is controlled by the vagus nerve. As Porges points out, the ventral vagal complex regulates facial muscle actions, head movements that enable gaze activity, and vocalizations, all of which are involved in positive emotions, such as love or compassion, that promote social connection (see Chapter 4).

Researchers usually record vagal tone (activation of the vagus nerve) by measuring heart rate and respiration to derive an index of parasympathetic influence on heart rate (Berntson, Cacioppo, & Quigley, 1993). Although the vagus serves many functions, some of these functions are emotional. In keeping with Porges's arguments, the vagus also reduces cardiac output, allowing for flexible thought and attention and greater social calm around others. People with elevated vagal tone have been found to experience greater positive emotions and stronger social connections. People who have elevated vagal tone reported higher levels of positive emotion and kindness and warmth toward others six to eight months after the assessment of vagal tone (Oveis et al., 2009). Resting vagal tone was associated with increases in spontaneous positive emotion during the Rorschach test (Kettunen et al., 2000). College students prone to mania reported extremely high levels of positive emotion in response to positive and negative films clips, and accompanying high levels of vagal response (Gruber et al., 2008).

A further line of evidence suggests that people with higher vagal tone enjoy more flexible thought processes and are thereby better able to regulate their emotions. For example, people

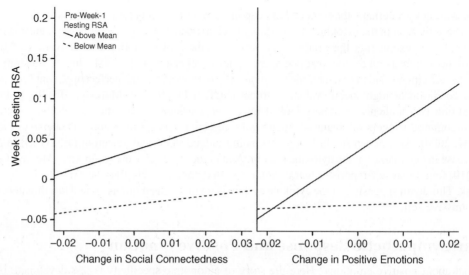

FIGURE 5.5 Participants who begin the study with elevated vagal tone or resting RSA (solid line) show greater increases over time in social connectedness and positive emotion, which in turn track increases in vagal tone (from Kok & Fredrickson, 2010).

with elevated vagal tone are better able to shift their attention from one task to another, they perform better on working memory tasks, and they respond with greater resilience, or less negative emotion, to stressful tasks (Kok & Fredrickson, 2010). Vagal activation seems to enable people to regulate their emotions more effectively.

In one of the richest studies to date, Kok and Fredrickson (2010) assessed people's vagal tone at the beginning and end of a nine-week study, and in between these two assessments they had participants report on their daily experience of positive emotions and the strength of their social connections. Over the nine-week period, people who at the start of the study had high levels of vagal tone experienced greater increases in positive emotion and social connection over the nine-week period of time. Just as importantly, increases in social connections over the nine weeks led to rises in vagal tone at the end of the study. Figure 5.5 represents these important findings. What you can see is that for people who begin with elevated vagal tone at the beginning of the study (solid line), with each increase in vagal tone over the nine weeks (the vertical axis) they enjoy better social connectedness (left graph) and increases in positive emotion (right graph). These findings make the important point that not only does vagal tone predict more positive emotion and social connection over time, but the complement holds as well: increases in positive emotion and social connection will increase vagal tone.

The Interplay Between Bodily Reaction and Emotional Experience

Alongside the thesis of physiological specificity, which we have just examined, William James made a second argument, that activation in the bodily systems of emotion should produce the experience of emotion. In James's own words from his influential essay: "Any voluntary arousal of the so-called manifestations of a special emotion ought to give us the emotion itself." Here James was arguing that if specific bodily systems of emotion are engaged, we will experience specific patterns of emotion.

Some 80 years after James, the influential theorist Sylvan Tomkins (1962) made a similar point, arguing that the experience of emotion closely tracks emotion-specific bodily responses:

> *Affects are sets of muscle and glandular responses located in the face and also widely distributed through the body, which generate sensory feedback which is either inherently "acceptable" or "unacceptable." These organized sets of responses are triggered at subcortical centers where specific "programs" for each distinct affect are stored. These programs are innately endowed and have been genetically inherited. They are capable of simultaneously capturing such widely distributed organs as the face, the heart, and the endocrines and imposing on them a specific pattern of correlated responses. (pp. 243–244)*

Empirical tests of this thesis face significant obstacles. How can scientists activate specific bodily systems? In spite of these difficulties, two kinds of evidence bear upon James's thesis, and Tomkins's as well, that bodily responses generate emotional experience.

Bodily Action Generates Emotional Response

One of the earliest and most memorable demonstrations that bodily changes can have a direct measurable influence on emotions was by Strack, Martin, and Stepper (1988). They found that getting subjects to hold a pen in the mouth, thus making the muscle movements characteristic of a smile without the subjects realizing it, gave rise to judgments of cartoons as funnier than for subjects not contracting these muscles. In another study along similar lines, Larsen, Kasimatis, and Frey (1992) induced subjects to draw their eyebrows together in a way that mimicked those of a sad face. They found that subjects' judgments of pictures indicated greater sadness, although they did not know that their eyebrow pose had implied sadness.

Let's make some predictions; think about what you know about fear. It engages specific facial muscles, vocal tones, patterns of touch, flight- or freezing-related movements in the hands, arms, and body, and patterned responses in the cardiovascular system. James and his followers would predict that with bodily changes like these, the experience of fear should arise, with comparable results for other emotions.

In keeping with this hypothesis, select studies find that when people move emotion-specific facial muscles, elements of the emotion arise. For example, in Levenson and Ekman's study using directed facial action, over 50% of people reported experiencing emotion in doing the directed facial action, and over 25% reported the target emotion—for example, sadness when moving their facial muscles into a sad expression—as very intense. Simply moving facial muscles associated with fear or anger or sadness in a laboratory setting triggered the experience of that emotion.

New studies are revealing that when we move our whole bodies in ways that conform to expressive patterns associated with specific emotions, elements of the emotion arise. For example, in Chapter 4 you learned that pride displays involve physical signs of strength—the expanded shoulders and chest and clenched fists raised high. Shame, by contrast, is signaled in the opposite pattern of behavior—drooping shoulders, constricted posture, and head

Reflection and cultivation: Developing emotional calmness

In this chapter you have learned about the profile of fear, anxiety, and stress: that it involves elevated activation of the sympathetic autonomic nervous system and the HPA axis. This study of emotion-related bodily responses just as readily reveals certain practical tips for finding emotional calm. Perhaps the most powerful is what you see on many bumper stickers: "Breathe." Many of the contemplative practices in human history found in meditation and yoga practices focus on patterns of deep breathing. In different meditation traditions, for example, people are encouraged to slow down their breathing through deep patterns of exhalation and inhalation.

One common technique, for example, is to breathe in for a count of six (while expanding the chest), and breathe out for a count of six (while pulling in the abdominal muscles), and to continue this for 10 or 20 times. A central focus in the different kinds of yoga is what is known as *pranayama* breathing, which emphasizes slower, deeper patterns of breathing, with a particular focus on deep exhalation. What you have learned in this chapter, and as anticipated by James's second prediction, is that these patterns of breathing engage the vagus nerve, which quiets stress-related physiology and opens up possibilities for greater calm and positive emotion.

movements down. Recent studies find that when individuals engage in such postures they experience pride-related and shame-related feelings. For example, when people are asked to make the closed fist, often a sign of strength and part of the pride display, they experience feelings of elevated self-esteem (Schubert & Koole, 2009). In still other research, when people held postures of strength and pride for one minute, they actually increased measures of testosterone, a hormone related to status-enhancing behaviors, but when people held their body in a shame-related posture, they underwent increased levels of cortisol (Carney, Cuddy, & Yap, 2010).

Even engaging in different patterns of breathing can alter an individual's emotional state. For example, fear and anxiety are accompanied by shallower and shorter patterns of exhalation—breathing characteristic of a strong sympathetic autonomic nervous system response. When we exhale slowly and deeply, by contrast, the parasympathetic autonomic nervous system is activated, in particular the branches of the vagus nerve. Might simply exhaling deeply lead to reduced fear and increased calm, as William James might have anticipated? In keeping with this possibility, several laboratory studies have found that highly anxious individuals who engage in patterns of deep breathing and exhalation experience reductions in anxiety (Brown & Gerbarg, 2005). These findings may shed light on one important, pervasive way that people find calm in times of stress: deep breathing.

Reduced Input from the Body and Diminished Emotional Experience

A second approach to examining James's thesis that engaging in bodily responses will produce emotional experience is to look at what happens when people do not receive input from the bodily responses of emotion. The clear prediction is that people with diminished input from their bodies should have diminished emotions. So what's the evidence? One relevant study is to look at what happens to the emotional lives of people who suffer spinal injuries that remove sensation, including bodily sensation, below the site of the injury. Hohmann (1966) interviewed 25 adult men who had suffered spinal injuries. Hohmann, a paraplegic himself, conducted the interviews, querying the men about sexual feelings, fear, anger, grief, sentimentality, and overall emotionality. Most of the men reported decreases in sexual feeling since their injury. Those with injuries at the neck level reported large decreases. Before injury, one single 29-year-old described his previous feelings in sexual encounters: "a hot, tense feeling all over my body," but said that since the injury "it doesn't do anything for me" (p. 148). Hohmann also found decreased feelings of fear. One man had his injury at the high chest level. One day he was fishing on a lake when a storm came up and a log punctured his boat. He said: "I knew I was sinking, and I was afraid all right, but somehow I didn't have that feeling of trapped panic that I know I would have had before" (p. 150).

As you read Hohmann's descriptions, you should wonder about certain confounds in the study. (Confounds are variables other than those at the focus of the study that might produce the results obtained.) What is the effect of disablement itself on people's reactions to emotion-inducing events? What is the effect of simply getting older (the time lapse since the injury ranged from 2 to 17 years with a mean of 10 years)?

In subsequent studies of individuals with spinal cord injuries, with improved methodologies different results have been found. Bermond et al. (1991) asked 37 patients with spinal injuries to rate fear, anger, grief, sentimentality, and joyfulness on scales indicating increases and decreases since their injury. Neither in the whole group nor in the 14 participants with injuries in the neck region (and hence the greatest sensory loss) was there any general decrease in rated emotional intensity. Most participants reported no change on most scales, though some reported some increases in intensity since their injury. In a study with 19 patients with spinal cord injuries and 19 uninjured people matched for age, sex, and education, Cobos et al. (2002) found that the spinally injured people either had no decrease, or in some cases an increase, of emotional experience since their injury. At the same time there was no difference in the abilities of injured as compared with non-injured people to identify emotional pictures.

In another route to this question, researchers have blocked specific bodily reactions and looked at emotion-related responses. One such method has been to study the effects of injections of botox, which paralyzes muscles. It can be injected into the eyebrow region, because it can prevent wrinkles from appearing in that region of the face: the allure of this treatment! Joshua Davis, Kevin Ochsner, and their colleagues (Davis et al., 2010) had middle-aged women view emotionally evocative film clips before and after a botox treatment and report on their positive and negative emotional responses to the clips. They found that women who received the botox injection overall reported diminished emotional responses to the film clips. They did report similar levels of emotion in response to intense positive and negative clips, but they showed diminished emotional responses to milder positive clips. These findings suggest that bodily responses—in this case facial muscle movements—can influence some, but not all, emotional experience.

Embodiment, Cognition, and Social Interaction

As you shall learn in different ways throughout this book, emotions are more than just brief responses contained within the body; they shape how we perceive the world, reason, reach moral judgments, and interact with others. This suggests that perhaps we have been thinking about

James's thesis in a narrow fashion. Instead, it may be that emotion-related bodily responses not only contribute to momentary experience as we have seen; the broader possibility is that bodily responses shape a broader class of cognitive and social processes.

This interest has led Paula Niedenthal (2007) to offer an important line of theorizing on what is called **embodiment**, which holds that not only are our conscious experiences of emotion rooted in bodily responses, but so, too, are complex ideas, concepts, thoughts, and metaphors that arise during emotional experiences, and by implication, our social interactions. Here the claim is that cognitive processes related to an emotion, for example, our memories of an emotional experience or understanding of an emotional passage in a book, will engage the bodily responses and sensations of that emotion. In this final section we shall see that emotion-related bodily responses contribute in important ways to how we categorize objects in our environment, make decisions, and understand other people.

Niedenthal and her colleagues have offered one set of studies on how emotion-related bodily responses influence categorization (Niedenthal et al., 2009). In one study they gave participants lists of words related to three different emotions—anger, joy, and disgust—and asked them to determine whether the word was related to one of the three emotion categories. For example, they would be presented with the word *vomit* or *sun* or *fight* and asked to determine which of the three emotion categories the word belonged to (i.e., "disgust" "anger" "joy"). This simple conceptual judgment led to the activation of emotion-specific facial muscle movements, as you can see in Figure 5.6. Categorizing words related to anger led to the activation of the corrugator muscles that furrow the eyebrows, categorizing words related to joy activated the zygomaticus major muscle that pulls the lip corners up and the orbicularis oculi muscle surrounding the eyes, and categorizing words related to disgust led to the activation of the levator muscle that pulls the upper lip upward. Categorizing words related to emotions engages aspects of the body related to those emotions.

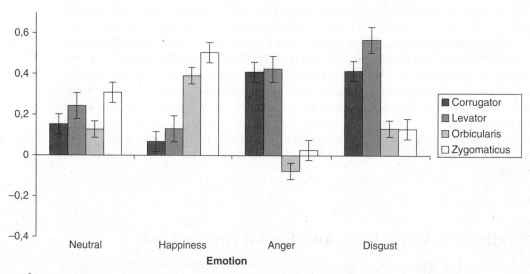

FIGURE 5.6 Processing concepts related to specific emotions activates emotion-specific facial muscles for happiness, anger, and disgust (adapted from Niedenthal et al., 2009).

In a further experiment in this series, Niedenthal et al. (2009) had participants hold a pen in their mouths while they made judgments about which of three emotion categories—disgust, joy, or anger—offered the best fit for emotion-related words. In holding the pen in their mouths, participants were prevented from moving facial muscles related to disgust (the upper lip raise) and joy (the smile). The researchers argued that without an embodied response people should find it harder to categorize disgust-related and joy-related words. This is indeed what they observed. Thus embodiment was found to have a causal effect on categorization, not just a correlational association.

Somatic Marker Hypothesis

Another variant on theorizing of the Jamesian kind is Antonio Damasio's (1994) somatic marker hypothesis. Recall Phineas Gage (discussed in Chapter 1), the railroad construction foreman whose frontal lobes were damaged when an iron bar was shot through them by an accidental explosion, and who became unable to organize his life. Hanna Damasio and colleagues (1994), using computer methods with Gage's skull, determined that the region of his brain that was destroyed was the lower-middle part of the frontal lobes. Antonio Damasio (1994) and his colleagues have now studied many patients with this kind of brain damage and have noticed that, like Phineas Gage, their emotions seem blunted. Along with the emotional deficit, these frontally damaged patients had great difficulties in planning ordinary life: they made disastrous social decisions such as associating with the wrong kinds of people, while dithering endlessly over issues that are inconsequential. They showed many deficits in the moral realm, for instance, inappropriate manners and a lack of concern for the well-being of others (Stuss & Benson, 1984). This syndrome has therefore sometimes been called *pseudo-psychopathy* or *acquired sociopathy*.

To explain this pattern of results, Damasio (1994) proposed the **somatic marker** hypothesis, which brings together much of the theorizing and findings we have encountered in this chapter. For patients with damaged ventromedial frontal cortex, they lack access to emotion-related bodily responses or symbolic representations of such reactions—somatic markers—that guide the individual in making judgments and decisions. For example, emotion-related bodily responses help us avoid risky actions, they help us respond to unfair actions or to help those who suffer, and emotion-related bodily actions help us focus on inspiring acts of virtue (see Chapter 10). When we damage the ventromedial frontal cortex, we no longer have access to these somatic markers. Our decision making in many realms suffers and life starts to be lived without the wisdom of the body.

What is the evidence for the somatic marker hypothesis? Several studies have documented that patients with damage to the ventromedial prefrontal cortex show little bodily response to emotional stimuli, and their judgment is affected. Compared to control participants, patients with damage to the ventromedial frontal cortex showed little galvanic skin response to emotionally evocative slides, such as nudes or scenes of mutilation (Tranel, 1994; Tranel & Damasio, 1994). Importantly, the group with ventromedial frontal damage also did show elevated galvanic skin response to other kinds of stimuli, such as a loud noise or taking a deep breath. Their particular deficit, it would seem, is in responding emotionally to events that ordinarily would prompt emotions.

In a paradigm known as the Iowa Gambling Task, patients with ventromedial frontal damage showed an inability to stay away from high-risk gambles (Bechara et al., 1997). In this task, patient groups and control participants were asked to choose cards from four different decks. Some cards gave monetary rewards; other cards signaled losses. Two of the decks were risky: they offered a chance of a big win, but when chosen repeatedly they led to overall loss of money. The other decks represented safer routes: they offered the chance of smaller wins, but when chosen repeatedly they led to small gains. Typical control participants eventually developed a heightened galvanic skin response (generated by the sympathetic nervous system) to the risky decks if they chose a card from those decks. Eventually they avoided these decks. In contrast, the group of patients with ventromedial frontal damage showed no such sympathetic system response to the risky decks. They tended to choose from the risky decks and lost money. Normal participants started to choose advantageously even before they could consciously articulate the best strategy. By contrast, patients continued to choose disadvantageously even after they consciously realized the best strategy.

The Iowa Gambling Task continues to be studied. In one independent replication with normal volunteers doing the task, Guillaume, Joliant, Jaussent, Lawrence, Malafosse et al. (2009) found skin conductance changes (described as an implicit measure) to be significantly correlated with choosing from the disadvantageous decks. At the same time, they found that participants' explicit recognition of the properties of the decks of cards was yet more strongly associated with decision making. Implicit and explicit measures were not associated with each other. The researchers found that both implicit and explicit pathways affected performance. In reviewing studies of the somatic marker hypothesis, Ohira (2010) concluded that although there is a correlation of decision making with raised galvanic skin responses in choosing from risky decks in the Iowa Gambling Task, it's still not clear what causal influence such bodily reactions have in decision making.

Embodied Cognition and Empathy

It is fitting that we end this chapter with a set of findings that are in keeping with the highly social emphasis of this book: recent studies suggest that embodied responses play an essential role in our understanding of others' emotion. For example, earlier you learned that botox treatments reduce our emotional experience. More recently, Neal and Chartrand (2011) found that after botox treatments people were less skilled at perceiving the emotions of others.

These findings suggest that the very foundation of empathy, of understanding others, is our own embodied responses. As we discussed in Chapter 1 with the work of de Vignmont and Singer (2006), when you are with someone else you don't just recognize that person's facial patterns, you create versions of their emotions in your own body, in yourself.

Several recent findings lend further credence to this view. A first important discovery that caused a big stir was by Giacomo Rizzolatti et al. (1996). The discovery was of **mirror neurons,** in the pre-motor cortex of monkeys' brains. They fired either when an intended action by another individual was perceived by the monkey or when the same action was carried out by the monkey itself.

In relation to human emotions, Wicker et al. (2003), in a paradigm like that which defined mirror neurons, found that an area of the brain called the insula was activated both when human participants saw someone else's facial expression of disgust and when participants themselves experienced disgust (see Chapter 6). Importantly, the insula is a region of the brain that tracks the individual's autonomic responses, suggesting that our understanding of others' emotions is based in part in the input of our own bodily response. Gallese, Keysers, and Rizzolatti (2004) say that these neural mechanisms "allow us to directly understand the meaning of the actions and emotions of others by internally replicating . . . them without any explicit reflective mediation" (p. 396). They call these mechanisms simulation systems.

One might think that in order to recognize an action, or an emotional expression, one just has to categorize a certain pattern (of the kind that behaviorists call a stimulus). The discovery of mirror neurons and the more general phenomenon of mirroring (or imitation) brings the issue much closer to home. We recognize intended actions by being able to do them ourselves in our own body; we can know what action words mean by being able to do the actions ourselves; we can recognize emotions by feeling them ourselves in our own bodies (Gallese, Gernsbacher, Heyes, Hickok, & Iacoboni, 2011).

Although this chapter has been about bodily changes, it is striking how frequently the emotional issues of human embodiment have pointed to the emotional issues of human relatedness.

SUMMARY

William James argued that emotional experience is the perception of emotion-specific bodily responses, especially those in the autonomic nervous system. We reviewed the two branches of the autonomic nervous system: the parasympathetic branch slows the body down, while the sympathetic branch is involved in arousal, in increased cardiac output to facilitate demanding actions like fight or flight. We next reviewed two theoretical proposals that followed on from James: Cannon's idea of nonspecific arousal in emotion and Schachter and Singer's idea that emotions derive from arousal plus a social appraisal. We followed this with a review of what is known about emotion-specific bodily responses, looking at recent studies of the directed facial action task, the blush, the HPA axis, the immune system, and the parasympathetic autonomic nervous system. Grounded in this understanding of emotion-related bodily responses, we then looked at how moving or blocking bodily responses influences emotional experiences. We concluded with recent theorizing known as embodiment, which helps illuminate how emotion-related bodily responses help us categorize objects in the world, make decisions, and understand others.

TO THINK ABOUT AND DISCUSS

1. One bodily response related to emotion that has just begun to be studied scientifically is the chills, or goosebumps. What emotions do you think are involved when you have goosebumps? How might you study the relationship between goosebumps and emotion? Can you come up with a Darwinian evolutionary account of the goosebumps?

2. Try to think of an occasion in a movie or novel in which a character blushed. What happened in the aftermath of the blush? How does it fit recent findings suggesting that the blush triggers increased trust and liking?

3. Try an experiment in embodiment and see how it influences your emotions. You might stand in the posture of pride with fists clenched and chest expanded. Or furrow your eyebrow and tighten your lips. What sensations and emotions seem to arise out of these postures for you?

FURTHER READING

This book, written for a nonspecialist readership, became a bestseller:

Antonio Damasio (1994). *Descartes' error*. New York, NY: Putnam.

For a review of the autonomic nervous system, and emotion-relevant findings, read:

Gerhard Stemmler (2003). Methodological considerations in the psychophysiological study of emotion. In R. J.

Davidson, K. R. Scherer, & H. H. Goldsmith (Eds.), *Handbook of affective sciences* (pp. 225–55). New York, NY: Oxford University Press.

Some of the most robust findings concerning physiological specificity are described by:

Robert Levenson, Paul Ekman, & Wallace Friesen (1990). Voluntary facial action generates emotion-specific autonomic nervous system activity. *Psychophysiology*, **27**(4), 363–84.

For an excellent treatment of embodiment and emotion, see P. M. Niedenthal, M. Mermillod, M. Maringer, and U. Hess (2010). The simulation of smiles (SIMS) model: Embodied simulation and the meaning of facial expression. *Behavioral and Brain Sciences*, **33**, 417–433.

Brain Mechanisms and Emotion

6

Photo Credit: From: Leah H. Somerville et al., "Anterior cingulate cortex responds differentially to expectancy violation and social rejection," *Nature Neuroscience 9,* 1007 -1008 (2006).

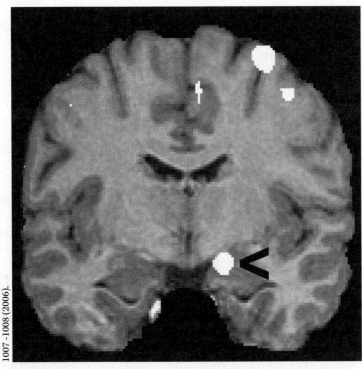

FIGURE 6.0 Image from a functional magnetic resonance imaging (fMRI) study by Leah Somerville and Bill Kelley: coronal slice through the brain showing greater blood oxygen level–dependent response in the right amygdala (the white region indicated by the black arrow) when participants viewed faces previously associated with emotional information, in contrast to faces previously associated with neutral information.

Herein too may be felt the powerlessness of mere Logic . . .
to resolve these problems which lie nearer to our hearts.

(George Boole, 1854, An Investigation of the Laws of Thought, p. 416)

In his book, *Awakenings* (1973), Oliver Sacks describes treatment of the survivors of the sleeping sickness (*encephalitis lethargica*), a disease that started in Europe in the winter of 1916–1917 and spread throughout the world. It continued for more than 10 years and affected five million people. It was caused by a virus that attacked the striatal regions of the brain, where there are networks of dopamine receptors, which, you shall learn, are important to motivation, action, and the feeling of pleasure. Victims fell into a suspended state: "they were as insubstantial as ghosts, as passive as zombies" (Sacks, p. 32), sitting motionless and speechless all day, observing but doing nothing. A few remained alive in hospitals for up to 50 years. In 1969, a precursor of the transmitter substance dopamine was discovered that became the drug L-Dopa. With its administration, transmitter functions in the striatal system were restored: Sacks described how, with L-Dopa, people in suspended animation experienced awakenings. They began to act spontaneously and schedule their daily activities.

With this restoration not only did there arise emotions of joy and excitement with emergence from decades of lethargy, but the drug gave rise to excitements, mood swings, and other emotional effects. Neural messages started to traverse long-dormant nerve pathways. In the case of the patient Frances D., Sacks writes, there occurred:

> . . . certain violent appetites and passions . . . [that] could not be dismissed by her as "purely physical" or "completely alien" to her "real self" but on the contrary were felt to be in some sense releases or exposures or confessions of very deep and ancient parts of herself.

Such emotions, passions, and appetites, sexual and otherwise, were common with the administration of L-Dopa in the cases Sacks describes; simple shifts in brain chemistry brought about profound changes in emotion. This story of the treatment of patients with sleeping sickness provides a vivid illustration of how brain regions and neurotransmitters are intimately involved in emotion. Understanding this is the task of this chapter.

Historical Approaches to the Neuroscience of Emotion

The human brain has about 100,000,000,000 neurons; typically each may have perhaps 10,000 synapses, some as many as 150,000 (Kandel, Schwartz, & Jessell, 1991). Imagine making sense of how the brain works given this kind of complexity. Neuroanatomists have mapped the brain into dozens of separate regions (for example, the cortex has been mapped into over 50 distinct regions known as Brodmann areas) and begun to trace pathways through which the different regions connect. The challenge is to map different emotion-related processes to these interacting regions of the brain.

Scientists do this with **neuroimaging** techniques. In these, a machine monitors biochemical events in a series of digitally animated slices through a person's brain, while a computer takes this information and constructs visual images to show which regions have been metabolically most active. These methods are noninvasive. They include positron emission tomography (PET) and functional magnetic resonance imaging (fMRI) in which pictures are constructed to show brain activity changing over time in the course, for instance, of different emotional states. Alongside these imaging methods, neuroscientists can study how accidental or disease-related damage to brain tissue influences emotional processes; some have made localized lesions in the brains of animals for experimental purposes. Neuroscientists who use electrophysiological methods have stimulated parts of the brain with electric currents or with magnetic fields (transcranial magnetic stimulation—TMS), and measured electric signals (electroencephalography—EEG) or magnetic signals (magnetoencephalography—MEG) generated by populations of neurons. Pharmacological neuroscientists use chemical substances that affect the mechanisms of neurons and either apply them generally as drugs or deliver them locally to small regions of the brain to examine their effects on mental functions and experiences. That is it: anatomy, lesions, stimulation, electrical and magnetic recording, and pharmacology.

With these methods researchers have begun to discover the functions of regions of the brain, which we portray in Figure 6.1. The hindbrain includes regions that control basic physiological

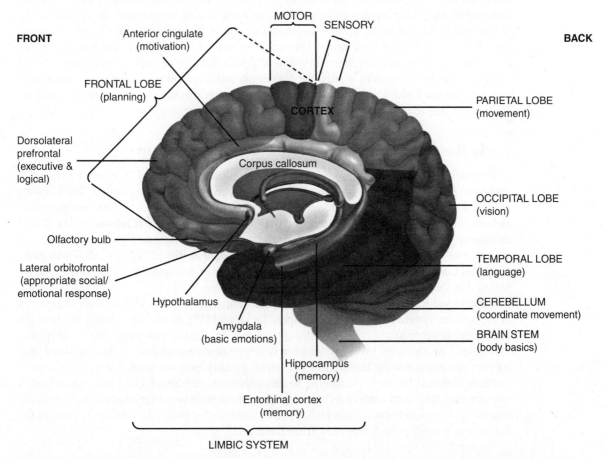

FIGURE 6.1 Exploded view of the human brain. This slice of the human brain brings into focus the areas you will learn about that are involved in emotion. Subcortical regions involved in emotion include the amygdala and hypothalamus (called the limbic system), as well as the ventral striatum and periaqueductal gray (not pictured). Cortical regions clearly involved in emotion include the orbitofrontal, dorsolateral, midline, and anterior cingulate, all located in the prefrontal region of the cerebral cortex.

processes: the medulla regulates cardiovascular activity, the pons controls sleep and breathing, and the cerebellum is involved in motor coordination and automatic movements, like blocking an incoming ball to the face. The so-called forebrain includes the thalamus, which is involved in integrating sensory information, the hippocampus, which is critical for memory processes, and the hypothalamus, which is involved with important biological functions like eating, sexual behavior, aggression, and bodily temperature. The forebrain also includes the limbic system—with structures like the **amygdala**—and the cerebral cortex, which, because it is so large in humans, sets our brains apart from those of other species. The exceptionally large size of our brains is almost certainly due to our profoundly social lives (Dunbar, 2003). We know, also, that frontal lobes of the cortex are involved in planning, decision making, and intentional action as well as in emotion regulation.

Over 350 years ago, Descartes (1649) proposed that sensory stimuli pulled little strings that ran inside the sensory nerves to open valves that would let fluids from a central reservoir in the brain run down tubes (the motor nerves) to inflate muscles (see Figure 7.0). This, he thought, was the mechanism underlying the human reflex. We now know that nerve messages are carried not by strings and hydraulics but by electric and chemical signals. Nevertheless, Descartes' analysis of the reflex—as involving events (stimuli) that excite sensory receptors, which send messages along the sensory nerves to the brain, which in turn send signals to motor nerves to work the muscles and organs of the body—remains a principal framework today. Emotions, however, are more than reflexes. We need additional concepts to understand brain mechanisms of emotion—concepts such as the individual's goals and appraisals of the social context.

Early Research on Brain Lesions and Stimulation

A substantial theory of the brain mechanisms of emotion was proposed by Cannon (whom we discussed in Chapter 1). Work in Cannon's laboratory, particularly by his student, Bard (1928), indicated that cats deprived of their cerebral cortex were liable to make sudden, inappropriate, and ill-directed attacks. The phenomenon was called "sham rage" (Cannon, 1931). If fed artificially and carefully tended, these cats could live for a long time, but would show few spontaneous movements except this angry sham rage (Bard & Rioch, 1937). Such observations prompted Cannon to propose that the cortex usually inhibits emotional expression, a theme we will revisit shortly in our discussion of emotion regulation.

Cannon and Bard's formulation was really the continuation of the 19th-century hypothesis of the nervous system proposed by Hughlings-Jackson (1959). In this view, lower levels of the brain (the hindbrain) are reflex pathways related to simple functions like posture and movement. At the next level are more recently evolved structures, including those that support the emotions. At the highest and most recently evolved level, the cerebral cortex controls all levels below it. According to this argument, children abound with uncontrolled emotion until their cortex develops sufficiently to inhibit their lower functions. Similarly, brain trauma (as with poor Phineas Gage) leads to the diminished activity of the higher regions of the brain, thus releasing the lower ones from inhibition.

The Limbic System

The neuroscience of emotion gained momentum with a theory proposed by MacLean (1990, 1993). His theory found inspiration in a speculative paper of Papez (1937), who argued that sensory impulses from the body and outside world reach the thalamus and are directed into three main pathways. One goes to the striatal region, the stream of movement. One goes to the most recently developed cerebral cortex, or neocortex, the stream of thought. One goes to the limbic system with its many connections to the hypothalamus, the stream of feeling.

In evolutionary terms, MacLean proposed that the human forebrain includes three distinct systems, each of which developed in a distinct phase of vertebrate evolution, with each system fulfilling new functions related to its species-characteristic repertoire. Apart from the hypothalamus, the earliest and most basic part of the forebrain is called the striatal region. This area became enlarged with the evolution of reptiles, argues MacLean, and it is devoted to scheduling and generating basic behaviors, including: preparation and establishment of a home site, marking and patrolling of territory, formalized fighting in defense of territory, foraging, hunting, hoarding, forming social groups including hierarchies, greeting, grooming, mating, flocking, and migration. When striatal areas are damaged in humans, for example, in the early stages of a hereditary disease called Huntington's chorea, patients become unable to organize daily activities; they tend to sit and do nothing, though they happily partake in activities planned for them. The striatal region was also damaged in the patients who suffered *encephalitis lethargica*, with whom we started this chapter.

MacLean (1993) next asked: "What do mammals do that reptiles do not?" His answer: maternal caregiving with infant attachment, vocal signaling, and play, all of which were served by a second subcortical region of the forebrain, the limbic system. Reptiles do interact with one other, but they hatch from eggs and start life on their own. In many reptile species, infants have to escape as soon as they hatch to avoid being eaten by parents. Though some species form aggregations, for the most part reptile lives are solitary. By contrast, every mammal is born in close association with another, and broadly speaking, mammals are social creatures.

The limbic system has close connections with the hypothalamus, which not only controls the autonomic nervous system (see Chapter 5) but, via the pituitary gland, also controls the body's hormonal system. As mammals diverged from reptiles in the course of evolution, the limbic system developed, according to MacLean (1993), to allow for mammals' increasing sociality.

MacLean's interests in the limbic system stemmed from several early discoveries. When large parts of the limbic system in wild monkeys housed in a laboratory were removed, the wild monkeys, normally aggressive, would become docile, hypersexual, and disinhibited, and approach everything without fear (Klüver & Bucy, 1937). When Olds and Milner (1954) implanted electrodes into septal regions of the limbic system in rats who were neither hungry nor thirsty, they would press a lever repeatedly for up to four hours a day to deliver stimulation to themselves, suggesting that such "pleasure centers" enable approach behavior and emotions that accompany such approach (Glickman and Schiff, 1967; Vaccarino, Schiff, & Glickman, 1989). Early analyses of temporal lobe epilepsy, caused by viruses or brain disease (Gibbs, Gibbs, & Fuster, 1948), found that the neural discharges contained within the limbic region triggered attacks defined by auras and suffused with strong emotions. The Russian novelist, Dostoevsky, who suffered from epilepsy, wrote of the aura of his attacks: "a feeling of happiness such as it is quite impossible to imagine in a normal state and which other people have no idea of . . . entirely in harmony with myself and with the whole world" (Dostoevsky, 1955, p. 8). About these feelings, MacLean says: "*Significantly, these feelings are free-floating, being completely unattached to any particular thing, situation, or idea"* (p. 79, emphasis in original).

These observations led MacLean to orient the field to the limbic system as a brain region likely to be centrally involved in emotion, and part of his hypothesis has been adopted and extended by Jaak Panksepp, a pioneer in the study of the neuroscience of emotion (1998, 2001, 2005). Let us call it the MacLean-Panksepp conjecture. It is that the experience of emotions is generated in the limbic system, and that each distinct emotion type is based on a particular system of limbic brain circuitry. For each emotion, its circuitry creates a readiness for a set of species-characteristic brain processes and behaviors, appropriate to the event that triggered them. It is in these processes that the experience of a particular emotion arises, and the experience—of happiness, anger, fear, and so on—is something we share with other animals. We shall encounter some support for this early theorizing, and some important modifications, most notably that the experience of emotion engages many different areas of the brain, both subcortical (i.e., limbic) and cortical.

Emotion and Subcortical Processes in the Brain

MacLean theorized that evolutionarily older regions of the brain give rise to simple emotional reactions that are in turn processed through the cortex. This claim has historical roots and converges with a central theme in this book, that emotions involve an unfolding of simpler and more complex processes. For example, you will learn in the next chapter that very fast appraisals of events in our environment give rise to initial emotional reactions, and then we elaborate upon those initial feelings with more complex deliberations about the meaning of the emotion (see Chapters 7 and 10).

This notion of an unfolding of simpler and more complex processes giving rise to emotion in essential ways corresponds to what has been learned about subcortical and cortical processes involved in emotion. In a recent synthesis of neuroscientific studies of emotion, Kober, Wager, and their colleagues brought together 162 neuroscientific studies in which participants were induced to feel emotion, most typically by watching slides or movies, and then had their brains scanned with imaging technologies (Kober et al., 2008). With complex statistical and brain-mapping techniques, Kober and Wager and colleagues identified six different brain regions consistently involved in emotional response. These include subcortical regions—the hypo-thalamus (discussed earlier), the amygdala, and the periaqueductal gray. Also activated across studies were several cortical regions: the visual cortex (the studies used visual means of eliciting emotion), regions to the back of the brain involved in understanding others and in bodily awareness, and regions in the frontal cortex.

In his own synthesis of neuroscientific studies of emotion, Kevin Ochsner takes a similar approach, arguing that basic social-emotional processes involved during emotion map onto different regions of the brain (Ochsner, 2008). These include regions of the brain that give emotional value to a stimulus, help us interpret the emotional cues of others, enable us to embody and feel the emotions of others, are involved in the conceptual understanding of others' states, and are involved in emotion regulation. Our task now is to drill down a little deeper and consider emotion processes engaged in subcortical and cortical regions of the brain.

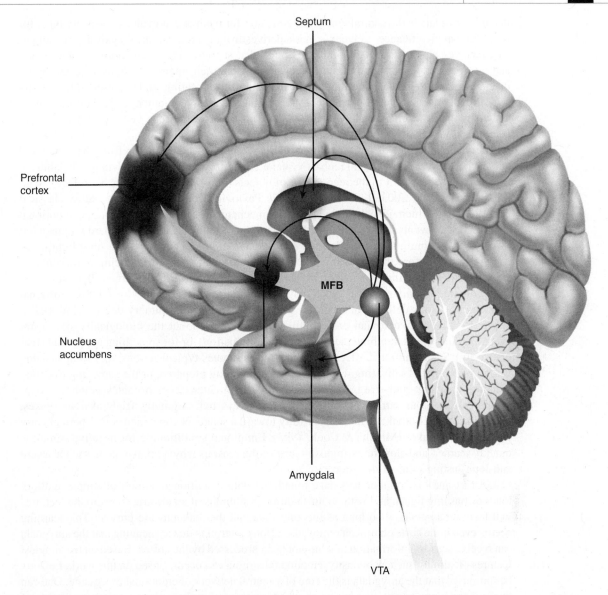

FIGURE 6.2   Subcortical regions involved in emotion, including the reward circuit (the nucleus accumbens, ventral tegmental area [VTA], and prefrontal cortex) and the amygdala.

The Amygdala as an Emotional Computer

In an important development in the study of emotion, Joseph LeDoux (1993, 1996; Rodriques, Sapolsky, & LeDoux, 2009) has called into question the idea of the limbic system because some of its functions can be more specifically localized to the amygdala. LeDoux has argued, indeed, that the amygdala is the central emotional computer for the brain: it **evaluates** sensory input for its emotional significance. LeDoux's thesis derives from neuroanatomical analysis. The amygdala receives inputs from regions of the cortex that support visual perception of objects and auditory perception of sounds. The amygdala also has rich interconnections with the hypothalamus, which regulates emotion-laden behaviors like sex, eating, and aggression. Rewarding self-stimulation can be demonstrated in the amygdala (Kane, Coulombe, & Miliaressis, 1991), and components of emotional behavior and autonomic responses can be elicited by electrical stimulation in this region (Hilton & Zbrozyna, 1963).

The distinctive part of LeDoux's hypothesis is that, as well as inputs from the visual and auditory cortex, the amygdala receives visual and auditory inputs directly via the thalamus—not via routes that result in the recognition of objects or events. Experiments by LeDoux (e.g., LaBar & LeDoux, 2003; LeDoux, 1990) use Pavlovian conditioning (also called classical conditioning), which is considered a basic mechanism of learning about the emotional significance of events that signal something pleasant or unpleasant. The standard arrangement involves two stimuli. One is called the *conditioned stimulus*, perhaps a flashing light or an auditory tone. Before the experiment, it has no significance other than being noticeable; its significance in signaling a reward or punishment is what will be learned. The so-called *unconditioned stimulus* is the event that has biological significance; in Pavlov's original experiments it was delivery of meat powder into the mouth of a hungry dog (Pavlov, 1927). What is learned in Pavlovian conditioning is an emotion about the biologically significant event: readiness for something pleasant (happy anticipation), or for something unpleasant (fear or anxiety). Such emotional effects are expressed as species-typical actions, for example, a dog wagging its tail and salivating when it sees its meal being prepared, or the same dog freezing, slinking, cringing, and struggling to escape when threatened. In primates emotional conditioning can occur purely by observation: monkeys not originally frightened of snakes, observing another monkey reacting fearfully toward a snake, become themselves permanently frightened of snakes (Mineka & Cook, 1993). Emotional conditioning for negative stimuli is quickly learned and slow to extinguish—one of the reasons why anxiety can be such a severe and long-lasting clinical disorder.

LeDoux and his collaborators have found that with conditioned stimuli of simple auditory tones or flashing lights, and with an unconditioned stimulus of an electric shock to the feet, rats will learn an association so long as the amygdala and the thalamus are present. This learning occurs even if the cortex has been removed. LeDoux interprets this as meaning that the amygdala can receive sensory information that has not been processed by the cortex. Based on the simplest features of stimuli, such as intensity, emotional learning can occur. Based on this work, LeDoux has proposed that the amygdala is the core of a central network of emotional processing. One can think of the amygdala as one region in which primary appraisals, or automatic evaluation of events in relation to goals, occur (see Chapters 1 and 7). In other words, the amygdala seems to be responsible for assigning emotional significance to events (see also Emery & Amaral, 2000; Rodrigues, Sapolsky, & LeDoux, 2009).

Three kinds of neuroimaging studies of humans support LeDoux's claims (Baxter & Murray, 2002; Gottfried, O'Doherty, & Dolan, 2003). A first is that the amygdala is often activated during momentary emotional reactions to evocative stimuli. The amygdala (along with other brain regions) has been found to increase activation in response to sad film clips (Levesque, Eugene et al., 2003) or erotic film clips (Beauregard, Levesque, & Bourgoin, 2001), disturbing slides (Lane et al., 1997; Phan, Taylor et al., 2004), and unpleasant tastes and odors (Zald et al., 1998).

The perception of faces that display fear activates regions in the left amygdala (Breiter et al., 1996; Phillips et al., 1997), even when the presentation of the fear faces is masked by the presentation of an immediately ensuing neutral expression, rendering the perception of the fear faces outside of conscious awareness (Whalen et al., 1998). The perception of sad faces activates the left amygdala and right temporal lobe (Blair et al., 1999).

A second line of studies focuses on individual differences in emotionality, and points to a role of increased amygdala activation in depression (Davidson et al., 2003). Some studies find that depressives suffering from bipolar disorders have enlarged amygdalae (Strakowski et al., 1999). Other studies find that at a resting baseline, depressives show elevated activation in the amygdala compared to control participants (Ho et al., 1996: Nofzinger et al., 1999). Still other studies find that depressives show elevated amygdala activation compared to controls in response to emotionally evocative stimuli such as fearful faces (Yurgelun-Todd et al., 2000).

Finally, a third kind of study has focused on the memory for emotional events and found that amygdala activation predicts whether people will recall emotionally evocative stimuli. For example, Turhan Canli et al. (1999) presented participants with slides evocative of positive emotion (for example, pictures of ice cream) and negative emotion (for example, pictures of guns or gore), and recorded brain activation in response to the slides. They later asked participants to try to recall the slides they had seen. Memory for the negative slides was correlated with activation in the amygdala and the insula (see also Hamman, Ely et al., 1999).

This early work on the amygdala led many to conclude that this region of the subcortex is central to appraisals of fear, or more generally, to appraisals of the valence (goodness or badness) of stimuli in our environments. More recently, this thesis has encountered some empirical difficulties. Most notably, in only 40 to 50% of studies designed to elicit fear was the amygdala activated (Kober et al., 2008). Just as problematic for the line of reasoning we have been developing is that the amygdala is activated by positive stimuli as well (Liberzon, Phan, Decker, & Taylor, 2003; see Zald, 2003, for a review). It seems as though the amygdala does more than simply respond to fear stimuli or negatively valenced stimuli.

In light of these concerns, Will Cunningham, Marcia Johnson, and their colleagues have hypothesized that the amygdala responds to the emotional intensity of a stimulus and not whether it is fear inducing or good as compared with bad. In one study that tested this formulation, participants made judgments of positively and negatively valenced concepts such as *murder*, *love*, *gun control*, and *abortion* while fMRI technologies captured activation in different areas of the brain (Cunningham et al., 2004). In their judgments of these emotionally evocative concepts, they rated the valence of the stimulus (how good and bad it was) as well as how emotionally intense it was. More intense stimuli—both good and bad—elicited greater activation in the amygdala. And the valence of the stimulus elicited activation in regions of the insula, a region we shall see later is involved in different emotional responses. In conceptually similar work, Cunningham and colleagues have looked at individual differences and found that people who look at life in terms of the potential rewards that situations offer showed greater amygdala activation to intense, positive stimuli, whereas people who look at life in terms of its costs and threats show greater amygdala activation in response to negative concepts (Cunningham et al., 2005). Here individuals, given their emotional profile, show greater amygdala activation in response to the intensity, and not the valence, of stimuli. In related research, Turhan Canli and his colleagues have found that highly extraverted individuals, defined by their tendencies toward social connection and positive emotion, show increased amygdala activation in response to pleasant images (Canli et al., 2001; Canli, Sivers, Whitfield, Gotlib, & Gabrieli, 2002).

Science advances thanks to debate and controversy, and here we see a vibrant one in play. A good deal of evidence suggests that the amygdala is responsive to the appraised fearfulness and valence of a stimulus, whereas new studies suggest it may be more precise to say that the amygdala responds to the emotional intensity or salience of the stimulus.

The Nucleus Accumbens, Dopamine, and the Opiates

Almost all living organisms must find rewarding objects in their environment—in humans, sources of food, beauty, comfort, security, and esteem—and act in ways that maximize those rewards. Emotions are essential to this most basic task of evolution, helping us approach and enjoy the rewards of life (Fredrickson, 1998). The feeling of enthusiasm propels us toward what we find rewarding. The feeling of contentment enables us to savor what is good. Feelings of pride or love signal more specific social rewards—the esteem of a valued friend or the affection of someone we cherish.

In a recent summary of the neuroscience of reward, Suzanne Haber and Brian Knutson (2010) detail what might be thought of as a reward circuit in the brain, likely involved in many positive emotions. One part of this reward circuit that is engaged by pleasing stimuli—nice tastes, pleasant touches, pleasing sounds, and the like—is in the ventral medial prefrontal cortex, part of the frontal lobes. A second is an older region of the subcortex known as the ventral striatum, and in particular, dopamine-rich networks in the nucleus accumbens and ventral tegmental areas (which manufacture dopamine). Importantly, the ventral striatum receives neural input from the prefrontal cortex, the amygdala, and the hippocampus and sends signals to regions such as the hypothalamus, which controls more basic bodily processes related to eating, sleep, and sex.

With this neuroanatomy as grounding, let's look more carefully at some empirical studies of this reward circuit. We'll focus on the nucleus accumbens. It is rich in dopamine and opioid neurotransmitter pathways and has long been thought central to the experience of positive affect (Panksepp, 1998; Rolls, 1999). For example, dopamine release and activation in the nucleus accumbens increase in response to pleasurable food (Schultz, Dayan, & Montague, 1997), the opportunity for sex (Fiorino, Coury, & Phillips, 1997), and conditioned neutral stimuli that have been repeatedly paired with food, sex, or rewarding drugs (Di Ciano, Blaha, & Phillips, 1998). People suffering from depression, when asked to maintain their positive emotion in response to positive slides, do not show sustained activation in the nucleus accumbens as non-depressives do; they have to struggle to keep the neural underpinnings of positive emotion active (Heller et al., 2009).

In light of this evidence, you might conclude that the nucleus accumbens and dopamine are central to the experience of pleasure. Careful work by Kent Berridge and colleagues offers a more subtle picture. They have found that activation of opioid receptors, but not dopamine receptors, enhances the **value** of the taste of sucrose, as measured by behavioral reactions in rats to sweet tastes (Berridge, 2000; Kringelbach & Berridge, 2009; Pecina & Berridge, 2000). This work has led Berridge to propose the following distinction between **wanting** and **liking**. You may consider, for instance, that in some kinds of drug addiction the urge to take the drug (wanting) persists even though the liking for the state it produces may no longer occur.

Dopamine and activation in the nucleus accumbens are central to wanting; they motivate the approach to rewards (see also, Depue & Collins, 1999; Panksepp, 1986), whereas (as we explain below) liking is rather different. Dopamine release and activation in the nucleus accumbens facilitate wanting: a variety of approach-related, goal-oriented behaviors, including exploration, affiliation, aggression, sexual behavior, food hoarding, and nursing. Lesions to the nucleus accumbens reduce the motivation to work for reward (Caine & Koop, 1993). Recent studies by Brian Knutson and his colleagues have elaborated upon this thinking, in particular documenting how the nucleus accumbens is involved in the anticipation of pleasure (see also Bowman et al., 1996; Schultz et al., 1997). In a gambling paradigm, Knutson and colleagues give participants the opportunities to win money. They consistently find that it is the anticipation of rewards that activates regions of the brain like the nucleus accumbens and the medial prefrontal cortex (Knutson & Greer, 2008). This research clearly suggests that activation of networks of dopamine neurons signals potential rewards in the environment—a clear motive for actions that are likely to bring about the pleasures of life.

In contrast, the opiates are central to our experience of liking stimuli. Liking is involved in consummatory process and in the enjoyment of rewards. The opiates are released by lactation, nursing, sexual activity, maternal social interaction, and touch (Insel, 1992; Keverne, 1996; Matheson & Bernstein, 2000; Nelson & Panksepp, 1998; Silk et al., 2003). The release of opiates makes consumption pleasurable and rewarding. In contrast to dopamine, it produces a state of pleasant calmness and quiescence, the kind of emotional experience you might enjoy after a great meal, a soothing massage, or a sunny picnic in a park.

What about rewards other than money or good tastes, social rewards like favorable attention, affectionate contact, or play, rewards so important to human emotional life? Matthew Lieberman and Naomi Eisenberger reason that the reward circuits we have been considering are also engaged when we enjoy the social rewards of life—the esteem of a friend, affection from a loved one, or praise from a superior (Lieberman & Eisenberger, 2009). In keeping with this line of reasoning, studies find that when people think about being in love, the nucleus accumbens is activated (Aron et al., 2005). When people cooperate in an economic game or when they give money to charity, they show activation in parts of a reward circuit (Harbaugh et al., 2007). The reward circuit is activated by more complex social rewards alongside pleasing tastes and money.

Let's now put these notions to use in understanding attachment processes, which are important to mammalian sociality and a source of several emotions. Richard Depue and Jeannine Morrone-Strupinsky (2004) have offered the following analysis of affilative bonding, which prioritizes the roles of dopamine and the opiates. They propose that distal affilative cues like smiles and gestures serve as incentive stimuli; they motivate approach-related tendencies served by dopamine release. These cues trigger dopamine, which promotes actions that bring individuals into close proximity with one another. As one illustration, the nucleus accumbens is activated in heterosexual males by viewing attractive female faces (Aharon et al., 2001).

Once in proximity, affilative behaviors like touch and soothing vocalizations elicit the release of opiates. The opiates in turn bring about the powerful feelings of warmth, calmness, and intimacy. For example, when the opiates are blocked in juvenile rats, they spend less time with their mothers after separation (Agmo et al., 1997). Human females given naltrexone, which blocks opiate release, spend more time alone and less time with friends and enjoy social interactions less (Jamner et al., 1998).

Periaqueductal Gray

Kober, Wager, and colleagues' review of the neuroscientific studies of emotion identified a final subcortical region implicated in emotion—the midbrain periaqueductal gray, which is situated above the hindbrain and below the forebrain. The periaqueductal gray appears to be involved in three different processes related to emotion. First, it is involved in the release of opioids, which you just learned about. These opioids, it is thought, inhibit ascending pain signals before they reach the cortex, which allows the individual to escape threat before attending to bodily harm (Heinricher et al., 2009; Lovick and Adamec, 2009). The periaqueductal gray, then, helps the individual regulate pain.

Second, it is increasingly clear that the periaqueductal gray is activated by images that evoke negative emotions, more broadly defined, along with pain. In one recent investigation relevant to this idea, participants showed increased activation in the periaqueductal gray in response to thermal pain as well as viewing distressing slides (Buhle et al., 2012). The periaqueductal gray, then, is activated by negatively valenced images of a distressing nature.

And finally, emerging evidence suggests that the periaqueductal gray may be part of a caregiving system in the mammalian brain (for review, see Swain, 2010). Studies of nonhuman mammals find that nurturant behaviors such as crouching over pups, retrieval to nest, licking, and prolonged nursing engage the periaqueductal gray (e.g., Stack et al., 2002). In humans, alongside other regions like the orbital frontal cortex and thalamus, periaqueductal gray activation has been reported in studies of mothers viewing images of their own versus acquainted or unknown infants, or viewing video clips of their own infants exhibiting attachment-figure-soliciting behaviors like smiling and crying (Noriuchi et al., 2008). Periaqueductal gray activation was also observed, along with activation in other empathy network regions, in participants instructed to generate unconditional love toward images of disabled people (Beauregard et al., 2009), while participants viewed sad facial expressions with instructions to extend a "compassionate attitude" toward them (Kim et al., 2009), and when participants viewed prototypical images of suffering and need (Simon-Thomas et al., 2011). These various studies begin to paint an interesting picture: the periaqueductal gray attenuates the pain response, it is activated by signs of distress and negative emotion, and it engages caregiving tendencies.

Taken together, the studies we have just reviewed bring into focus how three different subcortical regions generate basic elements of emotion. The amygdala seems to be involved in initial appraisals of the intensity or valence of the stimulus. The nucleus accumbens tracks the likelihood of reward that the stimulus promises. And periaqueductal gray activation relates to pain regulation, negative affect, and caregiving. Now we shall consider how different cortical regions of the brain transform these signals into more complex experiences.

Emotion and Cortical Processes in the Brain

Patients with brain damage have played a prominent role in the scientific study of emotion. What has been learned from the lives of Phineas Gage, for example, speaks volumes to the role that specific brain regions play in our social and emotional lives. Another such patient goes by the name of J.S. and has been studied by neuroscientist James Blair. One day in his mid-50s, J.S. collapsed and lost consciousness. He suffered damage to parts of his frontal lobes, most likely a region known as the orbitofrontal cortex, and his life changed in now-predictable ways. Although he retained his abilities to speak and reason, he became a textbook example of acquired sociopathy (see Chapter 1). During his recovery in a hospital, he was known for his emotional outbursts. He threw furniture at other patients. He groped female nurses. On one occasion he body-surfed on a gurney through the hallways of the hospital. In Blair's research, J.S. demonstrated normal capacities to learn, to recognize faces, and to identify whether faces are male or female. But he showed specific deficits in recognizing certain emotions and in responding to the emotions of others.

Our task in this section is build on our understanding of the social-emotional deficits of patients like J.S. toward a clearer picture of how different regions of the cortex are involved in emotion. According to MacLean (1993), after the emergence of the striatum and the limbic system, the third large step in the evolution of the human brain, perhaps distinctive to higher mammals, is the neocortex (often referred to as the cortex), which reaches its largest development in human beings. In humans, about 80% of the whole brain is taken up by it. The cortex (meaning "outer layer") of the brain is between 0.06 and 0.12 in. thick, but it is deeply folded. If spread out flat, it would have an area of about 310 square inches.

From early on in the study of the brain, scientists tended to assume that the cortex inhibits more "primitive" behaviors served by the lower regions, such as the amygdala, the ventral striatum, or the hypothalamus. More generally within cognitive neuroscience, the frontal lobes are seen as centers of regulation or executive control (Gazzaniga, Ivry, & Mangun, 2002). The thinking is that regions of the frontal lobes help individuals represent more basic feelings in ways available to consciousness. To start with, the argument goes, emotions are generated by regions like the amygdala, the nucleus accumbens, and the periaqueductal gray. Then representations of such feelings can be held in short-term memory and used to form plans, so that they can be guided in ways appropriate to the social context (e.g., Beer, Knight, & D'Esposito, 2006; Wallis, 2007).

Guided by these conceptual considerations, we will focus on central themes in the fast-growing literature on the cortex, examining how empathy, emotion regulation, social pain, and positive emotion are represented in the activation of different regions of the cortex.

Cortex and Empathy

In Chapter 1 we introduced you to a neuroscientist, Tania Singer, in search of the "empathy network" in the brain. Our ability to mimic others, to read others' mental states, and ultimately to feel what others feel is in many ways what makes us human and is central to social relationships (see Chapter 9). Recent neuroscientific studies are starting to chart how different empathic processes engage different regions of the cortex.

Numerous studies reviewed by Jean Decety and Claus Lamm (2006) and Kevin Ochsner and Jamil Zaki (in press) reveal that certain regions of the medial prefrontal cortex, in particular regions of the anterior insula and the anterior cingulate, are engaged when people respond empathically to the emotions of others. For example, when we feel a painful prick on the finger, the anterior insula and anterior cingulate are activated. And hearing that someone else is experiencing this same kind of pain activates those regions as well; our own experience of pain and our appraisal of another's pain can activate the same regions of the brain. This basic empathic process extends to other emotions: when we feel disgust, the anterior insula is activated; when we see other individuals feel disgust, the anterior insula is activated. These regions of the cortex are helping humans cross the gulf between self and other, ensuring we know what others feel.

A different form of empathy—the cognitive understanding of others' mental states, or what has been called **theory of mind**—engages different regions of the cortex. Singer refers to these regions of the brain as the empathy network and Rebecca Saxe as the theory-of-mind network (Bruneau et al., 2012). This cognitive empathy network includes the medial prefrontal cortex, the precuneus, and the temporal parietal junction, an associative region of the cortex that receives input from the prefrontal cortex. These cortical regions are more likely to be involved when we understand cognitively, in the abstract, what others are feeling, and that they feel different states than we do.

When the frontal lobes are damaged, then, as in the case of the patient J.S., abilities to feel empathically and to understand what other people feel may be lost, and social relationships can suffer profoundly (Beer, Shimamura, & Knight, 2004; Blair & Cipolotti, 2000; Hornak, Rolls, & Wade, 1996). For example, in one recent line of research, Howard Rosen and Robert Levenson (2009) have begun to characterize the emotional deficits that accompany one kind of dementia known as frontal temporal lobar dementia: it's an organic brain disease that strikes in the middle of life and devastates specific regions of the prefrontal cortex as well as the temporal lobes—regions involved in empathic processes, as we have been discussing. In keeping with a theme of this section, frontal temporal lobar dementia patients, compared to appropriate patient and matched control samples, show deficits in empathic behaviors: they are less accurate in reading the emotions of others; they engage in less mutual gaze with their romantic partners; and they don't show the usual levels of embarrassment—an emotion that is rooted in the understanding of others' judgments—when being put through the embarrassing exercise of watching themselves sing on videotape.

Prefrontal Cortex, Emotion, and Emotion Regulation

The prefrontal cortex includes three areas of relevance to emotion: the orbitofrontal region, the dorsolateral prefrontal region, and the medial prefrontal region. Recent advances in cognitive

Individual emotion: The feeling of beauty

Understanding our experience of beauty has long inspired poets and philosophers alike. We experience feelings of beauty in response to a wide array of stimuli. Scientists are now actively engaged in examining which faces we find beautiful, how music elicits the chills associated with aesthetic appreciation, how different kinds of natural scenes seem beautiful to people around the world, and how painting, architecture, and dance move us, sometimes literally. A small group of neuroscientists have taken up the call to understand beauty in a new field known as neuroaesthetics. A recent review of this field by Nadal and Pearce points to the promise of this inquiry (Nadal & Pearce, 2011). These neuroscientists first offer an important theoretical point: rather than finding the "beauty center" of the brain, it is much more likely that scientists will discover various regions activated in the brain that contribute to the experience of beauty. Very basic perceptual processes—for example, related to perceiving faces or sound—will be involved. So, too, will more integrative processes—for example, signals sent by the amygdala or nucleus accumbens—that give the perception of the

stimulus an affective quality. And higher-order cortical processes will certainly be involved in giving the experience conceptual meaning—for example, how the stimulus relates to the individual's self or identity. With this recommendation as conceptual background, Nadal and Pearce review what has been learned recently in neuroaesthetics. Here is a small sampling. Both beautiful paintings and pretty faces elicit activation in the nucleus accumbens and the orbitofrontal cortex, locations involved in basic reward processing and attaching social significance to the reward signal. Watching an inspiring dance performance activates parts of the visual cortex as well as the premotor cortex, as if the body is getting ready to dance. And music activates parts of the auditory cortex and either the amygdala or nucleus accumbens, depending on the emotional content of the music, as well as the orbitofrontal cortex. These preliminary discoveries on the feeling of beauty make contact with much that has been learned thus far in the neuroscience of emotion, and shed light on the neural underpinnings of one of the most mysterious sentiments—the feeling of beauty.

neuroscience highlight how this region of the cortex is important to emotion regulation. More specifically, the medial portions of the prefrontal cortex are centrally involved in self-representation, empathy (see Chapter 1), and experiences of reward, receiving input from the nucleus accumbens. The orbitofrontal region (see Figure 6.1), which receives input from different sensory modalities as well as the amygdala, is centrally involved in the representation of goals (Miller & Cohen, 2001), rewards (O'Doherty et al., 2001; Rolls, 1997, 1999; Rolls & Baylis, 1994; Rolls et al., 1998), and approach- and withdrawal-related tendencies (Davidson & Irwin, 1999; Davidson, Jackson et al., 2000), and is thought to represent anticipated rewards and punishments in consciousness. The orbitofrontal region may in turn send signals to the dorsolateral prefrontal region, which has more robust connections to motor cortex regions, which enable action.

It is quite clear, then, that the prefrontal cortex is doing much of the work of emotion regulation: it is receiving signals from basic emotion processing regions of the brain—the amygdala, as well as the nucleus accumbens—and representing those signals in ways that allow the individual to consider possible courses of action. This is central to emotion regulation, which refers to the different ways in which we modify our emotional responses once they are underway, in ways that fit the demands of the current social context (see Chapters 8 and 14 for fuller discussions). Two kinds of evidence suggest that the prefrontal cortex is important to the regulation of emotion.

First, patients with damage to the orbitfrontal cortex—the J.S.s and Gages of the world—have problems regulating their emotional behavior; their emotional reactions are often wildly inappropriate to the social context. Orbitofrontal patients like J.S., described above, have been observed to greet strangers by kissing on the cheek and hugging (e.g., Rolls, Hornak, Wade, & McGrath, 1994), to engage in tasteless joking and teasing (Stuss & Benson, 1984), and to disclose to a stranger in inappropriately intimate fashion (Beer, 2002). They often experience and express emotions that are inappropriate to the context, for example, showing a great deal of pride after teasing a stranger, when most people feel embarrassment, even mortification, at such an awkward social encounter (Beer et al., 2003).

Neuroimaging studies offer a second kind of evidence that speaks to how the prefrontal cortex is activated when people try to regulate their emotional responses (e.g., Levesque, Eugene et al., 2003). In one early study in this literature, Kevin Ochsner and his colleagues had 15 females view 114 photos, two-thirds of which were evocative of negative emotion, and one-third of which were relatively neutral in content (Ochsner, Bunge, Gross, & Gabrieli, 2002). For the negative photos, one-half of the participants were asked to reappraise the photo so that it would "no longer elicit a negative response." This reappraise condition led to greater activation in the dorsal and ventral regions of the left lateral prefrontal cortex and the dorsal medial prefrontal cortex.

That study inspired dozens of similar studies, and in a recent review of over 15 studies of this kind, Kevin Ochsner and James Gross summarize the evidence as follows (Ochsner & Gross, 2008). Simply thinking about emotions tends to activate amygdala response, as well as a region known as the insular cortex, a region that receives input from the autonomic nervous system and may be central to our experience of emotion. When people engage in a reappraisal of their emotional response, in the fashion described above, there tends to be activation in the dorsal prefrontal cortex, a region known to be involved in selecting what to attend to and where to focus attention, as well as left lateralized regions of the frontal cortex. Clearly this is in keeping with the core of reappraisal, which involves shifting attention away from one appraised meaning of a

Focus on film: *The Treasure of the Sierra Madre*

John Huston's *The Treasure of the Sierra Madre* from 1948 is a classic in American cinema, and speaks to the importance of the frontal lobes in emotion and emotion regulation. Humphrey Bogart plays expatriate Fred Dobbs, who is tired of bumming smokes and meals off expatriate Americans in Tampico, Mexico. He decides to encamp with two other down-on-their-luck prospectors in the arid mountains of Mexico's Sierra Madre. They are in search of gold. Initially they find success, and the social complexities of accumulating wealth. As their bags of gold dust mount in weight and number, the three men do their best to trust each other, in spite of the opportunities for exploitation. Still the band of desperate prospectors hold tight, bound together in cooperative spirit by the enthusiasm of their quest, the camaraderie of their work, the reverie of the meals and clothes and farms and white picket fences they envision with their newfound fortunes, and the

laughter, banter, back slapping, and firm handshakes of strangers trying to get along.

When a mineshaft collapses on Bogart, he suffers a blow to his head, in particular his frontal lobes. Like Phineas Gage, he loses his social-emotional talents and the story takes a dramatic turn. He misreads the intentions of his comrades and assumes erroneously that they are hiding gold from him. He comes to view his comrades as being guided by malicious intent. He becomes more remote and cold: the language of friendship— "buddy," "friend," and nicknames—shifts to the sharp, impersonal tones of last names. He becomes disregulated in his emotions and is prone to name-calling and gun-pointing confrontations. Even before the neuroscience of the frontal cortex really got off the ground, we see evidence of the importance of these regions of the brain to emotional functioning in classic tales like *The Treasure of the Sierra Madre*.

stimulus or event (e.g., how I do on this standardized test will determine which college I get into!) to another (this test is just one of many, and my future will be based on many of my talents and efforts). Another kind of emotion regulation that has been studied with neuroimaging techniques is taking a more distant, third-person perspective on current emotions. For example, in the heat of an emotional episode you might look upon yourself from a third-person perspective or as if you were an actor in a play or character in a novel, or from a distant point of view. This kind of regulation engages the medial prefrontal regions of the cortex, known to be involved in self-representation.

Anterior Cingulate and Social Pain

Thus far we have seen how cortical processes enable the social aspects of emotion, from empathic responses to others to regulating our emotions according to the demands of the current social context. What about other social dimensions of emotions and their representation in cortical process? One recent focus is the social pain of separation. The social pain of separation is manifest in the feeling of distress and sadness when separated from a romantic partner, the grief we feel when a loved one passes away, and even the feeling of shame at being socially rejected and excluded. John Bowlby, whom we introduced in Chapter 1, proposed in his attachment theory that the social pain of separation helps us stay close to attachment figures, so vital to our survival.

How might such social pain engage cortcal processes? In a fascinating line of theorizing, Naomi Eisenberger suggests an important role for the anterior cingulate cortex (see Figure 6.1), a region of the prefrontal cortex (Eisenberger & Lieberman, 2004). Eisenberger proposes that a specific region of the anterior cingulate might be thought of metaphorically as the mind's alarm system. This thesis draws upon several findings: the anterior cingulate cortex is thought of by cognitive scientists as a discrepancy detector, detecting conflicts between stimuli or the individual's goals or intentions. The dorsal region of the anterior cingulate cortex is also active during the experience of physical pain, or noxious physical senations, and in particular seems to track the felt unpleasantness of such pain. It is for this reason that surgeons at times may resort to ablating part of the anterior cingulate cortex when someone suffers from intractable pain. And you just learned that regions of the anterior cingulate cortex are activated (along with other regions like the insula) when we respond empathically to the pain of others.

Given these findings, Eisenberger suggests that our experiences of social pain likewise engage the anterior cingulate cortex, in particular its dorsal region. Here are some of the findings that bolster this conclusion. In mammalian species, ablating the dorsal region of the anterior cingulate cortex leads to a decline in distress calls when separated from family members, and reductions in affiliative behavior—classic attachment behaviors. Opiates can be used to reduce not only physical pain, but social pain as well. Building on this evidence and reasoning, Eisenberger posits that the dorsal region of the anterior cingulate cortex also helps humans detect and respond to cues of rejection, separation, and exclusion.

In one demonstration of this social rejection thesis, Eisenberger and her colleagues had participants play a ball-toss game on a computer with two other participants (Eisenberger et al., 2003). In this game, the participant tossed a virtual ball back and forth to the other participants. At a preset point in this playful exchange, the computer was programmed so that the two other players stopped tossing the ball to the participant, thus placing the participant in a situation of social rejection reminiscent of being ignored on the school playground. This act of social rejection triggered activation in the dorsal region of the anterior cingulate cortex, and partic-ipants' reported experiences of distress correlated with activation in this region. It would seem that in the course of human evolution, social connection became so important that social rejection recruited the use of ancient pain regions of the cortex for more social purposes.

Lateralization Effects, Approach and Withdrawal, and Emotion

Approach and withdrawal are basic tendencies at the core of broad swaths of emotional states. Some states—desire, compassion, enthusiasm—propel us toward goals and their delights. Other states—fear, shame, sadness—are defined by their withdrawal tendencies. Richard Davidson, one of the pioneers in the neuroscientific study of emotion, has proposed that the brain is lateralized in such a fashion that approach-related states, mostly positive, engage cortical processes in the left regions of the frontal lobes, whereas withdrawal-related states, mostly negative, are lateralized on the right side of the frontal cortex (Davidson, 1992a; 1998; Davidson et al., 2003).

Davidson's argument goes as follows. Approach-related emotions activate the left sides of the frontal lobes in part because language processes are enabled by regions of the left hemisphere, and language is central to carrying out planful, goal-directed behavior. By contrast, withdrawal-related tendencies are lateralized to the right frontal lobes. Given this analysis, states that enable the approach toward goals, mostly positive, should engage left frontal regions of the cortex. States that enable withdrawal responses should activate the right frontal regions.

In testing this formulation, Davidson and his colleagues have gathered two kinds of supportive evidence. A first bears upon whether positive, approach-related states and negative, withdrawal-related states are indeed lateralized as Davidson formulates. For example, in one study, Davidson et al. (1990) had subjects individually watch four short film clips. Two amusing films were of animals playing. Two gruesome ones were training films for nurses, one showing a burn victim and the other an amputation. While each subject watched, electroencephalogram (EEG) recordings were made from four positions on each side of the scalp, and facial expressions were videotaped. Expressions of happiness (indicated by Duchenne smiles as described in Chapter 4) and disgust (indicated by wrinkling of the nose) were observed. While the subjects were making happy expressions there was a significant average increase of activation in the left frontal region of the cortex as compared with the right frontal region. When expressing disgust there was greater right-sided activation in the frontal region.

In other similar studies of adults playing a video-type game in which they either gained monetary rewards or suffered monetary punishments for actions, and one in which 10-month-old infants were approached either by their mother or by a stranger, similar patterns are observed (Davidson, 1992a). Positive emotions were accompanied by more left-sided activation in the frontal region and negative emotions by more right-frontal activation. Subsequent studies have found that people showed greater activation in the left hemisphere in response to sweet tastes (Lane et al., 1997).

A second kind of evidence comes from studies of individual differences in emotionality, and again, one sees patterns of findings in keeping with Davidson's lateralization thesis. People who are prone to experience frequent positive emotions showed greater activation in the left hemisphere when they were in a resting or neutral state (Sutton & Davidson, 1997). Patients who have suffered left-sided strokes that damage the frontal regions have a high probability of becoming clinically depressed, while symptoms of mania are more common when a stroke damages the right frontal region (Starkstein & Robinson, 1991). Henriques and Davidson (1991) have found that patients who are depressed (without brain damage) have less activation in the left frontal regions than nondepressed people.

Genetically based asymmetries of function have been called by Davidson (1993) **affective styles**. One study that led to this formulation is one he carried out with Kagan and others (Davidson, 1992a). At 31 months of age, 386 children were tested in pairs with their mothers during 25-minute sessions in a large playroom with toys that included a play tunnel. Ten minutes after starting the session, an experimenter came in with a remote-controlled robot that moved toward each child and spoke. After three minutes the robot said it had to take a nap, and it was removed. Twenty minutes after starting, a stranger came into the room with a tray of interesting-looking toys, invited the children to play with them, and left three minutes later. From these sessions three groups of children were selected. In an inhibited group, the children (a) spent more than 9.5 minutes of the 25-minute session near their mothers, (b) did not touch a toy, (c) did not speak until more than three minutes after the start, (d) did not approach the robot, (e) did not approach the stranger, and (f) did not enter the play tunnel.

Then there was an uninhibited group. These children spent less than 30 seconds near their mother and did all the other activities (b to f) readily. There was a middle group of children who fell in between on these measures. Twenty-eight children were selected for each group, approximately balanced by sex. Seven months later, these children were tested for their resting EEG patterns. As can be seen from Figure 6.3, the inhibited children had much higher right-sided activation, the uninhibited much less. Children of the middle group were in between.

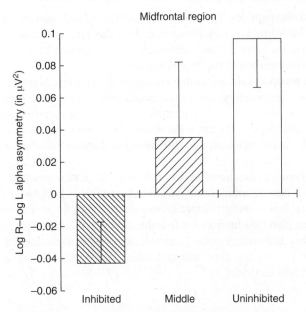

FIGURE 6.3 Mean scores at age 38 months on an index indicating relatively more EEG activation on the left as compared to the right hemisphere of children who at age 31 months had been classified as inhibited, middle, or uninhibited in a 25-minute play session (Davidson, 1992a).

Neurochemicals and the Emotions

One of the most important discoveries yet made about the nervous system was that nerve fibers work by electricity. This was Galvani's finding, part of Mary Shelley's inspiration in writing *Frankenstein* (Tropp, 1976). Nearly as momentous was the finding that chemicals carry messages from neuron to neuron. This was discovered when Otto Loewi was conducting experiments of electrically stimulating the vagus nerve of a frog; this stimulation slowed down its heart (Brazier, 1959). If during stimulation Loewi bathed the frog's heart in fluid and then applied this fluid to the heart of a second frog, then this second frog's heart slowed down, too. He inferred that some chemical substance was released into the fluid by the nerve endings of the first frog and was then responsible for slowing down the heart of the second. The substance was acetylcholine. Subsequently more than 50 substances have been discovered that are released by regions in the nervous system and have effects on other neurons, or on glands or muscles.

Neurochemicals can be thought of in three functional families that overlap with each other. The first family is neurotransmitters, which are released into the synapses of neurons. As well as acetylcholine they include norepinephrine, dopamine, serotonin, and gamma-amino butyric acid. Transmitter substances are released by nerve impulses from the end of a neuron's axon. They diffuse in milliseconds across the tiny synaptic gaps between cells to activate or inhibit the receiving neuron or muscle fiber.

Second, there are hormones: substances carried in the blood to affect organs that are sensitive to them. In their usual functions, hormones take longer to act than transmitter substances and their effects last longer. The substances include both small molecules like adrenaline and cortisol (see Chapter 5), and also peptides. The principal gland that controls most hormonal systems is the pituitary, which is joined to, and largely controlled by, the hypothalamus. Other glands remote from the brain such as the adrenal glands also release hormones that have effects on the body and in some cases also on neurons in the hypothalamus.

Third, there is a group of substances that are neuro-modulators. Many of them are peptides. Endogenous opiates (chemically similar to drugs like opium and heroin), for example, modulate the pain system, and other peptides (such as cholecystokinin) have important emotional effects. Some peptides are transmitters, but when they act as neuro-modulators they are released by some neurons, and diffuse some distance to affect many thousands of nearby neurons.

The study of different neurochemicals has helped us think how emotions are represented in the nervous system: neurochemicals are located anatomically in networks in regions of the brain and related to functionally distinct classes of behavior (e.g., Panksepp, 1986; 1998). Neurochemicals can also be administered to individuals in different ways, allowing researchers to study how they influence emotions, moods, and other psychological states. Here we'll review ideas about two of the most widely studied neurochemicals and their relevance to emotion: serotonin and oxytocin.

Serotonin

Serotonin is a neurotransmitter produced widely throughout the brain, in particular targeting subcortical areas (amygdala, ventral striatum, hypothalamus) as well as regions of the prefrontal cortex. It has come to be of interest because of the widespread use of serotonin-reuptake inhibitors like Prozac (chemical name, fluoxetine) as antidepressants, which are calculated to increase availability of brain serotonin. It is estimated that nearly 10% of Americans take antidepressants. As we shall see, however, in Chapter 13, it is likely that the efficacy of these substances in alleviating depression has been overestimated.

The question for this chapter is how serotonin may influence emotions and moods. In a synthetic review of the literature on serotonin, Charles Carver and his colleagues (2008) propose that brain mechanisms that use serotonin are involved in the balance between fast, emotional, associationistic processing in the subcortex and slower, deliberate, language-based processing in the frontal lobes. In cognitive terms, these have become known respectively as *heuristic* and *deliberative* processes—**fast and slow thinking** as Kahneman (2011) has called them—and we discuss them further in Chapter 10. When serotonin levels in the synapses of your brain are low, Carver et al. say your fast, intuitive subcortical reactions in regions like the amygdala or nucleus accumbens tend to predominate over the more deliberative, prefrontally based processes.

This framework may help to explain paradoxical findings related to serotonin. For example, low levels of serotonin are associated with two kinds of emotional disorders. The first is antisocial tendencies, in which the individual is prone to impulsive and aggressive outbursts. The second is depression, where the individual feels high levels of negative emotion. On the surface one might find contradiction in the idea that low levels of serotonin are associated with both antisocial and depressive tendencies. But in the treatment of Carver and colleagues, both antisocial behavior and depression reflect an imbalance in the influence of frontal lobes upon subcortical processes: in the case of antisocial people, the frontal lobes are not regulating aggressive tendencies; in depressives, the frontal lobes are not regulating negative emotions.

According to this idea, serotonin levels produce an imbalance in the interaction between subcortical and cortical regions of the brain that can lead to problematic aggression (if the person is prone to antisocial impulsivity) or depression (if the person is prone to negative affect and distress).

With respect to personality, Carver and colleagues summarize studies that fit with the notion that serotonin modulates the interaction between subcortical and cortical processes. Low levels of serotonin tend to correlate with certain personality traits that reflect diminished activation in prefrontal regions of the brain involved in emotion regulation: low levels of Agreeableness (that is to say hostility), high levels of Neuroticism (defined by increased emotional reactivity), and low levels of constraint (which reflect the individual's ability to be future oriented and able to modify impulses according to the current social context). Carver et al. argue that when serotonin levels are low, subcortical regions override the prefrontal regulation of impulses.

Carver et al. cite, for instance, experiments such as those of Brian Knutson and his colleagues (1998) in which a serotonin reuptake inhibitor (assumed to increase the brain's available serotonin) was given to some volunteers and a placebo was administered to others. Compared to participants in the placebo condition, those given the serotonin reuptake inhibitor were found to have decreased indices of hostility and negative affect as measured by personality tests, and showed more cooperation and affiliation as they played a puzzle game together. Carver et al. also cite subsequent studies in which, with experimental increases in serotonin, people were found to be less reactive to stressful events.

Oxytocin

Oxytocin is a peptide of nine amino acids. It is produced in the hypothalamus and released into both brain and bloodstream. Receptors for this peptide are found in the olfactory system, limbic-hypothalamic system, the periaqueductal gray, and regions of the spinal cord that regulate the autonomic nervous system, especially the parasympathetic branch (Uvnas-Moberg, 1994). Oxytocin is involved in lactation, maternal bonding, and sexual interaction (Carter, 1992). In the most general sense, oxytocin promotes bonding behavior possibly by reducing anxiety (Carter & Altemus, 1997; Taylor et al., 2000) and making social contact and affiliation pleasant (Insel, Young, & Zuoxin, 1997; Panksepp, 1998). Given these basic facts about oxytocin, early theorizing posited that oxytocin might be thought to be one biological substrate of love (Carter, 1998; Insel, 1993).

First, comparisons between prairie voles who display pair-bonding, and the closely related montane voles, who do not pair-bond, have revealed differences in the location of oxytocin receptors in the brains of each species (Carter, 1998; Insel et al., 1997). Moreover, in the prairie vole injections of oxytocin directly into specific areas of the brain have been found to increase preferences for a single partner over other partners, whereas injections of oxytocin antagonists depress single-partner preference (Williams, Insel, Harbaugh, & Carter, 1994). Other studies of voles find that mating stimulates oxytocin release (Carter, 1992), and blocking the activity of oxytocin prevents maternal behavior (Insel & Harbaugh, 1989; Pederson, 1997). Prosocial behavior was found to increase and aggression to decrease when female prairie voles were given oxytocin (Witt et al., 1990). Male and female prairie voles increase their social contact after oxytocin treatment (Witt et al., 1992).

Studies of other species likewise reveal similar social bonding functions of oxytocin. In primates, injections of oxytocin have led to increases in the frequency of touching and watching infants, and decreases in aggressive yawns and facial threats (Holman & Goy, 1995). Separation distress calls in isolated domestic chicks have been found to decrease after oxytocin treatment (Panksepp et al., 1997). Oxytocin injections have caused ewes to become attached to unfamiliar lambs (Keverne et al., 1997). Rat pups show preferences for odors of mothers, except when pretreated with oxytocin antagonists (Nelson & Panksepp, 1996).

In humans, early studies found suggestive evidence in support of the thesis that oxytocin promotes bonding. In studies of lactating women, it has been found that oxytocin reduces activity of the hypothalamic-pituitary axis (Carter & Altemus, 1997; Uvnas-Moberg, 1997, 1998). Massage leads to increased oxytocin release in the bloodstream (Turner et al., 1999, 2002). Oxytocin has been found to be released during sexual activity (Carmichael et al., 1987; Murphy, Seckl, Burton, Checkley, & Lightman, 1987). And when women were asked to recount an experience of warmth felt toward another person, their nonverbal display of love—evident in smiling, head tilts, and open-handed gestures—correlated with an increase in oxytocin released into the bloodstream (Gonzaga et al., 2006). And what's true of individuals is true of couples. Dietzen and colleagues have found that heterosexual couples who inhaled oxytocin through a nasal spray prior to discussing an issue of conflict, compared to couples in a control condition in which partners inhaled a neutral solution, showed more positive relational behaviors—validation, caring, eye contact, smiling—and they had lower levels of the stress hormone after the conflict (Dietzen et al., 2009).

These early findings relating oxytocin to bonding and love have led investigators to the thesis that oxytocin may promote prosocial behavior toward others more generally. Dozens of studies have focused on two more specific hypotheses. A first is that oxytocin promotes generosity. For example, in one seminal study in this literature, participants played the trust game with another player (Kosfeld et al., 2005). In the trust game, one participant, known as the "investor," makes contributions to another individual, known as the "trustee." The value of the money given to the trustee then triples, and the trustee then gives some amount back to the investor—as much or as little as he or she desires. In this particular study, participants either whiffed some oxytocin in a nasal spray, or a neutral control solution. As you can see in Figure 6.4, participants given oxytocin were

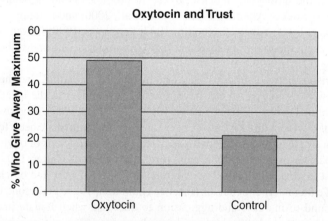

FIGURE 6.4 Participants given oxytocin are more likely to share the maximum amount of money in an economic game (adapted from Kosfeld et al., 2005).

more than twice as likely as those in the control condition to give away the maximum amount of money to a stranger.

A second interest is whether oxytocin increases our empathic responses to others. For example, in one study on this point, Domes and colleagues (Domes et al., 2007) had participants inhale oxytocin or a control solution in a nasal spray. They then were given 36 pictures in which people expressed different emotions in subtle expressions of the eyes—a task known as the Mind-in-the-Eyes task. Those participants who were given oxytocin performed better on this task, proving to be better able to read emotion in subtle expressions in the eyes, in particular more difficult expressions.

These studies relating oxytocin to increased love, positive communication, prosocial behavior, and empathy in humans generated a great deal of excitement—oxytocin was heralded as the love drug, as a potential cure for certain disorders defined by difficulties in social connection, such as autism, and a means by which to build trust and social ties in communities (there is even an oxytocin spray available in England!). More recent reviews and scientific studies raise some problems with this view. First of all, a recent review by Jennifer Bartz and her colleagues finds that whereas the influences of oxytocin upon increased prosocial behavior and empathy are often observed in studies, at other times they are not, suggesting that oxytocin does not promote a blind prosociality or empathy toward all (Bartz et al., 2011). Instead, the influences of oxytocin upon prosocial behavior and empathy depend on the specifics of the social context—for example, whether you are interacting with friend or foe—and the individual's personality. In their review, Bartz and colleagues suggest that oxytocin instead promotes a greater social sensitivity to salient social cues within the context.

Recent work by Carsten de Dreu and his colleagues (2010) also points to a more nuanced view of oxytocin, suggesting that oxytocin promotes a particular kind of prosociality—that directed toward the in-group, but not toward the out-group. A series of ingenious studies by de Dreu and his colleagues has found that oxytocin most potently promotes in-group favoritism, the preferential evaluation and treatment of one's own group relative to out-groups. In one series of studies, inhaling oxytocin compared to a control solution led participants to allocate more resources to their own group rather than to themselves (the preferred choice of control participants), to trust their in-group more, and, in conditions of high fear, to avoid cooperation with an out-group. In another investigation, participants who inhaled oxytocin relative to the control participants showed evidence of more automatic positive evaluations of their own group, they were more likely to assume their own group experienced complex moral emotions like embarrassment, and they were less likely to be willing to sacrifice a member of their own group to save the lives of several individuals in a moral decision-making task (de Dreu et al., 2011). It would appear that oxytocin promotes a more parochial form of altruism and empathy, one that benefits one's own group over others.

SUMMARY

In this chapter we turned toward the human brain to explore what regions might be involved in emotion, and in what ways. We reviewed current understandings of how the brain works and how different regions of the brain serve different functions. We considered different methods for the study of the brain, ranging from studies of patients with brain damage to the imaging of brain regional activity as humans respond to different stimuli, and the effects of psychoactive drugs. We then focused our attention on subcortical processes involved in emotion. In this section, we saw that a small portion of the forebrain, the amygdala, is involved in assigning, at an unconscious level, emotional significance to events, that the nucleus accumbens signals the potential rewards of different stimuli, and that the periaqueductal gray in the midbrain is related to the reduction of the experience of pain, and caregiving. We then looked at cortical processes related to emotion, focusing on regions of the cortex involved in empathy, emotion regulation, social pain, and positive emotion. Finally, we turned our attention to the role of two neurochemicals involved in emotion. Serotonin may be involved in balancing subcortical and cortical processes involved in emotion. Oxytocin has been thought of as a biological underpinning of love and devotion, although more recent studies suggest oxytocin may be more aptly thought of as a neurochemical that promotes social sensitivity.

TO THINK ABOUT AND DISCUSS

1. What would be definitive evidence for you to sort out whether the amygdala is activated by fear, valence, or the intensity of a stimulus?

2. What are some specific emotions that map onto wanting versus liking, or anticipating pleasure versus consuming pleasurable things?

3. Design a study that would clarify whether oxytocin is fundamentally related to social affection versus more general social sensitivity.

FURTHER READING

An excellent and wide-ranging introduction to affective neuroscience:

Panksepp, J., & Biven, L. (2012). *The archaelogy of mind: Neuroevolutionary origins of human emotions*. New York, NY. WW Norton.

For an outstanding recent review of affective neuroscience, read:

K. N. Ochsner (2008). The social-emotional processing stream: Five core constructs and their translational potential for schizophrenia and beyond. *Biological Psychiatry*, **64**, 48–61.

For the most recent summary of LeDoux's influential work, see:

S. M. Rodrigues, J. E. LeDoux, & R. M. Sapolsky (2009). The influence of stress hormones on fear circuitry. *Annual Review of Neuroscience*, **32**, 289–313.

Appraisal, Knowledge, and Experience

7

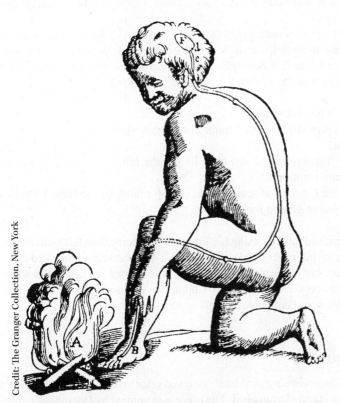

Credit: The Granger Collection, New York

FIGURE 7.0 Diagram from Descartes's book, *Traité de l'homme,* showing how the soul—which can be moved by emotions—can open valves to let vital fluids from the reservoir (labeled F) into the tubes to work the muscles and produce actions. The Granger Collection, New York

Herein too may be felt the powerlessness of mere Logic . . . to resolve these problems which lie nearer to our hearts.

(George Boole, 1854, An Investigation of the Laws of Thought, p. 416)

In 1961, a patient with epilepsy—a kind of electrical storm in the brain—had an operation to separate the left side of the cortex from the right, and hence to stop the spread of epileptic disturbances. (No other treatment had been effective.) This procedure is called a **split brain** operation, and in it the corpus callosum, a large bundle of nerve fibers that connects the left and right sides of the cortex, is severed. Despite the two sides being no longer in communication, the patient's IQ, personality, language, and ability to engage in meaningful interactions were not diminished. Twenty years after the first split-brain operation, Roger Sperry was awarded a Nobel Prize for his research with these patients, which showed in a strikingly new way the different functions of the left and right hemispheres.

If a picture or text is presented to the right side of the visual field, the information crosses over to the other side in the optic nerve and is processed by the left hemisphere. When anything is shown in the left visual field it is processed by the right hemisphere. But with a split brain, the two hemispheres do not communicate.

Here is an example from Michael Gazzaniga (1988), who worked with Sperry. He showed a frightening film about fire safety to the left visual field of a woman split-brain patient. Because the images were not accessible to the left hemisphere of her brain, she was not conscious of having seen the film. Gazzaniga then interviewed the patient, as follows.

M.G. (Michael Gazzaniga): What did you see?
V.P. (Patient): I don't really know what I saw. I think just a white flash.
M.G.: Were there people in it?
V.P.: I don't think so. Maybe just some trees, red trees like in the fall.
M.G.: Did it make you feel any emotion?
V.P.: I don't really know why, but I'm kind of scared. I feel jumpy. I think maybe I don't like this room, or maybe it's you. You're getting me nervous.

The patient seems to feel fear, and talks by using her linguistically competent left hemisphere. Fear has been processed by the unsplit subcortical regions, which have then communicated to the language-using right hemisphere, but without any indication of what caused the fear. When asked by Gazzaniga to explain her feelings, the patient draws upon her fear, and her narratizing left hemisphere offers a story about how Gazzaniga is making her feel nervous.

Appraisal and Emotion

What starts up our emotions? When events are evaluated, assigned value in terms of the individual's concerns, the evaluative process is called **appraisal**. The process is implied by Gazzaniga's split-brain patient. To start with, the process is automatic, something like a reflex, and need have nothing to do with language. This is **primary appraisal**. Emotions are then usually directed to particular objects and people and can often be described in words. This is **secondary appraisal**.

Historical Background and Concepts

As we explained in Chapter 1, the concept of evaluation of events in relation to an individual's concerns goes back 2,400 years, to Aristotle. He was followed by philosophers such as Epicurus and Chrysippus, who studied emotions to understand how to live in a good way. These and other philosophers in the schools of Epicurean and Stoic ethical philosophy, which have had an influence on Western thought, were—if one may put it like this—the first thoroughgoing Western emotion researchers. One of the most interesting analyses to emerge from this work was made by the Stoic, Chrysippus, who distinguished between what he called first movements of emotions, which are automatic, and second movements, which are mental and which involve judgment and decision. Chrysippus thought that one cannot avoid the first movements; they occur in the body and we can't do anything about them. But since second movements involve thought, they are more, as Stoic philosophers said, "up to us." The idea of second movements of bad emotions, such as giving in to angry revenge, or to greedy selfishness, was transformed in a later era to the Christian idea of seven deadly sins, all of which have an emotional quality (Oatley, 2011; Sorabji, 2000). Sin implies temptation, which in turn implies that we have choice. In the second stage of appraisal, there's the possibility of choice.

Magda Arnold and J.A. Gasson (1954; whose analyses we described in Chapter 1) discussed the work of the Stoics. Their paper is often taken as the founding of the modern notion that emotions are based on appraisals. An important figure in the development of the idea was Richard Lazarus, who studied challenges that people faced in their lives and the capacities they had to cope with them (Lazarus, 1991). Challenges produce vigilant attention and heightened activity in the sympathetic branch of the autonomic nervous system. But each kind of challenge promotes a different emotion, depending on how it is appraised. Here is how Lazarus describes these processes:

> This approach to emotion contains two basic themes: First, emotion is a response to evaluative judgments or meaning; second, these judgments are about ongoing relationships with the environment, namely how one is doing in the agenda of living and whether the encounter of the environment is one of harm or benefit.

Agreeing with Aristotle, and with Arnold and Gasson, Lazarus proposed that appraisals involve evaluative judgments of how good or bad an event is for the person. A second theme is that appraisals concern the individual's goals and aspirations, which Frijda (2007) calls "concerns." Emotions, then, could scarcely be more critical for psychology: emotions relate events in the outer world to one's inner self and one's concerns.

Agnes Moors (2007, 2009) has argued that the appraisal approach is critical to the study of emotions as processes that articulate events with people's goals, and that it is superior to any conceptualization that has no relation to goals, or a different relation to goals.

Stein, Trabasso, and Liwag (1994) have extended the idea of goals to plans that are generated from them and the beliefs on which they are based. They propose that aspects of emotion-related appraisal unfold as follows:

1. An event, usually unexpected, is perceived that changes the status of a valued goal.
2. Beliefs are often challenged. This can cause bodily changes and expressions to occur.
3. Plans are formed about what to do about the event to reinstate or modify the goal, and the likely results of the plans are considered.

These stages lead to questions that correspond to them:

1. What happened?
2. What do I think about it?
3. What can I do about it, and what might then happen?

Nancy Stein et al. (1994) give an example of a 5-year-old, Amy. Her kindergarten teacher had just told the class that she had a paint set for each child, and that after painting pictures for Parents' Night the children could take their paint sets home. When the children had been given their paint sets, Stein et al.'s research assistant noticed Amy looking apprehensive. She asked why. Amy said: "I'm jittery. I'm not sure why she wants to give me the paints. So do I have to paint all of the time at home? I really don't want to do this. I didn't think teachers made you paint at home. I don't like painting that much. Why does she want me to paint at home?"

Here we see that Amy has a goal that has been violated (1): she doesn't want to paint. The idea of being given something to do at home violates a belief about what teachers do (2). The conversation continues with Amy's plans (3):

Research assistant: What will you do, Amy?
Amy: I don't want to take the paints home. I want to know why I have to do this.
Research assistant: Well Amy, what are you going to do about this?
Amy: I'll take the paints home, but when I get home, I'll ask my mom why I have to do this.

Two weeks later the research assistant talked casually to Amy, who was still worried about the paints. She said she had used them only once. But she had not told the teacher, fearing that the teacher might be mad at her.

Stein et al. (1994) propose that how a person sees an event—which depends on the person's goals and values—will determine how the event is perceived and what emotions are elicited. This is consistent with Lazarus's treatment of appraisal. The same event can lead to different emotions in different people. Notice that the processes leading to specific emotions are thoughts or thought-like processes of the kind we are calling secondary appraisals.

Primary Appraisals, Good and Bad

Into our lives come events that have large effects. You arrive at your new college dorm and meet your roommate, who instantly fills you with a reassuring sense of comfort and familiarity. In the following year, you have to search for an apartment to rent, but the places trigger gut feelings of unease and discomfort. What appraisal processes give rise to these reactions?

As one answer to this question, Robert Zajonc (1980) has proposed that we process stimuli through several different systems. One system provides an immediate, unconscious evaluation of whether the stimulus is good or bad (LeDoux, 1993; Mischel & Shoda, 1995). This is a primary appraisal, an automatic emotional reaction to events and objects in the environment, which motivates rapid approach or avoidance responses. It corresponds to what Chrysippus (discussed above) called the first movement of an emotion. As you have learned in Chapter 6, the system that makes these appraisals probably involves the amygdala. This first appraisal system appears to give rise to our core feelings of positivity or negativity. Russell (2003) says the heart of any emotion is feeling good or bad, together with feeling enervated or excited. He calls this **core affect**, which we discuss later in the chapter. Other systems—which we are calling secondary appraisals, which Chrysippus called second movements—provide more deliberative, conscious, complex assessments to decide what to think and what to do about it.

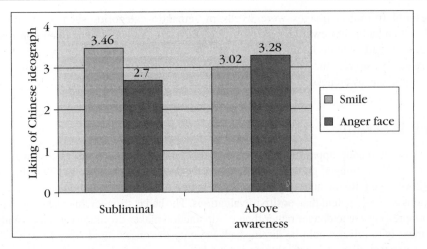

FIGURE 7.1 Unconscious appraisal. People liked Chinese ideographs more after they had first been subliminally presented with a smile, suggesting that the smile had activated positive feeling at an unconscious level. When presented with a smiling face long enough to be consciously aware of it, the smile did not lead participants to evaluate Chinese ideographs more positively (Source: Murphy & Zajonc, 1993).

To study automatic evaluations, Murphy and Zajonc (1993) presented participants with photos of people smiling or displaying facial anger. In a "suboptimal" condition, participants viewed these photos for four milliseconds and then looked at Chinese ideographs and rated how much they liked them. These participants had no idea whether they had seen a happy or angry face. In an "optimal" condition participants viewed the same faces for one second and were clearly aware of which faces they had viewed. Then they, too, looked at Chinese ideographs and rated how much they liked them.

As you can see in Figure 7.1, with suboptimal presentation, smiling faces prompted participants toward greater liking for the Chinese ideographs that followed them, and angry faces prompted less liking for the ideographs that followed them. No such priming effects emerged with the optimally presented faces. When we are consciously aware of emotionally charged stimuli, they are less likely to sway our judgments of other events that have nothing to do with them (Clore, Gasper, & Garvin, 2001; an effect that we discuss further in Chapter 10).

Is there evidence that automatic appraisals generate emotional experience as well as affecting preferences? Dimberg and Öhman (1996) suggest that there is. They first presented participants with photos of smiling faces and angry faces for extremely brief periods. These photos had been masked; that is to say each was immediately followed by other photos that prevented the possibility of consciously perceiving the original faces. Participants were not aware of having seen an angry or happy face, but a happy face prompted participants to smile, and an angry face prompted them to furrow their brow (see also Dimberg, Thunberg, & Elmehed, 2000; Whalen et al., 1998). In other work, Öhman and Soares (1994) presented people who had snake phobias with photos below their awareness and found that these photos of snakes generated a galvanic skin response and negative emotion. In further studies that used the technique of priming by subthreshold stimuli, Moors, De Houwer, and Eelen (2004) also found a phase of primary automatic appraisal about whether an event was good or bad. Their subthreshold (priming) images were words in semantic categories such as profession or animal, which had been rewarded and therefore had become good, or had been non-rewarded and therefore had become bad.

These studies suggest that there is a primary appraisal process that is fast and automatic and outside conscious awareness. It gives an immediate feeling of good or bad.

Which Is Stronger, the Good or the Bad?

Research on automatic appraisals of good and bad qualities of an event raises an intriguing question: which is stronger, good or bad? Reviews by Cacioppo and Gardner (1999), Baumeister et al. (2001), and Rozin and Royzman (2001) offer a perhaps unsettling answer: negative evaluations are more potent than positive evaluations. The bad is stronger than the good. This bias to be more responsive to danger rather than to satisfaction makes evolutionary sense. Without it, our chances of survival would be diminished; we only die once.

Negative stimuli, such as frightening sounds or disgusting smells, trigger more rapid, stronger physiological responses than positive stimuli, such as pleasing sounds or delicious tastes. In various experiments it has been shown that a loss, such as losing $10, is experienced as more intense than a pleasure, for instance, of gaining $10. Negative trauma, such as the death of a loved one or sexual abuse, can change the individual for a lifetime. It is hard to think of analogous positive life events that alter life in such profound and enduring ways. Or consider ideas about the workings of contamination, the process by which a disgusting object endows another object with its vile essence through simple contact (Rozin & Fallon, 1987). Brief contact with a cockroach will spoil a delicious meal (the negative contaminates the positive). The inverse—trying to make cockroaches delicious by touching them with a favorite food—is improbable at best, and probably impossible (Rozin & Royzman, 2001).

To address whether negative evaluations are more potent than positive evaluations, Ito et al. (1998) presented participants with positively valenced photographs (for example, of pizza or ice cream) and negatively valenced photographs (for example, of a mutilated face or of a dead cat). They recorded participants' electrocortical activity focusing on a region of brain activity associated with evaluative responses. They discovered a clear negativity bias in evaluation: negative slides prompted greater brain activity than positive or neutral slides.

Secondary Appraisals

What happens when we move beyond automatic primary appraisals to secondary appraisals? Modern research on appraisal has tended to be in two families: **discrete approaches**, which emphasize that appraisals give rise to distinct emotions, and **dimensional approaches**, which focus on the components of appraisals that can relate to several emotions.

Discrete Approaches

In his theory of discrete emotions, Lazarus discussed the two stages of the appraisal process (1991). In his version of the primary appraisal stage, which we show in Figure 7.2, the individual appraises the event in terms of its relevance to goals. Early in the process, the

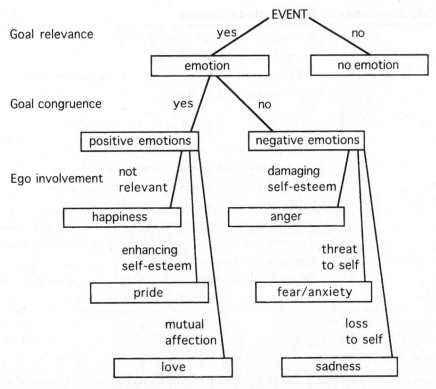

FIGURE 7.2 Decision tree of appraisals based on three features (goal relevance, goal congruence, and ego involvement), plus the emotions that can occur with these appraisals (Lazarus, 1991). Further differentiation among emotions occurs in secondary appraisals.

individual evaluates whether an event is relevant to personal goals. If it is, an emotion is elicited; if not, no emotion ensues. If an event is relevant, it is appraised as to whether it is congruent or incongruent with goals. Goal-congruent events elicit positive emotions, and goal-incongruent events produce negative emotions. These stages make up primary appraisal. Then the individual appraises the event in relation to more specific goals, or issues for the ego. This is secondary appraisal. Events can concern moral values, for example, to be kind, or to avoid doing to others what one would not want done to oneself. Events might bear upon issues of the self and identity, for example, whether one is excelling in areas that are central to self-definition, such as one's academic work, or performance in the arts or sport, or work for charities. Events can pertain to important ideals, for example, that societies should be fair and just. In light of emotions that occur to other people about whom we care, the goals and well-being of these people are also our concerns, and such events thus give rise to emotions in us also.

An approach to discrete emotions that is related to Lazarus's is that of Oatley and Johnson-Laird (1987, 2011). They postulate appraisals with two components, as we have been discussing. A primary appraisal of an event occurs in relation to goals. It is automatic and unconscious. It occurs not in terms of good and bad, but in terms of basic emotions (such as

Table 7.1   Emotions and core relational themes

Anger	A demeaning offense against me or mine
Anxiety	Facing an uncertain, existential threat
Fright	Facing an immediate, concrete, and overwhelming physical danger
Guilt	Having transgressed a moral imperative
Shame	Having failed to live up to an ego-ideal
Sadness	Having experienced an irrevocable loss
Envy	Wanting what someone else has
Jealousy	Resenting a third party for loss or threat to another's affection
Disgust	Taking in or being too close to an indigestible object or idea
Happiness	Making reasonable progress toward the realization of a goal
Pride	Enhancement of one's ego-identity by taking credit for self or in-group
Relief	Distressing goal-incongruent condition that has changed for the better
Hope	Fearing the worst but yearning for better
Love	Desiring or participating in affection, usually but not necessarily reciprocated
Compassion	Being moved by another's suffering and wanting to help

Source: Adapted from Lazarus (1991).

happiness, sadness, anger, fear, and disgust), each of which sets the brain into a mode adapted to deal with a recurring situation (respectively: progress toward a goal, loss, frustration by another, threat, and toxicity). Recall that Gazzaniga's patient, discussed at the beginning of the chapter, did not say she experienced something good or bad: she said she felt "kind of scared." Each mode is a set of states of **readiness** (Frijda, 1986, 2007) with a distinct phenomenological tone, but no necessary verbal meaning. The effect is a bit like having several sound devices in your house, say a doorbell, a telephone bell, a smoke detector, and a burglar alarm. If one goes off, you are alerted to something potentially important and your readiness changes accordingly, but initially you do not know exactly what the event was. You need to investigate. Similarly, an emotion can start, but its verbal meaning is supplied by a secondary process that occurs in awareness, in which you make a mental model of the event, what caused it, and how to act in relation to it.

In the second stage of appraisal the individual considers a causal attribution for the event, how to respond to the event, and future consequences of action. At this level Lazarus calls the process the **core relational theme** of the emotion: its essential meaning. In Table 7.1 we present Lazarus's analysis of several emotions.

You can think of emotions in relation to these core relational themes as summaries of the different classes of events that elicit them. In evolutionary terms, these themes map onto the problems and opportunities to which people respond with emotions—the slights (anger), dangers (fear), moral transgressions (guilt), losses (sadness), and sufferings of others (compassion), for example, that have been critical to human survival, reproduction, and cooperative group living. You can also think about these core relational themes as the language of our emotional experience: they capture the themes and issues that organize our emotional experience.

Dimensional Approaches

Can you think of aspects of emotional experience that are not well explained in terms of discrete emotions? Are there aspects of your emotional life that don't seem readily to follow from this approach? Phoebe Ellsworth (e.g., 1991) has suggested that we need to think about emotion-related appraisal in a way that's different from that of discrete emotions: the dimensional approach.

Approaches to emotions as discrete highlight differences between emotions in terms of their eliciting appraisals. Yet many emotions are similar in fundamental ways. Anger and fear, for example, at their core feel similar: they feel unpleasant and arousing. The same could be said about gratitude and love, which both feel quite pleasant and are marked by a feeling of devotion for others. An appraisal theory, Ellsworth contends, needs to account for the interesting similarities across emotions, as well as their differences.

A second gap in approaches to emotions as discrete, according to Ellsworth, is their inability to account for transitions between emotions. Very often in our emotional experience we move from one emotion to another; we shift from anger to guilt quite rapidly, or from sadness to hope, or (hopefully not often) from love to anger.

In light of such issues, Phoebe Ellsworth and Craig Smith (1985, 1988) developed a theory of appraisal that can account for interesting similarities among the emotions, as well as the many differences (for comparable accounts see Frijda, 1986; Ortony, Clore, & Collins, 1988; Roseman, 1984; Scherer, 1988; Weiner, 1986). Smith and Ellsworth reviewed numerous studies of the semantic content of emotions, and derived eight different dimensions of meaning that capture the appraisal processes that lead to various emotions. These dimensions are presented in Table 7.2. Think of these dimensions as units of meaning ascribed to events in your life: how positive or negative the event is, who is responsible for it, whether it is fair, how much energy is required, to what extent the stimulus requires intense attention, how certain things seem, and so on.

To document the patterns of appraisal associated with the different emotions, Smith and Ellsworth had 16 participants imagine experiencing 15 different emotions. The participants then rated the original emotional experience on the eight dimensions presented in Table 7.2. Each was defined by a pattern of appraisal. For example, interest was associated with appraisals of elevated pleasantness, the desire to attend, the sense that situational factors are producing events, the perceived need to expend effort, moderate certainty about future outcomes, together with little sense of perceived obstacle or illegitimacy of events. Hope was associated with appraisals of

Table 7.2 Dimensions of appraisal

1.	Attention: Degree to which you focus on and think about the event
2.	Certainty: Degree to which you are certain about what is going to happen
3.	Control/coping: Extent to which you have control over outcomes in the environment
4.	Pleasantness: Degree to which the event is positive or negative
5.	Perceived obstacle: Extent to which the pursuit of your goals is blocked
6.	Responsibility: Extent to which others, you, and situational factors are responsible for events
7.	Legitimacy: Extent to which the event is fair and deserved or unfair and undeserved
8.	Anticipated effort: Extent to which you must expend energy to respond to the event

Source: Adapted from Smith & Ellsworth (1985).

elevated attention and effort and situational agency, moderate pleasantness, and little certainty or sense of perceived obstacle or illegitimacy. Happiness was the emotion that was pleasant, associated with low effort, high certainty, and high attention.

A second important result found by Smith and Ellsworth was that certain dimensions stood out in their ability to differentiate among related emotions. They found that a combination of control and responsibility were at issue. Important was *agency*, a critical dimension identified by Roseman (1984), which, for instance, differentiates three negative emotions: anger, sadness, and guilt. When we blame others we become angry; when we attribute negative events to circumstances we become sad; when we attribute negative events to ourselves we become guilty. Agency also differentiates certain positive emotions. The same positive event attributed to the self is a source of pride, but when attributed to others it's a source of gratitude.

This importance of causality in emotion-related appraisal is likewise seen in the work of Weiner and Graham (1989). They found that some distinct emotions depend on **attributions**, the explanations of the causes of events that people give. They describe how children between the ages of 5 and 11 were given vignettes and asked to decide what emotion would occur. One was this:

> This is a story about a boy named Chris. Chris's teacher gave a spelling test and he got all the words right. Chris received an "A" on the test. (Weiner & Graham, 1989, p. 407)

If the children were told that Chris had studied all the words the night before (implying that the cause of his success was his own action), they tended to say that he would feel pride; but if the cause was that the teacher gave an easy test (a cause external to Chris), then the children, especially the older ones, thought Chris would not feel pride. Comparable results were found with guilt: if an event that caused damage could have been controlled, the children thought the person causing it would feel guilt, but if it was an accident, the older children thought the person would not feel guilt.

The finding that causal attributions differentiate among emotions has an important implication: a particular negative event may happen to you (perhaps you don't do as well on an exam as you had hoped), but which emotion you experience will depend on how you appraise the causes. Attribute the event to yourself and you're likely to feel guilt. Attribute it to others and you'll feel anger. Attribute it to circumstantial factors and you'll be more likely to experience sadness.

Extending Appraisal Research

Think about Smith and Ellsworth's study. In it, people remembered an emotional experience and then reported their appraisal. Several critiques have been leveled against this kind of retrospective, self-report study, for instance, by Parkinson, Fischer, and Manstead (2004). They pointed out that perhaps Smith and Ellsworth were really studying what people think about the causes of their emotions, rather than actual causes.

A study that is important because it showed experimentally that appraisals actually cause emotions was by Ira Roseman and Andreas Evdokas (2004). They assigned people to groups and told them to expect that they would experience either a pleasant or an unpleasant taste, and that either they would be in the taste group or they would be randomly assigned to this group or a neutral group. They found, for instance, as predicted by Roseman's (1984, 2001) theory, that when participants appraised the situation as one in which they would definitely avoid an unpleasant event, relief was caused, and when they appraised it as one in which they would probably experience a pleasant event, hope was caused.

Kuppens, van Mechelen, Smits, de Boeck, and Ceulemans (2007) found that appraisals can have different meanings for different people: although for some people anger is caused by frustration, for others it is usually caused by a sense of deliberate unfairness. For yet others it is caused by a threat to one's selfhood. Such meaningful appraisals can become habitual styles and hence aspects of personality (Power & Hill, 2010), and we discuss this further in Chapter 11.

Another approach is to identify appraisals as they occur, and ascertain whether emotion-specific appraisals relate to other measures of emotional response. For example, one might code appraisal-related themes, such as uncertainty or loss, or dimensions, such as responsibility or effort, in individuals' spontaneous speech, and ask whether those appraisals relate to measures of experience, or expression, or physiology. In one such study, Bonanno and Keltner (2004) coded the narratives of people who, six months previously, had experienced the death of their romantic partner. These narratives were complex, moving accounts of participants' lives with their partner, how they had met and fallen and love, how they raised families, and ultimately how their partner had died. The narratives included numerous references to loss, an appraisal theme related to sadness, and injustice, an appraisal theme at the heart of the experience of anger. These researchers coded spontaneous references to these two appraisal themes and related them to other measures of emotion gathered during the interview. They found that appraisals of loss correlated with facial expressions and self-reports of sadness but not anger, and that appraisals of injustice correlated with facial expressions and self-reports of anger but not sadness.

Cultural Variation in Appraisal

Rick Shweder and his colleagues (1997) conducted interviews to explore people's ideas about the kinds of events that they found morally repugnant, sources of anger and disgust. In Hindu India, they found that people are angered by kinds of events that would tend not to elicit much emotion in European cultures. These include the following: when a child cuts his hair after the death of his father, when a woman eats with her husband's elder brother, when a husband cooks for his wife or massages her legs, and when upper-caste individuals come into physical contact with lower-caste individuals.

Although the triggers for some kinds of emotions have been found to vary widely across different cultures (see Mesquita & Frijda, 1992), there are also substantial similarities. For instance, Roseman et al. (1995) compared appraisals of people living in America and people living in India. They found that in both countries appraisal of powerlessness prompted sadness and fear rather than anger, whereas an appraisal that someone else caused a negative event prompted anger rather than sadness or fear.

How, then, do cultures differ in the events that elicit emotion? Think back to our discussion of individualist, independent cultures and collectivist, interdependent cultures in Chapter 3, where you learned about culture-related differences in appraising emotions in terms of their capacity to engage or disengage with others. The important point is that culture shapes how we appraise emotion-eliciting events. Solitary and social experiences might have different meanings in individualist and collectivist cultures. Or consider being alone. Middle-class Europeans or Americans may appraise this in positive terms and experience contentedness. By contrast, Inuit people as studied by Briggs (1970) or the people of Ifaluk as studied by Lutz (1988) appraise being alone in terms of isolation, which elicits feelings of sadness (Mesquita & Ellsworth, 2001; Mesquita & Markus, 2004).

Being dependent upon others also appears to generate different appraisals and emotions across cultures. For example, among the Awlad'Ali, a nomadic tribe in Egypt, being in the presence of powerful others is the source of shame, or *hasham*, because such situations are reminders of one's dependence on others (Abu-Lughod, 1986). In contrast, it is reported that Japanese people sometimes experience a cozy and pleasurable emotion known as *amae* (Lebra, 1983). This is a comforting sense of dependence a less powerful person feels in relation to a more powerful person, which allows the less powerful person to be passive or helpless, in the manner of a small child, in the satisfying knowledge of being accepted.

A Third Phase of Appraisal: Verbal Sharing

Thus far we have spoken of appraisal as something that is inside the individual's head. Yet much of how we make sense of the world is in our conversations with others. In this sense, we might think of a third phase of appraisal that arises when we share and discuss our emotions with others. Using diary methods, Bernard Rimé and his colleagues have found that people have a strong tendency to confide their emotional experiences to others, which Rimé et al. (1991) call **social sharing**. In six studies they found that between 88 and 96% of emotions that could be remembered had been verbally shared with others. The rates were similar across the age range, for males and females, and for the interdependent Surinamese population living in the Netherlands as well as the highly individualistic Dutch. Sharing occurred even for emotions such as guilt and shame. When we share our emotions with others, we necessarily rely upon our knowledge of emotions, and we use specific words, concepts, categories, and narratives to convey our experiences to others.

As our experience of emotions is translated into verbal forms, as with other effects of language, we are enabled to extend the meanings and uses of our primary experiences. In this act something extraordinary occurs, which is available only to humans. Emotions and thoughts can themselves become objects of emotion and thought. We can turn them over in our minds, reflect on them, and share them with others. Rimé and his colleagues found that sharing does not decrease the intensity of emotions that are shared. Rimé (2009) argues that in sharing emotions verbally, relationships are extended, social support is enabled, and experience is compared with the experiences and intuitions of other members of our community.

Earlier in the chapter we described two phases of emotion: a brief initial phase that is largely involuntary and then an extended second phase that can be reflective. Sharing emotions is a third phase, a tertiary appraisal carried out with other people. It is just as much part of an emotion episode as primary and secondary appraisals, but now verbalized and coordinated with family members and friends.

The question of what emotions are really about, and how situations are appraised at the deepest level, may need to be coaxed out in verbal terms. James Pennebaker et al. (1988) had 50 students write either about emotionally significant issues or about superficial topics for 20 minutes on four consecutive days. Those who wrote about the deeper emotional issues showed improvements in immune function in the form of higher lymphocyte responses to an antigen challenge and fewer medical consultations at the University Health Center. Although participants who wrote about emotionally important issues found the actual writing more distressing than did control participants, three months later they were significantly happier than the controls and, looking back, they viewed the experience of confronting the emotional issues about which they wrote as a positive experience. These effects have been replicated many times, both in Pennebaker's laboratory and by other research groups. Pennebaker has found therapeutic effects of confronting traumatic experiences by writing or by talking. He understands the process in terms of alleviating a debilitation caused by suppressing traumatic experiences. He has concluded that the debilitation is relieved by confiding, turning the emotions over in consciousness, and by coming to understand the emotions and their implications (Pennebaker, 2012; Pennebaker & Chung, 2011; Pennebaker & Seagal, 1999).

Novels and films: *Vertigo*

Detective stories (mysteries) are based on the idea of an appraisal and then a radical reappraisal. Usually a crime has been committed and most people appraise it as appalling. Then a detective appears and reappraises the events to show that beneath the surface of things there is a very different world: at least one character will have appraised events differently and committed the crime. Before we've finished the story, our appraisals will have changed, too.

In the 1958 film, *Vertigo*, the director, Alfred Hitchcock, prepared not just one change of appraisal for the characters and for audience members, but several.

In the surface layer the film's protagonist, Scottie (played by James Stewart), was a San Francisco police detective. Chasing a suspect across rooftops, he was left hanging from a roof. A colleague who tried to save him fell to his death. Scottie takes early retirement, suffering from guilt, vertigo, and a phobia for heights. An old college friend gives him something on which he can employ his detective skills. It's to follow his wife, Madeleine (played by Kim Novak), who seems to have become mentally possessed by a dead person. Scottie starts to follow Madeleine and he sees her sitting for hours in an art gallery, gazing at a portrait of this dead person, her great-grandmother, Carlotta.

Now comes the second layer: a reappraisal by Scottie. His principal concern becomes no longer his friend's commission. It's the cool, blonde, sophisticated Madeleine. He falls in love with her. When she makes a suicide jump into San Francisco Bay, he rescues her and takes her to his apartment. When this film was made, sex could not be depicted on the screen. But we see Madeleine in Scottie's bed, waking up and asking how she got there while every bit of her clothing is hanging up to dry.

Now there is another layer: Scottie comes to be not just in love but obsessed, so he forgets his commission. Madeleine tells him of a dream of Carlotta at a place with a tower, south of San Francisco. Scottie drives her there because he thinks a visit might free her from her states of possession. When they arrive they declare their love for each other. But she breaks from him and runs up the steps of the tower. As Scottie follows her, he is overcome by his phobia for heights. A scream is heard. Through a window, we see her body hurtle downward. Then there is a shot of the dead Madeleine face-down on a rooftop.

Next comes yet another appraisal: Scottie in a state of depression and redoubled guilt wanders the city and sees a woman who reminds him of Madeleine: a brash redhead, Judy (also played by Kim Novak). They start going out. He coerces her to have her hair dyed blonde. He takes her to a dress shop and buys her a gray suit of the kind the dead Madeleine used to wear. Then, in one of the film's memorable scenes, Judy walks toward him through a luminous mist. She is Madeleine—as Scottie remembers her. Now he can love her.

But the film is not finished. We won't give the ending away but, in the next appraisal, we in the audience realize that Judy was indeed Madeleine and was hired by Scottie's college friend to impersonate his wife. As Goffman (1959) has said: "It is always possible to manipulate the impression the observer uses as a substitute for reality because a sign for the presence of a thing, not being that thing, can be employed in the absence of it" (p. 251).

An accomplishment of this film is its central question: "How far does that all-consuming emotion of sexual love depend on an appraisal based on projection, and how far does it derive from perceiving who the person actually is?

Emotion Words

An important component of reflection and sharing our emotions is our vocabulary of emotion words: the **emotion lexicon**. In English there are thousands of words to describe emotional experiences.

Some people have a condition called **alexithymia** (Taylor, Bagby, & Parker, 1997), which means having few emotion words; it's a difficulty in being able to identify or express emotions verbally. It is associated with a paucity of fantasies and a cognitive style oriented to outside events rather than to the inner world. Many studies have investigated associations between alexithymia and psychosomatic disorders, as if a lack of words for emotions channels emotional experience to be expressed in a bodily way that can affect immune function. Bird et al. (2010) found that responses of the insula region of the brain, which has been found to mediate empathy, were decreased in people who were alexithymic. Other researchers (Grynberg et al., 2010) have found that the association of alexithymia with decreased empathy may be due to anxiety.

Studies of emotion words reveal several different properties of the language of emotions. One of these is that applying a verbal label to an emotional experience helps identify its **intentional object**: what the emotion is specifically about (Ben Ze'ev & Oatley, 1996). (The philosophical term *intention* means "aboutness": thinking, knowing, and usually feeling are intentional in this sense because they are about something.) Emotion words direct us to the focus of the experience (Ben Ze'ev, 2000). For example, in the midst of a lively exchange at a party you might suddenly realize: "I'm feeling jealous." Recognizing a word for this experience is likely to sharpen the focus of your experience and guide you to attend to specific events: perhaps your partner is smiling flirtatiously at your best friend. The experience, the word, and the concept may evoke past experiences of a similar theme, perhaps with this current partner. Emotion words, then, appear to shape diffuse states into more specific emotional experiences. A study by Anderson et al. (2011) showed verbal emotional information can affect perception. When a piece of negative verbal emotional gossip was paired with a face, this face was recognized more easily in confusing circumstances than were faces that had been paired with neutral or positive gossip.

The emotion lexicon has structure. It is organized into categories at different levels, and implications of our categorizations are carried in our verbal discussions of emotions. In one important study, Shaver et al. (1987) gave participants 135 emotion terms written on cards and asked them to sort those words into as many or few categories as they thought appropriate. Based on this sorting, Shaver et al. captured English speakers' organization of emotion knowledge. What this task revealed, according to Shaver et al., is that there are three levels to our emotion knowledge.

At the superordinate level, there is a distinction between positive and negative emotions. This seems to fit well with how people appraise the goodness and badness of events immediately and automatically.

At the next level, known as the basic level of knowledge, are six emotion concepts: love, joy, surprise, anger, sadness, and fear. One might expect these terms to be those that people most frequently use to describe their emotional experience. It is interesting to note as well that many of the terms correspond to the emotions that appear to have universal facial expressions. This same list of emotions replicates (with slight variations) in analyses of other languages (Romney, Moore, & Rusch, 1997).

Below each of the basic emotion terms are many more specific states. This is known as the subordinate level of emotion knowledge. These are likely to be states that share properties of the basic emotion concept above them, and that are in important ways similar to one another. For example, below the basic emotion concept *love* is: love, compassion, lust, and longing. Below the concept *happiness* is: amusement, enthusiasm, pleasure, pride, hope, enthrallment, and relief. Below *sadness* is: agony, depression, disappointment, guilt, embarrassment, and pity.

Emotion words vary dramatically across cultures. Anna Wierzbicka (1999), a linguist who is fluent in many languages, has been critical of attempts to infer universal categories of emotion from intuitions by members of English-speaking cultures. She proposes, instead, universal concepts of emotions based on the following kind of (somewhat abbreviated) analysis that focuses on universal semantic elements. *Happiness*: (a) X was happy because X thought something, (b) X thought: "Some good things happened to me," (c) X thought: "I wanted things like this to happen," (d) X thought: "I don't want anything else now."

To explore how cultures vary in their language of emotion, Russell (1991) read hundreds of ethnographies written by anthropologists who had lived in different cultures and were familiar with the language and life of that culture. After observing that almost all languages have terms for anger, fear, happiness, sadness, and disgust, Russell paints a fascinating picture of how cultures vary in the language of emotion.

Cultures vary in the *number of words* that represent emotion. Researchers have identified 2,000 specific emotion-related words in English, 750 in Taiwanese, 58 in Ifaluk in Polynesia, and 8 in the Chewong of Malaysia.

Cultures vary in which states they represent with emotion terms. In the Gifjingali language of the Aborigines of Australia, fear and shame are captured by the same word, *gurakadj*. The distinction between shame and embarrassment is not made by the Japanese, Tahitians, Indonesians, or Newars of Nepal. There are states represented by a single word in other languages that are not represented by single English terms. For example, in Czech one finds *litost*, which means the sudden realization of life's tragic circumstances. In German there is the word *schadenfreude*, pleasure in the failure or suffering of another person. In a related way, some cultures represent kinds of experience with numerous words and concepts. For example, in Tahiti there are 46 separate terms that refer to anger. When this kind of effect occurs, people may be more likely to experience many shadings of meaning for certain kinds of emotion.

Many emotion words have metaphorical content. A **metaphor** is a concept that points to something other than itself. We might say, "This party is a blast." The image, the blast of a bomb, can characterize complex features of a party. Or we might say "Justice is blind" to characterize a hoped-for property of the abstract process of justice: to indicate it should be applied similarly to everyone, independently of who they are.

In their study of metaphor, George Lakoff, Mark Johnson, and Zoltán Kövesces have argued that there are five metaphors that speakers of English use frequently to describe emotional experience (Kövesces, 2003; Lakoff & Johnson, 1980). First, emotions can be *natural forces*. We speak of being swept away by our emotions as if they were waves. Second, emotions can be *opponents*. We struggle with our desire, grief, or frustration. Third, emotions can be *diseases*. We say that we are sick with love or envy. Fourth, we can think of emotions as fluids in containers. We simmer with rage or burst with joy. Fifth, we can think of emotions as animals. People who kiss a lot in public are "lovey-dovey."

Concepts of Emotion as Prototypes

How do we categorize emotions? Are there necessary and sufficient features of the concept of emotion, or of specific emotions? For some concepts we can give a correct definition with necessary and sufficient features—so a *grandmother* is "the mother of a person who is a parent." For most concepts exact definition is difficult or impossible because the natural world is not so neatly divided into categories, and for many objects we just do not know enough. So, when you say "tree," you mean that kind of thing called "tree" of which we all know typical examples but about which, if need be, those scientists in the Botany Department could tell us more.

Thus language and thought have the wonderful property of allowing us to talk and be understood even when we do not know very much. To do this we rely on thinking with **prototypes** that the hearer can summon into mind (Putnam, 1975). A prototype can be thought of as an example of an object in a category that shows off typical features of the category, so a prototypical bird is a robin. It flies, is of medium size, sings, builds nests, and so on. When invoking prototypes to explain things, we can also specify modifications. Although our prototype for *tree* might include the concept *large*, we can modify it and say, of a bonsai: "It's a tiny tree that has been grown in a pot and pruned to keep it small."

In several studies Fehr and Russell (1984) argued that people think about emotions in terms of prototypes. More specifically, people's everyday prototype of an emotion is something like a **script**, which refers to a characteristic outline of a sequence of events. Russell (1991b) has contrasted this kind of approach with approaches such as that of Johnson-Laird and Oatley (1989), who have offered a semantic analysis of the English lexicon in terms of primary emotions and their derivatives. Russell suggested that although in science we need to understand defining characteristics of emotions, perhaps in a manner such as that of semantic analysis, in ordinary life we think with prototypical examples of emotions with no sharp boundaries dividing off good from less good examples.

In one of the first studies systematically to explore prototypical scripts for different emotions, Shaver et al. (1987) had participants write about causes, thoughts, feelings, actions, and physical signs of different emotions. They coded these narratives and identified features of the emotion prototypes (namely, features that occurred in at least 20% of either the person's descriptions or the emotion's descriptions). The prototype for sadness is shown in Table 7.3.

By this narrative methodology, participants offer scripts, or as De Sousa (1987) calls them, **paradigm scenarios**, of different emotions (see also De Sousa, 2004). The idea has been useful for researchers in differentiating various emotions. Researchers using these narrative methods have sought to identify the distinct prototypes of the self-conscious emotions, including embarrassment, shame, and guilt (Keltner & Buswell, 1996; Miller & Tangney, 1994; Parrott & Smith, 1991). Embarrassment most typically follows violations of conventions that increase social exposure (e.g., after pratfalls or a loss of body control). Shame tends to follow the failure to live up to expectations, either one's own or those of significant others, that define the "core self,"

Table 7.3 **Prototype of sadness**

Causes:	Death, loss, not getting what one wants
Feelings:	Helpless, tired, run-down, slow
Expressions:	Drooping posture, saying sad things, crying, tears
Thoughts:	Blaming, criticizing self, reflection on past actions
Actions:	Negative talk to others, withdrawing from what was lost

Source: Adapted from Shaver et al. (1987).

"ego ideal," or character. Guilt appears to follow transgressions of moral rules that govern behavior toward others. The common antecedents of guilt, therefore, include lying, cheating, stealing, infidelity, and neglecting personal duties (Tangney, 1992; Tangney et al., 1996).

There are several interesting implications of taking a prototype perspective to emotion knowledge. First, it assumes there are no sharp boundaries between emotion categories. For example, there is going to be overlap in people's representations of sadness and anger, for example, or fear and guilt. Second, a prototype approach helps account for the varieties of experiences that are represented by one category of emotion. For example, there are numerous varieties of anger: some involving blame, others that are accidental; some directed at others, others directed at the self; some experiences of high intensity (like rage), others more modest (like irritation). A prototype perspective suggests that within each emotion category there are better examples of an emotion that possess the prototypical features of an emotion, such as those that we presented for sadness. Then there will be many variations of that emotion that have fewer of those features, or other features as well.

Categorical Properties of Emotion Knowledge

In other ways it appears that we do think about emotion in terms of **categories** with distinct boundaries between one another. A demonstration of this was provided by Nancy Etcoff and John Magee (1992). They argued that if there were basic emotions, then facial expressions would be recognized in categories. All happy faces would be sorted into one category, angry ones into another, and so forth. Perception of these expressions should be comparable to certain phenomena in the perception of speech. What distinguishes a spoken *b* from *p* in words like *bit* and *pit* is the time between the mouth opening and the onset of sound made by the larynx, called *voicing-onset time*. People are bad at making discriminations of voicing-onset time on either side of the *b–p* boundary, but they are excellent at discriminations across this boundary where time differences of a few milliseconds enable people to discriminate between *b* and *p*.

Etcoff and Magee created several series of faces ranging between pairs of states: happy to neutral, happy to sad, angry to disgusted, and so forth. To do this they traced faces from expressions of six basic emotions and a neutral face in photographs taken by Ekman and Friesen (1975) and used the caricature-generating computer program of Brennan (1985). For each pair of states they created 11-point scales with exactly equal increments of transition. You can see the series of 11 faces from happiness to sadness in Figure 7.3. They found that for these series there were abrupt shifts in discriminability between the faces, indicating a boundary between, for instance, happy and sad, angry and disgusted, and so forth. On either side of the boundary, people were not good at telling the difference between, for instance, the second and fourth faces in such series, but across the boundary, for instance between the fourth and sixth faces in the series, they were good. This experiment implies that functional categories of basic emotions affect discriminability of facial expressions.

A debate is in progress. On one side are those such as Ekman (1992), Panksepp (1992), Roseman (2011), and Oatley & Johnson-Laird (2011), who argue that there is a continuing usefulness in thinking of emotions in distinct categories. Researchers on the other side include Russell (2003), Barrett, Lindquist, Bliss-Moreau, Duncan, Gendron, Mize et al. (2007), and

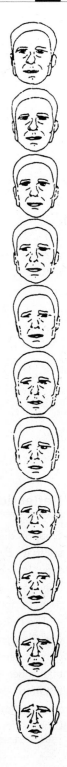

FIGURE 7.3   Series of faces in equal increments from happy to sad (from Etcoff & Magee, 1992).

Clore and Ortony (2008), who argue that emotions are not natural kinds, in the way that mammals and birds are naturally occurring kinds, because there is too much variation even in emotions that have the same name. It may be best to think of people on the different sides of this debate as focusing on different aspects of emotion. On the one side are those who focus on the functionality of emotions. On the other side are those who find more value in seeing emotions in terms of dimensions and cultural constructions.

Emotional Experience

How do we study the appraisals people make? One method has been in **diary studies**, in which people report on their everyday emotional experiences soon after they happen. Joanna Field (1934) kept a diary to see what it was in her life that made her happy. Here are some of her thoughts after falling in love, thinking about the man she would marry. "June 8th. I want us to travel together, exploring, seeing how other people live . . . sleeping at country inns, sailing boats, tramping dusty roads together . . . " (p. 48). Her thoughts take the form of plans of activities in a shared life of new experiences with the loved one.

In anxiety the thoughts are quite different. Here she is again:

> Oughtn't we to ask those people to tea? That's best, say, "Do you ever have time for a cup of tea? Will you come in any day?" Say we are free all the week, let them choose, will the maid answer the door? will she be too busy?

In this anxious little train of thought, Field wonders how to approach some people who are wealthier than she, rehearsing different forms of invitation and worrying about how she would feel if she called and a maid told her that the person she wanted to see was too busy.

Reflection and cultivation: Emotion diaries

Emotion diaries are ways of recording your emotions so that, by writing about what starts them, what thoughts you have during them, and what effects they have, you can reflect on them and understand them better.

The first psychologist to publish on emotion diaries was Georgina Gates (1926), who asked 51 women students to record instances of anger for a week; she found that anger in daily life was usually caused by being thwarted. Also in 1926, Marion Blackett, who had recently finished her psychology degree at the University of London, found herself wondering whether happiness

was important. She had started to work as an industrial psychologist, and she had the idea of keeping a diary of incidents that made her happy, and to relate them to her goals in life. The project took far longer than she expected, and she turned it into a book under the pen-name of Joanna Field (1934/1952). It produced the surprising discovery that much of her life was driven not by consciously recognized goals but by barely conscious anxieties. The project prompted a change of career. She became the distinguished psychoanalyst, Marion Milner. Her identification of anxieties on the edge of consciousness did not become widely known at the time; it was rediscovered decades later and became a cornerstone of cognitive-behavioral therapy.

One way to keep an emotion diary of your own is to look out for emotions that are distinct enough to recognize. Oatley and Duncan (1992) used this method, and told participants that indications of having an emotion were a bodily sensation such as the heart beating faster, or thoughts coming to mind that were hard to stop, or an urge to act emotionally. Among the questions we asked on a page made out like a questionnaire, were: What was the name of the emotion (or mood), how long did it last, what happened to start it, who was there, what thoughts came to mind during it, what urges were experienced, and what effects did it have? You can add to or delete from this list as you like.

Another way of keeping an emotion diary is to write down how you are feeling at certain moments in time. This method is called *experience sampling*, and it was invented by Csikszentmihalyi and Larson (1984), who asked adolescents to record how they were feeling when signaled at random moments. You can do this by keeping a timer in your pocket or purse, dialing up

some random time on it, maybe about 45 minutes ahead, and then recording how you feel when the timer goes off—what are you doing and how are you feeling at that moment?—then repeating the process as often as you like. You can write down as much or as little as you like in your diary entries.

Diary methods are often useful if there are aspects of your emotional life that you don't quite understand. They are a common technique in certain kinds of therapies to help people gain insight during difficult times (see Chapter 14). The work of James Pennebaker reviewed earlier speaks to the benefits of such reflection. Were you to keep an emotion diary you might learn interesting things. Do you, for instance, sometimes experience a wave of anxiety or despair for no obvious reason? Do you have some emotion more strongly than you think you should? Record when such incidents happen, what you are doing when they start, what just happened, and who else was there. Write what thoughts occur to you. Later, you can reflect on these thoughts: Are they still convincing? You might make some interesting discoveries about yourself.

Other people who have made diary studies of emotions are Oatley and Duncan (1994), who asked employed people to keep diaries of events that caused emotions, such as happiness, fear, anger, and so on. Oatley and Duncan (1992) reported a 20-year-old woman, Abigail, who was keeping such a diary and was then interviewed. She said the cause of an incident of anger with her boyfriend was a disagreement about preferences for different kinds of music. The argument lasted two-and-a-half hours, but intrusive thoughts continued for three days and kept her from sleeping for three nights. She said: "I just couldn't get through to him." Her thoughts included: "Is this going too far? If it goes too far, it [the relationship with the boyfriend] would end." Memories came to mind: the argument "reminded her of an ex-boyfriend" and made her "wonder if it [the relationship] was worth it" (p. 275).

Measuring Emotional Experience

A further question about emotional experience is how to measure it. Green, Goldman, and Salovey (1993) surveyed the different approaches to the assessment of positive and negative moods. One method is to construct **adjective checklists**, using items from lists of the following kind:

Positive	Negative
cheerful	blue
contented	depressed
happy	downhearted
pleased	gloomy
satisfied	sad
warmhearted	unhappy

Sets of adjectives that are synonyms of emotions and moods (as above) are offered to participants in a scrambled order. Participants are asked to check any adjective that applies to them. Points are given separately for positive and negative adjectives.

A second method is to offer statements like: "I am feeling sad and dispirited." Then ask people to indicate agreement on a scale—a common five-point scale is "strongly agree, agree, not sure, disagree, strongly disagree." Alternatively you can make up a scale indicating the extent to which each statement "Describes me."

A third method is to use a scale like the following:

Circle a number on the scale below to indicate how sad you feel:

Not at all 0–1–2–3–4–5–6–7–8–9–10 The most intense I have felt in my life

The ends of this kind of scale are marked with verbal expressions called *anchor points*, with which the participant can compare his or her current experience.

There are several established self-report scales that measure tendencies toward global positive and negative moods (Watson, Clark, & Tellegen, 1988), distinct positive emotions like awe and compassion (Shiota, Keltner, & John, 2006), the tendency to express specific emotions like anger (Spielberger, 1996), shame and guilt (Tangney, 1990), embarrassment (Miller, 1995), and fear (Spielberger, 1983), as well as emotions in relation to others such as gratitude (McCullough, Tsang, & Emmons, 2004) and empathy (Davis, 1983).

In a useful development of the diary method called experience sampling (see box), which minimizes forgetting, participants are beeped on a handheld device at random times during the day, and at that instant they provide information about their current feelings (Barrett & Barrett, 2001; Bolger, Davis, & Refaeli, 2003).

Specific Emotions and Core Affect

Appraisals give rise to emotional responses—facial expressions, vocalizations, movements of the body, and patterns of autonomic and central nervous system activation. We have experiences of anger, desire, or awe, for example, in all of their complexities. The nature of emotional experience—how it arises—in many ways remains mysterious to science. But we can ask two questions.

First, what are the fundamental elements of emotional experience? Reizensein (1992a) has pointed out that attempts to answer this question have taken two forms. In one form, the experience of certain basic emotions that include happiness, sadness, anger, and fear is taken as being irreducible. This, for instance, is the position of Oatley and Johnson-Laird (1987), and one that found support in diary studies of emotion (Oatley & Duncan, 1984) and observations that a small number of emotions or moods can occur in a **free-floating** form without any relation to external events, for instance, the emotional auras of certain kinds of epileptic seizure (MacLean, 1993) or the experience that Gazzaniga's (1988) split-brain patient had of being scared. The basic emotions cannot be reduced to lower-level components, although they can be labeled superordinately as pleasant or unpleasant. A related idea, based on the different states of readiness that emotions set up, is that of **ur-emotions**, states that are, as it were, primitive emotions that have some but not all the qualities of full emotions (Frijda & Parrott, 2011).

In the second form, Reizensein says that the experience of emotions might derive from elements that are not themselves emotions. So, for instance, Russell (2003) has proposed good versus bad (valence) and enervation versus energization (arousal) as the two underlying dimensions of emotional experience, which together make up core affect (which we discussed earlier in the chapter; see also Barrett & Bliss-Moreau, 2009). Good versus bad is something people can readily report. Enervation versus energization is a bit more problematic, but here Barrett et al. (2004) have found, by combining experience sampling with continuous autonomic measurement, that people can often report on this dimension, though some are more aware of it than others. Core affect, the reasoning goes, reflects the most fundamental and continuing assessments of how one is doing in the world. When experienced in more global terms, it is felt as more diffuse moods ("I feel unenthusiastic" or "I feel energetic").

If distinct basic emotions are primitives of experience (as argued by Oatley & Johnson-Laird, 1987), an emotion or mood is a basic state and a complex emotion derives from it by adding secondary appraisals about the emotion's cause, its object, and plans in relation to it. In the alternative scheme due to Russell (2003), primary appraisal is of core affect (good versus bad plus energization) and secondary appraisal is based on cognitive attributions of the core affect. In either case we have a primary stage, and in either case the secondary appraisal supplies meaning to the experience. The second stage is constructed: some of it is idiosyncratic, some is influenced by family upbringing, and some is influenced by culture.

A further question pertains to how other emotion-related responses enter emotional experience. Many researchers who pursue the idea of basic emotions follow *bottom-up* assumptions, and say that the experience of emotion tracks somatovisceral changes in the musculature of the body and peripheral physiological systems (e.g., Matsumoto, 1987). According to this view, somatovisceral changes serve as input into the online assessment of the individual's adaptation to the environment. This approach presupposes processes that are sensitive to interoceptive changes and to bodily movements such as facial muscle contraction. Over 20 studies indicate that experiences of specific emotions (e.g., anger, disgust, embarrassment, love, desire) covary with emotion-specific facial muscle movements (Hess et al., 1995; Keltner & Bonanno, 1997; for review, see Matsumoto et al., 2008). But although some studies find associations between bodily responses and emotional experience (e.g., Eisenberg et al., 1989; Shearn et al., 1990), others do not (Cacioppo et al., 2000). Mauss and Robinson (2009) review the three kinds of measures of emotion: (a) behavioral (including expressions), (b) physiological, and (c) self-reported conscious-experiential. They conclude that the underlying system of each is somewhat separate and that one of them cannot always be taken as standing for another.

The approach associated with core affect is more *top-down*. It holds that the experience of emotion is a conceptual act. Primary appraisals of goodness or badness and of energization trigger core affect, and this then becomes invested with attributions that arise from the situation, which can then be grounded in language (e.g., Barrett, 2006; Russell, 2003).

It is likely that both bottom-up and top-down processes offer important insights into understanding emotions. Phenomena of emotion range far in the brain and mind. Appraisals, intentions, and readiness occur in relation to events and to people in the social world. Emotional components of expression, physiology, and experience are not always aligned. Emotions are complex and are affected by context.

SUMMARY

Appraisals are evaluations of events in relation to an individual's goals or concerns. We started this chapter by thinking about how primary automatic appraisals occur unconsciously, when objects or events are evaluated in terms of the appropriateness of an event to a goal. Secondary appraisals then occur when we identify what caused an emotion and when we think what we might do about it. We showed how secondary appraisal varies across different cultures, and how there are arguments for both discrete and dimensional approaches. The important social process of tertiary appraisal starts when we turn our emotions into verbal forms and share them with others. Putting emotions into words helps focus emotional experience and enables us to explore implications, for instance, in metaphorical ways and in relation to others. Some aspects of emotions are best seen as prototypes or scripts, but at the same time there seem to be boundaries in people's representations of emotions. We introduced some of the approaches to measuring emotions: any emotion may have aspects of conscious experience that we can report and reflect on, behavioral expression, and physiological changes. These do not always cohere. They are best seen as different aspects of widely distributed processes.

TO THINK ABOUT AND DISCUSS

1. Think about a happy emotion that you are interested in, perhaps love or enjoyment of what you are doing, and reflect on what generally causes it for you. What concerns are at issue? Do the same for a negative emotion such as anger or sadness.

2. What functions for you has the expression of emotions in verbal forms?

3. There are three systems of emotion: behavioral (as in facial expressions and gestures), physiological (e.g., heart rate and skin conductance), and experiential (what you are conscious of). Why do you think these systems are not always closely coordinated?

FURTHER READING

For a cognitive account of emotions and their nature:
Nico Frijda (2007). *The laws of emotion.* Mahwah, NJ: Erlbaum.

An excellent review of appraisal is:
Agnes Moors (2009). Theories of emotion causation: A review. *Cognition and Emotion,* **23**, 625–662.

For a discussion of emotion in relation to language and metaphor:

Zoltán Kövesces (2003). *Metaphor and emotion.* Cambridge, MA: Cambridge University Press.

For a dimensional account of emotions:
James Russell (2003). Core affect and the psychological construction of emotion. *Psychological Review,* **110**, 145–172.

EMOTIONS AND SOCIAL LIFE

PART III

Development of Emotions in Childhood

8

This chapter written with Mark Wade

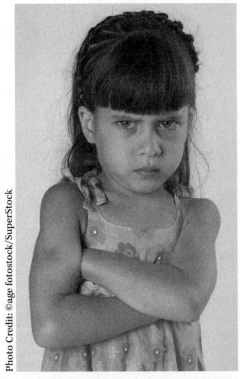

Photo Credit: ©age fotostock/SuperStock

FIGURE 8.0 The picture shows a little girl with characteristic facial and postural expressions of anger.

> . . . *for all the time of our infancy and child-hood, our senses were joint-friends in such sort with our Passions, that whatsoever was hurtfull to the one was enemy to the other* . . .
>
> *Thomas Wright,* The Passions of the Minde in Generall *(1604)*

Emotional development is social development. We think of children as emotional beings: they cry, they laugh, and they get angry, generally in relation to other people. What's known about the development of children's emotions? Are these emotions different from those of adults, or are they much the same?

Children's emotions contribute mightily to their overall development (e.g., Denham et al., 2003; Eisenberg, Spinrad, & Morris, 2002; Saarni, 1990). Abilities to express, recognize, and regulate emotions have profound effects on functioning in many areas of life. Although a newborn can be described as a bundle of reflexes, by the end of the first year, she or he is clearly a social being whose sociality is organized around emotions. A good introduction to infant development, including emotions and social life, is by Slater and Lewis (2007; see also Bremner & Slater, 2004). Kopp and Neufeld (2003) trace the patterns of research on infant emotions from the 1930s to recent times, including the role of emotions in social life.

In this chapter we examine children's emotional development in three main areas: emotional expression, emotion recognition, and emotion regulation, with a final section on genetics of emotion in relation to the environment. Themes of emotional development continue in Chapters 9 and 11.

Theories of Emotional Development

Emotion is the first language of us all. Within seconds of birth, the human baby makes its first communication: it starts crying. According to Paul MacLean, such sounds during evolution were momentous. Reptiles are largely silent. With the emergence of mammals, sounds signaled the beginnings of a new kind of adaptation in which social cooperation began to emerge (see Lambert, 2003 for review). Understanding emotional development includes understanding how emotional expressions enable infant and parent to communicate (Matsumoto, Keltner, Shiota, O'Sullivan, & Frank, 2008) and how such expressions take on the forms of culture and individuality.

Emotions such as joy, sadness, anger, and fear influence an individual's thoughts and behavior (e.g., Bechara, Damasio, & Damasio, 2000; Lerner & Keltner, 2000). Here, we briefly outline three theories of how such emotions emerge in the first years of life.

The first is **differential emotions theory** as articulated by Carroll Izard (1991, 2007, 2011). This describes discrete or basic emotions such as joy, sadness, anger, disgust, and fear as "natural kinds," based on hardwired systems that mature during development on a kind of developmental timetable. According to this theory, every basic emotion has a set of neural, expressive, and feeling components that occur automatically and nonconsciously in response to specific events (Izard, 2007). The response pattern that is generated by each emotion is rather restricted and stereotypical (see Öhman & Mineka, 2001), but it can be modified via information processing mechanisms (e.g., Cunningham et al., 2004; Oster, 2005). From this standpoint, emotional development is due to maturation and particular types of interaction that lead to distinct emotions.

A second and related perspective is based on **differentiation** theory. The idea is that infants start out with two basic emotion states of negativity/distress and positivity/pleasure. More differentiated emotions emerge later during development, perhaps as a result of changes in hedonic tone and general arousal. This view was originally conceptualized in 1932 by Katherine Bridges, who described infant emotion as a state of diffuse excitement, which would differentiate into positive and negative affect, and eventually into the discrete emotions of joy, sadness, anger, fear, and so on. The mechanism through which specific emotional states come to exist involves biological maturation (Lewis & Michalson, 1983) and interactive experiences with one's environment (Morris, Silk, Steinberg, Myers, & Robinson, 2007).

The third theory of emotional development is the **functionalist** view (e.g., Saarni, Campos, Camras, & Witherington, 2006). This theory describes emotions as relational processes in which children establish, alter, and maintain their relationship with the environment, especially the environment of caregivers, siblings, and other people. Under this model, an emotion is not simply an intrapersonal feeling: it has interpersonal consequences. Emotions are profoundly social. Joy may signal success toward a particular goal, sadness may connote a loss, and anger is a response to the blockage of one's goals, usually by someone else. Facial expressions are not conceived of as unconscious behavioral/physiological responses to emotional situations, but rather as signals that communicate to others. They differ depending on the audience, the event, and its personal relevance. Emotional development takes place as children establish new goal states and new ways of evaluating emotional events, and as their relationships with others change over time (Witherington & Crichton, 2007).

Emotional Expression

To examine the emotional experiences of young children, we rely on observations of behavior, such as facial expressions, vocal overtures, and gestures. We assume that these expressions are indicative of underlying emotions.

Basic Emotions: Developmental Emergence

Different kinds of emotions emerge at different stages of development. We can think of the first set of emotions that appear as basic, because they have been recognized by researchers who have experimented with specific kinds of events and tried to detect distinct kinds of emotion. The emergence of such emotions can be thought of as a sequence of steps in building an emotional repertoire that will support functioning in a complex social world.

Crying occurs in very young infants. One might take it to indicate a state of undifferentiated distress/irritability in response to a wide range of discomforts. Likewise, satiation, attention, and interest in the environment may represent a state of general pleasure (see Lewis, 1993). As far as expressions of distinct emotions go, the earliest seems to be disgust, which can be seen in newborns in response to sour tastes. Steiner et al. (2001) have shown that the expressions that human infants make to sour tastes are similar to those of other primates.

By the time babies are about 2 months old, expressions of joy/happiness occur (Lavelli & Fogel, 2005): smiles. Although babies occasionally give off smiles in their first month, they are probably not social as they are often made during sleep (Messinger, 2002). Properly social smiles emerge after the first month (Messinger & Fogel, 2007). In the second month smiles occur with gentle stroking, and by the third month they occur frequently in interaction with caregivers (Striano, Henning, & Stahl, 2005), and this is inferred to indicate positive emotion. Three-month-olds also smile in response to the same kinds of events that make older children smile: attention from others, invitations to play, and even mastery of goals (see Lewis, 2010; Lewis & Ramsay, 2005). Infant smiles are a source of interest and delight for parents, so that one function of smiling may be to engage caregivers. Recent evidence suggests that, during parent–child interactions, children's emotional displays affect their parent's emotions more than the reverse (Beebe et al.,

Photo Credit: ©Elizabeth Crews/The Image Works

Photo Credit: ©Robert Matton AB/Alamy

FIGURE 8.1   Babies showing emotional expressions: (a) a positive or happy expression, (b) a negative expression.

2007; Chow, Haltigan, & Messinger, 2010). These positive expressions may function to increase parents' talk, play, and interaction with their child (Huebner & Izard, 1988).

Some researchers have observed that infants show expressions of anger at 4 to 6 months (Stenberg, Campos, & Emde, 1983; Bennett, Bendersky, & Lewis, 2002a,b, 2005). Using a coding scheme for facial expressions developed by Izard, Bennett and colleagues (2002a,b) examined 4-month-olds' facial expressions in response to situations that are expected to produce certain emotions. Children showed more anger expressions during arm restraint than during any other situation (tickling, jack-in-the-box, and appearance of a masked stranger). However, during arm restraint more children demonstrated surprise than anger, which reveals that children respond emotionally in different ways to the same stimulus. In a follow-up study, Bennett et al. (2005) showed that, by 12 months, children exhibited more anger reactions in response to arm restraint than to any other situation, and arm restraint produced more expressions of anger than any other emotional display, except for joy, which occurred at a similar rate to anger. Also, the number of interest and surprise expressions in response to arm restraint declined between 4 and 12 months (see Figure 8.2). This suggests that distinct emotional expressions become more organized and differentiated over the first year of life, although by the end of this period they still do not have the specificity one sees in older children.

As to sadness, infants make sad faces at 4 months, but again we need to ask whether sadness in an infant has the same meaning as sadness in an adult. Michael Lewis and his colleagues (2005,

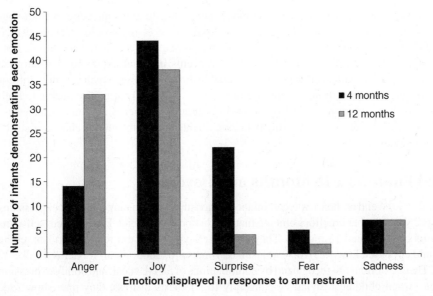

FIGURE 8.2 The number of children of 4 months and 12 months who exhibited different kinds of emotion in response to arm restraint in Bennett et al.'s (2005) study.

2006) found that facial expressions of sadness but not anger were accompanied by increased cortisol levels—a pattern that we might expect to see for adults. But we also see sad expressions in response to disgust elicitors (Bennett et al., 2005). Thus for sadness it is hard to be certain as to the age at which the emotional expression of sadness means the same thing as it does for an adult.

Most evidence indicates that fear emerges somewhat later in development, at about 7 months (see Lewis, 1993), perhaps in unison with children's growing ability to move in the physical environment (Campos et al., 2000). Bennett et al. (2002a,b) have shown that, in response to the fear-provoking situation of a masked stranger, 4-month-old children demonstrate more surprise, joy, and anger expressions than fear expressions. In their study, children showed fear expressions in response to a wide range of eliciting events that had nothing dangerous about them. Camras, Oster et al. (2007) found in a study of 11-month-old American, Chinese, and Japanese infants that cross-cultural differences in expression were small and that, although there was evidence that fear-eliciting and anger-eliciting events did produce the expected emotions, fear and anger expressions could not be reliably distinguished according to the context in which they occurred. In a recent study, Braungart-Rieker, Hill-Soderlund, and Karrass (2010) examined trajectories in children's fear expressions from 4 to 16 months. They showed that children exhibited fearful responses to strangers at 4 months, but this effect was weak. These fear responses increased over time, up until 12 months, and then leveled off between 12 and 16 months. Thus, the largest growth in fear expressions occurred between 4 and 12 months. Interestingly, these effects were moderated by children's temperament and mothers' level of sensitivity. Higher levels of temperamental fear predicted more fearful reactivity, whereas having a more sensitive mother was associated with a slower rate of increase in fear over time.

As to surprise, Bennett et al. (2002a,b) have shown that at 4 months expressions of this emotion are common in response to situations expected to elicit surprise, such as a jack-in-the-box.

However, surprise was also the most common reaction to situations intended to elicit anger and fear. This again points to a lack of specificity. In a sample of 11-month-olds, Camras et al. (2002) coded facial expressions of surprise to a surprising event and to a baseline condition. There was no difference between the surprise and baseline events in facial expressions of surprise. The surprising event was, however, frequently greeted by bodily stilling, which was only infrequently seen in the baseline condition. Scherer, Zentner, and Stern (2004) were also unable to find facial expressions of surprise in 5-to-14-month-old children. However, situations expected to elicit surprise were accompanied by freezing behavior. So this may be the unique characteristic of early surprise reactions.

Social Emotions: 18 Months and Beyond

Although, by the end of their first year, infants demonstrate a wide range of basic expressions, over the next 2 years further emotions emerge that are distinctively social. For instance, **self-conscious emotions** begin around 18 months. They include empathy, concern-related altruism, embarrassment, and envy (see Lewis, 2010; Warneken & Tomasello, 2006; Zahn-Waxler & Radke-Yarrow, 1990). These emotions are recognized by combinations of facial, vocal, and bodily expressions. For example, when children respond empathically to another's distress, they may show sad facial expressions, approach/comforting behaviors, and verbal concern, for instance, "You okay, Mommy?" Between 12 and 24 months children respond to another's distress by comforting, bringing a parent, or offering an object (Zahn-Waxler et al., 1992). At this age, children tend to offer comfort in ways that they themselves like to be comforted. By three years, however, children offer comfort in a manner tailored to the individual needs of others. For instance, children comfort a child in distress by fetching the child's mother. They are also more likely to respond with concern to distress that they have caused (Zahn-Waxler et al., 1992).

Sometime between the second and third year of life a more complex set of emotions is expressed, including pride, shame, guilt, and regret. These have been referred to as the **self-conscious evaluative emotions** (Lewis, 2010). For example, if a child is given a toy to play with by his mother, he may smile, suggesting happiness. If the child makes no attempt to pick up the toy, however, he doesn't show pride. Emotions such as pride require the ability to compare one's behavior with some social standard and to evaluate successes and failures. The capacity for such appraisals is not present before the third year of life (Lewis, 1997; Stipek, Recchia, & McClintic, 1992). Thus, by the time children are 3 years old they possess an extensive emotional repertoire.

Developmental Progression of Emotions

Now we consider the processes in children's cognitive development that enable the emergence of specific emotions. Let us begin with joy/happiness. Does some developing cognitive process contribute to the expression of this emotion? It appears that changes in visual attention parallel the emergence of smiling (Lavelli & Fogel, 2005; Messinger & Fogel, 2007). Lavelli and Fogel (2005) examined infants' expressions of happiness during mother–child interactions on a weekly basis from birth to 3 months. One-month-old infants switched between simple attention to their mother's face and neutral gazes away from the face. By 2 months, children showed more concentrated attention to the mother's face, with more fixations on the head, mouth, and eyes. This pattern of attention was closely followed by social smiling. Thus, the ability to attend to elicitors of happiness, for instance, Mom's face, may be required to experience that emotion.

By 3 to 4 months infants expect caregivers to respond to their overtures (Van Egeren, Barratt, & Roach, 2001). When there's no response to an overture, sadness tends to occur. Thus, in addition to hopelessness and loss of control, experiencing sadness is associated with a growing capacity to generate expectations for social events and to recognize violations of those expectations.

What about anger? This emotion usually emerges after happiness, at 4 to 6 months. Anger is a manifestation of frustration, and frustration is a response to the blockage of one's goals. Anger is usually conceptualized as an emotional reaction to obstacles. Unlike happiness, for instance, experiencing anger requires knowledge of the goal one is trying to achieve and understanding that one cannot successfully achieve this goal. Anger expressions are thus associated with children's means–end knowledge at around 6 months of age (Braungart-Rieker et al., 2010; Lewis, 1997). Further advances in cognitive development help to explain the emergence of fearfulness at around 8 months. Fearfulness requires the ability to compare a potentially threatening encounter with similar events in memory (Schaffer, 1974; Skarin, 1977). Therefore, fear reflects, among other things, an increase in memory capacity (see Lewis, 1997) and visual discrimination (Braungart-Rieker et al., 2010) over the first year of life.

As we discussed in Chapter 4, many researchers believe that appraisals cause emotions. For children, the prediction of appraisal theory is that when an event such as seeing Mom is consistent with a goal (wanting Mom to be present), joy will occur. If this event is predicted but is uncertain, then the child will experience hope rather than joy. If an event occurs such as Mom leaving, the child will experience sadness. If this same event may occur, but is not certain, the child may experience fear instead of sadness. Although there has been a good deal of research on types of elicitors in relation to types of emotion, being able to tie this to children's appraisals is of course very challenging because young children have a limited capacity to describe internal experience.

The development of **consciousness** and **mentalizing** abilities in the second year (Lewis, 1992) allows for experiences of empathy and embarrassment. These emotions entail two complementary processes. On the one hand, children must understand the subjectivity of others' experiences. For example, if a child responds empathically to the distress of an injured adult by asking questions or seeking help (Zahn-Waxler et al., 1992), she shows a rudimentary understanding that the other person is in a state that is different from her own. For other emotions, children must understand that they can be the object of another person's attention. To experience embarrassment, for instance, a child must realize that he is subject to social evaluations of other people. This entails an awareness of the objectivity of one's own body, that is to say self-recognition. This ability to self-recognize is typically assessed in the mirror-rouge paradigm (Amsterdam, 1972). In these tasks, children are marked with a spot of rouge and then look into a mirror. Children who detect the mark and demonstrate self-directed behavior are said to recognize the objectivity of their own body. This ability emerges around 18 months (Brownell, Zerwas, & Ramani, 2007; Nielsen & Dissanayake, 2004). Awareness of the self allows an individual to reflect on courses of action when making decisions, as well as to generate new solutions to problems. Lewis (1997) has called self-recognition the core marker of consciousness, permitting the onset of self-conscious emotions. In support of this claim, it has been shown that children who are capable of self-recognition are more likely to show both embarrassment (Lewis et al., 1989; see Table 8.1) and empathy (Bischof-Köhler, 1991). Also around 18 months, children become capable of understanding that they can be the target of others' emotional displays. For example, Repacholi and Meltzoff (2007) have shown that children are less likely to imitate another person's actions when these displays elicit negative reactions from others. Self-reflection and self–other differentiation represent key

Table 8.1 **Numbers of children who showed embarrassment as a function of whether they recognized themselves from the rouge-on-the-nose test (from Lewis et al., 1989)**

	Showed self-recognition	Did not show self-recognition
Showed embarrassment	19	5
Showed no embarrassment	7	13

cognitive milestones in the emergence of the self-conscious emotions in the second year of life.

The development of the last class of socially based emotions—pride, shame, guilt, regret, and the like—is accompanied by further cognitive development between the ages of 2 and 4. A major element of cognition contributing to emotional development at this stage is language. Dunn (2004) says that children have the "ability and propensity to talk about and reflect on emotions as soon as they begin to use language" (p. 307).

Children start talking about internal states around 18 months, and the proportion of time they spend talking about emotions gradually increases with age. By 2 years, children use the emotion words *happy*, *sad*, *mad*, and *scared* (Wellman, Harris, Banerjee, & Sinclair, 1995). Although they mainly talk about their own feelings at this age, they also attribute emotions of these same kinds to other people. So children as young as 2 years have mentalistic conceptions about emotions: they know that emotions are about certain kinds of events, and that consequences of emotions are different from the emotion itself (Widen & Russell, 2010). Two-year-olds also appear to understand the desires of others. For example, they are able to give an adult experimenter the food the experimenter likes even when it is different from the food the children themselves prefer (Repacholi & Gopnik 1997). They also understand that fulfillment of a desire will lead to positive emotions, and that a desire unfulfilled will give rise to negative emotions (Wellman & Woolley, 1990). This is an important step in understanding the experiences of others and why people behave the way they do. With this information, children become more capable of engaging in social activities such as cooperation.

A critical milestone around 18 months is children's capacity for both cooperation (Warneken, Chen, & Tomasello, 2006) and altruism (Warneken & Tomasello, 2006). Warneken and Tomasello have shown that 18-month-old children will engage in actions that are different from their partner in order to achieve a joint goal. For example, young children will hold up their end of a squishy trampoline in order to make an object bounce up and down. In this case the end goal of the object bouncing on the trampoline is satisfying to both partners. Interestingly, Tomasello and colleagues have also shown that, even when there is nothing to be gained by the 18-month-old child, she will still engage in an altruistic gesture to help someone else (see Table 8.2 and Figure 8.3). Figure 8.3 shows the helpfulness of the child in the experimental condition (the adult needs help to complete an action) and in the control condition (the adult does not require help).

It is not until the age of 3 or 4 that children begin to attribute representational states to people, such as beliefs, thoughts, and knowledge (Wellman, Cross, & Watson, 2001). For instance, they may reason that "John cheated because he believed the teacher was not in the room." According to Widen & Russell (2010), this conceptual shift in children's understanding of others' minds

Table 8.2   Problems used by Warneken & Tomasello (2006) in their study of altruism in 18-month-olds

Category	Task name	Problem
Out of reach	Marker	Adult accidentally drops marker on floor (experimental), versus throws marker down (control)
Obstacle	Cabinet	Adult wants to put magazines in cabinet but doors are closed and he bumps into them (experimental), versus bumps into doors as he tries to lift magazines onto the cabinet (control)
Wrong result	Books	Book slips from stack as adult tries to put it on top of stack (experimental) or puts book next to stack (control)
Wrong means	Flap	Spoon drops through hole in box and adult tries to reach through and get it, without knowing he could get it via a flap at the side of the box (experimental), versus throws spoon into hole in box (control)

"complements and perhaps underlies their fuller understanding of emotion concepts they already have in elementary form and their division of emotion into ever finer discrete categories" (p. 356). Indeed, a significant characteristic of the social emotions we observe in 3- and 4-year-olds is that they involve beliefs about eliciting situations. Pride, for example, is a feeling of accomplishment and joy based on the belief that one has successfully reached a goal. Shame involves feeling bad about something based on the belief that one has let down or disgraced others. Thus, the capacity to attribute beliefs to oneself or others between the third and fourth year of life closely parallels the development of these social emotions. This is consistent with the notion that social/moral emotions can be observed in preschool children (Aksan & Kochanska, 2005). However, it may not be until 5 or 6 years of age that children connect others' beliefs to their emotions. That is, although 3- and 4-year-olds may understand that people behave

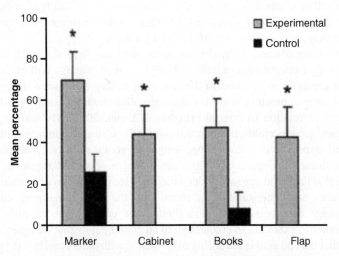

FIGURE 8.3   Mean percentage of 18-month-olds in Warneken and Tomasello's (2006) study who tried to help the adult experimenter in experimental and control conditions.

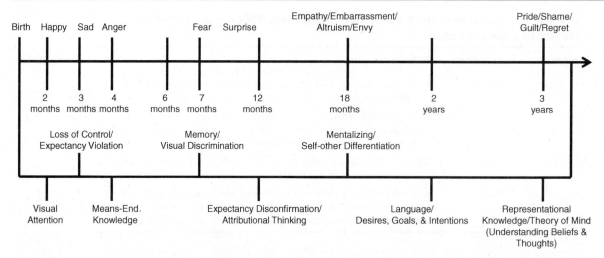

FIGURE 8.4 Summary timelines for the developmental progression of emotional expression. The top line shows the age at which certain emotions are expressed, and the bottom line shows the cognitive milestones associated with the emergence of various expressions across time.

according to beliefs, they may not fully understand that emotions are impacted by these beliefs (de Rosnay & Harris, 2002).

In general, the ability to understand oneself and others in terms of mental states (emotions, desires, and beliefs)—termed **theory of mind**—is critically important for children's socioemotional development. As this ability becomes more sophisticated across time, children acquire the mentalistic tools to understand the full range of emotions, thereby supporting their ability to participate in social interactions with others. Jenkins and Astington (2000) in a longitudinal study showed that theory of mind was responsible for children's increased capacity to engage in joint plans. Thus, the ability to represent the internal states of others, including their beliefs, paves the way to establishing and executing joint goals. See Figure 8.4 for a summary of the developmental progression in emotional expression from birth to preschool.

As children's theory of mind is developing, so are their language skills. By the time children are 3 years old, Judy Dunn and her colleagues (1991) have shown that half of the conversations they have about emotions are related to the causes of feelings. Between the ages of 3 and 7, children become more competent in talking about negative emotions, such as sadness in relation to loss and anger in relation to control (Hughes & Dunn, 2002). By learning to talk about emotions and their causes, children move well beyond the simple communication system that facial and vocal expressions allow. Here, language about emotions becomes part of the negotiation of relationships and enables the development of shared meanings about internal states (Stern, 1985). The child can talk about a feeling, give her version of its cause, refer back to emotions, and alter her understanding of them. It is the child's maturing cognitive system (including language development) that facilitates her engagement in complex evaluative, reflective, and analytical thought in connection to an emotional event. We agree with Tomasello and colleagues that the end goal is the ability to cooperate with others and that the human-specific motivation to share emotions, goals, and experience with others inspires the construction of culture and society (Tomasello, 2010; Tomasello, Carpenter, Call, Behne, & Moll, 2005).

Developmental Changes in Elicitation and Expression

In addition to developmental changes in children's capacities to signal different emotions across time, there are also changes in the kinds of events that elicit specific emotions. Let us consider the emotion of fear. Fear of loud or sudden movements and of unfamiliar toys begins at 7 months, reaches a peak at the end of the first year, and then declines across time (Scarr & Salapatek, 1970). By the age of 4 or 5, children are often frightened by the imaginary: monsters, ghosts, and scary dreams (Bauer, 1976). In the early school years, fear about bodily injury and physical danger begins; and in adolescence, social concerns become the predominant causes of fear and anxiety (Liang et al., 2009). Elicitors change for other emotions as well. An infant may be frustrated by restraint, whereas a preschooler might be angry when excluded from a game. In adolescence, failure to perform well in school or with peers may cause anger. Anger is usually a response to blocked goals, and goals change over development. In conjunction with children's maturing cognitive systems, their exposure to different eliciting situations across time creates a range of new emotional experiences.

Across developmental time, children's overall expression of emotions also changes. For example, Sallquist et al. (2009) have shown that the intensity of both positive and negative emotions based on parent and teacher ratings, as well as the degree of emotional expressivity in general, decreases across the elementary school years. Larson et al. (2002) used the experience sampling method in which children carried handheld devices and recorded their emotions through the day. Results show that there is a downward shift in positive affect (see Figure 8.5) as well as an increase in negative affect from pre-to-late adolescence. Weinstein et al. (2007) also present interesting data on changes of mood during adolescence.

Children's emotional expressions are not necessarily the same across cultures. Linda Camras and her colleagues (Camras, Oster, Campos, & Bakeman, 2003) have found that, as compared to American infants, Chinese infants were less expressive overall, showed a dampened distress response, and produced fewer smiles. Interestingly, Japanese infants were more similar to

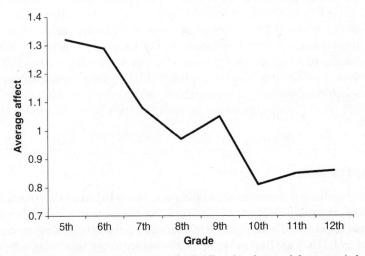

FIGURE 8.5 Average positive affect across middle childhood and into adolescence. (adapted from Larson et al., 2002).

American than to Chinese infants in their expressiveness. This finding challenges simplistic distinctions between Eastern and Western expressive behavior. Such differences may be due to parenting practices (Harkness & Super, 2002), including American mothers' propensity to encourage emotional expression compared to Chinese mothers. Further highlighting the contribution of culture is the finding that children living in the kibbutzim of Israel exhibited intense fear of strangers, whereas this fear was not seen in Israeli infants living in urban centers (Saarni et al., 2006). Thus, very specific elements of culture can be associated with emotion expression, even in seemingly similar populations.

To give a broad overall summary of the development of expression in children, we might say that when a 1-month-old baby cries, the mother tries to work out why: Is the child hungry, or sick, or wanting comfort? Parents do all the work. At age 2 the child has strong desires, which can get blocked, so the child can become very angry. At the same time this child can know when others are sad or angry, and with a vocabulary of several hundred words can ask about others' emotions, and can also learn what to do. At age 5, a child can take part happily in pretend play with a friend for hours, negotiating roles with concerns for fairness. In adolescence, kids can understand their own and others' emotions and can put aside their own feelings to respond to a friend.

Recognition of Emotions

For children to relate to others they must be able to recognize their emotions (Russell, Bachorowski, & Fernández-Dols, 2003). To this end, it has been suggested that emotion expression and recognition coevolved, such that both affect thoughts, emotions, and behavior (Izard, 2007).

Soon after birth, children begin to pick up information from others' faces, voices, and gestures. This ability is rooted in newborns' preference for human faces (de Haan, Pascalis, & Johnson, 2002) and voices (Grossman, Oberecker, Koch, & Friederici, 2010) compared to nonhuman stimuli. This preference is essential for newborns' ability to discriminate among people and to derive information about others' emotional states. According to Grossman (2010), emotion recognition relies on the interaction between the maturing perceptual system and the capacity to discriminate emotional information. For example, a newborn baby can only discriminate features of a face such as the nose, eyes, and mouth (Slater et al., 2000). As visual acuity improves over the first year (Gwiazda & Birch, 2011), infants become able to detect facial characteristics such as the distance between the brows and eyes or the width of the mouth (Cashon & Cohen, 2003). Thus, facial expressions become gradually more discernible (Leppänen & Nelson, 2008).

Facial Expressions

One method for studying recognition of facial expressions is **habituation**, based on the finding that infants look at patterns that are new to them for longer than patterns that are familiar. Infants can thus be presented with a picture of a facial expression (e.g., a happy face) until they no longer look at it. They are then presented with another happy face along with a new facial expression (e.g., a sad face). If they look at the new face more than the old face, this indicates that they can discriminate between the expressions. Using variations of this method, it has

Photo Credit: ©Elizabeth Crews/The Image Works

FIGURE 8.6 The visual cliff: visually the baby sees a steep drop—notice the finer grain of the checker-board pattern to the right of the baby's right knee—but actually a plate of thick glass supports the infant safely.

been shown that 2-to-3-month-old infants can discriminate happy, sad, and surprise expressions (Barrera & Maurer, 1981; Young-Browne et al., 1977). Four-to-six-month-olds can discriminate anger expressions (Montague & Walker-Andrews, 2001; Striano, Brennan, & Vanman, 2002), and 5-to-7-month-olds can discriminate fear (Bornstein & Arterberry, 2003). Notice that this pattern of development closely matches infants' expression of emotions.

By the end of the first year children start to move about independently. This is accompanied by **social referencing**, which is the ability to use the emotional displays of others to guide one's own behavior. The visual cliff provides an example (see Figure 8.6). In a classic experiment, Sorce, Emde, Campos, and Klinnert (1985) showed that 12-month-olds were likely to cross the visual cliff—a fear-provoking situation—when their mother looked happy (74% crossed), but were unlikely to cross when their mother looked fearful (none crossed). However, it is not totally clear that the children recognized specific emotions; they may have responded to the valence of the expression (positive or negative).

By preschool age, children have a modest ability to offer emotional labels for photographs, with happy, angry, and sad emerging first, followed by scared, surprised, and disgusted (Widen &

Russell, 2003). By school age, children are quite good at recognizing emotions in other people. Battaglia et al. (2004) found a 72% correct identification rate of pictures of emotional expressions—joy, fear, anger, disgust, sadness, surprise, and a neutral expression—by children in Grades 2 and 3. In general, recognition of facial emotions improves across the childhood years (Durand et al., 2007; Widen & Russell, 2008).

Vocal Expressions

Infants can recognize emotional expressions in their parents' voices, perhaps by prosodic aspects of speech, such as intonation (Morton & Trehub, 2001). For example, Mastropieri and Turkewitz (1999) have shown that newborns show more eye-opening behavior in response to happy versus sad or angry vocal expressions of their mothers, but only if the expressions are presented in their native language. Despite this early ability, it is not until about 5 months that infants can discriminate between happy, sad, and angry emotional voices (Flom & Bahrick, 2007).

Children's ability to recognize vocal expressions of emotion is also illustrated in studies of social referencing. Mumme et al. (1996) showed that, when shown a new toy, 12-month-old children demonstrated less engagement and more distress when their mothers expressed negative vocal emotions toward it. Vaish and Striano (2004) have also shown that infants are more likely to cross the visual cliff in response to positive vocal expressions or a combination of positive vocal and facial expressions, but not facial expressions alone. According to Mumme and Fernald (2003), 12-month-olds have the capacity to understand that emotions are object-directed, which may involve the ability to coordinate information about expressions and the directions of others' gaze. Thus, social referencing is based on the development of joint attention, which occurs in the second half of the first year (Carpenter et al., 1998; Moore & Dunham, 1995).

Postures and Gestures

Children's recognition of emotions from postures and gestures has been less studied than that of facial or vocal cues. A recent study by Nelson and Russell (2011a) tested 3-to-5-year-olds' ability to recognize happiness, sadness, anger, and fearfulness in three conditions. In the face-only condition, an actress produced expressions in which only the face and neck were visible to participants. In the voice-only condition, content-neutral vocal expressions were produced without any visual information. In the body posture–only condition, the actress's head and body were visible, but her face was blurred. The emotional postures were derived from previously validated displays of emotion (Aviezer et al., 2008). Results showed that children were most successful at recognizing emotions in the facial condition, then the postural condition, and finally the voice condition. It is also interesting to note that sadness was recognized earliest, followed by happiness, anger, and then fear (see Figure 8.7). These results show that postural cues are important for children in the recognition of emotion.

Multimodal Recognition of Emotions

How do children recognize emotions in their day-to-day lives? In the study by Nelson and Russell (2011a) described above, there was a condition in which children were required to

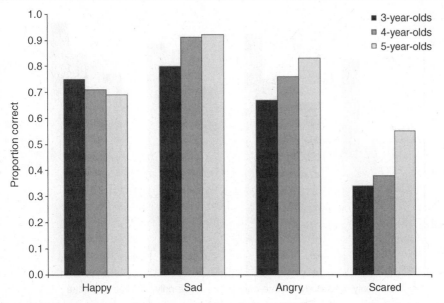

FIGURE 8.7 The proportion of correct responses to displays of discrete emotions as a function of age (from Nelson & Russell, 2011a).

label emotions after exposure to a combination of facial, vocal, and postural cues. This multi-cue condition enjoyed an advantage over the voice-only and body posture–only conditions, but not over the face-only condition; so no extra benefit was conferred from receiving information beyond that acquired from the face (see Figure 8.8). Perhaps, then, as children get older, they pick up cues from several sources but concentrate on the faces of others whose emotions they want to understand. In a study on social emotions, Nelson and Russell (2011b) showed that 6- and 7-year-olds were able to identify pride only when the expression contained both facial and postural cues together. By 8 years old, pride could be recognized by facial expressions alone.

Infants' Brain Mechanisms in the Recognition of Emotions

The amygdala (a brain structure discussed in Chapter 6) is fully developed in newborns and appears to have a role in directing infants' attention toward faces (see Johnson, 2005). The orbitofrontal cortex also has a role in the recognition of emotions, as seen by its activation in response to happy versus neutral faces in both 1-year-old infants and adults (Minagawa-Kawai et al., 2009). Findings of this kind point to certain early-developing brain mechanisms for recognition of facial expressions.

Humans have an evolved bias to attend to facial cues. The preparedness to process facial expressions may be specified by early-emerging neural circuits, but maturation of these circuits requires actual exposure to human facial expressions (Leppänen & Nelson, 2008). Individual experience, then, has an effect on the development of facial recognition. Pollack and colleagues provide a compelling example of this idea in their study of maltreated children. In their design,

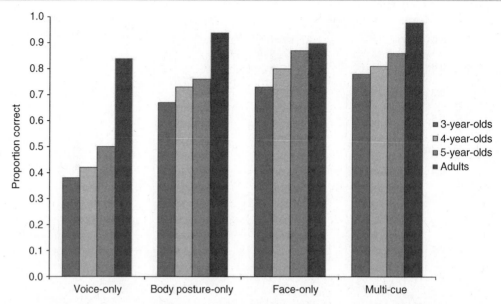

FIGURE 8.8 Proportion of emotional displays correctly recognized for different cue types (voice, posture, face, and multi-cue) by 3-to-5-year-old children and adults (from Nelson & Russell, 2011a).

faces with emotional expressions are presented to children, and the amount of useful visual information in the face is systematically manipulated by transforming the image from a structured to unstructured field (i.e., starting with an unstructured image that gains organization until, in the final image, it is a fully recognizable facial expression). Children who can recognize the emotion with less visual information are regarded as more sensitive to that expression. Using this method, it has been shown that children who have been maltreated show a heightened sensitivity to signals of anger and lower sensitivity to sadness (e.g., Pollack & Sinha, 2002; Pollack & Tolley-Schell, 2003; see Figure 8.9).

In the vocal domain Grossman et al. (2010) showed localized activity in the right temporal region of 7-month-old infants in response to happy or angry, but not neutral, voices. The amygdala was also activated in response to some vocal expressions of emotion, particularly fear (see Adolphs, 2002). Thus, the amygdala and the temporal regions may represent common areas associated with recognition of emotions across both facial and vocal modalities.

Grossman and colleagues (2006) presented facial and vocal expressions together, to 7-month-olds. They found stronger cortical activity when facial and vocal expressions were matched compared to when they were incongruent. These results are consistent with those of Flom and Bahrick (2007), who showed that infants could discriminate audiovisual expressions at 3 to 4 months, but could not discriminate vocal expressions alone until 5 months and could not discriminate facial expressions until 7 months. The finding that infants are better able to differentiate positive and negative vocal expressions, but not positive and negative facial expressions (see Fernald, 1992), lends support to the notion that the voice may convey more emotional information than the face early in development. As Nelson and Russell (2011a), described above, showed, however, the face may become more important for

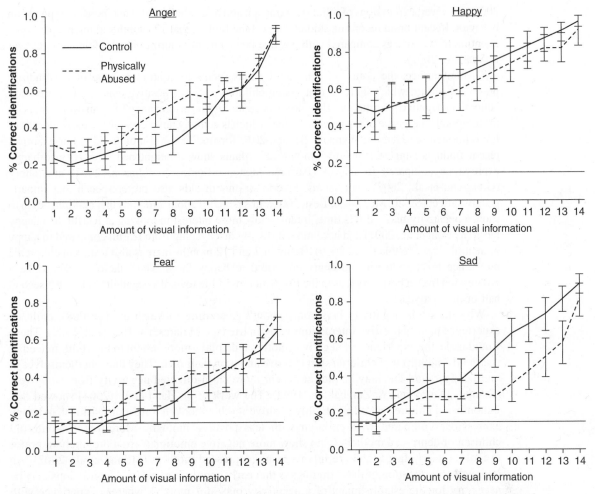

FIGURE 8.9 Numbers of correct identifications of four kinds of emotion as a function of the amount of visual information available in the face by children who were and were not physically abused (from Pollack & Sinha, 2002).

recognition once the visual system develops and children gain more experience with human faces.

The Negativity Bias

The negativity bias, which we discussed in Chapter 7, in which the bad affects us more strongly than the good, develops early in life and persists into adulthood. In support of this idea, Mumme and Fernald (2003) showed that 12-month-old infants were less likely to interact with a new object when an adult expressed a negative emotion toward it, but that positive expressions did not encourage children to interact with the object. Similar results show that infants are less likely to engage with an ambiguous toy when their mothers use kinaesthetic cues to convey fear (by increasing pressure around the child's abdomen and inhaling abruptly; Hertenstein & Campos,

2001); however, expressions of relief (relaxing tension and exhaling) did not increase exploration behavior. Recent brain recording studies support the finding that 12-month-old infants pay more attention to negative as compared with positive facial emotion during social referencing (Carver & Vaccaro, 2007).

On the surface, the notion of a negativity bias seems to contradict some of the findings presented earlier, which indicate that young children perceive positive emotional information better than negative information. How do we account for this discrepancy? The answer centers on the temporal emergence of the negativity bias, which is actually not present in the early months of life (although see Hamlin, Wynn, & Bloom, 2010 for findings in 3-month-olds). For example, recent findings suggest that 6-to-7-month-old infants show a heightened sensitivity to happy expressions compared to fearful (Farroni, Menon, Rigato, & Johnson, 2007) and angry (Grossman et al., 2007) expressions. Five-to-six-month-olds also prefer speech that imparts positive affect (Singh, Morgan, & Best, 2002). It is not until about 7 months that children begin to show a negativity bias. At this time, infants show more interest in looking at fearful than happy faces (Kotsoni et al., 2001) and have more difficulty disengaging from fearful compared to happy or neutral faces (Peltola et al., 2009). Between 7 and 12 months there is also a shift in children's preference to pay attention to angry compared to happy faces. Thus, there appears to be a progression from a positivity bias in the first 6 months of life toward a negativity bias in the second half of the first year.

Why does this negativity bias come about? According to Vaish et al. (2008), children experience mainly positive interactions early in life (see Malatesta & Haviland, 1982). These would make the experience of negative emotional displays more salient to the child. Indeed, it is around 7 months that children start to move about on their own. They thus put themselves in more danger, and this may be the reason for more child-directed negativity from caregivers (Campos, Kermoian, & Zumbahlen, 1992). The work of de Haan et al. (2004) showed that 7-month-old children who have highly positive mothers looked longer at fearful than happy expressions compared with children with less positive mothers. Moreover, 6-month-old children of depressed mothers (who show more negative emotions) are more likely to prefer to look at happy faces than are infants of nondepressed mothers (Striano et al., 2002). An interesting implication of these findings is that early exposure to positive interactions may be necessary for the establishment of a negativity bias at 7 months, whereas experience with negative affect may interfere with the development of this bias. These results emphasize the importance of interpersonal influences on emotional development.

Negativity bias has an evolutionarily adaptive function of prompting children to avoid potentially harmful circumstances. At the same time, interpersonal effects occur as children use the expressions of others to learn about the nature of objects and events. If children generalize the reactions of others, they come to know how to treat various objects and situations. When language emerges, talking about negative emotions with others (Lagattuta & Wellman, 2001) enables children to learn about other peoples' mental states, including their beliefs, desires, and intentions. Speaking about the reasons for certain outcomes enhances children's ability to think in mental terms about the causes of others' behavior. The negativity bias may, therefore, facilitate children's social-cognitive development. Finally, in learning about reasons for others' negative expressions, children can adjust their own behavior in ways that elicit more positive reactions from others. For example, by paying attention to the anger expressions of one's mother, learning about factors that cause the anger, and understanding the consequences of one's own behavior, a child may learn valuable lessons in emotion regulation.

Novels and Films: "My Oedipus Complex"

Although it's not a novel or a film, we're putting the short story, "My Oedipus Complex," by Frank O'Connor, in this box because, better than any other piece of fiction we know, it depicts the emotions of a young child. It's also one of the world's best short stories.

The story depicts the feelings and thoughts of 5-year-old Larry and his relationship with his parents. Larry recounts how his father would appear mysteriously from time to time, like Santa Claus, but mostly he was away during the war, so Larry has his mother to himself. He would get up in the morning, look from his window, then go to snuggle in his mother's bed and tell her his schemes for the day, which they would spend together. One day, father returns, and it's the end of the war, which the boy and his mother have been praying for. Out of uniform Larry's father seems altogether less interesting. During the day, Mother is looking anxious as Father talks to her. Naturally, Larry doesn't like his mother looking anxious, so he interrupts.

"'Do be quiet, Larry!' she said impatiently. 'Don't you hear me talking to Daddy?'"

"That was the first time I heard those ominous words, 'talking to Daddy.'"

Larry's mother gets his father to take the boy for a walk, but Larry finds this man is not good company. At teatime, "talking to Daddy" begins again, but Larry's father has an advantage. He reads pieces of the evening newspaper to Larry's mother.

"I felt this was foul play," thinks Larry.

Next morning, when Larry gets into his mother's bed, she reprimands him. "Don't wake Daddy." Another new development! He asks why.

"'Because poor Daddy is tired.' This seemed to me a quite inadequate reason, and I was sickened by the sentimentality of 'poor Daddy.' I never liked that sort of gush; it always struck me as insincere."

That night, Larry's mother gets the boy to promise not to come into the bed in the morning and wake his father. He promises. But, he can't keep the promise. Next morning, he gets into bed beside his mother. His mother says he can stay if he doesn't talk.

"But I want to talk," I wailed.

"'That has nothing to do with it,' she said with a firmness that was new to me . . . full of spite I gave father a kick."

Father wakes: "That damn child! Doesn't he ever sleep?"

Larry thinks the man looks very wicked, so he gets out of bed and dashes for the furthest corner, screeching.

"Father sat bolt upright in bed."

"'Shut up you little puppy!' he said in a choking voice."

"'Shut up you!' I bawled, beside myself."

Mother tries to intervene, and his father says: "He wants his bottom smacked."

"All his previous shouting was as nothing to these obscene words referring to my person. They really made my blood boil."

"'Smack your own!' I cried hysterically. 'Smack your own! Shut up! Shut up!'"

Life for Larry only gets worse when a new baby arrives. But there is a resolution in the end. Read this story; it's wonderful.

Regulation of Emotions

The concept of emotion regulation refers to the whole set of processes that modulate the onset, intensity, and duration of emotional experience, physiology, and expression (Eisenberg, Fabes, Guthrie, & Reiser, 2000; Eisenberg & Spinrad, 2004; Thompson, 2007). These processes may be automatic or voluntary. For example, a fearful experience may give rise automatically to physiological responses such as increased heart rate, yet a child may voluntarily decide to avoid making any expression that would indicate fear to others.

People often think of emotion regulation in individual terms: for instance, they might worry about how to control their anxiety. But emotion regulation is in many ways predominantly interpersonal. In childhood, caregivers are very concerned to modulate the emotions of their children: to soothe them when they are unhappy, to encourage them when they are joyful, to stop them having tantrums, to avoid occasions when fights might break out, and so on. As we will discuss when we approach emotion regulation in adulthood, in Chapter 14, an interpersonal emphasis continues to be the best way to conceptualize emotion regulation across the lifespan.

Regulatory Processes

Much research in developmental psychology has focused on interpersonal factors associated with emotion regulation (see Cole, Martin, & Dennis, 2004). For instance, as James Gross and Ross Thompson (2007) explain, regulation of emotions is often accomplished by means of changing the **situation**. The child's parents are usually responsible for managing a child's emotions by selecting play environments, creating predictable schedules, and offering a supportive emotional climate at home. A related process is trying to alter situations. A mother may help her child retrieve an out-of-reach toy, and so avoid a tirade. Children may prompt modifications by words and expressions. Indeed, when parents respond appropriately to their children's emotional displays, children are able to cope with their emotions more adaptively (Braungart-Rieker et al., 2010).

As children mature and experience different opportunities to learn to regulate their emotions, their abilities of **executive function** improve (Hughes, 2011). Executive function is the set of processes involved in being able to plan in relation to long-term goals and other people, to negotiate the unexpected, and to deal with dangers and with immediate emotions. An early-emerging example is managing attention. Rothbart, Ziaie, and O'Boyle (1992) found that children from 3 to 6 months pay attention to particular visual locations. Their ability to reorient is associated with less negative emotion and more soothability (see Rothbart, Sheese, Rueda, & Posner, 2011). Being able to disengage from an emotionally upsetting event by shifting attention elsewhere is an effective way for infants to regulate their social and emotional experience. Poor executive functioning is strongly linked in 4-year-olds to problem behaviors such as being unable to concentrate and being oppositional and difficult for parents (Hughes & Ensor, 2008). Executive functioning continues to develop well into adulthood.

Another method of regulating emotions is by **cognitive change**, which refers to altering the way an emotionally charged situation is appraised (Gross & Thompson, 2007). For example, a child may interpret an event as "Billy pushed me" or interpret it as "Billy bumped into me because the hallway was so crowded." Changing the meaning changes the emotional impact. This kind of reappraisal (Gross, 2002) can be fostered by parents' explanations of emotional situations (Root & Jenkins, 2005). However, the ability to appraise needs an understanding that events can be interpreted in different ways. This involves both beliefs and the ability to change one's beliefs. Children's power to make reappraisals and mental transformations depends on their cognitive maturation.

Finally, emotions can be regulated by **behavioral and physiological change**. Unlike the previous methods of regulation, this involves changing emotions once they are underway. Unfortunately, little research has been done on specific emotions that individuals attempt to regulate across the life span. However, there is evidence that controlling positive emotional experience is easier than controlling negative experience (Thompson, 1992). Attempts to mask emotions are common in adolescence and young adulthood, particularly in response to social situations (Gross, Richards, & John, 2006). These attempts to alter emotional expressions such as disgust increase sympathetic nervous system activation (Gross & Levenson, 1997). As a result, it is possible to have an incongruity between behavioral and physiological responses during an emotional event such that behaviors decrease while physiological responses rise.

Whereas a young child may be able only to look away from an upsetting event or close his eyes, a teenager may be able to select and modify the situation, distract himself, and cognitively reappraise the situation. Using multiple forms of regulation simultaneously may prove most effective at controlling one's emotions (Gross & Thompson, 2007).

Neurobiological Development of Emotion Regulation

Starting early in life, the diffuse excitatory processes that underlie arousal become more ordered. This includes changes in the hypothalamic-pituitary-adrenocortical (HPA) axis in response to stressful events (Gunnar & Quevedo, 2007), as well as maturational changes in the autonomic nervous system. This results in less marked changes of arousal, which allows other child- and parent-initiated regulatory processes to operate effectively. As mentioned earlier, one rudimentary strategy that infants use to regulate emotional experience is attentional control, which enables them to disengage from emotionally arousing situations (see Posner & Rothbart, 2000). The parasympathetic nervous system—which undergoes rapid development in the first year of life—is particularly important in this regard (Porges, 2003). As we discussed in Chapter 5, the vagus nerve lowers heart rate and is calming. During an emotionally arousing event good vagal tone implies successful regulation (Porges, 2003). It has been linked to attentional control and emotion regulation in infancy. DeGangi, DiPietro, Greenspan, and Porges (1991) have shown that regulatory-disordered infants—who have problems with behavioral control, sleep, feeding, self-calming, and regulation of mood—have lower vagal tone than children who regulate more successfully. Differences in vagal tone contribute to differences in emotion regulation in infants (Bazhenova, Plonskaia, & Porges, 2001) and preschoolers (Calkins, Graziano, & Keane, 2007; Calkins & Keane, 2004). Children with higher baseline vagal tone tend to be able to regulate their emotions more effectively.

Furthermore, cortical control over arousal develops across childhood, beginning with the growth of rudimentary forebrain inhibitory centers at 2 to 4 months (see Thompson, 1994; also see Chapter 6). This is manifested not only in improved attentional control, but also in the diminution of neonatal reflexes and the onset of more conventional sleep patterns. However, most of these inhibitory controls are not fully developed until well after birth. At about 9 to 10 months, response inhibition becomes more advanced as neural development (i.e., formation and connectivity) of the frontal lobes progresses (see Fox, 1991). Response inhibition affords children the ability to regulate overt expressions of emotions and tolerate arousing situations. In the second year of life, language becomes important in moderating emotions both through talk with others about the meaning and consequences of emotional experiences and, later in development, through self-directed calming (see Thompson, Lewis, & Calkins, 2008).

It has recently been shown that there is not much functional connectivity between brain structures during infancy, but that these connections become stronger by 2 years of age (Gao et al., 2009). By 2 years the functional brain network resembles the adult network, including the medial prefrontal cortex and posterior cingulate cortex. Whereas brain networks in infants are characterized by local anatomical connections, later in development these networks show longer range connectivity with separate regions of the brain being able to communicate with one another (Fair et al., 2009). For example, by age 2 the anterior cingulate cortex—which is critical for executive function (a theorized cognitive system that controls and manages other cognitive processes)—shows strong connectivity to the frontal and parietal areas, and this connectivity continues to increase throughout childhood (Rothbart et al., 2011).

By 3 to 5 years, development of the executive functioning system further contributes to emotion regulation through psychological processes such as inhibitory control, conscious self-reflection, reappraisal, and self-monitoring (Zelazo & Müller, 2002). A concept called **effortful control**—the ability to regulate attention and behavior deliberately and voluntarily—has become important. This ability develops strongly during the preschool period (Posner & Rothbart, 2007). Good effortful control is related to less negativity in children's emotional lives and to better attentional control, processes that are supported by neural development in prefrontal brain regions (Carlson & Wang, 2007; Rothbart & Rueda, 2005). Effortful control can be thought of as the emotional aspect of executive functioning. It is associated with activity of the ventromedial prefrontal cortex (MacDonald, 2008). This emotion related aspect of executive functioning is different from the aspect of executive functioning that is more deliberative and involves the dorsolateral prefrontal cortex. These brain areas develop progressively from infancy through adolescence into the early twenties (Giedd, 2004; Gogtay et al., 2004; Lenroot & Giedd, 2006; Shaw et al., 2008). We provide a summary timeline for the early development of emotion regulation in Figure 8.10.

Overall, there appears to be a developmental shift from simple orienting networks early in life to more sophisticated executive networks later in life (see Rothbart et al., 2011). Children and

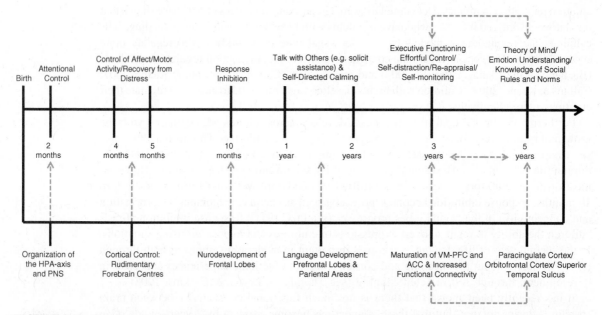

FIGURE 8.10 Summary timelines for the development of emotion regulation from infancy through mid-childhood. The top line represents approximate temporal onset of particular regulatory processes, and the lower line represents associated neurobiological underpinnings of those processes. Dashed arrows at age 3 to 5 indicate that these processes occur within this time frame, at roughly the same time.

adolescents become progressively more capable of using several means that are crucial for the establishment and maintenance of social relationships. Children with poor regulatory skills experience more psychosocial difficulties, including more aggression (Hill, Degnan, Calkins, & Keane, 2006), more peer rejection (Kim & Cicchetti, 2010), and worse school readiness (Bierman et al., 2008; Hughes, Ensor, Wilson, & Graham 2010). Without an ability to regulate emotions of the interpersonal kind, socioemotional well-being suffers.

Temperament

Although children develop regulatory skills through socialization and cognitive maturation, dispositions also contribute to development. One such set of characteristics is a child's **temperament**, defined as an inborn aspect of personality: for instance, to be generally shy, generally cheerful, generally negative, and so on, across situations. Temperament is presumed to have a neurobiological basis and is evident early in development.

Several conceptual models of temperament have been proposed; each conceptualization consists of temperamental dimensions associated with positive and negative outcomes related to emotion regulation. Thomas and Chess (1977) described the difficult temperament: a proneness to negative emotional expression, low adaptability, high activity, and low emotion regulation. Another classification identified resilient (good self-regulation and low negative affect), undercontrolled (impulsive, restless, and negative emotionality), and overcontrolled (fearful and socially reticent) styles of temperament (Asendorpf, Borkenau, Ostendorf, & Van Aken, 2001). Two other schemes come from Buss and Plomin (1975), who postulate four dimensions, and Rothbart (1981), who postulates six dimensions. In Table 8.3 you can see the dimensions of these two schemes and the ways in which they map onto aspects of emotions.

Table 8.3 Mapping of dimensions of temperament onto aspects of emotions for two well-known schemes of temperament: Buss and Plomin's (1975) and Rothbart's (1981)

Dimensions of temperament	Aspects of emotion onto which each dimension maps
Buss & Plomin (1975)	
Emotionality	Fear, anger, and distress
Activity	General arousal of the motor system
Sociability	Interest and positive emotions expressed toward people
Impulsivity	Time taken to express emotion or activity
Rothbart (1981)	
Activity	General arousal of the motor system
Smiling and laughter	Happiness or pleasure
Fear	Fear
Distress to limitations	Anger
Soothability	Recovery time from negative emotions when soothed
Persistence	Duration of interest

Source: Adapted from Campos et al. (1983).

Temperament is important for the study of emotion regulation for two reasons: (a) it is seen early in development, and (b) it is relatively stable and predictive of later outcomes. Highlighting early emergence, DiPietro, Hodgson, Costigan, and Johnson (1996) have found prenatal markers of temperament. These researchers showed that more fetal activity at 36 weeks prenatally is predictive of more difficult behavior in 3-to-6-month-old infants. In turn, these early temperamental differences are believed to provide a foundation for later personality and emotional development. For example, Rothbart, Derryberry, and Hershey (2000) have found that anger-frustration reactivity in infancy predicts higher impulsivity and activity level, a lack of soothability, and lower attentional control in childhood. Using Rothbart's model, Komsi et al. (2006) showed that positive affectivity—a combination of smiling and laughter, duration of orienting, and soothability—at 6 months was related to better effortful control at 5.5 years, whereas negative affectivity is not related to effortful control. Likewise, Kochanska and Knaack (2003) demonstrated that infants who were less prone to anger developed higher effortful control at 2 to 4 years, which in turn was associated with fewer externalizing problems (see Chapter 12 for definition) at about 6 years of age. Temperamental traits seen in infancy show some stability over the life-course. In a longitudinal study by Kagan, Snidman, Kahn, and Towsley (2007), children classified as high-reactive within the first year showed characteristic response patterns through childhood and adolescence, including reduced smiling behavior. Thus, early temperamental reactivity affects the mechanisms that are important for emotion regulation, and these effects may persist through life. In Chapter 11, we discuss continuities in temperament in more detail, including its relationship to later personality characteristics.

Genetic Contributions to Emotional Development

Understanding development requires a discussion of the genetic factors that influence emotionality. Here, we focus on genetic contributions to attentional control and effortful control; these play critical roles in children's development of a functional emotional repertoire. By examining differences between monozygotic twins (who share 100% of their genetic information) and dizygotic twins (who share 50% of their genetic information), we can get an idea about the importance of genetic influences. If monozygotic twins are more similar to one another than dizygotic twins on some emotional attribute, this implies a genetic influence. In studies of temperament and personality, the variance accounted for by any single gene is usually only 1 or 2% (see Yamagata et al., 2005). By contrast, **behavior genetic studies** of twins tell us of combinations of genes that all contribute to specific behaviors. These studies are useful because they give an overall picture of the heritability of certain traits (Plomin et al., 2009). In a sample of toddlers and preschoolers, Goldsmith, Buss, and Lemery (1997) found that monozygotic twins showed more similarity to each other than did dizygotic twins on measures of emotionality, activity, sociability, and impulsivity (see also Lemery & Goldsmith, 2002). More recently, Yamagata et al. (2005) showed that adult monozygotic twins were more similar to one another than were dizygotic twins on attentional control and effortful control. Heritability estimates were 0.45 for attentional control and 0.49 for effortful control. Studies of this kind suggest that there are moderate to strong genetic contributions to emotionality over early and middle childhood, and these effects extend into adulthood.

In studies of a different kind, based on **molecular genetics**, specific genes are sought that may be associated with certain kinds of behavior. The gene that has been most extensively studied in relation to emotional development is the serotonin transporter (5-HTT) gene. Studies of the 5-HTT gene began with the finding by Lesch et al. (1996) that an allele in which the promoter region of the 5-HTT gene was short in length was associated with reduced transcription, which in turn altered the level of serotonin uptake into lymphoblasts (immature precursor cells that differentiate into mature cells later in development). This short allele explained almost 10% of the variability in neurotic behavior (Lesch et al., 1996), a remarkable finding given that most single alleles explain only 1 or 2% of differences in behavior. Because we all have two sets of chromosomes, any particular allele can exist on one or both chromosomes. Hence, as far as the short allele of the serotonin-transporter-linked polymorphic region (called 5-HTTLPR) goes, it can exist on both chromosomes (called the short/short [s/s] version) or on one chromosome, paired with a long version of the allele (called short/long [s/l]). Individuals with either the s/s or the s/l version of the gene tended to show more amygdala activity in response to fearful or threatening stimuli than carriers of two long alleles, l/l (Hariri et al., 2002). Thus variation in the 5-HTT gene seems to be particularly important for processing emotional information.

A recent study by Grossman et al. (2011) examined how variations in both 5-HTTLPR and the catechol-O-methyltransferase (COMT) gene were associated with 7-month-old children's brain responsiveness to facial expressions of emotion. Variability in COMT was associated with differential brain responses to fearful faces in the centroparietal region, while variability in 5-HTTLPR was associated with differential brain reactivity to happy faces in the frontotemporal region. Moreover, COMT variation was linked to infant's recovery from distressing events, whereas variation in 5-HTTLPR was related to child laughter and smiling behavior. Thus, each of these genes appears to have a distinct role in the recognition of, and responsiveness to, positive and negative emotional information.

Recent evidence also implicates the 5-HTTLPR gene in emotion regulation. Beevers et al. (2011) showed that carriers of a short allele (s/s) of 5-HTTLPR paid more attention to positive emotional information than to sad, threatening, or neutral stimuli. On the other hand, carriers of two long alleles (l/l) of this gene were unbiased in their gaze fixation on positively and negatively valenced emotional information. These results suggest that carriers of the short 5-HTTLPR allele may experience greater reactivity to negative stimuli and thereby invoke effortful control mechanisms to shift attention away from negatively charged stimuli. These authors propose that, under circumstances in which the cognitive resources required to shift attention are not available, a focus on negative information may put individuals at risk for developing affective disorders. Interestingly, it has also been shown that carriers of a short allele also have more difficulty disengaging from positive and negative stimuli compared to carriers of the long allele, thus pointing to possible difficulties in emotion regulation (Beevers, Wells, Ellis, & McGeary, 2009).

Although genetic factors clearly influence emotional experience, they operate in conjunction with environmental effects. In general, variation in 5-HTTLPR seems to alter susceptibility to stress. For example, children who were carriers of the short allele of 5-HTTLPR had more depressive symptoms after experiencing maltreatment (Caspi et al., 2003). A recent study by Williams et al. (2009) revealed that individuals with the 5-HTTLPR short allele demonstrated greater startle responses, higher heart rate during fear-provoking situations, and heightened neural activation in the amygdala and prefrontal cortex compared with those who had the long allele. Interestingly, in combination with early life stress, individuals with a 5-HTTLPR short allele also showed a stronger negativity bias in emotion processing.

Child development can be understood in terms of an "experiential shaping of genetic potential" (Schore, 1999, p. 16), with genetic diversity being influenced by social experience.

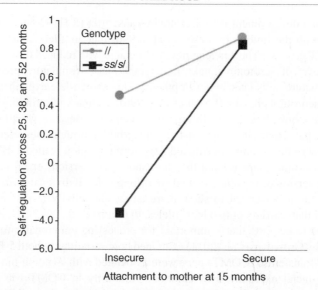

FIGURE 8.11 Self-regulation in infants between 25 and 52 months as a function of security of attachment and whether the child carried the short 5-HTTLPR allele (either s/s or s/l) as compared with those carrying two copies of the long 5-HTTLPR allele (l/l) (from Kochanska, Philibert, & Barry, 2009).

In other words, genetically programmed patterns involve transactions with the environment in order to be expressed (Plomin, 1983). Throughout infancy and early childhood, interactions with caregivers are fundamental kinds of environmental input, and many studies show how genetic dispositions interact with maternal characteristics to affect children's emotionality. For example, Fox et al. (2005) have shown that 7-year-old children are at risk for increased social reticence when they possess the 5-HTTLPR short allele, but only when their mothers report high levels of social stress. Another investigation by Barry, Kochanska, and Philibert (2008) showed that children who were carriers of the 5-HTTLPR short allele tended to have poor attachment relationships to their mothers at 15 months, but only if their mothers were less responsive to the infants at 7 months. In other words, the risk of insecurity was increased when children had a combination of genetic and environmental risks. A follow-up study by this research group showed that insecure attachment at 15 months along with the short 5-HTTLPR allele was associated with diminished self-regulation at 24 to 52 months (Kochanska, Philibert, & Barry, 2009; see Figure 8.11). Collectively, these studies provide striking evidence that emotional development is a function of genetic and experiential factors operating together.

Effects of gene–environment interactions have even been demonstrated when babies are in the womb. When mothers-to-be were anxious at 20 weeks (prenatally), their babies' negative emotionality (distress to limitations, fear, and recovery from distress) when they were 6 months old was greater, but only when they were carriers of the 5-HTTLPR short allele (Pluess et al., 2010). Pauli-Pott, Friedel, Hinney, and Hebebrand (2009) examined children's emotionality in the first year as a function of their genetic makeup and the quality of their attachment relationships. Children who carried the short 5-HTTLPR allele and who were categorized as having an insecure attachment showed more expressions of negative affect, less positive affect, and stronger fear responses compared to children with the long 5-HTTLPR allele, or than children with secure attachments.

These molecular genetic studies show that children's expression, recognition, and regulation of emotions are influenced by discrete genetic variants that act in combination with environmental experiences. Overall, these combinations will affect emotionality and relationships over the life-span.

SUMMARY

We began this chapter by giving three accounts of the development of emotions in children. Two of these propose that emotions emerge as a result of maturation, while the third stresses the importance of social interaction. We discussed the expression and recognition of emotions in three domains: facial, vocal, and gestural. These expressions are made at first in relation to caregivers. As children develop beyond 18 months, they include emotions that depend on achieving a sense of self, on recognizing emotions of other people, and of being able to make comparisons with these others. Within their first few years children are also able to talk about their own and others' emotions.

Regulation of emotions is an important topic in development, as children's emotions tend to be thought of at first as insistent and unsocialized. Regulation is first managed by parents, but within the preschool years children come to be able to regulate their emotions in relation to their goals and relationships. In a final section, we discuss the newly emerging science of how specific genes interact with environmental influences, such as whether a child has been physically maltreated. Gene–environment interactions are now understood as important in explaining temperament and emotion-based traits of personality.

TO THINK ABOUT AND DISCUSS

1. Arm restraint is sometimes used by psychologists to provoke anger in young children, and jack-in-the-boxes are used to provoke surprise. Why don't these stimuli always have the expected effects?

2. What aspects of children's emotional functioning develop so that by the time they attend school children can remain, on the whole, fairly even-tempered even when things don't go their way?

3. Given that both genes and environment affect the development of emotions, which do you think has the stronger effect: inborn genes and temperament, or the environmental influences of parents, family, and school?

FURTHER READING

The best general introduction we know to the development of emotions is:
Paul Harris (1989). *Children and emotion: The development of psychological understanding*. Oxford, UK: Blackwell.

On the significance of children's emotions in social interaction:
Judy Dunn (2003). Emotional development in early childhood: A social relationship perspective. In R. J. Davidson, K. R. Scherer, & H. H. Goldsmith (Eds.), *Handbook of affective sciences* (pp. 332–346). New York, NY: Oxford University Press.

On children's understanding of others' emotions:
Sherri Widen and James A. Russell (2007). Young children's understanding of others' emotions. In M. Lewis, J. Haviland Jones & L. F. Barrett (Eds.), *Handbook of emotions, third edition* (pp. 348–363). New York, NY: Guilford.

On the development of emotion regulation in childhood:
Mary Rothbart, Brad Sheese, M. Rosario Ruedo, & Michael Posner (2011). Developing mechanisms of self-regulation in early life. *Emotion Review*, **3**, 207–213.

9 Emotions in Social Relationships

CONTENTS

FIGURE 9.0 Auguste Renoir, "Dance at Bougival," 1882–83. This painting was used to illustrate a story, by Lhote, about an artist seeking to persuade a young woman to model for him. In the painting we see the man thrusting his face eagerly toward the young woman and grasping her possessively. We also notice from her ring that she is married. Keeping her polite social smile, she turns away.

Photo Credit: Dance at Bougival,1883 (oil on canvas), Renoir, Pierre Auguste (1841-1919) / Museum of Fine Arts, Boston, Massachusetts, USA / Picture Fund / The Bridgeman Art Library

To be means to be for another, and through the other, for oneself. A person has no internal sovereign territory, he is wholly and always on the boundary; looking inside himself, he looks into the eyes of another or with the eyes of another.

Mikhail Bakhtin, Problems of Dostoevsky's Poetics, p. 287

212

Tim Page is one of the most important music critics today. He has lived his life with Aspergers—a condition characterized by early single-minded preoccupations. As a child Page was obsessed with maps of towns in Massachusetts, obituaries, memorizing the 1961 edition of the *World Book Encyclopedia*, and the music of Scottish comedian Harry Lauder (he publicly declared his contempt for the Beatles in his school newspaper). Aspergers is sometimes seen as a mild form of autism. It is manifest in an unusual social style—often defined by the absence of many of the expressive behaviors of emotion we considered in Chapter 4. People with this condition often speak in a monotone voice, avoid making eye contact with others, and avoid touch. People with Aspergers, perhaps less aware of the judgments of others, often deviate from social conventions; Page liked to wear rabbits' feet in each button-hole of his shirt. No wonder he was reassured by Emily Post's *Etiquette*, a step-by-step manual for negotiating the social complexities of human relationships.

People with Aspergers often demonstrate prodigious talents. In the words of Hans Aspergers, the Viennese pediatrician who first characterized the condition: "For success in science or art, a dash of autism is essential." For Page, it led to deep insights into music. After hearing Steve Reich's *Music for 18 Musicians* in 1976, he was catapulted into a 5-year study of minimalism in contemporary music that led to his career as a music critic. He observed that Reich's music had achieved the equivalent of imposing a frame upon a moving river.

People with Aspergers or autism often reason like other people and their language is largely unaffected by their condition. They have trouble with expressing emotion and with feeling emotions for others. As a teenager, while most boys become romantically interested in young girls, Page would avoid making eye contact with them. Later he confessed that as a young adult, making love felt like being the Tin Man in the *Wizard of Oz*. In summing up his social life, Page writes: "I am left with the melancholy sensation that my life has been spent in a perpetual state of parallel play, alongside, but distinctly apart from, the rest of humanity."

Very often scientists turn to people who are at the ends of an emotional continuum to understand what emotions do. When researchers examine the correlates of extreme fear (see Chapter 13), we learn what fear does for the typical functioning person—it directs cognitive and social resources to attend to threats. In the case of people like Tim Page, who live with Aspergers syndrome, we learn what happens to social relationships when components of emotion are disrupted. Tim Page's life reveals the central theme of this chapter: emotions are vital to our social relationships.

The Interaction Between Emotions and Social Relationships

In summing up his observations of hunter-gatherer social life, ethologist Iraneus Eibl-Eibesfeldt concluded that emotions are the grammar of social relationships (1989). Emotional exchanges are the core elements of the interactions that make up our most meaningful relationships: the warm attachments between parents and children; sibling conflicts, play, and reconciliations; teasing flirtations of courtship; encounters of dominance and submissiveness between young male rivals; and the rage occasionally seen between groups. This emotional grammar is what Tim Page finds, at times, so difficult to grasp and practice.

Eibl-Eibesfeldt's observation is one variant of the central thesis of our book—that emotions are profoundly social (Tiedens & Leach, 2004). We are often struck by the internal qualities of emotion—how they feel, how they trigger memories from the past, how they serve as powerful guides to our decision making. But at the same time emotions are social. We quickly and often unconsciously communicate them to others with different signal behaviors in the face, in the voice, and in patterns of touch. Emotion-related responses in the autonomic nervous system enable social behaviors like social connection, as well as fighting or fleeing. Emotions are triggered by appraisals that relate to social goals. Emotions guide important social and moral judgments.

In the broadest sense, we can approach the social nature of emotions from two directions. The first is to think about how emotions create specific social relationships; they are indeed a grammar, the building blocks of social exchange. For example, emotional experiences help us assume specific roles within relationships (see Chapters 1 and 2). Feelings of romantic passion help us fold into long-term partnerships; feelings of sympathy and filial love enable us to take on the role of parent and care-provider (Shields, 1991). As you learned in Chapter 4, emotionally expressive behaviors help coordinate social interactions, and in so doing help us establish specific relationships (Aubé & Senteni, 1996; Oatley, 2004c). As we explained in Chapter 2, a smile is an invitation to a cooperative relationship. An angry expression is a declaration of conflict or a statement of one's power vis-à-vis others (Knutson, 1996). An expression of fear prompts everyone to join together in feeling wary. The social emotions are scripts for distinctive kinds of relationship. In this chapter you will learn how emotions help us establish romantic partnerships, friendships, and positions of rank within social hierarchies.

A second direction from which to approach the social dimensions of emotions is to ask how relationships shape them. As you move through the day you will find yourself in different relationships—with friends or romantic partners or bosses at work or parents (Moskowitz, 2004). Within these different relationships, our emotions are likely to shift. You may feel gratitude with friends and passion with a romantic partner. Your boss may trigger feelings of anxiety and modesty or inspiration. Your parents may trigger feelings of guilt, contentedness, or family pride. So how are appraisals, expressive behaviors, current feelings, and action tendencies shaped by the relationships we are in? We shall see in this chapter that emotional responses vary systematically according to whether we are among friends, whether we feel we have power, and even according to our class background.

To consider how emotions create specific relationships, and how relationships in turn shape our emotional lives, we will rely on a framework that we introduced in Chapter 2. There we proposed that three social goals and one antisocial goal are central to human emotion. We will organize what has been learned about emotions and social relationships according to the relationships related to these four goals. We will look at intimate relationships related to attachment and the place of emotions in those relationships. We'll see that relationships that center upon affiliation—friendships—are shaped by emotional processes that enable cooperation among non-kin. We'll next see that emotions are essential to hierarchical relationships related to the goal of assertion of power. And we shall see how emotions operate within groups, and also between groups, where they are often guided by the motive of hostility.

Emotions within Intimate Relationships

John Bowlby's (1969) influential theorizing about attachment in many ways is a theory about how emotions are at the core of intimate relationships from cradle to grave. In this section we focus on romantic partnerships. From the sparks of initial sexual attraction to the passions that enable enduring romantic love, emotions are central to intimate life. Based on the patterns of social goals that we introduced in Chapter 2, we can say that romantic love is founded jointly on the social motivations of attachment and affiliation: with attachment comes trustfulness and protection; with affiliation comes the ability—enormously expanded in humans as compared with other animals—for cooperation in joint projects. Phillip Shaver has been in the forefront of showing how romantic love has a basis in attachment (e.g., Shaver, 2006; Shaver & Mikulincer, 2002), and Helen Fisher (1992) has written engagingly on the joining of sex with cooperation.

Principles of Sexual Love

The human experiences of loving and of being loved are thought by many to give life its principal meaning. They are much celebrated in fictional literature. Here, for instance, is Laura Esquivel in the novel, *Like Water for Chocolate*:

> My Grandmother . . . said that each of us is born with a box of matches inside us but we can't strike them all by ourselves . . . the oxygen would come from the breath of the person you love; the candle could be any . . . music, caress, word, or sound that engenders the explosion.
>
> (Esquivel, 1992, Chapter 6)

For many people in Western society, love is what is most important in life. In one survey of 100,000 Americans, it was not wealth, not power, not youth, not health—but love in marriage that the respondents thought was the good that they most closely identified with happiness (Freedman, 1978). In this instance they would be correct: healthy relationships are one of the strongest determinants of happiness (Myers, 2000).

What brings individuals together into romantic partnerships? Two candidates are sexual desire and romantic love (Diamond, 2003; Djikic & Oatley, 2004; Hatfield & Rapson, 2002). To take a scientific approach, let's first consider the imaginative research of Eli Finkel and his colleagues on speed-dating (Finkel & Eastwick, 2008). In this research, much as would happen at a weekend social gathering, a dozen or so young women and a dozen or so young men arrive at the lab and engage in a series of 2-minute conversations with all the other members of the opposite sex. After each interaction, participants rate their sexual desire and felt chemistry for one another. From these data, Finkel and colleagues have uncovered important insights about initial passion and desire. First, when one individual feels unique desire and chemistry for another, those feelings are reciprocated by the person who is the object of attraction (Eastwick, Finkel, Mochon, & Ariely, 2007). Second, those speed daters who felt sexual attraction for many other people actually generated little desire or chemistry in those people themselves. Unlike our primate relatives—chimpanzees and bonobos—which show sexual responses to many others, we humans can feel romantic passion that locks onto one person and sets the stage for a more enduring relationship.

Our early feelings of sexual desire, as we detailed in Chapter 2, are responsive to specific cues: beautiful skin, full lips, and warm, glistening eyes; physical signs of youth, of strength in men and of fecundity in women (Miller, 2000). These feelings are depicted in common metaphors: young lovers can feel "knocked off their feet," "hungry" for each other, "mad" with desire, and "swept away" by passion (Lakoff & Johnson, 1980). These metaphors speak to the single-mindedness and loss of control characteristic of early sexual passion. We can become focused on just one person. Passion is then registered in specific patterns of touch, cuddling, and sexual signaling (see Chapter 4). Manifestations of sexual desire are tied, fittingly, to the woman's ovulation and fluctuating estrogen (Konner, 2003). Around the time of ovulation, women are more likely to initiate sex, masturbate, have affairs, and be accompanied by their husband. Ovulating pole dancers in bars even earn bigger tips (Miller, 2001; Miller et al., 2007).

As romantic partners spend more time together, the intense feelings of sexual desire they feel can give way to the experience of a second emotion—romantic love—defined by feelings of deep intimacy (Acevedo & Aron, 2009). The couple will feel comfort and security in being close, in knowing each other, and in the feeling of their identities coming to merge. As part of increasing intimacy, romantic partners come to include their partner's perspectives, experiences, and characteristics in their own self-concept (Aron & Aron, 1997; Aron, Aron, & Allen, 1989; Aron & Fraley, 1999). They may idealize their loved ones, attributing rare virtues to them that set them apart from others (Murray & Holmes, 1993, 1997).

One of the great writers of the Romantic period (whose novels are also romances in the day-to-day sense) was Jane Austen. In the accompanying box, you can see a brief description of her most famous novel, *Pride and Prejudice,* published in 1813. If you read the book or see the 1995 television miniseries, you encounter a challenging account of the transition between sexual attraction and love: you are asked to consider the idea that you can't love someone just by projecting your desire onto them, as a kind of hallucination. You can only love by getting to know who the person is, though this knowledge by no means precludes trying to change the person into who you would like them to be.

Several studies have differentiated sexual desire from romantic love (Chojnacki & Walsh, 1990; Sternberg, 1997; Whitley, 1993). For example, people often nominate love as a prototypical emotion, and sexual desire is believed to overlap only modestly with the content of love (Fehr & Russell, 1984; 1991; Shaver et al., 1987). In another study, participants were asked to exclude

Photo Credit: The Kobal Collection, Ltd./Picture Desk/Art Resource

FIGURE 9.1   Mr. Darcy (played by Matthew Macfadyen) and Elizabeth Bennet (played by Keira Knightley) in the 2005 film of *Pride and Prejudice.*

Novels and films: *Pride and Prejudice*

Jane Austen's *Pride and Prejudice* may still be the West's best love story. It's about Elizabeth Bennet, the daughter of an affectionate but silly mother and a clever but sardonic father. At a dance she is slighted by the rich, proud, and extremely eligible Mr. Darcy. Speaking to a friend, he says of Elizabeth, loudly enough for her to overhear: "She is tolerable, but not handsome enough to tempt *me*." In conversation with her sister (a few chapters after Darcy's snub), Elizabeth says: "I could easily forgive *his* pride if he had not mortified *mine*." Her love for Darcy has first to surmount this obstacle.

An important premise of any love story is that, to start with, neither of the lovers-to-be knows much about the other. Part of the beauty of Jane Austen's story is that Elizabeth's love for Darcy is not of the kind that is usual in the Western cultural script of falling in love, in which love comes into being in almost complete form with a meeting of the eyes between two strangers across a room. Rather, in this story, love grows only gradually as Elizabeth starts to know Darcy, at exactly the same time as we readers also come to know both him and Elizabeth.

Laura Vivanco and Kyra Kramer (2010) have noticed that a recurring theme in love stories is transformation, with *Pride and Prejudice* being an early example. The theme continues in romantic stories of today, for instance, those marketed by the publisher Harlequin. Although Jane Austen writes of Darcy's "utmost force of passion," he is not complete as a person. His pride prevents him from being a fully formed man. The story is about how Elizabeth, with her intelligence and determination, accomplishes his transformation. As she comes to know Darcy, he becomes able to know himself, becomes thereby able to admit his shortcomings, becomes more aware of others, and in the end becomes able to love. Only when Darcy's pride is transformed in this way does Elizabeth consent to marry him. At the same time, Elizabeth has to come to terms with and change her own prejudices. Vivanco and Kramer see this theme of transformation as a version of the ancient idea of alchemy in which, by means of the philosopher's stone, an alchemist would transform a base metal into gold. In *Pride and Prejudice*, Elizabeth becomes the alchemist who transforms the base metal of the imperfect Darcy into the gold of a man who is able to love her.

---

emotion terms that did not belong in the category of love (Fehr & Russell, 1991). Few participants excluded the words caring (8%), and affection (27%), but many participants excluded the words desire (59%), infatuation (82%), and lust (87%). Those people whom participants say they love overlap only partially with those for whom they say they feel sexual desire (Myers & Berscheid, 1997).

Emotions in Marriage

In many societies, feelings of sexual desire, and then of romantic love, lead to long-term commitments within marriage. Propelled by such feelings 80 to 90% of individuals in countries such as the United States and Canada marry, and yet more enter long-term romantic partnerships. The emotional lives of intimate partners will, however, change: not all of intimate life is lovely. With divorce rates in many industrialized nations hovering near 50%, and with levels of marital dissatisfaction also being high (Myers, 2000), it is essential to ask about sources of marital distress.

John Gottman and Robert Levenson sought an answer to this question: What emotional processes predict the demise of marriages? To find an answer, they studied the emotional

Photo Credit: Tetra Images/Getty Images, Inc.

FIGURE 9.2   Anger may be an important part of intimate relationships. It is typically less destructive in relationships than is contempt.

dynamics of married partners as they engaged in 15-minute conversations on conflictual problems, for example, unsatisfying sex, the husband's inability to get better-paying work, or a child's academic struggles. Gottman and Levenson then coded the interactions for several emotional behaviors and asked whether emotional patterns they found predicted whether the marriage would survive.

In one long-term study that started in 1983, Gottman and Levenson followed the marriages of 79 couples from Bloomington, Indiana. With the methods we just described they identified what they call "the Four Horsemen of the Apocalypse"—**toxic emotional behaviors** that are most damaging and most likely to predict divorce. First is *criticism*. Partners who are more critical, who continually find fault with their partners, have less satisfying marriages. The next two predictors are *defensiveness* and *stonewalling* (resisting dealing with problems). When romantic partners are unable to talk about their difficulties without being defensive, they are in trouble. The fourth is *contempt* expressed in sneers and eye-rolls and disparagement. Gottman and Levenson measured the four toxic behaviors in the 15-minute conversation about a conflict to predict who would stay together and who would be divorced. Some 93% of couples who showed evidence of toxic behaviors were divorced 14 years later (Gottman & Levenson, 2000).

More recent studies have identified several emotional patterns that help romantic partners stay committed and close. One such pattern is to share what is good in life with your partner, which Shelly Gable refers to as **capitalizing upon the good** (Gable, Gonzaga, & Strachman, 2006; Gable, Reis, Impett, & Asher, 2004). When romantic partners share their joys and respond to each other's good news with engaged enthusiasm, they are more likely to feel committed to one another many months later (Gable et al., 2006). Thus, instead of stonewalling or criticizing, it is wiser to express appreciation and encouragement for good things that happen in your partner's life.

Intimate relations also fare well when partners cultivate humor, amusement, and **play**. The middle phases of marriage often involve a great deal of drudgery: diaper changing, sibling squabbles, helping children with stomachaches, and coping with their children's adolescence. Not surprisingly, intimate relationships are least satisfied at this stage of the relationship (Myers, 2000). Romantic partners also often face their own problems: difficulties at work, health problems, financial difficulties, and, in 15 to 20% of marriages, infidelity.

Amusement, mirth, and play are emotional antidotes to these trends in intimate relationships. For example, more happily married couples often possess many playful nicknames for each other, and more readily playfully tease one another during conflict instead of directly criticizing (Keltner et al., 1998). Humor and laughter can deescalate intense conflicts to more peaceful exchanges (Gottman, 1993a,b). In one experiment, spouses who had been married several years who played silly games actually reported significant boosts in their satisfaction (Aron, Norman, Aron, McKenna, & Heyman, 2000). The moral for a happier intimate life: stay playful.

Another emotional tendency to cultivate is **compassionate love**: a positive regard for the partner and appreciation of the partner's foibles and weaknesses. In longitudinal research, partners who reported high levels of compassionate love for one another early in the relationship were less likely to divorce 4 years later (Neff & Karney, 2009).

Alongside compassionate love, it is also important to forgive. **Forgiveness** involves a shift in feeling toward someone who has done you harm, away from ideas about revenge and avoidance toward a more positive understanding of the humanity of the person (McCullough, 2000; McCullough, Sandage, & Worthington, 1997; Worthington, 1998). Forgiveness isn't a mindless glossing over the harm a partner has done; it involves recognizing that to err is human. Forgiving someone who has caused harm has been found to reduce blood pressure and anger (Snyder & Heinze, 2005; Witvliet, Ludwig, & Vander Laan, 2001).

Michael McCullough and his colleagues have studied how forgiveness influences the level of satisfaction in romantic partnerships and families (Hoyt, Fincham, McCullough, Maio, & Davila, 2005). They measured three dimensions related to forgiveness: the urge for revenge,

Individual emotion: Compassion

Is there a master social emotion, an emotion that helps you form stronger social relations of all kinds? Religious historian Karen Armstrong thinks so (2006). In her survey of the great traditions of religious and ethical thought that emerged some 2,500 years ago—Confucianism, Hinduism, Buddhism, Taoism, and early Greek and Judeo-Christian thought—she argues that compassion emerged as the cardinal emotion of virtue. Compassion is the feeling of concern for another, accompanied by a desire to enhance that person's welfare (Goetz et al., 2010). All of these great traditions center upon compassion, Armstrong argues, in their sayings and aphorisms and practices that encourage a concern for others, an interest in enhancing the welfare of others, of not causing harm, and a

devotion to treating others as you would have them treat you. Compassion is a pillar of the great ethical traditions.

The evidence seen in scientific studies supports this wisdom of the ages. People feeling compassion see greater common humanity with strangers (Oveis et al., 2010), they punish others less (Condon & DeSteno, 2011), and they are more generous and cooperative (Eisenberg et al., 1989). As you are learning in this chapter, compassion is a vital element of healthy relationships, from romantic bonds to nations with competing interests. It is perhaps for this reason that many meditation practices and prayers focus on instilling compassion, and it is considered by many to be the most social emotion.

the desire to avoid the partner, and a more compassionate view of the partner's mistake. They found that forgiveness promotes relationship satisfaction. For example, in one 9-week study (Tsang, McCullough, & Fincham, 2006), students who had suffered a recent transgression in a relationship reported classic kinds of harm: being cheated on, insulted, rejected, or left out of a social activity. Partners who were earlier to forgive reported greater closeness and commitment to their partner weeks later.

Emotions in Friendships

People often feel love, sometimes profound, for lifelong friends and for friends in the immediate moment. Whereas friendships are rarer in our nonhuman primate relatives, in humans they are central to our social life; they are based on the distinctively human social goal of affiliation, which affords friendly cooperation in accomplishing things together that we couldn't do alone. Most humans have a tight network of very close friends, say six or seven, and a broader network of people they feel supported by and connected to. In friendships, children learn their generation's morals and values (often to their parents' chagrin). In friendships, young adults sort out the difficulties of family and romantic life.

From an evolutionary perspective, friendships present something of a conundrum: they require cooperation with non-kin. In evolutionary terms it seems problematic for individuals to devote resources to others whose success brings no benefit to the benefactor's genes. As an answer to this puzzle, Trivers (1971) offered an influential analysis of the basis of friendships and focused his claims on reciprocity and gratitude. He proposed that cooperative alliances like friendships have emerged in human evolution, and are successful in our more immediate lives, to the extent that there is reciprocal giving and affection. Building upon this analysis, Randolph Nesse and Phoebe Ellsworth (1990, 2008) argued that emotions such as love and gratitude promote cooperative, affectionate alliances between friends. The scientific studies guided by this thinking have focused on gratitude, empathy and mimicry, and the broader benefits of feelings of social support.

Gratitude

When Adam Smith (1759) surveyed the new industries that were emerging in the British industrial revolution, he was struck by the tremendous cooperation that emerged within networks of people who worked together. He argued that gratitude was the sentiment that held people together, in the spirit of common cause. More recently, Michael McCullough, Robert Emmons et al. (2001) contend that gratitude is the glue of cooperative social living among non-kin; it is a moral emotion. How so? First, gratitude serves as a barometer; it helps us keep track of which friends are generous and which are not. It is much like the grooming between nonhuman primates; our feelings of gratitude track the cooperative non-kin.

Second, gratitude motivates altruistic and affectionate behavior. It produces the generosity, the favors, and the expressions of appreciation that are critical to long-term commitments among friends. As an illustration, David DeSteno and his colleagues (Bartlett & DeSteno, 2006; Desteno et al., 2010) have had participants engage in studies in which, out of the blue, they were helped by a confederate (to fix a computer problem). Being the recipient of generosity led participants to feel

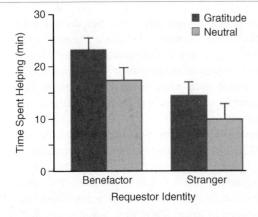

FIGURE 9.3 When feeling gratitude, people will give more of their time both to someone who's helped them (benefactor) and to a stranger (from Bartlett & DeSteno, 2006).

gratitude, and in this state they then proved to be more generous in allocating their time and resources to other strangers (see Figure 9.3). Gratitude is a powerful determinant of prosocial behavior.

McCullough and Emmons posit that the expression of gratitude, either verbally or non-verbally, acts as a reward; it reinforces affectionate, cooperative behavior. The gifts that we give gratefully, the simple statements of "thank you," the more elaborate ways in which we appreciate others, all serve to reward their generosity and increase the chances of further cooperative behavior. One might think of the kind of touching of another person to express gratitude (see Chapter 4) as inherently rewarding in this fashion, and a way to increase cooperative behavior among non-kin, as was found in Michael Kraus's study of teammates on basketball teams (see Chapter 4). Given all of these benefits of gratitude, Sara Algoe and her colleagues have begun to explore how gratitude promotes friendship and find that expressions of gratitude predict increased closeness among group members over time (Algoe, Haidt, & Gable, 2008).

Mimicry

Humans are an imitative species (Hatfield, Cacioppo, & Rapson, 1994). People imitate each other's facial expressions, postural movements, tones of voice, and styles of gait. In experiments, participants will unconsciously imitate smiles presented in photos so fast they do not know what they have seen (Dimberg & Ohman, 1996). We are especially likely to imitate the emotions of others. Simply hearing another person laugh can trigger laughter (Provine, 1992). If a friend blushes in an embarrassing situation, our cheeks will redden too (Shearn, Bergman, Hill, Abel, & Hinds, 1992).

Emotional mimicry is a central ingredient of friendship. Feelings of similarity are a basic driving force of the formation of friendships. We feel closer to other people who share our attitudes, our preferences, and our beliefs. Our interactions with similar others are often more gratifying and are more likely to develop into enduring friendships. Emotional mimicry is a basic way in which friends build common ground and become closer.

Consider the case of laughter. Jo-Anne Bachorowski has devoted years to studying laughter, analyzing the acoustic profiles—the rhythm, pitch, and variability—of different laughs (Bachorowski & Owren, 2001). She has catalogued different kinds of laughs—the hisses, snorts, guffaws, chuckles, and belly laughs that punctuate our days. She has documented surprising gender differences: men are more likely than women to produce "grunts" than women. With respect to friendship, in one study she and Moria Smoski studied the laughter of strangers and friends. They found that within milliseconds of participating in amusing tasks, the laughs of friends but not strangers began to mimic each other (Smoski & Bachorowski, 2003). The implication is that friends quickly imitate one another's signs of amusement and thereby enjoy the pleasure and perspective of humor and play.

Does emotional mimicry actually increase people's liking for potential friends? People engage in all sorts of rituals to increase their mimicry—from dance to clapping to marching in unison. The end result is likely to be greater friendship and cooperation among those who might otherwise become adversaries. In an ingenious test of this hypothesis, Piercarlo Valdesello and David DeSteno (2011) had participants and confederates sit across from one another and listen with earphones to rhythmic patterns of tones. They were asked to tap their finger to the tones. The participant and confederate either listened to the same patterns of tones, and therefore mimicked one another in their synchronous tapping, or they listened to different patterns of tones, and therefore tapped their fingers at different times. Participants whose tapping was mimicked by the confederate looked upon this confederate as more like a friend: they felt more similar to the confederate, had higher levels of compassion, and were more likely to help that person complete a long and uninteresting task later in the study. Physical mimicry is a basis of increased closeness among potential friends.

Complementing this experimental work, Cameron Anderson and his colleagues have found that emotional mimicry helps build close friendships (Anderson, Keltner, & John, 2003). In one study, new roommates came to the laboratory at the fall and spring and at each visit reported their emotional reactions to different evocative stimuli, such as humorous or disturbing film clips. As a demonstration of the tendency for friends to mimic one another, the roommates' emotions became increasingly similar (compared to two randomly selected individuals) over the course of the year. This emotional mimicry, furthermore, predicted increased closeness in friendships.

Social Support

Enjoying strong emotional connections to good friends gives individuals a sense of social support, which is defined by strong feelings of being surrounded by good friends during times of need. In Table 9.1 we present a widely used measure of social support. As evident in this measure, friends not only provide the delights and laughter of friendship but, as we saw in the last section, a strong network of friends gives the individual a sense that there are people to turn to in times of need—people with whom to share complex emotions.

Strong social support exercises powerful influences upon people's emotional lives. As we shall see in Chapter 13, it buffers people from emotional breakdowns, and it is also beneficial to physical health. A clearly documented effect is that social support reduces feelings of stress, anxiety, and uncertainty during difficult and challenging times. People with high social support show lower baseline levels of cortisol, which we considered in Chapter 5, suggesting that having many good friends calms the hypothalamic-pituitary axis (HPA), which is activated in fight and flight (Kiecolt-Glaser & Glaser, 1999). Shelley Taylor et al. (2008) have found that this same sense of social support reduces cortisol response to one of the most powerful triggers of anxiety: giving a public speech. Having friends present in stressful contexts likewise reduces

Table 9.1 **Measure of social support**

1. There is a special person who is around when I am in need.
2. There is a special person with whom I can share my joys and sorrows.
3. My family really tries to help me.
4. I get the emotional help and support I need from my family.
5. I have a special person who is a real source of comfort for me.
6. My friends really try to help me.
7. I can count on my friends when things go wrong.
8. I can talk about my problems with my family.
9. I have friends with whom I can share my joys and sorrows.
10. There is a special person in my life who cares about my feelings.
11. My family is willing to help me make decisions.
12. I can talk about my problems with my friends.

Source: From Zimet, Dalhem, Zimet, & Farley (1988).

stress-related physiology. In one illustrative study, women had to perform challenging tasks either in the presence of a friend or alone. Those with a friend showed less stress-related cardiovascular response to the challenging tasks (Kamarack, Manuch, & Jennings, 1990). Other studies find that if you are in networks of good friends, as assessed with scales like those of Table 9.1, you benefit in many ways. In one study in Alameda County, California, people who had fewer meaningful connections to others were 1.9 to 3.1 times more likely to have died 9 years later (Berkman & Syme, 1979).

Emotions in Hierarchical Relationships

In writing about power in 1938, the British philosopher Bertrand Russell offered the following:

> The fundamental concept in social science is Power, in the same sense that Energy is the fundamental concept in physics. . . . The laws of social dynamics are laws which can only be stated in terms of power. (p. 10)

In many individualistic Western countries, people believe that in most relationships no clear power differences are at play. Russell was arguing something quite different, that all social relationships—of children on the playground, romantic partners, siblings, parents and their children—are shaped by differences in power. Power is a motive that in Chapter 2 we called assertion, the desire to gain influence. It's part of every relationship, and perhaps part of most social interactions.

This begs the question of how assertive power influences emotion. Stephanie Shields has offered one broad answer to this question in her concept of "emotion politics," which refers to the processes by which people experience, express, and conceptualize emotion in ways that define their own **status** and that of others (Shields, 2005). Status, sometimes called rank, means the level one can occupy in a hierarchy. As we explained in Chapter 2, hierarchies are ubiquitous among mammals; they are evolved means of distributing resources unequally. Building upon the notion of emotion politics, we will look at how we rely on emotions to signal and negotiate our status in hierarchies. We will also consider how assertive power differences within social contexts influence emotional response.

Emotional Displays and the Negotiation of Social Rank

Conflicts over rank within hierarchies can be deadly affairs. In many species, from chimpanzees to Narwals out at sea, status conflicts can be violent and combatants can incur enormous costs. The same is true in humans, in particular in groups of young males as they jockey for position in social hierarchies. For example, in his fieldwork with the Yanomamö, a group who live in the forests of southern Venezuela and northern Brazil, Napoleon Chagnon observed how young men fought in duels where adversaries would take turns striking each other over the head, to assess their relative toughness (Chagnon, 1968).

Given the costs of status contests, many nonhuman species rely on nonverbal displays to negotiate and establish their positions within the hierarchy. Apes pound their chests, frogs croak, stags roar for hours, chimps flash their fangs, and deer lock up in their horns. These kinds of ritualized displays enable group members to establish who has power and who doesn't in less costly fashion than direct aggressive encounters. Humans, too, negotiate their places in hierarchies by emotional displays.

For example, anger is clearly a high-power emotion. It has force and strength behind it. Expressions of anger lead to gains in power within groups. People attribute elevated status and power to those who display anger (Knutson, 1996). People assume that high-power people respond to difficulties with anger (Tiedens, 2000; Tiedens, Ellsworth, & Mesquita, 2000). Larissa Tiedens found that people attributed greater power to leaders when they displayed anger as opposed to other emotions (Tiedens, 2001).

Many people think anger is destructive, and it can be, but in diary studies Averill (1982) found that episodes of anger happen for most people once or twice a week, and they usually occur between people who know and like each other—parent and child, friends, lovers. Anger typically occurs when a person has a sense of being wronged; the person's status or selfhood has been diminished. This person then feels empowered to confront the other, and the usual function of anger is to readjust something in the relationship.

Another power-related emotion is pride. Pride is signaled in dominance behaviors—chest expansions, arms akimbo, and backward head-tilts (as you learned in Chapter 4). Are people who experience pride more likely to rise in their status? Williams and DeSteno (2009) led people to experience pride before engaging in an interaction with a collection of other individuals. Those who experienced pride were judged by others to be more powerful. Their social rank within the group increased.

Is there a low-power emotional counterpart to anger and pride, which, when felt and expressed, would signal lower rank? One candidate is embarrassment. In experimental research, people who display embarrassment are judged to be of lower status and physically smaller (Ketelaar, 2005). Much as anger and pride signal power within groups, and allow people to occupy higher status positions, embarrassment signals submissiveness.

Our momentary displays of emotion, therefore, are one means by which we signal and occupy different positions of power within hierarchies. Highly emotional exchanges—confrontations, battles of wit, teasing and banter—allow group members to negotiate status differences through emotional display. One such interaction is teasing, a common means by which people playfully, and at times destructively, use emotion to negotiate social status

Table 9.2   **Teasing among foursomes of fraternity members**

	High power (HP)		Low power (LP)	
	Teasing LP	**Teased by LP**	**Teasing HP**	**Teased by HP**
Duchenne smiles[a]	83.3	95.8	56.5	95.8
Facial anger	8.3	25.0	0.0	0.0
Facial contempt	4.2	16.7	0.0	0.0
Facial fear	0.0	0.0	16.7	8.3
Facial pain	4.2	4.2	12.3	25.0

Notes: In groups of four, high-power (HP) and low-power (LP) fraternity members teased one another. During these interactions, high-power individuals were more likely to smile with delight, and to show facial displays of anger and contempt, especially when being challenged by a low-power member. Low-power fraternity members, in contrast, were more likely to show displays of fear and pain.

[a]Duchenne smiles involve the action of the *zygomatic* major muscle, which pulls the lip corners up, and the *orbicularis oculi* muscle surrounding the eye, and are closely tied to the experience of positive emotion.

(Keltner et al., 2001). For example, in one study, fraternity members teased each other by making up nicknames and embarrassing stories about each other in foursomes comprised of two low- and two high-power members (Keltner et al., 1998). The individual's power was defined according to his position in the fraternity. As you can see in Table 9.2, high-power members tended to display smiles of pleasure, anger, and contempt, emotions associated with high power. In contrast, the low-power members were more likely to show submissive emotions like fear and pain (see also Öhman, 1986). In their subtle emotional displays embedded within their banter and teasing, the group members were signaling their elevated or lower rank relative to one another.

Power and Emotion

We have seen that in our emotional display and experience, we navigate our rank within social hierarchies. Let's now look at the other side of the power-emotion equation, and ask how the power we experience within a social context influences our emotional tendencies. We know from studies of humans and nonhumans alike that individuals who occupy positions of low rank within a hierarchy face greater threats of most kinds and tend to be anxious, on guard, and vigilant of the actions of others (Keltner, Gruenfeld, & Anderson, 2003). Individuals of high status, by contrast, enjoy greater access to resources and freedom and are less dependent on others. These differences should have profound effects on the emotional lives of individuals who occupy high or low rank positions.

In keeping with this analysis, assertion, or power, has been found to influence in profound ways the emotions people feel moment by moment. Because power is associated with increased rewards and freedoms, those who enjoy positions of elevated power tend to experience greater positive emotion in different situations than do low-power people (Hecht & LaFrance, 1998). People in positions of low power, by contrast, attuned to potential threats in the social environment, are more likely to experience negative emotions like sadness, shame, guilt, and anxiety (Hecht, Inderbitzen, & Bukowski, 1998; Tiedens et al., 2000).

Power influences how individuals respond to the emotions of others. Because high-power people are less dependent on others, and low-power individuals tend to be careful in monitoring others' emotions, difference might be found in accuracy of judgments. In keeping with this theme, Galinsky, Magee, Inesi, and Gruenfeld (2006) found that having participants recall a time of being powerful made them less accurate in judging emotional expressions portrayed in photographs, and van Kleef, De Dreu, Pietroni, and Manstead (2006) found that high-power individuals were less responsive to others' emotions. On the other side of the equation, Anderson et al. (2003) found that low-power individuals were more likely to mimic their friends' emotions than vice-versa.

In a study of conversations between two strangers, Gerben van Kleef and his colleagues found that high-power individuals' compassion decreased as their partner disclosed more distressing experiences (van Kleef, Oveis, van der Löwe, LuoKogan, Goetz, & Keltner, 2008). When people speak of the social disconnect associated with elevated power, it is very likely to be observed in the lack of attention high-power individuals direct to the emotions of others.

Social Class and Emotion

In what many believe to be an apocryphal exchange, the writer F. Scott Fitzgerald observed to his colleague, Ernest Hemingway, that, "The rich are different from you and me." Hemingway's laconic response was: "Yes, they have more money."

Social scientists study the rich and poor in terms of **social class**, which refers to the wealth, education, and prestige of work that the individual enjoys within a particular society (Adler et al., 1994). Individuals think of their own social class and that of other people in terms of categories like rich and poor, or working class and bourgeoisie, or the 1% and the 99%. Scholars often write about how people from different class backgrounds live different lives in terms of their neighborhoods, the schools they attend, the clubs they belong to, the food they eat, and what entertainment they enjoy. Social class is a pervasive and powerful part of the individual's social identity.

Here we ask whether class influences the emotional lives of individuals. One answer to this question begins in the recognition that social class is imbued with a sense of rank, a sense of high and low, of who has influence and who does not (Adler et al., 1994). It is not necessarily the case that a person of power comes from the upper class. Nor do upper-class people always wield lots of power. But, the fact that social class expresses high and low rank helps illuminate profound differences in the emotional lives of the rich and the poor. One would expect social class to shape the emotional lives of individuals in ways that resemble how power influences emotion (Kraus, Piff, & Keltner, 2011).

In keeping with this argument, lower-class individuals tend to respond to situations with threat-related emotions such as anxiety. For example, in studies of children and adults, lower-class people tend to report greater anxiety, to respond with increased heart rate and blood pressure when reading ambiguous, socially threatening scenarios, and to show diminished reduction in daily cortisol levels over the course of the day relative to their upper-class counterparts (e.g., Chen & Mathews, 2001; Hajat et al., 2010). Regrettably, occupying a lower-class position in society is accompanied by more frequent and intense experiences of threat, anxiety, and stress-related physiology.

Because they are vigilant of the emotions of others, one would expect lower-class people to be better judges of others' emotions, much as we saw in the judgments of low-power individuals.

This hypothesis has received support in several studies. For example, people from lower-class backgrounds, or individuals experimentally prompted to think of how they are less well off than others, proved to be better judges of emotion from photographs of facial expressions (Kraus, Côté, & Keltner, 2010). Lower-class people tend to be better judges than upper-class people of their own friends' negative emotions (Kraus et al., 2011).

As with power, these class-related differences give rise to the tendency for lower-class, as compared with upper-class, people to respond to others' emotions empathically. In a study of friendship, Michael Kraus and his colleagues found that over the course of several interactions, the emotions of the lower-class friend came to resemble those of the upper-class friend, but this pattern of empathic response was not observed in how the upper-class friend responded to the emotions of the lower-class friend (Kraus et al., 2011). Lower-class people also respond with greater compassion, in terms of self-report and autonomic physiology (heart-rate deceleration), to the suffering of others (Stellar, Manzo, Kraus, & Keltner, 2011).

Emotions within and Between Groups

Humans belong to groups: we are male or female, we are members of a family, we have this nationality or that; perhaps we are members of a religious congregation or perhaps we're in the group of people who think of themselves as nonreligious. We feel close emotional connections and similarities with members of groups to which we belong, our **in-groups**, while we maximize and even exaggerate differences between us and other groups (Sherif & Sherif, 1953). Many groups work hard to increase similarities among their members, for instance, by clothing, rituals, and belief systems; sometimes fear and other forms of emotional pressure are used to increase conformity. At the same time, many groups have characteristic responses to members of **out-groups**.

Much of our membership in groups is essential to us. Groups are our principal arenas of the three principal social motivations we introduced in Chapter 1, which we've discussed further in this chapter. First, a group affords a focus of attachment, people to look up to, a place of safety, and a secure base. Second, it is based on the affiliative motivation of cooperation; groups are networks of cooperation. Third, a group is typically organized into a hierarchy of assertion in which high status connotes leadership and in which everyone has a place. Groups afford roles we can enact, a sense of identity, a set of relationships with others, feelings of connection and generosity to these people, and important feelings of purpose that extend beyond mere selfishness. As we discussed earlier in the chapter, the emotions of generosity and warmth are among the greatest strengths of our species.

The other side of affiliative emotion within groups is conflict between groups. Many conflicts with out-groups are benign and are ritualized into competition, not unlike the individual competition that occurs in hierarchies. Group competition has a worthwhile place in life: we enjoy it when our football team is victorious, we like it when a university to which we belong does well, we can feel proud when a company for which we work is successful or when a member of our nation wins a medal at the Olympic Games.

But some intergroup conflicts become violent, and this potentiality is probably the most destructive of our human proclivities. A capacity to act violently against members of out-groups is embedded deep in our nature.

Novels and films: *Harry Potter and the Philosopher's Stone*

In J.K. Rowling's *Harry Potter and the Philosopher's Stone* we meet Harry, a young wizard. His parents were killed by the wicked Lord Voldemort, who vanished after trying to kill Harry, leaving him with a distinctive scar on his forehead. Now Harry has been placed for safekeeping with relatives who are muggles (non-wizards), who neglect and mistreat him. At the age of 11 he discovers he is famous among wizards for having escaped Voldemort, and that he has been accepted at Hogwarts School for Witchcraft and Wizardry, a boarding school that is its own enclosed world with friends and adversaries.

As to emotions: under cover of a cloak of invisibility, Harry is able to search the school library, where he finds the Mirror of Erised. When Harry looks into it he sees his parents. He becomes addicted to this sight until he is rescued by the school's headmaster, Dumbledore, who explains that one sees in the mirror whatever one most desires. Readers of *Understanding Emotions* will know that this is Harry's attachment desire for his lost parents.

Emotional themes continue: so when Voldemort feels emotions, Harry's scar itches. Finally there is a confrontation with Voldemort. Harry ends up in a hospital, where Dumbledore tells him he survived Voldemort's attack because his mother sacrificed her life for him, and Voldemort could not understand such love.

How do we explain the emotional power of the Harry Potter books? As well as the attachment theme, part of the answer is that it's about identification with groups: wizards as compared with muggles, good people such as ourselves as compared with bad people, and as compared with outright wicked people such as Voldemort (in stories out-groups are often depicted as wicked). Gabriel and Young (2011) investigated this idea by asking people to read an extract either from *Harry Potter and the Philosopher's Stone*, or Stephanie Meyer's *Twilight* (which is about vampires). Readers were given a test of implicit associations to *wizard* and *vampire* words, and were also asked explicit questions such as "Do you think, if you tried really hard, you might be able to make an object move just using the power of your mind?" and "How sharp are your teeth?"

Gabriel and Young found that people who read the Harry Potter excerpt took on characteristics of a wizard, and those who read an excerpt from *Twilight* took on characteristics of a vampire. Readers' identification with wizards or vampires put them in a good mood and it prompted higher scores on a life-satisfaction scale. Such identification demonstrates a basic need for connection. It can alleviate loneliness by attaching people to a social group and can offer a rewarding psychological identity.

Anger and Intergroup Conflict

On the evening of April 6, 1994, a plane carrying President Juvenal Habyarimana of Rwanda, a Hutu, was shot down near Kigali, Rwanda's capital. The incident would fuel anti-Tutsi sentiment among the majority Hutus, and in the 100 days that followed, Hutus would massacre approximately 800,000 Tutsis and moderate Hutus. A United Nations force was committed to preventing violence, but was unable to do so (Dallaire, 2004). The rage and anger felt by Hutus toward Tutsis fueled the genocide. So, too, did other emotions. For example, in a widely read newspaper and on local radio stations, Hutus were fed propaganda about the Tutsis; rumors about disgusting habits and inhuman tendencies no doubt increased the contempt felt by Hutus toward their Tutsi compatriots. As we'll discuss in Chapter 14, some admirable people were able to resist the almost overwhelming emotional pressures: some Hutu women took care of Tutsi children, putting themselves at risk of death (Prunier, 1995).

Among ethnically motivated genocides of the 20th century were the killings of minorities for being minorities by the Pol Pot regime in Cambodia between 1975 and 1979 (Kiernan, 2008), and the 1995 massacre of Muslims in Srebrenica, Bosnia, by the Army of the Serbian Republic (Leyesdorff, 2011). The most egregious example occurred when, from 1933 onward, German citizens were induced to commit themselves to the Nazis' programs. The programs involved injecting propaganda into all levels of education and through the use of mass-communication media such as radio and film. The process was based on positive emotional appeals to national pride, and it included the happiness of leisure activities and recreation, made widely available in the Strength Through Joy movement. It was based, too, on the negative emotions of fear of denunciation by acquaintances, terror of imprisonment and death for nonconformity, and angry contempt toward out-groups (Evans, 2005, 2008; Larson, 2011). Conspicuous among the out-groups were Jews, of whom the Nazis killed six million in World War II's total death toll of 60 to 70 million.

How are we to think of such terrible events? Perhaps the most important starting point is the discovery by Jane Goodall (1986) that we described in Chapter 2 about how chimpanzees of a larger group systematically hunted down and killed chimpanzees from a smaller group who had previously been members of the whole group, but who had split off and started to live separately. These observations indicate that the potential for intergroup violence in humans is part of our primate heritage. The lessons of genocide challenge us to think about how emotions of anger and rage, which are potent in producing violent behavior, derive from antisocial motivations.

Leonard Berkowitz has devoted a career to studying the proximal determinants of violence (1993). His conclusion is that anger is the spark of violence. This thesis is borne out in studies of

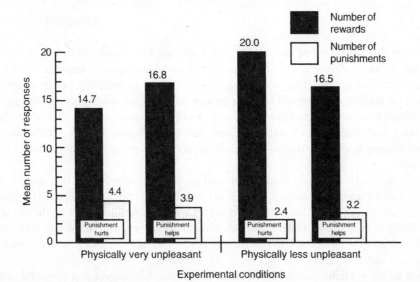

FIGURE 9.4 Mean numbers of rewards and punishments given to others by women who were in pain (physically very unpleasant condition) or not in pain (physically less unpleasant condition) (Berkowitz et al., 1981).

aggression. For example, Figure 9.4 portrays findings showing that when feeling angered by pain women are less likely to reward others and more likely to punish them. In studies of violent children and adults, it is high levels of anger felt by the individual that give rise to violence (see Chapters 12 and 13). With respect to violence between groups, Berkowitz has noted that many of the social conditions that increase the likelihood of aggression between groups —insults, humiliations, civil strife, inequality—increase violence when these conditions give rise to feelings of anger.

This analysis begs the question of what factors increase the likelihood of one group feeling rage and anger toward another and thus being more likely to act aggressively. Diane Mackie and Eliot Smith and their colleagues have offered an answer (Mackie et al., 2000; Mackie, Devos, & E. R. Smith, 2000; Mackie & Smith, 2002; E. R. Smith, 1993; see also Dumont et al., 2003; Yzerbyt et al., 2003). They have found that anger directed at the out-group is more likely when group members individually feel that their own group is strong as compared with the out-group, and when the members are very identified with the group. And regrettably, incidental feelings of anger, once set in motion, will increase prejudice and hatred toward out-groups (DeSteno et al., 2004).

Disgust and Us–Them Thinking

Violence between groups often includes anger, but it's also prompted by other feelings. Disgust is a clearly toxic emotion between groups, and can fuel violence. Here, for instance, is a description of the result of the Aztecs under Montezuma offering a gift of precious works of art in gold and other materials, hoping to buy off the aggression of Cortez and the Spaniard invaders:

> The Spaniards' faces grinned: they were delighted, they were overjoyed. They snatched up the gold like monkeys. ... . They were swollen with greed; they were ravenous; they hungered for that gold . . . They babbled in a barbarous language; everything they said was in a savage tongue.

> (Wright, 1992, p. 26)

While the Spaniards treated the Aztecs with contempt, the Aztecs, from whose eyewitness reports this is taken, observed the Spaniards' behavior with disgust: a response seen in many encounters between groups. They viewed those alien others as behaving not as people but as animals. This tendency to respond to other groups with disgust is common during periods of rising violence between groups. Groups in conflict will dehumanize one another with references to each other as disgusting rats or vermin. These feelings of disgust set the stage for laws—such as the anti-Semitic laws of the Nazis—that limit contact across group boundaries and set the stage for violence.

Early in the study of disgust, Paul Rozin and his colleagues proposed that disgust, though originally derived from taste, often extends from protecting the body from disease, to protection against contamination of all kinds, to anything that might harm our soul or the social order (Rozin, Haidt, & McCauley, 2008). This extends to others groups: people can feel disgusted with other groups and be guided by the irrational belief that contact renders one's own group contaminated and less pure.

Guided by these claims, recent work has documented that disgust is a powerful engine of prejudices toward out-groups. For example, people who report a trait-like tendency to experience high levels of disgust also report high levels of dislike for groups, and in particular homosexuals (Inbar et al., 2009; Tapias et al., 2007). Yoel Inbar and his colleagues have led people to experience disgust by spraying nearby trashcans with a foul odor. Smelling a disgusting scent led participants to express negative attitudes toward gays (Inbar et al., in press). Disgust can amplify prejudicial feelings, in particular toward homosexuals, and, more generally, can give rise to us-versus-them thinking.

Infrahumanization

The emotional preference for "us" and hostility to "them" is seen in many cultures (Brown, 1991). Even the random assignment of individuals to meaningless groups triggers preferential judgments and treatments of people in the in-group and derogation of individuals in the out-group (Tajfel & Turner, 1979). This tendency to think of one's own group as superior compared to other groups is amplified by different emotions, in particular anger, contempt, and disgust.

One emotion-related facet of the tendency to privilege the in-group compared to the out-group is known as infrahumanization (Cortes, Demoulin, Rodriguez, Rodriguez, & Leyens, 2005). **Infrahumanization** is the tendency for in-group members to attribute animal-like qualities to out-group members—that is, to deny them full human standing. Emotions play a critical role in infrahumanization. In many different parts of the world, group members assume that their own group is more likely than out-group members to experience more complex, sophisticated emotions such as pride or sympathy (Cortes et al., 2005). These more complex emotions involve more uniquely human cognitive capacities—a sense of self, taking others' perspectives, empathy—and are especially important in the value group members attach to their own identity (and by implication, how they might devalue other identities). By contrast, group members attribute similar levels of more basic emotions, such as anger or disgust, to their own group and different out-groups. As is evident in how conflicts escalate, this tendency toward infrahumanization can readily feed into violence toward out-group members.

Emotional Processes That Improve Group Relations

Much as emotions can readily accelerate divisions and violence between groups, emotional processes can also improve relations between groups. For example, friendships across group boundaries have been found to reduce the negative emotions that escalate tensions between people from different groups (Page-Gould & Mendoza-Denton, 2011).

Also important is joint projects that unite members of different groups. In one imaginative exploration of this thesis, Muzafer Sherif and his colleagues created surprisingly high levels of conflict between two groups of boys at a summer camp. To build stronger relations between the two groups of boys, the investigators engaged them in **joint project**s. One such project was when the investigators arranged that the water supply to the camp was cut off. The boys had to search for the problem in the long pipeline coming into the camp and then repair it. They could do this only by both groups cooperating. Another was when the boys were hungry and the investigators arranged that the truck, which was to go to town to get food, would not start. The boys used a rope—one that had been used in the tug-of-war competitions—to pull together to start the truck. Hostility did not cease immediately, but after a number of such cooperative activities it was much reduced (see Figure 9.5).

Another solution to conflict between groups is one that we have seen is powerful in intimate relations and families: **forgiveness**, which has its roots in the reconciliation processes nonhuman

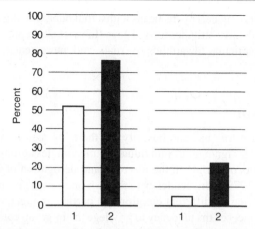

FIGURE 9.5 Hostility toward an out-group in Sherif's study. On the left the open histogram shows the proportion of boys in group 1 who thought that *all* (rather than some or none) in group 2 were cheaters, sneaks, and so forth, while the solid histogram shows the proportion of group 2 who thought that all members of group 1 were cheaters, sneaks, and so forth. On the right are comparable histograms after harmony had been restored by cooperative activities.

primates so routinely engage in to maintain peaceful communities. We saw earlier that forgiveness is important to marriages and family intimacy. Forgiveness has been a central process to repairing relations between groups in conflict. In South Africa, after the end of apartheid, the Truth and Reconciliation Commission set out to bring white perpetrators of violence face to face with their black victims with the intention of promoting forgiveness. In informal "truth and reconciliation" gatherings in Rwandan villages, Hutu perpetrators apologized to relatives of their victims, who were given a public arena to air their rage and sense of injustice. Today, although tensions and bitterness persist, levels of aggression between the Hutus and Tutsis are low.

Emotional Intelligence

We began this chapter with the story of Tim Page, the music critic who has struggled in personal relationships because of his Aspergers condition. We have seen throughout this chapter how important the expression and experience of different emotions is to intimate relations, friendships, hierarchical relationships, and even dynamics between groups. Emotions are a grammar of human relationships.

Is there a general concept that might capture the importance of emotion in relationships? John Mayer and Peter Salovey think so, and, in an important theoretical development, have outlined the concept of **emotional intelligence** (Salovey & Mayer, 1990). Their argument is that just as people vary in terms of verbal, quantitative, analytic, or artistic intelligence, they likewise vary in terms of their emotional intelligence.

Salovey and Mayer argue that emotional intelligence involves four different skills. First, it involves an ability to accurately perceive others' emotions through the careful reading of others' facial expressions, vocalizations, and posture and gesture. One way to think about the effects of power on emotion, then, is that when in positions of high power, this first component of emotional intelligence is compromised. Second, emotional intelligence involves an ability to understand one's own emotions, a skill that is compromised, for example, by particular kinds of brain damage (see Chapter 6). Third, emotional intelligence involves an ability to use current feelings in making decisions, which we describe in Chapter 10. Fourth, emotional intelligence includes the ability to manage one's emotions in ways that are fitting to the current situation, usually called emotion regulation (see Chapter 14).

Given the arguments of this section, one would expect individuals who score high on measures of emotional intelligence to fare better in their relationships. Several studies show this to be the case (Mayer et al., 2008). For example, 5-year-old children who scored higher on measures of emotional intelligence were better adjusted socially 3 years later. Adolescents who scored higher on emotional intelligence reported having more friends and better social support. Young adults who scored higher on emotional intelligence had more constructive and cooperative interactions with their romantic partners. Late in life, adults who scored higher on emotional intelligence enjoyed greater respect and rank at work and were perceived to be better workplace citizens. Emotional intelligence, then, benefits the four kinds of relationships we have considered in this chapter: intimate bonds, friendships, hierarchical relations, and relations with other group members.

SUMMARY

This chapter zeroed in on a central theme in this book: that emotions are social. We began by suggesting that there are two ways to think about the social nature of emotions: emotions can structure social relationships; and emotional responses are shaped by the relationships we are in. Within intimate relationships shaped by attachment goals, we looked at how desire and love help create intimate bonds, and at the negative emotional processes (e.g., contempt) and positive emotional processes (e.g., forgiveness) that contribute to the quality of the marital bond. In friendships defined by the goal of affiliation, gratitude, mimicry, and the general feeling of social support are ingredients for good friendships and the broader sense of being socially connected. In hierarchical relationships defined by the goals of power and assertion, emotional displays are one means by which we negotiate positions of rank, and our position of power and social class influence the emotions we feel and our capacity to empathize with others. Finally, we discussed how emotional processes bind us to groups, and how in-group/out-group dynamics are shaped by emotion, by feelings of rage and disgust, and by infrahumanization, but also how these can be moderated by the tendency to forgive. Putting these findings together, emotional intelligence, defined by four skills, proves to be a general benefit for many kinds of relationships.

TO THINK ABOUT AND DISCUSS

1. Consider yourself and someone you know well. How do you and this other person negotiate emotional transitions between sexual attraction and commitment?

2. Think of the different social hierarchies among the people you know: perhaps of intelligence, fashion sense, sporting ability, money, success with romantic partners, confidence when speaking. Which hierarchies are important to you? How do your emotions affect and respond to your movements up and down these hierarchies?

3. What social group(s) are you most identified with? Perhaps you are a feminist, a keen member of your university or college, or a supporter of a sports team. What feelings do you have of belonging, and what feelings do you have toward people who are not members of your group?

FURTHER READING

For an excellent review of research on emotions in social life:

Larissa Tiedens and Colin Leach (Eds.) (2004). *The social life of emotions*. New York, NY: Cambridge University Press.

Among the best single-author works on love is a book by an anthropologist:

Helen Fisher (1992). *Anatomy of love*. New York, NY: Norton.

An excellent book on anger is:

Carol Tavris (1989). *Anger: The misunderstood emotion, revised edition*. New York, NY: Simon & Schuster.

A fascinating account of an American family witnessing the changes that took place in Germany after the Nazis had come to power:

E. Larson (2011). *In the garden of the beasts: Love, terror, and an American family in Hitler's Berlin*. New York, NY: Crown.

Emotions and Cognition

10

Photo Credit: Toronto Rare Book Library

FIGURE 10.0 Reason, advised by Divine Grace, holds the Passions, Feare, Despaire, Choler, and others in chains. The caption starts: "Passions araing'd by Reason here you see/As she's Advis'd by Grace Divine. . . . " From Senault (1671).

CONTENTS

The heart has its reasons of which reason knows nothing.

           Blaise Pascal, Pensées, *iv*

On July 2, 1860, Eadweard Muybridge, a founding figure in photography, boarded a stagecoach for St. Louis, where he was to catch a train and make his way to Europe to buy rare books for his San Francisco bookstore. In northeastern Texas the driver of the stagecoach lost control of the horses, and the coach careened down a mountainside. In the crash, Muybridge was thrown headfirst into a tree. Miraculously he survived and, although he suffered serious brain damage, he made the trip to England, where he spent six vague years recuperating.

Muybridge returned to California in 1866, but he was not the same man. His photography had an eerily risky and often obsessive quality. He would take thousands of photographs of animals in motion. He took hundreds of photos of himself, often naked, with his characteristic furrowed brow glaring into the camera.

In 1872, Muybridge married Flora Shallcross Stone, 21 years his junior. Not long after the wedding, while Muybridge was away on assignment, Flora had an affair with a dashing young man, Harry Larkyns, and from this assignation she had a baby. At an acquaintance's house, Muybridge saw a photo of the baby he thought was his, and casually looked at the back of the photo. On it were written the words "Little Harry." The acquaintance confirmed Muybridge's suspicion that the baby was not his.

Muybridge went to the ranch in Calistoga, California, where Larkyns worked. He greeted the man by saying: "I am Muybridge, and this is a message from my wife." He raised a Smith & Wesson No. 2 six-shooter and shot and killed Larkyns.

At Muybridge's highly publicized trial, witnesses spoke of how different he seemed upon his return from England. Silas Selleck, a friend and fellow photographer, observed: "After his return from Europe he was very eccentric, and so very unlike his way before going." M. Gray noted that before the accident Muybridge was "much less irritable than after his return; was much more careless in dress after his return." J.G. Easland testified that after the accident Muybridge had "certain eccentricities of speech, manner, and action."

Passion and Reason

Eadweard Muybridge's orbitofrontal cortex had been damaged. In Chapters 1 and 5, we referred to Damasio's (1994) work with people who suffered a similar damage, with effects on their emotions and social lives. Here we extend that line of thought. Without a functioning orbitofrontal cortex and the social emotions that this brain area is involved in processing, people lack social judgment; their decision making is askew. It isn't that on the one hand there is rationality and on the other hand there is emotion. Without social emotions, these brain-damaged people become no longer rational. We see Muybridge's shooting of Larkyns as driven by jealousy. We can understand jealousy, and may have suffered it ourselves. Many people who have no disorder are driven by it, and their actions sometimes land them in criminal courts. In Muybridge's case, however, the jealousy was so magnified, so unaffected by other emotions—love for the child he had thought was his son, who was innocent of the events that upset Muybridge, compassion for his victim, fear of consequences for himself—that the jealousy seemed to have grown larger than the man himself. For us to be functioning members of society, our emotions need to be in working order in relation to each other so that they may guide our reasoning and action wisely.

One of the most striking qualities of emotions is how they influence reasoning. The philosopher Jean-Paul Sartre (1962) referred to this as **magical transformation** by the emotions of how we see the world. When angry, afraid, euphoric, or in love, we construe the world in different ways. Each emotion invokes its own world, almost never as completely as jealousy did for Eadweard Muybridge. Usually it's more temporary, but usually it's convincing at the time. We are aware of particular themes or events. We recall particular experiences from our past. We envision a certain future. Each emotion is its own lens through which we view the world.

In the Western philosophical tradition, emotions have often been regarded with suspicion. The position taken by the ethical philosophers of the third century BCE, the Epicureans and Stoics, was that to lead a good life, emotions should be extirpated altogether (Nussbaum, 1994). If Epicureans or Stoics heard about Muybridge's jealousy, they would say: "There, you see!" Drawing on these intuitions, many philosophers have assumed that the emotions are less sophisticated, more primitive ways of perceiving the world, especially when juxtaposed with loftier forms of reason (Haidt, 2001). The implication is that human society is better off when the more primitive passions are reigned in by rational thought. The rare exception was someone like the 18th-century moral philosopher, David Hume (1739–1740/1972), who contended in a famous statement that "Reason is and ought only to be the slave of the passions."

What do we mean when we ask whether emotions can be rational? A first meaning has to do with whether the emotions are based on substantive beliefs: do beliefs and appraisals that support our emotions correspond to actual events in the world? Although we often experience emotions in response to imaginary occurrences, most often our emotions meet this criterion of rationality. The literature on appraisal (see Chapter 7) suggests that emotions are often products of complex beliefs about events in the world.

A second meaning of rationality concerns whether emotions help individuals function effectively in the social world. We think of rational human beings as those who navigate their environment effectively. Delusional beliefs of grandiosity (overweening pride) or persecution (pervasive fear) are irrational in this sense. They make it difficult for the individual to be an effective member of society. A central assumption of this book is that emotions in many contexts are rational in that they help individuals respond adaptively to the environment. This is certainly not true all the time, as we shall see in Chapters 12 and 13, but many, if not most, occurrences of emotion help people act adaptively.

A third meaning is relevant to this chapter. Do emotions guide perception, attention, memory, and judgment in principled, organized, and constructive ways? Or do they interfere with and disrupt cognitive processes? Certain extreme levels of emotion can get the better of us. Extreme anger may prevent us from perceiving cooperative gestures of an ideological opponent or romantic partner. Yet 40 years of research—the focus of this chapter—indicates that emotions structure perception, direct attention, give preferential access to certain memories, and bias judgment in ways that generally help people in ways that we recognize as valuable to our humanity (Clore, Gasper, & Garvin, 2001; Clore & Palmer, 2009; Forgas, 2003).

Emotions Prioritize Thoughts, Goals, and Actions

The notion that emotions guide cognitive processes in an adaptive fashion emerged within a movement known as cognitive science, which matured in the 1960s and included among its methods the construction of mind-like processes in computers. The question is this: If you had to design a mind, what problems would you have to face and what principles would you need to embody?

In an influential paper, Simon (1967) argued that emotions would be necessary in any intelligent being; a human, a Martian, or—if we were ever able to create it—an intelligent computer. Emotions, Simon continued, are a solution to a general problem: they set priorities among the very many different goals that impinge upon individuals at any moment.

This need for some sort of interrupt and prioritization mechanism emerges in complex organisms like humans (De Sousa, 1987; Oatley, 1992). In very simple animals, behavior is controlled by reflexes. Take the behavior of the female tick as an example (Von Uexküll, 1934). After mating, she climbs a tree and hangs at the end of a lower twig. When she detects a particular stimulus—the smell of butyric acid—she lets go. Because tiny quantities of butyric acid are released into the air by mammals, letting go of the branch in response to this stimulus gives a fair probability of falling onto the back of a passing mammal, such as a browsing deer. If the tick lands on a mammal's back, another stimulus comes to control behavior: warm temperature causes the tick to climb through the fur toward the warmth. When she reaches the mammal's skin, another stimulus triggers burrowing into it, to suck the mammal's blood, which will be necessary for laying her eggs. In the simple world of the female tick, the perceptual system is tuned to just a few events. In the tick's world there is no need for emotions.

Now imagine a being at the other end of the scale of complexity, one vastly more intelligent than ourselves, perhaps a god. A god is often conceived of as omniscient and omnipotent or, as a cognitive scientist might say, having a perfect model of the universe and no limitations of resources. Such a being could predict the results of its every action. Again there is no need for emotions. Everything would be known, everything anticipated.

We are somewhere in between ticks and gods. Our world is complex and we act with purposes. But our actions sometimes produce effects we don't anticipate. We have limitations of knowledge and resources. Sometimes we need encouragement to continue what we are doing. Sometimes events occur—small successes, losses, frustrations, threats—for which we have no ready-prepared response and which may make it better to switch goals or change plans. Such events occur when we don't know enough to be certain what to do next. They are signaled by emotions. They don't tell us exactly what to do next. They prompt us and create an urge and a readiness to act in a certain way or in a range of ways that, on average during the course of evolution and our own development, have been better either than acting randomly or than becoming lost in thought trying to calculate the best possible action.

This notion that emotions signal conflict and redirect the individual's action was a focus of classical Greek dramas, of some of Aristotle's work, and of much of Freud's. What became new in the era of cognitive science was the idea of just how important emotions (or something like them) are for any complex being that has several motives and that operates in a complex world. Emotions guide action in a world that is always imperfectly known and that can never be fully controlled. It is not so much that emotions are irrational, but rather that in a complex world we often have no fully rational solution because we do not know enough. Emotions are bridges toward rationality.

In elaborating this view, Oatley and Johnson-Laird (1987, 2011) proposed that emotions involve two different kinds of signaling in the nervous system, which we discussed in Chapter 7. One kind occurs automatically and derives from primary appraisal. In evolutionary terms it is old, simple, and carries no specific information about objects in the environment. It's **organizational**. It sets the brain into a particular mode of organization, or readiness, along with an urge to act in line with this readiness, specific to the particular basic emotion (joy, anger, sadness, fear, etc.). It has the phenomenological feeling tone of an emotion but no other content. Such an emotion-related signal can have many sources, inside the body and outside in the environment (Izard, 1993). It is a quick prompt toward the kind of thing to do next. It is significant that phenomena of emotional priming, in which stimuli are shown subliminally (discussed in Chapter 7), operate at this automatic, unconscious level (Winkielman, Zajonc, & Schwarz, 1997) and are resistant to attributional interventions.

The second kind of signal derives from secondary appraisal. It is **informational**. The information it carries enables us to make mental models of the events and their possible causes and implications. On the basis of these two kinds of signal we act in accordance both with how we feel and with what we know.

Normally the organizational and informational signals occur together to produce an emotional feeling with a consciously known cause and object. But the two kinds of signal can be dissociated, as we discussed in relation to split-brain patients in Chapter 7. According to Oatley and Johnson-Laird (1996), the dissociation accounts for why we can sometimes have emotions with no objects, and how psychoactive drugs such as tranquillizers can change our emotional state without doing anything to events of the world. It is also how we can know about some events in the world without caring about them. Figure 10.1 is a diagram of the two kinds of signal.

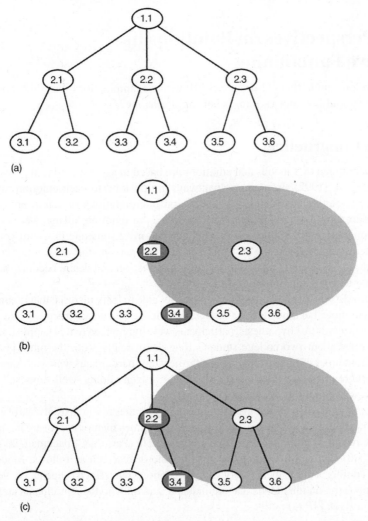

FIGURE 10.1 Modules of the brain and different kinds of messages that pass among them (to illustrate Oatley & Johnson-Laird's, 1987, theory). In (a) the signals are informational and travel along particular pathways. In (b) an emotion-control signal spreads diffusely from one module (2.3), turning some other modules on and some off, thereby setting the system into a distinctive mode. Normally (c) these two kinds of signals occur together.

To illustrate the organizational and informational aspects of an emotion, consider fear. In humans, the organizational part interrupts ongoing action. It makes ready physiological mechanisms and a repertoire of actions for flight or for defensive fight, and urges us toward this kind of action. It directs attention to the environment for any sign of danger or safety, and it induces checking of the results of actions just completed. In this mode, we can think of the brain's resources as marshaled to respond to danger. The emotion signal turns on this mode. Moods are based on the same organizational signals, but they maintain the brain in a certain mode despite events that might tend to switch it into some other mode. The informational part of fear is about what we are frightened of. And as we know, sometimes this can be quite insubstantial.

Three Perspectives on Emotions in Cognitive Functioning

How do emotions guide thought processes? How, for example, does fear shift your perception and judgment? And how do we think when we are happy?

Emotion Congruence

Gordon Bower argued that moods and emotions are based in associative brain networks (Bower, 1981; Mayer et al., 1992). In memory, pathways are devoted to each emotion, in which past experiences, images, related concepts, labels, and interpretations of sensations are interconnected in a semantic network. When you experience an emotion, all the associations of that emotion become more accessible. For example, if you meet someone in whom you once had a romantic interest and feel renewed attraction to that person, the past experiences, related concepts, images, and beliefs related to feelings of attraction and desire become more available and contribute to your interpretation of the event.

According to Bower's account, we should be better able to learn material that is **congruent** with our current emotion, because it is integrated into active memory structures and more easily retrieved. In one test of this hypothesis, participants were hypnotized to feel happy or sad; they then read a brief story about two college students, one doing really well, the other poorly (Bower, Gilligan, & Monteiro, 1981). In a memory test the next day, participants who were happy when they read the story remembered more facts about the student doing well, and sad participants remembered more about the student doing poorly.

The idea proposed by Bower about congruence still pervades research on effects of emotions, but not with the mechanism he proposed. For instance, sometimes memories that are incongruent with mood may be recalled better than those that are congruent (Parrott & Spackman, 2000). Eich and Macaulay (2000) summed up conclusions of this line of research as follows. Mood-dependent effects are certainly salient in memory and perception, but effects depend on the tasks that participants perform, on the moods that are induced, and on who the participants are. So as Eich, Macaulay, and Ryan (1994) put it:

> Two individuals—one happy, the other sad—are shown say, a *rose* and asked to identify and describe what they see. Both individuals are apt to say much the same thing and to encode the *rose* event in the same manner. After all, and with all due respect to Gertrude

Stein, a rose, is a rose is a rose . . . memory for the rose event will probably not appear to be mood dependent under these circumstances. Now imagine a different situation. Instead of identifying and describing the rose the subjects are asked to recall a specific episode, from any time in their personal past, that the object calls to mind. (p. 213)

When people recall an autobiographical event, Eich and his colleagues found that mood effects do occur, but they vary because people's experiences are different (Miranda & Kihlstrom, 2005).

A well-known modification of Bower's proposal is the Affect Infusion Model of Joseph Forgas (Forgas, 1995; Forgas & Laham, 2005). According to this model, emotions infuse into a cognitive task, and are more likely to influence memory and judgment, particularly if the task is complex. For instance, the mood of happiness infuses positive evaluations into judgment tasks. In a study of reasoning from syllogisms, Goel and Vartanian (2011) found an effect of mood infusion. Reasoning from syllogisms is usually found to be affected by prior beliefs, whereas, to be purely logical, people should just reason from the premises offered in a syllogism. Goel and Vartanian found that negative emotions could induce people to pay more attention to the problem as stated and draw conclusions in a way that their prior beliefs did not affect their reasoning.

Feelings as Information

A second approach to thinking, proposed by Gerald Clore, about how emotion influences cognition is of **affect as information** (Clore & Palmer, 2009; Clore & Pappas, 2007; Clore & Parrott, 1991; Martin & Clore, 2001; Schwarz, 2005). In this perspective, emotions themselves can be informative when we make judgments. The account rests on two hypotheses. The first is that emotions provide us with a signal. For example, anger can signal that an injustice has occurred and needs to be changed. A second hypothesis is that many of our judgments are too complex to enable us to review all the relevant evidence. For instance, to say how satisfied you are with your political leader you might think about environmental policy, the state of health care, unemployment and the national economy, global warming, and whether the leader is living up to his or her campaign promises. Given the complexity of so many judgments, we often rely on a simpler assessment based on our current feelings. In the case of evaluating a leader, we often think, more simply: "How do I feel about this person?" Only seldom can human beings act with full rationality, think through all the relevant evidence, and arrive at a justified conclusion. Emotions are **heuristics**, guesses that often work better than chance (Polya, 1957): shortcuts to making judgments or taking action.

One test of this affect-as-information perspective was by Schwarz and Clore (1983), who studied effects of bright sunny days and gloomy overcast days on people's emotional lives. They telephoned people in Illinois either on a cloudy or a sunny day and asked them: "All things considered, how satisfied or dissatisfied are you with your life as a whole these days?" In one condition participants were simply asked this question. In a second condition, participants were first asked: "How's the weather down there?" and only then asked the question about life satisfaction. Schwarz and Clore predicted that only those participants who had *not* been asked about the weather would use their current feelings as heuristics, or shortcut strategies to help make the complex judgment of how satisfied they were: those who were called on a sunny day would report greater life satisfaction than participants who were called on a gloomy day. Participants who *were* asked about the weather, Schwarz and Clore reasoned, would be less likely to be influenced by feelings that had been affected by the weather as they made their judgments of life satisfaction. As you can see from Figure 10.2, the results of this study confirm Schwarz and Clore's claim that people often use their

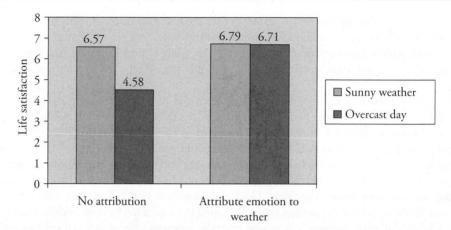

FIGURE 10.2   People say they're more satisfied with their life on sunny than on overcast days, except when they are explicitly asked to think about the weather (Schwarz & Clore, 1983).

emotions as heuristics in making judgments, but not when they can attribute those feelings to a specific source such as feeling happy because it's a nice day.

In 1992, Clore wrote: "The most reliable phenomenon in the cognition-emotion domain is the effect of mood on evaluative judgment" (p. 134); a mood acquired in one situation can affect a judgment made about something entirely different. One of the most striking studies of this effect was by Dutton & Aron (1974). It's one of the most imaginative studies in the whole of psychology. The researchers recruited young male passers-by who were not accompanied by a female, who crossed the Capilano suspension bridge (near Vancouver, Canada). This bridge is 450 feet long and has cables that act as handrails. One walks across on boards suspended from the cables. The whole bridge rocks and sways alarmingly, so one fears one will fall 200 feet to the rocks and rapids of the Capilano River below. The comparison group was of young men who crossed a fixed cedar bridge further upstream that is firm, wide, and only 10 feet above the river. At the other side of each bridge, each man was met either by a young woman or by a young man, who asked them to take part in a study she or he was conducting for a psychology class on the subject of scenic attractions. Participants were asked to fill out a short questionnaire and look at an ambiguous picture of a young woman covering her face with one hand and reaching out with the other. After the man had completed the questions, the interviewer wrote her or his phone number on a piece of paper, gave it to the participant, and asked him to phone if he wanted to talk further.

Sexual imagery in response to the ambiguous picture was significantly higher in the men who had crossed the high suspension bridge and were met by the female interviewer (as compared with those who crossed the low bridge, or who were met at either bridge by the male interviewer). Not only that, but many more phone calls to the female interviewer were made by men who crossed the high bridge than by those who crossed the low bridge. Dutton and Aron also reported a second field study and a laboratory experiment to show that the correct explanation of the effect was that anxious excitement had transformed to sexual attraction.

When in a positive or negative emotional state, feelings are likely to affect judgments, even when the objects being judged have no relation to the cause of the emotion. Positive and negative moods have been shown to influence a wide array of judgments, which include evaluations of consumer items (Isen, Shalker, Clark, & Karp, 1978), political leaders (Forgas & Moylan, 1987; Keltner, Lock, & Audrain, 1993), and evaluations of losses and gains (Ketelaar, 2004, 2005). In a positive emotional state we evaluate objects and events in a positive light. In a negative emotional state we evaluate the same events and objects in a negative light.

Do current moods and emotions affect judgments of the future? Indeed they do. Negative moods lead people to view the future pessimistically, whereas positive moods lead people to look at the future optimistically. Johnson and Tversky (1983) had participants read newspaper accounts about the death of a young man, which induced a negative mood. People in a negative mood (for instance, sad) judged negative life events in the future, like contracting a disease, to be more likely than people feeling a positive mood (such as feeling happy).

Different emotions are associated with more specific strains of **pessimism** or **optimism**. For example, Keltner, Ellsworth, and Edwards (1993) asked whether people feeling angry or sad would judge different events to be more likely in their future. They reasoned that angry people, attuned to the blameworthy actions of others, would judge unfair acts caused by others to be frequent in the future. In contrast, sad people, attuned to situational causes of negative outcomes, should judge negative life events caused by situational factors as more likely.

To test this hypothesis, they asked angry or sad participants to estimate the likelihood of different events, some of which were caused by other people (a pilot's error causes a friend to die in a plane crash) and some caused by situational factors (icy roads cause a car accident). Consistent with expectation, angry people judged the negative life events caused by other people to be more likely than sad people, who judged the events caused by situational factors to be more likely.

In similar work, DeSteno and colleagues (2000) asked people feeling anger or sadness to estimate the likelihood of "sad" events (of 60,000 orphans in Romania, how many will be malnourished) and "angry" or unfair events (of 20,000 violent criminals put on trial in the upcoming year, how many will be set free because of legal technicalities). Whereas sad participants judged the sadness-inducing events to be more likely, angry participants judged the anger-inducing events to be more likely. In similar work, fearful individuals have been shown to have heightened estimates that risky, dangerous events will be part of their future (Lerner & Keltner, 2001).

The theory of affect as information helps us understand social interactions (Clore & Huntsinger, 2007). With others, we carefully choose our actions and what we say to maintain a tone that is compatible with our identity and our role; our emotion supplies information that enables us to act in this identity-supporting fashion.

Styles of Processing

A third perspective is that different emotions and moods promote different **styles of processing**. When you feel guilty or angry, grateful or enthusiastic, you engage in different forms of reasoning, of weighing evidence, and of drawing conclusions.

One of the most important themes to emerge in cognitive psychology in the last 10 years is that when it comes to thinking, reasoning, and making decisions, two types of system are at work: **System 1** and **System 2**. This idea has been developed by Keith Stanovich (2004) and Daniel Kahneman (2011). System 1 is fast, involuntary, and based on heuristics. Here is a question. Please answer it as fast as you can: "What do cows drink?" For most of us the answer that comes to mind is "milk." It's triggered by the association of the words *cows* and *drink*. This is System 1 at work. But if we go at it more slowly and deliberatively, System 2 starts up and we may think something like: "Milk, perhaps. Well . . . some cows—calves actually—drink milk, but in the ordinary way I suppose cows must drink water." Both systems are good for particular kinds of problem.

In *Thinking Fast and Slow*, Daniel Kahneman (2011) describes the line of research with his colleague, Amos Tversky, in which they showed that when people are asked to do problems that require deliberative thinking, the heuristic response often gets in first. Although the deliberative System 2 is capable of overriding System 1, it is often effortful, and even a bit lazy. Our preference is often for System 1 to make decisions.

Damasio (1994) describes how he suggested to a patient with frontal-lobe damage two possible dates for his next visit, then: "For the better part of half an hour the patient enumerated reasons for and against each of the two dates" (p. 193). He couldn't decide. Damasio had to decide for him, and says he found it difficult to avoid pounding on the table and telling the patient to stop. We would now say the patient was using the deliberative System 2, which on its own couldn't reach a conclusion. For most of us, a System 1 emotion-heuristic would be all we need. We might say: "No difference for me; I'll take the first date." In terms of our emotional world, it's unimportant. Without an emotional world, how could one know?

Given these distinctions, we now might ask: What particular emotions are associated with heuristic thought based on System 1, and which emotions are more likely to engage the deliberative System 2? The answer is that it's been found that positive moods tend to facilitate use of heuristic rather than deliberative thinking. Anxious moods facilitate deliberative thought and careful attention to details (Bless, Schwarz, & Wieland, 1996; Lambert et al., 1997). It's probably a good idea to be anxious when doing one's income taxes!

But there are also differences among negative emotions. If people feel sad, they are less likely to rely on stereotypes than if they feel angry when they make social judgments of others (Bodenhausen, Sheppard, & Kramer, 1994). Stereotypes are heuristics for judging others: ideas like *foreign* or *tough*. They are more likely to be used when one is in an emotional state such as happiness or anger, and often they make us less systematic.

Positive moods can, however, prompt us to think in more flexible ways (Isen et al., 1987). In an important theory, Barbara Fredrickson (e.g., Fredrickson, 1998, 2003; Fredrickson & Branigan, 2005) has argued that the function of positive emotions is to **broaden and build** our resources. Positive emotions enable more creative thought and aid formation of important bonds. The creativity associated with positive emotion that Isen found builds schemas and intellectual resources by enhancing our perspective taking, our novel ideas, and our learning. Positive emotions also help us build interpersonal resources by motivating us to approach others, to cooperate, and to express affection. Research carried out by Fredrickson and her colleagues has found that when we experience positive emotions like joy, amusement, contentment, and relief we are more likely to see global patterns in stimuli rather than focus on specific details, we are more likely to see connections between our group and other groups, and within our close relationships we are more likely to see similarities between ourselves and our relationship partners (Fredrickson, 2001; Johnson & Fredrickson, 2005; Waugh & Fredrickson, 2006). These kinds of findings strongly suggest that we would be well advised not to look upon happiness and pleasure too skeptically, or consider happiness a luxury; it appears to be a wellspring of complex, integrative, and creative thought that is essential to learning, insight, and healthy social bonds.

Individual Emotion: Happiness

What is happiness? If we start to think about it, we might think of things we like: being on vacation on a beach, eating ice-cream, and laughing with a friend. Such activities are usually called pleasures. Pleasures certainly seem to be important to happiness, particularly if you compare them with their opposites, such as having too little money to afford a vacation, being in the throes of illness so that pain blots out other experiences, or feeling socially isolated. But in the course of human history, many writers have been skeptical of the idea that pleasure is the only contributor, or even the most important contributor, to happiness.

The subject of happiness received a big boost recently with the realization by psychologists such as Martin Seligman, Mihaly Csikszentmihaly, and Barbara Fredrickson that for a long time researchers on emotions had concentrated on negative emotions like fear and anger, but neglected positive emotions.

Seligman has proposed that happiness has three main components. Pleasure is one of them, the second is engagement in what one is doing, the third is the meaningfulness of one's activities. In a large Internet survey of 13,565 people, Schueller and Seligman (2010) asked about the extent of these three factors in people's lives. They found that pleasure, engagement, and meaning were all associated with people's subjective sense of well-being in their lives. But in relation to objective well-being, which included measures of educational and occupational attainment, only engagement and meaningfulness contributed positively, whereas pleasure made a negative contribution. These results suggest that engaging and meaningful activities have a stronger influence on well-being than the pursuit of pleasure.

With some colleagues, in 2008, Fredrickson ran a field experiment with 139 adults, half of whom were assigned to begin a practice of loving-kindness mediation. Over time this practice increased their amounts of positive emotion, which in turn produced increases of personal resources such as increased mindfulness, increased sense of purpose in life, and social support, as well as decreased symptoms of illness and depression.

Effects of Moods and Emotions on Cognitive Functioning

Let's now review the influence of emotions and moods on perception, attention, memory, judgment, and decision making. As we do this, we ask you to consider whether emotions are rational, and how the findings conform to the claims of the three accounts just given—congruence, feelings-as-information, and styles of processing.

Perceptual Effects

Do moods and emotions influence our perceptions? Experience suggests so. You may have gone to a family gathering and had your perception of the event shaped by your feelings. When feeling blue, you might have been more attuned to what has been lost, or the unfulfilled hopes that perhaps hover behind many such gatherings. In an exhilarated mood, the same event might strike you entirely differently, as full of conviviality and promise.

Are we attuned to perceiving things that are congruent with our mood? Niedenthal and Setterlund (1994) induced happy and sad moods by playing music throughout an experimental session. To put people in a happy mood they played pieces such as the allegro from Mozart's *Eine Kleine Nacht Musik.* To induce sadness they played pieces such as *Adagietto* by Mahler. Participants performed a standard psychological task, called a *lexical decision* task, in which strings of letters were flashed on a screen: some were words and some were non-words that can be pronounced in English, like *blatkin*. Participants were asked to press one button if the letters formed a word, another if it was a non-word. Words were from five categories: happy words such as *delight*, positive words unrelated to happiness such as *calm*, sad words like *weep*, negative words unrelated to sadness like *injury*, and neutral words like *habit*. Consistent with the hypothesis of emotion-congruence, when participants were in a happy mood they were quicker at identifying happy than sad words. When sad, they were quicker at identifying sad than happy words. But the effects of happy and sad moods did not extend to the positive or negative words that were unrelated to the specific emotions of happiness or sadness.

Baumann and DeSteno (2010) started their report of how emotions can affect perception with this:

> The death of 23-year-old Amadou Diallo, who was shot and killed on February 4, 1999 by New York City Police officers, stands in most people's memories as a tragic example of rapid threat detection gone wrong. When the young African American man reached into his jacket to produce his wallet and identification, police officers—believing that he was in fact reaching for a gun—opened fire, shooting Diallo 19 times. (p. 595)

Baumann and DeSteno conducted experiments in which participants first wrote about an emotional memory so that they came to feel the corresponding emotion, and then made a judgment. Under the influence of a specific emotion, participants judged whether a man, shown in a photograph for three-quarters of a second, was holding a gun or a neutral object. Anger increased the probability that neutral objects were misidentified as guns. It did not increase the probability that guns were seen as neutral objects. The effect was not one of negative emotions in general, but stemmed from cues of threat evoked by anger.

Our current moods and feelings lead us selectively to perceive emotion-congruent objects and events. This in part helps explain why emotions and moods can persist: because built into our experience is a tendency to perceive emotion-congruent objects and events, thus prolonging our experience.

Niedenthal (2007) explains that when one embodies a particular emotion in oneself, for instance, by making a facial expression or gesture appropriate to it, one is more likely to make judgments appropriate to that emotion (for other evidence, see Chapter 5). The findings reviewed in this section suggest that moods and emotions can redirect perception to objects and events that are relevant to current feelings; often this occurs in ways that are likely to guide action according to current goals and concerns.

Attentional Effects

In his textbook of psychology (1890, vol. 1, p. 402), William James wrote: "My experience is what I agree to attend to." It is also what we attend to even when we do not consciously agree to it. Emotions affect attention. The effects range from largely unconscious processes of filtering incoming information to conscious preoccupation of the kind that we have when we worry.

Among the most studied effects of emotions on attention are those that concern anxiety. Anxiety narrows attention (Mineka, Rafaeli, & Yovel, 2003). When we are anxious we focus on what we are anxious about. If we are doing a task that involves arithmetic and it's important not to make a mistake, a focusing anxiety can be useful. But if people persistently focus on feared events, or on keeping safe from them, they can come to disregard many, or even most, other issues (Eysenck, Derekshan, Santos, & Calvo, 2007). Anxiety can come to monopolize processing capacities and even whole lives. People for whom this is the case suffer from an anxiety disorder, which we discuss in Chapter 13.

Among several ways of exploring how an anxious-making threat can capture attention is the **emotional Stroop test**. Stroop (1935) found that if people were asked to look at words such as *red*, *yellow*, and *blue* that were printed in different colors, and to name the color of the *print* for each word, they were slowed down when the color of the print and the color word were different—they were slower if the word *red* was printed in blue ink and they had to say "blue," than if it were printed in red ink and they therefore had to say "red." The meaning of the word involuntarily captures attention, distracting subjects from naming the ink color. This idea of the emotional Stroop test is that words are shown that are neutral or that have emotional significance, to see if people are slowed down in naming the colors of words with emotional significance. Using this test, Foa et al. (1991) found that people who had been victims of rape were slowed down in naming the print-colors of words related to rape. People who had coped with their trauma better showed less capture of attention by these words.

In another kind of study, Calvo and Avero (2005) presented pictures of scenes that were either neutral or emotional (positive, harm related, or threat related). In each trial, a neutral and an emotional picture were presented side by side for three seconds and participants' eye movements were measured. As compared with non-anxious people, anxious participants more often looked first at the emotional picture than at the neutral one in a pair; then they looked longer at emotional pictures during the first half-second of viewing. In the later phase of viewing they tended to avoid looking at the emotional pictures.

An important implication of attention is that its effects of emotional prioritization enable us to concentrate on just those events and objects that are relevant to what we are doing. Fenske and Raymond (2006) review these effects, based on fMRI studies, and offer evidence for a reciprocal influence in which, when we concentrate on a task, patterns, objects, and even perhaps people irrelevant to that task, that previously were neutral, become less emotionally attractive. Sharot, Korn, and Dolan (2011) have found that optimistic people (about 80% of us, although we wouldn't necessarily label ourselves in this way) maintain our optimism by being biased to focus on positive rather than negative events in the future.

Effects on Remembering

To understand the effect of emotions on memory, we need first to explain how memory works. This is best seen in the groundbreaking work of Frederic Bartlett (1932). He asked people first to read a story and then to reproduce it as exactly as possible, both immediately after reading and at intervals up to several years later. In one famous experiment, Bartlett had people read a Native American folk story called "The War of the Ghosts" twice, at their normal reading speed. It starts like this:

> One night two young men from Egulac went down to the river to hunt seals, and while they were there it became foggy and calm. Then they heard war-cries, and they thought:

"Maybe this is a war party." They escaped to the shore, and hid behind a log. Now canoes came up, and they heard the noise of paddles, and saw one canoe coming up to them. There were five men in the canoe, and they said:

"What do you think? We wish to take you along. We are going up the river to make war on the people."

One of the young men said: "I have no arrows."

"Arrows are in the canoe," they said.

"I will not go along. I might be killed. My relatives do not know where I have gone. But you," he said, turning to the other, "may go with them."

So one of the young men went . . .

Then follow 11 lines about how the young man who went with the men in the canoe took part in a fight in which he was shot but did not feel sick, and thought, "Oh, they are ghosts." The story ends with his return home. Here are the story's last lines:

He told it all, and then he became quiet. When the sun rose he fell down. Something black came out of his mouth. His face became contorted. The people jumped up and cried.
He was dead.

Here is a reproduction by one of Bartlett's participants who had been asked to reproduce the story several times in the first months after reading it, but had then not thought of it for two-and-a-half years:

Some warriors went to wage war against the ghosts. They fought all day and one of their number was wounded.
They returned home in the evening, bearing their sick comrade. As the day drew to a close, he became rapidly worse and the villagers came round him. At sunset he sighed: something black came out of his mouth. He was dead.

Here, much has been lost and much has changed. In the remembered story the man dies at sunset rather than sunrise. But the emotionally charged detail "something black came out of his mouth" was preserved, as it was in most of the reproductions that Bartlett reported.

Bartlett concluded that when we remember a verbal account our words are never exact. What we perceive is assimilated into our own structure of meaning, which Bartlett called a **schema**, which includes a great deal of general knowledge. When a recall is asked for, the participant takes a few significant remembered details and a general emotional attitude to the story and from the schema constructs what the story must have been. So style becomes the participant's style, and things happen in ways appropriate to the culture of the person remembering, such as dying in the evening rather than at sunrise.

As Bartlett said, remembering:

. . . is an imaginative reconstruction, built out of the relation of our [emotional] attitude towards a whole active mass of organized past reactions or experience, and to a little outstanding detail. . . . It is thus hardly ever really exact . . . and it is not at all important that it should be. (1932, p. 213)

In one group of 20 participants, Bartlett reported that in their early reproductions only 10 remembered the excuse of the young man saying he had no arrows, but 18 remembered the excuse that the man's relatives would not know where he had gone. Bartlett ran this study toward the end of World War I, and he wrote that anxieties about separation from relatives were salient at this time. Was this, perhaps, why the idea of making an excuse about relatives could easily enter participants' minds, and why they remembered it?

How accurate are our memories? Waganaar (1986) recorded an event from his own life every day for four years. He made up standard forms, and for each event he wrote whom it concerned, what it was, where it happened, and when. He also described a critical detail about each event, and he rated the event on three scales: salience (how frequently events such as this occurred, from every day to once in a lifetime), emotional involvement, and pleasantness. A colleague transcribed all the events into typewritten booklets, so that on recall he could be given one, two, three, and then all four of the recall cues (who, what, where, when) in order. His task was to recall all the other cues, and when all four cues had been given, also to recall the critical detail. If he were unsuccessful in all these, the event was scored as completely forgotten. Over a period of five years, the numbers of events completely forgotten were about 20% but, as you can see from Figure 10.3, most events could not be remembered in all their details and recall deteriorated over time.

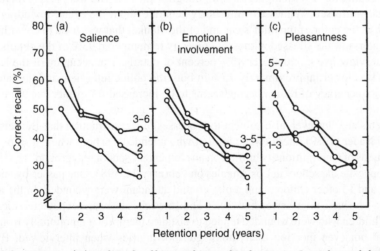

FIGURE 10.3 Wagenaar's (1986) study of his autobiographical memory. In each panel the percentage of events correctly recalled when all the cues were given is shown as a function of one of three variables over five years. In (a) the variable is salience; the graph marked 3–6 indicates events of the kind that happen once a month to once in a lifetime, 2 indicates the kind that happen once a week, and 1 indicates the kind that happen once a day. In (b) the variable of emotional involvement is shown by a graph marked 3–5 for moderately to extremely involving, one marked 2 indicating little involvement, and one marked 1 meaning no involvement. In (c) the variable of pleasantness, the graph marked 5–7 means pleasant to extremely pleasant, 4 means neutral, and 1–3 means unpleasant to extremely unpleasant.

Eyewitness Testimony

What if you were an eyewitness to a crime? How would your memory for the event be affected? Psychologists know from Bartlett's (1932) principles, and from research by Loftus and Doyle (1987), that eyewitness testimony is often mistaken. A sense of certainty does not mean the memory is correct. In Britain the Devlin Report (of an official committee set up to examine cases of wrongful conviction for crimes) recommended that it is not reliable to convict someone on the basis of eyewitness testimony unless the circumstances are exceptional or the testimony is corroborated by evidence of some other kind.

There has now been much research on memory for stressful events (Christianson, 1992). Here is an engaging and unusual study. Five months after a thief had held up a gun shop in a suburb of Vancouver, Yuille and Cutshall (1986) were able to re-interview 13 witnesses, previously interviewed by the police, about the event. The thief had tied up the owner of the shop and left with money and several guns. The owner had freed himself, taken a revolver, and gone out to take the thief's car number. The thief had not yet departed and, in full view of several people, shot the shop owner twice. After a pause the shop owner fired all six rounds of his revolver at the thief, who died. The shop owner recovered. Because the thief was dead, and there were no legal complications, Yuille and Cutshall were able to gain access to police files to reconstruct events from the rather complete forensic evidence of the event, including police photographs, and from the testimony of the witnesses where they corroborated each other. Yuille and Cutshall made a list of details of actions, of people present, and of objects.

In their research interview, Yuille and Cutshall found that witnesses who had contact with the store owner or the thief rated themselves as very stressed by this event and said they had difficulty sleeping for several nights after it, though witnesses who were less involved were not so emotionally stressed. Witnesses were fairly accurate about the event, including incidental details such as the color of the thief's car and of the blanket that was used to cover his body. At the police interview the stressed witnesses correctly remembered 93% of the details, and at the research interview five months later 88% percent of details. The accuracy of the less stressed individuals was lower: approximately 75% in both the police interview and the later research interview. So: accuracy of remembering seems to be increased for events that are emotionally involving.

Such events are, however, also subject to processes of reconstruction that Bartlett discussed. Pynoos and Nader (1989) interviewed children who attended a school where a sniper had "shot repeated rounds of ammunition at children on an elementary school playground" (p. 236) from an apartment opposite the school in Los Angeles on February 24, 1984. One passer-by and one child were killed and 13 other children and a playground attendant were wounded. In the accounts of 113 children who were interviewed between 6 and 16 weeks afterwards, characteristic distortions occurred. Children who were wounded tended to distance themselves emotionally from the event, and five did not even mention their minor gunshot injuries when interviewed. By contrast, children who were not at school that day, or who were on their way home, tended to place themselves nearer to the events.

A firm conclusion from research is that we are better able to recall events that were emotionally intense for us. This has been found in day-to-day life as well as in the laboratory (Levine & Pizarro, 2004; Levine & Edelstein, 2009). If an event is important and unusual, the condition is set both for an emotion and for recall. If an event is thought about often, or if flashbacks occur as they can do with traumatic events, then the event becomes salient in memory.

The question of whether there is some special form of repressed memory of especially intense and emotionally traumatic incidents, for instance, of childhood sexual abuse that can be recalled in therapy, has induced widespread controversy. Many researchers do not discount this possibility but are skeptical on the grounds that it is relatively easy to suggest, advertently or inadvertently, that certain events occurred in the past, and the person involved can then come to believe they really happened (Hardt & Rutter, 2004; Loftus & Davis, 2006).

Persuasion

In Chapter 1, we described how Aristotle wrote that emotions are important in persuasion. The relevant research offers a more complex message about emotion and **persuasion**, but in keeping with Aristotle's general emphasis on emotion.

Factors that affect persuasive messages include congruence of emotions in the receiver of the message with those of the message itself. If, for instance, a politician is running for office and trying to mobilize an angry group of supporters, it is most effective to frame the communication in anger-related terms, centering upon injustice and blame.

DeSteno, Petty, Rucker, Wegener, and Braverman (2004) induced participants to feel either sad or angry by reading hypothetical newspaper stories that elicited one of these emotions. Participants were then presented with one of two messages about raising taxes (not a popular message for many Americans). One message was sadness-framed, and emphasized how increasing taxes would help special-needs infants and the elderly. The other message was anger-framed, and emphasized how increasing taxes would keep criminals from getting off on legal technicalities and would prevent aggravating traffic jams. Sad people changed their attitudes more toward raising taxes when presented with the sadness-framed message, whereas angry people changed their attitudes toward increasing taxes more in response to the anger-framed message.

Briñol, Petty, and Barden (2007) found that emotion can affect persuasion in a different way by influencing the confidence people have in their thoughts. Participants first read a strong or weak persuasive message. After listing their thoughts about it, they were induced to feel happy or sad. People who became happy reported more confidence in their thoughts than those who became sad. As compared with those who were made sad, for happy participants the quality of the argument in the message had a greater effect on changes of attitudes.

Moral Judgment

We began this chapter with the tragic story of Eadweard Muybridge, and how the damage to his orbitofrontal cortex altered his emotions and his ability to live a moral life. The more general conclusion is that emotions, when they are properly functioning, act as guides to **moral judgment**, that is, to judgments about right and wrong and about character and virtue. This conclusion is in keeping with a central theme of this book: that emotions are bases for social life.

Although changes are now occurring, this view of moral judgment has not been widely accepted in philosophy and psychology. More prevalent has been the view that moral judgment is guided by deliberative processes like perspective taking, cost–benefit analyses, and considerations of rights and duties. Within this tradition, moral philosophers have been skeptical about the place of emotion in moral judgment. For example, intuitively you might think that feelings of sympathy and compassion are important to moral judgment, but not in the eyes of the influential philosopher, Immanuel Kant, who argued that sympathy should not be relied on in judgments of right and wrong because it is inherently subjective and blind and unreliable as a guide to moral judgment across context and culture.

More recently, however, researchers have argued that emotions act as social-moral intuitions (Haidt, 2001; McCullough et al., 2001), and that they act to amplify moral judgments (Horberg, Oveis, & Keltner, 2011). According to this perspective, fast, automatic experiences of specific emotions provide intuitions of right and wrong, virtue, and punishment without elaborate calculation at the conscious level (Greene & Haidt, 2002; Haidt, 2003). These emotional intuitions then can be followed by thought and discussion with others (Haidt, 2007).

Jonathan Haidt has made the case for several categories of moral intuition, which appear rapidly and effortlessly in consciousness and are emotional in nature (Haidt, 2007). First there are emotions related to *harm,* like sympathy and concern, which derive from perceptions of vulnerability and need for care. They motivate prosocial responding (Batson & Shaw, 1991; Eisenberg et al., 1989). These emotions likely arose during our evolution because of our mammalian heritage of taking care of offspring, and extending this care to others in families and in close social groups. Recent studies find that momentary feelings of compassion lead people to see their common humanity with others, and this encourages more prosocial behavior (Oveis, Horberg, & Keltner, 2010). People feeling compassion also are less punitive (Condon & DeSteno, 2011). Even infants have been found to have moral intuitions. Warneken and Tomasello (2009) observed 12-month-old children began to comfort victims in distress, and 14-to-18-month-olds began to help others in ways that were spontaneous and unrewarded.

Second there are emotions related to fairness, reciprocity, and justice, which perhaps have arisen during evolution in relation to what evolutionary theorists call reciprocal altruism. Thus we are exquisitely sensitive to who deserves what, and to cheaters. Many emotions here involve *condemnation of others* in anger, disgust, and contempt, when they are seen to do immoral actions such as those that lead to unfairness or harm to others (Lerner, Goldberg, & Tetlock, 1998). Buckholz et al. (2008) found in fMRI scans that activity in brain regions that included the amygdala and medial prefrontal cortex predicted the size of punishment that participants deemed appropriate for various crimes.

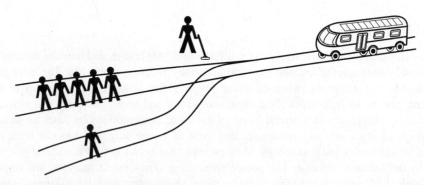

FIGURE 10.4   The trolley problem for testing moral intuitions by means of vignettes, invented by Philippa Foot (1967/1978).

Among the methods of the first line of research (on harm and caring) is "trolleyology," a paradigm invented by Foot (1967/1978) that involves giving people a vignette in which a trolley rolls out of control toward five people tied to the line who would be killed if the trolley were to hit them. Participants are asked whether they would switch some points and divert the trolley onto another line so that it would hit only one person.

Waldemann and Dieterich (2007) compared results using a vignette describing this scenario with one in which participants had to decide whether to push a very large person

Novels and Films: *Decalogue 8*

The Decalogue, written by Krzysztof Kieslowski and Krzysztof Piesiewicz and directed by Kieslowski, is a set of ten films inspired by the Ten Commandments. The films are about the effects of human actions on other people. The filmmakers said they wanted to make films about situations that could be recognized universally but at the same time were out of the ordinary, in which the characters would face difficult choices that could not be taken lightly.

In psychology the dilemmas of ethical decision making were studied by Kohlberg (1969). He constructed vignettes about which people could be asked questions. The most famous is about Heinz, whose wife is dying. A drug that might save her is being sold by the town druggist for ten times its cost. Heinz has no money and cannot borrow any. Kohlberg's question was, "Should Heinz steal the drug?" He then traced, in the course of child and adolescent development, the choices people made and the reasons they gave for these choices as they thought about this problem. Such vignettes were convenient to study the development of ethical thinking, but enormously better for understanding the emotions of ethical choice are novels and short stories, plays, and films. The *Decalogue* films were designed to put problems to us so that we could imagine ourselves into situations of ethical choice, and experience the social world in relation to our fears and our yearnings to do the right thing. One could imagine a psychology course on the emotions of morals and social actions in which, instead of using vignettes, each week, in class, students would watch one of these films and discuss it to understand

themselves better in their doing of good and doing of harm to others.

Decalogue 8 is based on the Commandment, "Thou shalt not bear false witness." It's about a professor of ethics who uses pieces of biography in exactly this way. It's about Zofia (played by Maria Koscialkowska), a senior professor of ethics at Warsaw University. A researcher from New York, Elzbieta (Teresa Marczewska), comes to visit and is invited to sit in on one of Zofia's classes. A class discussion begins and Elzbieta takes the opportunity to pose a problem, as follows. The time is 1943. The place is Warsaw, occupied by the Nazis. A family has said they will be godparents to a six-year-old Jewish girl, so that she can be christened and adopted rather than sent to a Nazi concentration camp. But the woman who had volunteered to be the godmother said she had changed her mind. She said that her religion forbade the bearing of false witness.

It looks as if, in this decision, the woman condemned the six-year-old to death. Was it right for her to change her mind after having made an undertaking? Did she refuse for the reason she gave?

In the story that Elzbieta tells, another family saved the six-year-old, who grew up and moved to America. The young girl is Elzbieta, who became the researcher. Zofia, the professor, is the woman who was expected to be her godmother. Why did Zofia refuse to adopt Elzbieta? Is there anything Zofia could now say that would satisfy Elzbieta, in this dramatic confrontation in the middle of a university class on ethics? The film is beautiful and emotionally moving. It puts the question in a way that engages us completely.

from a bridge onto the trolley line in such a way that this person would be killed but would halt the trolley before it could kill five people on the line. Although people were willing to switch the points so that the trolley, an inanimate object, would be affected, their intuitions made them reluctant to act on a person directly, by pushing in a way that condemned him or her to death, even if it were to result in saving a larger number of people. Greene et al. (2001) had people engage in moral dilemmas, including trolley problems, while undergoing brain scanning using functional magnetic resonance imaging (fMRI). They found that moral dilemmas varied systematically in the extent to which they engaged brain areas involved in emotional processing, and that these variations in emotional engagement were associated with moral judgments, a finding in keeping with Haidt's formulation of the emotional nature of moral judgment.

The second line of research (on fairness) has often employed the Ultimatum Game, in which there are two players: a proposer who offers to share a sum of money (provided by the experimenter) in a certain proportion, and a responder who decides to accept or reject the offer. If the responder decides to accept, the money is shared in the proportion proposed. If the responder rejects the offer, neither proposer nor responder gets anything. When proposers offer to share the money equally, such offers are typically seen as fair and are accepted. But contrary to conventional economic theory, when shares of money offered are in the proportions 7 to 3, 8 to 2, or 9 to 1 in the proposer's favor, responders are usually upset at their unfairness and they reject them. This behavior is often labeled irrational, because the responder gives up the chance of receiving some money. It is thought that this occurs for emotional reasons, and Osumi and Ohira (2009) found that, in comparison with effects of offers that would be accepted, offers that would be rejected slowed down the responders' heart rate: the more unfair the offer, the more the heart slowed. Gospic et al. (2011) monitored responders' brains in an fMRI machine as they played this game. They found that unfair offers that were rejected elicited a response in the amygdala, which the researchers labeled as an immediate aggressive response. They found, too, that giving responders a benzodiazepine drug decreased their rejection rate of unfair offers from 37.6 to 19%, and this decrease was associated with decreased amygdala activation. Harlé and Sanfey (2010) found that rejections of unfair offers in this game were more usually prompted by emotions of withdrawal such as disgust, than by emotions of approach such as anger. The idea of deservingness (Feather, 2007) has become important. Emotions affect our sense of who deserves what, and of what should happen when just deserts are not achieved.

Drawing upon cross-cultural research, Haidt has described further sets of moral emotions related to moral intuitions (Haidt, 2007). One set is directed toward oneself in a critical way that corresponds to the emotions that are sometimes directed at others for disliked actions. These are self-critical emotions, like shame, embarrassment, and guilt, which arise when we have violated moral codes or ideas about virtue and character, and they motivate moral behavior (Baumeister, Stillwell, & Heatherton, 1994; Keltner & Anderson, 2000; Keltner & Buswell, 1997; Tangney et al., 1996). Haidt has also described a set of other-praising emotions, most notably gratitude and "elevation" or awe, that signal our approval of others' moral virtues (Haidt, 2003; Keltner & Haidt, 2003).

Finally, concerns over bodily and spiritual purity are important in the moral frameworks of many cultures and engage the emotion of disgust. For example, people feeling disgust induced through hypnosis, through exposure to putrid smells, or through viewing disgusting images are more likely to condemn transgressive behaviors of others (Wheatley & Haidt, 2005) and people they regard as members of out-groups (Dasgupta, DeSteno, Williams, & Hunsinger, 2009). More generally, they tend to value bodily and spiritual purity in making moral judgments of others' actions (Horberg, Oveis, Keltner, & Cohen, 2009; Schnall, 2011). Still other moral intuitions that engage emotions pertain to the dynamics of in-groups and out-groups and the importance of loyalty, and to authority and the importance of respect and obedience. After an initial intuitive emotion, Haidt (2001, 2007) proposes that slow, effortful, and deliberative reasoning processes, followed by discussion, become influences on our moral judgment. Recall that we have earlier argued for a primary, heuristic, appraisal process (System 1), a slower, deliberative secondary appraisal (System 2), and a third stage of sharing and discussion with others. When we encounter morally relevant events, we contemplate the evidence, we consider logical and ethical principles, and we debate the consequences of different actions. Emotional intuitions feed into these deliberative and discursive processes.

Emotions and the Law

Marcus (2002) has argued that attainment of public ideals that include democracy and justice would be impossible without the emotions. Emotions and the law is a newly emerging field to which philosophers (Nussbaum, 2004), psychologists (Finkel and Parrott, 2006), and lawyers (Maroney, 2006) have contributed. Some issues in this field apply to questions of how emotions interact with our sense of morality and with our judgments of others. We also consider other aspects of how emotions and legal issues interact, for instance, of how people who work in the law are affected by their emotions, and how people make sense of evidence.

Terry Maroney's (2006) thoughtful article is a good place to start because, as she points out, different emotions are closely linked to different kinds of law.

> Criminal law reflects theories of fear, grief, and remorse; family law seeks (ideally) to facilitate love and attachment; tort law measures emotional suffering; litigants seek emotional satisfaction by invoking legal mechanisms; legal decision makers may have strong feelings about parties in their cases. (p. 120)

In this section, we concentrate on criminal law, an area of practical importance and of continuing interest.

Rules of Morality, Rules of Obligation

Some laws decree that we should do actions like stopping at a red light. Others decree that we should not do actions like assaulting people who have not harmed us. We generally regard such laws as good for most people. But there is another side to the law: coercion by fear of punishment, which can involve police, courts, and imprisonment.

The previous paragraph is largely descriptive, but what is law, in its essence? Is it a set of orders to act in certain ways? An analogy would be of a man who orders us to hand over our money, or he will shoot us. In his famous book, *The Concept of Law* (1961), H.L.A. Hart says this is a good starting point because it depicts behavior that is obligatory, with sanctions for non-compliance. Hart then spends the first half of his book showing how the analogy doesn't quite work. For instance, in the image of the gunman giving an order, there is only external constraint and only one participant is constrained, whereas in a law-abiding society there is also inward constraint, and the law applies to everyone. So, laws are best seen not as orders but as rules, and there are parallels between externalized rules of law, rules in games, and internalized psychological rules about how to live into which we have grown since infancy.

Hart continues that in law there isn't just one set of rules, but two. Primary rules are obligations to act and refrain from acting in particular ways: these rules are embodied in written laws. Secondary rules include procedures (for instance, for a legislature) about how to construct and discard primary rules. One function of secondary rules is to enable primary rules to keep in register with society's sense of morality. Laws prohibiting the killing of others without adequate cause occur worldwide; they depend on a sense of human vulnerability and our moral intuition of reducing harm. The parallel between our inner moral sense and certain laws has been shown in public surveys (Stylianou, 2003). It has been repeatedly found that people feel that deliberately killing someone (murder) is among the most heinous of offenses, and—as we all know—it carries the most severe penalties. There is also the sense that killing someone in the course of a robbery is worse than killing in a rush of jealous anger when one unexpectedly finds someone in bed with one's spouse. This difference is reflected in American law so that killing while committing another crime is murder, and killing someone in sudden anger can, under certain circumstances, be manslaughter, which carries a lesser penalty.

Laws are distillations of such attitudes. Based on the emotional-moral intuition of avoiding harm to others, discussed in the previous section, people feel it's right for those who behave badly to be punished. In some societies impulses to harm others are regulated by fear of revenge. This kind of regulation is well seen in some ancient literatures, for instance, in medieval Icelandic sagas as explained by Miller (2006). From Germanic and English law comes the tradition that angry vengeance should not, however, be enacted by individuals because feuds can be destructive to the whole of society and can continue indefinitely, so that special officers of the state should take over the function of apprehending and punishing criminals.

People tend to like, and to approve, those who behave well and to dislike and feel anger, disgust, or contempt toward those who behave badly. One may see this in fiction. Zillmann (2000) has proposed a highly regarded theory, called *disposition theory*, according to which we are disposed to like fictional characters who behave well and to dislike those who behave badly. Zillmann says that each person who engages with fiction is "a moral monitor who applauds or condemns the intentions and actions of characters" (p. 38). The criminal law enacts this in society.

There is useful evidence on these issues from fiction, in which people experience pleasure when a liked character behaves well and succeeds and experience displeasure when a disliked character behaves badly and succeeds (Weber, Tamborini, Lee, & Stipp, 2008). Also, when a good character achieves retribution for a wrong he or she has suffered, or when a bad character is punished, people are sensitive to the level of revenge or punishment that occurs. We enjoy stories more when this seems appropriate. There is even a name for this: poetic justice.

Politicians often say they will be tough on crime. This invariably means that they will increase punishments, and they do. This can resonate with voters because our emotional-intuitive sense is that punishments should be visited on people who do bad things. Although being tough is supposed to decrease crime, what politicians don't tell us is that the strong weight of evidence is that harsher judicial penalties do not diminish crime (Webster & Doob, 2011). A likelier route to decreasing crime would be to increase the certainty that crimes will be detected (Durlauf & Nagin, 2011), but this is more difficult to arrange.

People's feelings about good and bad behavior in life and fiction coincide in mystery stories, thrillers, and television shows that include courtroom scenes, like *Law and Order.* Watch one of these shows and observe your own likes, dislikes, and emotions in relation to criminals and their apprehension. Watch how the detectives in the show use a method used by actual police in the United States, called the Reid technique: first they assume guilt and verbally attack a suspect based on this assumption, then they detain the suspect to increase anxiety, then they confront the suspect with evidence of guilt (which may be fabricated), and finally they try to gain the suspect's trust by saying they understand (Gudjonsson & Pearse, 2011). How would you feel if subjected to this? It's a technique with a rate of false confessions that is higher than had been thought.

The basic appeal of mystery stories isn't so much in following a trail of clues, although this is enjoyable. It's the sense that seriously bad behavior, like murder or rape, causes a breach in the fabric of society, and that identification and punishment of criminals might repair the breach so that we can all go on living with each other. Similar emotions are projected into the larger world when international crimes are committed, as occurred, for instance, in the angry American response to the attacks on New York and Washington on September 11, 2001 (Hogan, 2009).

Dispassionate Judgments?

Here is a paradox. Although the roots of law and its enforcement could scarcely be more emotional, the traditional story in law is that apprehension and punishment of perpetrators should be "dispassionate," and that those concerned with administering the law should set aside their feelings. Maroney (2011) has written an informative review of the implications of this paradox. She describes, for instance, that in nominating a new member of the U.S. Supreme Court, President Obama said he wanted to nominate someone with empathy, and listed among the qualifications of his nominee, Judge Sonia Sotomayor, a sense of compassion. But Sotomayor knew the right thing to say at her hearings:

> "Judges can't rely on what's in their heart[s]," she testified before the Senate Judiciary Committee, because "[i]t's not the heart that compels conclusions in cases, it's the law."
> (Maroney, p. 639)

Maroney discusses how Obama's idea that empathy and compassion are important for a Supreme Court Judge was criticized by some, with sneers such as "touchy-feely." If people understood emotions better, for instance, about how they inform judgment and mediate relationships, they might sneer less.

A further area in which emotions enter processes of law is in the deliberations of jurors. Reid Hastie (2001) has written that emotional reactions of jurors in criminal trials include:

> . . . reactions to events that led to the trial, primarily anger; reactions to participants involved in the trial, primarily anger, sympathy and fear; and reactions to evidentiary exhibits, primarily disgust and horror. (p. 1007)

A cogent account of the psychology of jurors as they listen to a case in criminal court is by Pennington and Hastie (1988), who observe that jurors construct a story as a causal explanation of what happened and that, rather than basing their reasoning on some form of logic (such as Bayesian logic, as an alternative theory holds), they decide on the basis of this emotion-based story. In fact two stories are typically offered in court, one by the prosecution and one by the defense. As Hastie (2008) has argued, jurors are generally willing to convict if the prosecution's story has no large holes and no large pieces of counterevidence. But in the end, jurors have to construct their own version of the story. This version allows some inferences and prevents other inferences. Unlike the stories offered by prosecution and defense, which both end with a question mark, the story offered by the jury reaches a conclusion: guilty or not guilty.

Emotions that jurors feel as they listen to evidence change priorities because, as with any story, people have their own feelings as they construct their version (Oatley, 2011). Anger tends to make the constructed story aggressive and end in punishment. As we have discussed earlier in this chapter, anger has been found to lead people to blame others for actions, whereas sadness leads people to attribute events to impersonal, situational causes (Feigeson, Park, & Salovey, 2001; Keltner, Ellsworth, & Edwards, 1993; Lerner, Goldberg, & Tetlock, 1998; Quigley & Tedeschi, 1996). Empathy and sympathy are likely to make the constructed story protective and to focus on restitution.

Among jurors, Hastie describes anticipatory emotions of being able to feel satisfied after the trial that one has played one's part in punishing someone who was guilty or in freeing someone wrongly accused. Also anticipated may be feelings of regret and sadness at rendering a guilty verdict against a sympathetic person. We don't suggest that jurors should engage in some activity other than story-construction, but rather that justice would be better served by understanding more deeply how we make judgments that can convict people of crimes, or free them.

SUMMARY

Emotions are usually rational in relation to particular goals. We've described in this chapter how they can guide cognition in systematic ways that enable people to respond to immediacies of the environment when perfect rationality is impossible, for instance, because of insufficient knowledge. This view is in keeping with a central premise of this book: that although emotions are by no means infallible, they generally serve important social functions. They help the individual navigate complex and changing social relationships. Three theoretical perspectives offer explanations of how emotions can affect cognition: they exert effects upon cognition because of congruency, they can themselves be informative, and they can lead to different styles of reasoning. We presented evidence that emotions affect people's perceptions of events, and also affect attention. In terms of memory, people tend to recall emotionally salient events and, at the same time, current emotions can bias what is recalled from the past. Emotions also affect evaluative judgments, judgments of the future, and causal attribution. Moral intuitions are now understood as being affected by emotions, which can guide judgments of right and wrong in the social world, and we discussed how this connection between emotions and morality extends to the processes of law and the administration of justice.

TO THINK ABOUT AND DISCUSS

1. When does an emotion or mood affect your decision making? Does this effect make sense to you, or are there aspects you would like to change? Consider the same questions in relation to someone close to you: a parent or sibling or a boyfriend or girlfriend.

2. Think about how anxiety, or anger, or happiness affects your recall of past memories. What, for you, is the principal effect here? How does this effect work for you?

3. Think about some social arrangement with which you are familiar, perhaps the family, perhaps a work setting. How is emotion related to what gets said and decided in this setting?

FURTHER READING

An excellent introduction to the philosophy of emotions, providing a basis for understanding the sense in which emotions are rational:

Ronald De Sousa (1987). *The rationality of emotions*. Cambridge, MA: MIT Press.

A useful review of emotional biases, including clinical implications:

Paula Hertel & Andrew Mathews (2011). Cognitive bias modification: Past perspectives, current findings, and future applications. *Perspectives on Psychological Science*, **6**, 521–536.

A good review of the relation of emotion to memory:

Elizabeth Kensinger & Daniel Schachter (2008). Memory and emotion. In M. Lewis, J. Haviland Jones, & L. F. Barrett (Eds.), *Handbook of emotions, third edition* (pp. 601–617). New York, NY: Guilford.

An excellent statement of the role of emotion in moral judgment:

Jonathan Haidt (2001). The emotional dog and its rational tail: A social intuitionist approach to moral judgment. *Psychological Review*, **108**, 814–34.

EMOTIONS AND THE INDIVIDUAL

PART IV

Individual Differences in Emotionality

11

This chapter written with Heather Prime

FIGURE 11.0 A mother picks up her child after an absence. Notice the child clasping the mother and pushing away the babysitter.

Photo Credit: Erika Stone/Science Photo Library/Photo Researchers, Inc.

A child forsaken, waking suddenly,
  Whose gaze afeared on all things round doth rove
  And seeth only that it cannot see
  The meeting eyes of love.

                                    George Eliot

CONTENTS

From the first hours of life children show marked individual differences in their emotions. Early temperament contributes to what we think of as personality: those characteristics of an individual that remain stable over time and across circumstances. Many of these characteristics of personality are emotion-based. They are ways in which people are warm and outgoing toward others, fearful or easily angered, and so on. In this chapter we consider the ways in which individual differences in emotion become part of personality over the life course. We also think about the role of close relationships in influencing the development of individual differences in emotion.

Biases of Emotion in Temperament and Personality

Individual differences in emotion have been called *affective-cognitive structures* (Izard, 1971, 1977); they affect emotional information processing and behavior. Both temperament in babies (Campos et al., 1983) and personality in adulthood (Magai, 2008) can be thought of as affective biases that shape how people tend to feel, how they are likely to construe life events, and how they will usually act in the environment across the lifespan.

Individual Differences in Emotion Shape How We Construe the World

One of the lasting insights of the study of individual differences is that people actively construe situations in individual ways (Buss, 1987; Caspi & Bem, 1987). Several studies point to perceptual

Photo Credit: Image Source/Alamy

FIGURE 11.1   Most 3-to-5-year-olds are shy with strangers: notice this child clinging to her mother and looking apprehensive. Extreme shyness in childhood can continue into adulthood.

biases that derive from people's personality traits. A recent meta-analysis of the literature on threat-related biases conducted by Bar-Haim, Lamy, Pergamin, Bakermans-Kranenburg, & van Ijzendoorn (2007) demonstrated that the threat-related bias is a robust phenomenon: individuals high in anxiety are more sensitive to threat-related stimuli than they are to neutral stimuli, and they allocate more attention to such stimuli than do non-anxious individuals. This finding holds under a variety of experimental conditions and in different types of anxious populations (individuals with different clinical disorders, high-anxious nonclinical individuals, anxious children, and adults).

Biases in the way in which anxious individuals perceive their environments significantly affect day-to-day living. For instance, the "neurotic cascade" (Suls & Martin, 2005) involves neurotic individuals reporting more daily problems, reacting with more severe emotions, experiencing more mood spillover from prior occasions, and having stronger reactions to recurring problems, all of which reinforce one another.

Biases in construals of the world are seen in angry individuals as well. Hazebroek, Howells, & Day (2001) showed people video clips of social interaction scenarios that had negative conse-quences and asked them to rate how angry they would feel if they were faced with the same situation. Individuals who rated themselves as generally more angry perceived the scenarios differently from those who rated themselves as less angry. These biases were more apparent for ambiguous situations. In response to the same events, angry individuals exhibited higher levels of anger than less angry individuals. Further, they were more likely to blame the antagonist and identify another person as an antagonist than less angry individuals. This has been called the *hostile attribution bias*, a bias that has been demonstrated to contribute to aggressive behavior and problematic interactions (Dodge, 1999). A meta-analysis of 41 studies investigating the relation between children's aggressive behavior and hostile attribution of intent to peers demonstrated a robust significant association between the two (Orobio de Castro, Veerman, Koops, Bosch, & Monshouwer, 2002).

Reciprocal Processes in Emotion Expression

Individual differences are seen in the ways in which people react to other people's emotions. Although certain emotions do elicit typical responses (Jenkins & Ball, 2000), many reactions are varied. For one person a crying child will be an irritation; for another sympathy will be elicited. David Kenny has developed an imaginative and rigorous approach to examining the extent to which individuals elicit the same or different reactions from other people, using a model that he called the Social Relations Model. Think of a family (or indeed any social group). He suggested that by observing each family member in interaction with every other family member we could determine the extent to which individuals **expressed** the same emotions to different family members (called the person's *actor* effect) and **elicited** the same emotions from different family members (called the person's *partner* effect). Data are collected in a round-robin design in which each family member interacts with all other members.

Rasbash, Jenkins, O'Connor, Tackett, and Reiss (2011) used this model to examine emotion-based interactions within families. Six hundred and eighty seven families with two adolescents and two parents were observed interacting in all dyadic combinations across the family. Each dyad was videotaped for 10 minutes, during which they resolved two problematic issues (e.g., chores, sharing, curfew, money, etc.). Videos were subsequently coded for expressions of negative and positive emotions (based on voice tone, facial expression, and gesture) on a scale of 1–5. First, it was evident that individuals did show similar emotions across all family members.

The actor effect was stronger for positivity (explaining 28% of the variance) than it was for negativity (20% of the variance), meaning that family members' positive expressive style was more pronounced across family members than their negative expressive style. A partner effect was also evident for negativity (representing 9% of the variance) but not for positivity. This means that individuals do show characteristic emotion expressions in terms of both what they express to others and elicit from them. One of the most important findings in this study, though, was that around 50% of the variance for both negativity and positivity was unique to the specific combination of people in the dyad. How family members express their emotions depends critically upon the specific relationship: whether it was a younger or older sibling, for example, interacting with the mom. This means that there is a lot of variation in what we express to different people and what we elicit.

Attachment and Emotionality

Attachment theory has been extremely influential in thinking about emotion-based continuities in relationships (Shaver & Mikiluncer, 2003). John Bowlby, the founder of attachment theory (1971), saw attachment as an evolutionarily derived aspect of the parent–child relationship that is activated when the infant experiences a threat. Emotions function as signals: the infant cries, and this signals fear and a need for protection, which in turn summons the parent's attention. Over time, experiences with the caregiver, and the way in which the caregiver has responded to

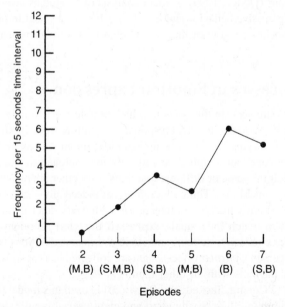

FIGURE 11.2   The frequency of crying per 15 seconds of observation in different episodes of the Strange Situation test (Ainsworth & Bell, 1970). Along the x-axis are the episodes as follows: M = Mother present, B = Baby present, S = Stranger present) 2. Mother sits quietly with Baby; 3. Stranger enters and sits quietly, then at the end of this episode Mother leaves unobtrusively; 4. Stranger tries to interact with Baby; 5. Mother returns and Stranger leaves unobtrusively, then at the end of the episode Mother leaves, saying "bye-bye"; 6. Baby alone; 7. Stranger returns to interact with Baby.

the child, become internalized. The child comes to expect that when he or she signals distress, the caregiver will be there (or not). Bowlby argued that this expectation, based on a mental model, is the basis of the child being able to explore the world confidently.

Mary Ainsworth developed a test of infants' responses to a situation that was strange to them—the **Strange Situation** test—based on observations of infants' emotional reactions to the fear-inducing circumstance of being separated from the mother, and then the experience of being reunited with her (see Figure 11.2).

Using this test, Ainsworth et al. (1978) identified three distinct **attachment styles**. Securely attached infants are distressed at separation, but when their caregivers return they seek them and can be comforted. Then there were two styles of insecure attachment. Ambivalently attached infants want to be near caregivers upon their return, but at the same time will not be comforted and show a great deal of angry and resistant behavior. Avoidantly attached infants make no effort to interact when their caregivers return.

Subsequently another style was added by Main and Solomon (1986). It is called the Disorganized style. It is seen in children who respond to parents in the strange situation with disorientation and contradictory behaviors. In a meta-analysis, van Ijzendoorn, Schuengel, & Bakermans-Kranenburg (1999) found that the percentage of disorganized infant attachment in middle-class, nonclinical groups in North America was 15%. This percentage increased to 25% in low socioeconomic samples and 23% in groups with teen mothers. In addition, the percentage of Disorganized children was elevated in clinical groups such as those with neurological abnormalities (35%), in groups of mothers with alcohol or drug abuse (43%), in groups with maltreating parents (48%), as well as in groups whose mothers were depressed (21%).

Attachment security is associated with many different aspects of socioemotional functioning later in childhood. For example, it has been associated with stronger peer relationships, enhanced emotion understanding and social problem-solving skills, as well as greater self-concept (see Thompson, 2008, for a review), making it a central concept for understanding children's emotional development.

Emotions Associated with Attachment Styles

Are different attachment styles associated with children's emotions? The answer to this question is *yes*, both for children's immediate emotions and for emotionality as they grow older. Observing infants in the strange situation and then coding their affective profiles reveals that each attachment style has a fairly specific pattern of emotional expression. Secure infants engage in positive, negative, and neutral emotions equally. In contrast, ambivalent infants show more negative emotions (i.e., anger) and avoidant infants show less negative emotions. Overall, avoidant infants showed the fewest emotions of all kinds, followed by the secure and then the ambivalent (Goldberg, MacKay-Soroka, & Rochester, 1994). One thought about Avoidant babies is that they feel negative emotions but they have adopted a strategy of only showing these emotions infrequently. One study found that Avoidant babies showed fewer facial and vocal displays of emotion during the strange situation than Secure babies. However, the Avoidant babies had similar heart rates as the Secure babies during the test, and higher cortisol levels after it (Spangler & Grossmann, 1993). This suggests that despite less overt distress, these Avoidant children may nevertheless experience physiological arousal and that their Avoidant behavior is not effective as a coping strategy (Spangler & Grossmann, 1993).

What is the link between attachment status and children's emotions as they age? Kochanska et al. (2001) sought an answer to this question in a study examining children from 1 year (when attachment status was assessed) to 3 years (when emotions to a standard set of elicitors were examined). As did Goldberg et al. (1994), they found that Avoidant infants expressed few negative emotions at 1 year, but by 3 years old they showed an increase in fearful expressions. Children initially classified as Ambivalent responded most fearfully not only to the fear-eliciting stimuli but also to the joy-eliciting stimuli. Furthermore, these children showed the greatest decrease in positive emotion from age 1 to age 3. Secure children's anger expression, which peaked at 14 months, decreased significantly by 33 months. The anger of Disorganized children increased over time.

A careful reading of attachment theory leads to another prediction: that Securely attached children cope better with stress than children in the other categories. Several studies have shown links between attachment status and physiological indicators of stress reactivity. Cortisol is a hormone that indicates response to stress. Researchers have shown that when the caregiver is present, toddlers classified as Securely attached do not show elevations in cortisol in distressing situations, whereas Insecure toddlers do (see Gunnar & Donzella, 2002, for review). We get a sense of how this works from a recent study by Bernard and Dozier (2010). They found that attachment Disorganization was related to increases in cortisol in response to a stressor task but not to a play task, whereas organized infants did not show cortisol reactivity to either task. This shows that cortisol responses are contingent not only on attachment status but also the type of eliciting circumstance with which the child is faced. Higher physiological stress responses to acute stress have been associated with attachment insecurity in adult populations as well, with both attachment-related stressors (Powers et al., 2006) as well as non-attachment-related stressors (Quirin et al., 2008).

Is attachment status associated only with reactivity to stresses, or are there individual differences in cortisol levels throughout the day? In general, the expected pattern of cortisol levels includes high morning levels, a sharp rise between 30 and 45 minutes after waking (called the *cortisol awakening response*), and then a gradual decline through the rest of the day (Adam & Gunnar, 2001; Quirin, Pruessner, & Kuhl, 2008). A recent study by Oskis, Loveday,

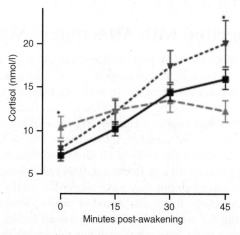

FIGURE 11.3   Means and standard errors of salivary-free cortisol in 9-to-18-year-old females in the first 45 minutes after waking. Secure participants ($n = 30$) are indicated by the solid line, Avoidant participants ($n = 17$) by the steeply rising dotted line, and Anxious participants ($n = 13$) by the flatter dotted line (Oskis et al., 2011).

Significant figures: John Bowlby and Mary Ainsworth

A renaissance of research on emotions began in the aftermath of World War II, in part inspired by John Bowlby and his theory of attachment. Bowlby trained in medicine. He became a psychiatrist and a psychoanalyst. His concerns were with children, for instance, in how they became maladapted. After the war these concerns focused on problems of children's separation from parents and he drew on observations of Anna Freud and Dorothy Burlingham (during the war) on children who had been evacuated and separated from their parents (for instance, in the *kindertransport* in which Jewish parents sent their children from Nazi Germany to be adopted in England).

Attachment theory was derived jointly from these concerns and from the new science of ethology. In her 1992 obituary of Bowlby, Mary Ainsworth wrote that when Robert Hinde and Julian Huxley introduced Bowlby to the idea of imprinting and to the works of Lorenz and Tinbergen, he quickly realized that in ethology and Darwinian evolution theory lay the key: "Attachment theory's main structure emerged whole in this first flash of insight and gave coherence to all that followed." Bowlby's book *Child Care and the Growth of Love,* published in 1951, was derived from a report he made on the importance of attachment to the World Health Organization. Attachment has become the most important single theme in the emotional development of children.

Mary Ainsworth, born in Ohio, grew up from the age of 5 in Canada, gained her PhD at the University of Toronto, and after the war worked there as a faculty member. When her husband moved to London, England, to complete his PhD, she accompanied him, and answered a job advertisement in the *Times*. She got the job. It was at the Tavistock Clinic, to work with Bowlby on separation of children from their mothers. She amplified attachment theory, making important observations of attachment behavior in Uganda, where the couple next moved, and then in Baltimore, in the United States. Ainsworth devised the Strange Situation Test to observe how infants behave when separated from their mothers. This test became the basis for understanding that people have different attachment styles.

From the time of the Romantic Movement in the 18th century, people knew that early relationships were important for the formation of character in the long-term, but it took Bowlby and Ainsworth to realize what the processes were and how they worked.

Hucklebridge, Thorn, and Clow (2011) found that female children and adolescents with Anxious Insecure attachment styles showed flattened cortisol awakening responses when compared to those who had Secure attachment styles, as you can see in Figure 11.3. Thus, attachment style is associated with long-lasting physiological effects in systems responsible for responding to stress.

Genetic Influences on Attachment

Are attachment styles genetic? Investigators have used twin designs of the kind we have discussed in Chapter 8, in which monozygotic twins, who share 100% of their genes, are compared to the attachment status of dizygotic twins, who share on average 50% of their genes. In Chapter 8 you learned that a child's temperament is influenced by his or her genetic inheritance. By contrast, three studies concerning the genetic underpinnings of attachment style find little influence of genes upon attachment style (Bokhorst et al., 2003; Fearon et al., 2006; O'Connor & Croft, 2001). They all find negligible genetic influences on attachment; instead, attachment style is influenced by what is known as the shared environment (the conditions in the family that were experienced by all the children in the family) and the non-shared environment (environmental experiences specific to an individual child). Fearon and colleagues (2006) extended these findings by measuring the parenting that children receive. They showed that the shared component of parental sensitivity (i.e., awareness and interpretation of baby's signals, appropriate and prompt responding) within families was able to explain part of the similarity of attachment security between twins.

Internal Working Models of Attachment

A core idea of Bowlby's theorizing was that children's emotional interactions with caregivers lead them to build an **internal working model** of relationships. It is a mental model, or set of beliefs, of what to expect in an intimate relationship. Can the other person be trusted? Can one expect comfort and love from others? The beginnings of such a model are evident before the child learns language, but if it could be spelled out in words, the model of a Secure child would be something like: "When I am in danger, I can trust my parent to protect me." For an Avoidant child it would be something like: "When I am in danger, I must be wary and rely only on myself." These internal models form the basis of a persisting emotional bias, which is at the heart of individual differences in emotion. They start in relationships with caregivers, they are somewhat resistant to change, and they affect all later intimate relationships (Bowlby, 1988; Mikulincer & Shaver, 2003). The striking idea conceived by Bowlby (and before him by Freud) is that each intimate relationship leaves an imprint. It becomes an element in the construction of selfhood—a template of how to understand intimate relationships and how to act in them subsequently.

In early work in this area, George, Kaplan, and Main (1985) developed the Adult Attachment Interview to examine how people think about their early attachment relationships. Using this method, people are asked about their relationship with their parents when they were children, and also in the present. The interview covers what they remembered doing when they were upset in childhood, whether they were ever rejected, and so forth. On the basis of fairly complicated coding of the responses in the interview, adults are classified into Secure/Autonomous, Preoccupied, or Dismissing adult attachment styles. These categories, furthermore, are thought respectively to derive from Secure, Ambivalent, and Avoidant attachment in infancy. Autonomous adults are those who talk about their childhood experiences with objectivity and balance. They give a coherent account of difficulties in their childhood experiences that may have been good or bad. Adults are rated as Preoccupied when they give incoherent accounts of their experiences and still seem overwhelmed by their memories of their often-traumatic childhood. Dismissing adults give a distant, abstract account of their childhood, characterized by inability to recall events, by idealization or by over-rationalization, and with little show of emotion.

A critical test of the idea that attachment forms a template for subsequent intimate relationships would be to measure attachment styles of children at age 1, and then use the Adult Attachment Interview to measure the **continuity** of styles of relating into adulthood. Everett Waters et al. (2000) found, among 50 white middle-class people who were classified in the strange situation as infants and given an Adult Attachment Interview at the age of 21, that 64% of them maintained the corresponding style of attachment. This result is portrayed in Table 11.1.

Table 11.1 **Numbers of people classified as Secure, Avoidant, or Resistant at age 1 in the Strange Situation Test, who were classified at age 21 as Secure, Dismissing, or Preoccupied in the Adult Attachment Interview**

Adult Attachment Interview	Infant attachment classification (Strange Situation Test)		
	Secure	Avoidant	Resistant
Secure	20	2	3
Dismissing	6	8	2
Preoccupied	3	2	4

Source: Waters et al. (2000).

Continuities of attachment style have not been found in all studies, however (Grossman et al., 2002; Weinfield, Sroufe, & Egeland, 2000), and this represents an important challenge to Bowlby's theorizing. To some extent, lack of continuity is explained by disruption in the individual's relational context. Thus negative life events such as loss of a parent, parental divorce, parental physical or psychiatric illness, and physical or sexual abuse of the child do explain changes in attachment (Waters et al., 2000; Weinfield et al., 2000).

When considering the lasting influences of early attachment, one needs to distinguish between cross-sectional studies and true longitudinal studies. The series of studies described above by Waters and colleagues are examples of true longitudinal studies, wherein participants are followed over time from infancy to adulthood and data are collected a number of times on a particular sample. In contrast, cross-sectional designs involve observation of a sample at one specific point in time. Whereas with longitudinal studies you can make conclusions regarding causality, one is unable to do so with cross-sectional data; a cause must precede its effect and there is no way to demonstrate this when data are collected at a single time point. An example may help with this distinction. As in Waters and colleagues' studies above, one might assess attachment styles at age 1 and then adult attachment 20 years later; this would be an example of a longitudinal study wherein one could make causal inferences regarding the effect of early attachment patterns on adult attachment. A cross-sectional study, however, might report the association between early attachment (measured in adulthood) and some other aspect of adult functioning (e.g., marital conflict). We cannot conclude that experiences in childhood influenced adult functioning, but rather that two constructs measured in adulthood are related to one another. When reading research or conducting it, it is important to note what conclusions can and cannot be made based on the research design.

Children classified as securely attached in infancy have been found, later in their preschool years, to be more self-reliant, independent, and self-confident. They exhibit higher levels of self-esteem, social competence, and emotion regulation (Sroufe, 2005). Longitudinal studies suggest that early attachment continues to be associated with personal adjustment in adolescence and early adulthood (see Grossmann, Grossmann, & Waters, 2005, for a review). For example, adolescents with histories of Secure attachment are more effective in their peer groups and in social encounters and have enhanced leadership qualities. Security of attachment in infancy has also been related to the emotional tone of adult romantic relationships (Sroufe, 2005). Cross-sectional studies have found associations between attachment styles and adults' intimate relationships (Collins & Feeney, 2000; Feeney & Collins, 2001), levels of contentment (e.g., Cooper, Shaver, & Collins, 1998; Shaver & Brennan, 1992), and general life problems (Mikulincer & Shaver, 2003). In general, securely attached individuals tend to fare well in several of life's domains.

If internal working models are important, and if they do influence later relationships, we would expect the experiences of childhood to influence parenting when individuals become adults and have babies of their own. The development of the Adult Attachment Interview and other instruments assessing adults' recollection of childhood attachment experiences (Benoit, Parker, & Zeanah, 2000) have allowed researchers to investigate how mothers' own attachment experiences influence the development of infant–mother attachment and thus the inter-generational patterns of these relationships.

So, how do adults with these different styles affect the attachment styles of their own babies? To answer this question, Fonagy, Steele, and Steele (1991) assessed women on the Adult Attachment Interview during their pregnancy, and then measured the attachment style of their babies at age 1 in the Strange Situation Test: 75% of the Secure/Autonomous women had securely attached 1-year-olds, and 73% of Preoccupied or Dismissing women had Insecurely attached 1-year-olds (Ambivalent or Avoidant).

What accounts for this intergenerational transmission of attachment patterns? The idea is that attachment representations affect parents' abilities to exhibit sensitive parenting (van Ijzendoorn, 1995), which in turn influences children's development of secure attachment (e.g., Ainsworth, Blehar, Waters, & Wall, 1978; Bakermans-Kranenburg, van Ijzendoorn, & Juffer, 2003). Although there is evidence that the influence of adult attachment on infant attachment is partly explained by maternal behavior (van Ijzendoorn, 1995), it is only a weak mediator and the transmission gap from parent attachment to children's attachment is not well understood.

So, although continuities of attachment styles do occur, they do not imply that internal working models of relating rigidly program later behavior. Life events, such as severe relational problems, can affect such models. Even people who have experienced early attachment failures can recover from them to build satisfactory attachment relationships later in their lives and with their children, as we shall see in the next chapter.

The Bridge Between Attachment and Emotions

How do we think about attachment within the more general frame of emotion? Emotions help us in the formation and negotiation of relationships. They allow a bridge to other minds as a means of fostering cooperation (Tomasello, 2010). Attachment styles represent a stable organization that is indicative of the way in which emotional interactions have been handled by the child and those people close to the child. One way to think of Secure attachment is as a mutually responsive orientation. Thus Kochanska (1997, 1999, 2002) has suggested that parent–child relationships characterized by mutual responsiveness, positivity, and harmony promote the child's eager, willing stance toward the other. This is a similar idea to Bowlby's (1971) idea of the "goal-corrected partnership." He saw that an ideal of early cognitive and emotional development was that parent and child would each let the other into their mind such that the goals, desires, and beliefs of each would be represented with an attitude of willingness and such that each would want to foster the goals of the other.

If you think back to Chapter 8, you may remember cognitive underpinnings of a mutually rewarding orientation. In the latter part of the first year of life infants can share mental states with others: they point in order to draw their partner's attention to an object, and they respond by looking at an object when others point to it (Carpenter, Nagell, & Tomasello, 1998). Kochanska & Aksan (2004) have shown that between 7 and 15 months, children increased the frequency of their attempts to influence their parents. Parents were more responsive to positive than to negative emotions, and the child's positivity increased over time. Over this same period, parents—evidently aware of their children's growing autonomy—decreased the frequency of their attempts to influence their children. By 18 months infants have developed the cognitive capacity to engage in a cooperative activity with another person, even when the interactional partners have to perform different roles in order to achieve the joint goal (Warneken & Tomasello, 2006). By 2 years, children are beginning to talk about their own and other people's desires, as we described in Chapter 8.

These developments are at the core of a mutually responsive orientation, which serves as the basis for cooperation across the life course. Forman, Aksan, and Kochanska (2004) showed that children exhibiting mutually responsive interactions with their mothers were more likely to develop subsequent conscience and moral conduct in the preschool years (see also Rothbart et al., 2003). This mutually rewarding orientation has also been found to predict lower levels of externalizing in children (Kochanska, Woodard, Kim, Koenig, Yoon, & Barry, 2010).

Parental Relationships in Children's Emotional Organization

Most of the processes that are important in the development of individual differences in children's emotions take place within close relationships. We'll start with the parent–child relationship, and in a later section discuss sibling and peer relationships.

Parents' Responsiveness to Children's Internal States

We divide the findings for parent–child processes into two broad areas, although there is overlap between them. The first area, which we call **parental responsiveness**, involves the ways in which parents are sympathetic and responsive to children's internal states, with the studies having been strongly influenced by attachment theory.

Parental Responsiveness

Because infants and toddlers have only rudimentary skills in being able to communicate their needs, the ways that parents respond to children's attempts at emotional communication are critical to the individual differences in emotions that we witness across the life-course. Several parental behaviors have been shown to be important in this regard.

One of the most extensively examined aspects of parental responsiveness is **parental sensitivity**. Ainsworth et al. (1978, p. 142) originally described a sensitive mother as "alert to perceive her baby's signals, interprets them accurately, and responds appropriately and promptly . . . temporally contingent upon the baby's signals." Parental sensitivity has been shown to be positively related to children's Secure attachment status in meta-analyses (Atkinson et al., 2000; DeWolff & van Ijzendoorn, 1997).

Supporting the causal role of maternal sensitivity, van Ijzendoorn et al. (2000) and Fearon and colleagues' (2006) have both demonstrated that similarities observed in sibling attachment styles

Table 11.2   Changes in attachment security in intervention and control groups as a result of sensitivity training in high-risk families

Attachment classifications	Intervention group (n = 35)		Control group (n = 32)	
	n	%	n	%
Secure to secure	8	22.9	4	12.5
Secure to insecure	1	2.8	3	9.4
Insecure to insecure	11	31.4	20	62.5
Insecure to secure	15	42.9	5	15.6

Source: Moss et al. (2011).

can be partially explained by similarities in parental sensitivity. A causal role is also supported by findings from intervention studies. Bakermans-Kranenburg, van Ijzendoorn, and Juffer (2003) conducted a meta-analysis investigating the efficacy of attachment-based interventions targeting parental sensitivity in clinical and nonclinical samples. Programs targeting parent sensitivity (i.e., assisting parents to become more accurate perceivers of children's signals) were shown to be effective in enhancing parental sensitivity and increasing children's attachment security, supporting the notion of a causal role of sensitivity in shaping attachment. Parent sensitivity training has been shown to be effective even in groups of children known to be at high risk of attachment failures. Moss et al. (2011) recruited 67 parent–child dyads wherein the parent was presently being monitored for child maltreatment. Children were approximately 3 years of age. The intervention group received an 8-week home-visiting program targeted at enhancing maternal sensitivity to promote greater child security. The intervention focused on reinforcing parental sensitive behavior by means of video feedback of parent–child interaction, as well as discussions of attachment/emotion regulation-related themes. Results from this randomized controlled trial showed a positive effect of sensitivity training on attachment status (see Table 11.2), as well as a reduction in child disorganization. There was also a positive effect of the intervention on externalizing and internalizing disturbances in older children.

Parental sensitivity is important in explaining a wide range of children's outcomes: children of parents who are more sensitive have demonstrated enhanced moral development (Kochanska Forman, Aksan, & Dunbar, 2005), better language and literacy (Tamis-LeMonda, Bornstein, & Baumwell, 2001; Wade, Prime, Browne, & Jenkins, 2011), fewer behavior problems (Belsky & Fearon, 2002), as well as a more developed theory of mind (Meins et al., 2002).

Contingent Responding

Exploring contingent responding, the moment-to-moment responses of a parent to a child and vice-versa, allows us to look at the **co-construction of parent–child relationships** and the role of individuals in the relationships. Beebe et al. (2010) observed face-to-face interactions between mothers and babies when babies were 4 months old and used these interactions to understand 12-month attachment styles. At 4 months, examining the effect of each person in the dyad on moment-to-moment interactions, they coded the mothers' behavior (e.g., gaze, facial affect, touch, and spatial orientation) a couple of seconds before the infant's behavior (e.g., gaze, facial affect, vocal affect, touch, and head orientation) and examined whether this predicted the infant's subsequent behavior. The same was done to examine whether the infants influenced the mothers' behavior. The most marked differences in the 4-month interaction were seen for babies who were later (at 12 months) classified as Disorganized, in contrast to Secure. At 4 months, the babies that were later classified as Disorganized showed more distress, more negative vocal affect, and more discrepancies in facial versus vocal expression (e.g., vocal distress while facially positive). Mothers of Disorganized babies were more likely to gaze avert, or to show behaviors that may have frightened the baby (for instance, bringing their face too close too quickly), and, when babies were distressed, they were more likely to show positive facial expressions. Both the babies and their mothers in this category changed their own behavior more across time: Disorganized babies showed less consistency of engagement, while mothers showed less predictable gaze patterns. Thus for both infants and their mothers, behavior was less predictable for babies who were later classified as Disorganized.

Maternal Interpretation of Child Emotion

The way that parents interpret and respond to children's expressions of emotion is central to the emotional patterns that children develop. Spangler, Maier, Geserick, & von Wahlert (2010) found that **parents' interpretations** of their children's emotions was associated with the parents' attachment styles. Secure parents, as compared to Insecure ones, showed a positive bias in their responses (i.e., overt facial activity) to infant pictures. The authors suggested that this general positive evaluation of infants' emotions in Secure parents may increase responsiveness to infant signals even in stressful caregiving situations. The absence of this bias in Insecure parents, however, may heighten the risk for a reduced responsiveness. Their findings also indicated a negative physiological response to negative infant emotion expressions in parents classified as Dismissive. Such a negative bias in evaluating infants' emotions was not seen in Secure and Preoccupied parents. The idea here is that Dismissing people may evaluate negative emotional expression as aversive and associated with threat and danger in being rejected themselves when they have expressed negative emotion during their own attachment history (Main et al., 1985). These findings highlight the importance of attachment experiences for emotional information processing in parents and, thus, parental behavior.

Synchronization

Synchronization is about timing one's own behavior in relation to a baby's. It refers to **moment-by-moment interactions**. Isabella, Belsky, and von Eye (1989) separated mothers into two categories. The mothers who were synchronized kept in tune and in time with their babies: when the babies vocalized, they did, too; when the babies wanted to gaze at the mother's face, the mother gazed back; when the baby wanted to explore, the mother assisted this, and so on. The interactions of the pair were reciprocal and mutually rewarding. By contrast, non-synchronized mothers would vocalize or try to stimulate when their babies were asleep or being quiet, remain quiet and unresponsive when the babies vocalized, and so forth. Isabella et al. (1989) found that mothers who kept more closely in time with their 1-month-olds and 3-month-olds during interactions with them had babies who were more likely to be securely attached at 1 year. There is obvious overlap in the concepts of synchronization and maternal sensitivity. It has been noted that when the definition of maternal sensitivity is expanded to include synchronization, it more strongly predicts children's attachment status than when sensitivity does not include synchronization (Nievar and Becker, 2008). This suggests that the development of emotions in children is influenced by the extent to which the moment-to-moment interactions between infants and their mothers are well-synchronized.

Mind-Mindedness and Reflective Functioning

A degree of interpretation on the parent's part is necessary to be sensitive toward an infant, as Elizabeth Meins (1999) has shown. Parents' responses must be not only prompt, but also appropriate. Thus, sensitive parents must first perceive their infant's cues and then interpret them correctly, necessitating that parents "treat [their] infant as an individual with a mind rather than merely as a creature with needs that must be satisfied" (Meins et al., 2001, p. 638). This ability to recognize and treat an infant as having his or her own desires, thoughts, and intentions has been termed **mind-mindedness** (Meins et al., 2001), and has been proposed as a prerequisite for parental sensitivity and hence subsequent infant attachment security (Meins, 1997, 1999).

Suppose a baby has just woken up from a nap and begins crying. A parent who responds by picking up her baby, turning on playful music, and dancing around the living room with her isn't exactly showing sensitive parenting. Is this what you want to be doing when you wake up from a nap? An infant can't tell her parents why she's crying or smiling, or ask questions about the world around her. It's up to her parents to interpret her body language and other cues to understand her needs and emotions. To figure out how to respond, the baby's parents need to try to see the world from her perspective. Then parents can respond in a way that will meet their baby's needs and foster the formation of a healthy attachment relationship. Indeed, the interrelatedness of mind-mindedness and both maternal sensitivity and infant attachment security has been supported (Laranjo, Bernier, & Meins, 2008; Lundy, 2003; Meins, Fernyhough, Fradley, & Tuckey, 2001). A recent study by Laranjo, Bernier, and Meins (2008) revealed that the relationship between mind-mindedness and attachment was partly mediated by maternal sensitivity, supporting Meins' (1999) suggestion that mind-mindedness is a prerequisite to mothers' abilities to respond appropriately to infants' cues.

There is evidence that adolescent mothers show lower levels of responsiveness when compared to adult mothers (Borkowski et al., 2002; Culp et al., 1996; Garcia Coll et al., 1986; Jaffee et al., 2001). Demers, Bernier, Tarabulsy, and Provost (2010) extended this finding by showing that adult mothers, as compared to adolescent mothers, used more appropriate and positive mind-related comments while interacting with their infants. Additionally, adult mothers had children who were more likely to be classified as Securely attached. Given what we know about the role of mind-mindedness in parents' abilities to parent sensitively, these findings suggest that the lower levels of sensitivity seen in young moms may stem in part from failures in accurately interpreting the meaning of their infants' signals, and this has implications for their children's attachment patterns.

Related to mind-mindedness is **reflective functioning**, a term coined by Peter Fonagy to indicate parents' abilities to reflect on their own and their child's internal mental experiences, to create both a physical and psychological experience of comfort and safety for their child (Fonagy et al., 1991, 1995). By reflecting on their own childhood experiences and relating them to that of their children, parents can better respond and exhibit sensitivity to their children. Let's say you remember having a miserable day at school. Your dad took you on his lap and just listened. Thinking about how that helped you enables you to see the world through your child's eyes. Reflecting on difficult experiences in childhood can also help you to parent. Grienenberger, Kelly, and Slade (2005) showed that mothers with higher levels of maternal reflective functioning had children with Secure attachment, and that maternal behavior mediated this relationship.

Parenting in the Socialization of Emotion

The second broad area of parent–child processes has less to do with attachment and more to do with parents inducting their children into the social norms of their family and of society. Socialization of emotions occurs in the emotions parents show to children, in how they respond to children's emotions, and in how they discuss emotions with children. Grusec (2011) highlights the importance of the bidirectionality of this socialization. Parents aren't always driving the process; children are active agents in it (Kuzynski, 2003), with some being temperamentally responsive to parental efforts while others are not.

The Emotions to Which Children Are Exposed

Children often model their behavior according to the behaviors they observe in their social environment (Bandura, 1977). In their experience and expression of emotions, parents teach children about what emotions are acceptable and how to express and regulate them (Denham, Mitchell-Copeland, Strandberg, Auerbach, & Blair, 1997; Parke, 1994). Three related processes are thought to be involved in this kind of **observational learning** of emotionality: modeling, social referencing, and emotion contagion.

There is great variability among families with respect to what emotions are emphasized; one family may be full of laughter, another full of fiery displays of anger, and another still committed to the avoidance of any emotional display. Frequency of expression of emotion within one person has been shown to predict the frequency of the same emotion in other family members. For instance, Barry and Kochanska (2010) looked at 102 parents' and children's emotion expression in family settings over the first years of life. They found that one person's positive emotions were associated with greater positive emotion within and across relationships, whereas one's anger was associated with greater anger within and across relationships. These findings suggest that emotions in one dyad are linked with emotions not only in a reciprocal way within the dyad, but also across relationships, reflecting the interconnectedness among family interactions. Emotions are contagious (see Chapter 10). Rasbash et al. (2011), looking at all dyads in the family (using a design described above), found that 16% of the variance in expressed negativity in different family relationships was at the family level. This means that although dyads interact with one another separately, there is a substantial similarity within families across dyads. Families have emotional climates: some of warmth, others of hostility.

Exposure to positive emotions in families has been found to be associated with children being more empathic and affectionate (Eisenberg, 1992), showing better affect regulation (Davidov & Grusec, 2006) and more affection in the sibling relationships (Jenkins et al., 2012). Using a three-wave longitudinal design, wherein data are collected on participants on three separate occasions, McCoy, Cummings, and Davies (2009) demonstrated a relationship between constructive marital conflict (characterized by cooperation and resolution) and children's positive social adjustment. Specifically, constructive marital conflict was positively related to children's emotional security surrounding their parents' marital relations, which was in turn related to children's prosocial behavior.

Exposure to negative emotions in the family is linked to children showing more negative emotions in other settings. So, for instance, when children see angry conflict between their parents, they are more likely themselves to show anger with their peers (Cummings & Davies, 2002; Jenkins et al., 2000, 2005). Denham et al. (2000) found that in families where there is more expressed anger and parental hostility, there are higher rates of externalizing behavior problems in children over time. It is important to note that modeling is not the only process involved in children showing similar emotions as their parents, an issue that we return to in Chapter 12.

These associations between the emotions of parents and children are evident very early. Malatesta and Haviland (1982) showed that if their own mothers' expressions include more anger than those of other mothers, then by 6 months their infants, too, show more anger than do other infants. If their mothers display more happiness, then by 6 months their infants show more happiness. Valiente, Eisenberg, Shepard et al. (2004) found that mothers' reports of their own negative emotions predicted their children's negative emotionality when watching a distressing film in a laboratory setting.

The way that children can produce the same emotions as people they observe has also been called *emotion contagion* (Hatfield, Cacioppo, & Rapson, 1994). Studies suggest that emotion contagion, or the catching of an emotion, occurs in early infancy and beyond (Saarni, Mumme, & Campos, 1998). Emotion contagion is said to occur when a facial, vocal, or emotional gesture generates a similar response in another person (Saarni et al., 1998).

Responding to Emotions and Emotion Coaching

As babies develop language, they learn many ways of communicating about internal states. As parents see their infants having more flexible ways of expressing their needs, they change how they respond to their children's emotions. They may pay attention to acceptable modes of expression and ignore other modes. Brooks-Gunn and Lewis (1982) found that mothers responded more to crying in their babies' first 6 months than in their second year. As their children reached a year and then 2 years, they increased their responding to their child's efforts to speak. Such behavior says: "I'll pay attention to you when you talk to me, but not just when you cry." They also found that mothers responded less to the crying of boys than to the crying of girls. Similarly, Dunn, Bretherton, and Munn (1987) found that mothers' references to feeling states following a child's distress decreased as the child aged from 18 to 24 months, presumably to deemphasize negative emotions (see also Kochanska & Aksan, 2004). By the time children are age 2, parents are decreasing their response to negative emotions and hence inducting their children into a culture in which it is less acceptable to cry to achieve goals.

We might think from our discussion about attachment and parental responsiveness that the best thing for parents to do as soon as a child is distressed is to respond immediately and sympathetically. Indeed, we discussed one study that did find that mothers of Secure infants responded to a wider range of infant's emotions than mothers of Insecure babies (Goldberg, Mackay, & Rochester, 1994). However, parents' goals are more complex than simply protecting or comforting children, particularly as children get older. As infants become toddlers, parents make complex evaluations about how distressed their child is, what the context is, how important the situation is in teaching a long-term lesson, and so forth (Dix, 1991; Mesman, Oster, & Camras, 2012).

Being negatively reactive to children's anger and sadness is the response most strongly associated with poor outcomes in children (Patterson 1982). When mothers respond to children's negative emotions in a problem-focused way, wherein the child is encouraged to, or helped to, deal with the source of a problem, they foster children's constructive coping (Eisenberg, Fabes, & Murphy, 1996). Punitive reactions are associated with escape and revenge-seeking (Eisenberg & Fabes, 1994; Eisenberg, Fabes, Carlo, & Karbon, 1992) and, as we'll see in Chapter 12, more externalizing behavior in children. Other parental reactions such as minimization of children's emotions, or negative and dismissing responses, have been linked to Avoidant emotion regulation and enhanced displays of anger in parent–child

Table 11.3 Means of children's use of emotional labels and of behavior problems recorded by teachers pre-intervention and at 6-month follow-up in the intervention study of Havighurst et al. (2010)

	Pre-intervention	Six-month follow-up
Child emotion labels		
Intervention group	25.5	30.5
Control group	26.2	29.2
Child behavior problems		
Intervention group	90.2	81.2
Control group	91.8	90.9

interactions (Eisenberg, Fabes, Carlo, & Karbon, 1992; Eisenberg, Fabes, & Murphy, 1996; Snyder, Stoolmiller, & Wilson, 2003).

We talked before about reflective functioning: parents' reflection on their own and their child's mental states. This has been found to be associated with emotion coaching (Gottman, Katz, & Hooven (1996, 1997). It involves parents using children's emotions as an opportunity for teaching. Parents help children identify their emotions, problem solve the eliciting circumstance, and empathize or validate those emotions (Gottman et al., 1997). Such activities are associated with better outcomes for children: fewer behavior problems, stronger social skills, and even less frequent physical illness (Eisenberg et al., 1998; Gottman et al., 1997).

Mothers who endorsed beliefs that valued children's negative emotions were more likely to discuss the September 11, 2001, terrorist attacks with their children than parents who did not endorse such beliefs (Halberstadt, Thompson, Parker, & Dunsmore, 2008). Similarly, parents accepting of children's negative emotions also encouraged their children to express such emotions (Wong, Diener, & Isabella, 2008).

The studies described above were correlational, limiting the conclusions that we can draw about causality. Havighurst et al. (2010) has shown, however, that teaching parents how to respond to children's emotions results in a significant increase in children's labeling of emotions and a significant decrease in their behavior problems. This was achieved through a six-session parenting group that targeted parents' responses to, and coaching of, their children's emotions. Results can be seen in Table 11.3.

Learning to Talk about Emotions

Through the learning of emotion language, parents and other caregivers structure a world that will contribute to the emotional experience of children. Parents do this in several ways. One way is to talk to children about the kinds of events that evoke emotions. For instance, a father says to his daughter, who is recoiling at the sight of a big dog: "You don't need to be scared of him." On another occasion she wanders into the cycle path and a bicyclist narrowly misses her. Her father rushes to her and says, "That's dangerous! You really frightened me." Such emotional communications teach children about *what events appropriately elicit emotions* in their community, inducting the child into the cultural rules of emotion. Emotion talk also structures the child's own internal experience and lets the child know about the internal experience of others.

Developmental psychologists talk of **scaffolding**, a process in which parents and teachers can help children take the next steps in their development. Parents can scaffold children's understanding of the mind and emotions by talking about the mind at a more advanced level than the child's independent ability. In this way parents can deepen their children's emotional understanding (Fernyhough, 1996; Meins et al., 2002; Taumoepeau & Ruffman, 2008). Taumoepeau & Ruffman (2006, 2008), over two studies, provided evidence for this kind of scaffolding process. The first study found that maternal use of desire language (e.g., *love, want, hope, wish, dream*) with 15-month-old children predicted children's mental state language and emotion task performance (i.e., their ability to discern how a person felt) at 24 months (Taumoepeau & Ruffman, 2006). In the second study, at 24 months of age, mothers' reference to others' thoughts and knowledge, a more advanced form of mental state talk, was the most consistent predictor of children's later mental state language at 33 months (Taumoepeau & Ruffman, 2008). Parents adjusted their sophistication of mental state talk according to their child's developmental stage; mothers' talk about more sophisticated mental states (i.e., thoughts and knowledge) increased significantly between 15 and 33 months and 24 and 33 months, while less sophisticated talk (i.e., about desires and emotions) remained relatively stable. These findings show parents' use of a systematic scaffolding process wherein, as a more knowledgeable conversation partner, they control children's exposure to mental state language according to their child's developmental stage.

Parental discourse with children has been identified as an important predictor of children's understanding of mind and emotion. As early as 18 months, young children and their mothers engage in discourse about emotions, initiating the socialization of children's use of language of emotion (Dunn, Brown, Slomkowski, Tesla, & Youngblade, 1991). The use of mental state terms has been of particular interest in the field. Indeed, parents who use more mental state terms when interacting with their children influence their children's understanding of emotion (e.g., Dunn, Bretherton, & Munn, 1987; Kuebli, Butler, & Fivush, 1995; Ontai & Thomson, 2002). Dunn, Brown, Slomkowski, Tesla, and Youngblade (1991) showed that mother–child discourse about feelings and causality at age 33 months predicted children's emotion understanding 7 months later. In another study, mothers' discourse about feelings and causal talk about emotions to 3-year-old children were related to their emotion understanding (i.e., their ability to recognize emotions in others when presented with tape-recordings coupled with pictures) 3 years later (Dunn, Brown, & Bearsdall, 1991). Meins and colleagues have contributed to this field by investigating mind-minded comments, which accurately reflect children's mental states; maternal mind-minded comments to 6-month-olds are predictive of children's mentalizing abilities several years later (Meins & Fernyhough, 1999). Laranjo, Bernier, Meins, and Carlson (2010) recently extended this to toddlers; mothers' mind-minded comments at children's age of 12 months were predictive of children's relational understanding at 2 years old.

Conversations about emotion when reminiscing occurs might be especially influential in promoting children's emotional and relational understanding (Laible, 2004; Laible & Panfile, 2009). By discussing children's emotions, parents directly coach children on ways to cope with emotions and help to clarify emotion causes (Gottman, Katz, & Hooven, 1996; Ramsden & Hubbard, 2002). Discussion about negative events appears to be of particular importance. In a recent study, Laible (2011) found that in negative event conversations, as opposed to positive event conversations, mothers were more likely to discuss the causes of emotions with children and have in-depth discussions about emotion with children, and were also more likely to confirm their emotional experiences. Furthermore, maternal elaboration during the discussion of negative events in particular was linked with children's emotional understanding as well as coherent representations of relationships. Given that children struggle with making sense of negative emotions (Laible & Panfile, 2009), it is possible that mothers' elaboration concerning their children's past negative emotional experiences may help them to construct rich memories of these experiences, scaffolding emotional understanding of the event (Laible, 2011). It is important to note that it is not just parents who influence children's talk about emotions. Older siblings are also a critical influence (Jenkins et al., 2003).

There appear to be cultural differences in parents' discourse on emotions. For example, during conversations with their children, Chinese mothers tend to emphasize external behaviors and actions, whereas European American mothers often focus on the child's internal attributes, thoughts, and feelings (Fivush & Wang, 2005; Wang, 2001). Consistent with other research in Western cultures, Doan and Wang (2010) found that, across the cultural groups, mothers' use of mental state language was predictive of 3-year-old children's emotion knowledge (i.e., their ability to describe situations that likely evoke different emotions such as happy, sad, angry, etc.). They also showed that maternal references to behaviors were negatively associated with children's emotion knowledge. Finally, mothers' use of mental state talk as opposed to behavior talk partially accounted for the cultural effect on children's emotion knowledge. That it only partially mediated the relationship, however, highlights that there may be a host of factors that play important roles in the development of children's emotional understanding (Doan & Wang, 2010).

Intergenerational Transmission and Genetics in Parenting

Earlier we presented evidence about the intergenerational transmission of attachment. What about intergenerational transmission of parenting? Do succeeding generations in a family show consistently warm or hostile parental behavior?

Several studies have observed the influence of parenting in one generation on the parenting carried out by offspring when they come to parent their own children. Individuals that have been parented with positivity and warmth in their childhoods grow up to be warm parents with their own children (Belsky, Jaffee, Sligo, Woodward, & Silva, 2005; Kovan, Chung, & Sroufe, 2009). The same effects have been shown for hostility. Individuals who have received harsh parenting in their own childhoods are more likely to parent their own children more harshly (Kovan, Chung, & Sroufe, 2009; Neppl, Conger, Scaramella, & Ontai, 2009). Intergenerational continuities of harsh parenting are affected by the individual's choice in marital partners. Conger et al. (2012) followed up children into adulthood. They showed that children who have been parented harshly are at increased risk of choosing partners who parent harshly. Thus, the risk of harsh parenting for someone who has been parented harshly themselves becomes even more marked because of the mate that the individual chooses. One parent's tendency toward aggression is augmented by the other parent's tendency.

Some intergeneration effects may be because of what people learned about caring for children when they were children themselves. Another likely cause of these intergenerational effects of parenting is **genetics**. It is important to remember that most of the studies of the kind discussed in the previous paragraph are based on correlational data. Each child shares approximately 50% of his or her genes with each parent, so at least some of the influence operating between parents and children is likely to be genetic. A meta-analysis by Kendler and Baker (2007), based on

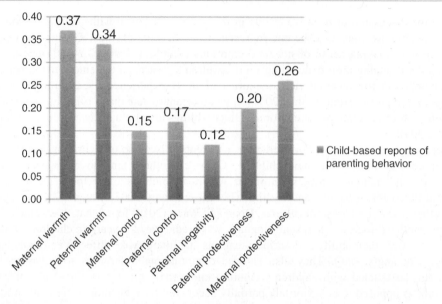

FIGURE 11.4   Weighted mean heritability of different elements of parenting as found by Kendler and Baker (2007).

children's reports of their parents' behavior toward them, has examined the influence of genetics on parenting. The studies included in the meta-analysis involve twins or siblings of varying degrees of genetic relatedness reporting on their parents' behavior toward them.

The heritability estimates shown in Figure 11.4 show that for several aspects of parenting there is a substantial genetic influence. There is a mechanism at play here beyond the genetic influence of parents passing on genes for positive and negative emotions to children. Parenting is, in part, elicited by genetically-based characteristics of children referred to as *gene–environment correlation* (Jaffee & Price, 2008; McGuire, 2012). Lucht et al. (2006) reported on two polymorphisms related to the dopaminergic and GABA-ergic systems. These were found to be related to the individual's temperamental trait of persistence and the individual's rating of parental rejection, suggesting that these gene polymorphisms were responsible for the difficulties in temperament that served to elicit paternal rejection.

Beyond Parenting: Influences of Siblings and Peers

Although parental interactions and genetics are the most important influences on emotionality in childhood and beyond, relationships with siblings and peers are important, too.

Siblings

Siblings have unique relationships characterized by high levels of intimacy, emotionality, and familiarity (Dunn, 1983). As such, they are afforded many shared reciprocal and complementary interactions in play (Dunn, 1983) and teaching (Azmitia & Hesser, 1993), both of which heighten opportunities for interpersonal and intrapersonal development. Research that has studied teaching in siblings reveals that younger children are more likely to solicit teaching from older siblings than from older peers, and that they are more active participants in the process (Azmitia & Hesser, 1993). In the same research it's been shown that older siblings are more likely to provide explanations and positive feedback, and give the learners more control of the task than do older peers. These results suggest a unique scaffolding process for siblings.

Children in multiple child families demonstrate better social skills (Downey & Condron, 2004) and better theory of mind development (Jenkins & Astington, 1996; Lewis, Freeman, Kyriakidou, Maridaki-Kassotaki, & Berridge, 1996; Perner et al., 1994). Furthermore, the presence of older siblings has been associated with relatively good mental health (i.e., lower hyperactivity, emotional, and peer problems; Lawson & Mace, 2010). Finally, there is research suggesting that siblings play a protective role for children facing early risk, which will be discussed in the next chapter (Gass, Jenkins, & Dunn, 2007a,b).

The interactions that occur between siblings appear to play an influential role. Karos, Howe, and Aquan-Assee (2007) examined sibling relationships in 40 Grade 5–6 children in relation to children's sociocognitive problem solving. Using sibling interviews, the authors coded interactions as reciprocal (i.e., companionship and emotional responsiveness) and/or complementary (i.e., instrumental support and competencies). Children were presented with a picture that had a story stem and were then asked to explain what was happening and possible outcomes. For example, with a picture of marital conflict an interviewer would say: "In this picture, the mother and father are having a fight. Can you tell a story about why the parents were fighting, what might happen, and what you might do in a similar situation?" Only reciprocal interactions were positively correlated with socioemotional problem solving. Furthermore, birth order moderated this relationship, suggesting that engaging in reciprocal interactions with an older sibling in particular may have positive developmental implications in promoting sociocognitive skills.

Kim, McHale, and Crouter (2007) investigated longitudinally the association between sibling relationships and change in adjustment from middle childhood through adolescence. They found that, after controlling for parent–child relationships and sibling–parent adjustment, increases in sibling conflict were predictive of an increase in depression symptoms, whereas increases in sibling intimacy were linked to an increase in peer competence and, for girls, decreases in depression symptoms.

Perhaps sibling intimacy could hinder rather than facilitate emotional competence. An interesting study comes from Deneault et al. (2008). They demonstrated that, despite having equivalent age, language abilities, parental SES, and maternal education, dizygotic twins showed better emotion understanding than that of monozygotic twins. A similar finding occurred for non-twin children who had one sibling: they outperformed monozygotic twins on emotion understanding. A similar pattern occurred for social competence. These findings may imply that affective closeness experienced by monozygotic twins might impede their ability to understand others' emotions.

Nonhuman species may also tell us something about the influence of siblings on development. Litter size is reported to be associated with differences in emotionality in adult laboratory rats, beyond differences in maternal behavior (Dimitsantos, Escorihuela, Fuentes, Armario, & Nadal, 2007). Specifically, rats reared in small litters were found to be more emotional: they showed more behaviors indicative of anxiety in a plus-maze task, and reduced coping strategies (i.e., active escape behavior) in a forced-swimming task, when compared to rats from large litters.

Peers

Over 50 years ago, Sullivan (1953) suggested that peer interactions in childhood and early adolescence provide opportunities for learning important social skills, such as cooperation, altruism, and empathy. There appears to be a unique response pattern among peers to children's emotions. Strayer (1980) observed 4- and 5-year-olds playing and documented how children's emotional expressions were responded to by their peers. During interactions children most frequently showed happiness (34%), then sadness (30%), then anger (22%), and least commonly hurt (13%). For the most part their companions just let them pass. Hurt was most often ignored, followed by anger, then sadness, then happiness, so the emotions that were most often displayed were also those to which other children most often responded. Children gave more empathic responses to happy expressions than to all other emotions combined, and fewer in response to anger than to all other emotions combined. Responses were different for different emotions: happy displays usually met with happiness, sad displays usually met with an attempt to share an activity or a toy, angry expressions most often met with verbal or physical acknowledgment like moving out of the way, and hurt expressions met with reassurance or a question such as "Are you okay?"

These reactions change with the age of the child. For instance, Denham (1986) found when she observed 2-to-3-year-old children that they were more responsive to other children's anger than they were to their sadness, a quite different result from that found by Strayer. It may be that as children get older they get better at responding to lower-intensity emotions (like sadness) in other people. In any case, such differential responding probably affects children's expressions of emotion with their peers. Children learn what results when they express various emotions within the context of their age group; they alter their own expressions accordingly.

Many key milestones in a child's development (i.e., false belief understanding) occur during a time when peer interactions increase dramatically for children (e.g., Wellman, Cross, & Watson, 2001). Peer relations are relevant to important processes in social and emotional development. For example, peer interactions provide a context for children to engage in pretend play, and children often use mental state talk in this play (e.g., Howes & Matheson, 1992; Lillard, 1993; Youngblade & Dunn, 1995). In line with this, Maguire and Dunn (1997) showed that earlier friendship interactions influence children's emotion understanding; children who had higher levels of play complexity at age 6 (including concessions and reassurances reflecting an appreciation of the other's interests) were more adept at understanding mixed emotions 7 months later.

The importance of peers to children's academic development, social functioning, and psychological well-being has been demonstrated (e.g., Nangle & Erdley, 2001; Wentzel, 2009). Positive peer relationships have been associated with emotional well-being, values for prosocial behaviors, as well as positive beliefs about the self (Rubin et al., 2006). There appears to be a particular importance of peer acceptance and rejection in children's well-being. Peer acceptance (i.e., the degree to which an individual is liked or disliked by his or her peers) is a known correlate of well-being, and has been found to predict adjustment problems in later adolescence and adulthood (Parker and Asher, 1993; Rubin et al., 2006).

In recent years, researchers have emphasized the importance of examining peer relations and emotionality in a bidirectional fashion (Dougherty, 2006; Oberle, 2010). The impact of social competence and emotional well-being on relationships, as well as the opposite, is apparent (Oberle et al., 2010). Dougherty (2006) conducted a meta-analysis and found a stable negative relationship between negative emotionality (i.e., anger, aggression) and social status, and a positive relationship between positive emotionality (i.e., happiness) and social status. In a recent study, Banerjee, Watling, and Caputi (2011) demonstrated a bidirectional model in the relationship between children's social understanding and their peer relations at school. This suggests that children's experience of peer rejection may impair the acquisition of social understanding, and also that, among older children, difficulties in understanding social concepts predict increased peer rejection.

Evidence for the impact of school environment on children's emotional outcomes is also present. Specifically, Milkie and Warner (2011) showed that children in more negative environments, characterized as classrooms with fewer material resources and with teachers who receive less respect from colleagues, have more learning, externalizing, interpersonal, and internalizing problems. Additionally, children in classrooms with low academic standards, excessive administrative paperwork, rowdy behavior, and low skill level of peers have more problems across one or more outcomes.

Emotionality Over the Lifespan

We've talked about how individual differences in emotionality emerge in the interaction between early relationships and genetic factors. Although people develop in adulthood in many different ways, and although some people do change radically in adulthood, early emotional styles form a kind of outline of the person we are likely to be.

The repertoires of emotion that we form in early relationships affect the relationships that we form over the life course. Jenkins, Shapka, and Sorenson (2006) reported on women initially seen when they were teenagers and followed up 12 years later in adulthood. The more angry these women were during their adolescence, the more likely they were 12 years later to fight with their partners and to experience romantic breakups. Similarly, both in adolescence and adulthood individuals who are antisocial and aggressive are more likely to befriend and partner with other people who are themselves hostile and aggressive (Dishion & Tipsord, 2011; Krueger, Moffitt, Caspi, Bleske, & Silva, 1998).

Continuities in Emotionality from Childhood to Adulthood

Consider how emotion changes over the life course for everyone. As people undergo the transition through their early-to-middle-adult years, they tend to become more comfortable with themselves, less inclined to moodiness and negative emotions, more responsible and caring, more focused on long-term tasks and plans, and less susceptible to extreme risk-taking (Caspi, Roberts, & Shiner, 2005; McAdams & Olson, 2010). Of course, these are simply normative trajectories in adult development. Variations in the rates and amounts of change people undergo still occur (Mroczek, Almeida, Spiro, & Pafford, 2006).

Are children who are angry and easily frustrated in childhood more likely to become hostile adults? Are inhibited, fearful children likely to develop into restrained, timid adults? Continuities certainly occur (Caspi et al., 2005). Associations between children's temperaments at 3 years old and personality traits nearly 20 years later (Caspi et al., 2003) have been demonstrated in a sample of 1,000 in New Zealand. Children who were impulsive, restless, and easily distracted grew up to score the highest on the trait of negative emotionality, and were described by their informants as disagreeable, tense, and anxious. Confident children grew up

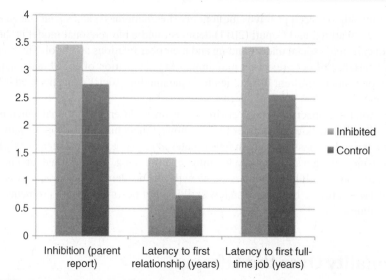

FIGURE 11.5 Outcome (means) of degree of inhibition, time until first relationship, and time until first full-time job of 23-year-olds who were inhibited or not inhibited at ages 4 to 6 (Asendorpf et al., 2008).

to be the most disinhibited (low constraint), had the highest scores on the Positive Emotionality factor, and had other people describe them as extraverted. Inhibited children (i.e., socially reticent and fearful), on the other hand, showed the highest levels of constraint as adults and demonstrated low levels of a positive emotional attitude.

A similar longitudinal study in Germany (Asendorpf, Denissen, & van Aken, 2008) followed children aged 4 to 6 years old until they were 23 (see Figure 11.5). They compared the 15% most inhibited children with controls who were below average in preschool inhibition. Their results demonstrated that the inhibited children were more likely to be rated by their parents as inhibited as young adults, and more likely to be delayed in entering their first stable relationship and finding a first full-time job. They also looked at the 15% most aggressive children and found that when they were followed up as young adults, they were more likely to be rated by their parents as more aggressive, less agreeable, less conscientious, and less open to experience. They were also more likely to be underachievers at school and at work, and show enhanced delinquency, when compared to controls. Here we see the pervasive effects of individual differences in emotionality that carry across the lifespan.

Later in adolescence we see continuities into middle age—again not one-to-one relationships but increased probabilities. Harker and Keltner (2001) rated the intensity of women's smiles in their college yearbook photos and looked at how these ratings related to their well-being over the next 30 years. The intensity of the yearbook smile was related positively to affiliation and competence and negatively to negative emotionality in middle age (see Table 11.4). Interestingly, yearbook smiles also related to relationships that they had formed with others. Women who displayed more positive emotion in their yearbook pictures were more likely to be married by age 27 and more likely to have satisfying marriages 30 years later. In the same way that we saw that emotional characteristics from early in childhood, such as shyness and anger, predicted ways of

Table 11.4 Positive emotionality, as assessed in the magnitude of the smile shown in a photograph at age 20, predicts adult personality, relationship satisfaction, and personal well-being 30 years later

Measure	Positive emotionality
Negative emotionality age 52	$-.27^{**}$
Affiliation age 52	.14
Competence age 52	$.29^{**}$
Well-being age 52	$.28^{**}$
Marital well-being age 52	$.20^{*}$

Source: Harker & Keltner (2001).
Note: $^{**} = p < .01$, $^{*} = p < .05$.

being in adult life, we see the same from late adolescence to middle age. Emotions matter to the ways that we construct our lives.

When we think about why these continuities occur, we have to think both about the individual and his or her context. Think of a smiley and approachable infant who elicits warm and friendly reactions from others. Over time, these environments reinforce and elaborate initial emotionality. In contrast, a child who is easily frustrated and irritable will elicit more coercive or negative reactions, perpetuating the child's intrinsic emotional tendencies. So, not only do children bring temperamental dispositions, but these dispositions also partially drive the environmental responses around them, thus building a path from childhood temperament to dispositional traits in adulthood (Caspi et al., 2005; Roberts, Wood, & Caspi, 2008).

Personality Traits and Emotionality

In adulthood, the **Big Five model of personality** (John, Naumann, & Soto, 2008; McCrae & Costa, 2008) has come to be very influential. Its five traits are: Neuroticism, which involves the emotions of anxiety, hostility, and depression; Extraversion, which includes warmth, gregariousness, and tendencies to positive emotions; Agreeableness, which includes trust, straightforwardness, and compliance; Conscientiousness, which includes achievement striving, self-discipline, and dutifulness; and Openness to fantasy, esthetics, feelings, ideas. Neuroticism, Extraversion, and Agreeableness are all straightforwardly emotional. Conscientiousness and Openness also involve emotions, but perhaps less obviously.

Individuals who score higher in Neuroticism react more strongly to negative events, whereas individuals high in Extraversion react more strongly to positive events (Larsen & Ketelaar, 1991). At the beginning of the chapter we discussed how emotionality can be seen in terms of a lasting bias towards certain kinds of appraisals. In these terms, Neuroticism is a bias toward making negative appraisals, especially those that promote fear, anxiety, anger, sadness, and guilt (Tong, 2010), and Extraversion is a bias toward making positive appraisals (Lucas & Baird, 2004).

The relationship between Extraversion and positive affect is so strong that some researchers claim that positive emotionality forms the core of the personality dimension of Extraversion

(Lucas, Diener, Grob, Suh, & Shao, 2000). Interestingly, when you tease apart positive emotionality into components such as joy, contentment, pride, love, compassion, amusement, and awe, it's the components of joy, pride, and contentment that are most strongly related to Extraversion (Shiota, Keltner, & John, 2006).

Emotion regulation, too, is associated with personality (Gross, 2008). People high in Neuroticism show less, and people high in Extraversion show more adaptive emotion-regulation strategies (Gross & John, 2003; Wood, Heimpel, & Michela, 2003). In a recent study, Ng and Diener (2009) found that Neuroticism was related to lower use of strategies to repair negative emotions and Extraversion was related to the perceived ability to maintain or savor positive emotions.

Several studies have shown that emotional dispositions to anxiety and to aggression shape how adults perceive emotional facial expressions (Dimberg & Thunberg, 2007; Hall, 2006; Rubino et al., 2007; van Honk, Tuiten, & de Haan, 2001). Biases in perception of emotional faces were demonstrated in adolescents and young adults not only for anxiety and aggressiveness, but for other personality traits (Knyazev, Bocharov, Slobodskaya, & Ryabichenko, 2008). Specifically, when asked to rate "happy," "neutral," or "angry" faces in terms of their friendliness or hostility (see Figure 11.6), Knyazev et al. found that anxious adults showed a tendency to perceive facial expressions as more hostile.

In this same study, high Agreeableness and high Conscientiousness predisposed individuals to perceiving all faces as more friendly, while Extraverts were sensitive to positive facial expressions only and rated "happy" faces as more friendly. These findings indicate that personality may systematically bias perception of facial expressions in other people.

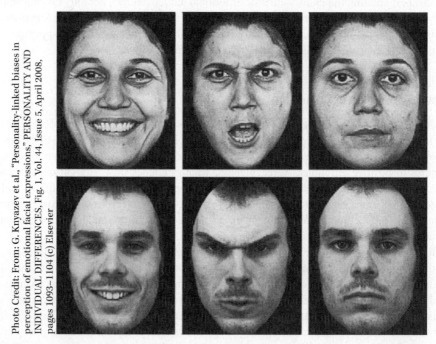

Photo Credit: From: G. Knyazev et al., "Personality-linked biases in perception of emotional facial expressions," PERSONALITY AND INDIVIDUAL DIFFERENCES, Fig. 1, Vol. 44, Issue 5, April 2008, pages 1093–1104 (c) Elsevier

FIGURE 11.6   Photos of a female and a male with, respectively, happy, angry, and neutral faces as used by Knyazev et al. (2008).

In a different kind of study, van Kleef et al. (2010) found that people who were low in Agreeableness responded more favorably to leaders who were angry, while those who were higher in Agreeableness responded more favorably to leaders who expressed positive emotions.

How might we explain the patterns of personality and emotionality? Hans Eysenck argued for a biological theory based on the brain's reticular activating system. He related Neuroticism to overactivity of this system. Neurotic individuals are more easily aroused by emotion-inducing events than are emotionally stable people: particularly they experience fear and anxiety. In contrast, Extraversion is associated with the reticulo-cortical circuit (Eysenck, 1990). Esyenck's hypothesis was that Extraverts have lower baseline levels of arousal than Introverts, leading them to seek out more arousing activities in social interaction and external events to maintain their ideal level of arousal.

Jeffrey Gray focused on neurobiological bases of personality. His reinforcement sensitivity theory proposed that differential sensitivities in the reward-oriented behavioral approach system, and in the behavioral inhibition system and the fight-flight-freezing system, can describe personality traits. According to this, Neuroticism is high sensitivity to threat based on behavioral inhibition and the fight-flight-freezing systems (Gray & McNaughton, 2000), while Extraversion is high sensitivity to positive cues in the behavioral approach system (Smillie, Pickering, & Jackson, 2006). Empirical evidence indicates a relationship of Neuroticism and anxiety with heightened skin conductance (Mardaga, Laloyaux, & Hansenne, 2006) and sensitivity to bodily sensation (Pollatos, Traut-Mattausch, Schroeder, & Schandry, 2007). Extroversion has been linked to increased sensitivity to positive emotional cues (Canli et al., 2001). Depue, Luciana, Arbisi, Collins, and Leon (1994) found trait levels of positive emotionality (central to Extraversion) to be positively related to brain dopamine functional activity, further supporting a physiological basis of personality.

Can Personality and Emotionality Change?

Our discussions so far have centered on continuities. But can we change our personality? This was the question that William James posed in his only large-scale research project, published as *Varieties of Religious Experience* (1902). He asked whether religious conversion could change people's personality, and he concluded that often it could. James introduced the idea of the once-and twice-born. One would think, James argued, that all the processes of socialization would ensure that people would be comfortable with who they are and the society they are in. They need to be born only once. But some people feel uncomfortable, distressed, and perplexed by the world. They want a different life, they want to be born again, and this is the impulse to conversion. James offered the metaphor that our personality is like that of a polyhedron, an object with several flat faces, lying on one of its faces on a table. If we lift it up a bit, it tends to fall back onto the same face that it had been on. That's how our personality is maintained even with perturbations. A conversion can occur when the polyhedron is levered up and falls onto a new face that it hasn't been on. And what do you think might cause such a momentous shift? Well, said James, it's an emotion: a strong emotional event, which is what a conversion experience is:

> Emotional occasions, especially violent ones, are extremely potent in precipitating mental rearrangements. The sudden and explosive ways in which love, jealousy, guilt, fear, remorse, or anger can seize upon one are known to everybody. Hope, happiness, security, resolve, emotions characteristic of conversion, can be equally explosive. (p. 198)

Strong emotions can tip us over into a new way of being. James's book is full of examples of people to whom this has occurred as a result of conversion.

In a discussion of James's research project, Oatley and Djikic (2002) argued that three kinds of event are most likely to cause the polyhedron of personality to tip onto a new face. One kind is personal. It's the kind on which James concentrated, but secular examples also occur, as in the case of Joanna Field (1934), who was able to give up a great deal of pervasive anxiety. (We'll continue this theme with the subject of therapy in Chapter 14.) A second kind occurs with a significant relationship, such as when one falls in love, or finds oneself devoted to someone who needs to be extensively cared for, or enters a new system of relationships, as one does in joining an organization such as the Army. Glenn Elder (1986) has shown the large changes in the lives of American men as a result of being in the armed forces during World War I. A third kind occurs when there is a large social upheaval. Oatley and Djikic give examples from the Holocaust and from the Bosnian war of 1995.

In less dramatic ways, Roberts and Mroczek (2008) have shown that although personality is supposedly fixed, it continues to change over the lifespan in relation to life events and experience. People tend to decrease in Neuroticism and increase in Extraversion and Conscientiousness. Changes of this kind occur especially in young adulthood—ages 20 to 40—but can continue into middle and old age. Ready and Robinson (2010) found that, whereas personality traits predicted younger people's experience of emotions, this kind of prediction ceased to work in older people, because as one gets older one seems to get better at regulating one's emotions and one's emotionality.

Stemmler and Wacker (2010) presented data from several large studies in which physiological measures (i.e., brain activity and bodily responses such as heart rate and respiratory rate) were taken. They asked whether personality traits (and the physiological activity related to them) were

Novels and films: *Casablanca*

Casablanca may be the most loved American film of all time. In lists of the world's best films it is consistently near or at the top.

The film stars Humphrey Bogart as Rick, who owns a bar in Casablanca, and Ingrid Bergman as Ilsa, who arrives in the bar one day with the famous and admirable freedom-fighter, Victor Laszlo (played by Paul Henried). The story starts with a map of Europe and a voiceover explaining how, at the beginning of World War II, people all over Europe were fleeing the Nazis. Casablanca, in North Africa, was a destination from where flights could be taken to Lisbon, and from there to America. But to leave Casablanca for Lisbon, an exit visa was needed. Early in the film we learn that two letters of transit, bearing irrevocable permission to leave Casablanca, have been stolen. They end up being given to Rick

for safekeeping. In a long flashback, we see that at the beginning of the war Rick and Ilsa had a passionate affair, and were due to leave together on the last train from Paris before the Nazis overran the city. Ilsa didn't show up. We movie-watchers now see that Rick's escape to run a bar in Casablanca, his sardonic statements, his lonely drinking, his self-protective attitude—"I stick my neck out for no-one"—derive from his having been deeply wounded by Ilsa.

We learn that Rick has been idealistic, but is now embittered. But we see him caring about those who work for him in his bar, and we see him, too, sticking his neck out for several people. Has his personality really changed? If you haven't seen this film, then you might watch and ponder these questions. If you have seen it, what do you think about Rick's personality?

the same across all situations or whether they were better thought of in interactional terms, as dispositions that were operative only in certain situational contexts. They found that for both brain and bodily measures, the interactional model matched the data best.

Emotionality and Biography

Among the exciting developments of understanding how emotionality affects **character** is the book by Carol Magai and Jeannette Haviland-Jones (2002). They combined the theory of styles of attachment (discussed earlier in this chapter), Tomkins's theory of scripts (see Chapter 8), and the theory of dynamic systems (see Chapter 8).

They studied three men: Carl Rogers, founder of client-centered counseling and therapy, Albert Ellis, founder of rational-emotive therapy, and Fritz Perls, founder of Gestalt therapy. Magai and Haviland analyzed, for emotional themes and content, these men's autobiographical writings and also three scholarly books by each, and their habitual facial expressions as seen in earliest movie made to demonstrate psychotherapy (Shostrom, 1966).

Here is part of Magai and Haviland-Jones's emotion-based biography of Carl Rogers, who was the fourth of six children and the baby of the family for 5 years. At the age of 22 he graduated from university and 2 months later began a long, and for the most part happy, marriage with a woman he had known in adolescence. In his autobiography he wrote: "As a person I see myself as fundamentally positive in my approach to life; somewhat of a lone wolf in my professional activities, socially rather shy, but enjoying close relationships" (C.R. Rogers, 1972). His wife wrote that as a teenager he had been "shy, sensitive, and unsocial" (H.E. Rogers, 1965). Many people found him a gentle person, remarkably devoid of anger. At the same time some professional colleagues found him "an irritant of monumental proportions" (Magai & Haviland-Jones, p. 57). During his academic career he moved to new positions several times, probably to escape interpersonal conflicts that had arisen in professional relationships.

These are conventional materials of biography. What binds them together, in a manner not previously offered by other approaches (including psychoanalysis), are the continuities of emotionality based in attachment theory, script theory, and dynamic systems theory. As Magai and Haviland-Jones put it:

> . . . it appears that Rogers's primary attachment relationship was secure . . . Yet, his interactions with other social partners could be fractious . . . . Rogers could also be painfully shy, and yet he was drawn to people and even did group encounter therapies. (p. 57)

Magai and Haviland-Jones explain how Carl Rogers was drawn to others and often made them the center of his existence, but that he also often found himself in conflicts, although he was not an angry kind of person.

Magai and Haviland-Jones see Rogers as having developed a script of longing for close relationships of the kind he had lost in the attachment relation with his mother, but the script also contained a great deal of shame, which had been induced frequently by his mother, always ready to recognize shortcomings as he grew older. In the family in which he was raised, emotions were not valued and anger was not tolerated. Rogers's emotional organization can be thought of (in terms of dynamic systems theory) as a large attractor area of interpersonal warmth and interest, with areas of shame repellors within it, and a very large region growing out of it (derived from family culture) by which anger is to be avoided. They saw evidence of some of these themes in the facial expressions Rogers showed in the psychotherapy film.

Whereas psychologists tend to talk about personality, biographers and novelists tend to talk about character. By relating personality and character to people's early attachment styles and their habitual ways of emotional relating, Magai and Haviland-Jones have redesigned the psychological bases of biography.

SUMMARY

In adulthood, researchers tend to agree that central personality traits, most notably Neuroticism, Extraversion, and Agreeableness, at their core involve individual differences in emotionality. Styles of emotionality become habitual. Continuities in these styles are evident from childhood to adulthood, influencing our choices in friends and lovers as well as how these relationships proceed over time. One way that researchers have thought about emotions in relationship is through an attachment framework. Four styles of attachment have been recognized: secure, ambivalent, avoidant, and disorganized. There is evidence that some aspects of these styles continue from age 1 to adulthood, and can be transmitted from parents to their offspring. Many aspects of parental caregiving have been found to shape children's emotions, including parental responsiveness to distress, contingent responding in infancy, and the ways in which parents talk to children about emotions and respond to some of their children's emotion displays but not others. Sibling and peer contexts are also important for understanding the development of emotion expression in children.

TO THINK ABOUT AND DISCUSS

1. What biases of appraisal do you have in your life, and how do these affect your relationships with others? Ask the same question for someone you know well.

2. Which do you think is the better way of thinking about the development of early styles of relating: attachment theory or parent's socialization of emotions?

3. Think about your emotional experiences in your family as you were growing up. How do you think these experiences will affect your own parenting?

FURTHER READING

A classic that is still stimulating in its thoughtful and wide-ranging treatment of fundamental issues of emotions in our human condition:

John Bowlby (1971). *Attachment and loss: Volume 1. Attachment.* London, UK: Hogarth Press (reprinted by Penguin, 1978).

Perhaps the best book on the emotional and interpersonal life of the very young:

Daniel Stern (1985). *The interpersonal world of the infant.* New York, NY: Basic Books.

The argument for emotional schemas of social interaction, with a review of how this idea has been approached from different perspectives:

Mark Baldwin (1992). Relational schemas and the processing of social information. *Psychological Bulletin*, **112**, 461–484.

A very good summary of the relation of emotion to personality:

R. Reisenzein & H. Weber (2009). Personality and emotion. In P. J. Corr & G. Matthews (Eds.), *The Cambridge handbook of personality psychology* (pp. 54–71). New York, NY: Cambridge University Press.

Emotion-Based Disorders of Childhood

12

This chapter written with Dillon Browne and Mark Wade

Photo Credit: PhotoAlto/Laurence Mouton /Getty Images, Inc.

FIGURE 12.0   These boys are in a tussle. Is it hostility or is it just play-fighting?

. . . we are obliged to pay as much attention in our case histories to the purely human and social circumstances of our patients as to the somatic data and symptoms of the disorder. Above all, our interest will be directed towards their family circumstances.

Sigmund Freud (1905, p. 47)

CONTENTS

Emotions and Mental Disorders

Most mental disorders of childhood and adolescence are impairments of emotional functioning. Extremes of anxiety, anger, or sadness can occur, making it hard for children to get along with friends and family or to learn at school. Emotion-based disorders in childhood are distinct from those in adulthood, as there are "changes in both magnitude and character as development progresses" (p. 102; Hudziak, Achenbach, Althoff, & Pine, 2008). As we show in this chapter, the emotion-based disorders of childhood and adolescence are more than just extreme emotions.

The Case of Peter

To get a sense of how emotions and emotion-based disorders overlap, we describe a boy with conduct disorder: a type of externalizing disorder. He is a composite of several boys who have been seen in the course of clinical work and research interviews by one of us (JJ). We have developed this composite to maintain anonymity and to illustrate the range of issues present in the child, family, and broader context that are discussed in the rest of the chapter.

> Peter, aged 11, lives in an apartment with one older sister, one younger sister, and his parents. He is often in trouble at school and was recently suspended for several days after fighting with another child. When a teacher intervened he picked up a chair and threw it at her. He screamed and swore at her, and only stopped the aggressive outburst when he was restrained by two adults. In the last two years Peter's school principal has complained about his quick temper, defiance, rudeness, aggression, and truancy. His parents have worried about his behavior at home since he was a toddler. He was born prematurely and, as a baby, was often crying and hard to comfort. As a toddler he was challenging to control and his language was slow to develop. His parents are frequently angry with him, and often capitulate to his demands because they get tired of arguing with him. Moreover, he is hostile and physically aggressive with his sisters, and his parents frequently fight with one another. When Peter is seen at the clinic, he describes frequent feelings of anger, anxiety, and loneliness.

Conceptualizing Childhood Disorders: Categories and Dimensions

Many boys and a smaller number of girls show disorders similar to Peter's. A term that you will see used for disorder in general is **psychopathology**. Two types of systems have been used for assessing and classifying these disorders. The first involves psychiatric diagnosis. To make a **diagnosis**, a child's behaviors, experiences, and emotions are evaluated by a trained clinician. The main scheme used to classify the psychiatric problems of adults and children in North America is the *Diagnostic and Statistical Manual of Mental Disorders* (American Psychiatric Association, 2012). In other parts of the world the *International Classification of Diseases* is more commonly used (World Health Organization, 2008). These classifications are based on a medical model of illness. Underlying the model are the ideas (1) that problems are discrete and well-differentiated from normal functioning, (2) that there is a specific and recognized etiology (causation) and corresponding treatment for certain disorders, and (3) that the course of illness is similar across children who suffer from it. For the most common mental

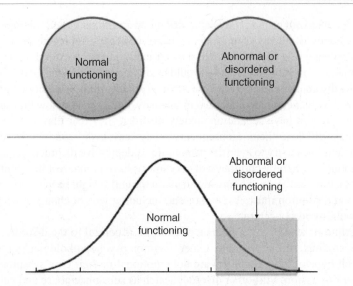

FIGURE 12.1   Contrast between the categorical (medical) idea of disorder (above) and the dimensional view (below).

health problems in childhood, these assumptions are not well met. The idea that disorders represent distinct entities that are qualitatively separate from one another and from normal functioning has been questioned in a growing body of research (Maser, Norman, Zislook, Everall, Stein, Schettler et al., 2009). The large number of mental disorders also calls the validity and utility of this system into question (Rutter, 2011). In addition, the excessive co-occurrence between multiple disorders, lack of attention to developmental, gender, cultural, and informant differences, and the inability to deal with subclinical emotional disturbance represent other criticisms of the categorical approach (Achenbach, 2009a; Hyman, 2010).

Another way of conceptualizing emotion-based disorders, often preferred by psychologists, is to view symptoms as varying on a **dimension**, such as the tendency to express anger, where there is a quantitative rather than qualitative distinction between psychopathology and normal functioning (Pickles & Angold, 2003). Information is usually gathered through *psychometric assessment*, where checklists and questionnaires are completed by clinicians, teachers, parents, or the children. Such measures provide a continuous range of symptom scores, permitting the identification of clusters of behaviors that overlap with the categorical diagnoses described above (Achenbach, 2009b; Achenbach & Rescorla, 2000, 2001). The differences in categorical and dimensional classification systems are presented in Figure 12.1.

How Is Emotion Involved in Children's Mental Disorders?

The most common emotion-based disorders of childhood are described along two dimensions, which, according to the widely accepted proposal by Thomas Achenbach (Achenbach & Rescorla, 2000, 2001), are known as **externalizing** and **internalizing**. The externalizing dimension is characterized by disruptive behavior (i.e., "acting out") and the internalizing dimension is characterized primarily by depressed mood and anxiety (i.e., "acting in") (Kovacs & Devlin, 1998; Lahey, Rathouz, Van Hulle, Urbano, Krueger, Applegate et al., 2008). Peter, described at the beginning of the chapter, showed many kinds of externalizing behavior and, within a psychiatric classification scheme, would be diagnosed as having conduct disorder (CD).

Internalizing disorders include problems related to anxiety and depression. Anxiety disorders are characterized by fears that are abnormal in intensity, duration, and how they are elicited. For example, when children have separation anxiety disorder, they fear that harm will befall their parents and they will lose them. Consequently, they may avoid school, birthday parties, or extracurricular activities to try to keep the parent safe. A depressive disorder is characterized by a marked shift in mood whereby children feel very low or have no interest in activities for at least two weeks. Sometimes rather than being low in mood the child might be very irritable. Symptoms apart from mood disruption must also be present, including weight changes, sleep disturbance, fatigue, and inability to concentrate.

In the descriptions above, a disturbance of emotion is central to the disorder: children may be aggressive, anxious, sad, or irritable. Other common psychopathologies of childhood (e.g., attention-deficit hyperactivity disorder) are not emotional in their core symptoms and are not included in our discussion. Still other disorders, such as substance abuse and eating disorders, do not involve emotions in their core symptoms but underlying emotional issues may contribute to the occurrence of the disorder. An adolescent may start engaging in substance abuse due to feelings of discontent (Dodge, Malone, Lansford, Miller, Pettit, & Bates, 2009). Similarly, depressed mood may precede an eating disorder (Stice, 2002; Weltzin, Weisensel, Franczyk, Burnett, Klitz, & Bean, 2005). However, no disturbance of emotions is needed for diagnosis. Our focus in this chapter is on the problems in childhood that have emotions at their core, and the correlates of emotional experiences that co-occur with psychopathology.

Emotion-based disorders are not necessarily as discrete as the above description may suggest. Indeed, it is common for children to experience both internalizing and externalizing forms of psychopathology. For example, children predisposed to anger and aggression, who are involved in lying, stealing, fighting, and cheating, are also very likely to experience anxiety and depression (Lahey et al., 2008). This was the case with Peter. Children who show high levels of both internalizing and externalizing disorders are particularly impaired, and these patterns are identifiable as early as 6 years of age (Essex, Kraemer, Slattery, Burk, Boyce, Woodward et al., 2009).

Emotions are central to how we define certain types of disorder in childhood. In Chapter 1 we described a continuum of emotional experience and expression. At one end are emotional expressions lasting for seconds, and emotional episodes lasting for minutes or hours. Near the other end are disorders like depression or conduct disorder, in which prolonged emotional states drastically affect life over a long period, even a whole lifetime (as in personality disorders).

Are Emotions Abnormal in Emotion-Based Disorders?

Predominance of One Emotion System

Probably the most common view of emotion-based disorders in childhood, articulated by Tomkins (1962, 1963, 1978) as well as Jenkins and Oatley (1996), is that one particular emotion or family of emotions becomes prominent and dominates other possible experiences. For example, depressed people would experience more sadness than other emotions, or experience more sadness than other people. Similarly, someone like Peter reverts too rapidly and too often to anger and aggression. According to this idea, disorders represent an **imbalance** among emotions, and these emotions become incongruent with what actually happens in the outside world.

Such biases in emotion are represented in several components of the emotion process that we discussed in Chapter 7 on appraisal. So, for instance, aggressive children make biased appraisals of events, and these appraisals make them angry. In a seminal study, Dodge and Coie (1987) read vignettes or showed videotapes that portrayed a negative social event: one child bumped into another or one child refused to let another child play. Aggressive children were more likely to say that the perpetrator was being intentionally hostile, while nonaggressive children saw the event as an accident (Dodge, 2006; Dodge, Bates, & Petit, 1991). A meta-analysis (de Castro, Veerman, Koops, Bosch, & Monshouwer, 2002) has shown that this kind of appraisal bias is indeed more common to aggressive children. It also predicts later aggressive behavior (Runions & Keating, 2007).

An equivalent for internalizing problems is a depressogenic style of appraisal (depressogenic means tending to cause depression). Children who are vulnerable to anxiety and depression show appraisal biases toward threat or misfortune (Frampton, Jenkins, & Dunn, 2010). Such styles are not likely to trigger internalizing problems on their own, but when they occur in a stressful environment they put children at risk (Abela, McGirr, & Skitch, 2007; Frampton et al., 2010; Hammen, 1988). Not only is the content of the thought risky, but depressed people are more likely to ruminate on negative events before and after. That is, they replay negative events or thoughts over and over again in their minds (Baars, 2010; Smith, Alloy, & Abramson, 2006). Additionally, an individual's goals, important in generating emotions and described in Chapter 7, are suggested to be more problematic among individuals with emotion-based disorders (Fontaine, 2010; Fontaine & Dodge, 2009). For example, depressed people are more likely to avoid negative situations or events (that is, are guided by what are known as avoidance goals), compared to non-depressed people, who often set goals for positive situations, events, or things they would like to see happen (or are guided by what are known as approach goals; Vergara & Roberts, 2011).

Inappropriate Emotional Responses

Another view is that children with a disorder react to events with **atypical emotional responses**: crying when nothing has happened, or being angry or contemptuous when someone makes a friendly gesture (Jenkins & Oatley, 2000). Their emotional responses are unsettling and other people have difficulty understanding them. In this view, it is not that children necessarily show more of one emotion than another, but that certain emotions seem unusual. For instance, a child of 11 might be shy of strangers, much like a child of 2; most children have grown out of this kind of shyness, making this an inappropriate or deviant response. Another child may be callous and unemotional. This trait is seen as unusual and is associated with externalizing disorders and a lack of the kind of empathy that is normally seen in children (Fontaine, McCrory, Boivin, Moffit, & Viding, 2011; Muñoz, 2009).

There are physiological mechanisms that may explain the relationship between atypical emotions and disorders. For example, one study exposed youths to popular film clips intended to elicit feelings of anger, sadness, fear, or happiness. Heart rate was measured during each clip and subsequently participants reported on their subjective experiences of emotion (Hastings, Nuselovici, Klimes-Dougan, Kendziora, Usher, Ho et al., 2009). Young people who exhibited externalizing symptoms had a lack of coherence between cardiac indicators of emotional reactivity and their internal subjective states. Those with internalizing problems demonstrated coherence between heart rate and subjective reports of negative affect. However, negative emotion in these individuals was elicited even by clips that were not intended to provoke negative affect. Moreover, in the internalizing children there was an atypical pattern of positive emotionality whereby feelings of happiness did not coincide with increased heart rate. These findings illustrate that emotional experiences have many components, and the relationship between these components may be a factor in the inappropriateness of emotions in disorder.

Poor Emotional Regulation

In Chapter 8 we discussed **regulation of emotions**; this important process offers another way of conceptualizing emotion-based disorders. This view suggests that children with disorders are not capable of regulating their emotions adequately to meet situational demands. This approach suggests that several internal and external risk factors contribute to the development of disorder by affecting the self-regulatory system, which is comprised of an integrated network of cognitive, executive, attentional, and affective controls (Cole & Deater-Deckard, 2009). Children who develop internalizing problems cannot inhibit self-blame and rumination. It's a struggle for them to reappraise difficult situations in a positive light, and this contributes to depression and anxiety. Similarly, children who develop externalizing problems find it hard to shift their focus to anything positive when they are frustrated, and so they remain angry (Garnefski, Kraaij, & van Etten, 2005).

Relative to normally developing youngsters, children with developmental delays have a harder time regulating their behavior in response to frustration (Gerstein, Pedersen, Crnic, Ryu, Baker, & Blacher, 2011). They are more likely to vent their frustration and less likely to use positive coping strategies. Overall, children with poor self-regulation develop ways of thinking and acting that perpetuate their tendencies for inappropriate emotional expression, while normally developing children can regulate their internal states and benefit from positive developmental experiences (Cole & Deater-Deckard, 2009).

Emotional Adaptation to Negative Environments

A final view of emotional disorder is very different. It is that psychological patterns that are viewed as disordered by society actually reflect strategic **adaptations to negative environments** that children have experienced (Ellis, Boyce, Belsky, Bakermans-Kranenburg, & van Ijzendoorn, 2011). Consistent with the evolutionary framework on which this model is based, stressful environments are viewed as contexts to which children must adjust in order to achieve reproductive success. Ellis and colleagues (2011) suggest that children reared in risky environments develop insecure attachment relationships, opportunistic ways of interacting with others, and rapid sexual development as ways of succeeding in the risky contexts that they will likely encounter. In another kind of example, a child who has angry outbursts and steals things from others may be (unconsciously) attempting to gain a survival and reproductive advantage over others who are similarly competitive. An extremely anxious child may have developed hyper-vigilance so that he or she is prepared to generate an appropriate response to potential negative events. When these children are not confronted with this degree of competition and adversity in their environments, their survival orientation is viewed as disruptive and maladaptive. Presumably, children reared in safe environments would not need such strategies and are, therefore, viewed as normally developing. Note that this is not a perspective of environmental determinism; different children respond to negative and positive environments differently. We outline this phenomenon in greater detail below.

The various explanations for the conceptualization of emotion-based disorders are presented in Figure 12.2.

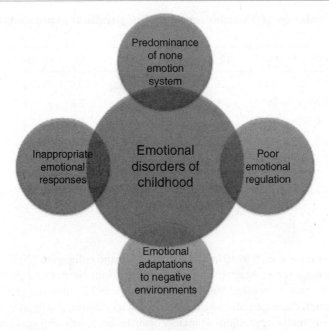

FIGURE 12.2 Complementary explanations of childhood emotion-based disorders.

Prevalence of Disorders in Childhood

The science of **epidemiology** is concerned with how frequently disorders occur in the population and the ways in which their patterns are explained. Epidemiologists are concerned with **prevalence**, the proportion of a population who suffer from some disorder over a particular time period, and **incidence**, the number of new onsets of a particular disorder in a given time period. We are primarily concerned with the former.

Population-based studies reveal that psychiatric problems in childhood and adolescence are surprisingly common. One study, involving a representative sample of kindergarten children in Massachusetts, found that one in five children met criteria for a disorder within the year prior to school entry (Carter, Wagmiller, Gray, McCarthy, Horowitz, & Briggs-Gowan, 2010), with boys showing more externalizing problems and girls more internalizing problems (see Table 12.1).

Table 12.1 Twelve-month prevalence of disorder among a representative sample of 6-year-olds

Type of disorder	Total	Boys	Girls
Internalizing	11.1	7.9	14.3
Externalizing	13.8	17.4	10.4
Any disorder	21.6	23.4	19.8
Comorbid (2+)	5.8	5.3	6.3

Source: Adapted from Carter et al. (2010).

Table 12.2 Three-month prevalence of disorder among a longitudinal representative sample of adolescents

Type of disorder	Total	9–10	11	12	13	14	15	16	Girls	Boys
Externalizing	7.0	5.7	4.4	5.3	5.2	6.3	10.0	10.3	4.5	9.5
Anxiety	2.4	4.6	2.6	0.9	2.0	1.8	2.8	1.6	2.9	2.0
Substance use	2.4	0.0	0.0	0.1	0.3	1.4	5.3	7.6	2.0	2.8
Depression	2.2	0.5	1.9	0.4	2.6	2.7	3.7	3.1	2.8	1.6
Any disorder	13.3	19.5	12.7	8.3	12.7	9.7	14.2	12.7	10.6	15.8

Source: Data from Costello et al. (2003a).

By middle childhood (i.e., 9 to 10 years old), Costello and colleagues (2003a) found that one in five children from a representative sample of children from North Carolina met criteria for a disorder within the past 3 months. You can see from Table 12.2 that the gender difference in prevalence continues, that externalizing disorders, substance abuse, and depression increase with age, whereas the internalizing problem of anxiety disorder decreases with age. National estimates reveal similar results.

By the time adolescence has been reached (13 to 18 years of age), Merikangas and colleagues (2010) suggest that nearly half of all children have met criteria for a diagnosis at some point in their lives. If the threshold is set at serious impairment, however, this estimate drops to 22%. Gender differences in psychopathology persist into adolescence, where girls experience higher rates of internalizing disorder (with female depression in particular increasing as adulthood is approached), whereas boys exhibit higher rates of externalizing disorder. Overall, behavioral disturbances of boys are picked up at an early age, whereas some of the emotional disturbances of females become noticeable only at later ages.

Relationship Between Risk Factors and Emotion-Based Disorders

As Alan Sroufe (2009) has emphasized, emotion-based disorders can be understood only within a complex, systemic framework that is dynamic in nature. Many small influences (including genetic or constitutional vulnerabilities and risky experiences in the environment) set children onto pathways that eventually result in compromised development. As we will see, the relationship between **risks** and **outcomes** is nondeterministic and nonspecific (Cicchetti & Rogosch, 1996). That is, the presence of a particular risk factor may increase the probability of a particular disorder, but its presence never guarantees disorder. Likewise, many environmental risks contribute to a single disorder and one environmental risk can lead to many types of disturbance. The processes involved in the development of mental disorders are also transactional (Sameroff, 2010). This means that children influence their contexts. Because Peter is so oppositional, he can make his parents very angry. This context in turn makes his disturbance worse: the angrier his parents are with Peter, the worse his behavior becomes over time.

People, Contexts, and the Multilevel Environment

A **multilevel perspective** is important for understanding the development of emotion-based disorders in children (Bronfenbrenner, 1977, 2005; Cicchetti & Valentino, 2007; Lerner, 2006). Children are influenced by multiple levels of their environments, including macro-influences such as cultures, neighborhoods, and schools (called **distal factors**), and those that are closer and more immediate to the child, such as their relationships with family and friends (called **proximal factors**). The multilevel structure of children's ecological systems is depicted in Figure 12.3.

Similarly, levels of organization within the child also range from macro (or large scale) to micro (small scale)—that is to say from a child's overall personality and IQ down to his or her neural circuitry, cells and synapses, and even down to the influence of genes. Distal and proximal risk factors influence all these levels of child functioning (Hertzman & Boyce, 2010).

One of the implications of thinking in terms of a multilevel structure is to recognize the indirect effects that occur between various aspects of a child's environment. For instance, neighborhood violence and disorganization have been found to increase the negativity that parents show children. When parents are negative with their children, children are more likely to get involved with deviant peers and become delinquent (Chung & Steinberg, 2006).

When we think about the development of psychopathology in children, we have to think about the relationship between persons and contexts, rather than just children or environments alone (Sameroff, 2010). Psychopathology can be thought of as **maladaptive person–context interactions**: the child is difficult for the environment and the environment is difficult for the child. Thus, children who are difficult elicit more harshness and negativity from their parents during interactions

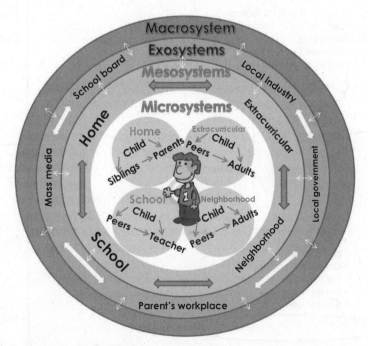

FIGURE 12.3   Multilevel nature of children's developmental contexts, based on Bronfenbrenner's (1979, 2005) bioecological model of human development.

(Lytton, 1990; Yagoubzadeh, Jenkins, & Pepler, 2010) and increase their parents' marital conflict (Jenkins, Simpson, Dunn, Rasbash, & O'Connor, 2005). Both harshness from the parents and marital conflict further increase the children's difficult behavior. Children with problematic emotions also choose friends who share their own characteristics. Thus, angry and aggressive children befriend other children who are angry and aggressive (Sijtsema, Ojanen, Veenstra, Lindenberg, Hawley, & Little, 2009). Depressed children befriend others who are depressed (Cassidy, Aikins, & Chernoff, 2003). Thus we can see that children co-create their family and peer environments and these environments go on to influence their subsequent development.

Sroufe (1997) offers a developmental framework for thinking about psychopathology. He suggests that initially the child's behavior may be only a little bit deviant: the child is a little more oppositional by temperament or shows poorer language development than other children. If the child's context cannot support him or her, the problematic behavior becomes more deviant over time. The child is on a pathway that makes it harder and harder for him or her to resume normal functioning.

In Figure 12.4 we have summarized these processes. The person's emotional functioning is at the center of the diagram. Above are the environmental risks that operate and below are the vulnerabilities that begin as endogenous risks within the child. Over time the interactions between the person and his or her context set children on a trajectory of good or poor mental health. In time the "psychopathology" takes on a life of its own such that a person's previous functioning is a much

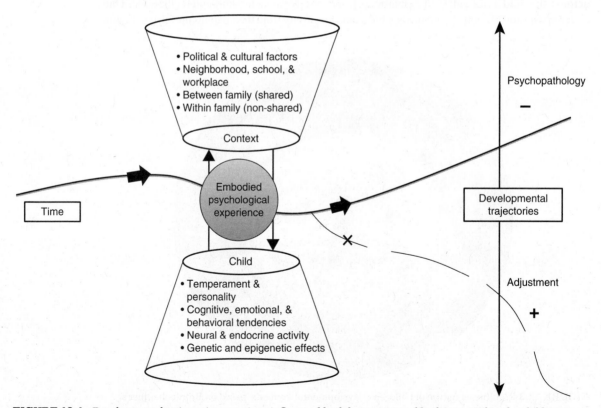

FIGURE 12.4 Developmental trajectories over time, influenced both by context and by factors within the child.

stronger predictor of subsequent behavior than anything related to his or her context (Luby, Xuemei, Belden, Tandon, & Spitznagel, 2009).

Risk and Resilience: The Combination of Risk and Protective Factors

The person who has been most influential in establishing our understanding of the emotion-based disorders of childhood is Michael Rutter, who was the first to undertake thoroughgoing epidemiological studies of children's disorders and who conceptualized children's emotional problems in terms of risks and resilience (e.g., Rutter 2005). There is increasing evidence that the risks that we describe below are not independent of one another.

When one environmental risk is present, other risks are likely to be present. For instance, in a study of childhood **adversities** (for example, experiencing abuse, poverty, mental health problems, or substance abuse in parents), Dong and colleagues (2004), found that 87% of respondents that reported one adversity in childhood reported a second adversity. When adversities in childhood were summed, the resulting distribution was significantly different from the distribution that would have occurred if adversities had been independent of one another. A count of the number of adversities faced by children is called cumulative risk. As the number of risks in the environment increases, so do the physiological indicators of stress (Badanes, Watamura, & Hankin, 2011; Evans, 2003) and the likelihood of showing emotion-based disorders (Deater-Deckard, Dodge, Bates, & Pettit, 1998; Rutter, 1979). Figure 12.5 shows this effect.

The most important element in understanding how risk factors influence emotion-based disorders is to see how they combine (Kumsta, Rutter, Stevens, & Sonuga-Barke, 2010). Peter, whose case we sketched at the beginning of the chapter, had several risk factors. He was born prematurely, which put him at increased risk of having a negative temperament. His parents always found him challenging. Consequently, they were harsh and reactive toward him so that he never learned appropriate emotion regulation. He and his sister had been close in early childhood but she now found his temper frightening. By the time Peter started to receive help from professionals, he had many bad things in

Significant Figures: Michael Rutter and George Brown

Michael Rutter trained in medicine. It was he who laid foundations for empirical child psychiatry. This work included (with George Brown, e.g., Brown & Rutter, 1966) working out how to interview families to understand their emotional characteristics. He also headed up the first large epidemiological study of childhood disorders. It's called the Isle of Wight study (Rutter, Tizard, & Whitmore, 1970) because it took place on the Isle of Wight, which is just off the English south coast. In this work, Rutter started systematically to define the risks for childhood emotional and behavioral disorders. His recent work has been on gene–environment interactions in the development of children. He is still a principal force in the field of child development and children's disorders.

George Brown trained as a sociologist, and after working with Michael Rutter, developed an interview that would enable him to conduct the first large-scale epidemiological study of depression among women. This work is published, with Tirril Harris (1978), as *Social Origins of Depression*. It's one of the most innovative and important studies of emotional disorder that has yet been made. We discuss it in Chapter 13.

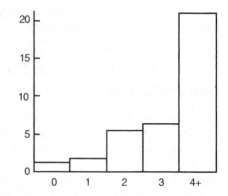

FIGURE 12.5 Effects of risk factors on developing a psychiatric disorder in children (Rutter, 1979): children with one risk factor are no more likely to develop a disorder than those with none, but with each added risk factor the prevalence of psychiatric disorder multiplies.

his life and few sources of nourishment and support. If he had experienced more support, he would have been less likely to become disordered. But remember that because of his aggression, it would not have been easy for family members or teachers to support him.

Although research shows us that endogenous strengths of children such as good temperament (Clark, 2005), IQ (Masten, 2007) and stable vagal tone (El-Sheikh, Harger, & Whitson, 2001) protect children, it's the quality of relationships in childhood and adulthood that is probably the most significant factor in helping people cope with adversity. In one longitudinal study by Gass, Jenkins, and Dunn (2007a, b), between baseline and follow-up measurements, a number of children were found to have suffered adverse life events. However, even when they had been exposed to many negative events, the presence of a close sibling relationship protected them, and they had fewer internalizing symptoms than would have been expected. Relationships with parents, teachers, grandparents, and siblings have all been shown to have protective effects (Jenkins & Smith, 1991).

This conceptualization of differential vulnerability to environmental risk has been called the **diathesis–stress** perspective. It assumes that the effects of positive environments will be similar for all persons. However, a recent alternative, called the theory of **differential susceptibility**, suggests that certain people are more influenced by both the positive (development-enhancing) and negative (psychopathology-promoting) environments that they encounter (Ellis, Boyce, Belsky, Bakermans-Kranenburg, & van Ijzendoorn, 2011). Children have been referred to as "orchids" or "dandelions." Orchids thrive under optimal circumstances, but will wither and die if not cultivated properly. Conversely, dandelions appear to develop equally well whether they are growing on the sidewalk or in a well-kept garden. Differential susceptibility is thought to be neurobiologically based. It reflects a heightened reactivity of the stress-response systems (see Chapters 5 and 6) whereby environments exert a greater influence on the psychophysiological states of highly susceptible people. Differential susceptibility is influenced by both heritable factors and early developmental experiences. Recall Darwin's principle of variation that we discussed in Chapter 1. Evolutionary differences in environmental reactivity will result in increased likelihood of some variations being successful.

Risk Factors

Outlined below are a variety of factors that can influence the development of emotion-based disorders. Thus atypical expressions of anger, sadness, and fear, pervasive enough to affect the child's everyday life, develop through a complex interaction of factors that are endogenous to the child and factors within their environments.

Risk Factors within Children

There are three main approaches to the study of genetic effects on emotion-based disorders: quantitative genetics, candidate gene studies, and genome-wide association studies. As we discussed in Chapter 8, **quantitative genetics** estimates the rates of heritability for particular disorders, and many studies have investigated the relative contribution of genes and environments in the development of psychopathology. This is often done by comparing the frequencies of a particular disorder between monozygotic twins (who share 100% genes) and dizygotic twins (who, on average, share 50% of their genes). Disorders can be recognized as highly heritable when monozygotic twins are more similar to each another (on presence or absence of the disorder) than are dizygotic twins. From these studies, heritability estimates are derived that indicate the amount of variation attributable to genetics.

One of the most comprehensive heritability studies of child and adolescent emotion-based disorders examined a representative sample of 1,571 pairs of twins between the ages of 9 and 17 years (Lahey, Van Hulle, Singh, Waldman, & Rathouz, 2011). Results are presented in Table 12.3.

Heritability estimates for all the most common childhood disorders ranged between 57% (for social phobia and inattention) and 71% (for generalized anxiety and major depression). Although separate genetic effects can be identified for both externalizing and internalizing disorders, the researchers also identified a genetic risk for distress that operated across both externalizing and internalizing disorders. This raises the important possibility that underlying different kinds of psychopathology is a genetic risk for something emotional and nonspecific such as distressed emotional responding.

Table 12.3 Proportion of genetic variance in childhood disorders attributable to genetic relatedness based on a sample of 1,571 twins

Disorder	Proportion of variance attributable to genetics
Major Depressive Disorder	0.71
Generalized Anxiety Disorder	0.71
Social Phobia	0.57
Agoraphobia	0.67
Separation Anxiety Disorder	0.56
Obsessive Compulsive Disorder	0.64
Conduct Disorder	0.76
Inattention	0.57
Hyperactivity-Impulsivity	0.62
Oppositional Defiant Disorder	0.69

Source: Data from Lahey et al. (2011).

Following the establishment of the human genome project, **candidate gene studies** have begun (Plomin & McGuffin, 2003). These have allowed us to see how variations in individual genes are related to particular emotion-based disorders. Striking findings have emerged from the Dunedin Birth Cohort in New Zealand, a study that has evaluated the mental health and environments of 1,000 people from birth to adulthood. Avshalom Caspi, Joseph McClay, Terrie Moffitt, and their colleagues (2002) tested male members for different forms of the mono-amine oxidase-A (MAOA) gene, which promotes an enzyme that deactivates a set of amine-based transmitter substances that include serotonin. Some alleles of the gene (giving rise to a low MAOA functioning group) are much less efficient in promoting the enzyme. In addition to genetic testing, each member of the Dunedin cohort was assessed for history of physical abuse from age 3 to age 11. Cohort members were categorized as not maltreated (64%), probably maltreated (28%), and severely maltreated (8%). Thirteen boys in the cohort had both the low MAOA gene and had been severely maltreated. Of these, 85% met diagnostic criteria for conduct disorder between the ages of 10 and 18. Comparatively, only 22% of children in the low MAOA group who experienced no maltreatment met criteria for conduct disorder. The males who had the low MAOA gene who had been maltreated (probably or severely) comprised 12% of the male cohort. By the age of 26 they had been responsible for 44% of the total cohort's convictions for violent crime. These boys grew up to show a far higher rate of aggression than the boys who had been maltreated but had the high MAOA gene. Results from the initial Dunedin study are presented in Figure 12.6. A meta-analysis confirmed this effect in aggressive behavior across five studies of approximately 1,000 children (Kim-Cohen, Caspi, Taylor, Williams, Newcombe, Craig, & Moffitt, 2006). Other genes have been implicated in the development of depression, again when individuals are exposed to negative life events. A meta-analysis has shown that individuals with a particular variant of the serotonin transporter (5-HTT) gene are more likely to become depressed if they are exposed to traumatic or disturbing life events such as child maltreatment (Karg, Burmeister, Shedden, & Sen, 2011).

The previous studies support the diathesis-stress model: when individuals are vulnerable they show a greater reaction to negative environmental influences. Bakermans-Kranenburg and van

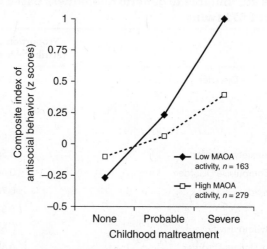

FIGURE 12.6 Antisocial behavior as a function of low or high MAOA activity and childhood maltreatment (Caspi et al., 2002).

Ijzendoorn (2011) tested the differential susceptibility theory. They examined whether certain individuals are more reactive or susceptible to the influences of negative *and* positive environments as a function of variation on dopamine-related genes. Their idea was that lower dopaminergic activity hinders learning in response to negative feedback, but enhances learning in response to immediate reinforcement. The meta-analysis included nine studies of negative-rearing environmental factors (prenatal smoking, poor maternal communication, parental loss and marital status, negative parenting), six studies of positive-rearing environment factors (elevated maternal sensitivity, attachment security), and a variety of outcomes (irritability, emotional regulation, attention-deficit hyperactivity disorder, attachment, externalizing behavior, and prosocial behavior as measured by donating and sharing). They found support for the differential susceptibility theory, as individuals with less efficient dopamine-related genes had better outcomes when they were in supportive environments. Now we turn to the effect of experience on the expression of genes themselves.

To understand individual genetic vulnerability, it is increasingly clear that we need to look beyond the variations in genes that we have described above. Recent studies show that **epigenetic processes** occur whereby environmental experience alters gene expression. *Epigenetic* literally translates as "upon the genome." Here's how it happens. The sequences of nucleotides, of which genes are composed, function to produce particular amino acids, and these form the neurochemicals and physiological systems that affect anatomy, physiology, and psychology. Neurotransmitters, for instance, affect the experience of emotions and are made up of these amino acids. Environments can affect the human genome without actually changing the nucleotide sequences of the genes. This happens when particular chemical groups are added or taken away from genes, which reside in the nuclei of cells in certain areas of the brain, thereby preventing or promoting the gene from producing the amino acid sequence that it usually produces. One way this occurs is through the addition of a methyl base to the DNA sequence in response to environmental exposure in a process called DNA methylation, thereby altering gene expression. In other words, aspects of the environment can switch the expression of genes on or off since areas with a lot of methylation are less active during gene transcription (Weaver, Cervoni, Champagne, D'Alessio, Sharma, Dymov et al., 2004; Weaver, Champagne, Brown, Dymov, Sharma, Meaney et al., 2005; Weaver, D'Alessio, Brown, Hellstrom, Dymov, Sharma et al., 2007).

Currently, most epigenetic research is conducted with rats, and the most commonly studied environmental effect is maternal licking and grooming of rat pups. The analog of this behavior in humans is maternal sensitivity during infancy. This maternal behavior affects the stress reactivity patterns of offspring through an environmental programming effect, where pups that experience less licking and grooming become more reactive to stress as adults (Bagot & Meaney, 2010; Weaver et al., 2004). The absence of licking and grooming alters the offspring's internal physiological environment and reduces the expression of genes that are required for normal stress responses, namely the glucocorticoid receptor gene (Belay, Burton, Lovic, Meaney, Sokolowski, & Fleming, 2011; Meaney, 2001). This effect of maternal behavior on offspring stress response is mediated by gene methylation (Weaver et al., 2004, 2005, 2007). Analogous patterns have been found in humans, whereby altered DNA methylation in the glucocorticoid receptor was observed among suicide victims as a function of their child abuse history (McGowan, Sasaki, D'Alessio, Dymov, Labonte, Szyf et al., 2009).

In a comparable way, Fleming and colleagues found that rat pups that were deprived of early maternal care had lower levels of neural proteins in brain areas associated with attention, impulsivity, and social behavior (Chatterjee, Chatterjee-Chakraborty, Rees, Cauchi, de Medeiros, & Fleming, 2007). Collectively, these proteins are involved with the complex symphony of neural development across early life, which includes axonal path finding, synaptic plasticity, and neuron survival, in limbic, cortical, and hypothalamic connections to the autonomic nervous system. When initially deprived rats are exposed to real or simulated care, the consequences of these effects are reversed. This pattern confirms the environmentally mediated nature of these effects.

Methylation of genes is one of several epigenetic processes that have been identified by examining genetic material from blood samples. One study looked at the methylation patterns in the whole genome among a sample of children who had been raised in institutional care (a circumstance known to increase psychopathology) and compared them to a group of children raised by their parents (Naumova, Lee, Koposov, Szyf, Dozier, & Grigorenko, 2011). Compared to children raised by biological parents, the institutionally raised children showed greater levels of gene methylation in regions that control immune and cellular functioning, the latter being specific to regions involving neural development and communication. The authors conclude that the institutionally reared group may have experienced altered hypothalamic-pituitary-adrenal axis development. This axis is partially responsible for the human stress response, and was discussed in Chapter 5. However, the link between gene methylation, gene expression, and, even further down the line, child emotion has yet to be studied systematically. Researchers have summarized epigenetic effects as ways in which rearing environments get "under the skin," contributing to the development of emotion-based disorders (Hertzman & Boyce, 2010).

Neurological and Endocrine Risk Factors

Certain neural and hormonal functions in children with emotion-based disorders are different from those of children without these conditions. Such differences are often rooted in altered patterns of brain development, resulting in various physiological and anatomical consequences for affected children. Indications of the relationship between abnormal brain functioning and emotion-based disorders include the much higher rate of emotion-based disorders among children who are born prematurely (Boyle, Miskovic, Van Lieshout, Duncan, Schmidt et al., 2011), and/or are exposed to a poor uterine environment through smoke (Huijbregts, Seguin, Zelazo, Parent, Japel, & Tremblay, 2007), poor nutrition (Janssens, Uvin, Van Impe, Laroche, Van Reempts, & Deboutte, 2009), and maternal depression or anxiety (O'Connor, Ben-Shlomo, Heron, Golding, Adams, & Glover, 2005; O'Connor, Heron, Golding, & Glover, 2003; O'Donnell, O'Conner, & Glover, 2009). Emotion-based disorders in children are also associated with hypothalamic-pituitary-adrenal axis function (El-Sheik & Hinnant, 2011), the size of the prefrontal cortex (Raine, 2000, 2002), the structure of the amygdala (Raine, 2011; Yang, Raine, Narr, Colletti, & Toga, 2009), vagal tone (Raine, 2002), and receptor densities of monoamine neurotransmitters in the prefrontal cortex, amygdala, nucleus accumbens, and hippocampus (Pollak, 2005, 2008). Neuro-imaging studies have shown that fearfulness and aggression relate to a heightened amygdala response and suppressed cortical negative feedback (Hariri, Mattay, Tessitore, Kolachna, Fera, Goldman et al., 2002; Hariri & Whalen, 2011; Meyer-Lindenberg, Buckholtz, Kolancha, Hariri, Pezawas, & Blasi, 2006). In other words, people with psychopathology can have neural structures that predispose them to impaired emotional regulation.

In addition to the influences of the prenatal environment, experiences after birth have also been demonstrated to affect brain development. Pollak (2012) presents data across multiple brain systems showing effects of abusive environments. Effects are evident in the volume of the orbital frontal cortex (which is smaller in individuals from abusive environments) as well as the cerebellum and the neuroendocrine system (including both oxytocin and the AVP systems), as well as in neural responses to the processing of anger. Perceptual and attentional biases develop such that abused children identify anger more rapidly, they attend to it more, they have trouble disengaging from angry faces, and, as a consequence of privileging anger within the cognitive system, other aspects of cognition become less efficient.

Initially described in Chapter 8, **temperamental traits** represent one of the ways that researchers think about the biological underpinnings of emotion-based disorders. Temperament, which can be thought of as the first sign of personality (Matthews, Deary, & Whiteman, 2003), is assumed to have a biological basis. Negative temperament in early childhood is a weak but consistent predictor of internalizing and externalizing psychopathology in childhood (Caspi, Henry, McGee, Moffitt, & Silva, 1995; Dougherty, Bufferd, Carlson, Dyson, Olino, Durbin et al., 2011; Lonigan, Phillips, & Hooe, 2003; Ruschena, Prior, Sanson, & Smart, 2005; Rydell, Berlin, & Bohlin, 2003). Bates and colleagues argue for a tripartite model of problematic temperaments consisting of: (1) "irritability-difficultness"; (2) "behavioral inhibition–fearfulness;" and (c) "impulsivity-unmanageability" (e.g., Bates & Petit, 2007). They suggest that the "impulsivity-unmanageability" type of negative emotionality is more likely to result in externalizing problems, whereas the "behavioral inhibition–fearfulness" style typically precedes internalizing problems. There are also indirect effects of temperament on later psychopathology through the effect of temperament on parenting. Children high on negative affect are much more difficult to parent than temperamentally easy children; consequently their temperament elicits higher levels of aversive parenting (Ganiban, Ulbricht, Saudino, Reiss, & Neiderhiser, 2011; Lengua & Kovacs, 2005).

Now that the within-child risk factors for emotion-based disorders have been discussed, our attention shifts to environmental risks while keeping in mind that factors in the person and the context are always in dynamic exchange.

Proximal Risk Factors

In Chapter 11 we considered the normative influences that are important for emotional development. Influences on the development of psychopathology are similar to those that we reviewed there, but they are more extreme (Hatch, Harvey, & Maughan, 2010). For instance, we saw that responsive and warm parenting resulted in positive emotions and secure attachment relationships for children. Now we examine more extreme versions of some of the same processes: parents being harsh or abusive, children being raised in foster care with the absence of an attachment relationship. Such influences are **proximal**, meaning near at hand: they bear directly on the child. Such extreme experiences are associated with the abnormal emotions that we see in emotion-based disorders (Jenkins, 2008) and carry over into adult life (Edwards, Holden, Felitti, & Anda, 2003). It is important to remember that there is never a one-to-one correspondence between particular risk factors and psychopathology (Rutter, 2009). The risks simply increase the probability of disorder.

One of the most-studied proximal contributors to emotion-based disorders is the **parent–child relationship**. In Chapter 11 dimensions of this relationship were considered (sensitivity, scaffolding, mind-mindedness). Only at the extreme do these experiences become important in psychopathology. Parental hostility is the element of parenting most clearly associated with children's disorders (Granic & Patterson, 2006; Maughn, Cicchetti, Toth, & Rogosch, 2006). Researchers are now attempting to understand the causal relationship between parental hostility and children's problems. For example, one longitudinal study of 1,479 children and mothers illustrated that externalizing behavior and maternal negativity predicted one another in a "recursive feedback loop" over time (Zadeh, Jenkins, & Pepler, 2010). Difficult child behavior made parents more negative toward them and harsh parenting resulted in children being more negative. Moreover, the effect of children on parents increased in size as children got older. The reciprocal connections between negative parenting and child externalizing behavior have been called "negative coercion cycles" (Granic & Patterson, 2006). In these cycles, parents respond to child misbehavior with hostility and punitive discipline. This escalates child misbehavior. Patterson (1982) noted a critical mechanism that reinforces the cycle. As children become more and more difficult, parents withdraw their demands, which functions to reinforce the child's aversive behavior.

Though the majority of research on parent–child relationships is observational, there has been some experimental research examining the effects of parental control on child emotions, adding strength to causal claims. One study trained parents to engage in (a) controlling and (b) autonomy-granting behavior while children were preparing to write a speech (Thirwall & Cresswell, 2010). The experiment was counterbalanced so that all children and parents experienced both conditions in an order that was randomly determined. When mothers were highly controlling, children had negative expectations of their performance. Moreover, children exhibited more anxious behavior during the speech, especially if they were temperamentally anxious in the first place. Researchers suggested that controlling parenting increases feelings of self-doubt, manifesting as anxiety in performance situations.

The absolute level of negative parenting a child receives is an important predictor of emotion-based disorders. However, the parenting received by a child's siblings is also influential on well-being. **Differential parenting** refers to one child experiencing more warmth, love, and affection, or more hostility, anger, and negative emotionality, than his or her siblings. In a sample of 565 five-year-old monozygotic twin pairs, Caspi and colleagues (2004) found that the twin who received more emotional negativity and less warmth from their mothers had more antisocial behavior problems, ruling out the possibility of genetic effects. Interestingly, all children in a family suffer when parents are very differential with siblings. Thus, the within-family standard deviation on the parenting of different children explains child behavior over and above the family average and child-specific influences (Boyle, Jenkins, Georgiades, Cairney, Duku, & Racine, 2004). As you can see in Figure 12.7, at high levels of differential parenting both favored and disfavored children show higher levels of disturbance (Meunier, Bisceglia, & Jenkins, 2011). This effect is strongest when children are closer in age (i.e., experiencing the greatest competition for parental resources). These findings suggest that dynamics of the family as a whole, not children's immediate relationships, are important for understanding emotion-based disorders.

Child maltreatment refers to the presence of physical abuse, sexual abuse, neglect, or emotional maltreatment (Barnett, Manly, & Cicchetti, 1993; Cicchetti & Toth, 2005). This represents an extreme and pathological relational environment that fails to provide the developmental experiences necessary for normal development. Problems among maltreated children are widespread, including delays with the development of affect regulation, higher-order cognition, self-representation, and social information processing. The problems of maltreated children increase with age as they fail to develop the necessary competencies at each stage of development and the deficits compound one another (Cicchetti & Toth, 2005).

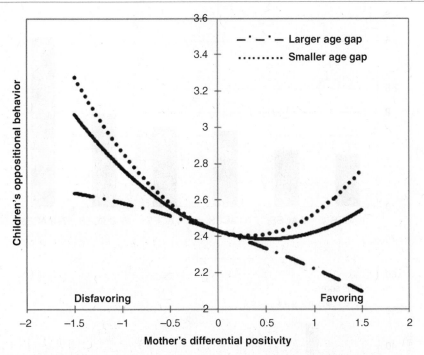

FIGURE 12.7 Children's oppositional behavior as a function of differential parenting: whether the children have been treated favorably or unfavorably (Meunier, Bisceglia, & Jenkins, 2011).

Children exposed to serious and prolonged **conflict between parents** are at increased risk of developing externalizing and internalizing disorders (Kitzman, Gaylord, Holt, & Kenny, 2003). Researchers have concluded that exposure to overt hostility, and the underlying stress reactivity in children, can lead to patterns that have long-term consequences for emotional development (El Sheikh & Hinnant, 2011). But externalizing problems in children occur before parents separate and are related to parental conflict before divorce (Block, Block, & Gjerde, 1986; Cherlin, Furstenberg, Chase-Lansdale, Kiernan, & Robins, 1991). Similarly, children's disorders after their parents' divorce have been found to be most strongly associated with continuing parental conflict (Emery, 1988). Authors of a meta-analysis of 118 studies, using a variety of different methodologies, suggested that outcomes are particularly poor when children have been exposed to domestic violence (Kitzman, Gaylord, Holt, & Kenny, 2003).

The mechanism of influence is hard to determine in observational studies. We know that child externalizing behavior contributes to parental conflict but we also know that parental conflict increases children's behavioral problems over time (Jenkins et al., 2005). Given the fact that parents and children share both environments and genes, it is important to try to determine whether the association that we see between parental conflict and child emotion-based disorders is attributable to their shared genes or whether the conflict itself causes problems for the child (D'Onofrio, Turkheimer, Emery, Slutske, Heath, Madden et al., 2005). Using a quantitative genetics design, D'Onofrio and colleagues demonstrated that there is an environmental effect of marital conflict on child externalizing behavior, even when controlling for genetic contributions. Such findings are consistent with a causal hypothesis. Consistent with this, researchers have

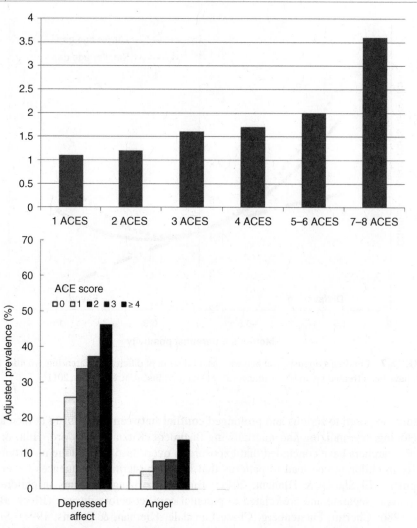

FIGURE 12.8 Risk of ischemic heart disease (top, odds ratios) and sad and angry emotions (bottom, adjusted prevalence) as a function of number of adverse childhood experiences (ACEs). ACEs include physical, emotional, and sexual abuse, poverty, parental separation, and having a mentally ill, criminal, or substance-abusing parent before the age of 16 years old. Dong et al., 2004.

found that the random assignment of couples to a marital conflict resolution and parental education intervention results in better adjustment for children relative to individuals in a control condition (Faircloth, Schermerhorn, Mitchell, Cummings, & Cummings, 2011).

What is the impact of a number of these risks in the environment occurring together? In Figure 12.8 you can see that the more adverse the childhood experiences, the more likely the individual is to suffer from ischemic heart disease as an adult. The data for these graphs are derived from the study of Adverse Childhood Experiences (ACEs), which have been linked in a rapidly growing body of literature to a wide range of adolescent and adult mental and physical health problems. In one study of 9,367 adult members of a health maintenance organization, links between the number of types of adverse early experiences (maltreatment, witnessing violence, poverty, parental separation) and a range of problematic health conditions have been noted, including substance abuse (Dube et al., 2003), smoking (Ford et al., 2011), poor mental health (Edwards, 2003), and heart disease (Dong et al., 2004). This relationship is partly explained by emotions. Feelings of anger and depression increase with the number of ACEs experienced. After accounting for these emotions, the relationship between ACEs and heart disease is much reduced.

Attachment status in early childhood has been linked to both internalizing and externalizing psychopathology based on a meta-analysis that included nearly 6,000 children. The strongest risk is for children in the Disorganized category, followed by Avoidant children and Ambivalent children, respectively (Fearon, Bakermans-Kranenburg, van Ijzendoorn, Lapsley, & Roisman, 2010). As we discussed in Chapter 11, disorganization is more common in high-risk families and the strongest single predictor of disorganization has been found to be maltreatment (Cyr, Euser, Bakermans-Kranenburg, & van Ijzendoorn, 2010).

Though problematic parenting has implications for the development of disorganized attachment, the absence of or **failure of an attachment relationship** is particularly damaging. Such is the case for children who are raised in orphanages without the opportunity to develop attachment relationships. After the fall of the Ceausescu regime in 1989, researchers became aware of many Romanian children, reared in orphanages, who were being adopted into British families. These children have been intensely studied, for instance, by Michael Rutter and his colleagues. The orphanage was described as "appalling"; children were confined to cots, were left alone without stimulation or much social contact to speak of, and were washed by being hosed down with cold water (Rutter, Sonuga-Barke, & Castle, 2010). Researchers have uncovered a dose–response relationship whereby the longer the period of institutionalization, the worse the emotional outcomes (O'Connor, Marvin, Rutter, Olrick, & Britner, 2003). Romanian orphans adopted into homes when compared to noninstitutionalized English adoptees were more likely to show (a) indiscriminate friendliness as compared with children's usual wariness of strangers, (b) more abnormal patterns of attachment to adoptive parents, and (c) more externalizing symptoms (see also Ellis, Fisher, & Zaharie, 2004). Although most environmental risk factors operate in a nonspecific way, increasing the risk of all kinds of disturbance (McMahon, Grant, Compas, Thurm, & Ey, 2003), there is some suggestion that the absence of an attachment relationship confers a specific kind of risk. In a follow-up of adoptees when they were 15 years old, a coherent syndrome was described, including four elements: quasi-autism, disinhibited or disorganized attachment, cognitive impairment, and inattention-overactivity (Kumsta, Kreppner, Rutter, Beckett, Castle, & Stevens, 2010).

Although the previous studies were all observational, one intervention study suggests that an absence of attachment relationships *causes* these emotional problems. Charles Nelson and colleagues worked with a population of children institutionalized in Romania prior to 31 months old (Nelson, Zeanah, Fox, Marshall, Smyke, & Guthrie, 2007). They randomly assigned 139 children to go to a foster family (intervention group) or to remain in institutional care (control group). They also tracked the development of 72 children who were being raised normally by their families (Ghera, Marshall, Fox, Zeanah, Nelson, Smyke et al., 2009). Results from this study are presented in Figure 12.9. The intervention group showed more positive emotion than the control children. Not surprisingly, the children with the best outcomes were those who had never gone into foster care. These results highlight the importance of the attachment relationship for the development of emotion.

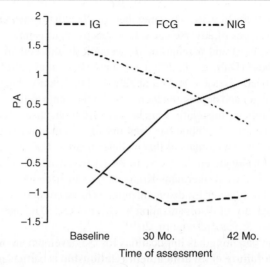

FIGURE 12.9 Positive affect in early-institutionalized children randomly assigned to a foster-care group (FCG) or who remained institutionalized (IG) as compared with a never-institutionalized group (NIG) (from Ghera et al., 2009).

Distal Risks: Parental Psychopathology, Neighborhood, Social Class, and Peer Groups

Risks that are thought of as **distal** (meaning distant) are more indirect than those that bear directly on children. Among distal risks for psychopathology in children are psychopathology and poverty of their parents. A Scandinavian population cohort study followed over 800,000 people for up to 28 years, examining the onset of mental illness in adolescence and young adulthood (Dean, Stevens, Mortensen, Murray, Walsh, & Pedersen, 2010). Serious mental disorders in parents, such as psychosis, increased the risk of children developing all forms of psychopathology. The strongest effects were observed when both parents had serious mental illness (in this study, psychosis). When this occurred, offspring were 13 times more likely to show schizophrenia, 8 times more likely to show substance abuse, and 3 times more likely to show any psychiatric disorder when compared to individuals with unaffected parents. However, the risk of psychopathology in offspring was elevated when parents had any form of mental illness, not strictly psychosis.

As depression is far more common in the population than schizophrenia, most of our understanding of the effects of psychiatric illness on children comes from studies of maternal depression. A recent meta-analysis of 193 studies indicated that maternal depression was associated with internalizing and externalizing psychopathology among children between 1 and 82 months. Effect sizes were small, with maternal depression explaining between 1 and 6% of the variance across studies (Goodman, Rouse, Connell, Broth, Hall, & Heyward, 2010). Some of this influence is explained by parental behavior (Lim, Wood, Miller, & Simmens, 2011), as depressed parents are more likely to be harsh and insensitive (Elgar, McGrath, Waschbusch, Stewart, & Curtis, 2004). Genetic risk, previously discussed, is also a critical mechanism in this association.

There is evidence that social processes within children's neighborhoods can also influence emotional problems. Two key social processes fall under the banner of social organization: (1) social control—the extent to which youth are monitored by the collective community; and (2) social cohesion—a measure of mutual trust and shared values (Silk, Sessa, Morris, Steinberg, & Avenevoli, 2004). Together, these processes comprise the concept of **collective efficacy** (see Sampson, Raudenbush, & Earls, 1997), which can be thought of as the extent to which communities have influence on child outcomes. Collective efficacy has a positive effect on levels of prosocial behavior in adolescents and involvement with non-delinquent friends, and is associated with reduced risk of behavior problems (Elliott, Wilson, Huizinga, Sampson, Elliot, & Rankin, 1996). Aneshensel and Sucoff (1996) provide evidence for a relationship between social cohesion and adolescent psychopathology wherein greater familiarity among individuals in a community predicts lower rates of adolescent depression. In this same study, social cohesion was inversely correlated with oppositional defiant disorder and anxiety problems. Xue, Leventhal, Brooks-Gunn, and Earls (2005) have also shown that social cohesion and informal social control are associated with more positive mental health outcomes in children, even after controlling for the level of social disadvantage.

Although neighborhood efficacy is a distal risk, it operates through more proximal influences; that is to say it affects parenting behavior and the amount of stimulation offered from the home environment (e.g., Klebanov, Brooks-Gunn, Chase-Lansdale, & Gordon, 1997). That is, social organizational institutions may function to socialize parents by providing neighborhood role models, improving relations among parents and children in the community, or affording opportunities for social interaction at local parks and libraries (Kohen, Leventhal, Dahinten, & McIntosh, 2008). A recent model by Kohen and colleagues (2008) relates distal environmental processes to child outcomes. This model supports a mechanism whereby structural disadvantage such as poverty relates to lower neighborhood social cohesion. In turn, lower cohesion is associated with poorer family functioning and more parental emotional distress. These variables then impact child outcomes by enhancing proximal influences such as inconsistent and punitive forms of parenting. A recent study has provided evidence for a direct effect of neighborhoods on children's outcomes as well, after controlling for parenting (Wade et al., 2011). It is possible that adults in the neighborhood are serving as socialization agents for children beyond the influence of their parents.

Socioeconomic conditions, including poverty, are among the best established predictors of mental and physical health in children and adults (Shokonoff, Boyce, & McEwen, 2009). A study of 2,800 children demonstrated that children who had experienced persistent food insecurity were twice as likely to suffer from externalizing problems compared to children without such insecurity (Slopen, Fitzmaurice, Williams, & Gilman, 2008). Researchers have argued that socioeconomic status (social class) influences development through three pathways: (a) inequitable allocation of **resources** like nutrition, healthcare, housing, and education; (b) **stress reactions** caused by parenting, environmental hazards, adverse life events, violence, and neighborhood problems, and (c) **health behaviors** like tobacco, alcohol, and illicit substance abuse and exercise (Bradley & Corwyn, 2002). Following an increase in the understanding of the physiological consequences of poor childrearing (e.g., Bagot & Meaney, 2010), researchers now suggest that biological stress reactions may be the most important link between emotion-based disorders and socioeconomic conditions (Repetti, Taylor, & Seeman, 2002).

The consequences of socioeconomic conditions are not just about absolute levels of income, however. It is also about social inequality. Wilkinson and Pickett (2009) have developed an inequality metric by examining the ratio of incomes for the top and bottom 20% of a particular nation or society (so, for instance, in the United States, the top 20% are 8.5 times more wealthy than the bottom 20%, whereas in Japan, the top 20% are only 3.4 times richer than the bottom 20%). This inequality relates to the rates of health problems in a society. The same patterns are observed for a number of social issues, including infant mortality, heart disease, homicides, mental illness, trust, and so on.

The United Nations Children's Fund (UNICEF) has developed a composite index of well-being based on subjective well-being, material well-being, health and safety, the quality of family and peer relationships, behaviors, and risks. If one looks at the relationship between levels of income inequality in different countries of the developed world and their scores on this index, a very striking relationship emerges.

In general, the greater the equality of personal incomes within a developed country, the higher the level on the UNICEF index of child well-being in that country. So countries with more equal incomes, such as Finland, Norway, Sweden, and Denmark, have the highest levels of child well-being. There are some exceptions, for instance incomes in Japan are among the most equal in the world, but this country is in the middle of the scale of child well-being, whereas the Netherlands, which has a somewhat more inequality of income than the Scandinavian countries, nonetheless has one of the best scores on the child well-being index. In general terms, again, at the other end of the scale, several countries with the most unequal incomes, such as USA and UK, are among those with the lowest levels of child well-being. Again, however, there are one or two exceptions to the general rule. For instance Portugal, which is among the highest on income inequality is about in the middle of the range of child well-being. Also, in general terms, in the middle of the range on both income inequality and scores on the index of child well-being is a group of countries that include Canada, France, and Germany.

In stark contrast to this strong relationship of income inequality with the index of child well-being in developed countries, there is no consistent relationship between average income in different countries and child well-being. Norway and USA are among the countries with the highest level of income per person, but on the scale of child well-being, Norway does far better than USA. Spain and New Zealand are at the low end of the scale of income per person, with their citizens having about the same average income, but the index of child well-being is far better in Spain than it is in New Zealand.

Poor socioeconomic conditions have been found to increase parenting problems. Parenting is a hard job, and when parents are worrying about the basics, such as not having enough money to feed and clothe children, or when they feel disadvantaged in their communities, they do not have the emotional resources to form optimal relationships with their children (Duncan, Ziol-Guest, & Kalil, 2010; Jenkins et al., 2003, Macmillan et al., 2004). The New Hope project in Milwaukee (Huston, Gupta, Bentley, Dowsett, Ware, & Epps, 2008) was an experiment in which working parents who lived in very poor neighborhoods were eligible to enroll in a study. They were then randomly assigned to an intervention group or a control group. The intervention group was given a wage supplement and a child-care subsidy for any child under age 13. The supplement could be used for childcare and subsidized health insurance. Two years later, children in the intervention and the control families were followed up. There were strong protective effects for boys as a result of the intervention (although these were not evident for girls) on externalizing problems, academic outcomes, and social skills.

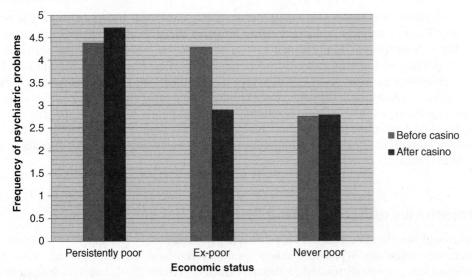

FIGURE 12.10 Frequency of psychiatric problems in children before and after a casino opened. Families were categorized into persistently poor, those who improved from being poor to being better off, and those who were never poor (adapted from Costello et al., 2003b).

A study based on a natural experiment showed similar findings. A casino was opened on a native reserve during the course of a longitudinal study. It alleviated the poverty experienced by many families. When families were no longer living in poverty, their parenting improved and, as a consequence, children's behavior improved. This can be seen in Figure 12.10. When parents have fewer financial worries, they are able to develop better relationships with their children, which in turn reduces their children's likelihood of psychopathology (Costello, Compton, Keeler, & Angold, 2003).

We are influenced by the behavior of people in our close environment. Thus adolescents have been found to engage in more smoking, drinking, drugs, and delinquent behavior when these behaviors are common in their peer group (Dishion & Tipsord, 2011). The effects of an aggressive peer group on the aggressiveness of an individual child have been demonstrated among preschool (Howes, 2000) and school-age children (Kellam & Hendricks-Brown, 1998) as well. These are effects of the **composition** of social groups; they have been shown for children's depression and anxiety (Schaefer, Kornienko, & Fox, 2011), for obesity (people's weight gain increases as a function of the weights of close relatives and friends; Christakis & Fowler, 2007), and for children's early language (Justice, Petscher, Schatschneider, & Mashburn, 2011). So, when we think about development of emotion-based disorders, we need to think not just about immediate influences but also about adults and peers in children's surroundings.

Trajectories of Disorders

How stable are disorders over time? We think of emotions as short-term reactions to events. When we look at psychopathology, however, although the emotional reactions themselves might be short-term, patterns of emotional reactivity can occur over months, years, or a lifetime. There is stability to the underlying **affective biases** in the same way that there is stability in temperament and personality. As a consequence, we do see strong continuities in internalizing and externalizing disorders among children: they confer significant risk of psychopathology later in life. While such **continuities** are evident, we also see **discontinuities**. Among discontinuities, some children show early signs of aggression but stop being aggressive as they mature. Similarly, some children who are sad and anxious in childhood do not continue to show these problems in adulthood. In the following section we consider the continuities and discontinuities in psychopathology and also examine why changes occur.

Trajectories of Externalizing Problems

Even though there are discontinuities in patterns of psychopathology, it is important to remember that earlier indications of disorder almost invariably represent the strongest risk factor for predicting later disorder (Ferdinand, Dieleman, Ormel, & Verhulst, 2007; Luby, Xuemei, Belden, Tandon, & Spitznagel, 2009). Half of disorders diagnosed in adulthood had an onset in adolescence (Belfer, 2007).

There is a strong consensus regarding the nature of developmental trajectories in conduct problems (Broidy et al., 2003; Colman et al., 2009; Fergusson & Horwood, 2002; Nagin & Tremblay, 1999; Odgers et al., 2008; Schaeffer, Petras, Ialongo, Poduska, and Kellam, 2003; Shaw, Gilliom, Ingoldsby, & Nagin, 2003). Studies find a group of children with high levels of conduct problems that persist across development and into adulthood. This persistent group generally represents less than 10% of the population but it is a highly problematic group who are responsible for a large proportion of violent crime (Colman, Ploubidis, Wadsworth, Jones, & Croudace, 2007; Farrington & Welsh, 2007; Huesmann, Dubow, & Boxer, 2009; Loeber & Farrington, 2000; Moffit, 1993). Another group of children start high or moderately high on aggression in early or middle childhood, but as they mature their conduct problems reduce. There is variation across studies in the size of this group as a function of the age of the sample. Another group of children are persistently low in their conduct problems. A fourth pattern is evident when adolescence to early adulthood is included in the follow-up period. This is a group of children referred to as "adolescent limited" who show conduct problems during adolescence, although these problems tend not to be as severe as those shown by children in the persistently high group. Their problems reduce as they enter adulthood but do not disappear entirely (Moffit, Caspi, Harrington, & Milne, 2002).

Trajectories of conduct problems can be seen in Figure 12.11. The people who experience the highest levels of such problems are in the high persistent group. This group is differentiated from other trajectory groups in their early emotions. As Terrie Moffit and her colleagues (2002) have shown, people in this group exhibit more negative affect, and were likely to have had high perinatal risk and more neurodevelopmental problems, greater family adversity, and poorer intrafamilial relationships. Shaw, Lacourse, and Nagin (2005) confirmed the effects of many of these factors, and showed, too, that people in this group showed less fear in childhood. The adolescent-limited males experience fewer risks in their

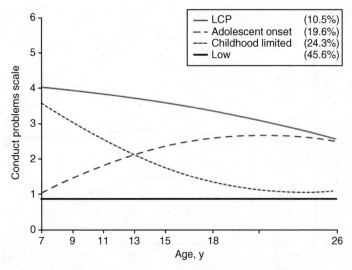

FIGURE 12.11 Conduct problems across childhood and early adulthood. Approximately 10% of individuals have life-course-persistent (LCP) conduct problems (Odgers et al., 2008).

backgrounds. Their delinquency seems to be driven largely by associating with deviant peers (Moffit et al., 2002).

Trajectories of Internalizing Problems

In general, continuities for internalizing disorders are less marked than those for externalizing problems (Esser, 1990; Offord et al., 1992). Between 70 and 75% of children with diagnoses of internalizing disorders when first interviewed were free of disorder at follow-up (Offord et al., 1992). Similar to the externalizing disorders there is a group of children who remain persistently high across childhood and into adulthood. As compared with externalizing disorders, internalizing disorders tend to be more episodic such that for some children the problems disappear and then reappear. This is evident from results of a study by Sterba, Prinstein, and Cox (2007). They examined continuities of anxiety from 2 to 11 years old. About two thirds of the children showed no anxiety across the whole follow-up period. The remaining one third were divided into an elevated-stable group, and a group characterized by an initial decline in problems from age 2 to age 6, followed by an increase from age 6 to age 11. This variable group indicates that there are periods of children's lives that are less anxiety-provoking even for those who are vulnerable.

What happens to internalizing problems from childhood to adulthood? Colman, Ploubidis, Wadsworth, Jones, and Croudace (2007) examined 4,627 individuals who were interviewed at 13, 15, 36, 43, and 53 years. Results of this are shown in Figure 12.12.

In Figure 12.12 you can see that some children experience serious or moderate problems in childhood, and that this level of disturbance persists into adult life. About 14% of children have significant problems in adolescence but these problems have disappeared by adulthood. Generally

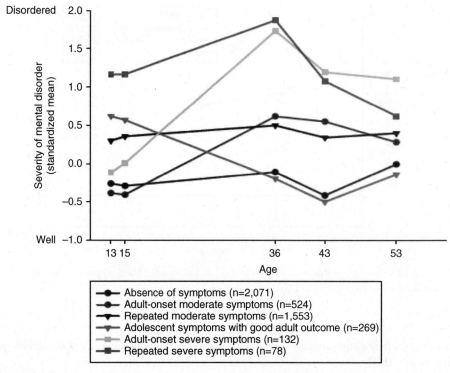

FIGURE 12.12 Life-course trajectories of internalizing disorders as a function of age in groups with different levels of symptoms. (Colman et al., 2007).

speaking, higher birthweights were associated with fewer internalizing problems, whereas delayed motor development was associated with more severe problems. The results suggest that there are neurodevelopmental contributions to the continuity of internalizing disorders.

In sum, some children exhibit an array of problems early in life, and many of these problems persist into adolescence and adulthood. In other children, early difficulties reduce over time, and sometimes children with few problems early on show steady increases across the life course. Most children, however, show persistently low problems. Whatever the course, there are a variety of individual, psychobiological, and contextual factors that contribute to these development trajectories.

Therapy and Prevention

There is a large field of clinical practice that aims to alleviate disorders in children and adolescents (Carr, 1999; Kazdin, 2004; Ollendick, 2004: Rutter & Taylor, 2002). Many of the treatment options used for adults—such as behavior therapy, cognitive-behavior therapy, and psychoanalytic therapy (to be discussed in Chapter 14)—are also used with children and adolescents. Nonetheless, there are important issues about the prevention and treatment of disorders that are specific to childhood.

Types of Treatment for Childhood Externalizing and Internalizing Problems

Perhaps the most important difference when children are involved in therapy is the emphasis on treating the child's relationships, most often in the family (see Carr, 2009), although interventions at school have also been found to be effective in reducing psychopathology in children (Polirstok & Gottlieb, 2006). One type of family therapy involves working with parents in **parent management training**. The theory behind this treatment approach is that child conduct problems are a result of maladaptive parent–child interactions. Gerald Patterson and colleagues (Patterson, Reid, & Dishion, 1992) have shown that antisocial behavior can begin in families when children are reinforced for aggressive and antisocial behavior and parents are reinforced for using hostile/coercive parenting techniques. In parent management training, parents can be taught to use more effective parenting practices aimed at consistently identifying, monitoring, and punishing problem behaviors and reinforcing prosocial child behaviors. Through various program components, such as didactic instruction, live or videotaped modeling, and role playing, parents learn proper use of commands, contingent reinforcement, differential attention, and timeouts (McMahon & Forehand, 2003).

A second method of treatment for both internalizing and externalizing disorders is **cognitive behavior therapy**, which focuses on children's cognitive distortions, emotion regulation, and social problem solving (e.g., Webster-Stratton, Reid, & Hammond, 2001a, b). An example of a cognitive distortion for aggressive children would be viewing the actions of others as hostile or malicious, though they may actually reflect accidents (e.g., a child bumping into another child in the hallway). There is evidence that cognitive behavior therapy improves psychological adjustment by changing negative appraisal biases in depression (Kaufman, Rohde, Seeley, Clarke, & Stice, 2005) and hostile appraisal biases for antisocial behavior (Lochman & Wells, 2002). This kind of therapy can also be delivered in the context of family sessions (Carr, 2009), thereby impacting child behavior directly through cognitive restructuring and indirectly by improving family relations.

Parent management training is a parent-focused treatment approach, whereas cognitive behavior therapy is family- or child-focused. However, given the findings that we described as risk factors, many different factors influence disorder. **Multisystemic treatment** addresses this issue. It is based on ecological systems theory, in which it is proposed that disorders are influenced by multiple layers of the child's environment, including his or her family, neighbourhood, peers, and school (Henggeler, Schoenwald, Borduin, Rowland, & Cunningham, 1998). The idea is that a combination of factors—for instance, cognitive distortions, ineffective parenting, and poor teacher management skills—may all contribute to problem behavior. Consider, for example, the treatment of conduct disorder. Elements from various approaches are combined into a multicomponent intervention that may include improving parental monitoring, child skill development, disengaging youth from delinquent peers, teacher training/consultation to improve classroom management, and creating a support network for families.

In general, there is evidence to support the efficacy of psychological therapies in the amelioration of emotion-based disorders of childhood. This evidence, which is most often derived from randomized experiments, is summarized in Figure 12.13. You can see the size of the effect for different therapies, culled from a number of sources. It is important to note that all therapies do not work equally well for all individuals. For example, in the case of conduct problems, intervention is

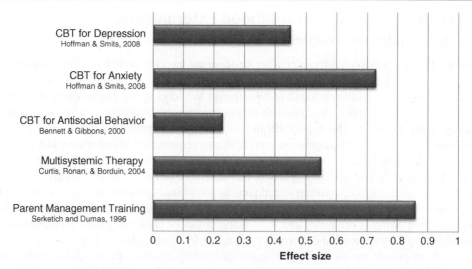

FIGURE 12.13   Effect sizes for different kinds of psychological therapy.

more effective at younger ages. By the time children are older, conduct problems are much more difficult to shift and it is much more expensive to try to do so.

Targeted versus Universal Approaches to Prevention and Intervention

A second issue in treatment concerns the implementation of targeted versus universal approaches. The treatments discussed earlier can be understood as **targeted** since they are aimed at assisting specific subgroups of individuals within the population who are believed to be at increased risk for negative developmental outcomes. Most interventions are of the targeted variety, since parents whose children receive services have tended to seek support for specific, individualized problems that have inflicted current emotional and psychological distress. Alternatively, **universal** interventions tend to be preemptive strategies that entire populations or communities use with the aim of preventing adverse child outcomes. There are benefits and drawbacks to both approaches. Universal interventions are beneficial in that they often address the social roots that underlie adverse outcomes, offer a potentially large benefit to the entire population or community, and can be integrated into everyday social activities. However, universal programs may provide little benefit to individuals who are especially vulnerable and some argue that they are unnecessarily expensive (as even those who don't need the service are offered it). Also, they may not attract community involvement, and may be less appealing to clinicians and frontline service providers who fail to witness tangible improvements. The targeted approach is advantageous in the sense that interventions can be tailored to each individual's needs. The individual and clinician are likely to be motivated and driven by clear treatment gains, and the cost-effective use of resources can be efficiently monitored. However, targeted programs require costly screening phases and are less likely to reach all affected individuals.

Individual Emotion: Bullying

Bullying may not be a very well-defined emotion, but the activity is certainly emotional. It's the victimization and humiliation of someone with less power who is lower down in the social hierarchy. Often it includes physical assault and many other aggressive forms of behavior such as vandalism and pinning children down on the ground. An important program was started by Dan Olweus and his colleagues (e.g., Olweus, 1993; Olweus, Limber, & Mihalic, 1999) to prevent bullying in Bergen, Norway, and it has been taken up in other European countries and in North America.

In one study using unobtrusive video recording of school playgrounds by O'Connell, Pepler, and Craig (1999), when bullying was seen by adolescents, about 54% supported the activity by simply watching while 21% joined in on the bully's side. Only 25% aided the victim. Bullies are common among antisocial offenders: at age 24, 35 to 40% of former bullies (as compared with 10% of non-bullies) had three or more criminal convictions.

In talks that he gives, Olweus sometimes says that preventing bullying is an important component of democracy. The bullying prevention program involves most of the adult members of a school, who become enthusiastically involved. The program requires adults to act with warmth to the children, but also to set firm limits to unacceptable behavior, to apply nonviolent consequences for breaking rules, and to act as authorities and positive role models. Children in the school stop thinking that they should connive at the bullying they see, and instead think that they should report it to adults. In terms of the social motivations that we discussed in Chapters 3 and 9, whereas bullies use assertion for their own psychological purposes, adults can be assertive in a non-hostile way, and at the same time act with warmth (affiliation) and humor to enlarge the attachment goal of safety and to promote fairness. In Bergen, this program reduced bullying by 50%, and elsewhere to a somewhat lesser extent.

In a Dutch study, Camodeca and Goossens (2005) studied children nominated by their peers as bullies, bully followers, victims, victim defenders, and outsiders. These children were assessed on aspects of their emotional lives. Both bullies and victims scored higher than other children on anger and on hostile interpretation, but proactive aggression was common only among the bullies. Victims were the saddest group.

So which approach is the most effective? In all likelihood, a combination of targeted and universal programs will engender the most positive, widespread effects. An example of this kind of program is **Triple-P (Positive Parenting Program)**, developed by Matt Sanders and his colleagues (e.g., Sanders, 1999). This program is geared toward improving parenting practices on a large scale in order to reduce child behavioral and emotional problems throughout entire communities. Under the Triple-P model, both universal and targeted approaches are integrated to provide the *minimally sufficient level* of support needed to parents. Triple-P provides intervention along a tiered continuum of increasing intensity and specificity. Level 1 is the broadest level, involving active provision of parenting information in the form of print and electronic media to the entire population. This strategy may include the dissemination of parenting tip-sheets, descriptions of common childhood problems, and information about where parents can seek additional help. Triple-P is believed to de-stigmatize parents' desire to seek help for their children. That is, instead of targeting "bad" parents, it provides parents with information that can empower them to take the necessary steps toward helping themselves and their children. The system increases in strength up to Level 5. This level may involve specific skills training to treat problems in at-risk children, as well as providing support to help parents deal with family-level stressors (e.g., relational conflict, parental psychopathology, etc.). To date, there have been almost 50 randomized controlled trials, 12 single-case experiments, 28 effectiveness studies, and four meta-analyses that have evaluated Triple-P. This program is effective at both improving parenting as well as reducing the number of clinically elevated behavioral and emotional problems in children (Sanders et al., 2008).

A principal issue for children and adolescents is prevention. The idea of prevention is a good one, but accomplishments have been modest. As Rutter (2002) has pointed out, during the past 50 years children's physical health has improved substantially. Over the same period, there have been no such improvements in children's socioemotional health. In fact, there are indications that during this time child psychopathology has actually become worse. Prevention is extraordinarily important, not only because of the misfortunes of human suffering that result from mental disorders, but also because of the economic cost to society. Think of it like this: there were 2,166,260 people in U.S. prisons during the middle of 2003, with an average cost of $21,400 for each person per year (Bruner, 2003). That works out to a total of more than $46 billion per year, despite there being no evidence that increased rates of imprisonment reduce rates of crime. But what if some proportion of that cost was spent alleviating known risks of externalizing disorders? Not only would this reduce the costs associated with incarceration and rehabilitation, but it would also reduce the incidence of disorders that cause emotional distress, thus improving community well-being.

Prevention programs that start prenatally and are carried out by registered nurses have been found to be most effective in reducing later psychopathology in children (Olds, Sadler, & Kitzman, 2007). Olds and colleagues (1998) have reported a 15-year follow-up of a randomized controlled trial of at-risk families based on visits by nurses while mothers were still pregnant (average 9 visits) and during the period between birth and the child's second birthday (average 23 visits). At age 15, children of the mothers who were visited in this way, as compared with children from control families, had fewer externalizing and serious antisocial behaviors, as measured by their own self-reports, by teachers' reports, and by criminal records. In a critical review, Olds, Sadler, and Kitzman (2007) have described the importance and effectiveness of parent-based interventions in the treatment and prevention of childhood problems.

SUMMARY

Emotion-based disorders in childhood and adolescence are complicated. Emotions are implicated in disorders in several ways, including a predominance of one emotion system, inappropriate expression of emotion, emotional dysregulation, and emotional adaptations to harmful environments. These patterns manifest through the inappropriate expression of emotions, projected outward in the case of externalizing disorders, or inward in the case of internalizing disorders. There are risk factors that operate at multiple levels of organization within the child and within his or her context. Also, there is an ongoing and transactional exchange between persons and their environments. Children who have experienced disorders in childhood are more likely to have psychological problems as adults, and continuities of disturbance are higher when there are riskier environments. Despite the complex nature of child and adolescent psychopathology, there are established intervention programs. These endeavors are most successful when they focus not only on processes presumed to be within the person, but also on the dynamic interplay between ever-changing persons and their contexts.

TO THINK ABOUT AND DISCUSS

1. What kinds of preventative measures do you think might have been most effective in helping Peter, the boy with externalizing problems whose case we introduced at the beginning of the chapter?

2. How do relationships with others help protect children from psychological problems?

3. How do biological processes within the child contribute to the development of mental health problems?

4. Why does experiencing poverty result in children showing mental health problems?

FURTHER READING

A comprehensive review article on the effects of orphanages and adoption is:

Kim Maclean (2003). The impact of institutionalization on child development. *Development and Psychopathology*, **15**, 853–84.

One of the first studies of child disorders of emotions to be based on the Human Genome Project, and one that will be of lasting importance:

Avshalom Caspi, Joseph McClay, Terrie Moffitt et al. (2002). Role of genotype in the cycle of violence in maltreated children. *Science*, **297**, 851–854.

On empirically based interventions for children:

Roth, A., Fonagy, P., Parry, G., Target, M., & Woods, R. (2005). *What works for whom? A critical review of psychotherapy research*. New York, NY: Guilford Press.

13 Mental Disorder and Well-Being in Adulthood

This chapter written with Hannah Oatley

Photo Credit: Image Source/Alamy

FIGURE 13.0 A striking result in psychiatric epidemiology is that the prevalence of depression is 50% higher in women than in men.

. . . human misery has awakened, stood before you, and today demands its proper place.

Jean Jaurès (1897) cited by Kleinman (1988, p. 53)

Into the lives of many people come periods of extreme negative emotion, such as hopeless depression or paralyzing anxiety. When such states reach levels at which a person can no longer function in ordinary life, they are referred to as emotional disorders. For an approach to the whole field of abnormal psychology you might turn to Kring, Johnson, Davison, and Neale (2012), and for an approach to psychiatry, the medical study of this field, to Gelder, Andreasen, Lopez-Ibor, and Geddes (2009).

When we refer to diagnoses in this chapter we generally use the criteria of the fourth edition of American Psychiatric Association's *Diagnostic and Statistical Manual of Mental Disorders* (*DSM-IV-TR,* 2000). The next version of this manual, *DSM-5,* is due to be published in 2013. More than half the disorders in *DSM-IV* have a prominent emotional component. In this chapter we concentrate on the two most frequently occurring such disorders, depression and anxiety states, with sections on psychopathy, on how patients with mental illnesses are emotionally affected by their families, on psychosomatics, and on emotional well-being.

Psychiatric Disorders: Symptoms and Prevalence

Depression, sometimes called affective disorder, or mood disorder, is intense sadness: a despair that can be painfully persecuting and can drain all meaning from life. Depression is not just sadness: according to *DSM-IV,* an episode of major depression is diagnosed when, for at least two weeks, the sufferer is unbearably sad or depressed, or has lost pleasure in nearly all activities, along with at least four other symptoms that include: being unable to sleep, being slowed down in one's actions, lack of energy to do ordinary things, inability to concentrate, feelings of worthlessness or guilt, and thoughts or plans of suicide. Major depression is the most prevalent single diagnosis among the emotional disorders.

Anxiety disorders come in several forms (described below), which usually involve protracted moods of disabling anxiety, often avoidance of what is most especially feared, and often a loss of personal confidence.

When someone has a nervous breakdown, usually this means suffering an episode of major depression with or without an accompanying anxiety disorder. In an emotional disorder, aspects of one's emotions become more difficult to understand than they normally would be (Oatley & Duncan, 1992).

Psychiatric Epidemiology

How common are emotional disorders? To answer this we turn to psychiatric epidemiology: the study of how frequently disorders occur, which we introduced in Chapter 12. Epidemiology is detective work: discovering from clues of **diagnosis** how people's lives have become disordered.

Modern medicine seems to owe its success to drugs like antibiotics, and to advances such as surgery without germs but with anesthetics. But infectious diseases were receding before these innovations. Really, the advances that were most important in improving general health were the epidemiological discoveries of how people caught diseases, and the prevention of infection by providing clean water and removing sewage from towns (Cartwright, 1977). Similarly, in psychiatry, the discovery of drugs for disorders has been important, but more important will be prevention (Dozois & Dobson, 2004; Munoz, Mrazek, & Haggerty, 1995).

Psychiatric epidemiology was slow to become established alongside the epidemiology of physical medicine, mainly because it was at first difficult to agree on criteria for diagnosis of disorders. Just as for the psychiatric epidemiology of childhood discussed in Chapter 12, there are now classification schemes and interviews to make diagnoses for both research and clinical purposes. Populations have been studied to find how common mental health problems are. The most substantial study in the United States, by Ronald Kessler and his colleagues (Kessler, Bergland, Demler, Jin, Merihangas, & Walters 2005), used a research interview to make diagnoses according to *DSM-IV-R* criteria, and to determine risks of disorder in the 48 contiguous United States. Interviews were carried out with 9,282 people of 18 years and upward, with a response rate of 70.9%. You can see some of its results in Table 13.1.

Depression was recognized in 2004 by the World Health Organization (WHO) as making the largest contribution to the burden of disease in middle- and high-income countries and it is the leading cause of years lost due to a disability worldwide. As explained in Chapter 12, the percentage of people suffering from a disorder over a specific time is called **prevalence**. Kessler et al. (2005) found a 16.6% lifetime prevalence of major depressive disorder in the United States, similar to estimates found by others (e.g., Marcotte, Wilcox-Gok, & Redmon, 1999).

While these studies used retrospective designs, Terrie Moffitt and her colleagues (Moffitt, Caspi, Taylor, Kokaua, Milne, Polanczyk et al., 2010) used a prospective design in a representative sample of 1,037 people who were followed up from birth with very little attrition up to the age of 32 in Dunedin, New Zealand. They found prevalence rates that were approximately twice those reported in Table 13.1, including a lifetime prevalence of 41.4% for depressive disorder, and 49.5% for anxiety disorder. Retrospective surveys are usually the best we have, and they continue to be fundamental. But they underestimate prevalence rates because respondents often fail to report symptoms as they think back over their lives. Although Moffitt et al.'s estimates of prevalence are much higher than those previously assumed, they probably offer a truer picture of the mental health problems that actually occur in people's lives.

As we discussed in Chapter 9, **gender differences** occur in normal emotions, but they are small in comparison to differences in prevalence of emotional disorders, which you can see in Table 13.2. Here we see that women are 1.5 times more likely than men to suffer an episode of major depression, and 1.6 times more likely to suffer an anxiety disorder. In confirmation of such trends for anxiety, Vesga-López et al. (2008) found that generalized anxiety disorder was almost twice as likely in women than in men. But women are less than half as likely to have an alcohol or drug disorder. These differences continue trends seen in childhood (see Chapter 12). Essau et al. (2010) have found that the increased prevalence of depression among females emerges in adolescence.

Many impulse-control disorders (a relatively new category of mental disorder in adulthood) can be thought of as expressions of anger or other resentful feelings, continuations of externalizing disorders in childhood (see Chapter 12). Attention-deficit/hyperactivity disorder, however, is not primarily a disorder of emotion, but of attention (see Chapter 12).

Alcohol is a drug that reduces anxiety, and in this sense overuse and abuse are related to emotions and their disorders: many people self-medicate with alcohol to control anxiety, shame, and other moods. Other drugs, of course, have various effects, and an excellent book on this subject is that of Lewis (2011). Keyes, Grant, and Hasin (2008) found that gender discrepancies in alcohol abuse decreased during the 20th century in the United States. Alcohol abuse used to be largely a male condition. For the cohort born between 1913 and 1932 the ratio of alcohol abusers was 7.1 men to one woman. For the cohort born between 1968 and 1984, this ratio had decreased to 1.6 to one.

Table 13.1 Lifetime prevalences (in percentages) of psychiatric conditions in people aged 18 and over in the 48 contiguous United States, using the World Health Organization World Mental Health Survey version of the Composite International Diagnostic Interview

		Total
Depressive (affective) disorder		
Major depressive episode		16.6
Bipolar disorder		3.9
Dysthymia		2.5
	Any depressive disorder	20.8
Anxiety disorder		
Panic disorder		4.7
Agoraphobia without panics		1.4
Social phobia		12.1
Generalized anxiety disorder		5.7
Specific phobia		12.5
Post-traumatic stress disorder		6.8
Obsessive-compulsive disorder		1.6
Separation anxiety disorder		5.2
	Any anxiety disorder	28.8
Impulse-control disorder		
Oppositional-defiant disorder		8.5
Conduct disorder		9.5
Attention-deficit/hyperactivity disorder		8.1
Intermittent explosive disorder		5.2
	Any impulse-control disorder	24.8
Substance use disorder		
Alcohol abuse		13.2
Alcohol dependence		5.4
Drug abuse		7.9
Drug dependence		3.0
	Any substance use disorder	14.6
	Any disorder	46.4

Source: Data from Kessler et al. (2005).

You can see from Table 13.2 that the likelihood that a black person in America will suffer a mental disorder of any kind is only 70% of the likelihood that a white person will do so. You can see, too, that having been divorced or separated doubles the rate of disorder as compared with being married or cohabiting.

Table 13.2 Relative lifetime prevalences of psychiatric disorders as a function of sex, race/ethnicity, and marital status

	Any depressive disorder	Any anxiety-control disorder	Any impulse or drug disorder	Any alcohol disorder	Any disorder
Sex					
Male	1.0	1.0	1.0	1.0	1.0
Female	1.5*	1.6*	0.7*	0.4*	1.1
Race/ethnicity					
White	1.0	1.0	1.0	1.0	1.0
Black	0.6*	0.8*	0.7	0.6*	0.7*
Hispanic	0.8*	0.7*	0.7	0.9	0.8
Other	1.1	1.2	1.1	1.2	1.0
Marital status					
Married/cohabiting	1.0	1.0	1.0	1.0	1.0
Previously married	1.9*	1.8*	1.8	3.9*	2.1*
Never married	1.0	1.0	1.4	1.4	1.0

Notes: In each section of the table one group is assigned a prevalence rate of 1.0. For other groups within the section prevalence rates are expressed as odds ratios: multiples of this. For instance, the rate for any depressive disorder in women is 1.5 times that for men. Asterisks indicate prevalences for which there was a significant difference ($p < 0.05$) from that of the standard value of 1.0.

Source: Data from Kessler et al. (2005).

Differences due to gender, to race or ethnicity, and to marital status, are huge—far larger than differences found in most of psychology. A fascinating aspect of epidemiology is that such a data set puzzles us. We must become detectives. Why do more women than men become depressed or chronically anxious? Why are men more likely than women to become alcoholics? Why are black people less susceptible to emotional disorder than white people? How does living with a partner protect one against emotional disorder?

The first hypothesis of the epidemiological detective is that such differences have less to do with how the brain works and more to do with how we live. This has been the subject of the most important research on the subject. But first let's say something more about the most common forms of emotional disorder.

Different Kinds of Depression and Anxiety

Major depression is to be distinguished from manic-depressive disorder, now called **bipolar disorder**, defined in terms of a person having experienced at least one period of mania (Johnson & Kizer, 2002). Mania is a disorder of happiness, exhilaration, and pride. In it, people are extremely happy and expansive. Their self-esteem is inflated. They sometimes become grandiose. They can work for long periods, need almost no sleep, and take unbounded pleasure in everything they do. Novelist Tom Wolfe said, in relation to an episode of hypomania (somewhat milder than full mania) that he experienced: "If I could only bottle that feeling . . . It was heaven on earth" (McGrath,

2004, p. 38). Wolfe thought he was very good company during this period, and people in such states can often be charming. But with severe mania, people can do alarming things such as run up huge debts that they can never repay. One of us remembers being in a car with someone who, in a manic episode, drove at 60 miles an hour the wrong way down a one-way street in the middle of town, laughing about how ludicrous social conventions were. Only rarely is the mood sustained. Often— and this is what happened to Wolfe—after a few weeks comes a plunge into depression. Gruber, Harvey, and Purcell (2011) found that when people with a diagnosis of bipolar disorder who were between episodes watched film clips, they had stronger positive experiences and less vagal regulation than people who were not bipolar. So, even between episodes there is a bias of emotional processing among people susceptible to bipolar disorder. A first-hand account of the disorder was written by Kay Jamison (1995), a professor of psychiatry.

Bipolar disorder has a lifetime prevalence of about 1% and no gender difference. Kessler et al. (2005) recently estimated that that prevalence could be as high as 4%. Genetics are discussed below, but here we can note that genetic risk for bipolar disorder, measured in terms of heritability of between 60 and 85% percent, is higher than for major depressive episodes (Smoller & Finn, 2003).

Anxiety disorders take several forms (*DSM-IV-TR*, American Psychiatric Association, 2000). They include **panic attacks** with sudden terror or dread, often with bodily symptoms such as racing heart, dizziness, and shortness of breath. The panic attack is a clear example of an emotion that is difficult to understand: people may have no idea why it occurs. Anxiety disorders include **phobias**, which are almost-irresistible urges to avoid certain places, objects, or activities. A disabling form is agoraphobia: the fear of being away from home (Fyer, Mannuzza, & Coplan, 1996; Mathews, Gelder, & Johnson, 1981). As you may see from Table 13.1, the lifetime prevalence of agoraphobia without panics is 1.4%; with panics the prevalence is higher. Often it starts when a person's life is in a precarious state. Then, perhaps in the supermarket (*agora* is Greek for "market"), the person has a panic attack, rushes home, and feels calm. A powerful learning script is established—away from home there has been unbearable fear; back at home is calmness—with a strongly conditioned anxiety about repeating the experience (Bouton, Mineka, & Barlow, 2001).

Some agoraphobic people fear being in places that they cannot leave without embarrassment. People with agoraphobia often find it more and more difficult to go out at all except perhaps with a partner (an attachment figure). The area in which they feel safe on their own can become much reduced. It can be just their own home. It can be just a bedroom. Often they lose social confidence and, as they isolate themselves from the world, confidence drains yet further. The restriction of life in agoraphobia can be treated successfully, for instance, by cognitive-behavior therapy (see Chapter 14). With treatment people can go out again, get a job, and visit friends. Whereas phobias for specific objects or activities such as spiders or flying are common, they are troublesome rather than disabling. Agoraphobia and social phobia (fear of being with other people) can, however, be severely disabling. Social phobia is more common than agoraphobia, with a lifetime prevalence of 12.1%. Generalized anxiety disorder, defined as at least six months of disabling and persistent anxiety or worry, has a lifetime prevalence of 5.7%.

A second group of anxiety disorders is of **obsessions and compulsions** (Jenike, 1996). Obsessions are intrusive anxious thoughts, for instance, of being contaminated by germs. The anxious thoughts occur repeatedly and the person cannot stop them even though he or she might know them to be irrational. Obsessions are repeated actions or rituals such as washing one's hands many times a day, or checking and rechecking that certain things have been done, like turning the stove off. Performing the action temporarily diminishes anxiety, but *only* temporarily. It is possible that the disorder is a defect in the emotional knowledge that a security-motivated action has been completed (Szechtman & Woody, 2004). In severe cases, many hours a day can be spent performing compulsive actions. The lifetime prevalence of obsessive-compulsive disorder has been estimated at between two and three percent.

Anxiety disorders include **post-traumatic stress disorder**, which involves intense anxiety, disturbed sleep, flashbacks in which a traumatic event is remembered and repeatedly reexperienced, together with avoidance of anything that might remind one of it (McNally, 2003; McNally et al., 1990). Traumas of the kind that can provoke this disorder occur in war (Grinker & Spiegel, 1945) when people have been in danger of their own lives and when companions have been killed and maimed. Elder and Clipp (1989) found that experience of combat in World War II and the Korean War was damaging and increased the risk of emotional and behavioral problems. The Vietnam War brought the damaging effects of combat to notice in the United States (see, e.g., Shay, 1995). Its repercussions on veterans include increased antisocial behavior, especially among those who have been in combat (Barrett et al., 1996). The syndrome can also result from natural and industrial disasters (Ironson et al., 1997), and from criminal assaults such as rape (Burnam et al., 1988). Brewin, Dalgleish, and Joseph (1996) define a trauma as anything that radically violates one's basic assumptions about the world. Such assumptions might be that the world is by and large a safe place, that one can achieve one's life goals, and that people including oneself will behave in reasonable and decent ways. Brewin et al. conclude that the chaotic nature of post-traumatic flashbacks and intense phobic anxiety can be explained in terms of two memory systems, one of which is verbal and subject to the making of meaningful sense of experience. The other is automatically triggered by aspects of situations, external or internal. The working of this system is not closely coupled to the verbal system, and its processes are far less voluntary. The traumas are represented in memory in both systems, which are repeatedly activated, and they do not necessarily correspond to each other. The confusion adds to the intense fears that are experienced.

How Disorders Are Caused

The most widespread general understanding of how emotional disorders are caused is the *stress-diathesis* hypothesis (Kring, Johnson, Davidson, & Neale, 2012; Monroe & Hadjiyannakis, 2002). In Chapter 12 we discussed this in relation to children's disorders. The hypothesis is that a disorder is typically caused by a stress—an adversity in the environment—in the presence of one or more inherent factors that make a person vulnerable, called diatheses. Examples of stresses are marital separation, job loss, or the death of someone close. Among diatheses are genetic factors and difficulties of early life.

Many emotional disorders would not happen without an adversity. For the most part, at least for the first occurrence of an emotional disorder, the adversity is severe. For psychotic disorders such as schizophrenia, less severe events can trigger psychotic breakdowns in which the person's predisposition (diathesis) is stronger.

Life Events and Difficulties

Perhaps the best example of the epidemiological detectives at work in the field of emotional disorders is by George Brown and Tirril Harris (1978). They interviewed 458 adult women in London, England, and found that 37 of them (8%) had suffered an onset of depression (some with anxiety) during the previous year at a level that was disabling, equivalent to major depressive disorder now defined by *DSM-IV-TR* (American Psychiatric Association, 2000). A further 9% of the women had a disabling psychiatric problem for more than a year (totaling 17% with a disorder during the year before interview).

In Brown and Harris's study, 89% of women with an onset of depression had a severe **life event or difficulty** shortly before their breakdown. By contrast, of women who did not have any disorder, only 30% had suffered a severe event or difficulty in the year before interview. Severe events included bereavement, marital separation, and job loss. Difficulties were long-lasting problems such as having to cope with a violent husband or looking after a demanding and chronically sick relative.

Brown and Harris developed a new method that gave better predictions than had previously been possible of who would get depressed. The method was a semistructured interview, the Life Events and Difficulties Schedule, which replaced the checklists of recent changes such as the originally popular version by Holmes and Rahe (1967). Checklists are far less accurate than the Life Events and Difficulties Interview Schedule (McQuaid et al., 2000; Thoits, 1995). Using the interview schedule, interviewers ask people about 40 areas of life: employment, finances, housing, children, relationships, and so on. Interviews are audio recorded, and each stressful event or difficulty is written up, with its date, so that its temporal relation to any onset of depression can be known (not possible with checklist methods). The description of the event is later read to the members of a research team, who make a rating of the degree of long-term threat (lasting more than a week) that this event or difficulty would cause in a woman living in the described circumstances. Ratings of long-term severity of an event or difficulty are made by people (the research team) who live in the same society. At the same time these ratings pass the tests of being reliable, because levels of severity are anchored by comparing them with dictionaries of previous ratings made by the research team over the years. The ratings are unbiased because raters do not know the woman's diagnosis. They also are independent of the woman's own evaluation of events, which might be affected by how depressed she was.

People become depressed when severe adversities occur. Here is the case of Mrs. Trent, one of the women in Brown and Harris's study.

Mrs. Trent (not her real name) had three small children and was married to a van driver. Her apartment had two rooms and a kitchen. Her third child was born eight months before the interview. Around that time her husband lost his job. She didn't worry too much, and he got another job quickly. But after two weeks he was fired from that job too, without explanation. Seven weeks later her worries had become so severe that she felt tense all the time, she felt miserable, did not sleep well and became irritable with the children. She found it difficult to do the housework, became unable to concentrate, and her appetite declined. In the next two months these symptoms worsened. She would often cry all day. She got some sleeping pills from her doctor. Her relationship with her husband deteriorated. She lost all interest in sex and thought her marriage finished. Three times she packed and walked out but returned because of the children. She felt self-deprecatory, felt she could not cope, and thought that she might end it all. By three weeks before the interview things had started to get better. She still tended to brood, though her concentration was now good enough for her to watch television which distracted her. Her sexual relationship with her husband had returned, and indeed was better than before. She had been depressed for five and a half months.

(paraphrased from Brown & Harris, 1978, pp. 28–30)

In this case the severely threatening event was her husband being fired for the second time, which left the family without income. Low mood, sleep disturbances, loss of weight, lack of concentration, self-deprecation, loss of interest in sex, and suicidal thoughts were symptoms of major depression. In Brown and Harris's method, Mrs. Trent's marital difficulty was not counted as an event that could have caused the depression because it could easily have been caused by it. Other researchers, too, have distinguished between events that one could have brought on oneself and those that were beyond one's control. Shrout et al. (1989) found that clinic patients suffering from depression were three times more likely than people in a non-depressed community sample to have suffered a negative and uncontrollable event. So, depression is not necessarily irrational. It involves sadness and hopelessness, brought on by events that have serious implications for our lives and our sense of ourselves. Since the early work of Brown and Harris, the association of depression with severe social adversity, particularly for the first onset of depression, has been well established around the world (Kinyanda et al., 2011; Korkeila et al., 2010).

An event that can cause depression is most typically **loss of a role** that is highly valued (Oatley & Bolton, 1985). Using life event interviews, Constance Hammen et al. (1989) found that people who valued their relationships became depressed when a social loss or social disruption occurred. This kind of loss is often related to the social motivations of attachment, and perhaps of affiliation. By comparison, those to whom autonomy and work were most important were more likely to become depressed when a **failure in achievement** occurred, related to assertive social motivations.

Anxiety can also be caused by a negative event or difficulty (Monroe & Wade, 1988). In one study of a community sample, 2,902 men and women were interviewed using standardized measures to diagnose generalized anxiety and to assess life events occurring over the previous year (Blazer, Hughes, & George, 1987). Severe negative events were associated with a threefold increase of anxiety disorder in both men and women.

What kinds of adversities cause depressive and anxiety breakdowns? Kenneth Kendler et al. (2003) offer a list that can be seen in Table 13.3. Compare the adversities in this table to the idea of appraisal, discussed in Chapter 7. People who have suffered both depression and anxiety have typically experienced events appraised as both **loss** and **danger**, and sometimes also as humiliation and/or entrapment.

Appraisal theory would predict that depression and anxiety are caused by different kinds of events. Finlay-Jones (1989), using Brown and Harris's method, interviewed women attending a general practice: 82% of cases with depression, 85% of cases of anxiety, and 93% of cases with mixed depression and anxiety had suffered a severe life event as compared with 34% of those who were not suffering from any emotional disorder. Depressive disorders were most

Table 13.3 **Adversities that cause depressive and anxiety disorders**

Loss: events such as deaths of loved ones, losses of means of livelihood

Humiliation: events such as separations in which there has been infidelity, or the delinquency of a child, rapes, putdowns and public humiliations by loved ones or persons in authority, which threaten core roles (this is related to the social motivation of assertion in relation to status, discussed in Chapter 9)

Entrapment: being stuck in an adverse situation with no way out

Danger: likelihood of future loss, or of an event that has yet to realize its full potential

Source: Kendler et al. (2003).

often precipitated by events that were losses. In contrast, other events were future directed, and involved danger, such as receiving a diagnosis of a cancer, unwanted pregnancy, or threat of eviction from home. Anxiety disorders were most often precipitated by such danger events. Some events involved both loss and danger: current problem and anticipation of further problems in the future.

Most episodes of major depression and some onsets of anxiety disorder occur when things go severely wrong in people's lives, and have serious long-term consequences. Like episodes of normal emotion, most emotional disorders are responses to events and circumstances. They affect what is important to us. When Mrs. Trent's husband lost his job, she experienced feelings of defeat, and of dread about not being able to live adequately or to provide for her family.

One should not think, however, that emotional disorders are only about losses and dangers. As Sheri Johnson (2005) has shown, people who have manic tendencies aren't involved with losses at all. Their disorder is to react to successes by becoming overenthusiastic, overconfident, and irrationally optimistic. They have a disorder of goal pursuit. It's not yet known whether people with these symptoms actually achieve more than the rest of us.

Cross-Cultural Differences

The World Health Organization (WHO, 2004) examined mental illness using *DSM-IV* in 14 countries and found broadly similar patterns in 12-month prevalence rates of disorder, with anxiety being the most frequent (as also found by Kessler et al., 2005), followed by depression (mood disorder). Rates of impulse-control disorder and substance abuse disorder were broadly similar to each other across countries, with generally lower rates than those of anxiety and depression. The United States had the highest overall prevalence rates of mental disorder (26.4%), with European countries being lower (France, 18.4%; Germany, 9.1%), and Asian and African countries having the lowest overall rates (Japan, 8.8%; Nigeria, 4.7%).

Although depression is a global phenomenon that affects 121 million people worldwide, its prevalence rates differ substantially among countries. For instance, in the WHO study, the 12-month prevalence of depression in the United States was 9.6%, in Spain 4.9%, and in China (Shanghai) 1.7%. Here is another striking clue for the epidemiological detective.

Could one reason why prevalence rates of depression are so different—more than five times higher in the United States than in China—be due to living in individualistic as compared with interdependent societies as discussed in Chapter 3? In the West, there are more kinds of competition and more opportunities for individual success, but even more possibilities of failure. Think of applying for a prestigious job. One person will get it, but how many won't? Perhaps 30, perhaps 100.

Some risk factors are common across different societies. For instance, Patel et al. (1999) found that in India, Zimbabwe, Chile, and Brazil, being female, being poor, and having little education were associated with depression. Kessler et al. (2005b) made a similar finding in their publication of 12-month prevalences in the United States: being depressed was associated with being female, having little education, being poor, and living in a city rather than in a smaller community.

Differences in prevalence, such as those due to gender, lack of education, and poverty, are all clues for the epidemiological detective. Some of these differences are large. But the evidence is **correlational**. For instance, epidemiological evidence does not tell us whether poverty causes depression, or whether being depressed makes it harder to hold a job. Next steps include starting with the clues of prevalence and then becoming more precise about what causes disorders.

Photo Credit: ©David Hoffman Photo Library/Alamy

FIGURE 13.1   Poverty is a fundamental cause of depression, which has hopelessness at its core.

Neurophysiology of Depression

From a neuroscience perspective, Davidson, Pizzagalli, Nitschke, and Kalin (2003) identify loss of pleasurable goal achievement as a principal emotional cause of depression. Three brain areas seem to be important to depression: the frontal lobe, the hippocampus, and the amygdala (Nestler et al., 2002).

Involvement of the frontal cortex in depression has been found by van Tol et al. (2010) who examined 68 patients with major depression and found that they had lower anterior cingulate

Photo Credit: From T. Yang et al., "Adolescents with Major Depression Demonstrate Increased Amygdala Activation." Fig. 2, Volume 49, Number 1, January 2010 (c) *Journal of the American Academy of Child and Adolescent Psychiatry*

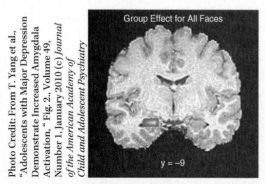

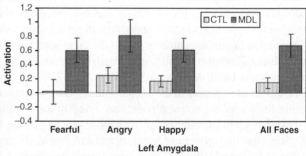

FIGURE 13.2   Activation of the left amygdala of adolescents in a control group (CTL) and in those with a major depressive disorder (MDD) who were shown fearful, angry, and happy faces (from Yang et al., 2010).

cortex volumes than 64 non-depressed controls. They found, too, that patients with early onsets of depression had smaller prefrontal cortex volumes.

As to the hippocampus, a meta-analysis examining 143 magnetic resonance imaging studies found that reductions in volume of the hippocampus and the basal ganglia are associated with major depression (Kempton et al., 2011). Additional evidence implicating the hippocampus in depression is that it modulates the function of the hypothalamic-pituitary axis.

As to the amygdala, Yang et al. (2010) found greater activation of the amygdala in depressed as compared with non-depressed adolescents when they viewed images of people making different emotional expressions. Siegle et al. (2002) found that in depressed patients' responses to negative comments, the amygdala remained activated for 30 seconds after such a comment, whereas the amygdala of non-depressed patients was activated for less than 10 seconds. Disner et al. (2011) proposed a neurobiological theory of depression, based on a role for the amygdala in encoding negative events. They argue that as the amygdala becomes hyperactivated in depression, it also causes connected areas such as the hippocampus to become more activated and thus more likely to recall negative events.

In this chapter we have suggested that the researcher is a detective. The most famous detective, of course, was Sherlock Holmes, and in the case entitled *Silver Blaze* he points out to a policeman who is working on a case: "the curious incident of the dog in the night-time." The policeman says: "The dog did nothing in the night-time," to which Holmes replies, "That was the curious incident" (Conan-Doyle, 1894, p. 347). Holmes inferred that the dog must have known the intruder whom they were seeking.

In the neurophysiology of depression, something similar has occurred. The main treatment for depression is drugs, of which the principal kinds, currently, are selective serotonin reuptake inhibitors (SSRIs), such as Prozac, widely prescribed and widely advertised. These drugs reduce reabsorption of the transmitter substance serotonin, so that it remains in synapses for longer. The idea of drug companies is that depression is caused by a lack of serotonin, or an imbalance of serotonin, in the brain, which can be rectified by daily doses of these drugs. The "curious incident" here is the absence of any evidence-based neurophysiological theory of depression based on this idea. The intruder has been the drug companies. The psychiatrists could have barked, but they haven't yet done so.

Irving Kirsch (2009) has found in meta-analyses of properly conducted trials that, as compared with placebos, serotonin reuptake inhibitor drugs show either no effect on depression, or only a tiny effect. Placebos show surprisingly large effects on the self-report scales of depression that are commonly used, and they have the advantage that they don't cause harmful side effects. Angell (2008) has made the case that drug companies now control most research on psychoactive drugs, and that "there is mounting evidence that they often skew the research they sponsor to make their drugs look better and safer" (p. 1069). As Kirsch has shown, knowing whether psychoactive drugs work as advertised requires far more than knowing whether they have reached a threshold set by the U.S. Food and Drug Administration.

Formation of new nerve cells (neurogenesis) in the hippocampus seems to be reduced in depression, and it has been found that antidepressants can reverse the diminution of neurogenesis in animals subjected to stress (Dranovsky & Hen, 2006). This suggests a possible way in which selective serotonin reuptake inhibitors may have their (probably small) effects on depression. But this is a new theory not yet applied to humans. It's a long way from the idea that depression is caused by a deficit or imbalance of serotonin in the brain.

Relation Between Emotions and Emotional Disorders

The way that severe life events elicit depression and anxiety is similar to the way that more ordinary events—setbacks to our projects and concerns—elicit negative emotions. We experience such emotions, and usually we deal with their implications. By contrast, severe events threaten fundamental life roles in ways that we cannot usually deal with. Imagine losing something fundamental to your life, to which you have given your best energy and aspiration: an important relationship, perhaps, or your place at university, or your expectation of a career. Losses of this kind can cause the despair of depression. When they occur they can drain all meaning from life (see Figure 13.3). No way forward seems possible, and the state can become **disabling**. Mrs. Trent experienced loss of her family's income, perhaps loss of faith in her husband and hence her hope for her family and the life they had made. She became unable to do things that had been important to her, such as care for her children.

In this chapter we have presented emotional disorders in the traditional way, in terms of diagnostic categories such as depression and anxiety states. A new approach is beginning, in which the relation of emotions to emotional disorders is conceptualized in a manner that Ann Kring (2008) has described, across a range of diagnoses. This approach is encouraged by the fact that many people have several diagnoses at the same time (comorbidity). In a comparable way, Gruber and Keltner (2007) have shown that we can see disorders as excesses of emotions, as diminished emotions, and as dysfunctions of emotions (see Table 13.4).

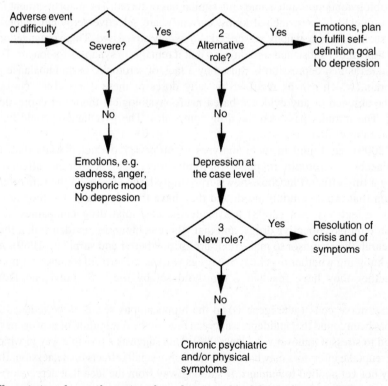

FIGURE 13.3   Differentiation of normal emotions from depressive breakdowns (Oatley, 1988).

Table 13.4 Disorders as excesses, deficits, and dysfunctions of emotions

Excess sadness: depression

Excess fear: phobias, general anxiety disorder, post-traumatic stress disorder, panic disorder, hypochondria (fear of disease), obsessional/compulsive disorders, self-medication of anxiety by alcohol and drugs

Excess happiness: mania, antisocial personality disorder

Excess anger: conduct disorder, oppositional-defiant disorder, intermittent explosive disorder

Excess disgust: anorexia

Excess self-conscious emotion: narcissistic pride

Lack of self-conscious emotion: adult autism (lack of embarrassment), psychopathy (lack of guilt or remorse)

Dysfunctions of emotion: schizophrenia, other psychoses

Source: Derived from Gruber & Keltner (2007).

How are depression and anxiety states related to normal sadness and fear (Flack & Laird, 1999; Kring & Werner, 2004; Power & Dalgleish, 2008)? We discussed in Chapter 6 the work of Mayberg et al. (2005), in which the researchers showed that the same brain regions involved in depression are also involved in normal sadness. So, although depression is not just sadness, the emotion of sadness is usually involved. As to anxiety, there is no question that its disorders are kinds of excessive fear. The main questions are why such fears can become entirely out of proportion to what the person seems to be frightened of (Öhman, 2000), and can be elicited by ambiguous events (McNally, 1999).

Overall, we can say that the emotions of sadness, happiness, fear, and anger correspond, respectively, to depression, mania, anxiety, and conduct disorder (Power & Dalgleish, 2008). Johnson-Laird, Mancini, and Gangemi (2006) found that emotional disorders are typically begun as elicitations of basic emotions such as sadness or fear that derive from the automatic appraisals that we have discussed. It is not the elicitations of emotions that are inappropriate; it is their intensity, which remains cognitively impenetrable and which tends to prolong the disorder.

In the end, the reasons we humans are subject to disabling emotional states remains a challenge for theories of emotions, especially when nowadays we tend to argue that most emotions have useful functions.

Individual emotion: Self-compassion

The search for how specific emotional states relate to mental health has led Kristin Neff to important work on self-compassion (2011). Self-compassion involves three different appraisals: the ability to treat one's own failures kindly and not critically; the ability to see oneself as part of humanity; and the ability to accept pain and suffering with equanimity. In her research Neff is finding that this state of self-compassion is an important buffer to depression and anxiety; it consistently correlates with reports of reduced depression, anxiety, rumination, and perfectionism. Cultivating self-compassion is one focus of many contemplative practices we discuss in the next chapter. If you are interested in this rich emotional state and how to measure it or cultivate it in yourself or people you are close to, you might visit Neff's website: www.self-compassion.org.

Vulnerability Factors

Although depression is often caused by a severe event or difficulty, not everyone who suffers a serious adversity of this kind has a breakdown. Some people are more vulnerable to disorder than others. What is the difference between responding to an event with a negative emotion and responding with a disabling emotional disorder of depression and/or anxiety?

Gene–Environment Interaction

Many studies of twins support the theory that interactions between a person's genes and the environment can lead to depression and/or anxiety. Studies of **gene–environment interaction** occupy much attention among geneticists.

Some people are genetically at higher risk than others for depression. But whether they become depressed depends also on the environment, including such happenings as events and difficulties. How large is the genetic risk? Sullivan, Neale, and Kendler (2000) did a meta-analysis on five methodologically sound twin studies and found that the likelihood of a person and that person's twin both having a diagnosis of depression was highly significant. Monozygotic twins showed higher rates than dizygotic twins of both having the condition. These five twin studies together yielded an aggregate estimate for genetic liability to depression of 37%. In a Swedish sample of 15,493 complete twin pairs, Kendler et al. (2006) made a similar estimate of 38% for the heritability of depression.

Genetic biases have also been found for anxiety disorders (Hamm, Vaitl, & Lang, 1990; Scherer et al., 2000). A high genetic sensitivity of a mechanism that associates certain cues to schemas of danger may explain why some people are generally more fearful than others, independently of whether they have experienced serious danger in their lives. Boomsma, Van Beijsterveldt, and Hudziak (2005) and Kendler, Gardner, and Lichtenstein (2008) studied twin pairs in childhood, adolescence, and early adulthood. They found that genetic factors influenced anxiety and depression in younger children, but that by age 20 this influence was much diminished.

Genetic influences on depression seem not to affect depression directly; among mediating factors is the experience of adverse life events. Robert Plomin et al. (1990b) and Kendler et al. (1993a) found that monozygotic twin pairs were more similar to each other than were dizygotic twin pairs in the number of life events they experienced. In other words, some people are genetically more likely than others to experience adverse life events, so this would be part of the causal process in making them more likely to become depressed. Federenko et al. (2006) found in a sample of 180 twin pairs that genetic risk of encountering a larger number of life events was higher if the events were personal (for instance, lack of social recognition), if they were negative rather than challenging, and if they were enduring.

Could people with some kinds of genetically influenced personality put themselves in the way of life events, as well as experiencing them more intensely? Using a sample of 542 twin pairs, Kendler and Myers (2010) examined the Big Five personality traits: Neuroticism, Extraversion, Openness, Conscientiousness, and Agreeableness, and found heritability estimates for these traits that ranged between 0.44 and 0.64 (similar to other published estimates). Middeldorp et al. (2008) examined a large sample of twin pairs and found that Neuroticism increased the rate of exposure to life events, and that there was also a substantial correlation between Neuroticism and depression.

Beginning with the draft of the Human Genome Project in 2001, there has been an extension of this research into **genomics**, the attempt to understand what particular genes are responsible for human traits. The longitudinal study by Avshalom Caspi et al. (2003) of the 1,000-strong birth cohort in Dunedin, New Zealand, and its follow-ups have been discussed in Chapter 12. They indicate that low serotonin production, genetically influenced by the 5-HTT gene, interacts with life events to increase likelihood of depression. Although there is still some controversy about these results (Wankerl, Wüst, & Otte, 2010), the weight of evidence from several fields, including animal research and human neuroimaging, supports Caspi et al.'s conclusion.

There is consensus that depression is influenced by a combination of several genes that each have small effects and that interact to produce susceptibility (Plomin & Davis, 2009). The hypothalamic-pituitary axis (HPA) is the final common pathway in regulating stress responses (see Chapter 5), and it may be involved in genetic risk for depression. There is support for this hypothesis from animal models of depression (Müller & Holsboer, 2006; Uriguen et al., 2008).

Over the past decade the genetics of depression has become more complex with the rise of epigenetics, discussed in Chapter 12. A recent review of the epigenetics of depression is by Schroeder et al. (2010).

Social Support

Relationships affect whether people develop major depression in response to adversities. The general term for relationships that can protect people from disorder is **social support**; typical measures are presence of an intimate relationship with someone in whom one can confide, lack of interpersonal friction, interpersonal appreciation, integration in a social network, and accessibility of practical assistance (see Chapter 9 for an example).

People with good social support are less likely to become depressed than those without support when they suffer an adverse life event. This was shown in women in the community by Brown and Harris (1978), and subsequently in different populations, such as men who suffered unemployment (Bolton & Oatley, 1987), adolescents (Stice et al., 2004), women psychiatric outpatients (Ali, Oatley, & Toner, 2002), and men with HIV (Johnson et al., 2001). By contrast, however, in a large study of female twin pairs, Wade and Kendler (2000) found that although life events and absence of social support were both independently associated with depression, an interaction effect, of social support protecting against the impact of life events, was not found.

In this book we argue that humans are social beings; our most important emotions concern relationships. The study of life events and depression throws additional light on these issues because, first, the events that induce depression are most often losses of relationship, and second, social support has an additional effect.

With loss of important relationships, some of life's meaning drains away. We lose part of our selfhood. A life lived without support of attachment and affiliation is far more difficult than with this kind of support.

Early Experience

Early experience affects people's susceptibility to emotional disorders in adulthood. A person who loses a mother in childhood is more likely than a person who has not lost his or her mother to develop depression (Brown & Harris, 1978). Originally it was thought that it was loss of the attachment figure that left the individual vulnerable. It now seems that it is not this loss as such, but the lack of parental care that is likely to follow such a loss that has the most negative effect. Women in Brown and Harris's study who suffered **neglect** during childhood, or who experienced physical or sexual abuse, were at increased risk of both depression and anxiety as adults (Brewin, Andrews, & Gotlib, 1993; Brown & Harris, 1993).

Poor care in childhood tends to induce people to put themselves into situations of higher risk for life events. So, Quinton, Rutter, and Liddle (1984, discussed in Chapter 12) found that girls raised in institutions had earlier pregnancies, had poorer sexual relationships, and became less competent parents than normal (see also Fleming et al., 2002, discussed in Chapter 9). Hammen (1991) found that women who have a history of major depression experienced more life events than did women without a history of depression. Most such events were interpersonal, such as conflicts with a spouse or with children.

The vulnerability of early neglect may include damage to people's sense of themselves as being valuable and worthy of love. Negative emotion schemas of self-in-relationship can increase people's risk of depression by increasing chances of events that turn out badly. People who have experienced lack of care may have yearnings for love, which prompt them toward hasty or early marriages, in which there is higher risk of being badly treated. This can confirm expectations of defeat and loss, which become part of the self-deprecating pattern of depression.

Recurrence, Recovery, and Prolongation of Disorders

People who experience one depressive episode are more likely than never-depressed people to experience another, and vulnerability to depression increases with subsequent episodes. Backs-

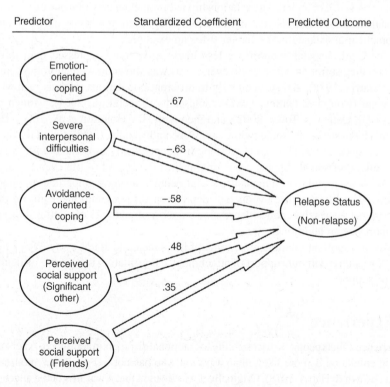

FIGURE 13.4 Standardized coefficients of factors that predicted relapse of depression in the study of Backs-Dermott, Dobson, and Jones (2010).

Dermott, Dobson, and Jones (2010) found, in a longitudinal study, that within a year of an episode of depression coming to an end, women were more likely to relapse into another episode of depression if they had avoidant coping styles, interpersonal difficulties, and/or lacked social support (see Figure 13.4).

Recurrence

The mechanism by which people become progressively more vulnerable to depression with each episode is called **kindling** (Stroud et al., 2011). Segal, Williams, Teasdale, and Gemar (1996) describe it in terms of mental patterns becoming established as habits, so that after each episode future activation is made more likely by progressively less severe events.

Kendler, Thornton, and Gardner (2001) also observed the decline in association between life events and depression across episodes, and found that this effect was most marked for those at low genetic risk. By contrast, those at high genetic risk frequently experienced a first depression without a severe adversity. Kendler et al. proposed that these highly vulnerable people could be thought of as "prekindled." Among the pathways to experiencing depression in the absence of major life stressors are genetic vulnerability and adversity begun in childhood.

Recovery and Fresh Starts

In the National Institute of Mental Health Collaborative Depression Study, most episodes of depression were found to resolve. Within a year of onset of depression, about 70% of people had recovered. By 5 years, 12% of people remained depressed (Mueller et al., 1996), and by 10 years the proportion was 7% (Keller & Boland, 1998).

When one is depressed, one can become trapped in a cognitive **bias** of negativity, which drains one of hope (Gotlib & Joormann, 2010). In Chapter 7 we showed that emotions change the organization of the brain to produce biases of processing. Emotional disorders prolong such changes. Because depressed people have a tendency to recall memories of loss and failure, Teasdale (1988) suggested that these memories lower mood and prolong depression (see Figure 13.5). The negative bias of depression makes people less likely to generate new life plans; then this lack of initiative can contribute to extending periods of depression.

Parrott and Sabini (1990) point out that most people do not get trapped in such inescapable cycles. Even when one is low, some memories can come to mind that are not depressing. We

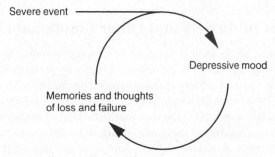

Severe event

Depressive mood

Memories and thoughts
of loss and failure

FIGURE 13.5 A vicious circle: depression caused by a life event may elicit memories of previous losses and failures, which in turn tend to make the person more depressed, and so on.

might say that in an episode of depression, people can start to reconceptualize their lives and make plans for the future (Nesse, 2000; Oatley, 1992). Such recoveries constitute what Brown, Lemyre, and Bifulco (1992) call "fresh starts," which may involve a new relationship, a new role, a new life project to replace what was lost. Any of these may enable a person to feel worthwhile and purposeful. In a longitudinal study of recovery from diagnosed depression, Oatley and Perring (1991) found that whether an episode of depression ended or remained unresolved depended on whether new plans made by the depressed person went well or went wrong.

Susan Nolen-Hoeksema asked whether depression is prolonged by **rumination**: dwelling on symptoms of distress in a passive and repetitive manner rather than in a problem-solving way. Nolen-Hoeksema and Morrow (1991) studied emotional responses to a natural disaster—the earthquake in the San Francisco Bay area in 1989 that killed 62 and left 12,000 people homeless—and found that those who ruminated on the event had lower mood up to seven weeks afterwards. In a study of people who had a close relative who had died in a hospice, Nolen-Hoeksema et al. (1994) found that the mood of people with a ruminative style was no lower than that of others a month after the death, but six months after the event their mood was still low, whereas that of non-ruminators had started to lift. Nolen-Hoeksema, Wisco, and Lyubomirsky (2008) reviewed the continuing program of research on rumination. Subsequent to this review, Cooney, Joormann, Eugène, Dennis, and Gotlib (2010) found that depressive rumination affected specific parts of the brain.

Not all thinking in depression is the same. Joormann, Dkane, and Gotlib (2006) showed that rumination has two aspects. One is brooding, which is maladaptive. But there is also reflective pondering, thinking through problems that led to incidents that caused depression, and this can resolve and shorten episodes of depression.

Alongside cognitive explanations, a second explanation of how depression is prolonged has been proposed by Hammen and her colleagues (Daley et al., 1997; Hammen, 1999), and by Joiner (2002). This explanation is in terms of relationships. Depression tends to make relationships deteriorate, and this deterioration tends to prolong depression. Hokanson et al. (1991) tracked mood and interactions between pairs of roommates at college. In one group one member of the pair had prolonged depressed mood as indicated by a continuously high score on the Beck Depression Inventory (Beck, Steer, & Garbin, 1988, the most widely used questionnaire to measure depression). In another group one person was generally cheerful, with a continuously low score on the Beck Inventory. As compared with roommates of cheerful people, those living with continuously depressed people became more depressed themselves over the year. They reported becoming more managerial and saw their roommate as becoming more dependent.

Cognitive Biases in Anxiety and Other Emotional Disorders

Anxiety states are more likely than depression to become chronic. Whereas the cognitive mechanism for sustaining depression is influenced strongly by memory of events and circumstances, mechanisms that sustain anxiety are mostly based on attention (Mogg & Bradley, 2004). As Andrew Mathews (1993) showed, people with anxiety traits and disorders are biased to attend to events that cause anxiety, especially their own particular kind of anxiety. So, a person anxious about health, or with hypochondriacal concerns, attends to bodily events by thinking them to be symptoms of illness (Stretton & Salovey, 1998). Such a person also tends to notice newspaper articles about health, attend to other people's accounts of health issues, and build up mental schemas and habits of mind that heighten anxiety. So, fear produces a focus on fear-inducing items and events that in turn produce more fear. Fear also causes avoidance, so socially anxious people tend to isolate themselves, which makes them more anxious about presenting themselves in public, which further drains confidence.

Following the 9/11 attacks in the United States in 2001, symptoms of post-traumatic stress disorder occurred among those who were closely involved (Galea et al., 2002). Fear derived from the attacks caused further anxiety symptoms, some of which made it impossible for people to return to work and caused disruptions of personal relationships. Lindstrom, Mandell, Musa, Britton, Sankin, Mogg et al. (2011) found that parents who were closely exposed to the 9/11 trauma in New York showed greater attention bias toward threat than parents with low trauma exposure.

Beyond Depression and Anxiety

We don't cover the whole field of abnormal psychology in this chapter, but in the following sections we discuss three further topics that focus on the relation of emotion to psychological disorder.

Psychopathy

Although the proportion of people who can be diagnosed as psychopaths is less than 2% of the population, it was found in a British survey by Coid and Yang (2011) that these people were responsible for 18.7% of violent incidents reported in the survey. Psychopathy is an emotional disorder with strong links to aggression. It has two core components: (i) callousness together with lack of emotional connection to others, and (ii) antisocial behavior. It is associated with thrill seeking, sadism, fearlessness, impulsivity, lack of anger control, antisocial lifestyle, and lack of guilt or remorse. The prototypical psychopath is male and socially antagonistic. He lacks social constraints of shame or worry about what others might think. He is not the usual young person diagnosed with conduct disorder or explosive anger disorder. He is not reflective in general, and in particular does not reflect on negative consequences of actions. Think of Robert Louis Stevenson's *Dr. Jekyll and Mr. Hyde,* in which the kind-hearted Dr. Jekyll starts taking a potion that transforms him into Mr. Hyde: purely selfish, free of all conscience. Most of us are Dr. Jekylls, mindful of convention and considerate of others. Psychopaths are the Mr. Hydes of this world.

Psychopathy starts at an early age and predicts adult criminal offending (Lynam, Miller, Vachon, Loeber, & Stouthamer-Loeber (2009). It is usually identified by a score on the Psychopathy Check-List, or some variant of it (Hare, Clark, Grann, & Thornton, 2000).

A psychopath seems unable to form emotional commitments with others and displays a lack of empathy. Although psychopathy seems to share with autism a deficit in empathy and theory of mind, the two syndromes differ (Blair, 2008). The psychopath is cruel, whereas the typical autistic person is not. Although it is possible for an autistic person also to be a psychopath, such a person would have two difficult traits, not one trait that is an aspect of the other (Baron-Cohen, 2011).

There are two principal theories about the psychopathic deficit. One is of attentional bias (Hiatt & Newman, 2006). Whereas anxious people are attuned to signs of danger, and switch attention from what they are doing to any new threat, the psychopath focuses only on what he or she is doing and is less affected by new information. According to this view, the impulsivity and poor avoidance of psychopaths is due to this deficit. In the second kind of theory (Blair & Mitchell, 2009), there is a deficit of emotional processing that involves dysfunctions of the amygdala and prefrontal cortex. In this view the effects of past or potential punishment are disrupted.

Psychopaths are fascinating to us in thrillers and murder-mysteries. They are not common in ordinary society, but they are common in prison populations. As yet, there has been little success in finding effective treatments for them, or in finding how to avoid their attaining positions of power in organizations or politics.

Schizophrenia and Expressed Emotion

The psychotic disorder of **schizophrenia** has a lifetime prevalence of 0.87% (Perälä et al., 2007) with slightly more females than males being affected. Whereas emotional disorders are largely provoked by the adversities of life, schizophrenia is determined more closely by genetics, and can occur in the absence of adversity. For a diagnosis according to *DSM-IV*, a disturbance has to last for at least six months, and to cause severe dysfunction socially and at work. Symptoms of schizophrenia include delusions, hallucinations, disorganized behavior, deteriorating relationships, and blunted emotions. The blunting of emotions is a difficulty in social functioning that is accompanied by being poor at recognizing emotional expressions in others (Hooker & Park, 2002). Important work by Ann Kring and her colleagues has revealed more specific nuances to the emotional blunting of those suffering from schizophrenia: they often report emotional experiences similar to people functioning well, but they show less emotion in their outward expressive behavior (e.g., Kring, 1999).

A major influence on schizophrenia occurs with emotions expressed by family members of patients. The term used is **expressed emotion**, a measure taken in family interviews with the patients' relatives. The original measure (Brown, Birley, & Wing, 1972) was of (a) the number of critical comments made by the relative, (b) the degree of relatives' hostility in nonverbal aspects and in content, and (c) the degree of over-involvement, such as treating the patient as a child. Vaughn and Leff (1976) found that among schizophrenic patients the degree of expressed emotion in relatives predicted whether the patient would relapse within the next nine months. For patients who came home from hospital to a family that was low in expressed emotion, irrespective of whether the patients took their antipsychotic medication, there was a low rate of relapse. But of those returning to a high–expressed emotion family, who spent more than 35 hours a week with them, and did not take their medication, 92% relapsed within nine months (see Figure 13.6).

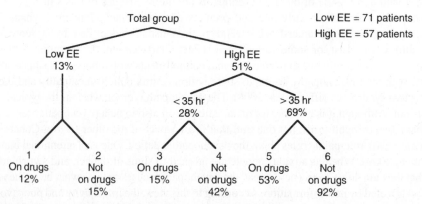

FIGURE 13.6 Percentages of schizophrenic patients who relapsed within 9 months of leaving hospital as a function of high and low expressed emotion, the amount of time they spent with their family, and whether they took their medication (Vaughn & Leff, 1976).

In a meta-analysis of studies of expressed emotion Butzlaff and Hooley (1998) found that high expressed emotion was associated with relapse of schizophrenia, and low expressed emotion was associated with low rates of relapse. All but three of the 27 studies that reached methodological criteria for inclusion in the meta-analysis showed the effect, with about 65% of patients who relapsed being in high–expressed emotion families, and 35% being in low–expressed emotion families. Butzlaff and Hooley found also that effects of expressed emotion for depressive disorders were larger than those for schizophrenia, and larger still for relapse of eating disorders such as anorexia.

Psychiatric disorders are not just disturbances within the sufferer. They are disturbing to others, and families differ in how they cope with these disturbances. For instance, Grice et al. (2009) found that high–expressed-emotion relatives of psychotic patients tended to blame the patients for negative events, whereas low–expressed-emotion relatives were focused more on positive events. Expressed emotion research has shown that with acceptance of the patient's condition and some flexibility in coping with it, not only may the lives be eased of families in which someone has a disorder, but the cycle of being emotionally critical and hostile, and hence provoking the patient into ever more difficult behavior and relapse, may be cut.

Psychosomatic Effects

There has been much research on emotional factors that affect physical health. Do adversities that can cause emotional disorders also make for physical ill-health by affecting the **immune system**? This system extends throughout the body and includes the bone marrow, spleen, thymus, lymph nodes, and the white cells of the blood such as lymphocytes and macrophages. The study of effects of stressors on the immune system is known as *psychoneuroimmunology*. Useful reviews are by Byrne-Davis and Vedhara (2008) and Kiecolt-Glaser (2009).

In this field findings have at first been epidemiological, and two kinds of study have been particularly significant. One significant series was the Whitehall Studies, by Michael Marmot and his colleagues, in which health was studied in men in the British Civil Service, all with the same health benefits and job security, but different status: Administrative at the top, then Professional/Executive, then Clerical, then Other. In the first study it was found that the higher people's grade in the civil service, the longer they lived (Marmot & Shipley, 1996). In the second Whitehall Study, Kuper and Marmot (2003) found that work stress, typified by low control at work, was associated with increased risk of heart disease. It seems that high status, of the kind studied in other primates, has health benefits. Following up the same population of civil servants, Boehm, Peterson, Kivimaki, and Kubzansky (2011) found that life satisfaction had a positive effect in protecting people from risk of heart disease.

In a second type of study, Richard Wilkinson and Kate Pickett (2009) offer extensive evidence on effects of social inequality as it occurs in different societies. Within developed countries, both mortality and the prevalence of specific diseases have striking associations with disparities of income.

In Chapter 12 we introduced the important work of Richard Wilkinson and Kate Pickett (2009), who have measured the inequality of personal incomes in different countries and studied the relationships of this personal economic inequality in these countries with a large array of indicators of psychological, social, and physical health. First, they present data nation-by-nation, with their measure of income inequality being the ratio of the top 20% of after-tax incomes to the bottom 20% of after-tax incomes in a nation. In Japan and the Scandinavian countries, for instance, this ratio is about 4 to 1. In France and Canada it is about 6 to 1. The United States is one of the developed countries with the highest income inequality: about 8.5 to 1.

Wilkinson and Pickett show that income inequality is strongly and consistently related to very wide array of psychological, social, and health indicators. These include lack of psychological well-being, low levels of trust in society, high prevalence of emotional disorders, low educational performance in children, high numbers of teenage births, high murder rate, and high prison populations. In one of their graphs (Figure 2.2, p. 20) they give an overall summary of their findings by plotting income inequality in different countries against a combined index of the psychological, social, and health problems, of the kind mentioned in the previous sentence.

The graph is a straight line from the lower left corner to the upper right corner, with very little scatter of countries around this line. At the bottom left end of the line are the four developed countries with the lowest income inequality, Finland, Norway, Sweden and Japan. They have the lowest scores on the combined index of psychological, social, and health problems. At the other end of this line, in the top right hand corner of the graph, are three developed countries with the most unequal incomes, UK, Portugal, and USA. These countries have the highest scores on the combined index of psychological, social, and health problems. Actually USA is way at the far end of the scales of both income inequality and the combined index of problems. In the middle of the graph, midway on both income inequality and the combined index of problems, are countries such as Canada, France, Switzerland, and Spain. You might note, too, that although some countries such those in Scandinavia achieve more equality through a system of progressive income tax, in which richer people pay higher rates of tax, Japan achieves a similar effect of more personal economic equality by having pre-tax salaries that are more equal.

In developing societies, measures of health and well-being relate to the national average income. In these countries, people who are poor have inadequate diets and few resources. In developed nations this mechanism is no longer at work; most people have enough, physically, to sustain themselves. But once a country reaches the level of development attained by Europe, North America, and Japan, health and well-being no longer relate to average national income. They relate instead to inequality. In developed nations, lower levels of physical health and lower psychological well-being—not just for the poor but for almost everyone in each nation— become far more closely associated with inequality of income. To counter the idea that unrecognized features of different countries might be responsible, Wilkinson and Pickett did similar analyses of U.S. states, in which people have the same American ideals, live in the same kinds of accommodation, eat the same kinds of food, and have their children go to similar schools. Louisiana and California, which are among states with the highest income inequality, have overall poorer physical health and well-being than the average. New Hampshire and Utah, which have lower income inequality, have better physical health and well-being. Oishi, Kesebir, and Diener (2011) have shown that in years of greater income inequality in the United States, people were more unhappy, and that their unhappiness was due to perceived unfairness and lower trust. Across nations, Oishi, Schimmack, and Diener (2012) found that people in nations where income taxes are progressive (so people who earn more, pay higher rates of tax) evaluated their lives as closer to the ideal, and reported having more positive and less negative daily experiences than did respondents living in nations with less-progressive taxation.

Since the large effects of inequality on health and social indicators do not relate to whether one has access to food and other resources, it can only be psychological. Is it that living in hierarchies makes people ashamed to be at the bottom of the heap, unable to bring up their children as they would like? Does envy of others affect not just one's mind but one's immune system? Does the distrust engendered by inequality adversely affect us all? These are pressing questions.

Janice Kiecolt-Glaser and her colleagues (2002) also started epidemiologically, and then took their detective work into the laboratory. They have found that negative emotions are risk factors, and supportive relationships are protective in a range of illnesses. They distinguish between short-term (acute) stress and long-term (chronic) stress. Kiecolt-Glaser has carried out a series of studies on acute stress, taking as a model students' acute anxiety and stress at exams. She and her colleagues have found that acute stress decreases immune responses to vaccinations (Glaser et al., 1998), and that students who have a surgical wound administered three days before an exam have a 40% lower rate of healing than those with the same kind of wound made during the summer vacation (Maroucha, Kiecolt-Glaser, & Favegehi, 1998).

Well-Being

The American Declaration of Independence speaks of inalienable rights, among which are "life, liberty, and the pursuit of happiness." But what is happiness? The World Health Organization defines it in terms of well-being. Happiness is:

> . . . a state of well-being in which the individual realizes his or her own abilities, can cope with the normal stresses of life, can work productively and fruitfully, and is able to make a contribution to his or her community.
>
> (WHO, 2001)

Happiness seems to be very positive, but Gruber, Mauss, and Tamir (2011) have shown that it needs to be of the right degree, about the right kinds of things, and in the right circumstances, otherwise it can be harmful. Many researchers see beneficial aspects of happiness/well-being as having three components: life satisfaction, positive affect, and a lack of negative affect (Nettle 2005). It's a state in which we can live our lives meaningfully and take part in our relationships in good heart. Diener and Diener (2002) found positive mental health across 43 countries to be the norm, with above-neutral levels of happiness in 86% of these countries.

Questions of happiness and its consequences have become central not just in psychology, but also in economics and sociology. The interest in economics has occurred because happiness can lead to greater productivity, achievement of financial success, the creation of supportive relationships, and increased longevity (Lyubomirsky, King, & Diener, 2005).

Sonja Lyubomirsky et al. (2005) have suggested three factors in thinking about happiness or well-being. The first is a genetic set point that regulates temperament and personality. Several twin studies have shown personality-based sense of happiness accounts for about 50% of the variation in long-term happiness, and that although life events may cause fluctuations around this point, most people return to their baseline level. The second factor is of circumstantial but long-term elements of a person's life such as gender, cultural background, income level, and marital status. Circumstantial factors account for an additional 10% of the variability of happiness.

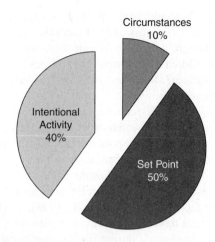

FIGURE 13.7   Determinants of happiness and well-being (Lyubomirsky et al., 2005).

Although achieving a desired job, or finding oneself having to live with less money than anticipated, seems, at the time, to make all the difference, these kinds of circumstance make less difference than one assumes, because people adapt to conditions. The third factor involves intentional activity: how people organize their activities in families, friendships, work, and leisure time. Intentional activities account for about 40% of the variability in well-being. The next sections are about these three factors.

Inherited Influences

A positive temperament predicts well-being. Cohn et al. (2009) found that the association between positive emotions and greater life satisfaction is mediated by greater ego resilience (a mental resource that helps a person deal with life stressors). According to this idea, positive emotions build resources to help people attain success in various life domains. For example, sharing joy and caring for another can lead to supportive relationships, and excitement about the world opens one to various work opportunities (Fredrickson & Cohn, 2008). Richards and Huppert (2011) followed up 2776 people in a British 1946 birth cohort. Teachers had rated these people at age 16 on domains that included energy level, happiness, popularity, and ease at making friends. As compared with those who received no positive teacher ratings in these domains, those who received positive ratings on two or more domains were 60% less likely to have mental health problems later in life. They were also more likely to be in frequent contact with family and friends and more likely to be satisfied at work.

Personality influences well-being through positive and negative mood. Abbott et al. (2008), for instance, found that Neuroticism and Extroversion, measured during adolescence, together accounted for between 13 and 18% of the variance in well-being measured more than three decades later. Stewart, Ebmeier, and Deary (2005) found a positive correlation between Extroversion and positive mood, and propose that effects of Extroversion on mood occur by creating conditions for positive experiences. Associations of Neuroticism with well-being are generally less consistent across samples from different societies. Neuroticism includes susceptibility to depression and anxiety. It involves a focus on immediate problems, and this contributes to emotional maladjustment.

Circumstance

A repeated finding within economic research is that moderate wealth is significantly associated with subjective well-being both within and between countries. This association is most marked between higher- and lower-income groups. Kahneman et al. (2006) found that as compared with those who earned less than $20,000 per year, nearly twice as many people were "very happy" who earned between $50,000 and $89,999. But earning $90,000 or more made almost no extra difference to happiness. Kahneman et al. propose that well-being does not continue to increase with increased income because it is influenced by judgments of *relative* wealth, and a person's position in the economic hierarchy is likely to persist. People with above-average incomes tend to be more tense and do not spend more time doing particularly enjoyable activities.

In global comparisons of well-being, Diener, Vitterso, and Diener (2005) found that the large majority of Kenyan Maasai, the U.S. Amish, and the Greenlandic Inughuit, who live traditional lifestyles without modern comforts or luxuries, scored above neutral on all scales of well-being. Their scores were comparable to those of people living in conventional ways in the United States. Happiness is not reliant on modernization and goods of industrialized societies. Among consistent factors that predict happiness cross-culturally are health, marriage, and employment.

Factors such as income inequality and victimization vary in their influence on well-being based on the context. For example, in high-crime areas there is a weaker association between loss of happiness and victimization than in low-crime areas (Graham, 2009). Graham (2009, 2010) argues that people are remarkably adaptable to their contexts and base their happiness on the *status quo* of the region in which they live. Tay and Diener (2011) found in a sample of 123 countries that fulfillment of basic needs was strongly associated with subjective well-being across cultures. Social needs and respect predicted positive affect, whereas lack of respect and lack of autonomy predicted negative affect across cultures. Tay and Diener also found that whereas being able to meet basic needs was dependent on the society in which a person lived, meeting psychosocial needs was possible in many different kinds of societies, and an ability to meet such needs enables people to adapt even to lives in which they are unable to meet basic needs.

Reflection and Cultivation: Flow

Mihalyi Csikszentmihalyi (1990) found that although many people's emotions were principally affected by the accidents of life, others conceived the world quite differently. Rico Medelin, for instance, worked on an assembly line in a factory that made movie projectors. His task was supposed to take 43 seconds, and he had to do it some 600 times a day. Although we could probably imagine grumbling if we had to earn our living at such a job, and had been doing it for as long as Rico—5 years— the samples of his experience on the production line were of happiness. He had consciously analyzed his task and worked out how to use his tools to become better and faster. His best average for the day was 28 seconds per unit. "It is better than anything else," said Rico. "It's better than watching TV" (pp. 39–40).

Through Rico and people like him, Csikszentmihalyi discovered a state he called flow. Another of his participants, who lived in the Italian Alps, enjoyed tending her cows and her orchard. She said, "I find a special satisfaction in caring for the plants. I like to see them grow each day" (p. 55). A dancer described how in a performance her attention was very complete, without any wandering of the mind. She was completely involved in what she was doing. A young mother described the time she and her small daughter spent together in similar ways.

Csikszentmihalyi also calls the state of flow *optimal experience*, and says it is characterized by a sense of creativity, of purpose, and of being deliberately and fully engaged so that self and the activity merge. To cultivate this state we can choose to do what we are doing, and turn it into a project in which we are engaged. Csikszentmihalyi has described some of the conditions for doing this and for achieving the state of engagement. It is not a matter of waiting for pleasurable events in the world. One needs to be creative (Csikszentmihalyi, 1996).

The best way is to accept or choose an activity and make it meaningful. It might be to learn the piano, or to become better at understanding what others are thinking. It's best to set yourself a goal, and set yourself specific problems and try to solve them on the way to reaching the goal. The goal and problems should be sufficiently specific so that that you can observe your own actions and their effects (feedback) to know whether you are progressing.

Activity

What kinds of activities enable people to experience their lives as worthwhile? Friendship has been repeatedly shown to be a source of joy and satisfaction. What is it about friendship that promotes happiness? In a study of 423 university students, Demir and Weitekamp (2007) found that the quality of friendships, especially companionship and self-validation, had significant effects on happiness. Although on its own, friendship accounted for 58% of the variance in happiness, most of this effect was due to personality variables. When these variables were controlled for, quality of friendship added a small independent effect to happiness. So, the activity of taking part in friendships and nurturing them is important.

Another important aspect of well-being is work. The founding piece of research on this subject was written by Marie Jahoda in 1932, originally published anonymously in 1933, and later published as Jahoda, Lazarsfeld, and Zeisel (1971). The book was about the devastating effects of unemployment in Marienthal, an Austrian village near Vienna, in which the main means of employment, a textile mill, closed down in 1930 during a depression that was far more severe than anything felt in the United States. This book became a model of comprehensive social research. Jahoda and her colleagues, in a team that included social researchers, physicians, and lawyers, drew on conversations, interviews, many kinds of observations including numbers of books loaned from the local library (which declined even though people had more time on their hands), as well as on diaries kept by the inhabitants. Poverty became severe, but the devastating loss of well-being was perhaps even worse: it was a sense of demoralization, apathy, and depersonalization. Jahoda et al. concluded that although the income that work provides is important, the most important benefits of work are social. Clark and Oswald (1994) found that among severe stressors that include divorce, being unemployed is the greatest depressor of well-being. Work structures our time and provides a sense of social purpose and personal worth. Several studies have now shown that people who take part in social activities, including paid work and volunteer work, report higher levels of well-being than those who have no work (e.g., McMunn et al. 2009). Associations between joblessness and well-being remain significant when income is kept constant, thus implying that unemployment influences well-being by exerting a negative psychological effect.

Among other activities that contribute to well-being is learning. In infancy we can't help doing it. In childhood we are pretty much compelled to do it at school. In young adulthood we can choose to do it, as perhaps you are doing now. We hope that your learning with this book is worthwhile and contributes to your well-being.

SUMMARY

In this chapter, we have shown that the emotional disorders of depression and anxiety, related to sadness and fear, are the most common psychiatric conditions worldwide, with women being more frequently afflicted than men. By contrast, men suffer more often from abuse of alcohol, and from impulse-control disorders that continue the externalizing disorders of childhood. We have explained how the first episode of major depression and/or clinical anxiety in a person's life is usually caused by a stress, which is typically a severely adverse event or difficulty, often in the presence of a genetic predisposition, or an environmental predisposition such as neglect in childhood. We then showed how an episode of major depression makes further episodes of depression more likely. Just as with emotions and moods, emotional disorders affect people's relationships. Beyond depression and anxiety, we discussed how some kinds of personality disorders, such as psychopathy, involve disorders of emotions. Critical and hostile emotions in the family can provoke relapse in schizophrenia and other disorders. Psychosomatic illnesses are affected by the same kinds of stresses that provoke depression and anxiety. Psychological well-being is the opposite of emotional disorder: it's a condition we generally strive for. It's affected by genetics, by long-term circumstances, and by intentional activities such as the maintenance of friendships, and work.

TO THINK ABOUT AND DISCUSS

1. Think back to a time of intense emotion for you, perhaps of sadness, or anxiety, or anger, or elation. What did you feel urged to think of at this time? What did you feel urged to do?

2. Do you know anyone, perhaps a family member or friend, who has suffered or is suffering a psychological disorder? What are the most important issues in caring for this person?

3. What are the most important principles of well-being in your life?

FURTHER READING

One of the most important books published on emotional disorders and engaging to read is:

George W. Brown & Tirril Harris (1978). *Social origins of depression: A study of psychiatric disorder in women.* London, UK: Tavistock.

An article on the importance of interpersonal emotions in psychopathology:

June Gruber & Dacher Keltner (2011). Too close for comfort? Lessons from excesses and deficits of compassion in psychopathology. In S. Brown, M. Brown, & L. Penner (Eds.), *Moving beyond self-interest: Toward a new understanding of human caregiving.* New York, NY: Oxford University Press.

An interesting and comprehensive article on physical health in relation to emotions is:

Janice Kiecolt-Glaser et al. (2002). Emotions, morbidity, and mortality: New perspectives from psychoneuro-immunology. *Annual Review of Psychology,* **53,** 83–107.

A good summary article on well-being:

Ed Diener, Shigehiro Oishi, & Richard Lucas (2003). Personality, culture, and subjective well-being: Emotional and cognitive evaluations of life. *Annual Review of Psychology,* **54,** 403–425.

14 Consciousness, Regulation, Psychotherapy

CONTENTS

Photo Credit: Thomas E. Hill, Manual of Business and Social Forms, 1885

FIGURE 14.0 Ronald De Sousa used these pictures for his book, *The Rationality of Emotions*. They are from Thomas Hill's (1885) book on etiquette—a making conscious of how to perform social customs with the right emotional tone.

There is, I assure you, a medical art for the soul. It is philosophy, whose aid need not be sought, as in bodily diseases, from outside ourselves. We must endeavor with all our resources and all our strength to become capable of doctoring ourselves.

Cicero: Tusculan Disputations, *III*, 6

Emotion may have been the original form of consciousness. So proposes Jaak Panksepp (2005). Most human brain networks that support the emotions are shared with other mammals. It seems likely, therefore, that something like the conscious feeling of fear when threatened by a predator and the enjoyment of play with another species-member occur in our close relatives, apes and monkeys, who have these same networks. We humans, however, not only experience emotions, we can experience them at a second level by consciously reflecting on the experiences. This kind of recursive consciousness is related to language whereby we can talk about our emotions with others and ourselves (see Chapter 7).

Reasons why consciousness might start as an emotional matter might be guessed from the statement of Paulhan (1887/1930) that emotions fill the field of consciousness, and from the observation of Mead (1913) that we become conscious when habit fails, and when sometimes "different tendencies appear in reflective thought as different voices in conflict" (p. 147). When the unexpected happens, when we are faced by a challenge in an argument that becomes heated, or by meeting a potential sexual partner with whom we make a connection, we tend to experience an emotion that fills our consciousness, both directly and reflectively.

Consciousness

Consciousness seems to be a process by which we can decide what to do and then do it. But recent evidence suggests this is misleading. As Libet (1985) has shown, action is often initiated before the corresponding conscious voluntary decision to act occurs. This finding has been repeatedly verified, for instance, by recording from single neurons implanted into the brains of patients (in order to make tests in the treatment of epilepsy; Fried, Mukamel, & Kreiman, 2011). If consciousness is not in the causal chain of deciding the simplest kind of action, such as pressing a key in an experiment, how much less may it be in the causal chain if we suddenly have an emotional urge? James's (1884) idea that when we see a bear in the woods we first run and only then feel the emotion becomes relevant in a new way.

In terms of the proposal introduced in Chapter 2 that our bodies are vehicles for our genes, our conscious selves may be passengers rather than the drivers of these vehicles. The question for this chapter is how we might sometimes be able to take the steering wheel.

The Function of Consciousness

Baumeister and Masicampo (2010) have proposed that the function of consciousness is to maintain an ongoing simulation of ourselves that interrelates memory, current social and emotional understandings, and evaluation of possible future actions. Here is a telling experiment by Galdi, Arcuri, and Gawronski (2008). At the time of their study, a proposal had been made to enlarge an American Forces base in Vincenza, Italy. This was a matter of emotional concern and an occasion of controversy. Galdi et al. made three measures of 129 residents of Vincenza: (a) whether they were for or against the proposal, or as yet undecided, (b) what their conscious beliefs were, gathered from a ten-item questionnaire on environmental, social, and economic consequences of the proposal, and (c) how they made automatic associations in an implicit association test in which they pressed buttons in response to pictures of the military base and evaluative words. Implicit association tests of this kind are difficult to control consciously and are not necessarily consistent with conscious reports. A week later, the researchers repeated the same

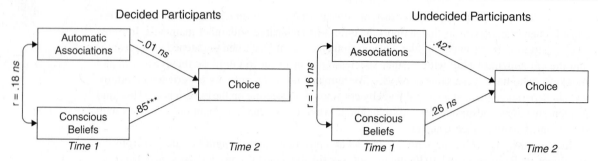

FIGURE 14.1 Automatic associations and conscious beliefs of choices at Time 2 by participants who at Time 1 were decided ($n = 96$) and undecided ($n = 33$). Significance values: $* = 0.05$, $*** = 0.001$, ns = not significant (Galdi et al., 2008).

measurements. For both decided and undecided participants, conscious thoughts and automatic associations did not correlate with each other either at either time 1 or time 2. The main results were that among the decided, conscious thoughts at time 1 predicted both the choice they would make and automatic associations at time 2, whereas among the undecided, automatic associations at time 1 predicted both the choice they would make and conscious thoughts at time 2. Conscious thinking was able to affect automatic associations and decision-making, but not immediately: only after an interval. You may see these results in Figure 14.1.

Using a paradigm known as **affective forecasting**, a shocking gap has been found between what we consciously think about ourselves and our less-conscious, automatic emotional processes. Kawakami et al. (2009) asked self-identified white and Asian people to complete a survey that included asking whether they would be upset by a racist act. They predicted they would be. Not long afterward, with the experimenter out of the room, they saw a black man (an experimenter's confederate) say he had to go and get his cell-phone and, as he left the room, gently bump the knee of a white man (another confederate). In different experimental conditions, and with the black man now out of the room, the white man either made no comment, or made a moderately racist remark, "Typical, I hate it when black people do that," or an extreme racist remark, "Clumsy n-----!" Within minutes, the experimenter and the black man returned to the room and participants were asked to rate the intensity of a list of emotions. Those who had heard either of the racist remarks were no more upset than those in the condition in which no comment had been made. When later asked whom they would choose to collaborate with, participants were found also to have overestimated the degree to which they would reject the man who made the racist remark.

Affective forecasting has become a distinct area of investigation (Lowenstein, 2007). Researchers often play up how bad we are at it, but a meta-analysis of studies has shown that although people's predictions of their future feelings are often somewhat inaccurate, people are quite good at knowing whether they would be more or less upset by some kinds of future events.

Our conscious thoughts can be affected by processes of which we are not consciously aware—including the unconscious processes that produce our emotions—and, rather than conscious thoughts being always able immediately to control what we feel, think, and decide, they can, as with the decided people in Galdi et al.'s study, affect the automatic structure of our minds over a longer term as we think about an issue, become aware of our emotions about it, and discuss it with others. It's also the case—as with the undecided people in Galdi et al.'s experiment—that unconscious processes, including those that give rise to emotions, can affect future consciously held beliefs, usually after a while.

According to Baumeister and Masicampo's theorizing, conscious thought enables us to understand the perspectives of others, learn from memories of our own actions and emotions, explore possibilities for future action, and share pieces of our ongoing simulation with others in conversation (including conversation about our emotions, as Rimé, 2009, has shown). So, although consciousness may not control immediate action, it can and does affect action indirectly by influencing the settings of our automatic thought processes—joggling them, perhaps, until they are in register with one another and with our conscious simulation.

In Chapter 7 we discussed how, when we experience an emotion, we tend first to do so in terms of a primary appraisal, which has attributes of a reflex. Only then, in secondary appraisal, does it become conscious, so that we can understand what caused it and think what to do about it. Though primary appraisal is brief, conscious experiences of emotion extend in time. Frijda, Mesquita, Sonnemans, and van Goozen (1991) had subjects draw graphs to indicate the changes of intensity of emotion experiences. They found that 69% of conscious emotions lasted an hour or more, and 22% lasted more than a day. The conclusion that conscious emotions extend in time was confirmed by Oatley and Duncan (1992) in a study of 57 undergraduates asked to record emotions in an emotion diary. As we described in Chapter 7, as found by Rimé (2009), most episodes of emotion are discussed with others, making emotions conscious in more elaborate ways.

Consciously Making Sense of Emotions

When we talk to a friend about an emotion, we narrate a story. Bruner (1986) has contrasted the narrative mode of thinking with what he calls the paradigmatic mode, which is used in explanations, for instance, in science. Narrative is the mode in which we understand ourselves and others as people who have intentions that meet vicissitudes.

Vicissitudes, or problems with goals and intentions, are the events that tend to cause emotions. Meaning-making occurs by casting emotional events into narratives about the social world, into stories with settings, characters, conflicts, and character development. Narrative meaning-making occurs with turning over emotions in our minds or with a friend, and also in reading novels and poetry and watching plays and movies, which can also help us represent our emotions in narrative form.

Emotions can be mere stirrings or unshaped movements of the mind. We have presented evidence that there is a biological basis for them (see Chapters 6 and 7), that emotions are embodied in physiological systems seen in mammals. If that were all, we would have emotions like those of our relatives the apes. But we are born not just into the biological world, but into society, which includes people to whom we may become attached in friendship or with whom we may become involved in conflict. In every society, in every community, in every family, narrative histories are recounted, with their characters and their traditions of custom: human meanings about what we people are up to with each other. In such traditions, emotions and our understandings of them are the pivotal points.

Emotions in Ritual, Drama, and Stories

In all societies, people enact rituals that include such group activities as singing, dancing, processions, presentations, and theater or its equivalents. In all, there can be the telling of stories, some historical and some fictional. Some rituals, such as birthday parties, mark events. Others create new social facts: the words of the marriage ceremony change the civil status of a couple. Perhaps the most potent rituals are based on emotions; one could almost say that a ritual is an emotion turned into a public form.

The oldest such ritual for which we have evidence is the funeral; archaeological findings of people's possessions that were buried with them (grave goods) imply that ritual burial may have dated back as far as 100,000 years. So, from early times, as part of grieving, such rituals must have been accompanied by stories: a person who is dead lives in memories that can be symbolically recognized by interring some of the person's possessions, or the person continues to live on another plane.

We can think of emotion-based rituals as events in which emotions in a person meet with a community, when people have similar emotions as at a funeral, when someone brings an emotion, as happened in the early church when regretful confession was made to a group, or when the ritual itself prompts emotions in those who attend it, as in ancient Greek drama. Sometimes an event of emotional significance for a particular group of people is reenacted to enable the people who take part in a ritual to reflect on it and make it mentally part of themselves. In this way, Holy Communion for Christians is a reenactment of Christ's Last Supper and is intended to induce personal transformation.

Turner (1974) has proposed stages through which an emotionally significant event can pass to create a ritual: (a) a breach of ordinary social relations occurs, which can lead to (b) a crisis that may escalate, and be followed by (c) redressive social action that may vary from personal advice to action within a formal legal system, and end with (d) the ritual that accomplishes reintegration of the disturbed person or people back into the community, or the recognition of irreparable schism.

How do we understand this? One explanation is given by Scheff (1979). He argues that many rituals have at their center the possibility of experiencing emotions at what he calls a best aesthetic distance (see Cupchik, 2002). Scheff argues that if emotionally intense events or difficulties are experienced as overwhelming (as in a trauma), or if we distance ourselves from them too much (as when we defend ourselves by blocking emotions out), then we accumulate a kind of emotional arrears or debt, which distorts our lives. Scheff argues that ritual, drama, and narrative provide memory cues that will bring emotions to mind, but in a safe context where we can experience them at a best aesthetic distance.

When we cry over the fates of Romeo and Juliet, we are reliving our own personal experiences of overwhelming loss, but in a context in which the self is momentarily free of duties or responsibilities. The experience of vicarious loss, in a properly designed drama, is sufficiently distressful to reawaken the old distress. It is also sufficiently vicarious, however, that the emotion does not feel overwhelming (Scheff, 1979, p. 13).

The issue does not end here, because fiction invites the reader of a novel, or the watcher of a film or play, to enter an imagined world and become involved in it. The imagined world is the kind of space in adulthood that play is in childhood. It's what Winnicott (1971) called a "space in between" oneself and others with whom we engage. Events in a novel, play, or film are not experienced in quite the same way as they are in quotidian life. They are experienced in a kind of simulation that runs not on computers but on minds (Oatley, 1999), or as an older metaphor had it, in a kind of dream (Miall & Kuiken, 2002). In this imaginative space we experience emotions, not those of fictional characters, but our own (Oatley, 2011). And just as we change somewhat when in the morning we arrive at our workplace, or in the evening we join a group of friends, we may be changed when we enter a space of emotional imagination. Just as we are careful whom we choose as friends, we should be judicious about what we read (Booth, 1988) and what movies we see.

Becoming Conscious of Emotions in Literature

"There is no history of mankind, there is only an indefinite number of histories of all kinds of aspects of human life," wrote Karl Popper. The history most of us learn at school, he continued, is largely "the history of power politics [which] is nothing but the history of international crime" (Popper, 1962b, p. 270). In our terms this means international power assertion. Among the many histories that would be more edifying—the history of ideas, the history of technology, the history of the family—might be counted histories of consciousness and of the emotions, which can be approached via written stories where emotions and their effects are typically at the center of the narratives.

From the earliest times, it is extraordinary that emotion has been a principal focus of poetic, fictional, and folk-historical narratives. From the Sumerians come epics from 4,000 years ago about Gilgamesh, who experiences a loss of meaning in his life and becomes depressed when his friend, Enkidu, dies. From Egypt comes "The dispute between a man and his soul," dating from about 3,700 years ago, in which a man complains to his soul of his misery and his longing for death. His soul becomes irritated with this grumbling and says that death will occur in due time (Lichtheim, 1973). From India, from 3,500 years ago, comes the *Mahabharata* (Vyasa, c. 1500 BCE) about the angry hostility that becomes a war between the Kauravas and the Pandavas, two branches of a dynastic family. From the Hebrews come the first five books of the Bible, written about 2,800 years ago, with their theme of a family history in which the human protagonists oscillate between fear of, and hopeful dependence on, their god, Yahweh (Rosenberg & Bloom, 1990). From the same period, from the Greeks comes the *Iliad*, whose first words are: "Of rage sing, goddess." This work was central to Greek culture. It's a tale of the repercussions of a sulk by Achilles during the long and angry war triggered by the abduction of Helen by the Trojan prince Menelaos (Homer, 850 BCE).

Hogan (2003) has surveyed stories from all round the world, from before the age of European colonization. He found that three prototypical stories, all based on emotions, are so common as to be universals. Most common is the love story, in which two lovers long to be united but are impeded by a male relative or a powerful suitor. Shakespeare's *Romeo and Juliet* is the most famous story of this kind. Second most common is the story of angry conflict, usually between two male members of a family. The *Mahabharata* is an example. Third most common is the story of a community, disintegrating in terrible distress until someone arises to diagnose the problem and sacrifice himself or herself for the good of the community. The Christian Gospel is an example. So from the first, and still continuing, in stories—crafted pieces of narrative consciousness—originally told orally and then written down, we find the intense preoccupation to understand and reflect upon emotions and to augment our consciousness of them in narrative.

In the 19th century, novels such as those by Gustave Flaubert and Émile Zola in France, by Jane Austen and George Eliot in England, by Leo Tolstoy and Fyodor Dostoevsky in Russia, and by Herman Melville and Harriet Beecher Stowe in America came to be means of enjoyment, ways of experiencing emotions so that they could be assimilated, and ways of identification with others so that the experiences of taking part emotionally in lives beyond the boundaries of our personal lot could become, as George Eliot put it, "the raw material of moral sentiment" (Eliot, 1883, p. 193). Hunt (2007) argues that novels were important in the invention of human rights—an idea that didn't exist before the 18th century—as people started to read about others in more difficult circumstances than their own and to identify with them emotionally and to experience moral intuitions about the sanctity of the individual.

By the 1920s, novels had become more inward, and the idea—not new but beginning at least with Shakespeare—became common: that becoming a whole person was concerned with being able to understand oneself in terms of an emotionally informed narrative of one's life.

Stories provide possibilities of mental action, as well as pieces of solutions to the problems of how to be a person in society. It has been found, too, by Mar, Oatley, and Peterson (2009) that reading fiction is associated with better empathy for others, and Johnson (2011) has confirmed that the causal direction here is that reading improves empathy. In a related way, Djikic et al. (2009) have shown that reading literary fiction can enable people to change their personality in small and self-determined ways, with the change being mediated by emotions. Stories in print and film are externalized cultural objects that offer examples that we can think about and discuss of emotions and their implications over a wider range than anyone could have in a single life (Oatley, 2011). They help us to reflect on and become part of the cultural tradition in which we live. As Baumeister and Masicampo (2011) suggest, by making the unconscious conscious, and enabling conscious thoughts to affect our automatic associations, we can align ourselves with ourselves and with the community of those with whom we live.

Regulation

Intense thought about **regulation** of emotions goes back to ancient times. In the East, the question of how to live without being affected by emotions of suffering was the problem that practices of meditation were developed to solve (as introduced in the final box in this chapter). In the West, regulation was the problem on which Epicureans and Stoics worked, more than 2,000 years ago. We have already begun our discussion of regulation in Chapter 7 and seen some of its neural correlates in Chapter 6; in this section we aim to show how regulation can work in adulthood.

Distraction, Reappraisal, Suppression, Augmentation

Most often the term *emotion regulation* refers to changing an emotion's intensity or duration. If you are in a traffic jam on the way to an appointment, you might try to feel less anxious: listen to music, think how to take care of being late, take deep breaths. If you work at a customer interface, you can increase your enjoyment of your job by being pleasant with customers or clients.

One approach to regulation is to think of emotions as having a dimension of pleasantness, as described by Russell (2003). Regulation can then be the attempt to move from the unpleasant toward the pleasant.

Nico Frijda (1988) and James Gross (1998) have argued that regulatory processes affect every stage of the emotion process. Gross, Sheppes, and Urry (2011) propose five stages at which regulation can work: situational selection, situational modification, attentional deployment, cognitive change, and response modulation. Selecting and modifying situations were discussed in Chapter 8. Among regulatory interventions at the attentional stage is distraction. As to cognitive change, the appraisal one makes of an event affects both the type of emotion and its intensity. Further along in the process comes response modulation: people can seek to suppress or emphasize expression of an emotion, usually by behaving or not behaving in particular ways. When one seeks to enhance an emotion, one can take William James's advice and explicitly enact what we want to feel so that, by means of the inner feedback from expressive processes, we feel it more strongly.

Several studies have been performed to examine the effects of different kinds of intervention. Thus in an electroencephalographic (EEG) study, Thiruchselvam et al. (2011) found that distraction operates early in the emotion process. In an fMRI study, Goldin et al. (2008) found that next in the chain of events is appraisal, or reappraisal, which affects the prefrontal cortex.

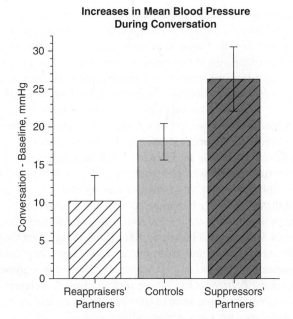

Increases in Mean Blood Pressure During Conversation

FIGURE 14.2 Increases in blood pressure by partners of those instructed to reappraise or to suppress their emotions, and control participants, in the study by Butler et al. (2003).

Suppression, for instance, by not expressing an emotion, although it, too, can affect the prefrontal cortex, tends to come later in the process and affects the insula and amygdala.

Different kinds of regulation can have different repercussions. Butler et al. (2006) had women view an unpleasant film clip. Then each woman met with another woman she did not know. Some women who had viewed the clip were asked to suppress their emotions by not expressing them. Others were asked simply to respond naturally. Yet others were asked to reappraise the experience by thinking of their current situation. Women who were asked to suppress, and the women they met, were found to have increased blood pressure as compared with those who responded naturally and those who reappraised (see Figure 14.2).

Suppression also reduced rapport, probably because emotional responsiveness is important for communication. It made the people to whom the women spoke less willing to take part in a friendship. Instructions to suppress an emotion in experiments have generally been found to be ineffective in decreasing the intensity of emotions that are experienced in the experiments (Ehring et al., 2010).

In another study of reappraisal and suppression, van't Wout, Chang, and Sanfey (2010) looked at regulation of emotional reactions to unfairness in the Ultimatum Game (discussed in Chapter 10, in which a responder decides whether to accept a proposer's suggested division of a sum of money). Participants worked through 24 trials of the game. Some people received no instructions as to regulating their emotions. Some received instructions to suppress, which included the phrase: "It is very important to us that you try your best not to show any signs of emotional feelings and suppress any emotional feelings as you watch the offers" (p. 817). Others were given instructions to reappraise: "It is very important to us that you try your best to adopt a neutral attitude as you watch the offers. To do this, we would like for you to view the offers with detached interest or try to come up with possible reasons why someone might give you a certain offer" (p. 817). As compared with those who were asked to suppress their emotional reactions, those asked to reappraise were less likely to reject unfair offers. So, van't Wout et al. argue that their results extend previous findings: "Emotional reappraisal as compared to expressive suppression, is a powerful regulation strategy that influences and changes how we interact with others even in the face of inequity" (p. 815).

Laboratory studies of regulation have been informative, but how do people regulate emotions in their day-to-day lives? Some tend to reappraise, and have developed the habit of making the best of things. Others tend to suppress. Yet others distract themselves. Here, too, there can be repercussions. It has been often suspected that people who habitually try to suppress their emotions make themselves vulnerable to depression and, in a study in which suppression was compared with reappraisal in people who had a history of depressive episodes as compared with people who had not, Ehring et al. (2010) studied recovered-depressed and never-depressed people and found that those who had experienced depression tended to suppress their emotions. But there are differences of culture: Soto, Perez, Kim, Lee, and Minnick (2011) asked European Americans in the United States and Chinese people in Hong Kong about their use of expressive suppression, their life satisfaction, and their depressed mood. They found that expressive suppression was associated with poorer psychological effects for European Americans but not for Chinese participants. Politeness in Chinese society involves different rules than in social interaction in America. Chinese people seem to have become more skilled at suppression in ways that are not at odds with how one lives in that culture.

Emotion and Free Will

Sometimes we enjoy being taken over by a strong emotion such as love. But sometimes an emotion such as anxiety or anger or despair can take us over and be persecuting. The idea of regulation is that we can modify some emotions, or some aspects of emotions, by means of our will.

In Chapter 2, on evolution, we showed that some emotions are closely programmed by the genes we humans carry. This emotion-programming is the genes' way of improving the chances of survival of the bodies that transport them toward the next generation. The problem of regulation of emotions can be seen in terms of how far we are compelled by this programming. The problem becomes yet more pressing because, along with the programming of our genes, we are affected by families in which we were raised (Chapters 8 and 11) and by constraints of society (Chapter 3). Do we really have choices? Or, in the end, do our genes and environment control us? Is there any free will left to us by which we can influence our emotional lives?

One form of argument, offered by Prinz (2007), is that free will has no place in science: one may as well ask a zoologist to describe unicorns. In the criminal justice system there are concepts such as guilt, but such ideas may not mean people have free will. Assignment of responsibility and verdicts of guilt may merely be mechanisms that society has developed to remove certain people from our midst. As Prinz puts it, "Scientific psychology has no room for a theoretical construct called the freedom of the will" (p. 74). According to Prinz, the scientific conclusion is that emotions and behavior are caused by neurons programmed by genes and environment. People don't act because of reasons—they behave because neurons fire in certain patterns.

But there is a counter argument. If we subject the "scientific" anti-free-will argument to Prinz's own analysis, the argument can't be meaningful because it's just a set of neurons firing. The holders of any position of this kind can mean no more than my computer can mean it when its silicon chips cause a pattern such as "Welcome" to appear on its screen.

Photo Credit: Alexandra Milgram

FIGURE 14.3   Stanley Milgram leaning on the apparatus by which participants in his experiments thought they were delivering electrical shocks to learners.

A second kind of argument is that although we may think we choose what to do in our lives, really we behave because of our genes, our upbringing, and social constraints. We defer to people higher in the status hierarchy, we take on group norms, and we obediently enact roles afforded by society.

Some of the most famous and important experiments in the whole of psychology—by Stanley Milgram (1963) and by Philip Zimbardo and his colleagues (Haney, Banks, & Zimbardo, 1973)—bear on this issue.

In Milgram's study, 40 men (skilled and unskilled workers, men in business occupations, and professionals) were recruited by newspaper advertisements and direct mail. They were asked to come to a laboratory at Yale University to take part in a memory experiment. They were told they would be paid for coming to the laboratory and that payment would not depend on anything that happened there. Their instructions were to help in an important experiment on effects of punishment on learning by training a man to learn associations between words. When they arrived at the laboratory another man was present, supposedly also a participant, but actually an experimenter's accomplice. The men were asked to draw slips of paper from a hat to see who would be the teacher and who would be the learner. In fact the participant was always the teacher, because the slips both bore the word "teacher." The participant did not see the slip of paper of the accomplice, who would always draw second. The participant saw the other man, in the role of learner, taken into a room and strapped into a chair. The participant was told to speak aloud from a written protocol pairs of words to be learned by association. The learner was to respond by pressing one of four keys. If a wrong key were pressed or no response occurred the participant was to punish the learner with increasingly severe electric shocks. Punishments were to be delivered by a machine with a graded set of switches the lowest of which was labeled "15 volts, Slight Shock." When the teacher pressed a switch, a light came on and an electric buzz sounded. The settings of the switches rose in 15-volt intervals to the range 375 to 420 volts, labeled "Danger, Severe Shock, with two switches beyond this point (435 and 450 volts), labeled "XXX." To deliver each successive punishment the teacher was to go to the level above the previous one, announce the voltage, and then press the appropriate switch. At 300 volts and at 315 volts the learner (the accomplice who did not actually receive shocks) was heard pounding on the wall, and from this point on he made no more responses. Many participants asked the experimenter whether it was all right to carry on after the learner stopped responding. In response to such questions the experimenter, dressed in a gray technician's coat, explained again that absence of a response was to be punished, and that the teacher should deliver the punishment and speak the next words to be associated. The experimenter used such phrases as: "It is absolutely essential that you continue," and 26 of the participants (65%) continued obediently to say the words to be learned, to announce the voltage, and to administer shocks up to the highest level, 450 volts. In doing so, some of them exhibited extreme emotional disturbance, shown by profuse sweating, trembling, and stuttering. Fourteen participants (35%) refused to continue either when they reached the point just before the 315–360 volt range labeled "Extreme Intensity Shock," or when they were within that range, or when they were at the 375-volt level just beyond it. In all, Milgram conducted nearly 40 studies, either as pilot studies or replications (Reicher & Haslam, 2011), in which, under varying conditions, he observed levels of conformity that ranged from 0 to 100%.

The Stanford Prison Experiment has been discussed in Zimbardo's (2007) book, *The Lucifer Effect: Understanding How Good People Turn Evil.* The experiment was in a simulated prison for which men were recruited in Stanford, California, from an advertisement in a local newspaper and randomly assigned to be either guards or prisoners. From the original 75 volunteers, five with psychiatric disorders or histories of crime or drugs were excluded. From the remainder, 24 men—all college students—were selected for inclusion as the most stable and psychologically healthy. In the end, 11 volunteers took part as guards, on eight-hour shifts, and 10 as whole-time prisoners. Among the prisoners, loss of identity occurred along with passivity, depression, and helplessness. Five of the 10 suffered such severe emotional reactions that the experimenters released them. Among those assigned to be guards, 9 of the 11 acted as their roles required, and 4 of these became cruel, enjoyed their new-found power, and constantly invented new forms of harassment. (This can't occur in normal prisons in civilized countries, where procedures are carefully regulated.) Two of the men assigned to be guards (18%) refused to go along with the cruelty that developed among some of the guards, and were kind to the prisoners. The experimenters were so alarmed at how the experiment developed that it was terminated after six days instead of the 14 days that had been planned.

Milgram and Zimbardo created alternative worlds, pieces of theater in which the participants were cast as actors, although they were the only ones who did not know the script. Among psychological explanations of why participants acted as they did are that they were led into these alternative worlds, of which they had no previous experience, by small steps, and that having found themselves acting in certain ways, compelled by obedience and by the roles they had willingly entered, they continued.

Although most accounts of Milgram's and Zimbardo's studies stress other aspects, emotions were central. In both studies, the emotional state of cruelty is evident, and in both, many participants experienced severe emotional conflicts.

These studies are significant in our understanding of how, after Hitler came to power in Germany, in 1933, with the establishment of a Nazi state, a chain of events occurred that led to the deaths of 50 to 70 million people in World War II. Two thirds of the deaths were civilians, including between five and six million Jews and several hundred thousand others defined by the Nazis as undesirables, including mentally retarded people, Gypsies, and homosexuals. Milgram's and Zimbardo's experimental studies are to be compared with a historical study by Christopher Browning (1992) in his book, *Ordinary Men,* which is about Battalion 101 of the Nazi Order Police. Browning's research was based on judicial interrogations, after the war, of

125 of the 486 men in this battalion. Some of the battalion's 11 officers received high-school education. Men of other ranks were recruited from the skilled and unskilled workforce in Hamburg and, although some of these had vocational training, most had no education beyond age 15. Two-and-a-half years after recruitment, it became their job, starting in 1942, to massacre Jews in Polish towns and villages. As in the Stanford Prison Experiment (with which Browning compares his study), the large majority went along with the roles they were given. Between 10 and 20% of them, however, refused to take part in the shootings. They were not court-martialed.

In his discussions of free will in the regulation of emotions, Frijda (2010, 2011) proposes that the minority of the men in the studies by Milgram, Zimbardo, and Browning who did not just draw on their primate repertoire of cruelty, who did not just go along obediently with social pressures, exercised their free will. Instead of being emotionally coerced by deference to authority or fear of consequences, they were able to act in a way that they felt to be right, according to their empathetic concern for others. In the same way, Frijda gives examples of non-Jewish people who harbored Jewish people in Nazi-occupied territories, and in the 1994 genocide in Rwanda, of some Hutu women who sheltered Tutsi children, putting themselves at risk of death (Prunier, 1995). As Simon Baron-Cohen (2011) shows in his book, *The Science of Evil*, some people do lack empathetic concern for others and are low on theory-of-mind, the ability to understand others' thoughts and feelings, as we discussed in Chapter 8. They need to be looked after, by society, in ways that they are not themselves able to look after others. It is a dire mistake for any society to put such people in positions of power over others. For the rest of us, part of emotion regulation is the cultivation of empathetic concern for others.

So what are we to think of free will, and the possibility of giving priority to empathetic concern above other kinds of emotion? We can, if we wish, smile at the naïveté of imagining the self, sitting inside our head, freely making decisions. But the real issue is to consider our own lives in relation to what we would do if we were confronted by coercions of the kind faced by participants in Milgram's or Zimbardo's experiment, or if we were recruits to Battalion 101 of the Order Police. Would we just do what we were told? Or would empathetic concern be more important?

Gailliot et al. (2007) have found that, whether you believe in free will or not, exercising the will reduces levels of blood glucose: it is effortful. Belief in free will is associated with thoughtfulness and helpfulness to others, and it can be expensive not only in the expenditure of energy but in many other ways, as shown by those who stood out against genocidal policies in their societies. Baumeister, Masicampo, and DeWall (2009) have shown that people who are induced to decrease their belief in free will become more aggressive and cruel. So, whatever you may want to call the ability to exercise conscious free will, it can be measured psychologically (Baumeister, Masicampo, & Vohs, 2011). Certainly, it affects how we live and it affects the societies we live in.

Another way to estimate our ability to exercise free will is to consider mental health, as discussed in Chapter 13. The voluntariness of those who suffer from serious anxiety and depressive disorders, and those in the grip of addictions, is seriously curtailed. Their area of free will is narrowed. They can no longer act as they would wish and their lives are thereby diminished.

Free will may not be an ideal term, but it refers to something important. This something is the ability to make meaning in our lives. Perhaps we should call it meaning-making. By taking part in it we can move toward the meaningful, rather than simply acting in response to biologically based urges and social compulsions. In this way, by understanding our own makeup we can, as Stanovich (2004) has put it, join the robots' rebellion. Although we necessarily continue to be robot-vehicles for our genes, we need no longer be compelled by all of these genes' emotional programming or by coercive aspects of societal groupthink. Because our evolution has also afforded us consciousness and verbal discussion, we can strive for human purposes rather than be compelled by mere gene-survival and group-survival purposes. By understanding that our relationship with the rest of humankind is one of interdependence, we can perhaps become more empathetic and compassionate. And by understanding our relation to the future of our planet, we can perhaps become less greedy and less thoughtless toward our successors. This had better become a possibility or we will go the way of the dinosaurs. To move toward this possibility, we need to give human purposes priority over emotional urgencies of our genes, and over the group-aspirational contempt that can arise in a society that comes into conflict with another society.

Conscious thought is the usual way in which meaning-making occurs. In this book we argue, as Baumeister and Masicampo propose, that consciousness is an inner simulation that relates past memories, the current social-emotional world, and future possibilities of action. Within this simulation we can make meanings with which we can decide that it is better to do one thing rather than another. Free will does not mean acting outside the laws of neural causality. It means being able to act for reasons that are considered and meaningful, such as empathetic concern for others. Once conscious meaning has been established, it can generate reasons that affect the more automatic processes that govern action. Even though it generally takes time and a willing search for understanding, in order for adjustments to be made in the association structure of our minds, choice and responsibility, in concern for others and ourselves, become possibilities.

No one yet understands consciousness. It's not known how biological beings can make human meaning. It could be an emergent property of our sociality. Whatever the explanation, instead of just behaving, we can act meaningfully and act in certain ways for reasons that we can articulate consciously and discuss with others. Human actions are—of course—constrained in ways that we have tried to articulate in this book. Free will is assisted by understanding our emotions. With such understanding we are more likely to be able to act for human reasons, rather than simply to behave at the behest of genes or of social coercion.

What Is Regulated?

The ancient Epicureans and Stoics argued that we can't fight our emotions because they are too strong. We must move, as it were, upstream, and concentrate on our desires, or as psychologists now say, on our goals or concerns. In terms of the two movements of emotions recognized by the Stoic Chrysippus, the first movement, physiological and perhaps expressive, is automatic. But in the second movement of reflection, and the third movement of social sharing with others, although we may experience an urge, we can say: "Do I really want to do this? Or would it be better to do something different?"

Joseph Campos et al. (2011) propose that we should regard emotions not in terms of the individual mind, but in terms of our relationships. They point out that, with an interpersonal view of emotions, the issue in regulation is not to adjust the personal pleasantness of emotions but to balance our interpersonal concerns. As they put it:

> . . . emotion regulation is typically the process of negotiating or coordinating the various goals and strivings of an individual who is in a relational encounter with another individual or groups of individuals with sometimes similar but quite often different strivings to that of the individual. (p. 27)

The relevance of this idea is reinforced by the examples discussed by Frijda (2010, 2011) of people in genocidal wars who, although they feared their own deaths, sheltered others from different social groups than themselves.

In this chapter, we have started to think about the idea of regulation as the attempt to avoid the unpleasantness of certain emotions and to enhance our pleasant experience. With the above discussion we can move to a more sophisticated concept. Tamir, Mitchell, and Gross (2008) proposed that regulation of an emotion can either be about pleasantness, or that it can be about concerns (goals). In an experiment they compared these two. They found that when people anticipated acting in pursuit of a confrontational goal, but not a non-confrontational one, they preferred activities that would increase their level of anger, although it was unpleasant. They also found that anger improved people's performance in a confrontational task, though not in a non-confrontational one. Gross, Sheppes, and Urry (2011) therefore define emotion regulation as "the activation of a goal to modify the emotion-generative process" (p. 767), that is to influence what emotions are started up and how they are directed.

Regulation of emotions is often a by-product of conducting our relationships. Emotions function to give priority to some concerns rather than others. As Mesquita and Frijda (2011) have pointed out: unlike in the laboratory, most real-life emotions are mixed, so we can usually decide what aspect to attend to. Their example is that, if at our birthday party friends sing "Happy Birthday," we might be embarrassed but, rather than running from the room, we stay with our friends because we are fond of them, and we smile. In the same way, if we are upset, but decide it's important to devote our attention to the concerns of a friend rather than to sink into gloom, we do so. We may thereby feel less upset in ourselves. If we are enjoying a success but don't want to make another person envious, we can give priority to the relational concern and avoid anything that may seem like boasting. If we feel afraid of someone in authority, we focus on implications of this relationship and act judiciously. If a friend has hurt us so that we are angry, we might move to forgive that person and thereby give priority to maintaining the relationship rather than to the blame we are tempted to express.

Psychological Therapies

Psychotherapy is a practice in which a therapist listens to a patient (or client) and makes occasional remarks. Whereas regulation is about management of particular episodes of emotion, therapy extends the idea: how one might manage one's personality to deal with emotional life generally.

It's useful to begin thinking about psychotherapy with Sigmund Freud's first form of therapy, which focused on emotionally traumatic events in a patient's earlier life. We briefly presented the idea of it in Chapter 1: Freud's case of Katharina (reported in Freud & Breuer, 1895). This therapy was aimed at having the patient recall the trauma, in this case of sexual abuse, enabling its details to become conscious, and allowing the emotions associated with it to be experienced and expressed. The idea of this was to free the patient from the trauma's continuing harmful effects.

Not long after he had published his first papers on this method, however, Freud came to believe he had been mistaken in thinking that emotional disorders were typically caused by childhood sexual abuse. The center of his new idea, the basis of psychoanalysis since then, was that people can suffer from **inner conflict**, for instance, feeling sexually attracted to someone in a way they are not quite aware of and at the same time inhibited by the prohibitions of society.

Photo Credit: Van Bucher/Science Photo Library/Photo Researchers, Inc.

FIGURE 14.4 Almost all forms of psychological therapy involve a therapist listening and coming to understand a client who talks about his or her emotional life.

Almost from its beginning, psychoanalysis attracted both adherents and detractors. Detractors argued that psychoanalysis was less a therapeutic procedure, more a matter for the police! The debate continues: psychoanalytic therapy continues to flourish and has become part of Western culture. Among attacks have been those of Grünbaum (1986) and Crews (1994). Other lines of attack on Freud's form of psychotherapy have come from cases in which people report having recovered memories of childhood sexual-emotional traumas and abuse (see Ochsner & Schachter, 2003) that, although they may have been repressed, may have been suggested to them by therapists.

Most enduringly, however, it was Freud who established the idea of therapy as including listening carefully, with respect, and with what he called "evenly hovering attention," to patients who suffered from emotional disorders. In Western psychiatric practice, all psychological therapies with individuals owe something to this practice of active listening.

Focus on Emotions

Many clinical psychologists and psychiatrists describe themselves as eclectic, which means they incorporate aspects from different kinds of therapy into their practice (Kring, Johnson, Davison, & Neale, 2012; Lambert, 2004). Most therapies involve a relationship with a therapist, conversation, and suggestion. Nearly all involve emotions in a more-or-less explicit way (Greenberg & Safran, 1989). Therapy, then, is an interaction with another person in which, as patient or client, a person can discover some of the properties of his or her emotion schemas—most typically schemas that can lead to anxiety, anger, or despair—and can to some extent change how these schemas operate. Therapy provides the context of a relationship in which these schemas may be better understood, and taken responsibility for, so that aspects of behavior and feeling might be modified.

The medical approach to emotional disorders is that of trying to relieve the suffering and anguish of emotional symptoms with prescription drugs. **Antidepressant** and **tranquilizer** medications, which we discussed in Chapters 6 and 13, are aimed, respectively, at decreasing the intensity of depression and anxiety states. Drugs are the treatments of choice for many psychiatrists because they are relatively cheap, convenient for the clinician, and frequently, also, preferred by patients.

Psychological therapies try to enable the client to exert some free will in the domain of the emotions. First we introduce four basic forms. Then we'll review evidence for their efficacy.

Psychoanalysis: Unconscious Schemas of Relating

The distinctive feature of psychoanalytic therapy is the recognition and interpretation of **transference**. The idea of transference was discussed by Freud (1905) in the case of Ida Bauer, to whom Freud gave the name, "Dora." She came every day except Sunday to see him at his consulting rooms at Berggasse 19, in Vienna (Bernheimer & Kahane, 1985). In his case history of Dora, Freud explained his new method: the patient was to lie on a couch, narrate the story of her life, and say whatever else came spontaneously to mind. Freud suggested interpretations to fill gaps in her story. One of the gaps Dora left was that, as she denounced her father for having an affair with another woman, Frau K., she omitted to say that, partly facilitated by her father's affair, she herself enjoyed the courtly attentions of Herr K., the woman's husband.

Transference is the manifestation of emotion schemas, mental models that embody ways of relating to others that have become habitual. It is perhaps best thought of as a set of emotional attitudes toward significant others from the past. Such attitudes and emotions are projected onto people in the present, including the therapist. "What are transferences?" asked Freud (1905). "They are new editions or facsimiles of the impulses and phantasies which . . . replace some earlier person [such as a parent] by the person of the physician" (p. 157). Thus Dora, in Freud's case, said her father "always preferred secrecy and roundabout ways." Her relationship with him was one of distrust. For instance, when he started his affair with Frau K., he diverted Dora's attention from it by arranging for Herr K. to pay courtly attention to her. In her analysis, Dora's transference included treating Freud as she had treated her father: with distrust. She took this to the point of dumping Freud by leaving therapy after three months, just as she had emotionally detached herself from her father.

Significant Figure: Sigmund Freud

Sigmund Freud was born in 1856 of an impecunious wool merchant and his wife. From the age of four until a year before he died, he lived in Vienna. Soon after qualifying as a doctor in 1881, he met Martha Bernays, fell deeply in love, and began a chaste four-year engagement, the frustrations of which may have contributed to his theories of sexuality. After various more-or-less unsuccessful attempts to make his way in biology and neurology, Freud started treating patients by hypnosis, at which he said he was not very good. Then he began the treatment that has become famous as psychoanalysis, listening to the stories people tell about their lives in order to discover inner conflicts, which, as they become conscious, can be resolved.

In 1902, Freud was promoted to professor extraordinarius (equivalent to associate professor) at the University in Vienna. Although he was always touchy about the recognition he felt he deserved, in retrospect one can see that from this time his fortunes improved, and his influence spread until, in his own lifetime, he became the world's most famous psychologist.

In 1938, Freud and his family fled from the Nazis to England. His last year, before he died of cancer in September 1939, was spent in London. Freud's work was not only foundational to psychology and psychiatry, but important in art and literature. He affected the very texture of 20th-century thinking: ideas such as the unconscious, anxiety, neurosis, and psychotherapy would not have the meanings they have today without Freud. (Biographical information: Gay, 1988; Sulloway, 1979.)

Psychoanalytic therapy is designed to recognize transferences and to bring them to the patient's consciousness. Transference occurs in many kinds of relationship (Miranda & Andersen, 2010). It occurs in almost every consultation with a physician, as we find ourselves hoping he or she will make everything better, as once a caregiver could. It occurs, as even therapists who are not analysts admit, in every kind of psychological therapy. It occurs in relationships of students with teachers. It occurs in encounters with people who have power or influence, so-called authority figures. It occurs in romantic relationships, in which we may be needy, or demanding, or irritable, or unavailable, or controlling as we once were with our parents. These transferential styles have been demonstrated by the attachment styles of infancy carrying forward into adulthood (Waters et al., 2000), as we discussed in Chapter 11.

The idea of psychoanalytic therapy is that our relationships are so fundamental to our emotional health that, if they are based on figures from the past rather than on real people in the present, there will be at best misunderstandings and at worst intractable problems. Emotion schemas that are problematic are often based on intense wishes bound tightly to beliefs that people hold about what is wrong with them, or how they can never be satisfied (Dahl, 1991). So, a woman might have an emotion schema derived from childhood in which she knows that only bad things can ever happen if she is angry. She tries more-or-less unsuccessfully to suppress her anger, perhaps restricting her life so that occasions for anger occur infrequently, but then finds her life narrow and unsatisfying. Or, from experiences with his parents, a man may feel it's too dangerous to have any strong emotion because of the likelihood of losing control; so, his personality becomes rigid like a stone. Yet another person may long for intimacy but be terrified of being taken over by the other.

The idea of psychoanalysis as the interpretation of transference is that effects of the emotion-relational schema are brought directly into the therapeutic relationship. As Strachey (1934) has written, from the viewpoint of the therapist:

> Instead of having to deal as best we may with conflicts of the remote past, which are concerned with dead circumstances and mummified personalities, and whose outcome is already determined, we find ourselves involved in an actual and immediate situation in which we and the patient are the principal characters. (p. xx)

Then, as Strachey continues, there is the possibility that, when the partly unconscious terms of the schema in which the client is lodged become conscious, the client can choose a new solution in the relationship with the therapist, and this kind of new solution can generalize to other relationships outside therapy.

An innovative form of psychodynamic therapy has been pioneered by Fonagy and Luyten (2009). It is called *mentalizing therapy* and it has been particularly important for people with borderline personality disorders, who have difficulties in regulating their emotions and are often self-mutilating and suicidal. It's based on attachment, which for these people has not been strong, so that they have grown up with a very meager sense of others and of themselves. It has the aim of enabling such people to develop empathy and theory-of-mind.

Among empirical studies of transference in therapy are those of Luborsky and Crits-Christoph (1990), who devised a method to recognize Core Conflictual Relationship Themes in transference. Using this method, Henry et al. (1994) found that when therapists recognize and interpret occurrences of these themes, the patient makes better progress in therapy. In an fMRI study, Loughead et al. (2010) found that autobiographical narratives preferentially activate areas of the brain concerned with theory-of-mind, self-referential processing, and emotion, and that the higher the content of Core Conflictual Relationship Themes in these autobiographical narratives the stronger was the activation of areas concerned with memory.

Rogerian Counseling: Empathetic Support

The father of counseling therapy was Carl Rogers (1951). Starting in the late 1930s, Rogers formulated the principles of what at first he called *nondirective therapy*. The aim is for the client to experience a relationship with the therapist that is genuine and non-judgmental. The aim for the therapist is to enter into the relationship, be emotionally warm, and listen to the client with empathy. In the absence of threat, and in the presence of this kind of therapist, a client can experience incongruencies in the self and start to change.

Rogers's revised name for his form of therapy was "person-centered." He believed that only the person him- or herself could initiate change in response to experienced incongruencies. It wasn't a matter of a therapist offering interpretations (as in psychoanalysis), or of any kind of teaching or coaching (as in the behaviorally based therapies). Although it arose separately, Rogers's form of humanistic therapy is related to the tradition of existentialist and phenomeno-logical therapies (Binswanger, 1963).

Rogers was among the first to take audio recorders into therapy sessions for research purposes.

Cognitive-Behavioral Therapy: Changing Emotional Life by Thought

The idea that we can change our emotions by thinking about them in the right way can be traced back to the ancient Epicureans and Stoics, introduced in Chapter 1; just as they took thought to avoid being influenced by desires that were worthless, so cognitive-behavioral therapy, founded by Beck (1976), works on thoughts in a comparable way. It is based on enabling people to recognize and avoid errors of evaluation of incidents that lead to emotions. For instance, clients who suffer anxiety and depression are asked to keep an emotion diary. In it, when they experience a negative emotion, they are to write in their diary what incident preceded the upset, what emotions occurred, and what thoughts. Then they have to write some alternative thoughts, not necessarily what they believe, just something different. In this way clients can gain some distance on their emotions, see some of the repetitive causes, and understand some of the cycles of thoughts-causing-emotions that bring to mind thoughts that cause more of the same emotions (Teasdale, 1988). Writing, it turns out, has, in all cultures that have used it, become one of the main means for reflecting on and becoming conscious of the meanings of emotions.

In this therapy, Beck (e.g. Beck, 1976; Beck et al., 1979) found that patterns of appraisal that cause anxiety and depression tend to involve evaluations that are arbitrary, absolute, and personalizing: if clients can make evaluations of other kinds—attributions that are external rather than internal, local rather than global, impermanent rather than permanent—then different emotions can occur that will break vicious cycles. Cognitive-behavioral therapy then allows revision both of core beliefs and of plans, changing the answer to the question that Stein et al. (1994) propose as central to the evaluation of an emotion-prompting event: "What can I do about it?"

In an extension of cognitive-behavioral therapy, a number of practitioners and theorists have now added mindfulness meditation (Philippot & Segal, 2009). One combination of mindfulness and cognitive-behavioral therapy, called *dialectical-behavioral therapy*, has been used with patients who are suicidal and/or self-injuring (Linehan, Comtois, Murray et al., 2006). One of the properties of mindfulness meditation is that it enables people to learn how to disconnect emotions from urges to act.

Emotion-Focused Therapy: Changing Emotional Life by Emotions

Why have emotions such a central role in therapy? Greenberg (1993) argues that making emotions explicit confers on emotion schemas a sense of clarity and possibility of control. Greenberg (2002) cites Spinoza (1661–1675) as saying that the only way to change an emotion is by means of another emotion, and this is the goal of emotion-focused therapy. In therapy, emotions can be explored. For instance, a person who in life and in therapy is angry, angry, angry may suddenly find her anger change to sadness as she realizes that she, too, has been partly responsible for some of what she is angry about.

In the course of life we take on many goals and many projects. Some, like attachment, are formed without words. Others formed later may have arisen more explicitly, but without us realizing how our goals may affect each other, so some of their implications may be unconscious. Emotions signal that some goal or concern is affected. If it is only partly known, an emotion may be our best clue to the importance of this concern. One of the tasks of emotion-focused therapy, then, is to work on such clues to build a consciously comprehended model of our goal structure as part of our sense of self.

Part of the task of therapy, and life, is to recognize emotions that we have not allowed ourselves to experience fully enough. Therapy, in this case, consists of encouraging a fuller experience of such emotions, which Greenberg (2002) calls primary emotions. So, clients may recognize that they are angry, although they had not allowed themselves to be so, or full of grief that they had not recognized. With recognition and expression, primary emotions and their origins become more comprehensible. They become, as philosophers say, more intentional, and the implications for relationships become clearer.

Focus on Emotion: Gratitude

The Ancient Greeks believed that reverence—the deep appreciation of all in life that is given to you—is essential to healthy individuals and societies, and as important as a sense of justice. Reverence is a form of consciousness, an awareness of the extraordinary things that are given to us—the chance to learn, enjoy good health, be surrounded by loved ones, travel the world, and give to society. One emotion intimately intertwined with reverence is gratitude. Robert Emmons, the world's leading researcher in this area, defines gratitude as a reverence for things that are given to you (Emmons, 2007). Throughout this book you have learned how we express gratitude through touch and how important it is to building strong connections.

Michael McCullough and Robert Emmons have found that a simple gratitude practice of taking a moment once a week to write down a few things you're grateful for leads to a 25% boost in well-being and physical health (McCullough et al., 2003). Based on these findings, several kinds of gratitude interventions or practices have been tested and are proving to yield important benefits. In his book, *Thanks*, Emmons reviews all the ways in which gratitude practices are becoming an important form of reflection, helping children socially and academically in schools, and helping boost the morale of workers in organizations, the satisfaction of couples in relationships, and individuals going through tough times (Emmons, 2007).

In addition, however, clients can experience some emotions too much. Greenberg calls these secondary emotions. They are what psychoanalysts call defenses. Secondary emotions derive from, or have emerged to cover up, certain primary emotions that were unacceptable. So, women who have been taught to be submissive may feel sad when really they are angry, but then their feeling of impotence makes them despairing and yet more sad. Men who have been brought up never to be afraid may have covered up their fear with anger, and their angry disposition has distanced them from others and become a cause of isolation. Often when primary emotions are not known or accepted they can metamorphose into secondary emotions rather easily (cf. Elster, 1999). Here the therapeutic task is not to encourage clients to experience secondary emotions—they do that too much already—but to understand that these emotions conceal something more authentic.

A third category is of instrumental emotions—the emotions that people have learned will help them get their way: the tears that elicit sympathy, the easy irritation that makes others hesitate to challenge or to be close.

Both the process and outcome of emotion-focused therapy have been objects of empirical research, and a recent review is Greenberg (2010).

Outcomes of Therapy

Does therapy work? We live in an era of evidence-based interventions and empirically supported psychotherapies (Hunsley & Lee, 2010). Health-care systems are unwilling to devote resources to treatments for which there is no evidence of effectiveness.

There have now been thousands of trials of different kinds of psychotherapy, assigning clients randomly to groups, or comparing outcomes for people who received one kind of therapy with those who received a different kind or with members of a control group. Among the best of such studies was that of Sloane et al. (1975). One of the first applications of the now-widespread statistical technique of meta-analysis was by Smith, Glass, and Miller (1980), who used it to estimate the effects of psychotherapy. Smith et al. found that in over 475 studies, the average effect size over a range of kinds of psychotherapy was 0.85 of a standard deviation. What this means is that the average person receiving therapy was better off than 80% of the members of control groups who did not receive therapy. In a review of meta-analyses of psychotherapeutic trials and of educational interventions, Lipsey and Wilson (1993) broadly confirmed these results. In comparison with educational interventions, a relatively modest amount of time in psychotherapy—typically of the order of a dozen sessions—has been found to be more effective than the majority of educational interventions designed, for instance, to produce more effective learning of mathematics. Ten years after this finding, Lambert and Ogles (2004) offered an extensive review of meta-analyses of different kinds of psychotherapy and came to similar conclusions. Outcome studies have been performed for many established psychological therapies, usually with positive results. Despite partisan commitments, therapists of different persuasions often produce effects of similar size.

Not all therapy is effective, however, and not all therapists are helpful. Though psychotherapy can be helpful, it can sometimes be harmful. Orlinsky and Howard (1980) reviewed case files of 143 women seen by 23 therapists. Six therapists were good: overall, 84% of the clients they saw were improved at the end of therapy and none were worse. Five therapists were not good: for these, less than 50% of their clients were improved and 10% were worse. A review of the outcome literature by Westen, Novotny, and Thompson-Bremner (2004), moreover, concluded that even with empirically supported therapies, many patients do not get better and many more do not maintain the gains they make.

An important area of research is on whether therapy can maintain well-being and increase resilience to the natural shocks that we humans are heir to. Fava and Tomba (2009) have shown that well-being therapy has been validated in randomized controlled trials, with outcomes of positive evaluations of oneself, a sense of continued growth and development, and the belief that life is purposeful and meaningful, especially in relations with others.

As to psychoanalysis: because it has been energetically attacked by certain critics, and because it takes a long time, there has been skepticism about its efficacy. Efficacy has, however, been found in a large study by Blomberg, Lazar, & Sandell (2001), in Stockholm, Sweden, with over 400 patients who received national insurance-funded psychodynamic treatment for up to three years: either full psychoanalysis, five times a week, or what is called psychoanalytic psychotherapy, once or twice a week. The authors argued that measuring outcomes as a function of the duration and frequency of treatment was equivalent to assigning people randomly to treatment groups (Sandell, Blomberg, & Lazar, 2002): the more psychodynamic treatment, the better the outcome. Follow-ups after three years of full psychoanalysis of 156 patients who were symptomatic when they started showed substantial improvement with treatment. They continued to improve after treatment to the point at which their mental health scores had become the same as those of a non-clinical sample.

In an extensive review of results of randomized controlled trials published between 1960 and 2008, Leichsenring and Rabung (2008) found that long-term psychodynamic psychotherapy had significantly better outcomes in overall effectiveness, target problems, and personality functioning than shorter forms of psychotherapy, so that patients with complex mental disorders were on average better off than 96% of the patients in comparison groups. A follow-up review by Leichsenring and Rabung (2011), which included newer studies, confirmed that longer term

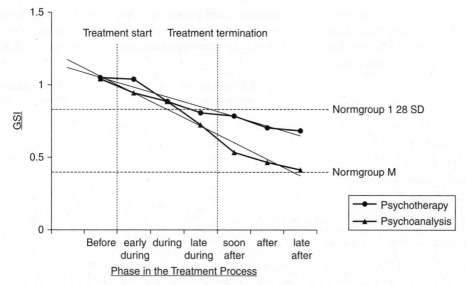

FIGURE 14.5 Global Symptom Index (GSI) over different phases of psychoanalytic therapy and psychoanalysis in the study by Blomberg, Lazar, and Sandell (2001), as compared with norm for the case level (upper dotted line) and a norm group who were without significant symptoms.

psychodynamic therapy was more effective than shorter therapies. A meta-analysis of random controlled trials by Smit et al. (2012) found that although long-term psychoanalytic therapy did better than control groups without any therapeutic input, it was no better than other kinds of psychological therapy.

As to cognitive-behavioral therapy: studies of the effectiveness of relatively short periods of this kind of therapy have been performed repeatedly and convincingly, especially for depression and anxiety. It tends, therefore, to be a preferred choice (Hollon & Beck, 2004). Gloaguen et al. (1998) found in a meta-analysis that in cases of depression it was more effective than antidepressant medication, and associated with a lower rate of relapse. Hollon and Ponniah (2010) found in a review of 125 published studies that cognitive-behavioral therapy, including variants that included mindfulness meditation, was effective for depression and other mood disorders. Stewart and Chambless (2009) found in a meta-analysis that for anxiety disorders cognitive-behavioral therapy was effective, not just in specially arranged trials but in clinical practice.

Emotion-focused therapy is newer than cognitive-behavioral therapy, so there is less research on it. It has, however, been found to produce gains of approximately the same size as those of cognitive-behavioral therapy (Elliott, Greenberg, & Lietaer, 2004).

Client-centered therapy (counseling) on its own has been found to be not as effective as cognitive-behavioral therapy (Watson, Gordon, Stermac et al., 2003). Nor was it as effective as emotion-focused therapy (Goldman, Greenberg, & Angus, 2006; see Table 14.1).

In a study of 291 psychiatric in-patients, Watzke et al. (2010) compared the results of random assignment to psychodynamic or cognitive-behavioral therapy with selection of patients as especially suitable for one or the other kind of therapy. For cognitive-behavioral therapy, selection showed no advantage over random assignment. For psychodynamic therapy there was an advantage: selection of patients for this form of therapy improved the treatment effect.

Table 14.1   **Pre-treatment and post-treatment means on two symptom measures for clients receiving client-centered therapy or emotion-focused therapy; post-treatment differences between the two treatments was significant at $p < .05$ for both symptom measures**

	Client-centered therapy ($n = 36$)	Emotion-focused therapy ($n = 36$)
Beck Depression Inventory		
Pre-treatment	24.6	26.1
Post-treatment	9.5	6.2
Global Symptom Index		
Pre-treatment	1.4	1.5
Post-treatment	0.7	0.5

Source: Goldman, Greenberg, & Angus (2006).

Kallestad et al. (2010) conducted a randomized controlled trial in which cognitive therapy was compared with psychodynamic therapy in 49 patients with personality disorders of the anxious or fearful type. Among those in psychodynamic therapy, insight was found to increase and to predict improvement of symptoms and of interpersonal functioning during a two-year follow-up period. Among patients assigned to cognitive therapy, measures of insight did not improve substantially during therapy and insight did not predict improvement.

Therapy does seem to require a supportive relationship with the therapist (of the kind emphasized by counseling therapies), but such a relationship alone has not been found especially effective for improvement.

Although short-term therapies, perhaps especially cognitive-behavioral therapy, have been found useful in improving symptoms, the kinds of therapies that enable people to gain insight into their emotional life—to come consciously to understand something of the functioning of their own emotion schemas—do better over the long term than those that merely improve symptoms over the short term.

Psychotherapy Without Professionals

A serious problem for therapy is its availability. Look at the prevalence of psychiatric disorder in the United States, described by Kessler et al. (2005a, 2005b) and discussed in Chapter 13. Consider the most common disorders, depression and anxiety. Now do some arithmetic: multiply the prevalence rates by the population of the United States, about 312 million in 2011, more than half of whom are between 15 and 54, the age-band of these prevalence figures. You will conclude that each year several tens of millions of Americans suffer from clinically significant depression or anxiety or both. Even in such a highly resourced society there are just not enough mental health professionals to go round. Kessler et al. indeed found that in any year in which people suffered a disorder, only about one fifth of them consulted a professional, and for only about half of those was this a mental health professional. Psychoanalysis, four or five times a week for several years, is obviously available only to the few. Even short treatments, such as 8 to 12 sessions of cognitive-behavioral therapy, are not available to all.

What is the answer? One is that alongside ideas of individual therapy developed by psychologists and psychiatrists there is another kind of therapy that involves people meeting in groups. Its founders included Jane Addams, who opened a house for group social work in 1889 and was later awarded a Nobel Prize. Not many years later, Joseph Pratt discovered that tuberculosis patients, whom he arranged to meet together in groups of 20 or so, formed supportive social structures among themselves that had important therapeutic effects on the course of illness. In terms of outcomes, group therapy, like individual therapy, has generally been found effective (Lambert & Ogles, 2004; Tillitski, 1990). Many self-help organizations such as Alcoholics Anonymous base their practices on group processes arranged around emotionally salient issues.

Still, there is not enough to go round. It is therefore not surprising that when people are surveyed about those to whom they turn in times of emotional crisis, they name a wide variety of persons, including priests, rabbis, doctors—but principally friends. Recall from Chapter 13 that one factor most widely found to be protective against emotional disorder is relationships with other people—close relationships with relatives and friends, known as social support.

In Chapter 7, we introduced the finding by Rimé et al. (1998) that most emotions are socially shared. At the beginning of this research, Rimé et al. thought that such sharing had a regulatory function so that the intensity of emotions that were shared would diminish as compared with those that were unshared, but no such difference was found. When an injustice has been experienced, talking about it does not diminish the anger one feels! People do want to share their emotions and, when asked, say they benefit from doing so. We suggest the benefit comes from being able in conversation to make meaningful sense of their emotions. This sense includes the implications of the emotions for the speaker and others, as seen both from the inside and from the outside in terms of implications of the commentary of the friend or relative. It seems likely that this is an important aspect of social support.

Cultivation and Reflection: Meditation

For thousands of years the great spiritual and ethical traditions of different cultures have been refining one approach for individuals to handle the complex emotions of social living: meditation. Today scientific studies are underway to look at whether meditation can serve as a means by which people can overcome clinical levels of anxiety and depression, and the results are encouraging. Across the different kinds of contemplation and meditation, there are core practices, all of which are undertaken in a quiet place where one can be in a comfortable posture (e.g., sitting on a chair or on the ground).

One practice that we talked about in Chapter 5 is mindfully to slow down your breathing to a healthy, steady rhythm with deep exhalations, which reduces stress-related cardiovascular arousal. A second one is to take brief moments to mindfully attend to sensations in the body. For example, an anxious child might be taught to tighten specific muscles and then relax them, to be aware of the sensations of tension and relaxation. Or someone might be encouraged to do a body scan, moving one's attention over different parts of the body, beginning, for example, in the toes and moving progressively up to the facial muscles and crown of the head. And finally, most meditation practices—for example, those popularized by the Dalai Lama in Tibetan Buddhism—encourage training the mind in lovingkindness or compassion. Here the meditator extends feelings of compassion to family members, friends, loved ones, strangers, the self, and ultimately adversaries to encourage a more compassionate stance toward fellow human beings.

Does meditation work? A wave of studies in the past 10 years suggests it does. One of the best-known is by Richard Davidson and Jon Kabat Zinn and their colleagues, who had software engineers train in the techniques of mindfulness meditation—an accepting awareness of the mind, lovingkindness toward others. Six weeks later, these individuals showed increased activation in the left frontal lobes, a region of the cortex associated with increased positive emotion and reduced anxiety and depression (see Chapter 6). They also showed enhanced immune function as evident in the magnitude of the immune response in the skin to a flu shot (Davidson et al., 2003). In similarly motivated work, Barbara Fredrickson and her colleagues have found that practicing mindfulness meditation, with a focus on being mindful of breathing and extending lovingkindness to others, boosts happiness several weeks later (Fredrickson, Cohn, Coffey, Pek, & Finkel, 2008).

Among the aims of psychiatric health care, then, should be that of enabling civil society to evolve so that fewer people become socially marginalized. At the same time, where practices have been discovered by mental health professionals that have been helpful in therapy for emotional suffering, arguably, rather than distributing these services for fees, the job of mental health professionals might better be seen as giving them away, diffusing them into the community.

This brings us to the close of our book. If emotions are the joints and sinews of our relationships, the deepest clues to our identity, and signals of how things are going between one person and another, they are the means by which we articulate our lives with each other.

SUMMARY

Emotions usually prompt us to become conscious of someone or something, to become aware of a feeling about what has happened. Consciousness enables us to make sense of our emotions, and often to bring them into register with other people. Conscious understanding of our emotions involves becoming more knowledgeable about the narratives that we and others tell about the self and its doings. Regulation is the process by which we modulate the intensity of emotions; some ways of doing this are more effective than others. Regulation presupposes that we can exert willpower over our emotions, and we discuss the extent to which free will is available to us. Psychological therapies have existed in the religious practices and rituals of many societies. In general they aim to reintegrate people whose relations with their community have become strained. In the 20th century many forms of psychotherapy were developed and most have an emotional base: the principal forms are psychoanalytic therapy, cognitive-behavioral therapy, and emotion-focused therapy. Benefits of many, though not all, forms of psychological therapy have been found empirically; however, not every therapist is helpful with every client.

TO THINK ABOUT AND DISCUSS

1. How far do psychological studies of consciousness correspond to your own conscious experience? What conclusions might you draw from correspondences and discrepancies?

2. What is your view of free will? Imagine yourself as one of the participants in Zimbardo's Stanford Prison Experiment. First imagine yourself to be a prisoner; next imagine yourself to be a guard. How would you have responded in each role?

3. If you were to enter therapy, what kind would you prefer, and why?

FURTHER READING

On emotions, consciousness, and the arts:

Keith Oatley (2003). Creative expression and communication of emotion in the visual and narrative arts. In R. J. Davidson, K. R. Scherer, & H. H. Goldsmith (Eds.), *Handbook of affective sciences* (pp. 481–502). New York, NY: Oxford University Press.

On emotions and free will:

Nico Frijda (2009). Not passion's slave. *Emotion Review*, **2**, 68–75.

A very useful discussion of emotional regulation and how to think about it:

James Gross & Ross Thompson (2007). Emotion regulation: Conceptual foundations. In J. Gross (Ed.), *Handbook of emotion regulation* (pp. 3–24). New York, NY: Guilford.

A handbook that shows how different approaches to psychotherapy have been integrated and empirically studied:

John Norcross & Marvin Goldfried (Eds.) (2005). *Handbook of psychotherapy integration, second edition*. New York, NY: Oxford University Press.

REFERENCES

References are for the most part cited in the format recommended by the American Psychological Association, except that for older books we cite the date of the original publication in the text, and in this reference list we generally give the date of a publication available in libraries and/or bookshops as (current edition 19xx) at the end of the reference.

Abbott, R. A., Croudace, T. J., Ploubidis, G. B., Kuh, D., Richards, M., & Huppert, F. A. (2008). The relationship between early personality and midlife psychological well-being: Evidence from a UK birth cohort study. *Social Psychiatry and Psychiatric Epidemiology, 43,* 679–687.

Abela, J.R.Z., McGirr, A., & Skitch, S. A. (2007). Depressogenic inferential styles, negative events and depressive symptoms in youth: An attempt to reconcile past inconsistent findings. *Behaviour Research and Therapy, 45,* 2397–2406.

Abramson, L. Y., Metalsky, G. I., & Alloy, L. B. (1989). Hopelessness depression: A theory-based subtype of depression. *Psychological Review, 96,* 358–372.

Abramson, L. Y., Seligman, M. E. P., & Teasdale, J. D. (1978). Learned helplessness in humans: Critique and reformulation. *Journal of Abnormal Psychology, 87,* 49–74.

Abu-Lughod, L. (1986). *Veiled sentiments.* Berkeley: University of California Press.

Abu-Lughod, L., & Lutz, C. A. (1990). *Introduction to language and the politics of emotion.* New York, NY: Cambridge University Press.

Acevedo, B. P., & Aron, A. (2009). Does a long-term relationship kill romantic love? *Review of General Psychology, 13,* 59–65.

Achenbach, T. M. (2009a). Some changes needed in the *DSM-V*: But what about children? *Clinical Psychology: Science and Practice, 16*(1), 50–53.

Achenbach, T. M. (2009b). *The Achenbach System of Empirically Based Assessment (ASEBA): Development, findings, theory, and applications.* Burlington: University of Vermont Research Center for Children, Youth and Families.

Achenbach, T. M., & Rescorla, L. A. (2000). *Manual for the ASEBA preschool forms & profiles.* Burlington: University of Vermont, Research Center for Children, Youth, & Families.

Achenbach, T. M., & Rescorla, L. A. (2001). *Manual for the ASEBA school-age forms & profiles.* Burlington: University of Vermont, Research Center for Children, Youth, & Families.

Adam, E. K., & Gunnar, M. R. (2001). Relationship functioning and home and work demands predict individual differences in diurnal cortisol patterns in women. *Psychoneuroendocrinology, 26*(2), 189–208.

Adler, N. E., Boyce, T., Chesney, M. A., Cohen, S., Folkman, S., & Kahn, R. L. (1994). Socioeconomic status and health: The challenge of the gradient. *American Psychologist, 49,* 15–24.

Adolphs, R. (2002). Neural systems for recognizing emotion. *Current Opinion in Neurobiology, 12*(2), 169–177.

Aggleton, J. P. (Ed.). (2000). *The amygdala* (2nd ed.). Oxford, UK: Oxford University Press.

Agmo, A., Barreau, S., & Lemaire, V. (1997). Social motivation in recently weaned rats is modified by opiates. *Developmental Neuroscience, 19,* 505–520.

Aharon, I., Etcoff, N., Ariety, D., Chabris, C., O'Connor, E., & Breiter, H. (2001). Beautiful faces have variable reward value: fMRI and behavioral evidence. *Neuron, 32,* 537–551.

Ainsworth, M. D. S., & Bells, S. M. (1970). Attachment, exploration, and separations: Illustrated by the behavior of one-year-olds in a stranger situation. *Child Development, 41*, 49–67.

Aksan, N., & Kochanska, G. (2005). Conscience in childhood: Old questions, new answers. *Developmental Psychology, 41*(3), 506–516.

Algoe, S. B., Haidt, J., & Gable, S. L. (2008). Beyond reciprocity: Gratitude and relationships in everyday life. *Emotion, 8*, 425–429.

Ali, A., Oatley, K., & Toner, B. (2002). Life stress, self-silencing, and domains of meaning in unipolar depression: An investigation of an outpatient sample of women. *Journal of Social and Clinical Psychology, 21*, 669–685.

Allen, J., McElhaney, K. B., Land, D., et al. (2003). A secure base in adolescence: Markers of attachment security in the mother–adolescent relationship. *Child Development, 74*, 282–307.

Alloy, L., Abramson, L. Y., Hogan, M. E., et al. (2000). The Temple-Wisconsin cognitive vulnerability to depression (CVD) project: Lifetime history of Axis-I psychopathology in individuals at high and low cognitive risk for depression. *Journal of Abnormal Psychology, 109*, 403–418.

Alloy, L., Abramson, L. Y., Murray, L. A., Whitehouse, W. G., & Hogan, M. E. (1997). Self-referent information processing in individuals at high and low cognitive risk for depression. *Cognition and Emotion, 11*, 539–568.

Ambadar, Z., Schooler, J., & Cohn, J. F. (2005). Deciphering the ambiguous face. *Psychological Science, 16*, 403–410.

American Psychiatric Association (2000). *Diagnostic and statistical manual of mental disorders* (4th ed., Text revision, *DSM-IV-TR*). Washington, DC: American Psychiatric Association.

Andalmann, P. K., & Zajonc, R. B. (1989). Facial efference and the experience of emotion. *Annual Review of Psychology, 40*, 249–280.

Anderson, A. K., & Phelps, E. A. (2000). Expression without recognition: Contributions of the human amygdala to emotional communication. *Psychological Science, 11*, 106–111.

Anderson, A. K., & Phelps, E. A. (2002). Is the human amygdala critical for the subjective experience of emotion?: Evidence of intact dispositional affect in patients with amygdala lesions. *Journal of Cognitive Neuroscience, 14*, 709–720.

Anderson, C., Keltner, D., & John, O. P. (2003). Emotional convergence between people over time. *Journal of Personality and Social Psychology, 84*, 1054–1068.

Anderson, E., Siegel, E., Bliss-Moreau, E., & Barrett, L. F. (2011). The visual impact of gossip. *Science, 332*, 1446–1448.

Anderson, S. M., & Chen, S. (2002). The relational self. *Psychological Review, 109*, 619–645.

Andersen, S. M., & Saribay, S. A. (2005). The relational self and transference: Evoking motives, self-regulation, and emotions through activation of mental representations of significant others. In M. W. Baldwin (Ed.), *Interpersonal cognition* (pp. 1–32). New York, NY: Guilford.

Andrew, R. J. (1963). The origin and evolution of the calls and facial expressions of the primates. *Behavior, 20*, 1–109.

Andrew, R. J. (1965, October). The origin of facial expressions. *Scientific American, 213*, 88–94.

Aneshensel, C. S., Fielder, E. P., & Becerra, R. M. (1989). Fertility and fertility-related behavior among Mexican-American and non-Hispanic white female adolescents. *Journal of Health and Social Behavior, 30*, 56–76.

Aneshensel, C. S., & Sucoff, C. A. (1996). The neighborhood context of adolescent mental health. *Journal of Health and Social Behavior, 37* (4), 293–310.

Angell, M. (2008). Industry-sponsored clinical research: A broken system. *Journal of the American Medical Association, 300*, 1069–1071.

Anisfeld, E., Casper, V., Nozyce, M., & Cunningham, N. (1990). Does infant carrying promote attachment? An experimental study of the increased physical contact on the development of attachment. *Child Development, 61*, 1617–1627.

Ardrey, R. (1966). *The territorial imperative*. New York, NY: Dell.

Aristotle (1984). *Complete works. Revised Oxford translation in 2 volumes* (J. Barnes, Ed.) Princeton, NJ: Princeton University Press.

Armstrong, K. (2001). *Buddha*. London, UK: Penguin.

Armstrong, K. (2006). *The great transformation: The beginning of our religious traditions*. New York, NY: Knopf.

Arnold, M. B., & Gasson, J. A. (1954). Feelings and emotions as dynamic factors in personality integration. In M. B.

Arnold & S. J. Gasson (Eds.), *The human person* (pp. 294–313). New York, NY: Ronald.

Aron, A., & Aron, E. N. (1997). Self-expansion motivation and including the other in self. In S. Duck (Ed.), *Handbook of personal relationships: Theory, research, and interventions* (2nd ed., pp. 251–270). Chichester, UK: Wiley.

Aron, A., & Aron, E. N. (1998). Love and sexuality. In K. S. McKinney (Ed.), *Sexuality and close relationships* (pp. 25–48). Hillsdale, NJ: Lawrence Erlbaum.

Aron, A., Aron, E. N., & Allen, J. (1989). *The motivation for unrequited love: A self-expansion perspective.* Paper presented at the International Conference on Personal Relationships, Iowa City, IA.

Aron, A., Aron, E. N., Tudor, M., & Nelson, G. (1991). Close relationships as including other in self. *Journal of Personality and Social Psychology, 60,* 241–253.

Aron, A., Fisher, H., Mashek, D., Strong, G., Li, H., & Brown, L. (2005). Reward, motivation and emotion systems associated with early-stage intense romantic love. *Journal of Neurophysiology, 93,* 327–337.

Aron, A., Norman, C. C., Aron, E. N., McKenna, C., & Heyman, R. E. (2000). Couples' shared participation in novel and arousing activities and experienced relationship quality. *Journal of Personality and Social Psychology, 78,* 273–284.

Arsenio, W. F., & Lemerise, E. A. (2004). Aggression and moral development: Integrating social information processing and moral domain models. *Child Development, 75,* 987–1002.

Asendorpf, J. B., Borkenau, P., Ostendorf, F., & Van Aken, M.A.G. (2001). Carving personality description at its joints: Confirmation of three replicable personality prototypes for both children and adults. *European Journal of Personality, 15*(3), 169–198.

Asendorpf, J. B., Denissen, J.J.A., & van Aken, M. (2008). Inhibited and aggressive preschool children at 23 years of age: Personality and social transitions into adulthood. *Developmental Psychology, 44,* 997–1011.

Atkinson, L., Goldberg, S., Raval, V., et al. (2005). On the relation between maternal state of mind and sensitivity in the prediction of infant attachment security. *Developmental Psychology, 41,* 42–53.

Atkinson, L., Niccols, A., Paglia, A., Coolbear, J., Parker, K.C.H., Guger, S., Poulton, L., Guger, S., & Sitarenios, G. (2000). A meta-analysis of time between maternal sensitivity and attachment assessments: Implications for internal working models in infancy/toddlerhood. *Journal of Social and Personal Relationships, 17*(6), 791–810.

Atkinson, R. L., Atkinson, R. C., Smith, E. E., & Bem, D. M. (1989). *Introduction to psychology* (10th ed.). Belmont, CA: Wadsworth.

Aubé, M., & Senteni, A. (1996). Emotions as commitments operators: A foundation for control structure in multi-agents systems. In W. V. de Velde & J. W. Perram (Eds.), *Agents breaking away: Proceedings of the 7th European Workshop on MAAMAW, Lecture notes on artificial intelligence, No. 1038* (pp. 13–25). Berlin, Germany: Springer.

Augustine (c. 400). *Confessions* (R. S. Pine-Coffin, Trans.). Harmondsworth, UK: Penguin (current edition 1960).

Aureli, F., Preston, S. D., & De Waal, F.B.M. (1999). Heart rate responses to social interactions in free-moving Rhesus Macaques (*Macaca mulatta*): A pilot study. *Journal of Comparative Psychology, 133,* 59–65.

Aurelius, M. (c. 170). *Meditations* (M. Staniforth, Trans.). London, UK: Penguin (1964).

Averill, J. R. (1985). The social construction of emotion: With special reference to love. In K. J. Gergen & K. E. Davis (Eds.), *The social construction of the person* (pp. 89–109). New York, NY: Springer Verlag.

Averill, J. R. (1999). Creativity in the domain of emotion. In T. Dalgleish & M. Power (Eds.), *Handbook of cognition and emotion* (pp. 765–782). Chichester: Wiley.

Averill, J. R., & Nunley, E. P. (1992). *Voyages of the heart: Living an emotionally creative life.* New York, NY: Free Press.

Aviezer, H., Hassin, R. R., Ryan, J., Grady, C., Susskind, J., Anderson, A., et al. (2008). Angry, disgusted, or afraid? *Psychological Science, 19*(7), 724.

Axelrod, R. (1984). *The evolution of cooperation.* New York, NY: Basic Books.

Azmitia, M., & Hesser, J. (1993). Why siblings are important agents of cognitive-development: A comparison of siblings and peers. *Child Development, 64*(2), 430–444.

Baars, B. J. (2010). Spontaneous repetitive thoughts can be adaptive: Postscript on "mind wandering." *Psychological Bulletin, 136*(2), 208–210.

Bachorowski, J. A. (1999). Vocal expression and perception of emotion. *Current Directions in Psychological Science, 8,* 53–57.

Bachorowski, J. A., & Owren, M. J. (2001). Not all laughs are alike: Voiced but not voiced laughter readily elicits positive affect. *Psychological Science, 12,* 252–257.

Bachorowski, J. A., Smoski, M. J., & Owren, M. J. (2001). The acoustic features of human laughter. *Journal of Acoustic Society of America, 110,* 1581–1597.

Backs-Dermott, B. J., Dobson, K. S., & Jones, S. (2010). An evaluation of an integrated model of relapse in depression. *Journal of Affective Disorders, 124,* 60–67.

Badanes, L. S., Watamura, S. E., & Hankin, B. L. (2011). Hypocortisolism as a potential marker of allostatic load in children: Associations with family risk and internalizing disorders. *Development and Psychopathology, 23,* 881–896.

Bagot R. C., & Meaney M. (2010). Epigenetics and the biological basis of gene *x* environment interactions. *Journal of the American Academy of Child and Adolescent Psychiatry, 49*(8), 752–771.

Bakermans-Kranenburg, M. J., & van Ijzendoorn, M. H. (2011). Differential susceptibility to rearing environment depending on dopamine-related genes: New evidence and a meta-analysis. *Development and Psychopathology, 23,* 39–52.

Bakhtin, M. (1963). *Problems of Dostoevsky's poetics* (C. Emerson, Trans.) Minneapolis, MN: University of Minneapolis Press (current edition 1984).

Banerjee, R., Watling, D., & Caputi, M. (2011). Peer relations and the understanding of faux pas: Longitudinal evidence for bidirectional associations. *Child Development, 82*(6), 1887–1905.

Banse, R., & Scherer, K. (1996). Acoustic profiles in vocal emotion expression. *Journal of Personality and Social Psychology, 70,* 614–636.

Barbato, A., & D'Avanzo, B. (2000). Family interventions in schizophrenia and related disorders: A critical review. *Acta Psychiatrica Scandinavica, 102,* 81–97.

Bard, P. (1928). A diencephalic mechanism for the expression of rage with special reference to the sympathetic nervous system. *American Journal of Physiology, 84,* 490–513.

Bard, P., & Rioch, D. M. (1937). A study of four cats deprived of neocortex and additional portions of the forebrain. *Johns Hopkins Medical Journal, 60,* 73–153.

Bar-Haim, Y., Lamy, D., Pergamin, L., Bakermans-Kranenburg, M., & van IJzendoorn, M. H. (2007). Threat-related attentional bias in anxious and nonanxious individuals: A meta-analytic study. *Psychological Bulletin, 133*(1), 1–24.

Barnett, D., Manly J. T., & Cicchetti, D. (1993). Defining child maltreatment: The interface between policy and research. In D. Cicchetti & S. L. Toth (Eds.), *Child abuse, child development, and social policy* (pp. 7–73). Norwood, NJ: Ablex.

Baron, R. A. (1987). Interviewer's mood and reaction to job applicants. *Journal of Applied Social Psychology, 17,* 911–926.

Baron-Cohen, S. (2011). *The science of evil: On empathy and the origins of cruelty.* New York, NY: Basic Books.

Barrera, M. E., & Mauer, D. (1981). The perception of facial expressions by the three-month-old. *Child Development, 52* (2), 203–206.

Barrett, D. H., Resnick, H. S., Foy, D. W., Dansky, B. S., Flanders, W. D., & Stroup, N. E. (1996). Combat exposure and adult psychosocial adjustment among U.S. Army veterans serving in Vietnam, 1965–1971. *Journal of Abnormal Psychology, 105,* 575–581.

Barrett, L. F. (2006). Solving the emotion paradox: Categorization and the experience of emotion. *Personality and Social Psychology Review, 10,* 20–46.

Barrett, L. F., & Bliss-Moreau, E. (2009). Affect as a psychological primitive. *Advances in Experimental Social Psychology, 41,* 167–218.

Barrett, L. F., Lindquist, K. A., Bliss-Moreau, E., et al. (2007). Of mice and men: Natural kinds of emotions in the mammalian brain? A response to Panksepp and Izard. *Perspectives on Psychological Science, 2,* 297–311.

Barrett, L. F., Ochsner, K. N., & Gross, J. J. (2007). On the automaticity of emotion. In J. A. Bargh (Ed.), *Social psychology and the unconscious: The automaticity of higher mental processes* (pp. 173–217). New York, NY: Psychology Press.

Barry, R. A., & Kochanska, G. (2010). A longitudinal investigation of the affective environment in families with young children: From infancy to early school age. *Emotion, 10*(2), 237–249.

Barry, R. A., Kochanska, G., & Philibert, R. A. (2008). G × E interaction in the organization of attachment: Mothers' responsiveness as a moderator of children's genotypes. *Journal of Child Psychology and Psychiatry, 49*(12), 1313–1320.

Bartlett, F. C. (1932). *Remembering: A study in experimental and social psychology.* Cambridge, UK: Cambridge University Press.

Bartlett, M. Y., & DeSteno, D. (2006). Gratitude and prosocial behavior: Helping when it costs you. *Psychological Science, 17*, 319–325.

Bartz, J. A., Zaki, J., Bolger, N., & Ochsner, K. N. (2011). Social effects of oxytocin in humans: Context and person matter. *Trends in Cognitive Sciences, 15*, 301–309.

Bateman, A. (2004). Psychoanalysis and psychiatry: Is there a future? *Acta Psychiatrica Scandinavica, 109*, 161–163.

Bates, J. E., & Pettit, G. S. (2007). Temperament, parenting, and socialization. In J. Grusec & P. Hastings (Eds.), *Handbook of socialization* (pp. 153–177). New York, NY: Guilford.

Bateson, P. (1990). Obituary: Konrad Lorenz (1903–1989). *American Psychologist, 45*, 65–66.

Bateson, P.P.G. (1983). *Mate choice.* Cambridge, UK: Cambridge University Press.

Batson, C. D., & Shaw, L. L. (1991). Evidence for altruism: Toward a pluralism of prosocial motives. *Psychological Inquiry, 2*, 107–122.

Battaglia, M., Ogliari, A., Zanoni, A., Villa, F., Citterio, A., Binaghi, F., et al. (2004). Children's discrimination of expressions of emotions: Relationship with indices of social anxiety and shyness. *Journal of the American Academy of Child & Adolescent Psychiatry, 43*(3), 358–365.

Bauer, D. H. (1976). An exploratory study of developmental changes in children's fear. *Journal of Child Psychology and Psychiatry, 17*, 69–74.

Bauer, P. M., Hanson, J. L., Pierson, R. K., Davidson, R. J., & Pollak, S. D. (2009). Cerebellar volume and cognitive functioning in children who experienced early deprivation. *Biological Psychiatry, 66*, 1100–1106.

Baumann, J., & DeSteno, D. (2010). Emotion guided threat detection: Expecting guns where there are none. *Journal of Personality and Social Psychology, 99*(4), 595–610.

Baumeister, R., & Masicampo, E. J. (2010). Conscious thought is for facilitating social and cultural interactions: How mental simulations serve the animal-culture interface. *Psychological Review, 117*, 945–971.

Baumeister, R., Masicampo, E. J., & DeWall, C. N. (2009). Prosocial benefits of feeling free: Disbelief in free will increases aggression and reduces helpfulness. *Personality & Social Psychology Bulletin, 35*, 260–268.

Baumeister, R., Masicampo, E. J., & Vohs, K. (2011). Do conscious thoughts cause behavior? *Annual Review of Psychology, 62*, 331–361.

Baumeister, R. F., Bratslavsky, E., Finkenauer, C., & Vohs, K. D. (2001). Bad is stronger than good. *Review of General Psychology, 5*, 323–370.

Baumeister, R. F., Stillwell, A. M., & Heatherton, T. F. (1994). Guilt: An interpersonal approach. *Psychological Bulletin, 115*, 243–267.

Baxter, M. G., & Murray, E. A. (2002). The amygdala and reward. *Nature Reviews Neuroscience, 3*, 563–574.

Bazhenova, O. V., Plonskaia, O., & Porges, S. W. (2001). Vagal reactivity and affective adjustment in infants during interaction challenges. *Child Development, 72*(5), 1314–1326.

Bear, R. A., & Nietzel, M. T. (1991). Cognitive and behavioral treatment of impulsivity in children: A meta-analytic review of the outcome literature. *Journal of Clinical Child and Adolescent Psychology, 20*(4), 400–412.

Beauregard, M., Courtemanche, J., Paquette, V., & St-Pierre, E. L. (2009). The neural basis of unconditional love. *Psychiatry Research, 172*(2), 93–8.

Beauregard, M., Levesque, J., & Bourgouin, P. (2001). Neural correlates of conscious self-regulation of emotion. *The Journal of Neuroscience, 21*, 1–6.

Bechara, A., Damasio, H., & Damasio, A. R. (2000). Emotion, decision making and the orbitofrontal cortex. *Cerebral Cortex, 10*(3), 295–307.

Bechara, A., Damasio, H., Tranel, D., & Damasio, A. (1997). Deciding advantageously before knowing the advantageous strategy. *Science, 275*, 1293–1295.

Beck, A. T. (1976). *Cognitive therapy and the emotional disorders.* New York, NY: Meridian.

Beck, A. T. (1983). Cognitive therapy of depression: New perspectives. In P. J. Clayton & P. E. Barrett (Eds.), *Treatment of depression: Old controversies, new approaches* (pp. 265–284). New York, NY: Raven Press.

Beck, A. T., & Emery, G. (1985). *Anxiety disorders and phobias: A cognitive perspective.* New York, NY: Basic Books.

Beck, A. T., Rush, A. J., Shaw, B. F., & Emery, G. (1979). *Cognitive therapy of depression.* New York, NY: Guilford.

Beck, A. T., Steer, R., & Garbin, M. (1988). Psychometric properties of the Beck Depression Inventory: Twenty-five years of evaluation. *Clinical Psychology Review, 8*, 77–100.

Beebe, B., Jaffe, J., Buck, K., Chen, H., Cohen, P., Blatt, S., et al. (2007). Six-week postpartum maternal self-criticism and dependency and 4-month mother-infant self- and interactive contingencies. *Developmental Psychology, 43*(6), 1360–1376.

Beebe, B., Jaffe, J., Markese, S., Buck, K., Chen, H., Cohen, P., et al. (2010). The origins of 12-month attachment: A microanalysis of 4-month mother-infant interaction. *Attachment & Human Development, 12*(1–2), 6–141.

Beer, J., Heerey, E. A., Keltner, D., Knight, R., & Scabini, D. (2003). The regulatory function of self-conscious emotion: Insights from patients with orbitofrontal damage. *Journal of Personality and Social Psychology, 85*, 594–604.

Beer, J. S. (2002). Self-regulation of social behavior. *Unpublished dissertation.* University of California, Berkeley.

Beer, J. S., Knight, R. T., & Esposito, M. (2006). Integrating emotion and cognition: The role of the frontal lobes in distinguishing between helpful and hurtful emotion. *Psychological Science, 17*, 448–453.

Beer, J. S., Shimamura, A. P., & Knight, R. T. (2004). Frontal lobe contributions to executive control of cognitive and social behavior. In M. S. Gazzaniga (Ed.), *The newest cognitive neurosciences* (3rd ed., pp. 1091–1104). Cambridge, UK: MIT Press.

Beevers, C. G., Marti, C. N., Lee, H. J., Stote, D. L., Ferrell, R. E., Hariri, A. R., et al. (2011). Associations between serotonin transporter gene promoter region (5-HTTLPR) polymorphism and gaze bias for emotional information. *Journal of Abnormal Psychology, 120*(1), 187–197.

Beevers, C. G., Wells, T. T., Ellis, A. J., & McGeary, J. E. (2009). Association of the serotonin transporter gene promoter region (5-HTTLPR) polymorphism with biased attention for emotional stimuli. *Journal of Abnormal Psychology, 118*(3), 670–681.

Beier, E. G., & Sternberg, D. P. (1977). Marital communication. *Journal of Communication, 27*, 92–97.

Belay, H., Burton, C. L., Lovic, V., Meaney, M. J., Sokolowski, M., & Fleming, A. S. (2011). Early adversity and serotonin transporter genotype interact with hippocampal glucocorticoid receptor mRNA expression, corticosterone, and behavior in adult male rats. *Behavioral Neuroscience, 125*(2), 150–160.

Belfer, M. L. (2007). Critical review of world policies for mental healthcare for children and adolescents. *Current Opinion in Psychiatry, 20*(4), 349.

Belsky, J., Jaffee, S. R., Sligo, J., Woodward, L., & Silva, P. A. (2005). Intergenerational transmission of warm-sensitive-stimulating parenting: A prospective study of mothers and fathers of 3-year-olds. *Child Development, 76*(2), 384–396.

Belsky, J., Spritz, B., & Crnic, K. (1996). Infant attachment security and affective-cognitive information processing at age 3. *Psychological Science, 7*(2), 111–114.

Bennett, D. S., Bendersky, M., & Lewis, M. (2002a). Children's intellectual and emotional-behavioral adjustment at 4 years as a function of cocaine exposure, maternal characteristics, and environmental risk. *Developmental Psychology, 38*(5), 648–658.

Bennett, D. S., Bendersky, M., & Lewis, M. (2002b). Facial expressivity at 4 months: A context by expression analysis. *Infancy, 3*, 97–113.

Bennett, D. S., Bendersky, M., & Lewis, M. (2005). Does the organization of emotional expression change over time? Facial expressivity from 4 to 12 months. *Infancy, 8*(2), 167–187.

Benoit, D., Parker, K. C., & Zeanah, C. H. (1997). Mothers' representations of their infants assessed prenatally: Stability and association with infants' attachment classifications. *Journal of Child Psychology and Psychiatry, and Allied Disciplines, 38*(3), 307–313.

Ben-Ze'ev, A. (2000). *The subtlety of emotions.* Cambridge, MA: MIT Press.

Ben-Ze'ev, A., & Oatley, K. (1996). The intentional and social nature of human emotions: Reconsideration of the distinctions between basic and non-basic emotions. *Journal for the Theory of Social Behaviour, 26*, 81–92.

Berk, M. S., & Anderson, S. M. (2000). The impact of past relationships on interpersonal behavior: Behavioral confirmation in the social-cognitive process of transference. *Journal of Personality and Social Psychology, 79*, 546–562.

Berkman, L. F., & Syme, S. L. (1979). Social networks, host resistance, and mortality: A nine year follow-up study of Alameda County residents. *American Journal of Epidemiology, 100*, 186–204.

Berkowitz, L. (1989). The frustration–aggression hypothesis: An examination and reformulation. *Psychological Bulletin, 106*, 59–73.

Berkowitz, L. (1990). On the formation and regulation of anger and aggression: A cognitive-neoassociationistic analysis. *American Psychologist, 45*, 494–503.

Berkowitz, L., Cochran, S., & Embree, M. (1981). Physical pain and the goal of aversively stimulated aggression. *Journal of Personality and Social Psychology, 40,* 687–700.

Bermond, B., Bleys, J. W., & Stoffels, E. J. (2005). Left hemispheric preference and alexithymia: A neuropsychological investigation. *Cognition and Emotion, 19,* 151–160.

Bermond, B., Fasotti, L., Nieuwenhuyse, B., & Schuerman, J. (1991). Spinal cord lesions, peripheral feedback and intensities of emotional feelings. *Cognition and Emotion, 5,* 201–220.

Bernard, K., & Dozier, M. (2010). Examining infants' cortisol responses to laboratory tasks among children varying in attachment disorganization: Stress reactivity or return to baseline? *Developmental Psychology, 46*(6), 1771–1778.

Bernheimer, C., & Kahane, C. (1985). *In Dora's case: Freud, hysteria, feminism.* New York, NY: Columbia University Press.

Berntson, G. G., Cacioppo, J. T., & Quigley, K. S. (1993). Respiratory sinus arrhythmia: Autonomic origins, physiological mechanisms, and psychophysiological implications. *Psychophysiology, 30,* 183–196.

Berridge, K. C. (2000). Taste reactivity: Measuring hedonic impact in human infants and animals. *Neuro-science and Biobehavioral Reviews, 24,* 173–198.

Berridge, K. C. (2003). Comparing the emotional brains of humans and other animals. In R. J. Davidson, K. Scherer, & H. H. Goldsmith (Eds.), *Handbook of affective sciences* (pp. 25–51). New York, NY: Oxford University Press.

Berscheid, E. (1985). Interpersonal attraction. In G. Lindzey & E. Aronson (Eds.), *Handbook of social psychology* (3rd ed., pp. 413–484). New York, NY: Random House.

Berscheid, E. (1988). Some comments on love's anatomy; Or, whatever happened to old-fashioned lust? In R. J. Sternberg & M. L. Barnes (Eds.), *The psychology of love* (pp. 359–374). New Haven, CT: Yale University Press.

Berscheid, E., & Ammazzalorso, H. (2004). Emotional experience in close relationships. In M. B. Brewer & M. Hewstone (Eds.), *Emotion and motivation. Perspectives on social psychology* (pp. 47–69). Malden, MA: Blackwell.

Bharata Muni. (200 BCE). *Natyasastra; English translation with critical notes* (A. Rangacharya, Trans.). Bangalore: IBH Prakashana (current edition 1986).

Bierman, K. L., Domitrovich, C. E., Nix, R. L., Gest, S. D., Welsh, J. A., Greenberg, M. T., et al. (2008). Promoting academic and social-emotional school readiness: The head start REDI program. *Child Development, 79*(6), 1802–1817.

Biglan, A., Hops, H., Sherman, L., Friedman, L. S., Arthus, J., & Osteen, V. (1985). Problem-solving interactions of depressed women and their husbands. *Behavior Therapy, 16,* 431–451.

Binswanger, L. (1963). *Being in the world: Selected papers* (J. Needleman, Ed. and Trans.). New York, NY: Basic Books.

Bird, G., Silani, G., Brindley, R., White, S., Frith, U., Singer, T., et al. (2010). Empathic brain responses in insula are modulated by levels of alexithymia but not autism. *Brain: A Journal of Neurology, 133,* 1515–1667.

Birdwhistell, R. L. (1970). *Kinesics and context.* Philadelphia: University of Pennsylvania Press.

Bischof-Köhler, D. (1991). The development of empathy in infants. In M. Lamb & H. Keller (Eds.), *Infant development: Perspectives from German-speaking countries* (pp. 1–33): Hillsdale, NJ: Erlbaum.

Biswas-Diener, R., & Diener, E. (2001). Making the best of a bad situation: Satisfaction in the slums of Calcutta. *Social Indicators Research, 55,* 329–352.

Biswas-Diener, R., Vitterso, J., & Diener, E. (2005). Most people are pretty happy, but there is cultural variation: The Inughuit, the Amish, and the Masai. *Journal of Happiness Studies, 6,* 205–226.

Blair, R.J.R. (2008). Fine cuts of empathy and the amygdala: Dissociable deficits in psychopathy and autism. *Quarterly Journal of Experimental Psychology, 61,* 157–170.

Blair, R.J.R., & Cipolotti, L. (2000). Impaired social response reversal: A case of acquired sociopathy. *Brain, 123,* 1122–1141.

Blair, R.J.R., & Mitchell, D.G.V. (2009). Psychopathy, attention and emotion. *Psychological Medicine, 39,* 543–555.

Blair, R.J.R., Morris, J. S., Frith, C. D., Perrett, D. I., & Dolan, R. (1999). Dissociable neural responses to facial expressions of sadness and anger. *Brain, 122,* 883–893.

Blascovich, J., Spencer, S., Quinn, D., & Steele, C. (2001). African-Americans and high blood pressure: The role of stereotype threat. *Psychological Science, 12,* 225–229.

Blazer, D., Hughes, D., & George, L. K. (1987). Stressful life events and the onset of a generalized anxiety syndrome. *American Journal of Psychiatry, 144,* 1178–1183.

Bless, H., Schwarz, N., & Wieland, R. (1996). Mood and the impact of category membership and individuating information. *European Journal of Social Psychology, 26,* 935–959.

Block, J. H., Block, J., & Gjerde, P. F. (1986). The personality of children prior to divorce: A prospective study. *Child Development, 57,* 827–840.

Blomberg, J., Lazar, A., & Sandell, R. (2001). Long-term outcome of long-term psychoanalytically oriented psychotherapies: First findings of the Stockholm outcome of psychotherapy and psychoanalysis project. *Psychotherapy Research, 11,* 361–382.

Bloom, H. (1989). *Ruin the sacred truths: Poetry and belief from the Bible to the present.* Cambridge, MA: Harvard University Press.

Bodenhausen, G., Sheppard, L., & Kramer, G. (1994). Negative affect and social judgment: The different impact of anger and sadness. *European Journal of Social Psychology, 24,* 45–62.

Boehm, J. K., Peterson, C., Kivimaki, M., & Kubzansky, L. D. (2011). *Heart health when life is satisfying: Evidence from the Whitehall II cohort study.* (*European Heart Journal,* online).

Boesch, C., & Boesch, H. (1989). Hunting behavior of wild chimpanzees in the Tai National Park. *American Journal of Physical Anthropology, 78,* 547–573.

Boesch, C., Head, J., Tagg, N., Arandjelovic, M., Vigilant, L., et al. (2007). Fatal chimpazee attack in Loango National Park. *International Journal of Primatology, 28,* 1025–1034.

Bolger, N., Davis, A., & Rafaeli, E. (2003). Diary methods: Capturing life as it is lived. *Annual Review of Psychology, 54,* 579–616.

Bolton, W., & Oatley, K. (1987). A longitudinal study of social support and depression in unemployed men. *Psychological Medicine, 17,* 453–460.

Bonanno, G. A., & Keltner, D. (2004). The coherence of emotion systems: Comparing "on-line" measures of appraisal and facial expressions, and self-report. *Cognition and Emotion, 18,* 431–444.

Boole, G. (1854). *An investigation of the laws of thought.* New York, NY: Dover.

Boomsma, D. I., Van Beijsterveldt, C.E.M., & Hudziak, J. J. (2005). Genetic and environmental influences on anxious/depression during childhood: A study from the Netherlands Twin Register. *Genes, Brain and Behavior, 4,* 466–481.

Booth, W. C. (1988). *The company we keep: An ethics of fiction.* Berkeley: University of California Press.

Borelli, J. L., Crowley, M. J., David, D. H., Sbarra, D. A., Anderson, G. M., & Mayes, L. C. (2010). Attachment and emotion in school-aged children. *Emotion, 10*(4), 475–485.

Borkowski, J. G., Bisconti, T., Weed, K., Willard, C., Keogh, D. A., & Whitman, T. L. (2002). The adolescent as parent: Influences on children's intellectual, academic, and socioemotional development. In J. G. Borkowski, S. L. Ramey, & M. Bristol-Power (Eds.), *Parenting and the child's world: Influences on academic, intellectual, and social-emotional development* (pp. 161–184). Mahwah, NJ: Erlbaum.

Bornstein, M. H., & Arteberry, M. E. (2003). Recognition, discrimination and categorization of smiling by 5-month-old infants. *Developmental Science, 6*(5), 585–599.

Borod, J. C. (2000). *The neuropsychology of emotion.* New York, NY: Oxford University Press.

Boucher, J. D., & Brandt, M. E. (1981). Judgment of emotion: American and Malay antecedents. *Journal of Cross-Cultural Psychology, 12,* 272–283.

Bouton, M. E., Mineka, S., & Barlow, D. H. (2001). A modern learning theory perspective on the etiology of panic disorder. *Psychological Review, 108,* 4–32.

Bouzouggar, A., Barton, N., Vanhaeren, M., et al. (2007). 82,000-year-old shell beads from North Africa and implications for the origins of modern human behavior. *Proceedings of the National Academy of Sciences of the USA, 104,* 9964–9969.

Bower, G. H. (1981). Mood and memory. *American Psychologist, 36,* 129–148.

Bower, G. H., Gilligan, S. G., & Monteiro, K. P. (1981). Selectivity of learning caused by affective states. *Journal of Experimental Psychology: General, 110,* 451–473.

Bowlby, J. (1979). *The making and breaking of affectional bonds.* London, UK: Tavistock.

Bowlby, J. (1991). *Charles Darwin: A new life.* New York, NY: Norton.

Bowler, J. M., et al. (2003). New ages for human occupation and climatic change at Lake Mungo, Australia. *Nature, 421,* 837–840.

Bowman, E., Aigner, T., & Richmond, B. (1996). Neural signals in the monkey ventral striatum related to motivation for juice and cocaine rewards. *Journal of Neurophysiology, 75,* 1061–1073.

Boyle, M. H., Jenkins, J. M., Hadjiyannakis, K., Cairney, J., Duku, E., & Racine, Y. A. (2004). Differential maternal parenting behavior: Estimating within and between family effects on children. *Child Development, 75,* 1457–1476.

Boyle, M. H., Miskovic, R., Van Lieshout, R., Duncan, L., Schmidt, L. A., Hoult, L., Paneth, N., & Saigal, S. (2011). Psychopathology in young adults born at extremely low birth weight. *Psychological Medicine, 41*(8), 1763–1774.

Bradley, R. H., & Corwyn, R. F. (2002). Socioeconomic status and child development. *Annual Review of Psychology, 53,* 371–399.

Braungart-Rieker, J. M., Hill-Soderlund, A. L., & Karrass, J. (2010). Fear and anger reactivity trajectories from 4 to 16 months: The roles of temperament, regulation, and maternal sensitivity. *Developmental Psychology, 46*(4), 791–804.

Brazier, M.A.B. (1959). The historical development of neurophysiology. In *Handbook of physiology Section 1* (Vol. 1, pp. 1–58). Bethesda, MD: American Physiological Association.

Breiter, H. C., Etcoff, N. L., Whalen, P. J., et al. (1996). Response and habituation of the human amygdala during visual processing of facial expression. *Neuron, 17,* 875–887.

Bremner, J. G., & Slater, A. (Eds.). (2004). *Theories of infant development.* New York, NY: Blackwell.

Brennan, S. (1985). The caricature generator. *Leonardo, 18,* 59–87.

Brestan, E. V., & Eyberg, S. M. (1998). Effective psychosocial treatments of conduct-disordered children and adolescents: 29 years, 82 studies, and 5,272 kids. *Journal of Clinical Child Psychology, 27*(2), 180–189.

Brewin, C. R., Andrews, B., & Gotlib, I. H. (1993). Psychopathology and early experience: A reappraisal of retrospective reports. *Psychological Bulletin, 133,* 82–98.

Brewin, C. R., Dalgleish, T., & Joseph, S. (1996). A dual representation theory of posttraumatic stress disorder. *Psychological Review, 103,* 670–686.

Briñol, P., Petty, R. E., & Barden, J. (2007). Happiness versus sadness as determinant of thought confidence in persuasion: A self-validation analysis. *Journal of Personality and Social Psychology, 93,* 711–727.

Broadbent, D. E., & Broadbent, M. (1988). Anxiety and attentional bias: State and trait. *Cognition and Emotion, 2,* 165–183.

Brody, L. R., & Hall, J. A. (2000). Gender, emotion, and expression. In M. Lewis & J. Haviland-Jones (Eds.), *Handbook of emotions, second edition* (pp. 338–349). New York, NY: Guilford.

Broidy, L. M., Nagin, D. S., Tremblay, R. E., Bates, J. E., Brame, B., Dodge, K. A., et al. (2003). Developmental trajectories of childhood disruptive behaviors and adolescent delinquency: A six-site, cross-national study. *Developmental Psychology, 39*(2), 222.

Bronfenbrenner, U. (1977). Toward an experimental ecology of human development. *American Psychologist, 32*(7), 513–531.

Bronfenbrenner, U. (2005). Ecological systems theory. In U. Bronfenbrenner, *Making human beings human: Bioecological perspectives on human development* (pp. 106–173). London, UK: Sage.

Brown, D. E. (1991). *Human universals.* Philadelphia, PA: Temple University Press.

Brown, G. W., Adler, Z., & Bifulco, A. (1988). Life events, difficulties and recovery from chronic depression. *British Journal of Psychiatry, 152,* 487–498.

Brown, G. W., Birley, J.L.T., & Wing, J. K. (1972). Influence of family life on the course of schizophrenic disorders. *British Journal of Psychiatry, 121,* 241–258.

Brown, G. W., & Harris, T. O. (1978). *Social origins of depression: A study of psychiatric disorder in women.* London, UK: Tavistock.

Brown, G. W., & Harris, T. O. (1993). Aetiology of anxiety and depressive disorders in an inner-city population. 1: Early adversity. *Psychological Medicine, 23,* 143–154.

Brown, G. W., Harris, T. O., & Hepworth, C. (1995). Loss, humiliation and entrapment among women developing depression: A patient and non-patient comparison. *Psychological Medicine, 25,* 7–21.

Brown, G. W., Lemyre, L., & Bifulco, A. (1992). Social factors and recovery from anxiety and depressive disorders: A test of specificity. *British Journal of Psychiatry, 161,* 44–54.

Brown, G. W., & Moran, P. (1994). Clinical and psychosocial origins of chronic depressive episodes. 1: A community study. *British Journal of Psychiatry, 165,* 447–456.

Brown, G. W., & Moran, P. (1998). Emotion and the etiology of depressive disorders. In W. F. Flack & J. D. Laird

(Eds.), *Emotions in psychopathology: Theory and research* (pp. 171–184). New York, NY: Oxford University Press.

Brown, R. P., & Gerbarg, P. L. (2005). Sudarshan Kriya Yogic breathing in the treatment of stress, anxiety, and depression, Part I: Neurophysiologic model. *Journal of Alternative and Complementary Medicine, 11,* 189–201.

Brownell, C. A., Zerwas, S., & Ramani, G. B. (2007). "So Big": The development of body self-awareness in toddlers. *Child Development, 78*(5), 1426–1440.

Browning, C. R. (1992). *Ordinary men: Reserve Police Battalion 101 and the final solution in Poland.* New York, NY: HarperCollins.

Bruneau E., Pluta A., & Saxe R. (2012) Distinct roles of the "shared pain" and "theory of mind" networks in processing others' emotional suffering. *Neuropsychologia, 50*(2), 219–231.

Bruner, J. (1986). *Actual minds, possible worlds.* Cambridge, MA: Harvard University Press.

Bruner, J. S. (2003, September 25). Do not pass go. Review of *The culture of control: Crime and social order in contemporary society,* by David Garland. *New York Review of Books, 50.*

Buck, R. (1999). The biology of affects: A typology. *Psychological Review, 106,* 301–336.

Buck, R. (2002). The genetics and biology of true love: Prosocial biological affects and the left hemisphere. *Psychological Review, 109,* 739–744.

Buck, R., & Ginsberg, B. E. (1997). Communicative genes and the evolution of empathy: Selfish and social emotions as voices of selfish and social genes. In C. S. Carter, I. I. Lederhendler, & B. Kirkpatrick (Eds.), *The integrative neurobiology of affiliation* (pp. 481–483). New York, NY: New York Academy of Sciences.

Buckholz, J. W., Asplund, C. L., Dux, P. E., Zald, D. H., Gore, J. C., et al. (2008). The neural correlates of third-party punishment. *Neuron, 60,* 930–940.

Buckley, T. C., Blanchard, E. B., & Neill, W. T. (2000). Information processing and PTSD: A review of the empirical literature. *Clinical Psychology Review, 20*(8), 1041–1065.

Buhle, J., Kober, H., Ochsner, K., Mende-Siedlecki, P., Weber, J., Hughes, B., Kross, E., Atlas, L., McRae, K., & Wager, T. (in press). Common representation of pain and negative emotion in the midbrain periaqueductal gray. *Social Cognitive and Affective Neuroscience.*

Burgess, E. W., & Wallin, P. (1953). *Engagement and marriage.* Philadelphia, PA: Lippincott.

Burnam, M. A., Stein, J. A., Golding, J. M., Siegel, J. M., Sorenson, S. B., Forsythe, A. B., & Telles, C. A. (1988). Sexual assault and mental disorders in a community population. *Journal of Consulting and Clinical Psychology, 56,* 843–850.

Buss, A. H., & Plomin, R. (1975). *A temperament theory of personality development.* Oxford, UK: Wiley-Interscience.

Buss, D. (1992). Mate preference mechanisms: Consequences for partner choice and intrasexual competition. In J. H. Barkow, L. Cosmides, & J. Tooby (Eds.), *The adapted mind* (pp. 267–288). New York, NY: Oxford University Press.

Buss, D. M. (1994). *The evolution of desire: Strategies of human mating.* New York, NY: Basic Books.

Buss, D. M., Larsen, R., Westen, D., & Semmelroth, J. (1992). Sex differences in jealousy: Evolution, physiology, and psychology. *Psychological Science, 3,* 251–255.

Butler, A. C., Chapman, J. E., Forman, E. M., & Beck, A. T. (2006). The empirical status of cognitive-behavioral therapy: A review of meta-analyses. *Clinical Psychology Review, 26*(1), 17–31.

Butler, E. A., Egloff, B., Wilhelm, F. H., Smith, N. C., Erickson, E. A., & Gross, J. J. (2003). The social consequences of expressive suppression. *Emotion, 3,* 48–67.

Byrne-Davis, L.M.T., & Vedhara, K. (2008). Psychoneuroimmunology. *Social and Personality Psychology Compass, 2,* 751–764.

Cacioppo, J. T., & Gardner, W. L. (1999). Emotion. *Annual Review of Psychology, 50,* 191–214.

Cacioppo, J. T., Klein, D. J., Berntson, G. C., & Hatfield, E. (1993). The psychophysiology of emotion. In M. Lewis & J. M. Haviland (Eds.), *Handbook of emotions* (pp. 119–142). New York, NY: Guilford.

Caine, S., & Koob, G. (1993). Modulation of cocaine self-administration in the rat through D-3 dopamine receptors. *Science, 260,* 1814–1816.

Calkins, S. D., Graziano, P. A., & Keane, S. P. (2007). Cardiac vagal regulation differentiates among children at risk for behavior problems. *Biological Psychology, 74*(2), 144–153.

Calkins, S. D., & Keane, S. P. (2004). Cardiac vagal regulation across the preschool period: Stability, continuity, and implications for childhood adjustment. *Developmental Psychobiology, 45*(3), 101–112.

Call, J., & Tomasello, M. (2008). Does the chimpanzee have a theory of mind? 30 years later. *Trends in Cognitive Science, 12*, 187–192.

Calvo, M. G., & Avero, P. (2005). Time course of attentional bias to emotional scenes in anxiety: Gaze direction and duration. *Cognition and Emotion, 19*, 433–451.

Cameron, J. (Writer & Director). (2009). *Avatar* [Movie]. USA.

Campos, B., Shiota, M., Keltner, D., Gonzaga, G., & Goetz, J. (in press). What is shared, what is different?: Core relational themes and expressive displays of eight positive emotions. *Cognition and Emotion.*

Campos, J. J., Barrett, K. C., Lamb, M. E., Goldsmith, H. H., & Stenberg, C. (1983). Socioemotional development. In M. M. Haith & J. J. Campos (Eds.), *Handbook of child psychology* (4th ed., Vol. II, pp. 783–915). New York, NY: Wiley.

Campos, J. J., Bertenthal, B. I., & Kermoian, R. (1992). Early experience and emotional development: The emergence of wariness of heights. *Psychological Science, 3*(1), 61–64.

Campos, J. J., Kermoian, R., & Zumbahlen, M. R. (1992). Socioemotional transformations in the family system following infant crawling onset. In N. Eisenberg & R. A. Fabes (Eds.), *Emotion and its regulation in early development. (New Directions in Child Development No. 55,* pp. 25–40). San Francisco, CA: Jossey-Bass.

Campos, J. J., Walle, E. A., Dahl, A., & Main, A. (2011). Reconceptualizing emotion regulation. *Emotion Review, 3*, 26–35.

Camras, L., Meng, Z., Ujiie, T., Dharamsi, S., Miyake, K., Oster, H., et al. (2002). Observing emotion in infants: Facial expression, body behavior, and rater judgments of responses to an expectancy-violating event. *Emotion, 2*(2), 179–193.

Camras, L., Oster, H., Campos, J. J., & Bakeman, R. (2003). Emotional facial expressions in European-American, Japanese, and Chinese infants. *Annual New York Academy of Science, 1000*, 135–151.

Camras, L. A., Oster, H., Ujiie, T., Campos, J. J., Bakeman, R., & Meng, Z. (2007). Do infants show distinct negative facial expressions for fear and anger? Emotional expression in 11-month-old European American, Chinese, and Japanese infants. *Infancy, 11*(2), 131–155.

Canli, T., Zhao, Z., Desmond, J. E., et al. (1999). FMRI identifies a network of structures correlated with retention of positive and negative emotional memory. *Psychology, 27*, 441–462.

Canli, T., Zhao, Z., Desmond, J. E., Kang, E., Gross, J., & Gabrieli, J. D. (2001). An fMRI study of personality influences on brain reactivity to emotional stimuli. *Behavioral Neuroscience, 115*(1), 33–42.

Cannon, W. B. (1927). The James–Lange theory of emotion: A critical examination and an alternative theory. *American Journal of Psychology, 39*, 106–124.

Cannon, W. B. (1929). *Bodily changes in pain, hunger, fear and rage* (2nd ed.). New York, NY: Appleton.

Cannon, W. B. (1931). Again the James–Lange and the thalamic theories of emotion. *Psychological Review, 38*, 281–295.

Carlson, E., Sroufe, A., & Egeland, B. (2004). The construction of experience: A longitudinal study of representation and behavior. *Child Development, 75*(1), 66–83.

Carlson, N. (2004). *Foundations of physiological psychology* (6th ed.). Boston, MA: Allyn & Bacon.

Carlson, S. M., & Wang, T. S. (2007). Inhibitory control and emotion regulation in preschool children. *Cognitive Development, 22*(4), 489–510.

Carmichael, M. S., Dixen, J., Palmisano, G., et al. (1987). Plasma oxytocin increases in the human sexual response. *Journal of Clinical Endocrinology and Metabolism, 64* (1), 27–31.

Carney, D., Cuddy, A., & Yap, A.J. (2010). Power posing: Brief nonverbal displays affect neuroendocrine levels and risk tolerance. *Psychological Science, 21*, 1363–1368.

Carpenter, M., Nagell, K., & Tomasello, M. (1998). Social cognition, joint attention, and communicative competence from 9 to 15 months of age. *Monographs of the Society for Research in Child Development, 63*(4), 1–174.

Carr, A. (2009). The effectiveness of family therapy and systemic interventions for child-focused problems. *Journal of Family Therapy, 31,* 3–45.

Carter, A. S., Wagmiller, R. J., Gray, S. A. O., McCarthy, K. J., Horowitz, S. M., & Briggs-Gowan, M. J. (2010). Prevalence of DSM-IV Disorder in a Representative, Healthy Birth Cohort at School Entry: Sociodemographic Risks and Social Adaptation. *Journal of the American Academy of Child and Adolescent Psychiatry, 49*(7), 696–699.

Carter, C. S. (1998). Neuroendocrine perspectives on social attachment and love. *Psychoneuroendocrinology, 23*(8), 779–818.

Carter, C. S., & Altemus, M. (1997). Integrative functions of lactational hormones in social behavior and stress management. In C. S. Carter & I. I. Lederhendler (Eds.), *Annals of the New York Academy of Sciences, 807,* 164–174.

Cartwright, F. F. (1977). *A social history of medicine.* London, UK: Longman.

Carver, C. S., Johnson, S. L., & Joormann, J. (2008). Serotonergic function, two-mode models of self-regulation, and vulnerability to depression: What depression has in common with impulsive aggression. *Psychological Bulletin, 134*(6), 912–943.

Carver, L. J., & Vaccaro, B. G. (2007). 12-month-old infants allocate increased neural resources to stimuli associated with negative adult emotion. *Developmental Psychology, 43*(1), 54–69.

Cashon, C. H., & Cohen, L. B. (2003). The construction, deconstruction, and reconstruction of infant face perception. In O. Pascalis & A. Slater (Eds.), *The development of face processing in infancy and early childhood: Current perspectives* (pp. 55–68). New York, NY: Nova Science.

Caspi, A., Harrington, H. L., Milne, B., Amell, J. W., Theodore, R. F., & Moffitt, T. E. (2003). Children's behavioral styles at age 3 are linked to their adult personality traits at age 26. *Journal of Personality, 71,* 495–513.

Caspi, A., McClay, M., Moffitt, T. E., Mill, J., Martin, J., Craig, I. W., et al. (2002). Role of the genotype in the cycle of violence in maltreated children. *Science, 297,* 851–854.

Caspi, A., Moffitt, T. E., Morgan, J., Rutter, M., Taylor, A., Arseneault, L., et al. (2004). Maternal expressed emotion predicts children's antisocial behavior problems: Using MZ-twin differences to identify environmental effects on behavioral development. *Development Psychology, 40,* 149–161.

Caspi, A., Roberts, B. W., & Shiner, R. L. (2005). Personality development: Stability and change. *Annual Review of Psychology, 55,* 453–484.

Caspi, A., Henry, B., McGee, R. O., Moffitt, T. E., & Silva, P. A. (1995). Temperamental qualities at age 3 predict personality traits in young adulthood: Longitudinal evidence from a birth cohort. *Child Development, 66,* 486–498.

Caspi, A., Sugden, K., Moffitt, T. E., Taylor, A., Craig, I.W., Harrington, H., et al. (2003). Influence on life stress on depression: Moderation by a polymorphism in the 5-HTT gene. *Science, 301*(5631), 386–389.

Cassidy, J., Aikins, J. W., & Chernoff, J. J. (2003). Children's peer selection: Experimental examination of the role of self-perceptions. *Developmental Psychology, 39*(3), 495–508.

Chagnon, N. A. (1968). *Yanomamö: The fierce people.* New York, NY: Holt, Rinehart & Winston.

Chaiken, S., Lieberman, A., & Eagly, A. H. (1989). Heuristic and systematic information processing within and beyond the persuasion context. In J. S. Uleman & J. A. Bargh (Eds.), *Unintended thought: Limits of awareness, intention and control* (pp. 212–252). New York, NY: Guilford.

Chamberlain, P., Price, J., Leve, L. D., Laurent, H., Landsverk, J. A., & Reid, J. B. (2008). Prevention of behavior problems for children in foster care: Outcomes and mediation effects. *Prevention Science, 9*(1), 17–27.

Chapman, H. A., Kim, D. A., Susskind, J. M., & Anderson, A. K. (2009). In bad taste: Evidence for the oral origins of moral disgust. *Science, 323,* 1222–1226.

Chatterjee, D., Chatterjee-Chakraborty, M., Rees, S., Cauchi, J., de Medeiros, C. B., & Fleming, A. S. (2007). Maternal isolation alters the expression of neural proteins during development: "Stroking" stimulation reverses these effects. *Brain Research, 1158,* 11–27.

Chen, E., & Matthews, K. A. (2001). Cognitive appraisal biases: An approach to understanding the relation between socioeconomic status and cardiovascular reactivity in children. *Annals of Behavioral Medicine, 23,* 101–111.

Cherlin, A. J., Furstenberg, F. F., Chase-Lansdale, P. L., Kiernan, K. E., & Robins, P. K. (1991). Longitudinal studies of effects of divorce on children in Great Britain and the United States. *Science, 252,* 1386–1389.

Cheyney, D. L., & Seyfarth, R. M. (1990). *How monkeys see the world: Inside the mind of another species.* Chicago, IL: University of Chicago Press.

Chimpanzee Sequencing and Analysis, Consortium (2005). Initial sequence of the chimpanzee genome and comparison with the human genome. *Nature, 437,* 69–87.

Chivers, M. L., Seto, M. C., Lalumière, M. L., Laan, E., & Grimbos, T. (2010). Agreement of genital and subjective measures of sexual arousal in men and women: A meta-analysis. *Archives of Sexual Behavior, 39,* 5–56.

Chojnacki, J. T., & Walsh, W. B. (1990). Reliability and concurrent validity of the Sternberg Triangular Love Scale. *Psychological Reports, 67,* 219–224.

Chow, S. M., Haltigan, J. D., & Messinger, D. S. (2010). Dynamic infant–parent affect coupling during the face-to-face/still-face. *Emotion, 10*(1), 101–114.

Chrétien de Troyes. (1180). The knight of the cart. In D. Staines (Ed.), *The complete romances of Chrétien de Troyes* (pp. 170–256). Bloomington: Indiana University Press (1990).

Christakis, N. A., & Fowler, J. H. (2007). The spread of obesity in a large social network over 32 years. *New England Journal of Medicine, 357*(4), 370–379.

Christian, D. (2004). *Maps of time: An introduction to big history.* Berkeley: University of California Press.

Christianson, S.-Å., & Loftus, E. (1991). Remembering emotional events: The fate of detailed information. *Cognition and Emotion, 5,* 81–108.

Chung, H. L., & Steinberg, L. (2006). Relations between neighborhood factors, parenting behavior, peer deviance and delinquency among serious juvenile offenders. *Developmental Psychology, 42*(2), 319–331.

Cicchetti, D., & Rogosch, F. A. (1996). Equifinality and multifinality in developmental psychopathology. *Development and Psychopathology,* 597–600.

Cicchetti, D., & Toth, S. (2005). Child maltreatment. *Annual Review of Clinical Psychology, 1,* 409–438.

Cicero. (45 BCE). *Tusulan disputations.* Loeb ed., Cicero Vol. 18. (J. E. King, Ed. and Trans.). Cambridge, MA: Harvard University Press (current edition 1927).

Cikara, M., Botvinick, M. M., & Fiske, S. T. (2011). Us versus them: Social identity shapes neural responses to intergroup competition and harm. *Psychological Science, 22,* 306–313.

Cikara, M., Bruneau, E. G., & Saxe, R. R. (2011). Us and them: Intergroup failures of empathy. *Current Directions in Psychological Science, 20,* 149–153.

Clark, A. E., & Oswald, A. J. (1994). Unhappiness and unemployment. *Economic Journal, 104,* 648–659.

Clark, C. (1990). Emotions and the micropolitics in everyday life: Some patterns and paradoxes of "Place. " In T. D. Kemper (Ed.), *Research agendas in the sociology of emotions* (pp. 305–334). Albany, NY: State University of New York Press.

Clark, L. A. (2005). Temperament as a unifying basis for personality and psychopathology. *Journal of Abnormal Psychology, 114*(4), 505–521.

Clark, M. S., & Finkel, E. J. (2005). Willingness to express emotion: The impact of relationship type, communal orientation, and their interaction. *Personal Relationships, 12,* 169–180.

Clark, M. S., Fitness, J., & Brissette, I. (2004). Understanding people's perceptions of relationships is crucial to understanding their emotional lives. In M. Brewer & M. Hewstone (Eds.), *Emotion and motivation. Perspectives on social psychology* (pp. 21–46). Malden, MA: Blackwell.

Clark, M. S., & Williamson, G. M. (1989). Moods and social judgments. In H. Wagner & A. Manstead (Eds.), *Handbook of social psychophysiology* (pp. 347–370). Chichester, UK: Wiley.

Clore, G. L. (1992). Cognitive phenomenology: Feelings and the construction of judgment. In L. L. Martin & A. Tesser (Eds.), *The construction of social judgment* (pp. 133–163). Hillsdale, NJ: Erlbaum.

Clore, G. L., & Gasper, K. (2000). Feeling is believing: Some affective influences on belief. In N. H. Frijda, A.S.R. Manstead, & S. Bem (Eds.), *Emotions and beliefs: How feelings influence thoughts* (pp. 10–44) Cambridge, MA: Cambridge University Press.

Clore, G. L., Gasper, K., & Garvin, E. (2001). Affect as information. In J. P. Forgas (Ed.), *Handbook of affect and social cognition* (pp. 121–144). Mahwah, NJ: Erlbaum.

Clore, G. L., & Huntsinger, J. R. (2007). How emotions inform judgments and regulate thought. *Trends in Cognitive Sciences, 11,* 393–399.

Clore, G. L., & Ortony, A. (2008). Appraisal theories: How cognition shapes affect into emotion. In M. Lewis, J. Haviland Jones, & L. F. Barrett (Eds.), *Handbook of emotions* (3rd ed., pp. 628–642). New York, NY: Guilford.

Clore, G. L., & Palmer, J. (2009). Affective guidance of intelligent agents: How emotion controls cognition. *Cognitive Systems Research, 10,* 21–30.

Clore, G. L., & Pappas, J. (2007). The affective regulation of social interaction. *Social Psychology Quarterly, 70,* 333–339.

Cohen, S., & Wills, T. A. (1985). Stress, social support, and the buffering hypothesis. *Psychological Bulletin, 98,* 310–357.

Cohen, S., Frank, E., Doyle, W. J., et al. (1998). Types of stressors that increase susceptibility to the common cold in healthy adults. *Health Psychology, 17,* 214–223.

Cohn, M. A., Fredrickson, B. L., Brown, S. L., Mikels, J. A., & Conway, A. M. (2009). Happiness unpacked: Positive emotions increase life satisfaction by building resilience. *Emotion, 9,* 361–368.

Coid, J., & Yang, M. (2011). The impact of psychopathy on violence among the household population of Great Britain. *Social Psychiatry and Psychiatric Epidemiology, 46,* 473–480.

Cole, P. M., & Deater-Deckard, K. (2009). Emotion regulation, risk and psychopathology. *Journal of Child Psychology and Psychiatry, 50*(11), 1327–1330.

Cole, P. M., Martin, S. E., & Dennis, T. A. (2004). Emotion regulation as a scientific construct: Methodological challenges and directions for child development research. *Child Development, 75*(2), 317–333.

Collingwood, R. G. (1938). *The principles of art.* Oxford, UK: Oxford University Press.

Collins, R. C. (1990). Stratification, emotional energy, and the transient emotions. In T. D. Kemper (Ed.), *Research agendas in the sociology of emotions* (pp. 27–57). Albany, NY: State University of New York Press.

Colman, I., Murray, J., Abbott, R. A., Maughan, B., Kuh, D., Croudace, T. J., et al. (2009). Outcomes of conduct problems in adolescence: 40 year follow-up of national cohort. *BMJ, 338,* 2981.

Colman, I., Ploubidis, G. B., Wadsworth, M.E.J., Jones, P. B., & Croudace, T. J. (2007). A longitudinal typology of symptoms of depression and anxiety over the life course. *Biological Psychiatry, 62*(11), 1265–1271.

Conan-Doyle, A. (1894). Silver Blaze. In *The Penguin complete adventures of Sherlock Holmes* (pp. 335–350). London, UK: Penguin (current edition 1981).

Condon, P., & DeSteno, D. (2011). Compassion for one reduces punishment for another. *Journal of Experimental Social Psychology, 47,* 698–701.

Conway, M. A. (1990). Conceptual representation of emotions: The role of autobiographical memories. In K. J. Gilhooly, M. T. G. Keene, R. H. Logie, & G. Erdos (Eds.), *Lines of thinking: Reflections on the psychology of thought, Vol. 2: Skills, emotion, creative processes, individual differences and teaching thinking.* Chichester, UK: Wiley.

Conway, M. A., & Bekerian, D. A. (1987). Situational knowledge and emotions. *Cognition and Emotion, 1,* 145–191.

Cooney, R. E., Joormann, J., Eugène, F., Dennis, E. L., & Gotlib, I. H. (2010). Neural correlates of rumination in depression. *Cognitive, Affective and Behavioral Neuroscience, 10,* 470–478.

Corter, C. M., & Fleming, A. S. (1990). Maternal responsiveness in humans: Emotional, cognitive, and biological factors. *Advances in the Study of Behavior, 19,* 83–136.

Cortes, B. P., Demoulin, S., Rodriguez, R. T., Rodriguez, A. P., & Leyens, J. P. (2005). Infrahumanization or familiarity? Attribution of uniquely human emotions to the self, the ingroup, and the outgroup. *Personality and Social Psychology Bulletin, 31*(2), 243–253.

Costello, E. J., Compton, S. N., Keeler, G., et al. (2003b). Relationships between poverty and psychopathology: A natural experiment. *Journal of the American Medical Association, 290,* 2023–2029.

Costello, E. J., Mustillo, S., Erkanli, A., Keeler, G., & Angold, A. (2003a). Prevalence and development of psychiatric disorders in childhood and adolescence. *Archives of General Psychiatry, 60,* 837–844.

Coyne, J. C. (1976). Depression and response to others. *Journal of Abnormal Psychology, 85,* 186–193.

Coyne, J. C. (1994). Self-reported distress: Analog or ersatz depression. *Psychological Bulletin, 116,* 29–45.

Coyne, J. C. (1999). Thinking interactionally about depression: A radical restatement. In T. Joiner & J. C. Coyne (Eds.), *The interactional nature of depression* (pp. 365–392). Washington, DC: American Psychological Association.

Coyne, J. C., & Gotlib, I. H. (1983). The role of cognition in depression: A critical appraisal. *Psychological Bulletin, 94,* 472–505.

Coyne, J. C., Kessler, R. C., Tal, M., Turnbull, J., Wortman, C., & Greden, J. (1987). Living with a depressed person: Burden and psychological distress. *Journal of Consulting and Clinical Psychology, 55,* 347–352.

Coyne, J. C., & Whiffen, V. E. (1995). Issues in personality as diathesis for depression: The case of sociotropy–dependency and autonomy-self criticism. *Psychological Bulletin, 118,* 358–378.

Craddock, N., & Jones, I. (1999). Genetics of bipolar disorder. *Journal of Medical Genetics, 36,* 585–594.

Crews, F. (1994, November 18). The unknown Freud. *New York Review of Books, 40,* 55–66.

Cronin, H. (1991). *The ant and the peacock.* New York, NY: Cambridge University Press.

Crowell, J., Treboux, D., & Waters, E. (2002). Stability of attachment representations: The transition to marriage. *Developmental Psychology, 38,* 467–479.

Csikszentmihalyi, M. (1990). *Flow: The psychology of optimal experience.* New York, NY: Harper Collins.

Csikszentmihalyi, M. (1996). *Creativity: Flow and the psychology of discovery and invention.* New York, NY: Harper Collins.

Culp, A., Osofsky, J. D., & O'Brien, M. (1996). Language patterns of adolescent and older mothers and their one-year-old children: A comparison study. *First Language, 16*(46), 61–75.

Cummings, E. M., & Davies, P. T. (2002). Effects of marital conflict on children: Recent advances and emerging themes in process-oriented research. *Journal of Child Psychology and Psychiatry, and Allied Disciplines, 43* (1), 31–63.

Cummings, E. M., Davies, P. T., & Campbell, S. T. (2000). *Developmental psychopathology and family process: Theory, research, and clinical implications.* New York, NY: Guilford.

Cunningham, W. A., Johnson, M. K., Raye, C. L., Gatenby, J. C., Gore, J. C., & Banaji, M. R. (2004). Separable neural components in the processing of black and white faces. *Psychological Science, 15*(12), 806–813.

Cunningham, W. A., Raye, C. L., & Johnson, M. K. (2004). Implicit and explicit evaluation: fMRI correlates of valence, emotional intensity, and control in the processing of attitudes. *Journal of Cognitive Neuroscience, 16,* 1717–1729.

Cunningham, W. A., Raye, C. L., & Johnson, M. K. (2005). Neural correlates of evaluation associated with promotion and prevention regulatory focus. *Cognitive, Affective, & Behavioral Neuroscience, 5,* 202–211.

Cupchik, G. C. (2002). The evolution of psychical distance as an aesthetic concept. *Culture and Psychology, 8,* 155–187.

Cutlip, W. D., II, & Leary, M. R. (1993). Anatomic and physiological bases of social blushing: Speculations from neurology and psychology. *Behavioural Neurology, 6,* 181–185.

Cyr, C., Euser, E. M., Bakermans–Kranenburg, M. J., & van Ijzendoorn, M. H. (2010). Attachment security and disorganization in maltreating and high-risk families: A series of meta-analyses. *Development and Psychopathology, 22,* 87–108.

Dahl, H. (1991). The key to understanding change: Emotions as appetitive wishes and beliefs about their fulfillment. In J. D. Safran & L. S. Greenberg (Eds.), *Emotions, psychotherapy, and change* (pp. 130–165). New York, NY: Guilford.

Daley, S. E., Hammen, C. L., Burge, D., et al. (1997). Predictors of the generation of episodic stress: A longitudinal study of late adolescent women. *Journal of Abnormal Psychology, 105,* 251–259.

Damasio, A. R. (1994). *Descartes' error.* New York, NY: Putnam.

Damasio, A. R. (2003). *Looking for Spinoza: Joy, sorrow, and the feeling brain.* Orlando, FL: Harcourt.

Damasio, H., Grabowski, T., Frank, R., Galaburda, A. M., & Damasio, A. R. (1994). The return of Phineas Gage: The skull of a famous patient yields clues about the brain. *Science, 264,* 1102–1105.

Dante Alighieri. (1295). *La vita nuova (The new life)* (B. Reynolds, Ed. & Trans.). Harmondsworth: Penguin (1969).

Dante Alighieri. (1307–1321). *La divina comedia (The divine comedy)* (M. Musa, Ed. & Trans.). Harmondsworth: Penguin (1984).

Darwin, C. (1859). *On the origin of species by means of natural selection*. London, UK: Murray.

Darwin, C. (1872). *The expression of the emotions in man and animals*. Chicago, IL: University of Chicago Press (current edition 1965).

Darwin, C. (1872/1998). *The expression of emotions in man and animals* (3rd ed.). New York, NY: Oxford University Press.

Dasgupta, N., DeSteno, D., Williams, L. A., & Hunsinger, M. (2009). Fanning the flames: The influence of specific incidental emotions on implicit prejudice. *Emotion, 9*, 585–591.

Davidov, M., & Grusec, J. E. (2006). Untangling the links of parental responsiveness to distress and warmth to child outcomes. *Child Development, 77*(1), 44–315.

Davidson, R. J. (1992). Anterior cerebral asymmetry and the nature of emotion. *Brain and Cognition, 20*, 125–151.

Davidson, R. J. (1993). The neuropsychology of affective style. In M. Lewis & J. M. Haviland (Eds.), *Handbook of emotions* (pp. 143–154). New York, NY: Guilford.

Davidson, R. J., Ekman, P., Saron, C. D., Senulis, J. A., & Friesen, W. V. (1990). Approach–withdrawal and cerebral asymmetry: Emotional expression and brain physiology I. *Journal of Personality and Social Psychology, 58*, 330–341.

Davidson, R. J., & Irwin, W. (1999). The functional neuroanatomy of emotion and affective style. *Trends in Cognitive Sciences, 3*, 11–21.

Davidson, R. J., Jackson, D. C., & Kalin, N. H. (2000). Emotion, plasticity, context, and regulation. *Psychological Bulletin, 126*, 890–906.

Davidson, R. J., Kabat-Zinn, J., Schumacher, J., Rosenkrantz, M., Muller, D., Santorelli, S. F., et al. (2003). Alterations in brain and immune function produced by mindfulness meditation. *Psychosomatic Medicine, 65*, 564–570.

Davidson, R. J., Pizzagalli, D., Nitschke, J. B., & Kalin, N. H. (2003b). Parsing the subcomponents of emotion and disorders: Perspectives from affective neuroscience. In R. J. Davidson, K. Scherer, & H. H. Goldsmith (Eds.), *Handbook of affective sciences* (pp. 8–24). New York, NY: Oxford University Press.

Davis, J. D., Senghas, A., & Ochsner, K. N. (2010). The effects of Botox injections on emotional experience. *Emotion, 10*, 433–440.

Davis, M. H. (1983). Measuring individual differences in empathy: Evidence for a multidimensional approach. *Journal of Personality and Social Psychology, 44*, 113–126.

Dawkins, R. (1976). *The selfish gene*. Oxford, UK: Oxford University Press.

Dawkins, R. (1986). *The blind watchmaker*. New York, NY: Norton.

De Castro, B. O., Veerman, J. W., Koops, W., Bosch, J. D., & Monshouwer, H. J. (2002). Hostile attribution of intent and aggressive behaviour: A meta-analysis. *Child Development, 73*(3), 916–934.

De Dreu, C.K.W., Greer, L. L., Handgraaf, M.J.J., Shalvi, S., van Kleef, G. A., Baas, M., ten Velden, F. S., van Dijk, E., & Feith, S.W.W. (2010). The neuropeptide oxytocin regulates parochial altruism in intergroup conflict among humans. *Science, 328*(5984), 1408–1411.

De Dreu, C.K.W., Greer, L. L., Handgraaf, M.J.J., van Kleef, G. A., & Shalvi, S. (2011). Oxytocin promotes human ethnocentrism. *Proceedings of the National Academy of Sciences of the United States of America, 108*(4), 1262–1266.

De Haan, M., Belsky, J., Reid, V., Volein, A., & Johnson, M. H. (2004). Maternal personality and infants' neural and visual responsivity to facial expressions of emotion. *Journal of Child Psychology and Psychiatry, 45*(7), 1209–1218.

De Haan, M., Pascalis, O., & Johnson, M. H. (2002). Specialization of neural mechanisms underlying face recognition in human infants. *Journal of Cognitive Neuroscience, 14*(2), 199–209.

De Lorris, G., & De Meun, J. (1237–1277). *The romance of the rose* (H. W. Robbins, Trans.). New York, NY: Dutton (current edition 1962).

De Rosnay, M., & Harris, P. L. (2002). Individual differences in children's understanding of emotion: The roles of attachment and language. *Attachment & Human Development, 4*(1), 39–54.

De Sousa, R. (1987). *The rationality of emotions*. Cambridge, MA: MIT Press.

De Sousa, R. (2004). Emotions: What I know, what I'd like to think I know, and what I'd like to think. In R. C. Solomon (Ed.), *Thinking about feeling: Contemporary philosophers on emotions* (pp. 61–75) New York, NY: Oxford University Press.

De Vignemont, F., & Singer, T. (2006). The empathetic brain: How, when, and why. *Trends in Cognitive Sciences, 10,* 435–441.

De Waal, F. (1982). *Chimpanzee politics.* New York, NY: Harper & Row.

De Waal, F. (1989). *Peacemaking among primates.* Cambridge, MA: Harvard University Press.

De Waal, F. (1996). *Good natured: The origins of right and wrong in humans and other animals.* Cambridge, MA: Harvard University Press.

De Waal, F. (2011). Interview, http://www.wonderlance.com/february2011_scientech_fransdewaal.html

De Waal, F., & Lanting, F. (1997). *Bonobo: The forgotten ape.* Berkeley, CA: University of California Press.

De Waal, F.B.M. (1995, March). Bonobo sex and society. *Scientific American, 272,* 82–88.

De Waal, F.B.M. (2000). Primates: A natural heritage of conflict resolution. *Science, 289,* 586–590.

De Wolff, M. S., & van Ijzendoorn, M. H. (1997). Sensitivity and attachment: A meta-analysis on parental antecedents of infant attachment. *Child Development, 68*(4), 571–591.

Del Carmen, R., Pedersen, F. A., Huffman, L. C., & Bryan, Y. E. (1993). Dyadic distress management predicts subsequent security of attachment. *Infant Behavior & Development, 16*(2), 131–147.

Dean, K., Stevens, H., Mortensen, P. B., Murray, R. M., Walsh, E. & Pedersen, C. B. (2010). Full spectrum of psychiatric outcomes among offspring with parental history of mental disorder. *Archives of General Psychiatry, 67*(8), 822–829.

Deater-Deckard, K., Dodge, K. A., Bates, J. E., & Pettit, G. S. (1998). Multiple risk factors in the development of externalizing behavior problems: Group and individual differences. *Developmental Psychopathology, 10,* 469–493.

Deci, E. L., & Ryan, R. M. (2000). The "what" and "why" of goal pursuits: Human needs and the self-determination of behavior. *Psychological Inquiry, 11*(4), 227–268.

DeGangi, G. A., DiPietro, J. A., Greenspan, S. I., & Porges, S. W. (1991). Psychophysiological characteristics of the regulatory disordered infant. *Infant Behavior and Development, 14*(1), 37–50.

Deleaveau, P., Jabourian, M., Lemogne, C., Guionnet, S., Bergouignan, L., Fossati, P., et al. (2011). Brain effects of antidepressants in major depression: A meta-analysis of emotional processing studies. *Journal of Affective Disorders, 130,* 66–74.

Demers, I., Bernier, A., Tarabulsy, G. M., & Provost, M. A. (2010). Mind-mindedness in adult and adolescent mothers: Relations to maternal sensitivity and infant attachment. *International Journal of Behavioral Development (Print), 34*(6), 529–537.

Demir, M., & Weitekamp, L. A. (2007). I am so happy 'cause today I found my friend: Friendship and personality as predictors of happiness. *Journal of Happiness Studies, 8,* 181–211.

Deneault, J., Ricard, M., Décarie, T. G., Morin, P. L., Quintal, G., Boivin, M., et al. (2008). False belief and emotion understanding in monozygotic twins, dizygotic twins and non-twin children. *Cognition and Emotion, 22*(4), 697–708.

Denham, S. A., Blair, K. A., DeMulder, E., Levitas, J., Sawyer, K., Auerbach-Major, S., et al. (2003). Preschool emotional competence: Pathway to social competence? *Child Development, 74,* 238–256.

Denham, S. A., Mitchell-Copeland, J., Strandberg, K., Auerbach, S., & Blair, K. (1997). Parental contributions to preschoolers' emotional competence: Direct and indirect effects. *Motivation and Emotion, 21*(1), 65–86.

Denham, S. A., Workman, E., Cole, P., Weissbrod, C., Kendziora, K., & Zahn-Waxler, C. (2000). Prediction of externalizing behavior problems from early to middle childhood: The role of parental socialization and emotion expression. *Development and Psychopathology, 12,* 23–45.

Dennis, T., Talih, M., Cole, P. M., Zahn-Waxler, C., & Mizuta, I. (in press). The socialization of autonomy and relatedness: Sequential verbal exchanges in Japanese and U.S. mother-preschooler dyads. *Journal of Cross-Cultural Psychology.*

Dentan, R. K. (1968). *The Semai: A nonviolent people of Malaya.* New York, NY: Holt, Rinehart & Winston.

Depue, R. A., & Collins, P. F. (1999). Neurobiology of the structure of personality: Dopamine, facilitation of incentive motivation, and extraversion. *Behavioral and Brain Sciences, 22,* 491–569.

Depue, R. A., & Morrone-Strupinsky, J. V. (2005). A neurobehavioral model of affiliative bonding: Implications for conceptualizing a human trait of affiliation. *Behavioral and Brain Sciences. 28,* 313–395.

Descartes, R. (1649). Passions of the soul. In E. L. Haldane & G. R. Ross (Eds.), *The philosophical works of Descartes*. New York, NY: Dover (current edition 1911).

DeSteno, D., Bartlett, M., Baumann, J., Williams, L., & Dickens, L. (2010). Gratitude as moral sentiment: Emotion-guided cooperation in economic exchange. *Emotion*, *10*, 289–293.

DeSteno, D., Dasgupta, N., Bartlett, M. Y., & Cajdric, A. (2004). Prejudice from thin air: The effect of emotion on automatic intergroup attitudes. *Psychological Science*, *15*, 319–324.

DeSteno, D., Petty, R. E., Rucker, D. D., Wegener, D. T., & Braverman, J. (2004). Discrete emotions and persuasion: The role of emotion-induced expectancies. *Journal of Personality and Social Psychology*, *86*, 43–56.

DeSteno, D., Petty, R., Wegener, D., & Rucker, D. (2000). Beyond valence in the perception of likelihood: The role of emotion specificity. *Journal of Personality and Social Psychology*, *78*, 397–416.

DeSteno, D. A., & Salovey, P. (1996). Jealousy and the characteristics of one's rival: A self-evaluation maintenance perspective. *Personality and Social Psychology*, *22*, 920–932.

Detert, N. B., Llewelyn, S., Hardy, G. E., Bakham, M., & Stiles, W. B. (2006). Assimilation in good- and poor-outcome cases of very brief psychotherapy for mild depression: An initial comparison. *Psychotherapy Research*, *16*, 393–407.

Di Ciano, P., Blaha, C. D., & Phillips, A. G. (1998). Conditioned changes in dopamine oxidation currents in the nucleus accumbens of rats by stimuli paired with self-administration or yoked-administration of d-amphetamine. *European Journal of Neuroscience*, *10*(3), 1121–1127.

Diamond, J. (1997). *Guns, germs, and steel: The fates of human societies*. New York, NY: Norton.

Diamond, L. M. (2003). What does sexual orientation orient?: A biobehavioral model distinguishing romantic love and sexual desire. *Psychological Review*, *110*(1), 173–192.

Dickerson, S. S., Gable, S. L., Irwin, M. R., Aziz, N., & Kemeny, M. E. (2009). Social-evaluative threat and proinflammatory cytokine regulation: An experimental laboratory investigation *Psychological Science*, *20*(10), 1237–1244.

Dickerson, S. S., Gruenewald, T. L., & Kemeny, M. E. (2004). Immunological effects of induced shame and guilt. *Psychosomatic Medicine*, *66*, 124–131.

Dickerson, S. S, & Kemeny, M. E. (2004). Acute stressors and cortisol responses: A theoretical integration and synthesis of laboratory research. *Psychological Bulletin*, *130*, 355–391.

Diener, E., & Biswas-Diener, R. (2002). Will money increase subjective well-being? A literature review and guide to needed research. *Social Indicators Research*, *57*, 119–169.

Dimberg, U., Thunberg, M., & Elmehed, K. (2000). Unconscious facial reactions to emotional facial expressions. *Psychological Science*, *11*, 86–89.

Dimberg, U., & Thunberg, M. (2007). Speech anxiety and rapid emotional reactions to angry and happy facial expressions. *Scandinavian Journal of Psychology*, *48*(4), 321–328.

Dimberg, U., Thunberg, M., & Grunedal, S. (2002). Facial reactions to emotional stimuli: Automatically controlled emotional responses. *Cognition and Emotion*, *16*, 449–471.

Dimitsantos, E., Escorihuela, R. M., Fuentes, S., Armario, A., & Nadal, R. (2007). Litter size affects emotionality in adult male rats. *Physiology & Behavior*, *92*(4), 708–716.

DiPietro, J. A., Hodgson, D. M., Costigan, K. A., & Johnson, T.R.B. (1996). Fetal antecedents of infant temperament. *Child Development*, *67*(5), 2568–2583.

Dishion, T. J., & Tipsord, J. M. (2011). Peer contagion in child and adolescent social and emotional development. *Annual Review of Psychology*, *62*, 189–214.

Disner, S. G., Beevers, C. G., Haigh, E.A.P., & Beck, A. T. (2011). Neural mechanisms of the cognitive model of depression. *Nature Reviews: Neuroscience*, *12*, 467–477.

Ditzen B., Schaer M., Gabriel B., Bodenmann G., Ehlert U., & Heinrichs M. (2009). Intranasal oxytocin increases positive communication and reduces cortisol levels during couple conflict, *Biological Psychiatry*, *65*, 728–731.

Djikic, M., & Oatley, K. (2004). Love and personal relationships: Navigating on the border between the ideal and the real. *Journal for the Theory of Social Behaviour*, *34*, 199–209.

Djikic, M., Oatley, K., Zoeterman, S., & Peterson, J. (2009). On being moved by art: How reading fiction transforms the self. *Creativity Research Journal*, *21*, 24–29.

Doan, S. N., & Wang, Q. (2010). Maternal discussions of mental states and behaviors: Relations to emotion situation knowledge in European American and immigrant Chinese children. *Child Development*, *81*(5), 1490–1503.

Dodge, K. A. (2006). Translational science in action: Hostile attributional style and the development of aggressive behaviour problems. *Development and Psychopathology, 18,* 791–814.

Dodge, K. A., Bates, J. E., & Pettit, G. S. (1990). Mechanisms in the cycle of violence. *Science, 250,* 1678–1683.

Dodge, K. A., & Coie, J. D. (1987). Social-information-processing factors in reactive and proactive aggression in children's peer groups. *Journal of Personality and Social Psychology, 53,* 1146–1158.

Dodge, K. A., Malone, P. S., Lansford, J. E., Miller, S., Pettit, G. S., & Bates, J. E. (2009). A dynamic cascade model of the development of substance-use onset. *Monographs of the Society for Research in Child Development, 74*(294), 1–120.

Dodge, K. A., & Pettit, G. S. (2003). A biopsychosocial model of the development of chronic conduct problems in adolescence. *Developmental Psychology, 39*(2), 349–371.

Dohrenwend, B. P., Link, B. C., Kern, R., Shrout, P. E., & Markowitz, J. (1990). Measuring life events: The problem of variablity within event categories. *Stress Medicine, 6,* 179–187.

Doi, T. (1973). *The anatomy of dependence* (J. Beste, Trans.). Tokyo: Kodansha.

Doll, R., & Peto, R. (1981). *The causes of cancer.* Oxford, UK: Oxford University Press.

Dollard, J., Doob, L. W., Miller, N. E., Mowrer, O. H., & Sears, R. R. (1939). *Frustration and aggression.* New Haven, CT: Yale University Press.

Domes, G., Heinrichs, M., Michel, A., Berger, C., and Herpertz, S. C. (2007). Oxytocin improves "mind-reading" in humans. *Biological Psychiatry, 61,* 731–733.

Dong, M., Anda, R. F., Felitti, V. J., Dube, S. R., Williamson, D. F., Thompson, T. J., Loo, C. M., & Giles, W. H. (2004). The interrelatedness of multiple forms of childhood abuse, neglect and household dysfunction. *Child Abuse & Neglect, 28,* 771–784.

D'Onofrio, B. M., Turkheimer, E., Emery, R., Slutske, W., Heath, A. C., Madden, P. A., & Martin, N. G. (2005). A genetically informed study of marital instability and its association with offspring psychopathology. *Journal of Abnormal Psychology, 114*(4), 570–586.

Dostoevsky, F. (1955). Introduction by D. Magarshak (Trans.). *The Idiot.* Harmondsworth: Penguin.

Dougherty, L. R. (2006). Children's emotionality and social status: A meta-analytic review. *Social Development, 15*(3), 394–417.

Dougherty, L. R., Bufferd, S. J., Carlson, G. A., Dyson, M. W., Olino, T. M., & Klein, D. N. (2011). Preschoolers' observed temperament and *DSM-IV* psychiatric disorders assessed with a parent diagnostic interview. *Journal of Clinical Child and Adolescent Psychology, 40,* 295–306.

Downey, D. B., & Condron, D. J. (2004). Playing well with others in kindergarten: The benefit of siblings at home. *Journal of Marriage and Family, 66*(2), 333–350.

Dozois, D.J.A., & Dobson, K. S. (Eds.). (2004). *The prevention of anxiety and depression: Theory, research, and practice.* Washington, DC: American Psychological Association.

Dranovsky, A., & Hen, R. (2006). Hippocampal neurogenesis: Regulation by stress and antidepressants. *Biological Psychiatry, 59,* 1136–1143.

Dube, S. R., Felitti, V. J., Dong, M., Chapman, D. P., Giles, W. H., & Anda, R. F. (2003). Childhood abuse, neglect, and household dysfunction and the risk of illicit drug use: The adverse childhood experiences study. *Pediatrics, 111*(3), 564–572.

Dumont, M., Yzerbyt, V. Y., Wigboldus, D., & Gordijn, E. (2003). Social categorization and fear reactions to the September 11th terrorist attacks. *Personality and Social Psychology Bulletin, 29,* 1509–1520.

Dunbar, K. (1993). How scientists really reason: Scientific reasoning in real-world laboratories. In R. J. Sternberg & J. Davidson (Eds.), *Mechanisms of insight.* Cambridge, MA: MIT Press.

Dunbar, R.I.M. (1993). Coevolution of neocortical size, group size, and language in humans. *Behavioral and Brain Sciences, 16,* 681–735.

Dunbar, R.I.M. (1996). *Grooming, gossip and the evolution of language.* London, UK: Faber & Faber.

Dunbar, R.I.M. (2001). Brains on two legs: Group size and the evolution of intelligence. In F.B.M. De Waal (Ed.), *Tree of origin: What primate behavior can tell us about human social evolution* (pp. 173–191). Cambridge, MA: Harvard University Press.

Dunbar, R.I.M. (2003). The social brain: Mind, language, and society in evolutionary perspective. *Annual Review of Anthropology, 32,* 163–181.

Dunbar, R.I.M. (2004). *The human story: A new history of mankind's evolution*. London, UK: Faber.

Duncan, G., Ziol-Guest, K., & Kalil, A. (2010). Early-childhood poverty and adult attainment, behavior and health. *Child Development, 81*(1), 306–325.

Dunn, B. D., Billotti, D., Murphy, V., & Dalgliesh, T. (2009). The consequences of effortful emotion regulation when processing distressing material: A comparison of suppression and acceptance. *Behavior Research and Therapy, 47*, 761–773.

Dunn, J. (1983). Sibling relationships in early childhood. *Child Development, 54*(4), 787.

Dunn, J. (2004). The development of individual differences in understanding emotion and mind: Antecedents and sequillae. In N. H. Frijda, A.S.R. Manstead, & A. Fischer (Eds.), *Feelings and emotions: The Amsterdam Symposium* (pp. 303–320). New York, NY: Cambridge University Press.

Durand, K., Gallay, M., Seigneuric, A., Robichon, F., & Baudouin, J. Y. (2007). The development of facial emotion recognition: The role of configural information. *Journal of Experimental Child Psychology, 97*(1), 14–27.

Durlak, J. A., Fuhrman, T., & Lampman, C. (1991). Effectiveness of cognitive-behavior therapy for maladapting children: A meta-analysis. *Psychological Bulletin, 110*(2), 204.

Durlauf, S. N., & Nagin, D. (2011). Imprisonment and crime: Can both be reduced? *Criminology and Public Policy, 11*, 9–54.

Dutton, D. (2009). *The art instinct: Beauty, pleasure, and human evolution*. London, UK: Bloomsbury.

Dutton, D. G., & Aron, A. P. (1974). Some evidence for heightened sexual attraction under conditions of high anxiety. *Journal of Personality and Social Psychology, 30*, 510–517.

Eagly, A., & Wood, W. (1999). The origins of sex differences in human behavior: Evolved dispositions versus social roles. *American Psychologist, 54*, 408–423.

Eales, M. J. (1992). Shame and guilt: Instincts and their vicissitudes in human evolution (Unpublished manuscript).

Easterling, D. V., & Leventhal, H. (1989). Contribution of concrete cognition to emotion: Neutral symptoms as elicitors of worry about cancer. *Journal of Applied Psychology, 74*, 787–796.

Eastwick, P. W., Finkel, E. J., Mochon, D., & Ariely, D. (2007). Selective versus unselective romantic desire: Not all reciprocity is created equal. *Psychological Science, 18*, 317–319.

Edelmann, R. J. (1990). Embarrassment and blushing: A component-process model, some initial descriptive and cross-cultural data. In W. R. Crozier (Ed.), *Shyness and embarrassment: Perspectives from social psychology* (pp. 205–229). Cambridge, MA: Cambridge University Press.

Edelmann, R. J., & Hampson, S. E. (1979). Changes in nonverbal behavior during embarrassment. *British Journal of Social and Clinical Psychology, 18*, 385–390.

Edelmann, R. J., & Hampson, S. E. (1981). Embarrassment in dyadic interaction. *Social Behavior and Personality, 9*, 171–177.

Edwards, V. J., Holden, G. W., Felitti, V. J., & Anda, R. F. (2003). Relationship between multiple forms of childhood maltreatment and adult mental health and community respondents: Results from the adverse childhood experiences study. *American Journal of Psychiatry, 160*, 1453–1460.

Egeland, B., & Farber, E. A. (1984). Infant-mother attachment: Factors related to its development and changes over time. *Child Development, 55*(3), 753–771.

Ehring, T., Tuschen-Caffler, B., Schnulle, J., Fischer, S., & Gross, J. J. (2010). Emotion regulation and vulnerability to depression: Spontaneous versus instructed use of emotion suppression and reappraisal. *Emotion, 10*, 563–572.

Eibl-Eibesfeldt, I. (1970). *Ethology: The biology of behavior*. New York, NY: Holt, Rinehart & Winston.

Eibl-Eibesfeldt, I. (1989). *Human ethology*. New York, NY: Aldine de Gruyter.

Eich, E., & Macaulay, D. (2000). Fundamental factors in mood-dependent memory. In J. Forgas (Ed.), *Feeling and thinking: The role of affect in social cognition* (pp. 109–130). New York, NY: Cambridge University Press.

Eich, E., Macaulay, D., & Ryan, L. (1994). Mood dependent memory for events of the personal past. *Journal of Experimental Psychology (General), 123*, 201–215.

Eisenberg, N. (1992). *The caring child*. Cambridge, MA: Harvard University Press.

Eisenberg, N., Cumberland, A., & Spinrad, T. L. (1998). Parental socialization of emotion. *Psychological Inquiry, 9*, 241–273.

Eisenberg, N., Fabes, R. A., Carlo, G., & Karbon, M. (1992). Emotional responsivity to others: Behavioral correlates and socialization antecedents. *New Directions in Child Development*, *55*, 57–73.

Eisenberg, N., Fabes, R. A., Guthrie, I. K., & Reiser, M. (2000). Dispositional emotionality and regulation: Their role in predicting quality of social functioning. *Journal of Personality and Social Psychology*, *78*(1), 136–157.

Eisenberg, N., Fabes, R. A., Miller, P. A., Fultz, J., Shell, R., Mathy, R. M., & Reno, R. R. (1989). Relation of sympathy and distress to prosocial behavior: A multimethod study. *Journal of Personality and Social Psychology*, *57*, 55–66.

Eisenberg, N., Fabes, R. A., & Murphy, B. C. (1996). Parents' reactions to children's negative emotions: Relations to children's social competence and comforting behavior. *Child Development*, *67*, 2227–2247.

Eisenberg, N., & Spinrad, T. L. (2004). Emotion-related regulation: Sharpening the definition. *Child Development*, *75*(2), 334–339.

Eisenberg, N., Spinrad, T. L., & Morris, A. S. (2002). Regulation, resiliency, and quality of social functioning. *Self and Identity*, *1*(2), 121–128.

Eisenberger, N. I., & Lieberman, M. D. (2004). Why rejection hurts: A common neural alarm system for physical and social pain. *Trends in Cognitive Sciences*, *8*, 294–300.

Eisenberger, N. I., Lieberman, M. D., & Williams, K. D. (2003). Does rejection hurt? An fMRI study of social exclusion. *Science*, *302*, 290–292.

Ekman, P. (1972). Universals and cultural differences in facial expressions of emotion. In J. Cole (Ed.), *Nebraska Symposium on Motivation, 1971* (pp. 207–283). Lincoln: University of Nebraska Press.

Ekman, P. (1984). Expression and the nature of emotion. In K. R. Scherer & P. Ekman (Eds.), *Approaches to emotion* (pp. 319–344). Hillsdale, NJ: Erlbaum.

Ekman, P. (1992). An argument for basic emotions. *Cognition and Emotion*, *6*, 169–200.

Ekman, P. (1993). Facial expression and emotion. *American Psychologist*, *48*, 384–392.

Ekman, P. (1994). Strong evidence for universals in facial expressions: A reply to Russell's mistaken critique. *Psychological Bulletin*, *115*, 268–287.

Ekman, P., & Friesen, W. V. (1969). The repertoire of nonverbal behavior: Categories, origins, usage and coding. *Semiotica*, *1*, 49–98.

Ekman, P., & Friesen, W. V. (1971). Constants across culture in the face and emotion. *Journal of Personality and Social Psychology*, *17*, 124–129.

Ekman, P., & Friesen, W. V. (1975). *Pictures of facial affect*. Palo Alto, CA: Consulting Psychologists Press.

Ekman, P., & Friesen, W. V. (1984). *Emotion facial action coding system (EM-FACS)*. Obtainable from Paul Ekman, University of California, San Francisco.

Ekman, P., Friesen, W. V., & Ellsworth, P. C. (1982). *Emotion in the human face*. Cambridge, MA: Cambridge University Press.

Ekman, P., Levenson, R. W., & Friesen, W. V. (1983). Autonomic nervous system activity distinguishes among emotions. *Science*, *221*, 1208–1210.

Ekman, P., & Rosenberg, E. L. (1997). *What the face reveals*. New York, NY: Oxford University Press.

Ekman, P., Sorenson, E. R., & Friesen, W. V. (1969). Pan-cultural elements in the facial displays of emotions. *Science*, *164*, 86–88.

Elder, G. H. (1986). Military times and turning points in men's lives. *Developmental Psychology*, *22*, 233–245.

Elder, G. H., & Clipp, E. C. (1989). Combat experience and emotional health: Impairment and resilience in later life. *Journal of Personality*, *57*, 311–341.

Elfenbein, H. A., & Ambady, N. (2002). On the universality and cultural specificity of emotion recognition: A meta-analysis. *Psychological Bulletin*, *128*, 203–235.

Elfenbein, H. A., & Ambady, N. (2003). Universals and cultural differences in recognizing emotions. *Current Directions in Psychological Science*, *12*, 159–164.

Elgar, F. J., McGrath, P. J., Waschbusch, D. A., Stewart, S. H., & Curtis, L. J. (2004). Mutual influences on maternal depression and child adjustment problems. *Clinical Psychology Review*, *24*, 441–459.

Elias, N. (1939). *The history of manners: The civilization process, Vol. 1* (E. Jephcott, Trans.). New York, NY: Pantheon (1978).

Eliot, G. (1860). *The mill on the floss*. Edinburgh, UK: Blackwood (current edition Penguin, 1973).

Eliot, G. (1871–1872). *Middlemarch: A study of provincial life*. Edinburgh, UK: Blackwood (The Works of George Eliot Standard Edition, 1883).

Elliott, R., Greenberg, L. S., & Lietaer, G. (2004). Research on experiential psychotherapies. In M. J. Lambert (Ed.), *Bergin and Garfield's handbook of psychotherapy and behavior change* (5th ed., pp. 493–539). New York, NY: Wiley.

Elliott, D., Wilson, W. J., Huizinga, D., Sampson, R., Elliott, A., & Rankin, B. (1996). The effects of neighborhood disadvantage on adolescent development. *Journal of Research in Crime and Delinquency, 33*, 389–426.

Ellis, B. H., Fisher, P. A., & Zaharie, S. (2004). Predictors of disruptive behavior, developmental delays, anxiety, and affective symptomatology among institutionally reared Romanian children. *Journal of the American Academy of Child and Adolescent Psychiatry, 43*, 1283–1292.

Ellis, B. J., Boyce, W. T., Belsky, J., Bakermans-Kranenburg, M. J., & van Izjendoorn, M. H. (2011). Differential susceptibility to the environment: An evolutionary-neurodevelopmental theory. *Development and Psychopathology, 23*, 7–28.

Ellsworth, P. (1991). Some implications of cognitive appraisal theories of emotion. In K. T. Strongman (Ed.), *International review of studies on emotion* (pp. 143–161). Chichester UK: Wiley.

Ellsworth, P. C., & Smith, C. A. (1985). Patterns of cognitive appraisal in emotion. *Journal of Personality and Social Psychology, 48*, 813–838.

Ellsworth, P. C., & Smith, C. A. (1988). From appraisal to emotion: Differences among unpleasant feelings. *Motivation and Emotion, 12*, 271–302.

Elmadjian, F. J., Hope, M., & Lamson, E. T. (1957). Excretion of E and NE in various emotional states. *Journal of Clinical Endocrinology, 17*, 608–620.

El-Sheikh, M., & Hinnant, J. B. (2011). Marital conflict, respiratory sinus arrhythmia and allostatic load: Interrelations and associations with the development of children's externalizing behaviour. *Development and Psychopathology, 23*, 815–829.

Elster, J. (1999). *Alchemies of the mind: Rationality and the emotions*. Cambridge, MA: Cambridge University Press.

Emery, N. J., & Amaral, D. G. (2000). The role of the amygdala in primate social cognition. In R. D. Lane & L. Nadel (Eds.), *Cognitive neuroscience of emotion* (pp. 156–191). New York, NY: Oxford University Press.

Emmons, R. A. (2007). *Thanks! How the new science of gratitude can make you happier*. Boston, MA: Houghton-Mifflin.

Emmons, R. A., & McCullough, M. E. (2003). Counting blessings versus burdens: An experimental investigation of gratitude and subjective well-being in daily life. *Journal of Personality and Social Psychology, 84*, 377–389.

Epictetus. (c. 100). *Discourses and Encheiridion* (English translation by W. A. Oldfather). Cambridge, MA: Loeb-Harvard University Press (1998).

Erikson, E. H. (1950). *Childhood and society*. London, UK: Penguin (reissued 1965).

Esquivel, L. (1992). *Like water for chocolate* (T. & C. Christensen, Trans.). New York, NY: Doubleday.

Essau, C. A., Lewinsohn, P. M., Seeley, J. R., & Sasagawa, S. (2010). Gender differences in the developmental course of depression. *Journal of Affective Disorders, 127*, 185–190.

Essex, M. J., Kraemer, H. C., Slattery, M. J., Burk, L. R., Boyce, T. W., Woodward, H. R., et al. (2009). Screening for childhood mental health problems: Outcomes and early identification. *Journal of Child Psychology and Psychiatry, 50*(5), 562–570.

Esteves, F., Dimberg, U., & Öhman, A. (1994). Automatically elicited fear: Conditioned skin conductance responses to masked facial expressions. *Cognition and Emotion, 8*, 393–413.

Etcoff, N. L., & Magee, J. J. (1992). Categorical perception of facial expressions. *Cognition, 44*, 227–240.

Etkin, A., Klemenhagen, K. C., Dudman, J. T., Rogan, M. T., Hen, R., Kandel, E. R., et al. (2004). Individual differences in trait anxiety predict the response of the basolateral amygdala to unconsciously processed fearful faces. *Neuron, 44*(6), 1043–1055.

Evans, G. W. (2003). A multimethodological analysis of cumulative risk and allostatic load among rural children. *Developmental Psychology, 39*(5), 924–933.

Eysenck, M., Derakshan, N., Santos, R., & Calvo, M. G. (2007). Anxiety and cognitive performance: Attentional control theory. *Emotion, 7*, 336–353.

Eysenck, M. W. (1992). *Anxiety: The cognitive perspective*. Hove, UK: Erlbaum.

Fair, D. A., Cohen, A. L., Power, J. D., Dosenbach, N. U. F., Church, J. A., Miezin, F. M., et al. (2009). Functional brain networks develop from a "local to distributed" organization. *PLoS Computational Biology, 5*(5), e1000381.

Faircloth, W. B., Schermerhorn, A. C., Mitchell, P. M., Cummings, J. S., & Cummings, E. M. (2011). Testing the long-term efficacy of a prevention program for improving marital conflict in community families. *Journal of Applied Developmental Psychology.*

Farrington, D. P., & Welsh, B. C. (2007). *Saving children from a life of crime: Early risk factors and effective interventions.* Oxford, UK: Oxford University Press.

Farroni, T., Menon, E., Rigato, S., & Johnson, M. H. (2007). The perception of facial expressions in newborns. *European Journal of Developmental Psychology, 4*(1), 2–13.

Faulkner, D., & Miell, D. (1993). Settling into school: The importance of early friendships for the development of children' social understanding and communicative competence. *International Journal of Early Years Education, 1*, 23–46.

Fava, G. A., & Tomba, E. (2009). Increasing psychological well-being and resilience by psychotherapeutic methods. *Journal of Personality, 77*, 1903–1934.

Fearon, R. M., van Ijzendoorn, M. H., Fonagy, P., Bakermans-Kranenburg, M. J., Schuengel, C., & Bokhorst, C. L. (2006). In search of shared and nonshared environmental factors in security of attachment : A behavior-genetic study of the association between sensitivity and attachment security. *Developmental Psychology, 42*(6), 1026–1040.

Fearon, R.M.P., Bakermans-Kranenburg, M. J., Van Ijzendoorn, M. H., Lapsley, A., & Roisman, G.I. (2010). The significance of insecure attachment and disorganization in the development of children's externalizing behavior: A meta-analytic study. *Child Development, 81*, 435–456.

Feather, N. T. (2006). Deservingness and emotions: Applying the structural model of deservingness to the analysis of affective reactions to outcomes. *European Review of Social Psychology, 17*, 38–73.

Federenko, I., Schlotz, W., Kirschbaum, C., Bartels, M., Hellhammer, D. H., & Wust, S. (2006). The heritablity of perceived stress. *Psychological Medicine, 36*, 375–385.

Fehr, B., & Russell, J. A. (1984). Concept of emotion viewed from a prototype perspective. *Journal of Experimental Psychology: General, 113*, 464–486.

Fehr, B., & Russell, J. A. (1991). The concept of love viewed from a prototype perspective. *Journal of Personality and Social Psychology, 60*, 425–438.

Feigeson, N., Park, J., & Salovey, P. (2001). The role of emotions in comparative negligence judgments. *Journal of Applied Social Psychology, 31*, 576–603.

Feldman-Barrett, L. (1997). The relationship among momentary emotional experiences, personality descriptions, and retrospective ratings of emotion. *Personality and Social Psychology Bulletin, 23*, 1100–1110.

Feldman-Barrett, L., & Barrett, D. J. (2001). Computerized experience-sampling: How technology facilitates the study of conscious experience. *Social Science Computer Review, 19*, 175–185.

Feldman-Barrett, L., Quigley, K. S., Bliss-Moreau, E., & Aronson, K. R. (2004). Interoceptive sensitivity and self-reports of emotional experience. *Journal of Personality and Social Psychology, 87*, 684–697.

Feldman-Barrett, L., & Russell, J. A. (1999). Structure of current affect. *Current Directions in Psychological Science, 8*, 10–14.

Fenske, M. L., & Raymond, J. E. (2006). Affective influences of selective attention. *Current Directions in Psychological Science, 15*, 312–316.

Ferdinand, R. F., Dieleman, G., Ormel, J., & Verhulst, F. C. (2007). Homotypic versus heterotypic continuity of anxiety symptoms in young adolescents: Evidence for distinctions between *DSM-IV* subtypes. *Journal of Abnormal Child Psychology, 35*(3), 325–333.

Fergusson, D. M., & Horwood, L. J. (2002). Male and female offending trajectories. *Development and Psychopathology, 14*(1), 159–177.

Fernald, A. (1992). Human maternal vocalizations to infants as biologically relevant signals: An evolutionary perspective. In J. H. Barkow, L. Cosmides, & J. Tooby (Eds.), *The adapted mind: Evolutionary psychology and the generation of culture* (pp. 391–428). New York, NY: Oxford University Press.

Fernandez-Dols, J. M., & Ruiz-Belda, M. A. (1995). Are smiles a sign of happiness? Gold medal winners at the Olympic Games. *Journal of Personality and Social Psychology, 69*, 1113–1119.

Fernandez-Dols, J. M., & Ruiz-Belda, M. A. (1997). Spontaneous facial behavior during intense emotional episodes: Artistic truth and optical truth. In J. A. Russell & J. M. Fernandez-Dols (Eds.), *The psychology of facial expression* (pp. 255–294). Cambridge, MA: Cambridge University Press.

Fernyhough, C. (1996). The dialogic mind: A dialogic approach to the higher mental functions. *New Ideas in Psychology, 14*(1), 47–62.

Ferrari, M., & Koyama, E. (2002). Meta-emotions about anger and *amae. Consciousness and Emotion, 3,* 197–212.

Field, J. (1934). *A life of one's own.* Harmondsworth, UK: Penguin (current edition 1952).

Field, T. (2001). *Touch.* Cambridge, MA: MIT Press.

Field, T., Healy, B., Goldstein, S., Perry, S., Bendell, D., Schanberg, S., Zimmerman, E. A., & Kuhn, C. (1988). Infants of depressed mothers show "depressed" behavior even with nondepressed adults. *Child Development, 59,* 1569–1579.

Finkel, E. J., & Eastwick, P. W. (2008). Speed-dating. *Current Directions in Psychological Science, 17,* 193–197.

Finkel, N. J., & Parrott, W. G. (2006). *Emotions and culpability: How the law is at odds with psychology, jurors, and itself.* Washington, DC: American Psychological Association.

Finkenauer, C., Engels, R., & Baumeister, R. F. (2005). Parenting behaviour and adolescent behavioural and emotional problems: The role of self-control. *International Journal of Behavioral Development, 29,* 58–69.

Finlay-Jones, R. (1989). Anxiety. In G. W. Brown & T. O. Harris (Eds.), *Life events and illness* (pp. 95–112). London, UK: Unwin Hyman.

Fiorino, D. F., Coury, A., & Phillips, A. G. (1997). Dynamic changes in nucleus accumbens dopamine efflux during the Coolidge effect in male rats. *Journal of Neuroscience, 17* (12), 4849–4855.

Fischer, A. H. (2000). *Gender and emotion: Social psychological perspectives.* Cambridge, MA: Cambridge University Press.

Fischer, A. H., & Manstead, A.S.R. (2000). The relation between gender and emotions in different cultures. In A. H. Fischer (Ed.), *Gender and emotion: Social psychological perspectives* (pp. 71–93). Cambridge, MA: Cambridge University Press.

Fisher, H. E. (1992). *Anatomy of love.* New York, NY: Norton.

Fiske, A. P. (1991). *Structures of social life.* New York, NY: Free Press.

Fiske, A. P., Kitayama, S., Markus, H. R., & Nisbett, R. E. (1998). The cultural matrix of social psychology. In D. T.

Gilbert, S. T. Fiske, & G. Lindzey (Eds.), *Handbook of social psychology* (4th ed., pp. 915–981). Boston, MA: McGraw-Hill.

Fiske, S. T. (2010). Interpersonal stratification: Status, power, and subordination. In S. T. Fiske, D. T. Gilbert, & G. Lindzey (Eds.), *Handbook of social psychology* (5th ed., pp. 941–982). New York, NY: Wiley.

Fivush, R., & Wang, Q. (2005). Emotion talk in mother-child conversations of the shared past: The effects of culture, gender, and event valence. *Journal of Cognition and Development, 6*(4), 489–506.

Flack, W. F., & Laird, J. D. (Eds.). (1998). *Emotions in psychopathology: Theory and research.* New York, NY: Oxford University Press.

Flack, W. F., Laird, J. D., Cavallaro, L. A., & Miller, D. R. (1998). Emotional expression and experience: A psychosocial perspective on schizophrenia. In W. F. Flack & J. D. Laird (Eds.), *Emotions in psychopathology: Theory and research* (pp. 315–322). New York, NY: Oxford University Press.

Fleming, A. S., & Corter, C. (1995). Psychobiology of maternal behavior in nonhuman mammals: Role of sensory, experiential and neural factors. In M. Bornstein (Ed.), *Handbook of parenting.* Hillsdale, NJ: Erlbaum.

Fletcher, G. J.O., Tither, J., O'Loughlin, C., Friesen, M., & Overall, N. (2004). Warm and homely or cold and beautiful? Sex differences in trading off traits in mate selection. *Personality and Social Psychology Bulletin, 30,* 659–672.

Flinn, M., & Alexander, R. (2007). Runaway social selection in human evolution In S. W. Gangestad & J. A. Simpson (Eds.), *The evolution of mind: Fundamental questions and controversies* (pp. 249–255). New York, NY: Guilford.

Flom, R., & Bahrick, L. E. (2007). The development of infant discrimination of affect in multimodal and unimodal stimulation: The role of intersensory redundancy. *Developmental Psychology, 43*(1), 238–252.

Foa, E. B., Feske, U., Murdoch, T. B., Kozak, M. J., & McCarthy, P. R. (1991). Processing of threat-related information in rape victims. *Journal of Abnormal Psychology, 100,* 156–162.

Fonagy, P. (2000). The outcome of psychoanalysis: The hope of a future. *The Psychologist, 13,* 620–623.

Fonagy, P., & Luyten, P. (2009). A developmental, mentalization-based approach to the understanding and treatment of borderline personality disorder. *Development and Psychopathology, 21,* 1355–1381.

Fonagy, P., Steele, M., Steele, H., Leigh, T., Kennedy, R., Mattoon, G., et al. (1995). Attachment, the reflective self, and borderline states: The predictive specificity of the Adult Attachment Interview and pathological emotional development. In S. Goldberg, R. Muir, & J. Kerr (Eds.), *Attachment theory: Social, developmental and clinical perspectives* (pp. 233–278). Hillsdale, NJ: Analytic Press.

Fonagy, P., Steele, M., Steele, H., Moran, G. S., & Higgitt, A. C. (1991). The capacity for understanding mental states: The reflective self in parent and child and its significance for security of attachment. *Infant Mental Health Journal, 12*(3), 201–218.

Fontaine, N.M.G., McCrory, E.J.P., Boivin, M., Moffit, T. E., & Viding, E. (2011). Predictors and outcomes of joint trajectories of callous-unemotional traits and conduct problems in childhood. *Journal of Abnormal Psychology, 120*(3), 730–742.

Fontaine, R. G. (2010). New developments in developmental research on social information processing and antisocial behavior. *Journal of Abnormal Child Psychology, 38,* 569–573.

Fontaine, R. G., & Dodge, K. A. (2009). Social information processing and aggressive behavior: A transactional perspective. In A. J. Sameroff (Ed.), *The transactional model of development: How children and contexts shape each other* (pp. 117–135). Washington, DC: American Psychological Association.

Foot, P. (1978). The problem of abortion and the doctrine of the double effect. In P. Foot (Ed.), *Virtues and vices and other essays in moral philosophy* (pp. 19–32). Oxford, UK: Blackwell (originally published 1967).

Forgas, J. (1994). Sad and guilty. Affective influences on the explanation of conflict episodes. *Journal of Personality and Social Psychology, 66,* 56–68.

Forgas, J., & Laham, S. M. (2005). The interaction between affect and motivation in social judgments and behavior. In J. Forgas, K. Williams, et al. (Eds.), *Social motivation: Conscious and unconscious processes* (pp. 168–193). New York, NY: Cambridge University Press.

Forgas, J. P. (2003). Affective influences on attitudes and judgments. In R. J. Davidson, K. R. Scherer, & H. H. Goldsmith (Eds.), *Handbook of affective sciences* (pp. 596–618). New York, NY: Oxford University Press.

Forgas, J. P., & Moylan, S. (1987). After the movies: The effect of mood on social judgments. *Personality and Social Psychology Bulletin, 13,* 465–477.

Forman, D. R., Aksan, N., & Kochanska, G. (2004). Toddlers' responsive imitation predicts preschool-age conscience: 1. *Psychological Science, 15*(10), 699–704.

Foster, C. A., Witcher, B. S., Campbell, W. K., & Green, J. D. (1998). Arousal and attraction: Evidence for automatic and controlled processes. *Journal of Personality and Social Psychology, 74,* 86–101.

Fox, E., Mathews, A., Calder, A. J., & Yiend, J. (2007). Anxiety and sensitivity to gaze direction in emotionally expressive faces. *Emotion (Washington, DC), 7*(3), 478–486.

Fox, E., Russo, R., & Georgiou, G. A. (2005). Anxiety modulates the degree of attentive resources required to process emotional faces. *Cognitive, Affective, & Behavioral Neuroscience, 5*(4), 396–404.

Fox, N., & Davidson, R. A. (1987). Electroencephalogram asymmetry in response to the approach of a stranger and maternal separation in 10-month-old infants. *Developmental Psychology, 23,* 233–240.

Fox, N. A., Henderson, H. A., Marshall, P. J., Nichols, K. E., & Ghera, M. M. (2005). Behavioral inhibition: Linking biology and behavior within a developmental framework. *Annual Review of Psychology, 56,* 235–262.

Fox, R. (1991). Aggression then and now. In M. H. Robinson & L. Tiger (Eds.), *Man and beast revisited* (pp. 81–93). Washington, DC: Smithsonian Institute Press.

Frampton, K. L., Jenkins, J. M., & Dunn, J. (2010). Within-family differences in internalizing behaviors: The role of children's perspectives of the mother-child relationship. *Journal of Abnormal Child Psychology, 38,* 557–568.

Francis, D., & Meaney, M. J. (1999). Maternal care and the development of stress responses. *Development, 9,* 128–134.

Frank, M., Ekman, P., & Friesen, W. V. (1993). Behavioral markers and recognizability of the smile of enjoyment. *Journal of Personality and Social Psychology, 64,* 83–93.

Frank, M. G., & Stennet, J. (2001). The forced-choice paradigm and the perception of facial expressions of emotion. *Journal of Personality and Social Psychology, 80,* 75–85.

Frank, R. H. (1988). *Passions within reason: The strategic role of the emotions.* New York, NY: W. W. Norton.

Fredrickson, B. L. (2001). The role of positive emotions in positive psychology: The broaden-and-build theory of positive emotions. *American Psychologist, 56,* 218–226.

Fredrickson, B. L. (2003). The value of positive emotions. *American Scientist, 91,* 330–335.

Fredrickson, B. L., & Branigan, C. (2005). Positive emotions broaden the scope of attention and thought–action repertoires. *Cognition and Emotion, 19,* 313–332.

Frederickson, B. L., & Cohn, M. A. (2008). Positive emotions. In M. Lewis, J. Haviland Jones & L. F. Barrett (Eds.), *Handbook of emotions* (3rd ed., pp. 777–796). New York, NY: Guilford.

Fredrickson, B. L., Cohn, M. A., Coffey, K. A., Pek, J., & Finkel, S. M. (2008). Open hearts build lives: Positive emotions, induced through loving-kindness meditation, build consequential personal resources. *Journal of Personality and Social Psychology, 95,* 1045–1062.

Fredrickson, B. L., & Levenson, R. W. (1998). Positive emotions speed recovery from the cardiovascular sequelae of negative emotions. *Cognition and Emotion, 12,* 191–220.

Fredrickson, B. L., Tugade, M. M., Waugh, C. E., & Larkin, G. R. (2003). What good are positive emotions in crises? A prospective study of resilience and emotions following the terrorist attacks on the United States on September 11th, 2001. *Journal of Personality and Social Psychology, 84,* 365–376.

Freedman, J. L. (1978). *Happy people: What happiness is, who has it, and why.* New York, NY: Harcourt Brace Jovanovich.

Freud, A. (1937). *The ego and the mechanisms of defense.* London, UK: Hogarth Press.

Freud, S. (1901). *The psychopathology of everyday life. The Pelican Freud Library, Vol. 5* (J. Strachey, A. Richards, & A. Tyson, Eds., A. Tyson, Trans.). Harmondsworth: Penguin (current edition 1975).

Freud, S. (1904/1985). Psychopathic characters on the stage. In A. Dickson (Ed.), *The Pelican Freud Library, Vol. 14: Art and literature* (pp. 119–127). London, England: Penguin.

Freud, S. (1905). *Fragment of an analysis of a case of hysteria (Dora). The Pelican Freud Library, Vol. 9: Case histories, II* (J. Strachey & A. Richards, Eds.) Harmondsworth, UK: Penguin (current edition 1979).

Freud, S. (1920). *Beyond the pleasure principle. The Pelican Freud Library: Vol. 11: On metapsychology: The theory of psychoanalysis* (J. Strachey & A. Richards, Eds., pp. 1–64). Harmondsworth, UK: Penguin (current edition 1974).

Freud, S., & Breuer, J. (1895). *Studies on hysteria. The Pelican Freud Library, Vol. 3* (J. Strachey, A. Strachey, & A. Richards, Eds.). Harmondsworth, UK: Penguin (current edition 1974).

Fridlund, A. J. (1992). The behavioral ecology and sociality of human faces. *Review of Personality and Social Psychology, 13,* 90–121.

Fridlund, A. J. (1994). *Human facial expression: An evolutionary view.* San Diego, CA: Academic Press.

Fried, I., Mukamel, R., & Kreiman, G. (2011). Internally generated preactivation of single neurons in human medial frontal cortex predicts volition. *Neuron, 69,* 548–562.

Friesen, W. V. (1972). *Cultural differences in facial expressions in a social situation. An experimental test of the concept of display rules.* Doctoral thesis, University of California, San Francisco.

Frijda, N. H. (1988). The laws of emotion. *American Psychologist, 43,* 349–358.

Frijda, N. H. (1993a). Moods, emotion episodes, and emotions. In M. Lewis & J. M. Haviland (Eds.), *Handbook of emotions* (pp. 381–403). New York, NY: Guilford.

Frijda, N. H. (Ed.). (1993b). Appraisal and beyond: The issue of cognitive determinants of emotion. *Cognition and Emotion, 7,* 225–387.

Frijda, N. H. (1994). The Lex Talionis: On vengeance. In S.H. M. Van Goozen, N. E. Van der Poll, & J. A. Sergeant (Eds.), *Emotions: Essays on emotion theory* (pp. 263–289). Hillsdale, NJ: Erlbaum.

Frijda, N. H. (2005). Emotion experience. *Cognition and Emotion, 19,* 473–497.

Frijda, N. H. (2007). *The laws of emotion.* Mahwah, NJ: Erlbaum.

Frijda, N. H. (2010). Not passion's slave. *Emotion Review, 2,* 68–75.

Frijda, N. H. (in press). Emotion regulation and free will. In T. Vierkant, A. Clark, & J. Kiverstein (Eds.) *Decomposing the will.* Oxford, UK: Oxford University Press.

Frijda, N. H., Kuipers, P., & ter Schure, E. (1989). Relations among emotion, appraisal, and emotional action readiness. *Journal of Personality and Social Psychology, 57,* 212–228.

Frijda, N. H., & Mesquita, B. (1994). The social rules and functions of emotions. In S. Kitayama & H. R. Markus (Eds.), *Emotion and culture: Empirical studies of mutual influence* (pp. 51–87). Washington, DC: American Psychological Association.

Frijda, N. H., & Parrott, W. G. (2011). Basic emotions or ur-emotions. *Emotion Review, 3,* 416–423.

Fyer, A., Mannuzza, S., & Coplan, J. D. (1996). Panic disorders and agoraphobia. In H. I. Kaplan & B. J. Saddock (Eds.), *Comprehensive textbook of psychiatry* (6th ed., Vol. 1, pp. 1191–1204). Baltimore, MD: Williams & Wilkins.

Gabbay, F. H., Krantz, D. S., Kop, W., et al. (1996). Triggers of myocardial ischemia during daily life in patients with coronary artery disease: Physical and mental activities, anger, and smoking. *Journal of the American College of Cardiology, 27,* 585–592.

Gable, S. L., Gonzaga, G., & Strachman, A. (2006). Will you be there for me when things go right? Social support for positive events. *Journal of Personality and Social Psychology, 91,* 904–917.

Gable, S. L., Reis, H. T., Impett, E., & Asher, E. R. (2004). What do you do when things go right? The intrapersonal and interpersonal benefits of sharing positive events. *Journal of Personality and Social Psychology, 87,* 228–245.

Gabrielsson, A., & Juslin, P. N. (2003). Emotional expression in music. In R. Davidson, K. Scherer, & H. H. Goldsmith (Eds.), *Handbook of affective sciences* (pp. 503–534). London, UK: Oxford University Press.

Gailliot, M. T., Baumeister, R., DeWall, C. N., Maner, J. K., Plant, A., Tice, D. M., et al. (2007). Self-control relies on glucose as a limited energy source: Willpower is more than a metaphor. *Journal of Personality and Social Psychology, 92,* 325–336.

Galdi, S., Arcuri, L., & Gawronski, B. (2008). Automatic mental associations predict future choices of undecided decision-makers. *Science, 321,* 1100–1102.

Galea, S., Ahern, J., Resnick, H., Kilpatrick, D., Bucuvalas, M., Gold, J., et al. (2002). Psychological sequelae of the September 11 terrorist attacks in New York City. *New England Journal of Medicine, 346,* 982–987.

Galinsky, A. D., Magee, J. C., Inesi, M. E., & Gruenfeld, D. H. (2006). Power and perspectives not taken. *Psychological Science, 17,* 1068–1074.

Gao, W., Zhu, H., Giovanello, K. S., et al. (2009). Evidence on the emergence of the brain's default network from 2-week-old to 2-year-old healthy pediatric subjects. *Proceedings of the National Academy of Sciences, 106,* 6790–6795.

Garcia Coll, C., Vohr, B. R., Hoffman, J., & Oh, W. (1986). Maternal and environmental factors affecting developmental outcome of infants of adolescent mothers. *Journal of Developmental and Behavioral Pediatrics:JDBP, 7*(4), 230–236.

Gardner, H. (1993). *Creating minds: An anatomy of creativity seen through the lives of Freud, Einstein, Picasso, Stravinsky, Eliot, Graham, and Ghandi.* New York, NY: Basic Books.

Garnefski, N., Kraaij, V., & van Etten, M. (2005). Specificity of relations between adolescents' cognitive emotion regulation strategies and internalizing and externalizing psychopathology. *Journal of Adolescence, 28*(5), 619–631.

Gasper, K., & Clore, G. L. (1998). The persistent use of negative affect by anxious individuals to estimate risk. *Journal of Personality and Social Psychology, 74,* 1350–1363.

Gasper, K., & Clore, G. L. (2000). Do you have to pay attention to your feelings in order to be influenced by them? *Personality and Social Psychology Bulletin, 26,* 698–711.

Gass, K., Jenkins, J. M., & Dunn, J. (2007a). Are sibling relationships protective? A longitudinal study. *Journal of Child Psychology and Psychiatry, and Allied Disciplines, 48*(2), 167–175.

Gass, K., Jenkins, J. M., & Dunn, J. (2007b) The sibling relationship as protective for children experiencing life events: A longitudinal study. *Journal of Child Psychology and Psychiatry, 48,* 167–175.

Gay, P. (1988). *Freud: A life for our time.* London, UK: Dent.

Gazzaniga, M. S. (1985). *The social brain.* New York, NY: Basic Books.

Gazzaniga, M. S. (1988). Brain modularity: Towards a philosophy of conscious experience. In A. J. Marcel & E. Bisiach (Eds.), *Consciousness in contemporary science* (pp. 218–238). Oxford, UK: Oxford University Press.

Gazzaniga, M. S., Ivry, R. B., & Mangun, G. R. (2002). *Cognitive neuroscience.* New York, NY: Norton.

Geertz, C. (1973). *The interpretation of cultures*. New York, NY: Basic Books.

Gelder, M., Andreasen, N., Lopez-Ibor, J., & Geddes, J. (Eds.). (2009). *New Oxford textbook of psychiatry* (2nd ed.). Oxford, UK: Oxford University Press.

Gewertz, D. (1981). A historical reconsideration of female dominance among the Chambri of Papua New Guinea. *American Ethnologist*, 8, 94–106.

Ghera, M. M., Marshall, P. J., Fox, N. A., Zeanah, C. H., Nelson, C. A., Smyke, A. T., & Guthrie, D. (2009). The effects of foster care intervention on socially deprived institutionalized children's attention and positive affect: Results from the BEIP study. *Journal of Child Psychology and Psychiatry*, 50(3), 246–253.

Gibbs, E. L., Gibbs, F. A., & Fuster, B. (1948). Psychomotor epilepsy. *Archives of Neurology and Psychiatry*, 60, 331–339.

Giedd, J. N. (2004). Structural magnetic resonance imaging of the adolescent brain. *Annals of the New York Academy of Sciences*, 1021(1), 77–85.

Gilbert, P. (1998). What is shame? Some core issues and controversies. In P. Gilbert & B. Andrews (Eds.), *Shame: Interpersonal behavior, psychopathology, and culture* (pp. 3–38). New York, NY: Oxford University Press.

Gilbert, P. (2000). The relationship of shame, social anxiety and depression: The role of the evaluation of social rank. *Clinical Psychology and Psychotherapy*, 7, 174–189.

Givens, D. B. (1983). *Love signals: How to attract a mate*. New York, NY: Crown.

Gladwell, M. (2005). *Blink*. New York, NY: Little, Brown & Co.

Glaser, R., Kiecolt-Glaser, J. K., Malarkey, W. B., & Sheridan, J. F. (1998). The influence of psychological stress on the immune response to vaccines. *Annals of the New York Academy of Sciences*, 840, 656–663.

Glickman, S. E., & Schiff, B. B. (1967). A biological theory of reinforcement. *Psychological Review*, 74, 81–109.

Gloaguen, V., Cottraux, J., Cucherat, M., & Blackburn, I. (1998). A meta-analyisis of the effects of cognitive therapy in depressed patients. *Journal of Affective Disorders*, 49, 59–72.

Goel, V., & Vartanian, O. (2011). Negative emotions can attenuate the influence of beliefs on logical reasoning. *Cognition and Emotion*, 25, 121–131.

Goethe, J. W. von. (1774). *The sorrows of young Werther* (M. Hulse, Trans.). Harmondsworth, UK: Penguin (current edition 1989).

Goetz, J., Simon-Thomas, E., & Keltner, D. (2010). Compassion: An evolutionary analysis and empirical review. *Psychological Bulletin*, 136(3), 351–374.

Gogtay, N., Giedd, J. N., Lusk, L., Hayashi, K. M., Greenstein, D., Vaituzis, A. C., et al. (2004). Dynamic mapping of human cortical development during childhood through early adulthood. *Proceedings of the National Academy of Sciences of the United States of America*, 101(21), 8174–8179.

Goldberg, S., Grusec, J. E., & Jenkins, J. M. (1999). Confidence in protection: Arguments for a narrow definition of attachment. *Journal of Family Psychology*, 13, 475–483.

Goldberg, S., Perrotta, M., Minde, K., & Corter, C. (1986). Maternal behavior and attachment in low-birth-weight twins and singletons. *Child Development*, 57(1), 34–46.

Goldin, P. R., McRae, K., Ramel, W., & Gross, J. J. (2008). The neural bases of emotion regulation: Reappraisal and suppression of negative emotion. *Biological Psychiatry*, 63, 577–586.

Goldman, R. N., Greenberg L. S., & Angus L. (2006). The effects of adding emotion-focused interventions to the client-centered relationship conditions in the treatment of depression. *Psychotherapy Research*, 16, 537–549.

Goldsmith, H. H., & Alansky, J. A. (1987). Maternal and infant temperamental predictors of attachment: A meta-analytic review. *Journal of Consulting and Clinical Psychology*, 55, 805–816.

Goldsmith, H. H., Buss, K. A., & Lemery, K. S. (1997). Toddler and childhood temperament: Expanded content, stronger genetic evidence, new evidence for the importance of environment. *Developmental Psychology*, 33(6), 891–905.

Gombrich, E. H. (1972). *The story of art* (12th ed.). London, UK: Phaidon.

Gonzaga, G. C., Keltner, D., Londahl, E. A., & Smith, M. (2001). Love and the commitment problem in romantic relations and friendship. *Journal of Personality and Social Psychology*, 81, 247–262.

Gonzaga, G. C., Turner, R., Keltner, D., Campos, B., & Altemus, M. (2006). Romantic love and sexual desire in close bonds. *Emotion*, 6, 163–179.

Goodall, J. (1986). *The chimpanzees of Gombe: Patterns of behavior.* Cambridge, MA: Harvard University Press.

Goodall, J. (1992). Unusual violence in the overthrow of an alpha male chimpanzee at Gombe. In T. Nishida, W. C. McGrew, P. Marler, M. Pickford, & F. B. M. De Waal (Eds.), *Topics in primatology, Vol. 1: Human origins* (pp. 131–142). Tokyo: University of Tokyo Press.

Goodman, S. H., Rouse, M. H., Connell, A. M., Broth, M. R., Hall, C. M., & Heyward, D. (2010). Maternal depression and child psychopathology: A meta-analytic review. *Clinical Child and Family Psychology Review, 14*(1), 1–27.

Gospic, K., Mohlin, E., Fransson, P., Petrovic, P., Johannesson, M., Ingvar, M., et al. (2011). Limbic justice: Amygdala involvement in immediate rejection in the ultimatum game. *PLoS Biology, 9*(5), 1–8.

Gotlib, I. H., & Joormann, J. (2010). Cognition and depression: Current status and future directions. *Annual Review of Clinical Psychology, 6,* 285–312.

Gottfried, J. A., O'Doherty, J., & Dolan, R. J. (2003). Encoding predictive reward value in human amygdala and orbitofrontal cortex. *Science, 301,* 1104–1107.

Gottlieb, J., & Polirstok, S. (2006). The impact of positive behavior intervention training for teachers on referral rates for misbehavior, special education evaluation and student reading achievement in the elementary grades. *International Journal of Behavioral Consultation 2*(3), 354–361.

Gottman, J. M. (1993a). *Why marriages succeed or fail.* New York, NY: Simon & Schuster.

Gottman, J. M. (1993b). The roles of conflict engagement, escalation, and avoidance in marital interaction: A longitudinal view of five types of couples. *Journal of Consulting and Clinical Psychology, 61,* 6–15.

Gottman, J. M., Katz, L. F., & Hooven, C. (1996). Parental meta-emotion philosophy and the emotional life of families: Theoretical models and preliminary data. *Journal of Family Psychology, 10*(3), 243–268.

Gottman, J. M., Katz, L. F., & Hooven, C. (1997). *Meta-emotion.* Mahwah, NJ: Lawrence Erlbaum.

Gottman, J. M., & Levenson, R. W. (1992). Marital processes predictive of later dissolution: Behavior, physiology and health. *Journal of Personality and Social Psychology, 63,* 221–233.

Gottman, J. M., & Levenson, R. W. (2000). The timing of divorce: Predicting when a couple will divorce over a 14-year period. *Journal of Marriage and the Family, 62,* 737–745.

Granic, I., & Patterson, G.R. (2006). Toward a comprehensive model of antisocial development: A dynamic systems approach. *Psychological Review, 113,* 101–131.

Gray, J. A., & McNaughton, N. (2000). *The neuropsychology of anxiety: An enquiry into the functions of the septohippocampal system* (2nd ed.). Oxford, UK: Oxford University Press.

Gray, L., Watt, L., & Blass, E. M. (2000). Skin-to-skin contact is analgesic in healthy newborns. *Pediatrics, 105,* 1–6.

Green, D. P., Goldman, S. L., & Salovey, P. (1993). Measurement error masks bipolarity in affect ratings. *Journal of Personality and Social Psychology, 64,* 1029–1041.

Greenberg, L. S. (1993). Emotion and change processes in psychotherapy. In M. Lewis & J. M. Haviland (Eds.), *Handbook of emotions* (pp. 499–508). New York, NY: Guilford.

Greenberg, L. S. (2002). *Emotion focused therapy: Coaching clients to work through their feelings.* Washington, DC: American Psychological Association.

Greenberg, L. S. (2010). Emotion focused therapy: A clinical Synthesis. *Focus: Journal of Lifelong Learning in Psychiatry, 8,* 32–42.

Greenberg, L. S., & Safran, J. D. (1989). Emotion in psychotherapy. *American Psychologist, 44,* 19–29.

Greene, J., & Haidt, J. (2002). How (and where) does moral judgment work? *Trends in Cognitive Sciences, 6,* 517–523.

Greene, J. D. (2007). Why are VMPFC patients more utilitarian?: A dual-process theory of moral judgment explains. *Trends in Cognitive Sciences, 11*(8), 322–323.

Greene, J. D., Sommerville, R. B., Nystrom, L. E., Darley, J. M., & Cohen, J. D. (2001). An fMRI investigation of emotional engagement in moral judgment. *Science, 75,* 2105–2108.

Grice, S. J., Kuipers, E., Bebbington, P., Dunn, G., Fowler, D., et al. (2007). Carers' attributions about positive events in psychosis relate to expressed emotion. *Behavior Research and Therapy, 47,* 783–789.

Grienenberger, J. F., Kelly, K., & Slade, A. (2005). Maternal reflective functioning, mother-infant affective communication, and infant attachment: Exploring the link between mental states and observed caregiving behavior in the intergenerational transmission of attachment. *Attachment & Human Development, 7*(3), 299–311.

Griffiths, P. E. (1997). *What emotions really are.* Chicago, IL: University of Chicago Press.

Grinker, R. R., & Spiegel, J. P. (1945). *Men under stress.* New York, NY: Blakiston.

Gross, J. (2008). Emotion and emotion regulation: Personality processes and individual differences. In O. P. John, R. W. Robins, & L. A. Pervin (Eds.), *Handbook of personality: Theory and research* (3rd ed., pp. 701–724). New York, NY: Guilford.

Gross, J. J. (1998). Antecedent- and response-focused emotion regulation: Divergent consequences for experience, expression, and physiology, *Journal of Personality and Social Psychology, 74,* 224–237.

Gross, J. J. (2002). Emotion regulation: Affective, cognitive, and social consequences. *Psychophysiology, 39*(3), 281–291.

Gross, J. J., & John, O. P. (2003). Individual differences in two emotion regulation processes: Implications for affect, relationships, and well-being: Implications for affect, relationships, and well-being. *Journal of Personality and Social Psychology, 85*(2), 348–362.

Gross, J. J., & Levenson, R. W. (1997). Hiding feelings: The acute effects of inhibiting negative and positive emotion. *Journal of Abnormal Psychology, 106*(1), 95–103.

Gross, J. J., Richards, J. M., & John, O. P. (2006). Emotion regulation in everyday life. In D. K. Synder, J. Simpson, & J. N. Hughes (Eds.), *Emotion regulation in couples and families: Pathways to dysfunction and health* (pp. 13–35). Washington, DC: American Psychological Association.

Gross, J. J., Sheppes, G., & Urry, H. L. (2011). *Cognition and emotion.* Lecture at the 2010 SPSP Emotion Preconference. Emotion generation and emotion regulation: A distinction we should make (carefully). *Cognition and Emotion, 25,* 765–781.

Gross, J. J., & Thompson, R. A. (2007). Emotion regulation: Conceptual foundations. In J. J. Gross (Ed.), *Handbook of emotion regulation* (pp. 3–24). New York, NY: Guilford Press.

Grossmann, K., Grossmann, K. E., Kindler, H., & Zimmermann, P. (2008). A wider view of attachment and exploration. In J. Cassidy & P. R. Shaver (Eds.), *Handbook of attachment: Theory, research, and clinical applications* (2nd ed.). New York, NY: Guilford.

Grossmann, K., Grossmann, K. E., Spangler, G., Suess, G., & Unzner, L. (1985). Maternal sensitivity and newborns' orientation responses as related to quality of attachment in northern Germany. In I. Bretherton & E. Waters (Eds.), *Growing points in attachment theory and research. Monographs of the Society for Research in Child Development, 50,* 233–256.

Grossmann, K. E., Grossmann, K., & Waters, E. (2005). *Attachment from infancy to adulthood: The major longitudinal studies.* New York, NY: Guilford.

Grossmann, K. E., Grossmann, K., Winter, M., & Zimmerman, P. (2002). Attachment relationships and appraisal of partnership: From early experience of sensitive support to later relationship representation. In L. Pulkkinen & A. Caspi (Eds.), *Paths to successful development: Personality in the life course* (pp. 73–105). New York, NY: Cambridge University Press.

Grossmann, T., Oberecker, R., Koch, S. P., & Friederici, A. D. (2010). The developmental origins of voice processing in the human brain. *Neuron, 65*(6), 852–858.

Grossmann, T., Striano, T., & Friederici, A. D. (2006). Crossmodal integration of emotional information from face and voice in the infant brain. *Developmental Science, 9*(3), 309–315.

Grossmann, T., Striano, T., & Friederici, A. D. (2007). Developmental changes in infants' processing of happy and angry facial expressions: A neurobehavioral study. *Brain Cognition, 64*(1), 30–41.

Gruber, H. E., & Barrett, P. H. (1974). *Darwin on man: A psychological study of scientific creativity, together with Darwin's early and unpublished notebooks.* New York, NY: Dutton.

Gruber, J., Harvey, A. G., & Purcell, A. (2011). What goes up can come down? A preliminary investigation of emotion reactivity and emotion recovery in bipolar disorder. *Journal of Affective Disorders, 133,* 457–466.

Gruber, J., Johnson, S. L., Oveis, C., & Keltner, D. (2008). Risk for mania and positive emotional responding: Too much of a good thing? *Emotion, 8,* 23–33.

Gruber, J., & Keltner, D. (2007). Emotional behavior and psychopathology: A survey of methods and concepts. In J. Gruber & D. Keltner (Eds.), *Emotion and psychopathology: Bridging affective and clinical science* (pp. 35–52). Washington, DC: American Psychological Association.

Gruber, J., & Keltner, D. (2011). Too close for comfort? Lessons from excesses and deficits of compassion in psychopathology. In S. Brown, M. Brown, & L. Penner (Eds.), *Moving beyond self-interest: Toward a new understanding of human caregiving*. New York, NY: Oxford University Press.

Gruber, J., Mauss, I. B., & Tamir, M. (2011). A dark side of happiness? How, when, and why happiness is not always good. *Perspectives on Psychological Science, 6*, 222–133.

Grünbaum, A. (1986). Precis of *The foundations of psychoanalysis: A philosophical critique*. *Behavioral and Brain Sciences, 9*, 217–284.

Grusec, J. E. (2011). Socialization processes in the family: Social and emotional development. *Annual Review of Psychology, 62*, 243.

Grusec, J. E., Goodnow, J. J., & Kuczynski, L. (2000). New directions in analyses of parenting contributions to children's acquisition of values. *Child Development, 71*(1), 205–211.

Grynberg, D., Luminet, O., Corneille, O., Grèzes, J., & Berthos, S. (2010). Alexithymia in the interpersonal domain: A general deficit of empathy? *Personality and Individual Differences, 49*, 845–850.

Gudjonsson, G., & Pearce, J. (2011). Subject interviews and false confessions. *Current Directions in Psychological Science, 20*, 33–37.

Gunnar, M. R., & Donzella, B. (2002). Social regulation of the cortisol levels in early human development. *Psychoneuroendocrinology, 27*(1), 199–220.

Gunnar, M. R., Mangelsdorf, S., Larson, M., & Hertsgaard, L. (1989). Attachment, temperament, and adrenocortical activity in infancy: A study of psychoendocrine regulation. *Developmental Psychology, 25*(3), 355–363.

Gunnar, M. R., & Quevedo, K. M. (2007). Early care experiences and HPA axis regulation in children: A mechanism for later trauma vulnerability. *Progress in Brain Research, 167*, 137–149.

Haber, S. N., & Knutson, B. (2010). The reward circuit: Linking primate anatomy and human imaging. *Neuropsychopharmacology, 35*, 4–26.

Haidt, J. (2001). The emotional dog and its rational tail: A social intuitionist approach to moral judgment. *Psychological Review, 108*, 814–834.

Haidt, J. (2003). The moral emotions. In R. Davidson, K. Scherer, & H. H. Goldsmith (Eds.), *Handbook of affective sciences* (pp. 852–870). London, England, Oxford University Press.

Haidt, J. (2007). The new synthesis in moral psychology. *Science, 316*, 998–1002.

Haidt, J., & Keltner, D. (1999). Culture and facial expression: Open ended methods find more faces and a gradient of universality. *Cognition and Emotion, 13*, 225–266.

Haidt, J., Koller, S. H., & Dias, M. G. (1993). Affect, culture, and morality, or Is it wrong to eat your dog? *Journal of Personality and Social Psychology, 65*, 613–628.

Haight, G. S. (Ed.). (1985). *Selections from George Eliot's letters*. New Haven, CT: Yale University Press.

Hajat, A., Diez-Roux, A., Franklin, T. G., Seeman, T., Shrager, S., Ranjit, N., Castro, C., Watson, K., Sanchez, B., & Kirschbaum, C. (2010). Socioeconomic and race-/ethnic differences in daily salivary cortisol profiles: The multi-ethnic study of atherosclerosis. *Psychoneuroendocrinology, 35*, 932–943.

Halberstadt, A. G., Thompson, J. A., Parker, A. E., & Dunsmore, J. C. (2008). Parents' emotion-related beliefs and behaviours in relation to children's coping with the 11 September 2001 terrorist attacks. *Infant and Child Development, 17*, 557–580.

Hall, C. W. (2006). Self-reported aggression and the perception of anger in facial expression photos. *The Journal of Psychology, 140*(3), 255–267.

Hallion, L. S., & Ruscio, A. M. (2011). A meta-analysis of the effect of cognitive bias modification on anxiety and depression. *Psychological Bulletin, 137*, 940–958.

Hamlin, J. K., Wynn, K., & Bloom, P. (2010). Three-month-olds show a negativity bias in their social evaluations. *Developmental Science, 13*(6), 923–929.

Hamm, A. O., Vaitl, D., & Lang, P. J. (1990). Fear conditioning, meaning and belongingness: A selective association analysis. *Journal of Abnormal Psychology, 98*, 395–406.

Hammen, C. (1988). Self cognitions, stressful events and the prediction of depression in children of depressed mothers. *Journal of Abnormal Child Psychology, 16*, 347–360.

Hammen, C. (1991). Generation of stress in the course of unipolar depression. *Journal of Abnormal Psychology, 100,* 555–561.

Hammen, C. (1999). The emergence of an interpersonal approach to depression. In T. Joiner & J. C. Coyne (Eds.), *The interactional nature of depression* (pp. 21–35). Washington, DC: American Psychological Association.

Hammen, C., Ellicott, A., Gitlin, M., & Jamison, K. R. (1989). Sociotropy/autonomy and vulnerability to specific life events in patients with unipolar depression and bipolar disorders. *Journal of Abnormal Psychology, 98,* 154–160.

Haney, C., Banks, C., & Zimbardo, P. (1973). Interpersonal dynamics in a simulated prison. *International Journal of Criminology and Penology, 1,* 69–97.

Hankin, B., Abramson, L. Y., Miller, N., & Haeffel, G. J. (2004). Cognitive vulnerability-stress theories of depression: Examining affective specificity in the prediction of depression versus anxiety in three prospective studies. *Cognitive Therapy and Research, 28,* 309–345.

Harbaugh, B. T., Mayr, U., & Burghart, D. (2007). Neural responses to taxation and voluntary giving reveal motives for charitable donations. *Science, 316,* 1622–1655.

Hardt, J., & Rutter, M. (2004). Validity of adult retrospective reports of adverse childhood experiences: Review of the evidence. *Journal of Child Psychology and Psychiatry, 45,* 260–273.

Hare, R. D., Clark, D., Grann, M., & Thornton, D. (2000). Psychopathy and the predictive validity of the PCL-R: An international perspective. *Behavioral Sciences and the Law, 18,* 623–645.

Hare, T. A., Tottenham, N., Galvan, A., Voss, H. U., Glover, G. H., & Casey, B. J. (2008). Biological substrates of emotional reactivity and regulation in adolescence during an emotional go-nogo task. *Biological Psychiatry, 63*(10), 927–934.

Hariri, A. R., Mattay, V. S., Tessitore, A., Kolachana, B., Fera, F., Goldman, D., et al. (2002). Serotonin transporter genetic variation and the response of the human amygdala. *Science,* 297–400.

Hariri, A. R., & Whalen, P. J. (2011). The amygdala: Inside and out. *F1000 Reports Biology, 3,* 2.

Harker, L. A., & Keltner, D. (2001). Expressions of positive emotion in women's college yearbook pictures and their relationship to personality and life outcomes across adulthood. *Journal of Personality and Social Psychology, 80,* 112–124.

Harlé, K. M., & Sanfey, A. G. (2010). Effects of approach and withdrawal motivation on interactive economic decisions. *Cognition and Emotion, 24,* 1456–1465.

Harris, C. R. (2001). Cardiovascular responses of embarrassment and effects of emotional suppression in a social setting. *Journal of Personality and Social Psychology, 81,* 886–897.

Harris, C. R. (2003). A review of sex differences in sexual jealousy, including self-report data, psychophysiological responses, interpersonal violence, and morbid jealousy. *Personality and Social Psychology Review, 7,* 102–128.

Harris, C. R., & Christenfeld, N. (1996). Gender, jealousy, and reason. *Psychological Science, 7,* 364–366.

Harris, P. L. (1989). *Children and emotion: The development of psychological understanding.* Oxford, UK: Blackwell.

Harrison, P. J. (2002). The neuropathology of primary mood disorder. *Brain, 125,* 1428–1449.

Hart, A. J., Whalen, P. J., Shin, L. M., et al. (2000). Differential response of the human amygdala to racial outgroup vs. ingroup face stimuli. *Neuroreport, 11,* 2351–2354.

Hart, H.L.A. (1961). *The concept of law.* Oxford, UK: Oxford University Press.

Hastie, R. (2001). Emotions in jurors' decisions. *Brooklyn Law Review, 66,* 991–1009.

Hastie, R. (2008). Conscious and non-conscious processes in jurors' decisions. In C. Engel & W. Singer (Eds.), *Better than conscious: Decision making, the human mind, and implications for institutions* (pp. 371–390). Cambridge, MA: MIT Press.

Hastings, P. D., Nuselovici, J. N., Klimes-Dougan, B., Kendziora, K. T., Usher, B. A., Ho, M. R., et al. (2009). Dysregulated coherence of subjective and cardiac emotional activation in adolescence with internalizing and externalizing problems. *Journal of Child Psychology and Psychiatry, 50*(11), 1348–1356.

Hatch, S. L., Harvey, S. B., & Maughan, B. (2010). A developmental-contextual approach to understanding mental health and well-being in early adulthood. *Social Science & Medicine, 70*(2), 261–268.

Hatfield, E., & Rapson, R. L. (2002). Passionate love and sexual desire: Cultural and historical perspectives. In A. L. Vangelista, H. T. Reis, & M. A. Fitzpatrick (Eds.), *Stability and change in relationships* (pp. 306–324). New York, NY: Cambridge University Press.

Hauser, M. D. (1996). *The evolution of communication.* Cambridge, MA: MIT Press.

Havighurst, S. S., Wilson, K. R., Harley, A. E., Prior, M. R., & Kehoe, C. (2010). Tuning in to kids: Improving emotion socialization practices in parents of preschool children—Findings from a community trial. *Journal of Child Psychology and Psychiatry and Allied Disciplines*, *51*(12), 1342–1350.

Hazan, C., & Shaver, P. (1987). Romantic love conceptualized as an attachment process. *Journal of Personality and Social Psychology*, *52*, 511–524.

Hazebroek, J. F., Howells, K., & Day, A. (2001). Cognitive appraisals associated with high trait anger. *Personality and Individual Differences*, *30*(1), 31–45.

Hecht, D. B., Inderbirtzen, H. M., and Bukowski, A. L. (1998). The relationship between peer status and depressive symptoms in children and adolescents. *Journal of Abnormal Child Psychology*, *26*, 153–160.

Hecht, M., and LaFrance, M. (1998). License or obligation to smile: The effect of power and sex on amount and type of smiling. *Personality and Social Psychology Bulletin*, *24*, 1332–1342.

Heelas, P. (1986). Emotion talk across cultures. In R. Harré (Ed.), *The social construction of emotions* (pp. 234–266). Oxford, UK: Blackwell.

Hejmadi, A., Davidson, R. J., & Rozin, P. (2000). Exploring Hindu Indian emotion expressions: Evidence for accurate recognition by Americans and Indians. *Psychological Science*, *11*, 183–187.

Heinrichs, M., von Dawans, B., and Domes, G. (2009). Oxytocin, vasopressin, and human social behavior. *Frontiers in Neuroendocrinology*, *30*, 548–557.

Heller A. S., Johnstone, T., Shackman, A. J., Light, S., Peterson, M., Kolden, G., Kalin, N., & Davidson, R. J. (2009). Reduced capacity to sustain positive emotion in major depression reflects diminished maintenance of fronto-striatal brain activation. *Proceedings of the National Academy of Sciences*, *106*(52), 22445–22450.

Henggeler, S. W. (2002). *Serious emotional disturbance in children and adolescents: Multisystemic therapy.* New York, NY: Guilford.

Henggeler, S. W., Melton, G. B., & Smith, L. A. (1992). Family preservation using multisystemic therapy: An effective alternative to incarcerating serious juvenile offenders. *Journal of Consulting and Clinical Psychology*, *60*(6), 953.

Henggeler, S. W., Schoenwald, S. K., Borduin, C. M., Rowland, M. D., & Cunningham, P. B. (1998). *Multisystemic treatment of antisocial behavior in children and adolescents.* New York, NY: Guilford.

Henriques, J. B., & Davidson, R. J. (1991). Left frontal hypoactivation in depression. *Journal of Abnormal Psychology*, *100*, 535–545.

Henry, W. P., Strupp, H. H., Schacht, T. E., & Gaston, L. (1994). Psychodynamic approaches. In A. E. Bergin & S. L. Garfield (Eds.), *Handbook of psychotherapy and behavior change* (4th ed., pp. 467–508). New York, NY: Wiley.

Henshilwood, C. S., & Dubreuil, B. (2009). Reading the artifacts: Gleaning language skills from the Middle Stone Age in southern Africa. In R. P. Botha & C. Knight (Eds.), *The cradle of language: Studies in the evolution of language* (pp. 41–61). New York, NY: Oxford University Press.

Hertel, P., & Mathews, A. (2011). Cognitive bias modification: Past perspectives, current findings, and future applications. *Perspectives on Psychological Science*, *6*, 521–536.

Hertel, P. T., & Hardin, T. S. (1990). Remembering with and without awareness in a depressed mood. *Journal of Experimental Psychology: General*, *119*, 45–59.

Hertenstein, M. J. (2002). Touch: Its communicative functions in infancy. *Human Development*, *45*, 70–94.

Hertenstein, M. J., & Campos, J. J. (2001). Emotion regulation via maternal touch. *Infancy*, *2*(4), 549–566.

Hertenstein, M. J., Holmes, R., McCullough, M., & Keltner, D. (2009). The communication of emotion via touch. *Emotion*, *9*, 566–573.

Hertzman, C., & Boyce, W. T. (2010). How experience gets under the skin to create gradients in developmental health. *Annual Review of Public Health*, *31*, 329–347.

Hess, U., Adams, R. B., & Kleck, R. E. (2005). Who may frown and who should smile? Dominance, affiliation, and the display of happiness and anger. *Cognition and Emotion*, *19*, 515–536.

Hess, U., Banse, R., & Kappas, A. (1995). The intensity of facial expression is determined by underlying affective states and social situations. *Journal of Personality and Social Psychology, 69,* 280–288.

Hess, U., & Thibault, P. (2009). Darwin and emotion expression. *American Psychologist, 64,* 120–128.

Hetherington, E. M., Stanley-Hagan, M., & Anderson, E. R. (1989). Marital transitions: A child's perspective. *American Psychologist, 44,* 303–312.

Hiatt, K., & Newman, J. P. (2006). Understanding psychopathy: The cognitive side. In C. J. Patrick (Ed.), *Handbook of psychopathy* (pp. 334–352) New York, NY: Guilford.

Hibbs, E. D., Zahn, T. P., Hamburger, S. D., Kruesi, M.J.P., & Rapoport, J. L. (1992). Parental expressed emotion and psychophysical reactivity in disturbed and normal children. *British Journal of Psychiatry, 160,* 504–510.

Hill, A. L., Degnan, K. A., Calkins, S. D., & Keane, S. P. (2006). Profiles of externalizing behavior problems for boys and girls across preschool: The roles of emotion regulation and inattention. *Developmental Psychology, 42* (5), 913–928.

Hilton, S. M., & Zbrozyna, A. W. (1963). Amygdaloid region for defense reactions and its efferent pathway to the brainstem. *Journal of Physiology, 165,* 160–173.

Hirata, S. (2009). Chimpanzee social intelligence: Selfishness, altruism, and the mother–infant bond. *Primates, 50,* 3–11.

Hitchcock, A. (Writer and Director). (1958). *Vertigo* [Movie]. USA.

Ho, A. P., Gillin, J. C., Buchsbaum, M. S., Wu, J. C., Abel, L., & Bunney, W. E., Jr., (1996). Brain glucose metabolism during non-rapid eye movement sleep in major depression. A positron emission tomography study. *Archives of General Psychiatry, 53,* 645–652.

Hochschild, A. R. (1983). *The managed heart: Commercialization of human feeling.* Berkeley: University of California Press.

Hochschild, A. R. (1990). Ideology and emotion management. In T. D. Kemper (Ed.), *Research agendas in the sociology of emotions* (pp. 117–142) Albany, NY: State University of New York Press.

Hofmann, W., & Baumert, A. (2010). Immediate affect as a basis for intuitive moral judgement: An adaptation of the affect misattribution procedure. *Cognition and Emotion, 24,* 522–535.

Hofstede, G. (1980). *Culture's consequences: International differences in work-related values.* Beverley Hills, CA: Sage.

Hogan, P. C. (2003). *The mind and its stories.* Cambridge, MA: Cambridge University Press.

Hogan, P. C. (2009). *Understanding nationalism: On narrative, cognitive science, and identity.* Columbus: Ohio State University Press.

Hogarty, G. E., Anderson, C. M., Reiss, M. A., et al. (1986). Family psychoeducation, social skills training, and maintenance chemotherapy in the aftercare treatment of schizophrenia. One-year effects of a controlled study of relapse and Expressed Emotion. *Archives of General Psychiatry, 43,* 633–642.

Hohmann, G. W. (1966). Some effects of spinal cord lesions on experienced emotional feelings. *Psychophysiology, 3,* 143–156.

Hokanson, J. E., Hummer, J. T., & Butler, A. C. (1991). Interpersonal perceptions by depressed college students. *Cognitive Therapy and Research, 15,* 443–457.

Hollon, S. D., & Beck, A. T. (2004). Cognitive and cognitive-behavioral therapies. In M. J. Lambert (Ed.), *Bergin and Garfield's handbook of psychotherapy and behavior change* (5th ed., pp. 447–492). New York, NY: Wiley.

Hollon, S. D., & Ponniah, K. (2010). A review of empirically supported psychological therapies for mood disorders in adults. *Depression and Anxiety, 27,* 891–932.

Holman, S. D., & Goy, R. W. (1995). Experiential and hormonal correlates of care-giving in rhesus macaques. In C. R. Pryce & R. D. Martin (Eds.), *Motherhood in human and nonhuman primates: Biosocial determinants* (pp. 87–93). Basel, Switzerland: Karger.

Holmes, T. H., & Rahe, R. H. (1967). The social readjustment rating scale. *Journal of Psychosomatic Research, 11,* 213–218.

Hom, H. L., & Arbuckle, B. (1988). Mood induction effects upon goal setting and performance in young children. *Motivation and Emotion, 12,* 113–122.

Homer. (c. 850 BCE). *The Iliad* (M. Hammond, Ed. and Trans.). Harmondsworth, UK: Penguin (current edition 1987).

Hooker, C., & Park, S. (2002). Emotion processing and its relationship to social functioning in schizophrenia patients. *Psychiatry Research, 112,* 41–50.

Hooley, J. M., & Teasdale, J. D. (1989). Predictors of relapse in unipolar depressives: Expressed emotion, marital distress and perceived criticism. *Journal of Abnormal Psychology, 98*, 229–237.

Horberg, E. J., Oveis, C., Keltner, D., & Cohen, A. B. (2009). Disgust and the moralization of purity. *Journal of Personality and Social Psychology, 97*, 963–976.

Hou, J., Wu, W., Lin, Y., Wang, J., Zhou, D., et al. (2012, in press). Localization of cerebral functional deficits in patients with obsessive–compulsive disorder: A resting-state fMRI study. *Journal of Affective Disorders.*

Howell, S. (1981). Rules not words. In P.H.A. Lock (Ed.), *Indigenous psychologies: The anthropology of the self* (pp. 133–143). London, UK: Academic Press.

Howes, C. (2000). Social-emotional classroom climate in child care, child-teacher relationships and children's second grade peer relations. *Social Development, 9*(2), 191–204.

Howes, C., & Matheson, C. C. (1992). Sequences in the development of competent play with peers: Social and social pretend play. *Developmental Psychology, 28*(5), 961–974.

Hoyt, W. T., Fincham, F. D., McCullough, M. E., Maio, G., & Davila, J. (2005). Responses to interpersonal transgressions in families: Forgivingness, forgivability, and relationship-specific effects. *Journal of Personality and Social Psychology, 89*, 375–394.

Hrdy, S. B. (1999). *Mother nature.* New York, NY: Ballantine.

Hsu, H.-C., & Fogel, A. (2003). Stability and transitions in mother–infant face-to-face communication during the first 6 months: A microhistorical approach. *Developmental Psychology, 39*(6), 1061–1082.

Hudziak, J. J., Achenbach, T. M., Althoff, R. R., & Pine, D. S. (2007). A dimensional approach to developmental psychopathology. *International Journal of Methods in Psychiatric Research, 16*(1), 16–23.

Huebner, R. R., & Izard, C. E. (1988). Mothers' responses to infants' facial expressions of sadness, anger and physical distress. *Motivation and Emotion, 12*, 185–196.

Huesmann, L. R., Dubow, E. F., & Boxer, P. (2009). Continuity of aggression from childhood to early adulthood as a predictor of life outcomes: Implications for the adolescent-limited and life-course-persistent models. *Aggressive Behavior, 35*, 136–149.

Huey S. J., Jr., Henggeler, S. W., Brondino, M. J., & Pickrel, S. G. (2000). Mechanisms of change in multisystemic therapy: Reducing delinquent behavior through therapist adherence and improved family and peer functioning. *Journal of Consulting and Clinical Psychology, 68*(3), 451.

Huey S. J., Jr., Henggeler, S. W., Rowland, M. D., Halliday-Boykins, C. A., Cunningham, P. B., Pickrel, S. G., et al. (2004). Multisystemic therapy effects on attempted suicide by youths presenting psychiatric emergencies. *Journal of the American Academy of Child & Adolescent Psychiatry, 43*(2), 183–190.

Hughes, C. (2011). Changes and challenges in 20 years of research into the development of executive functions. *Infant and Child Development, 20*(3), 251–271.

Hughes, C., & Dunn, J. (2002). "When I say a naughty word": A longitudinal study of young children's accounts of anger and sadness in themselves and close others. *British Journal of Developmental Psychology, 20*(4), 515–535.

Hughes, C., & Ensor, R. (2008). Does executive function matter for preschoolers' problem behaviors? *Journal of Abnormal Child Psychology, 36*(1), 1–14.

Hughes, C., Ensor, R., Wilson, A., & Graham, A. (2010). Tracking executive function across the transition to school: A latent variable approach. *Developmental Neuropsychology, 35*(1), 20–36.

Hughlings-Jackson, J. (1959). *Selected writings of John Hughlings-Jackson* (J. Taylor, Ed.). New York, NY: Basic Books.

Huijbregts, S.C.J., Seguin, J. R., Zelazo, P. D., Parent, S., Japel, C., & Tremblay, R. E. (2006). Interrelations between maternal smoking during pregnancy, birthweight and sociodemographic factors in the prediction of early cognitive abilities. *Infant and Child Development, 15*, 593–607.

Hume, D. (1972). *A treatise of human nature.* London, UK: Fontana/Collins (original publication 1739–1740).

Hunsley, J., & Lee, C. M. (2010). *Introduction to clinical psychology: An evidence-based approach.* Hoboken, NJ: Wiley.

Hunt, L. (2007). *Inventing human rights.* New York, NY: Norton.

Hupka, R. B. (1991). The motive for the arousal of romantic jealousy: Its cultural origin. In P. Salovey (Ed.), *The psychology of jealousy and envy* (pp. 252–270). New York, NY: Guilford.

Huron, D. (2003). Is music an evolutionary adaptation? In I. Peretz & R. Zatorre (Eds.), *The cognitive neuroscience of music* (pp. 57–75). Oxford, UK: Oxford University Press.

Huston, A. C., Gupta, A. E., Bentley, A. C., Dowsett, C., Ware, A., & Epps, S. R. (2008). *New hope's effect on social behavior, parenting, and activities at eight years.* New York, NY: MDRC.

Hyman, S. E. (2010). The diagnosis of mental disorders: The problem of reification. *Annual Review of Clinical Psychology, 6,* 155–179.

Inbar, Y., Pizarro, D. A., & Bloom, P. (in press). Disgusting smells cause decreased liking of gay men. *Emotion.*

Inbar, Y., Pizarro, D. A., Knobe, J., & Bloom, P. (2009). Disgust sensitivity predicts intuitive disapproval of gays. *Emotion, 9,* 435–439.

Insel, T. (1992). Oxytocin—A neuropeptide for affiliation: Evidence from behavioral, receptor autoradiographic, and comparative studies. *Psychoneuroendocrinology, 17*(1), 3–35.

Insel, T., Young, L., & Wang, Z. (1997). Molecular aspects of monogamy. *Annals of the New York Academy of Sciences, 807,* 302–316.

Insel, T. R. (1993). Oxytocin and the neuroendocrine basis of affiliation. In J. Schulkin (Ed.), *Hormonally induced changes in mind and brain* (pp. 225–251). San Diego, CA: Academic Press.

Insel, T. R., & Harbaugh, C. R. (1989). Lesions of the hypothalamic paraventricular nucleus disrupt the initiation of maternal behavior. *Physiology and Behavior, 45,* 1033–1041.

Ironson, G., Wynings, C., Schneiderman, N., et al. (1997). Post traumatic stress symptoms, intrusive thoughts, loss and immune function after Hurricane Andrew. *Psychosomatic Medicine, 59,* 128–141.

Isabella, R. A. (1993). Origins of attachment: Maternal interactive behavior across the first year. *Child Development, 64*(2), 605–621.

Isabella, R. A., Belsky, J., & von Eye, A. (1989). Origins of infant-mother attachment: An examination of interactional synchrony during the infant's first year. *Developmental Psychology, 25*(1), 12–21.

Isen, A. (1970). Success, failure, attention and reactions to others: The warm glow of success. *Journal of Personality and Social Psychology, 15,* 294–301.

Isen, A. M. (1987). Positive affect, cognitive processes and social behavior. In L. Berkowitz (Ed.), *Advances in experimental social psychology* (Vol. 20, pp. 203–253). New York, NY: Academic Press.

Isen, A. M. (1993). Positive affect and decision making. In M. Lewis & J. M. Haviland (Eds.), *Handbook of emotions* (pp. 261–278). New York, NY: Guilford.

Isen, A. M., Daubman, K. A., & Nowicki, G. P. (1987). Positive affect facilitates creative problem solving. *Journal of Personality and Social Psychology, 52,* 1122–1131.

Isen, A. M., Shalker, T., Clark, M., & Karp, L. (1978). Affect, accessibility of material in memory and behavior: A cognitive loop? *Journal of Personality and Social Psychology, 36,* 1–12.

Isley, S. L., O'Neil, R., Clatfelter, D., & Parke, R. D. (1999). Parent and child expressed affect and children's social competence: Modeling direct and indirect pathways. *Developmental Psychology, 35*(2), 547–560.

Isley, S., O'Neil, R., & Parke, R. (1996). The relation of parental affect and control behaviors to children's classroom acceptance: A concurrent and predictive analysis. *Early Education and Development, 7*(1), 7–23.

Ito, T. A., Larsen, J. T., Smith, N. K., & Cacioppo, J. T. (1998). Negative information weighs more heavily on the brain: The negativity bias in evaluative categorizations. *Journal of Personality and Social Psychology, 75,* 887–900.

Izard, C. E. (1971). *The face of emotion.* New York, NY: Appleton-Century-Crofts.

Izard, C. E. (1977). *Human emotions.* New York, NY: Plenum.

Izard, C. E. (1991). *The psychology of emotions.* New York, NY: Plenum.

Izard, C. E. (1993). Four systems for emotion activation: Cognitive and non-cognitive processes. *Psychological Review, 100,* 68–90.

Izard, C. E. (1994). Innate and universal facial expressions: Evidence from developmental and cross-cultural research. *Psychological Bulletin, 115,* 288–299.

Izard, C. E. (2007). Basic emotions, natural kinds, emotion schemas, and a new paradigm. *Perspectives on Psychological Science, 2*(3), 260–280.

Izard, C. E. (2010). The many meanings/aspects of emotion: Definitions, functions, activation, and regulation. *Emotion Review, 2,* 363–370.

Izard, C. E. (2011). Forms and functions of emotions: Matters of emotion–cognition interactions. *Emotion Review, 3*(4), 371–378.

Jaffee, S., Caspi, A., Moffitt, T. E., Belsky, J., & Silva, P. (2001). Why are children born to teen mothers at risk for adverse outcomes in young adulthood?: Results from a 20-year longitudinal study. *Development and Psychopathology, 13*(2), 377–397.

Jaffee, S. R., & Price, T. S. (2007). Gene-environment correlations: A review of the evidence and implications for prevention of mental illness. *Molecular Psychiatry, 12*, 432–442.

Jahoda, M., Lazarsfeld, P. F., & Zeisel, H. (1971). *Marienthal: The sociography of an unemployed community*. Chicago, IL: Aldine.

James, W. (1884). What is an emotion? *Mind, 9*, 188–205.

James, W. (1890). *The principles of psychology*. New York, NY: Dover (current edition 1950).

Jamison, K. R. (1993). *Touched with fire: Manic-depressive illness and the artistic temperament*. New York, NY: Free Press.

Jamison, K. R. (1995). *An unquiet mind*. New York, NY: Knopf.

Jamner, L. D., Alberts, J., Leigh, H., & Klein, L. C. (1998, March). Affiliative need and endogenous opiods. Paper presented at the annual meeting of the Society of Behavioral Medicine. New Orleans, LA.

Janssens, A., Uvin, K., Van Impe, H., Laroche, S.M.F., Van Reempts, P., & Deboutte, D. (2009). Psychopathology among preterm infants using the Diagnostic Classification Zero to Three. *Acta Paediatrica, 98*, 1988–1993.

Janig, W. (2003). The autonomic nervous system and its coordination by the brain. In R. Davidson, K. Scherer, & H. H. Goldsmith (Eds.), *Handbook of affective sciences* (pp. 135–186). London, UK: Oxford University Press.

Jankowiak, W. R., & Fischer, E. F. (1992). A crosscultural perspective on romantic love. *Ethos, 31*, 149–155.

Jaynes, J. (1990). *The origin of consciousness in the breakdown of the bicameral mind*. London, UK: Penguin.

Jenike, M. A. (1996). Obsessive-compulsive disorder. In H. I. Kaplan & B. J. Saddock (Eds.), *Comprehensive textbook of psychiatry* (6th ed., Vol. 1, pp. 1218–1227). Baltimore, MD: Williams & Wilkins.

Jenkins, J. M. (2008). Psychosocial adversity. In M. Rutter, D. Bishop, D. Pine, S. Scott, J. Stevenson, E. Taylor, & A. Thapar (Eds.), *Rutter's child and adolescent psychiatry* (5th ed.). New York, NY: Blackwell.

Jenkins, J. M., & Astington, J. W. (1996). Cognitive factors and family structure associated with theory of mind development in young children. *Developmental Psychology, 32*(1), 70–78.

Jenkins, J. M., & Astington, J. (2000). Theory of mind and social behavior: Causal models tested in a longitudinal study. *Merrill Palmer Quarterly, 46*, 203–220.

Jenkins, J. M., & Ball, S. (2000). Distinguishing between negative emotions: Children's understanding of the social-regulatory aspects of emotion. *Cognition and Emotion, 14*, 261–282.

Jenkins, J. M., Dunn, J., O'Connor, T. G., Rasbash, J., & Simpson, A. (2005). The mutual influence of marital conflict and children's behavior problems: Shared and non-shared family risks. *Child Development, 76*(1), 24–39.

Jenkins, J. M., & Oatley, K. (1996). Emotional episodes and emotionality through the life span. In C. Magai & S. H. McFadden (Eds.), *Handbook of emotion, adult development, and aging* (pp. 421–441). San Diego, CA: Academic Press.

Jenkins, J. M., & Oatley, K. (1998). The development of emotion schemas in children: The processes underlying psychopathology. In W. F. Flack & J. D. Laird (Eds.), *Emotions and psychopathology* (pp. 45–56). New York, NY: Oxford University Press.

Jenkins, J. M., & Oatley, K. (2000). Psychopathology and short-term emotion: The balance of affects. *Journal of Child Psychology and Psychiatry, 41*, 463–472.

Jenkins, J. M., Rasbash, J., Leckie, G., Gass, K., & Dunn, J. (2012, in press). The role of maternal factors in sibling relationship quality: A multilevel study of multiple dyads per family. *Journal of Child Psychology & Psychiatry*.

Jenkins, J. M., Shapka, J., & Sorenson, A. (2006). Teenage mothers' anger over twelve years: Partner conflict, partner transitions and children's anger. *Journal of Child Psychology & Psychiatry, 47*, 775–782.

Jenkins, J. M., Simpson, A., Dunn, J., Rasbash, J., & O'Connor, T. G. (2005). Mutual influence of marital conflict and children's behavior problems: Shared and nonshared family risks. *Child Development, 76*(1), 24–39.

Jenkins, J. M., Smith, M. A., & Graham, P. (1989). Coping with parental quarrels. *Journal of the American Academy of Child and Adolescent Psychiatry, 28,* 182–189.

Jenson, P. S., Xenakis, S. N., Davis, H., & Degroot, J. (1988). Child psychopathology rating scales and interrater agreement: II. Child and family characteristics. *Journal of the American Academy of Child and Adolescent Psychiatry, 27,* 451–461.

John, O. P., Naumann, L. P., & Soto, C. J. (2008). Paradigm shift to the integrative Big Five trait taxonomy: History, measurement, and conceptual issues. In O. P. John, R. W. Robins, & L. A. Pervin (Eds.), *Handbook of personality: Theory and research* (pp. 114–58). New York, NY: Guilford.

Johnson, D. R. (2012). Transportation into a story increases empathy, prosocial behavior, and perceptual bias toward fearful expressions. *Personality and Individual Differences, 52,* 150–155.

Johnson, M. H. (2005). Subcortical face processing. *Nature Reviews Neuroscience, 6*(10), 766–774.

Johnson, E. J., & Tversky, A. (1983). Affect, generalization, and the perception of risk. *Journal of Personality and Social Psychology, 45,* 20–31.

Johnson, J. G., Alloy, L., Panzarella, C., et al. (2001). Hopelessness as a mediator of the association between social support and depressive symptoms: Findings of a study of men with HIV. *Journal of Consulting and Clinical Psychology, 69,* 1056–1060.

Johnson, K. J., & Fredrickson, B. L. (2005). "We all look the same to me": Positive emotions eliminate the own-race bias in face recognition. *Psychological Science, 16,* 875–881.

Johnson, S. L. (2005). Mania and dysregulation in goal pursuit: A review. *Clinical Psychology Review, 25,* 241–262.

Johnson, S. L., & Kizer, A. (2002). Bipolar and unipolar depression: A comparison of clinical phenomenology and psychosocial predictors. In I. H. Gotlib & C. L. Hammen (Eds.), *Handbook of depression* (pp. 141–165). New York, NY: Guilford.

Johnson-Laird, P. N., Mancini, F., & Gangemi, A. (2006). A hyper-emotion theory of psychological illnesses. *Psychological Review, 113,* 822–841.

Johnson-Laird, P. N., & Oatley, K. (1989). The language of emotions: An analysis of a semantic field. *Cognition and Emotion, 3,* 81–123.

Joiner, T. (2002). Depression in its interpersonal context. In I. H. Gotlib & C. L. Hammen (Eds.), *Handbook of depression* (pp. 295–313). New York, NY: Guilford.

Jonas, H. (1958). *The gnostic religion: The message of the alien God and the beginnings of Christianity.* Boston, MA: Beacon.

Jones, S., Eisenberg, N., & Fabes, R. (2002). Parents' reactions to elementary school children's negative emotions: Relations to social and emotional functioning at school. *Merrill-Palmer Quarterly, 48,* 133–159.

Joormann, J., Dkane, M., & Gotlib, I. H. (2006). Adaptive and maladaptive components of rumination? Diagnostic specificity and relation to depressive biases. *Behavior Therapy, 37,* 269–280.

Jung, C. G. (1925). Marriage as a psychological relationship. In J. Campbell (Ed.), *The portable Jung* (pp. 163–177). New York, NY: Viking-Penguin (current edition 1971).

Juslin, P. N., & Laukka, P. (2003). Communication of emotions in vocal expression and music performance: Different channels, same code? *Psychological Bulletin, 129,* 770–814.

Juslin, P. N., Liljeström, S., Västfjäll, D., Barradas, G., & Silva, A. (2008). An experience sampling study of emotional reactions to music: Listener, music, and situation. *Emotion, 8,* 668–683.

Justice, L. M., Petscher, Y., Schatschneider, C., & Mashburn, A. (2011). Peer effects in preschool classrooms: Is children's language growth associated with their classmates' skills? *Child Development, 82*(6), 1768–1777.

Kagan, J., Snidman, N., Kahn, V., & Towsley, S. (2007). The preservation of two infant temperaments into adolescence. *Monographs of the Society for Research in Child Development, 72*(2), 1–95.

Kahneman, D. (2011). *Thinking fast and slow.* Toronto: Doubleday Canada.

Kahneman, D., Kreuger, A. B., Schkade, D. A., Schwarz, N., & Stone, A. (2006). Would you be happier if you were richer? A focusing illusion. *Science, 312,* 1908–1910.

Kallestad, H., Valen, J., McCullough, L., Svartberg, M., Hoglend, P., & Stiles, T. C. (2010). The relationship between insight gained during therapy and long-term outcome in short-term dynamic psychotherapy and cognitive therapy for cluster C personality disorders. *Psychotherapy Research, 20,* 526–534.

Kamarack, T. W., Manuch, S., & Jennings, J. R. (1990). Social support reduces cardiovascular reactivity to psychological challenge: A laboratory model. *Psychosomatic Medicine, 52,* 42–58.

Kandel, E. R., Schwartz, J. H., & Jessell, T. M. (1991). *Principles of neural science* (3rd ed.). Norwalk, CT: Appleton & Lange.

Kane, F., Coulombe, D., & Miliaressis, E. (1991). Amygdaloid self-stimulation: A movable electrode mapping study. *Behavioral Neuroscience, 105,* 926–932.

Kano, T. (1992). *The last ape: Pygmy chimpanzee behavior and ecology* (E. O. Vineberg, Trans.). Stanford, CA: Stanford University Press.

Kant, I. (1764, 1960). Observations on the feeling of the beautiful and the sublime. Translated by J.T. Goldthwait. Berkeley: University of California Press.

Kappas, A., Bherer, F., & Thériault, M. (2000). Inhibiting facial expressions: Limitations to the voluntary control of facial expressions of emotion. *Motivation and Emotion, 24,* 259–270.

Karg, K., Burmeister, M., Shedden, K., & Sen, S. (2011). The serotonin transporter promoter variant (5-HTTLPR), stress and depression meta-analysis revisited: Evidence of genetic moderation. *Archives of General Psychiatry, 68*(5), 444–454.

Karos, L., Howe, N., & Aquan-Assee, J. (2007). Reciprocal and complementary sibling interactions, relationship quality and socio-emotional problem solving. *Infant and Child Development, 16*(6), 577–596.

Katkin, E. S. (1985). Blood, sweat, and tears: Individual differences in autonomic self-perception. *Psychophysiology, 22,* 125–137.

Katkin, E. S., Blascovich, J., & Godband, S. (1981). Empirical assessment of visceral self-perception: Individual and sex differrences in the acquisition of heart rate discrimination. *Journal of Personality and Social Psychology, 40,* 1095–1101.

Kaufman, N. K., Rohde, P., Seeley, J. R., Clarke, G. N., & Stice, E. (2005). Potential mediators of cognitive-behavioral therapy for adolescents with comorbid major depression and conduct disorder. *Journal of Consulting and Clinical Psychology, 73*(1), 38.

Kawabata, H., & Zeki, S. (2004). Neural correlates of beauty. *Journal of Neurophysiology, 91,* 1699–1705.

Kawakami, K., Dunn, E., Karmali, F., & Davidio, J. F. (2009). Mispredicting affective and behavioral responses to racism. *Science, 323,* 276–278.

Kazdin, A. E. (1986). Comparative outcome studies of psychotherapy: Methodological issues and strategies. *Journal of Consulting and Clinical Psychology, 54,* 95–105.

Kazdin, A. E. (2004). Evidence-based treatments: Challenges and priorities for practice and research. *Child and Adolescent Psychiatric Clinics of North America, 13*(4), 923–940.

Keegan, J. (1994). *A history of warfare.* New York, NY: Vintage.

Kellam, S. G., & Hendricks-Brown, C. (1998). The effect of level of aggression in the first grade classroom on the course and malleability of aggressive behavior into middle school. *Development and Psychopathology, 10,* 165–185.

Keller, M. B., & Boland, R. J. (1998). Implications of failing to achieve successful long term maintenance treatment of recurrent unipolar major depression. *Biological Psychiatry, 44,* 348–360.

Keltner, D. (1995). Signs of appeasement: Evidence for the distinct displays of embarrassment, amusement, and shame. *Journal of Personality and Social Psychology, 68,* 441–454.

Keltner, D. (2004). The compassionate instinct. *Greater Good, 1,* 6–9.

Keltner, D., & Anderson, C. (2000). Saving face for Darwin: Functions and uses of embarrassment. *Current Directions in Psychological Science, 9,* 187–191.

Keltner, D., & Bonanno, G. A. (1997). A study of laughter and dissociation: The distinct correlates of laughter and smiling during bereavement. *Journal of Personality and Social Psychology, 73,* 687–702.

Keltner, D., & Buswell, B. (1996). Evidence for the distinctness of embarrassment, shame, and guilt: A study of recalled antecedents and facial expressions of emotion. *Cognition and Emotion, 10*(2), 155–172.

Keltner, D., & Buswell, B. N. (1997). Embarrassment: Its distinct form and appeasement functions. *Psychological Bulletin, 122,* 250–270.

Keltner, D., Capps, L. M., Kring, A. M., Young, R. C., & Heerey, E. A. (2001). Just teasing: A conceptual analysis and empirical review. *Psychological Bulletin, 127,* 229–248.

Keltner, D., Ellsworth, P. C., & Edwards, K. (1993). Beyond simple pessimism: Effects of sadness and anger on social perception. *Journal of Personality and Social Psychology, 64,* 740–752.

Keltner, D., & Gross, J. J. (1999). Functional accounts of emotions. *Cognition and Emotion, 13*, 467–480.

Keltner, D., Gruenfeld, D. H., & Anderson, C. (2003). Power, approach, and inhibition. *Psychological Review, 110*(2), 265–284.

Keltner, D., & Haidt, J. (1999). Social functions of emotions at four levels of analysis. *Cognition and Emotion, 13*, 505–521.

Keltner, D., & Haidt, J. (2001). Social functions of emotions. In T. Mayne & G. Bonanno (Eds.), *Emotions: Current issues and future directions* (pp. 192–213). New York, NY: Guilford.

Keltner, D., & Haidt, J. (2003). Approaching awe, a moral, spiritual, and aesthetic emotion. *Cognition and Emotion, 17*(2), 297–314.

Keltner, D., Haidt, J., & Shiota, M. N. (2006). Social functionalism and the evolution of emotions. In M. Schaller, J. A. Simpson, & D. T. Kenrick (Eds.), *Evolution and social psychology* (pp. 115–142). Madison, CT.: Psychosocial Press.

Keltner, D., Haidt, J., & Shiota, M. (in press). Social functionalism and the evolution of emotions.

Keltner, D., & Harker, L. A. (1998). The forms and functions of the nonverbal display of shame. In P. Gilbert & B. Andrews (Eds.), *Interpersonal approaches to shame* (pp. 78–98). Oxford, England: Oxford University Press.

Keltner, D., & Kring, A. (1998). Emotion, social function, and psychopathology. *General Psychological Review, 2*, 320–342.

Keltner, D., Locke, K. D., & Audrain, P. C. (1993). The influence of attributions on the relevance of negative emotions to personal satisfaction. *Personality and Social Psychology Bulletin, 19*, 21–29.

Keltner, D., & Shiota, M. N. (2005). New facial displays of emotions (Unpublished manuscript).

Keltner, D., Young, R., & Buswell, B. N. (1997). Appeasement in human emotion, personality, and social practice. *Aggressive Behavior, 23*, 359–374.

Keltner, D., Young, R. C., Heerey, E. A., Oemig, C., & Monarch, N. D. (1998). Teasing in hierarchial and intimate relations. *Journal of Personality and Social Psychology, 75*, 1231–1247.

Kemeny, M. (2009). Psychobiological responses to social threat: Evolution of a psychological model in psychoneuroimmunology. *Brain, Behavior, and Immunity, 23*, 1–9.

Kemper, T. D. (1978). *A social-interactional theory of emotions.* New York, NY: Wiley.

Kemper, T. D. (2006). Power and status and the power-status theory of emotions. In J. Turner & J. Swets (Eds.) *Handbook of the Sociology of Emotions* (pp. 87–113). Boston, MA: Springer.

Kemper, T. D. (2011). *Status, power and ritual interaction.* Ashgate. Burlington, VT.

Kempton, M. J., Salvador, Z., Munafo, M. R., Geddes, J. R., Simmons, A., et al. (2011). Structural neuroimaging studies in major depressive disorder: Meta-analysis and comparison with bipolar disorder. *Archives of General Psychiatry, 68*, 675–690.

Kendler, K. S., & Baker, J. H. (2007). Genetic influences on measures of the environment: A systematic review. *Psychological Medicine, 37*(5), 615–626.

Kendler, K. S., Gatz, M., Gardner, C. O., & Pedersen, N. L. (2006). A Swedish national twin study of lifetime major depression. *American Journal of Psychiatry, 163*, 109–114.

Kendler, K. S., Gardner, C. O., & Lichtenstein, P. (2008). A developmental twin study of symptoms of anxiety and depression: Evidence for genetic innovation and attenuation. *Psychological Medicine, 38*, 1567–1575.

Kendler, K. S., Heath, A., Martin, A., & Eaves, I. J. (1986). Symptoms of anxiety and depression in a volunteer twin population. *Archives of General Psychiatry, 43*, 213–221.

Kendler, K. S., Hettema, J. M., Butera, F., Gardner, C. O., & Prescott, C. A. (2003). Life event dimemsions of loss, humiliation, entrapment, and danger. *Archives of General Psychiatry, 60*, 789–796.

Kendler, K. S., & Myers, J. (2010). The genetic and environmental relationship between major depression and the five-factor model of personality. *Psychological Medicine, 40*, 801–806.

Kendler, K. S., Neale, M. C., Kessler, R. C., Heath, A. C., & Eaves, L. J. (1993a). A twin study of recent life events. *Archives of General Psychiatry, 50*, 789–796.

Kendler, K. S., Neale, M. C., Kessler, R. C., Heath, A. C., & Eaves, L. J. (1993b). A longitudinal twin study of 1-year prevalence of major depression in women. *Archives of General Psychiatry, 50*, 843–852.

Kendler, K. S., Thornton, L. M., & Gardner, C. O. (2000). Stressful life events and previous episodes in the etiology of major depression in women: An evaluation of the "kindling" hypothesis. *American Journal of Psychiatry, 157*, 1243–1251.

Kendler, K. S., Thornton, L. M., & Gardner, C. O. (2001). Genetic risk, number of previous episodes, and stressful life events in predicting onset of major depression. *American Journal of Psychiatry, 158*, 582–586.

Kensinger, E., & Schachter, D. (2008). Memory and emotion. In M. Lewis, J. Haviland Jones, & L. F. Barrett (Eds.), *Handbook of emotions, third edition* (pp. 601–617). New York, NY: Guilford.

Kessler, H., Taubner, S., Buchheim, A., Münte, T. F., Stasch, M., Kächele, H., et al. (2011). Individualized and clinically derived stimuli activate limbic structures in depression: An fMRI study. *PLoS ONE, 6*(1).

Kessler, R. C., Bergland, P., Demler, O., Jin, R., Merihangas, K. R., & Walters, E. E. (2005). Lifetime prevalence and age-of-onset distributions of *DSM-IV* disorders in the National Comorbidity Survey replication. *Archives of General Psychiatry, 62*, 593–602.

Kessler, R. C., Zhao, S., Blazer, D. G., & Swarz, M. (1997). Prevalence, correlates, and course of minor depression and major depression in the national comorbidity study. *Journal of Affective Disorders, 45*, 19–30.

Ketelaar, T. (2004). Ancestral emotions, current decisions: Using evolutionary game theory to explore the role of emotions in decision-making. In C. Crawford & C. Salmon (Eds.), *Evolutionary psychology, public policy and personal decisions* (pp. 145–168). Mahwah, NJ: Erlbaum.

Ketelaar, T. (2006). The role of moral sentiments in economic decision making. In DeCremer, D., Zeelenberg, M., & Murnighan, K. (Eds.) *Social Psychology and Economics.* Lawrence Erlbaum Associates, pp. 97–116.

Ketelaar, T., & Clore, G. L. (1997). Emotions and reason: The proximate effects and ultimate functions of emotions. In G. Matthews (Ed.), *Advances in personality* (pp. 355–396). Amsterdam, The Netherlands: Elsevier.

Ketelaar, T., Gross, J. J., & Sutton, S. K. (1998). Relations between affect and personality: Support for the affect-level and affective-reactivity views. *Personality and Social Psychology Bulletin, 24*(3), 279–288.

Keverne, E. B. (1996). Psychopharmacology of maternal behaviour. *Journal of Psychopharmacology, 10*, 16–22.

Keverne, E. B., Nevison, C. M., & Martel, F. L. (1997). Early learning and the social bond. In C. S. Carter, I. I. Lederhendler, & B. Kirkpatrick (Eds.), *The integrative neurobiology of affiliation, Vol. 807.* New York, NY: New York Academy of Sciences.

Keyes, K. M., Grant, B. F., & Hasin, D. S. (2008). Evidence for a closing gender gap in alcohol use, abuse, and dependence in the United States population. *Drug and Alcohol Dependence, 93*, 21–29.

Kiecolt-Glaser, J. K. (2009). Psychoneuroimmunology. *Perspectives on Psychological Science, 4*, 367–369.

Kiecolt-Glaser, J. K., & Glaser, R. (1999). Chronic stress and mortality among older adults. *Journal of the American Medical Association, 282*, 2259–2260.

Kiecolt-Glaser, J. K., McGuire, L., Robles, T., & Glaser, R. (2002). Psychoneuroimmunology: Psychological influences on immune function and health. *Journal of Consulting and Clinical Psychology, 70*, 537–547.

Kiecolt-Glaser, J. K., Robles, T. F., Heffner, K. L., Loving, T. J., & Glaser, R. (2002). Psycho-oncology and cancer: Psychoneuroimmunology and cancer. *Annals of Oncology, 13*(Suppl. 4), 166–169.

Kieslowski, K. (Writer and Director). (1991). *Decalogue: The Ten Commandments* [Movie]. Poland.

Kim, J., & Cicchetti, D. (2010). Longitudinal pathways linking child maltreatment, emotion regulation, peer relations, and psychopathology. *Journal of Child Psychology and Psychiatry, 51*(6), 706–716.

Kim, J., McHale, S. M., & Crouter, A. C. (2007). Longitudinal linkages between sibling relationships and adjustment from middle childhood through adolescence. *Developmental Psychology, 43*(4), 960–973.

Kim, J. W., Kim, S.-E., Kim, J.-J., et al. (2009). Compassionate attitude towards others' suffering activates the mesolimbic neural system. *Neuropsychologia, 47*(10), 2073–2081.

Kim-Cohen, J., Caspi, A., Taylor, A., Williams, B., Newcombe, R., Craig, I. W., & Moffit, T. E. (2006). MAOA, maltreatment and gene-environment interaction predicting children's mental health: New evidence and a meta-analysis. *Molecular Psychiatry, 11*, 903–913.

Kinyanda, E., Woodburn, P., Tugumisirize, J., Kagugube, J., Ndanabangi, S., & Paatel, V. (2011). Poverty, life events and the risk for depression in Uganda. *Social Psychiatry and Psychiatric Epidemiology*, *46*, 35–44.

Kirsch, I. (2009). Antidepressants and the placebo response. *Epidemiology and Psychiatric Sciences*, *18*, 318–322.

Kitayama, S., Karasawa, M., & Mesquita, B. (2003). Collective and personal processes in regulating emotions: Emotion and self in Japan and the United States. In P. Philipott & R. S. Feldman (Eds.), *The regulation of emotion*. Hillsdale, NJ: Erlbaum.

Kitayama, S., Markus, H. R., & Kurokawa, M. (2000). Culture, emotions, and well-being: Good feelings in Japan and the United States. *Cognition and Emotion*, *14*, 93–124.

Kitayama, S., Mesquita, B., & Karasawa, M. (2006). The emotional basis of independent and interdependent selves: Socially disengaging and engaging emotions in the U.S. and Japan. *Journal of Personality and Social Psychology*, *91*, 890–903.

Kitzman, K. M., Gaylord, N. K., Holt, A. R., & Kenny, E. D. (2003). Child witness to domestic violence: A meta-analytic review. *Journal of Consulting and Clinical Psychology*, *71*(2), 339–352.

Klasmeyer, G., & Sendlmeier, W. F. (1999). Voice and emotional states. In R. Kent & M. Ball (Eds.), *Voice quality measurement* (pp. 339–359). San Diego, CA: Singular.

Klaus, M. H., & Kennell, J. H. (1976). *Maternal—infant bonding*. St Louis, MO: Mosby.

Klebanov, P. K., Brooks-Gunn, J., Chase-Lansdale, L., & Gordon, R. (1997). Are neighborhood effects on young children mediated by features of the home environment? In J. Brooks-Gunn, G. Duncan, & J. L. Aber (Eds.), *Neighborhood poverty: Context and consequences for children* (Vol. 1, pp. 119–145). New York, NY: Russell Sage.

Klüver, H., & Bucy, P. C. (1937). "Psychic blindness" and other symptoms following bilateral temporal lobectomy. *American Journal of Physiology*, *119*, 352–353.

Knutson, B. (1996). Facial expressions of emotion influence interpersonal trait inferences. *Journal of Nonverbal Behavior*, *20*, 165–182.

Knutson, B., Burgdorf, J., & Panksepp, J. (2002). Ultrasonic vocalizations as indices of affective states in rats. *Psychological Bulletin*, *128*, 961–977.

Knutson, B., & Greer, S. M. (2008). Anticipatory affect: Neural correlates and consequences for choice. *Philosophical Transactions of the Royal Society B*, *363*, 3771–3786.

Knutson, B., Wolkowitz, O. M., Cole, S. W., et al. (1998). Selective alteration of personality and social behavior by serotonergic intervention. *American Journal of Psychiatry*, *155*, 373–379.

Knyazev, G. G., Bocharov, A. V., Slobodskaya, H. R., & Ryabichenko, T. I. (2007). Personality-linked biases in perception of emotional facial expressions. *Personality and Individual Differences*, *44*(5), 1093–1104.

Kochanska, G. (1997). Mutually responsive orientation between mothers and their young children: Implications for early socialization. *Child Development*, *68*(1), 94–112.

Kochanska, G. (2001). Emotional development in children with different attachment histories: The first three years. *Child Development*, *72*(2), 474–490.

Kochanska, G. (2002). Mutually responsive orientation between mothers and their young children: A context for the early development of conscience. *Current Directions in Psychological Science*, *11*(6), 191–195.

Kochanska, G., & Aksan, N. (2004). Development of mutual responsiveness between parents and their young children. *Child Development*, *75*(6), 1657–1676.

Kochanska, G., Forman, D. R., Aksan, N., & Dunbar, S. B. (2005). Pathways to conscience: Early mother-child mutually responsive orientation and children's moral emotion, conduct, and cognition. *Journal of Child Psychology and Psychiatry, and Allied Disciplines*, *46*(1), 19–34.

Kochanska, G., Forman, D. R., & Coy, K. C. (1999). Implications of the mother-child relationship in infancy for socialization in the second year of life. *Infant Behavior & Development*, *22*(2), 249–265.

Kochanska, G., & Knaack, A. (2003). Effortful control as a personality characteristic of young children: Antecedents, correlates, and consequences. *Journal of Personality*, *71*(6), 1087–1112.

Kochanska, G., Philibert, R. A., & Barry, R. A. (2009). Interplay of genes and early mother-child relationship in the development of self-regulation from toddler to preschool age. *Journal of Child Psychology and Psychiatry*, *50*(11), 1331–1338.

Kochanska, G., Woodard, J., Kim, S., Koenig, J. L., Yoon, J. E., & Barry, R. A. (2010). Positive socialization mechanisms in secure and insecure parent child dyads: Two longitudinal studies. *Journal of Child Psychology and Psychiatry*, *51*(9), 998–1009.

Kohen, D. E., Brooks-Gunn, J., Leventhal, T., & Hertzman, C. (2002). Neighborhood income and physical and social disorder in Canada: Associations with young children's competencies. *Child Development, 73*(6), 1844–1860.

Kohen, D. E., Leventhal, T., Dahinten, V. S., & McIntosh, C. N. (2008). Neighborhood disadvantage: Pathways of effects for young children. *Child Development, 79*(1), 156–169.

Kohlberg, L. (1969). Stage and sequence: The cognitive developmental approach to socialization. In D. A. Goslin (Ed.), *Handbook of socialization theory and research* (pp. 347–480). Chicago, IL: Rand McNally.

Kok, B. E. & Fredrickson, B. L. (2010). Upward spirals of the heart: Autonomic flexibility, as indexed by vagal tone, reciprocally and prospectively predicts positive emotions and social connectedness *Biological Psychology, 85,* 432–436.

Komsi, N., Räikkönen, K., Pesonen, A. K., et al. (2006). Continuity of temperament from infancy to middle childhood. *Infant Behavior and Development, 29*(4), 494–508.

Kopp, C. B., & Neufeld, S. J. (2003). Emotional development during infancy. In R. J. Davidson, K. R. Scherer, & H. H. Goldsmith (Eds.), *Handbook of affective sciences* (pp. 347–374). New York, NY: Oxford University Press.

Korkeila, J., Vahtera, J., Nabi, H., Kivimaki, M., Korkeila, K., et al. (2010). Childhood adversities, adulthood life events, and depression. *Journal of Affective Disorders, 127,* 130–138.

Kosfeld, M., Heinrichs, M., Zak, P., Fischenbacher, U., & Fehr, E. (2005). Oxytocin increases trust in humans. *Nature, 435,* 673–676.

Kotsoni, E., De Haan, M., & Johnson, M. (2001). Categorical perception of facial expressions by 7-month-old infants. *Perception, 30*(9), 1115–1125.

Kovacs, M., & Devlin, B. (1998). Internalizing disorders in childhood. *Journal of Child Psychology and Psychiatry, 39*(1), 47–63.

Kovan, N. M., Chung, A. L., & Sroufe, L. A. (2009). The intergenerational continuity of observed early parenting: A prospective, longitudinal study. *Developmental Psychology, 45*(5), 1205–1213.

Kövesces, Z. (2003). *Metaphor.* London, UK: Oxford University Press.

Kraepelin, E. (1899). *Psychiatrie: Ein Lehrbuch für Studirende und Aerzte* (2nd ed.). Leipzig, Germany: Barth.

Kramer, P. D. (1993). *Listening to Prozac.* New York, NY: Viking.

Kraus, M. W., Côté, S., & Keltner, D. (2010). Social class, contextualism, and empathic accuracy, *Psychological Science, 21,* 1716–1723.

Kraus, M. W., Huang, C., & Keltner, D. (2010). Tactile communication, cooperation, and performance: An ethological study of the NBA, *Emotion, 10,* 745–749.

Kraus, M. W., Piff, P. K., & Keltner, D. (2011). Social class as culture: The convergence of resources and rank in the social realm. *Current Directions in Psychological Science.*

Kraut, R. E., & Johnson, R. E. (1979). Social and emotional messages of smiling: An ethological approach. *Journal of Personality and Social Psychology, 37,* 1539–1553.

Krebs, J. R., & Davies, N. B. (1993). *An introduction to behavioural ecology.* Oxford, UK: Blackwell.

Kreitler, H., & Kreitler, S. (1972). *Psychology and the arts.* Durham, NC: Duke University Press.

Kring, A., Johnson, S. L., Davison, G. C., & Neale, J. M. (2012). *Abnormal psychology* (12th ed.). Hoboken, NJ: Wiley.

Kring, A., & Werner, K. H. (2004). Emotion regulation and psychopathology. In P. Philippot & R. S. Feldman (Eds.), *The regulation of emotion* (pp. 359–385). Mahwah, NJ: Erlbaum.

Kring, A. M. (1999). Emotion in schizophrenia: Old mystery, new understanding. *Current Directions in Psychological Science, 8,* 160–163.

Kring, A. N. (2008). Emotion disturbances as transdiagnostic processes. In M. Lewis, J. Haviland-Jones, & L. F. Barrett (Eds.), *Handbook of emotions* (3rd ed., pp. 691–705). New York, NY: Guilford.

Kringelbach, M. L., & Berridge, K. C. Toward a functional neuroanatomy of pleasure and happiness. *Trends in Cognitive Sciences, 13*(11) 479–487 (2009).

Krpan, K., Coombs, R., Zinga, D., et al. (2005). Experiential and hormonal correlates of maternal behavior in teen and adult mothers. *Hormones and Behavior, 47,* 112–122.

Krumhuber, E., & Manstead, A.S.R. (2009). Can Duchenne smiles be feigned? New evidence on felt and false smiles. *Emotion, 9,* 807–820.

Kuczynski, L. (Ed.). (2003). *Parent-child relationships as a dyadic process.* Thousand Oaks, CA: Sage.

Kuebli, J., Butler, S., & Fivush, R. (1995). Mother-child talk about past emotions: Relations of maternal language and child gender over time. *Cognition and Emotion, 9*(2-3), 265–283.

Kuipers, L., & Bebbington, P. (1988). Expressed emotion research in schizophrenia: Theoretical and clinical implications. *Psychological Medicine, 18*, 893–909.

Kumsta, R., Kreppner, J., Rutter, M., Beckett, C., Castle, J., Stevens, S., et al. (2010). III. Deprivation-specific psychological patterns. *Monographs for the Society of Research in Child Development, 75*(1), 48–78.

Kumsta, R., Rutter, M., Stevens, S., & Sonuga-Barke, E. J. (2010). IX. Risk, causation, mediation and moderation. *Monographs of the Society for Research in Child Development, 75*(1), 187–211.

Kuper, H., & Marmot, M. (2003). Job strain, job demands, decision latitude, and risk of coronary heart disease within the Whitehall II study. *Journal of Epidemiology and Community Health, 57*, 147–153.

Kuppens, P., Van Mechelen, I., Smits, D.J.M., De Boeck, P., & Caulemans, E. (2007). Individual differences in patterns of appraisal and anger experience. *Cognition and Emotion, 21*, 689–713.

La Bar, K. S., & LeDoux, J. E. (2003). Emotional learning circuits in animals and humans. In R. J. Davidson, K. R. Scherer, & H. H. Goldsmith (Eds.), *Handbook of affective sciences* (pp. 52–65). New York, NY: Oxford University Press.

La Rochefoucauld (1665). *Maxims* (L. Tancock, Trans.). Harmondsworth: Penguin (current edition 1959).

Lagattuta, K. H., & Wellman, H. M. (2001). Thinking about the past: Early knowledge about links between prior experience, thinking, and emotion. *Child Development, 72*(1), 82–102.

Lahey, B. B., Rathouz, P. J., Van Hulle, C., Urbano, R. C., Krueger, R. F., Applegate, B., et al. (2008). Testing of structural models of *DSM-IV* symptoms of common forms of child and adolescent psychopathology. *Journal of Abnormal Child Psychology, 36*, 187–206.

Lahey, B. B., Van Hulle, C. A., Singh, A. L., Waldman, I. D., & Rathouz, P. J. (2011). Higher order genetic and environmental structure of prevalent forms of child and adolescent psychpathology. *Archives of General Psychiatry 68* (2), 181–189.

Laible, D. (2004). Mother-child discourse in two contexts: Links with child temperament, attachment security, and socioemotional competence. *Developmental Psychology, 40*(6), 979–992.

Laible, D. (2011). Does it matter if preschool children and mothers discuss positive vs. negative events during reminiscing? Links with mother-reported attachment, family emotional climate, and socioemotional development. *Social Development, 20*(2), 394–411.

Laible, D., & Panfile, T. (2009). Mother-child reminiscing in the context of secure attachment relationships: Lessons in understanding and coping with negative emotion. In J. Quas & R. Fivush (Eds.), *Emotion and memory in development: Biological, cognitive, and social considerations. Oxford series in affective science* (pp. 166–195). Oxford, UK: Oxford University Press.

Laible, D. J., & Thompson, R. A. (1998). Attachment and emotional understanding in preschool children. *Developmental Psychology, 34*(5), 1038–1045.

Lambert, A. J., Khan, S. R., Lickel, B. A., & Fricke, K. (1997). Mood and the correction of positive versus negative stereotypes. *Journal of Personality and Social Psychology, 72*, 1002–1016.

Lambert, K. G. (2003). The life and career of Paul MacLean: A journey toward neurobiological and social harmony. *Physiology & Behavior, 79*(3), 343–349.

Lambert, M. J. (2004). *Bergin and Garfield's handbook of psychotherapy and behavior change* (5th ed.). New York, NY: Wiley.

Lambert, M. J., & Ogles, B. M. (2004). The efficacy and effectiveness of psychotherapy. In M. J. Lambert (Ed.), *Bergin and Garfield's handbook of psychotherapy and behavior change* (5th ed., pp. 139–193). New York, NY: Wiley.

Lambie, J., & Marcel, A. J. (2002). Consciousness and emotion experience: A theoretical framework. *Psychological Review, 109*, 219–259.

Lancaster, J. B., & Kaplan, H. (1992). Human mating and family formation strategies: The effects of variability among males in quality and the allocation of mating effort and parental investment. In T. Nishida, W. C. McGrew, et al. (Eds.), *Topics in primatology: Vol. 1. Human origins* (pp. 21–33). Tokyo: University of Tokyo Press.

Lane, R. D., Fink, G. R., Chau, P. M., & Dolan, R. J. (1997). Neural activation during selective attention to subjective emotional responses. *Neuroreport, 8*, 3969–3972.

Lang, P. J., Greenwald, M. K., Bradley, M. M., & Hamm, A. O. (1993). Looking at pictures: Affective, facial, visceral, and behavioral reactions. *Psychophysiology, 30,* 261–273.

Lange, C. (1885). The emotions. In E. Dunlap (Ed.), *The emotions.* Baltimore, MD: Williams & Wilkins (current edition 1922).

Langer, S. K. (1957). *Philosophy in a new key: A study in the symbolism of reason, rite, and art.* Cambridge, MA: Harvard University Press.

Laranjo, J., Bernier, A., & Meins, E. (2008). Associations between maternal mind-mindedness and infant attachment security: Investigating the mediating role of maternal sensitivity. *Infant Behavior and Development, 31*(4), 688–695.

Larsen, R. J., Kasimatis, M., & Frey, K. (1992). Facilitating the furrowed brow: An unobtrusive test of the facial feedback hypothesis applied to unpleasant affect. *Cognition and Emotion, 6,* 321–338.

Larson, R. W., Moneta, G., Richards, M. H., & Wilson, S. (2002). Continuity, stability, and change in daily emotional experience across adolescence. *Child Development, 73*(4), 1151–1165.

Lavelli, M., & Fogel, A. (2005). Developmental changes in the relationship between the infant's attention and emotion during early face-to-face communication: The 2-month transition. *Developmental Psychology, 41*(1), 265–280.

Lawler, K. A., Younger, J. W., Piferi, R. L., Billington, E., Jobe, R., Edmondson, K., et al. (2003). A change of heart: Cardiovascular correlates of forgiveness in response to interpersonal conflict. *Journal of Behavioral Medicine, 26,* 373–393.

Lawson, D. W., & Mace, R. (2010). Siblings and childhood mental health: Evidence for a later-born advantage. *Social Science & Medicine (1982), 70*(12), 2061–2069.

Lazarus, R. S. (1991). *Emotion and adaptation.* New York, NY: Oxford University Press.

Lazarus, R. S., & Lazarus, B. N. (1994). *Passion and reason: Making sense of our emotions.* New York, NY: Oxford University Press.

Leakey, R., & Lewin, R. (1991). *Origins.* Harmondsworth: Penguin.

Leary, M. R., Britt, T. W., Cutlip, W. D., & Templeton, J. L. (1992). Social blushing. *Psychological Bulletin, 112,* 446–460.

Lebra, T. S. (1983). Shame and guilt: A psychological view of the Japanese self. *Ethos, 11,* 192–209.

LeDoux, J. (1996). *The emotional brain: The mysterious underpinnings of emotional life.* New York, NY: Simon & Schuster.

LeDoux, J. E. (1993). Emotional networks in the brain. In M. Lewis & J. M. Haviland-Jones (Eds.), *Handbook of emotions* (pp. 109–118). New York, NY: Guilford.

Lee, R. B. (1984). *The Dobe !K ung.* New York, NY: Holt, Rinehart & Winston.

Leichsenring, F., & Rabung, S. (2008). Effectiveness of long-term psychodynamic psychotherapy. *Journal of the American Medical Association, 300,* 1551–1565.

Leichsenring, F., & Rabung, S. (2011). Long-term psychodynamic psychotherapy in complex mental disorders: Update of a meta-analysis. *British Journal of Psychiatry, 199,* 15–22.

Leick, G. (2001). *Mesopotamia: The invention of the city.* London, UK: Penguin.

Lemery, K. S., & Goldsmith, H. H. (2002). Genetic and environmental influences on preschool sibling cooperation and conflict: Associations with difficult temperament and parenting style. *Marriage & Family Review, 33,* 77–99.

Lengua, L. J., & Kovacs, E. A. (2005). Bidirectional associations between temperament and parenting and the prediction of adjustment problems in middle childhood. *Journal of Applied Developmental Psychology, 26,* 21–38.

Lenroot, R. K., & Giedd, J. N. (2006). Brain development in children and adolescents: Insights from anatomical magnetic resonance imaging. *Neuroscience and Biobehavioral Reviews, 30*(6), 718–729.

Leppänen, J. M., & Nelson, C. A. (2008). Tuning the developing brain to social signals of emotions. *Nature Reviews Neuroscience, 10*(1), 37–47.

Lerner, J. S., Goldberg, J. H., & Tetlock, P. E. (1998). Sober second thoughts: The effects of accountability, anger, and authoritarianism on attributions of responsibility. *Personality and Social Psychology Bulletin, 24,* 563–574.

Lerner, J. S., & Keltner, D. (2000). Beyond valence: Toward a model of emotion-specific influences on judgement and choice. *Cognition & Emotion, 14*(4), 473–493.

Lesch, K. P., Bengel, D., Heils, A., et al. (1996). Association of anxiety-related traits with a polymorphism in the serotonin transporter gene regulatory region. *Science, 274* (5292), 1527–1531.

Levenson, R. W., Carstensen, L. L., Friesen, W. V., & Ekman, P. (1991). Emotion, physiology, and expression in old age. *Psychology and Aging, 6,* 28–35.

Levenson, R. W., Ekman, P., & Friesen, W. V. (1990). Voluntary facial action generates emotion-specific autonomic nervous system activity. *Psychophysiology, 27,* 363–384.

Levenson, R. W., Ekman, P., Heider, K., & Friesen, W. V. (1992). Emotion and autonomic nervous system activity in the Minangkabau of West Sumatra. *Journal of Personality and Social Psychology, 62,* 972–988.

Levesque, J., Eugene, F., Joanette, Y., Paquette, V., Mensour, B., Beaudoin, G., Leroux, J. M., Bourgouin, P., & Beauregard, M. (2003). Neural circuitry underlying voluntary suppression of sadness. *Biological Psychiatry, 53,* 502–510.

Levi, P. (1958). *If this is a man* (S. Woolf, Trans.). London, UK: Sphere (current edition 1987).

Levine, L. (1997). Reconstructing memory for emotions. *Journal of Experimental Psychology: General, 126,* 165–177.

Levine, L., & Pizarro, D. (2004). Emotion and memory research: A grumpy overview. *Social Cognition, 22,* 530–554.

Levine, L., Whalen, C. K., Henker, B., & Jamner, L. D. (2005). Looking back on September 11, 2001: Appraised impact and memory for emotions in adolescents and adults. *Journal of Adolescent Health, 20,* 497–523.

Levine, L. J., & Edelstein, R. S. (2009). Emotion and memory narrowing: A review and goal relevance approach. *Cognition and Emotion, 23,* 833–875.

Levine, L. J., & Safer, M. A. (2002). Sources of bias in memory for emotions. *Current Directions in Psychological Science, 11,* 169–173.

Levine, S., & Stanton, M. E. (1984). The hormonal consequences of mother-infant contact in primates and rodents. In C. C. Brown (Ed.), *The many facets of touch: The foundation of experience, its importance through life, with initial emphasis for infants and young children* (pp. 51–58). Skillman, NJ: Johnson & Johnson Baby Products Co.

Levy, R. J. (1984). Emotion, knowing, and culture. In R. A. Shweder & R. A. Levine (Eds.), *Culture theory: Essays on mind, self, and emotion* (pp. 214–237). Cambridge, MA: Cambridge University Press.

Lewis, C., Freeman, N., Kyriakidou, C., Maridaki-Kassotaki, K., & Berridge, D. (1996). Social influences on false belief access: Specific sibling influences or general apprenticeship? *Child Development, 6,* 2930–2947.

Lewis, C. S. (1936). *The allegory of love: A study in medieval tradition.* Oxford, UK: Oxford University Press.

Lewis, M. (1992). *Shame: The exposed self.* New York, NY: Free Press.

Lewis, M. (1993). Self-conscious emotions: Embarrassment, pride, shame, and guilt. In M. Lewis & J. M. Haviland-Jones (Eds.), *Handbook of emotions* (pp. 563–573). New York, NY: Guilford.

Lewis, M. (1997). The self in self-conscious emotions. *Annals of the New York Academy of Sciences, 818*(1), 119–142.

Lewis, M., Haviland-Jones, J. M., & Barrett, L. F. (Eds.). (2008). *Handbook of emotions* (3rd ed.). New York, NY: Guilford.

Lewis, M., & Michalson, L. (1983). *Children's emotions and moods: Developmental theory and measurement.* New York, NY: Plenum Press.

Lewis, M., & Ramsay, D. (2002). Cortisol response to embarrassment and shame. *Child Development, 73,* 1034–1045.

Lewis, M., & Ramsay, D. (2005). Infant emotional and cortisol responses to goal blockage. *Child Development, 76*(2), 518–530.

Lewis, M., Sullivan, M. W., Stanger, C., & Weiss, M. (1989). Self-development and self-conscious emotions. *Child Development, 60,* 146–156.

Lewis, M. D. (2010). Desire, dopamine, and conceptual development. In S. D. Calkins & M. A. Bell (Eds.), *Child development at the intersection of emotion and cognition.* (1st ed.). Washington, DC: American Psychological Association.

Lewis, M. D. (2011). *Memoirs of an addicted brain.* Toronto: Doubleday Canada.

Lewis, M. D., & Granic, I. (Eds.). (2000). *Emotion, development, and self-organization: Dynamic systems approaches to emotional development.* New York, NY: Cambridge University Press.

Lewis, M. D., & Ramsay, D. (2005). Infant emotional and cortisol responses to goal blockage. *Child Development, 76*, 518–530.

Li, J., Wang, L., & Fischer, K. W. (2004). The organization of Chinese shame concepts. *Cognition and Emotion, 18*, 767–797.

Li, M., & Fleming, A. S. (2003). The nucleus accumbens shell is critical for normal expression of pup-retrieval in postpartum female rats. *Behavioural Brain Research, 145*, 99–111.

Libet, B. (1985). Unconscious cerebral initiative and the role of conscious will in voluntary action. *Behavioral and Brain Sciences, 8*, 529–566.

Lichtenstein, J., & Cassidy, J. (1991, April). *The Inventory of Adult Attachment (INVAA): Validation of a new measure of adult attachment.* Paper presented at the biennial meeting of the Society for Research in Child Development, Seattle, WA.

Lichtheim, M. (1973). *Ancient Egyptian literature: Vol. 1. The Old and Middle Kingdoms.* Berkeley: University of California Press.

Lieberman, M. D., & Eisenberger, N. I. (2009). Pains and pleasures of social life. *Science, 323*, 890–891.

Liebowitz, M. R. (1983). *The chemistry of love.* Boston, MA: Little, Brown.

Lillard, A. (1993). Pretend play skills and the child's theory of mind. *Child Development, 64*, 348–371.

Lim, J., Wood, B. L., Miller, B. D., & Simmens, S. J. (2011). Effects of paternal and maternal depressive symptoms on child internalizing symptoms and asthma disease activity: Mediation by interparental negativity and parenting. *Journal of Family Psychology, 25*(1), 137–146.

Lindsley, D. B. (1951). Emotions. In S. S. Stevens (Ed.), *Handbook of experimental psychology* (pp. 473–516). New York, NY: Wiley.

Lindstrom, K. M., Mandell, D. J., Musa, G. J., Britton, J. C., Sankin, L. S., Mogg, K., et al. (2011). Attention orientation in parents exposed to the 9/11 terrorist attacks and their children. *Psychiatry Research, 187*, 261–266.

Linehan, M. M., Comtois, K. A., Murray, A. M., Brown, M. Z., Gallop, R. J., et al. (2006). Two-year randomized controlled trial and follow-up of dialectical behavior therapy vs therapy by experts for suicidal behaviors and borderline personality disorder. *Archives of General Psychiatry, 63*, 757–766.

Lipps, T. (1962). Empathy, inner imitation, and sense feeling. In M. Rader (Ed.), *A modern book on esthetics: An anthology, 3rd edition* (pp. 374–382). New York, NY: Holt, Rinehart & Winston.

Lipsey, M. W., & Wilson, D. B. (1993). The efficacy of psychological, educational, and behavioral treatment. *American Psychologist, 48*, 1181–1209.

Lochman, J. E., & Wells, K. C. (2002). Contextual social-cognitive mediators and child outcome: A test of the theoretical model in the coping power program. *Development and Psychopathology, 14*(4), 945–967.

Lodi-Smith, J., & Roberts, B. W. (2007). Social investment and personality: A meta-analysis of the relationship of personality traits to investment in work, family, religion, and volunteerism. *Personality and Social Psychology Review, 11*, 68–86.

Loeber, R., & Farrington, D. P. (2000). Young children who commit crime: Epidemiology, developmental origins, risk factors, early interventions, and policy implications. *Development and Psychopathology, 12*, 737–762.

Loftus, E. F., & Davis, D. (2006). Recovered memories. *Annual Review of Clinical Psychology, 2*, 469–498.

Loftus, E. F., & Doyle, J. M. (1987). *Eyewitness testimony: Civil and criminal.* New York, NY: Kluwer.

Lonigan, C. J., Phillips, B. M., & Hooe, E. S. (2003). Tripartite model of anxiety and depression in children: Evidence from a latent variable longitudinal study. *Journal of Consulting and Clinical Psychology, 71*, 465–481.

Lopez, S. R., Nelson-Hipke, K., Polo, A. J., Jenkins, J. H., et al. (2004). Ethnicity, expressed emotion, attributions, and course of schizophrenia: Family warmth matters. *Journal of Abnormal Psychology, 113*, 428–439.

Lorenz, K. (1937). Über die Bildung des Instinktbegriffes. *Die Naturwissenschaften, 25*, 289–331. [The conception of instinctive behavior.] In C. Schiller (Ed. & Trans.), *Instinctive behavior: Development of a modern concept* (pp. 176-208). London, UK: Methuen.

Lorenz, K. (1967). *On aggression* (M. Latzke, Trans.). London, UK: Methuen.

Loughead, J. W., Luborsky, L., Weingarten, C. P., Krause, E. D., German, R. E., Kirk, D., et al. (2010). Brain activation during autobiographical relationship episode narratives:

A core conflictual relationship theme approach. *Psychotherapy Research, 20,* 321–336.

Lovejoy, C. O. (1981). The origin of man. *Science, 211,* 341–350.

Lowenstein, G. (2007). Affect regulation and affective forecasting. In J. Gross (Ed.), *Handbook of emotion regulation* (pp. 180–203). New York, NY: Guilford.

Lowenstein, G., & Lerner, J. S. (2003). The role of affect in decision making. In R. J. Davidson, K. R. Scherer, & H. H. Goldsmith (Eds.), *Handbook of affective sciences* (pp. 619–642). New York, NY: Oxford University Press.

Luborsky, L., & Crits-Christoph, P. (1990). *Understanding transference.* New York, NY: Basic Books.

Luby, J. L., Xuemei, S., Belden, A. C., Tandon, M., & Spitznagel, E. (2009). Preschool depression: Homotypic continuity and course over 24 months. *Archives of General Psychiatry, 66*(8), 897–905.

Lucas, R. E., & Baird, B. M. (2004). Extraversion and emotional reactivity. *Journal of Personality and Social Psychology, 86*(3), 473–485.

Lucas, R. E., Diener, E., Suh, E. M., Shao, L., & Grob, A. (2000). Cross-cultural evidence for the fundamental features of extraversion. *Journal of Personality and Social Psychology, 79*(3), 452–468.

Luminet, O., Rimé, B., Bagby, R. M., & Taylor, G. J. (2004). A multimodal investigation of emotional responding in alexithymia. *Cognition and Emotion, 18,* 741–766.

Lundy, B. L. (2003). Father- and mother-infant face-to-face interactions: Differences in mind-related comments and infant attachment? *Infant Behavior & Development, 26* (2), 200–212.

Lutz, C. (1990). Engendered emotion: Gender, power, and the rhetoric of emotional control in American discourse. In C. A. Lutz & L. Abu-Lughod (Eds.), *Language and the politics of emotions* (pp. 69–91). New York, NY: Cambridge University Press.

Lutz, C., & White, G. M. (1986). The anthropology of emotions. *Annual Review of Anthropology, 15,* 405–436.

Lynam, D. R., Miller, D. J., Vachon, D., Loeber, R., & Stouthamer-Loeber, M. (2009). Psychopathy in adolescence predicts official reports of offending in adulthood. *Youth Violence and Juvenile Justice, 7,* 189–207.

Lytton, H. (1990). Child and parent effects in boys' conduct disorder. A reinterpretation. *Developmental Psychology, 26*(5), 683–704.

Lyubomirsky, S., King, L., & Diener, E. (2005). The benefits of frequent positive affect: Does happiness lead to success? *Psychological Bulletin, 131,* 803–855.

MacDonald, K. (1992). Warmth as a developmental construct: An evolutionary analysis. *Child Development, 63,* 753–773.

MacDonald, K. B. (2008). Effortful control, explicit processing, and the regulation of human evolved predispositions. *Psychological Review, 115*(4), 1012–1031.

Macintyre, M. (1986). Female autonomy in a matrilineal society. In N. Grieve & A. Burns (Eds.), *Australian women: New feminist perspectives* (pp. 248–256). Melbourne: Oxford University Press.

Mackie, D. M., Devos, T., & Smith, E. R. (2000). Intergroup emotions: Explaining offensive action tendencies in an intergroup context. *Journal of Personality and Social Psychology, 79,* 602–616.

Mackie, D. M., & Worth, L. T. (1989). Processing deficits and the mediation of positive affect in persuasion. *Journal of Personality and Social Psychology, 57,* 27–40.

Mackie, D. M., & Worth, L. T. (1991). Feeling good but not thinking straight: The impact of positive mood on persuasion. In J. P. Forgas (Ed.), *Emotion and social judgments* (pp. 181–200). Oxford, UK: Pergamon Press.

MacLean, P. D. (1949). Psychosomatic disease and the "visceral brain": Recent developments bearing on the Papez theory of emotion. *Psychosomatic Medicine, 11,* 338–353.

MacLean, P. D. (1990). *The triune brain in evolution.* New York, NY: Plenum.

Macmillan, R. et al. (2004). Linked lives: Stability and change in maternal circumstances and trajectories of antisocial behavior. *Child Development, 75*(1), 205–220.

Magai, C. (2008). Long-lived emotions: A life course perspective on emotional development. In M. Lewis, J. M. Haviland-Jones, & L. Feldman Barrett (Eds.), *Handbook of emotions* (3rd ed.). New York, NY: Guilford.

Maguire, M. C., & Dunn, J. (1997). Friendships in early childhood, and social understanding. *International Journal of Behavioral Development, 21,* 669–686.

Main, M. (1990). *Parental aversion to infant-initialed contact is correlated with the parent's own rejection during childhood: The effects of experience on signals of security with respect to attachment.* In K. E. Barnard & T. B. Brazelton (Eds.), *Touch: The foundation of experience* (pp. 461–495). Madison, CT: International Universities Press.

Main, M., & Stadtman, J. (1981). Infant response to rejection of physical contact by the mother. *Journal of the American Academy of Child Psychiatry, 20,* 292–307.

Malatesta, C. Z., & Haviland, J. M. (1982). Learning display rules: The socialization of emotion expression in infancy. *Child Development, 53*(4), 991–1003.

Mandler, G. (1964). The interruption of behavior. In *Nebraska Symposium on Motivation* (Vol. *12).* Lincoln: Nebraska University Press.

Mandler, G. (1984). *Mind and body: Psychology of emotions and stress.* New York, NY: Norton.

Manstead, A.S.R., & Wagner, H. L. (1981). Arousal, cognition, and emotion: An appraisal of two-factor theory. *Current Psychological Reviews, 1,* 35–54.

Mar, R. A., Oatley, K., & Peterson, J. B. (2009). Exploring the link between reading fiction and empathy: Ruling out individual differences and examining outcomes. *Communications: The European Journal of Communication, 34,* 407–428.

Mardaga, S., Laloyaux, O., & Hansenne, M. (2006). Personality traits modulate skin conductance response to emotional pictures: An investigation with Cloninger's model of personality. *Personality and Individual Differences, 40*(8), 1603–1614.

Marks, J. (1992). The promises and problems of molecular anthropology in hominid origins. In T. Nishida, W. C. McGrew, P. Marler, M. Pickford, & F.B.M.De Waal (Eds.), *Topics in primatology: Vol. 1. Human origins* (pp. 441–453). Tokyo: University of Tokyo Press.

Markus, H. R., & Kitayama, S. (1994). The cultural construction of self and emotion: Implications for social behavior. In S. Kitayama & H. R. Markus (Eds.), *Emotion and culture: Empirical studies of mutual influence* (pp. 89–130). Washington, DC: American Psychological Association.

Marmot, M. G., & Shipley, M. J. (1996). Do socioeconomic differences in mortality persist after retirement?: 25-year follow-up of civil servants from first Whitehall study. *British Medical Journal, 313,* 1177–1180.

Maroney, T. A. (2006). Law and emotion: A proposed taxonomy. *Law and Human Behavior, 30,* 119–142.

Maroney, T. A. (2011). The persistent cultural script of judicial dispassion. *California Law Reviews, 99,* 629–681.

Maroucha, P. T., Kiecolt-Glaser, J. K., & Favegehi, M. (1998). Mucosal wound healing is impaired by examination stress. *Psychosomatic Medicine, 60,* 362–365.

Marshall, L. (1976). *The !Kung of Nyae Nyae.* Cambridge, MA: Harvard University Press.

Martin, L. L. (2000). Moods do not convey information: Moods in context do. In J. Forgas (Ed.), *Feeling and thinking: The role of affect in social cognition* (pp. 153–177). New York, NY: Cambridge University Press.

Martin, L. L., & Clore, G. L. (2001). *Theories of mood and cognition: A user's guidebook.* Mahwah, NJ: Erlbaum.

Maruskin, L. A., Thrash, T. M., & Elliot, A. J. (in press). The chills as a psychological construct: Content universe, factor structure, affective composition, elicitors, trait antecedents, and consequences. *Journal of Personality and Social Psychology.*

Maser, J. D., Norman, S. B., Zislook, S., Everall, I. P., Stein, M. B., Schettler, P. J., et al. (2009). Psychiatric nosology is ready for a paradigm shift in *DSM-V. Clinical Psychology: Science and Practice, 16,* 24–40.

Mason, W. A., & Mendoza, S. P. (Eds.). (1993). *Primate social conflict.* Albany, NY: State University of New York Press.

Masten, A. S. (2007). Resilience in developing systems: Progress and promise as the fourth wave rises. *Development and Psychopathology, 19*(3), 921–930.

Mastropieri, D., & Turkewitz, G. (1999). Prenatal experience and neonatal responsiveness to vocal expressions of emotion. *Developmental Psychobiology, 35*(3), 204–214.

Masuda, T., Ellsworth, P. C., Mesquita, B., Leu, J., Tanida, S., & van de Veerdonk, E. (2008). Placing the face in context: Cultural differences in the perception of facial emotion. *Journal of Personality and Social Psychology, 94,* 365–381.

Masuda, T., Gonzalez, R., Kwan, L., & Nisbett, R. E. (2008). Culture and aesthetic preference: Comparing the attention to context of East Asians and European Americans. *Personality and Social Psychology Bulletin, 34,* 1260–1275.

Matarazzo, O. (2008). Use and effectiveness of three modalities of emotion regulation after negative life events: Rumination, distraction and social sharing. In A. B. Turley & G. C. Hoffman (Eds.), *Life style and health research progress* (pp. 87–138). Hauppauge, NY: Nova Biomedical Books.

Matas, L., Arend, R. A., & Sroufe, L. A. (1978). Continuity of adaptation in the second year: The relationship between quality of attachment and later competence. *Child Development, 49*, 547–556.

Matheson, M. D., & Bernstein, I. S. (2000). Grooming, social bonding, and agonistic aiding in rhesus monkeys. *American Journal of Primatology, 51*, 177–186.

Mathews, A., Gelder, M. G., & Johnson, D. W. (1981). *Agoraphobia: Nature and treatment*. London, UK: Tavistock.

Mathews, A., & Klug, F. (1993). Emotionality and interference with color-naming in anxiety. *Behavior Research and Therapy, 29*, 147–160.

Mathews, A., Yiend, J., & Lawrence, A. (2004). Individual differences in the modulation of fear-related brain activation by attentional control. *Journal of Cognitive Neuroscience, 16*, 1683–1694.

Matsumoto, D. (1989). Cultural influences on the perception of emotion. *Journal of Cross-Cultural Psychology, 20*(1), 92–105.

Matsumoto, D. (1990). Cultural similarities and differences in display rules. *Motivation & Emotion, 14*(3), 195–214.

Matsumoto, D., & Ekman, P. (1989). American-Japanese cultural differences in intensity ratings of facial expressions of emotion. *Motivation & Emotion, 13*(2), 143–157.

Matsumoto, D., & Ekman, P. (2004). The relationship between expressions, labels, and descriptions of contempt. *Journal of Personality and Social Psychology, 87*(4), 529–540.

Matsumoto, D., & Hwang, H. S. (2012). Culture and emotion: The integration of biological and cultural contributions. *Journal of Cross-Cultural Psychology, 43*(1), 91–118.

Matsumoto, D., Keltner, D., Shiota, M. N., O'Sullivan, M., & Frank, M. (2008). Facial expressions of emotion. In M. Lewis, J. M. Haviland-Jones, & L. F. Barrett (Eds.), *Handbook of emotions* (3rd ed., pp. 211–234). New York, NY: Guilford Press.

Matsumoto, D., Seung, H. Y., Nakagawa, S., et al. (2008). Culture, emotion regulation, and adjustment. *Journal of Personality and Social Psychology, 94*(6), 925–937.

Matsumoto, D., Weissman, M., Preston, K., Brown, B., & Kupperbusch, C. (1997). Context-specific measurement of individualism-collectivism on the individual level: The IC Interpersonal Assessment Inventory (ICIAI). *Journal of Cross-Cultural Psychology, 28*, 743–767.

Maughn, A., Cicchetti, D., Toth, S. L., Rogosch, F. A. (2006). Early-occurring maternal depression and maternal negativity in predicting young children's emotion regulation and socioemotional difficulties. *Journal of Abnormal Child Psychology, 35*, 685–703.

Mauro, R., Sato, K., & Tucker, J. (1992). The role of appraisal in human emotions: A cross-cultural study. *Journal of Personality and Social Psychology, 62*, 301–317.

Mauss, I. B., Butler, E. A., Roberts, N. A., & Chu, A. (2010). Emotion control values and responding to an anger provocation in Asian-American and European-American individuals. *Cognition and Emotion, 24*, 1026–1043.

Mauss, I. B., Levenson, R. W., McCarter, L., et al. (2005). The tie that binds? Coherence among emotion experience, behavior, and physiology. *Emotion, 5*, 175–190.

Mauss, I. B., & Robinson, M. D. (2009). Measures of emotion: A review. *Cognition and Emotion, 23*, 209–237.

Mayberg, H. S., Lozano, A. M., Voon, V., McNeely, H. E., Seminowicz, D., et al. (2005). Deep brain stimulation for treatment-resistant depression. *Neuron, 45*, 651–660.

Mayer, J. D., Barsade, S. G., & Roberts, R. D. (2008). Human abilities: Emotional intelligence. *Annual Review of Psychology, 59*, 507–536.

Mayer, J. D., Gaschke, Y. N., Braverman, D. L., & Evans, T. W. (1992). Mood-congruent judgment is a general effect. *Journal of Personality and Social Psychology, 63*, 119–132.

McAdams, D. P., & Olson, B. D. (2010). Personality development: Continuity and change over the life course. *Annual Review of Psychology, 61*(1), 517–542.

McCoy, K., Cummings, E. M., & Davies, P. T. (2009). Constructive and destructive marital conflict, emotional security and children's prosocial behavior. *Journal of Child Psychology and Psychiatry and Allied Disciplines, 50*(3), 270–279.

McCrae, R. R., & Costa, P. T. (2008). The five-factor theory of personality. In O. P. John, R. W. Robins, & L. A. Pervin

(Eds.), *Handbook of personality: Theory and research* (pp. 159–81). New York, NY: Guilford.

McCullough, M. E. (2000). Forgiveness as human strength: Theory, measurement, and links to well-being. *Journal of Social and Clinical Psychology, 19*, 43–55.

McCullough, M. E., Kilpatrick, S. D., Emmons, R. A., & Larson, D. B. (2001). Is gratitude a moral affect? *Psychological Bulletin, 127*, 249–266.

McCullough, M. E., Sandage, S. J., & Worthington, E.L.J. (1997). *To forgive is human*. Downers Grove, NJ: InterVarsity.

McCullough, M. E., Tsang, J., & Emmons, R. A. (2004). Gratitude in "intermediate affective terrain": Grateful moods and their links to personality and daily life events. *Journal of Personality and Social Psychology, 86*, 295–309.

McFarland, C., & Ross, M. (1987). The relation between current impressions and memories of self and dating partners. *Personality & Social Psychology Bulletin, 13*, 228–238.

McGrath, C. (2004, Oct. 31). Wolfe's world. *New York Times, Magazine Section*, pp. 34-39.

McGowan, P. O., Sasaki, A., D'Alessio, A. C., Dymov, S., Labonte, B., Szyf, M., Turecki, G., & Meaney, M. J. (2009). Epigenetic regulation of the glucocorticoid receptor in human brain associates with childhood abuse. *Nature Neuroscience, 12*(3), 342–348.

McGuffin, P., & Sargeant, M. P. (1991). Genetic markers and affective disorder. In P. McGuffin & R. Murray (Eds.), *The new genetics of mental illness* (pp. 165–181). Oxford, UK: Butterworth-Heinemann.

McMahon, R. J., Forehand, R. L., & Foster, S. L. (2005). *Helping the noncompliant child: Family-based treatment for oppositional behavior*. New York, NY: Guilford.

McMahon, S. D., Grant, K. E., Compas, B. E., Thurm, A. E., & Ey, S. (2003). Stress and psychopathology in children and adolescents: Is there evidence of specificity? *Journal of Child Psychology and Psychiatry, 44*, 107–133.

McMunn, A., Nazroo, J., Wahrendorf, M., Breeze, E., & Zaninotto, P. (2009). Participation in socially-productive activities, reciprocity and well-being in later life: Baseline results in England. *Ageing and Society, 29*, 765–782.

McNally, R. J. (1999). Panic and phobias. In T. Dalgleish & M. Power (Eds.), *Handbook of cognition and emotion* (pp. 479–496). Chichester, UK: Wiley.

McNally, R. J. (2003). Progress and controversy in the study of posttraumatic stress disorder. *Annual Review of Psychology, 54*, 229–252.

McNally, R. J., Kaspi, S. P., Riemann, B. C., & Zeitlin, S. B. (1990). Selective processing of threat cues in posttraumatic stress disorder. *Journal of Abnormal Psychology, 99*, 398–402.

McNeill, D. (Ed.). (2000). *Language and gesture*. New York, NY: Cambridge University Press.

McQuaid, J. R., Monroe, S. M., Roberts, J. E., Kupfer, D. J., & Frank, E. (2000). A comparison of two life stress assessment approaches: Prospective prediction of treatment outcome in recurrent depression. *Journal of Abnormal Psychology, 109*, 787–791.

Meaney, M. J. (2001). Maternal care, gene expression, and the transmission of individual differences in stress reactivity across generations. *Annual Review of Neuroscience, 24*, 1161–1192.

Meins, E. (1997). *Security of attachment and the social development of cognition*. Howe: Psychology Press.

Meins, E. (1999). Sensitivity, security and internal working models: Bridging the transmission gap. *Attachment & Human Development, 1*(3), 325–342.

Meins, E., & Fernyhough, C. (1999). Linguistic acquisitional style and mentalising development: The role of maternal mind-mindedness. *Cognitive Development, 14*(3), 363–380.

Meins, E., Fernyhough, C., Fradley, E., & Tuckey, M. (2001). Rethinking maternal sensitivity: Mothers comments on infants' mental processes predict security of attachment at 12 months. *Journal of Child Psychology and Psychiatry, 42*(5), 637–648.

Meins, E., Fernyhough, C., Wainwright, R., Das Gupta, M., Fradley, E., & Tuckey, M. (2002). Maternal mind-mindedness and attachment security as predictors of theory of mind understanding. *Child Development, 73*(6), 1715–1715.

Mellars, P. (2004). Neanderthals and the modern human colonization of Europe. *Nature, 432*, 461–465.

Mellars, P., & French, J. C. (2011). Tenfold population increase in Western Europe at the Neanderthal-to-modern human transition. *Science, 333*, 623–627.

Mendes, W. B., Major, B., McCoy, S., & Blascovich, J. (2008). How attributional ambiguity shapes physiological and emotional responses to social rejection and acceptance. *Journal of Personality and Social Psychology, 94*, 278–291.

Menon, U., & Shweder, R. A. (1994). Kali's tongue: Cultural psychology, cultural consensus and the meaning of "shame" in Orissa, India. In H. Markus & S. Kitayama (Eds.), *Emotion and culture: Empirical studies of mutual influence* (pp. 241–284). Washington, DC: American Psychological Association.

Mesman, J., Oster, H., & Camras, L. (2012). Parental sensitivity to infant distress: What do discrete negative emotions have to do with it? *Attachment and Human Development*.

Mesquita, B. (2001). Culture and emotion: Different approaches to the question. In T. J. Mayne & G. A. Bonanno (Eds.), *Emotions: Current issues and future directions. Emotions and social behavior* (pp. 214–250). New York, NY: Guilford.

Mesquita, B. (2003). Emotions as dynamic cultural phenomena. In J. Davidson Richard, K. R. Scherer, & H. H. Goldsmith (Eds.), *Handbook of affective sciences* (pp. 871–890). New York, NY: Oxford University Press.

Mesquita, B., & Ellsworth, P. C. (2001). The role of culture in appraisal. In K. R. Scherer & A. Schorr (Eds.), *Appraisal processes in emotion. Theory, methods, research*. New York, NY: Oxford University Press.

Mesquita, B., & Frijda, N. (1992). Cultural variations in emotions: A review. *Psychological Bulletin, 112*, 179–204.

Mesquita, B., & Frijda, N. H. (2011). An emotion perspective on emotion regulation. *Cognition and emotion, 25*, 782–784.

Mesquita, B., Frijda, N. H., & Scherer, K. R. (1997). Culture and emotion. In P. R. Dasen & T. S. Saraswathi (Eds.), *Handbook of cross-cultural psychology, Vol. 2: Basic processes and human development* (pp. 255–297). Boston, MA: Allyn & Bacon.

Mesquita, B., & Markus, H. R. (2004). Culture and emotion: Models of agency as sources of cultural variation in emotion. In N. H. Frijda, A. S. R. Manstead, & A. Fischer (Eds.), *Feelings and emotions: The Amsterdam Symposium* (pp. 341–358). New York, NY: Cambridge University Press.

Messinger, D. (2002). Positive and negative: Infant facial expressions and emotions. *Current Directions in Psychological Science, 11*(1), 1–6.

Messinger, D., & Fogel, A. (2007). The interactive development of social smiling. *Advances in Child Development and Behaviour, 35*, 328–366.

Meunier, J. C., Bisceglia, R., & Jenkins, J. M. (2012, in press). Differential parenting and children's behavioral problems: Curvilinear associations and mother-father combined effects. *Developmental Psychology, 48*, 987–1002.

Meyer-Lindenberg, A., Buckholtz, J. W., Kolancha, B., Hariri, B., Pezawas, L., Blasi, G., et al. (2006). Neural mechanisms of genetic risk for impulsivity and violence in humans. *Proceedings from the National Academy of Sciences of the United States of America, 103*(16), 6269–6274.

Miall, D. S., & Kuiken, D. (2002). A feeling for fiction: Becoming what we behold. *Poetics, 30*, 221–241.

Middeldorp, C. M., Cath, D. C., Beem, A. L., Willemsen, G., & Boomsma, D. I. (2008). Life events, anxious depression and personality: A prospective and genetic study. *Psychological Medicine, 38*, 1557–1565.

Milgram, S. (1963). Behavioral study of obedience. *Journal of Abnormal and Social Psychology, 67*, 371–378.

Milkie, M. A., & Warner, C. H. (2011). Classroom learning environments and the mental health of first grade children. *Journal of Health and Social Behavior, 52*(1), 4–22.

Miller, E. K., & Cohen, J. D. (2001). An integrative theory of prefrontal cortex function. *Annual Review of Neuroscience, 24*, 167–202.

Miller, G. F. (2001) *The mating mind: How sexual choice shaped the evolution of human nature*. New York, NY. Doubleday.

Miller, G. F., Tybur, J., & Jordan, B. (2007). Ovulatory cycle effects on tip earnings by lap-dancers: Economic evidence for human estrus? *Evolution and Human Behavior*.

Miller, R. S. (1995). On the nature of embarrassability: Shyness, social-evaluation, and social skill. *Journal of Personality, 63*, 315–339.

Miller, R. S., & Tangney, J. P. (1994). Differentiating embarrassment from shame. *Journal of Social and Clinical Psychology, 13*, 273–287.

Miller, W. I. (2006). *An eye for an eye*. Cambridge, MA: Cambridge University Press.

Miller, W. L. (1994). The politics of emotion display in heroic society. In N. Frijda (Ed.), *Proceedings of the 8th conference of the International Society for Research on Emotions, Cambridge*, July 14–17. Storrs, CT: ISRE Publications (pp. 43–46).

Minagawa-Kawai, Y., Matsuoka, S., Dan, I., Naoi, N., Nakamura, K., & Kojima, S. (2009). Prefrontal activation associated with social attachment: Facial-emotion recognition in mothers and infants. *Cerebral Cortex, 19*(2), 284–292.

Mineka, S., & Cook, M. (1993). Mechanisms involved in the observational conditioning of fear. *Journal of Experimental Psychology: General, 122*, 24–38.

Mineka, S., & Gilboa, E. (1998). Cognitive biases in anxiety and depression. In W. F. Flack & J. D. Laird (Eds.), *Emotions in psychopathology: Theory and research* (pp. 216–228). New York, NY: Oxford University Press.

Mineka, S., Rafeali, E., & Yovel, I. (2003). Cognitive biases in emotional disorders: Information processing and social-cognitive perspectives. In R. J. Davidson, K. R. Scherer, & H. H. Goldsmith (Eds.), *Handbook of affective sciences* (pp. 976–1009). New York, NY: Oxford University Press.

Miranda, R., & Andersen, S. M. (2010). The social psychology of transference. In J. E. Maddux & J. P. Tangney (Eds.), *Social psychological foundations of clinical psychology* (pp. 476–496). New York, NY: Guilford.

Miranda, R., & Kihlstrom, J. F. (2005). Mood congruence in childhood and recent autobiographical memory. *Cognition and Emotion, 19*, 981–998.

Mischel, W., & Shoda, Y. (1995). A cognitive-affective system theory of personality: Reconceptualizing situations, dispositions, dynamics, and invariance in personality structures. *Psychological Review, 102*, 244–268.

Mithen, S. (1996). *The prehistory of the mind: The cognitive origins of art and science*. London, UK: Thames and Hudson.

Mithen, S. (2001). The evolution of imagination: An archeological perspective. *SubStance* (# 94/95), 28–54.

Miyake, K., Campos, J., Kagan, J., & Bradshaw, D. L. (1986). Issues in socioemotional development. In H. Stevenson, H. Azuma, & K. Hakuta (Eds.), *Child development and education in Japan* (pp. 239–261). New York, NY: Freeman.

Miyamoto, Y., Uchida, Y., & Ellsworth, P. C., (2010). Culture and mixed emotions: Co-occurrence of positive and negative emotions in Japan and the United States. *Emotion, 10*(3), 404–415.

Moffitt, T. E. (1993). Adolescence-limited and life-course-persistent antisocial behavior: A developmental taxonomy. *Psychological Review, 100*, 674–701.

Moffitt, T. E., Caspi, A., Harrington, H., & Milne, B. J. (2002). Males on the life-course persistent and adolescence-limited antisocial pathways: Follow-up at age 26 years. *Development and Psychopathology, 14*(1), 179–207.

Moffitt, T. E., Caspi, A., Taylor, A., Kokaua, J., Milne, B. J., Polanczyk, G., et al. (2010). How common are common mental disorders? Evidence that lifetime prevalence rates are doubled by prospective versus retrospective ascertainment. *Psychological Medicine, 40*, 899–909.

Mogg, K., & Bradley, B. P. (1999). Selective attention and anxiety: A cognitive-motivational perspective. In T. Dalgleish & M. Power (Eds.), *Handbook of cognition and emotion* (pp. 145–170). Chichester, UK: Wiley.

Mogg, K., & Bradley, B. P. (2003). Selective processing of nonverbal information in anxiety: Attentional biases for threat. In P. Philippot (Ed.), *Nonverbal behavior in clinical settings* (pp. 127–143). London, UK: Oxford University Press.

Mogg, K., & Bradley, B. P. (2004). A cognitive-motivational perspective on the processing of threat information and anxiety. In J. Yiend (Ed.), *Cognition, emotion, and psychopathology: Theoretical, empirical and clinical directions* (pp. 68–85). New York, NY: Cambridge University Press.

Mogg, K., & Bradley, B. P. (2005). Attentional bias in generalized anxiety disorder versus depressive disorder. *Cognitive Therapy and Research, 29*(1), 29–45.

Monroe, S. M., & Hadjiyannakis, K. (2002). The social environment and depression. In I. H. Gotlib & C. L. Hammen (Eds.), *Handbook of depression* (pp. 314–340). New York, NY: Guilford.

Monroe, S. M., & Simons, A. D. (1991). Diathesis stress in the context of life stress research: Implications for the depressive disorders. *Psychological Bulletin, 110*, 406–425.

Monroe, S. M., & Wade, S. L. (1988). Life events. In C. G. Last & M. Hersen (Eds.), *Handbook of anxiety disorders* (pp. 293–305). New York, NY: Pergamon Press.

Montagne, B., Kessels, R. P., Frigerio, E., de Haan, E. H., & Perrett, D. I. (2005). Sex differences in the perception of affective facial expressions: Do men really lack emotional sensitivity? *Cognitive Processing, 6*(2), 136–141.

Montague, D.P.F., & Walker-Andrews, A. S. (2001). Peekaboo: A new look at infants' perception of emotion expressions. *Developmental Psychology, 37*(6), 826–838.

Montepare, J. M., Goldstein, S. B., & Clausen, A. (1987). The identification of emotions from gait information. *Journal of Nonverbal Behavior, 11*, 33–42.

Moons, W. G., Eisenberger, N. I., & Taylor, S. E. (2010). Anger and fear responses to stress have different biological profiles. *Brain, Behavior, and Immunity, 24*, 215–219.

Moore, C., & Dunham, P. J. (1995). *Joint attention: Its origins and role in development*. Mahwah, NJ: Lawrence Erlbaum.

Moors, A. (2007). Can cognitive methods be used to study the unique aspect of emotion: An appraisal theorist's answer. *Cognition and Emotion, 21*, 1238–1269.

Moors, A. (2009). Theories of emotion causation: A review. *Cognition and Emotion, 23*, 625–662.

Moors, A., De Houwer, J., & Eelen, P. (2004). Automatic stimulus-goal comparisons: Support from motivational affective priming studies. *Cognition and Emotion, 18*, 29–54.

Morris, A. S., Silk, J. S., Steinberg, L., Myers, S. S., & Robinson, L. R. (2007). The role of the family context in the development of emotion regulation. *Social Development, 16*(2), 361–388.

Morris, D., Collett, P., Marsh, P., & O'Shaughnessy, M. (1979). *Understanding emotions from gestures: Their origin and distribution*. London, UK: Cape.

Morton, J. B., & Trehub, S. E. (2001). Children's understanding of emotion in speech. *Child Development, 72*, 834–843.

Moskowitz, A. K. (2004). "Scared stiff": Catatonia as an evolutionary based fear response. *Psychological Review, 111*, 984–1002.

Moss, E., Dubois-Comtois, K., Cyr, C., Tarabulsy, G. M., St-Laurent, D., & Bernier, A. (2011). Efficacy of a home-visiting intervention aimed at improving maternal sensitivity, child attachment, and behavioral outcomes for maltreated children: A randomized control trial. *Development and Psychopathology, 23*(1), 195–210.

Mueller, T. I., Keller, M. B., Leon, A., Solomon, D. A., Shea, M. T., Coryell, W., et al. (1996). Recovery after five years of unremitting major depressive disorder. *Archives of General Psychiatry, 53*, 794–799.

Müller, M. B., & Holsboer, F. (2006). Mice with mutations in the HPA-system as models for symptoms of depression. *Biological Psychiatry, 59*, 1104–1115.

Mumme, D. L., & Fernald, A. (2003). The infant as onlooker: Learning from emotional reactions observed in a television scenario. *Child Development, 74*(1), 221–237.

Mumme, D. L., Fernald, A., & Herrera, C. (1996). Infants' responses to facial and vocal emotional signals in a social referencing paradigm. *Child Development, 67*(6), 3219–3237.

Muñoz, L. C. (2009). Callous-unemotional traits are related to combined deficits in recognizing afraid faces and body poses. *Journal American Academy of Child and Adolescent Psychiatry, 48*(5), 554–562.

Munoz, R. F., Mrazek, P. J., & Haggerty, R. J. (1995). Institute of Medicine report on prevention of mental disorders: Summary and commentary. *American Psychologist, 51*, 1116–1122.

Murphy, M. R., Seckl, J. R., Burton, S., Checkley, S. A., & Lightman, S. L. (1987). Changes in oxytocin and vasopressin secretion during sexual activity in men. *Journal of Clinical Endocrinology and Metabolism, 65*(4), 738–742.

Murphy, S. T., & Zajonc, R. B. (1993). Affect, cognition, and awareness: Affective priming with optimal and suboptimal stimulus exposures. *Journal of Personality and Social Psychology, 64*, 723–739.

Murray, S. L., & Holmes, J. G. (1993). Seeing virtues in faults: Negativity and the transformation of interpersonal narratives in close relationships. *Journal of Personality and Social Psychology, 65*, 707–723.

Murray, S. L., & Holmes, J. G. (1997). A leap of faith? Positive illusions: Idealization and the construction of satisfaction in close relationships. *Journal of Personality and Social Psychology, 70*, 79–98.

Myers, D. G., & Diener, E. (1996, May). The pursuit of happiness. *Scientific American, 274*, 54–56.

Myers, S. A., & Berscheid, E. (1997). The language of love: The difference a preposition makes. *Personality and Social Psychology Bulletin, 23*, 347–362.

Nadal, M., & Pearce, M. T. (2011). The Copenhagen neuroaesthetics conference: Prospects and pitfalls for an emerging field. *Brain and Cognition, 76*, 172–183.

Nagin, D., & Tremblay, R. E. (1999). Trajectories of boys' physical aggression, opposition, and hyperactivity on the path to physically violent and nonviolent juvenile delinquency. *Child Development*, *70*(5), 1181–1196.

Nakota, T., & Trehub, S. (2004). Infants' responsiveness to maternal speech and singing. *Infant Behavior and Development*, *27*, 455–464.

Nance, J. (1975). *The gentle Tasaday*. New York, NY: Harcourt Brace Jovanovich.

Nangle, D. W., & Erdley, C. A. (2001). Editors' notes. In D. W. Nangle & C. A. Erdley (Series Eds.) & W. Damon (Volume Ed.), New directions for child and adolescent development. *The role of friendship in psychological adjustment*. San Francisco, CA: Jossey-Bass.

Naumova, O. Y., Lee, M., Koposov, R., Szyf, M., Dozier, M., & Grigorenko, E. L. (2011). Differential patterns of whole-genome DNA methylation in institutionalized children and children raised by their biological parents. *Development and Psychopathology* (Online preprint).

Neal, D. T., & Chartrand, T. (2011). Embodied emotion perception: Amplifying and dampening facial feedback modulates emotion perception accuracy. *Psychological Science*, *2*, 673–678.

Neff, K. (2011). *Self-compassion*. New York, NY: William Morrow.

Nelson, E., & Panksepp, J. (1996). Oxytocin mediates acquisition of maternally associated odor preferences in preweaning rat pups. *Behavioral Neuroscience*, *110*(3), 583–592.

Nelson, E. E., & Panksepp, J. (1998). Brain substrates of infant–mother attachment: Contributions of opioids, oxytocin, and norepinephrine. *Neuroscience and Biobehavioral Reviews*, *22*(3), 437–452.

Nelson, N. L., & Russell, J. A. (2011a). Preschoolers' use of dynamic facial, bodily, and vocal cues to emotion. *Journal of Experimental Child Psychology*, *110*(1), 52–61.

Nelson, N. L., & Russell, J. A. (2011b). Putting motion in emotion: Do dynamic presentations increase preschooler's recognition of emotion? *Cognitive Development*, *26*(3), 248–259.

Nelson, N. L., & Russell, J. A. (2011c). When dynamic, the head and face alone can express pride. *Emotion*, *11*(4), 990–993.

Neppl, T. K., Conger, R. D., Scaramella, L.V., & Ontai, L. L. (2009). Intergenerational continuity in parenting behavior: Mediating pathways and child effects. *Developmental Psychology*, *45*(5), 1241–1256.

Nesse, R. M. (1990). Evolutionary explanations of emotions. *Human Nature*, *1*, 261–283.

Nesse, R. (2000). Is depression an adaptation? *Archives of General Psychiatry*, *57*, 14–20.

Nesse, R. (2006). Why so many people with selfish genes are pretty nice, except for their hatred of *the selfish gene*. In A. Grafen & M. Ridley (Eds.), *Richard Dawkins: How a scientist changed the way we think: Reflections by scientists, writers, and philosophers* (pp. 203–212). New York, NY: Oxford University Press.

Nesse, R., & Ellsworth, P. C. (2009). Evolution, emotions, and emotional disorders. *American Psychologist*, *64*, 129–139.

Ng, W., & Diener, E. (2009). Personality differences in emotions does emotion regulation play a role? *Journal of Individual Differences*, *30*(2), 100–106.

Niedenthal, P. M. (2007). Embodying emotion. *Science*, *316*, 1002–1005.

Niedenthal, P. M., & Halberstadt, J. H. (2000). Grounding categories in emotional response. In J. Forgas (Ed.), *Feeling and thinking: The role of affect in social cognition* (pp. 357–386). New York, NY: Cambridge University Press.

Niedenthal, P. M., Mermillod, M., Maringer, M., & Hess, U. (2010). The Simulation of Smiles (SIMS) model: Embodied simulation and the meaning of facial expression. *Behavioral and Brain Sciences*, *33*, 417–433.

Niedenthal, P. M., & Setterlund, M. B. (1994). Emotion congruence in perception. *Personality and Social Psychology Bulletin*, *20*, 401–411.

Niedenthal, P. M., Winkielman, P. Mondillon, L., & Vermeulen, N. (2009). Embodiment of emotional concepts: Evidence from EMG measures. *Journal of Personality and Social Psychology*, *96*, 1120–1136.

Nielsen, M., & Dissanayake, C. (2004). Pretend play, mirror self-recognition and imitation: A longitudinal investigation through the second year. *Infant Behavior and Development*, *27*(3), 342–365.

Nievar, M. A., & Becker, B. J. (2008). Sensitivity as a privileged predictor of attachment: A second perspective on de Wolff and van Ijzendoorn's meta-analysis. *Social Development, 17*(1), 102–114.

Nishida, T., Hasegawa, T., Hayaki, H., Takahata, Y., & Uehara, S. (1992). Meat-sharing as a coalition strategy by an alpha male chimpanzee. In T. Nishida, W. C. McGrew, P. Marler, M. Pickford, & F.B.M.De Waal (Eds.), *Topics in primatology, Vol. 1: Human origins* (pp. 159–174) Tokyo: University of Tokyo Press.

Nofzinger, E. A., Nichols, T. E., Meltzer, C. C., et al. (1999). Changes in forebrain function from waking to REM sleep in depression: Preliminary analyses of [18F] FDG PET studies. *Psychiatry Research, 91*, 59–78.

Nolen-Hoeksema, S. (2000). The role of rumination in depressive disorders and mixed anxiety/depressive symptoms. *Journal of Abnormal Psychology, 109*, 504–511.

Nolen-Hoeksema, S. (2002). Gender differences in depression. In I. H. Gotlib & C. L. Hammen (Eds.), *Handbook of depression* (pp. 492–509). New York, NY: Guilford.

Nolen-Hoeksema, S., & Jackson, B. (2001). Mediators of the gender difference in rumination. *Psychology of Women Quarterly, 25*, 37–47.

Nolen-Hoeksema, S., Larson, J., & Grayson, C. (1999). Explaining the gender difference in depression. *Journal of Personality and Social Psychology, 77*, 1061–1072.

Nolen-Hoeksema, S., & Morrow, J. (1991). A prospective study of depression and post traumatic stress symptoms after a natural disaster: The 1989 Loma Prieta earthquake. *Journal of Personality and Social Psychology, 61*, 115–121.

Nolen-Hoeksema, S., Morrow, J., & Fredrickson, B. J. (1993). Response styles and the duration of episodes of depressed mood. *Journal of Abnormal Psychology, 102*, 20–28.

Nolen-Hoeksema, S., Parker, L. E., & Larson, J. (1994). Ruminative coping with depressed mood following loss. *Journal of Personality and Social Psychology, 67*, 92–104.

Nolen-Hoeksema, S., Wisco, B. E., & Lyubomirsky, S. (2008). Rethinking rumination. *Perspectives on Psychological Science, 3*, 400–424.

Norcross, J. C., & Goldfried, M. R. (Eds.). (2005). *Handbook of psychotherapy integration* (2nd ed.). New York, NY: Oxford University Press.

Noriuchi, M., Kikuchi, Y., & Senoo, A. (2008). The functional neuroanatomy of maternal love: Mother's response to infant's attachment behaviors. *Biological Psychiatry, 63*(4), 415–23.

Nussbaum, M. (2001). *Upheavals of thought: The intelligence of emotions*. New York, NY: Cambridge University Press.

Nussbaum, M. C. (1986). *The fragility of goodness: Luck and ethics in Greek tragedy and philosophy*. Cambridge, MA: Cambridge University Press.

Nussbaum, M. C. (1994). *The therapy of desire: Theory and practice in Hellenistic ethics*. Princeton, NJ: Princeton University Press.

O'Connor, F. (1963). *My Oedipus complex and other stories*. London, UK: Penguin Books.

O'Connor, T. G., Ben-Shlomo, Y., Heron, J., Golding, J., Adams, D., & Glover, V. (2005). Prenatal anxiety predicts individual differences in cortisol in pre-adolescent children. *Biological Psychiatry, 58*(3), 211–217.

O'Connor, T. G., Heron, J., Golding, J., & Glover, V. (2003). Maternal antenatal anxiety and behavioural/emotional problems in children: A test of a programming hypothesis. *Journal of Child Psychology and Psychiatry, 44*, 1025–1036.

O'Connor, T. G., Marvin, R. S., Rutter, M., Olrick, J. T., & Britner, P. A. (2003). Child-parent attachment following early institutional deprivation. *Development and Psychopathology, 15*, 19–38.

O'Doherty, J., Kringelbach, M., Rolls, E., et al. (2001). Abstract reward and punishment representations in the human orbitofrontal cortex. *Nature Neuroscience, 4*, 95–102.

O'Donnell, K., O'Connor, T. G., & Glover, V. (2009). Prenatal stress and neurodevelopment of the child: Focus on the HPA axis and role of the placenta. *Developmental Neuroscience, 31*, 285–292.

Oatley, K. (1988). Life events, social cognition and depression. In S. Fisher & J. Reason (Eds.), *Hand-book of life stress, cognition and health* (pp. 543–557). New York, NY: Wiley.

Oatley, K. (1992). *Best laid schema: The psychology of emotions*. New York, NY: Cambridge University Press.

Oatley, K. (1999). Why fiction may be twice as true as fact: Fiction as cognitive and emotional simulation. *Review of General Psychology, 3*, 101–117.

Oatley, K. (2002). Emotions and the story worlds of fiction. In M. C. Green, J. J. Strange, & T. C. Brock (Eds.), *Narrative impact: Social and cognitive foundations* (pp. 39–69). Mahwah, NJ: Erlbaum.

Oatley, K. (2003). Creative expression and communication of emotion in the visual and narrative arts. In R. J. Davidson, K. R. Scherer, & H. H. Goldsmith (Eds.), *Handbook of affective sciences* (pp. 481–502). New York, NY: Oxford University Press.

Oatley, K. (2004a). From the emotions of conversation to the passions of fiction. In A.S.R. Manstead, N. Frijda, & A. Fischer (Eds.), *Feelings and emotions: The Amsterdam Symposium* (pp. 98–115). Cambridge, MA: Cambridge University Press.

Oatley, K. (2004b). Scripts, transformations, and suggestiveness, of emotions in Shakespeare and Chekhov. *Review of General Psychology, 8*, 323–340.

Oatley, K. (2004c). *Emotions: A brief history*. Malden, MA: Blackwell.

Oatley, K. (2009). Other bodies, other minds. Review of *Avatar* (2009), dir. James Cameron, *PsycCRITIQUES, 55*(5).

Oatley, K. (2011). *Such stuff as dreams: The psychology of fiction*. Oxford, UK: Wiley-Blackwell.

Oatley, K., & Bolton, W. (1985). A social-cognitive theory of depression in reaction to life events. *Psychological Review, 92*, 372–388.

Oatley, K., & Djikic, M. (2002). Emotions and transformation: Varieties of experience of identity. *Journal of Consciousness Studies, 9–10*, 97–116.

Oatley, K., & Duncan, E. (1992). Incidents of emotion in daily life. In K. T. Strongman (Ed.), *International review of studies on emotion* (pp. 250–293). Chichester, UK: Wiley.

Oatley, K., & Duncan, E. (1994). The experience of emotions in everyday life. *Cognition and Emotion, 8*, 369–381.

Oatley, K., & Jenkins, J. M. (1992). Human emotions: Function and dysfunction. *Annual Review of Psychology, 43*, 55–85.

Oatley, K., & Johnson-Laird, P. N. (1987). Towards a cognitive theory of emotions. *Cognition and Emotion, 1*, 29–50.

Oatley, K., & Johnson-Laird, P. N. (1995). The communicative theory of emotions: Empirical tests, mental models, and implications for social interaction. In L. L. Martin &

A. Tesser (Eds.), *Striving and feeling: Interactions among goals, affect, and self-regulation* (pp. 363–393). Mahwah, NJ: Erlbaum.

Oatley, K., & Johnson-Laird, P. N. (2011). Basic emotions in social relationships, reasoning, and psychological illnesses. *Emotion Review, 3*, 424–433.

Oatley, K., & Perring, C. (1991). A longitudinal study of psychological and social factors affecting recovery from psychiatric breakdown. *British Journal of Psychiatry, 158*, 28–32.

Oberle, E., Schonert-Reichl, K., & Thomson, K. C. (2010). Understanding the link between social and emotional well-being and peer relations in early adolescence: Gender-specific predictors of peer acceptance. *Journal of Youth and Adolescence, 39*(11), 1330–1342.

Ochsner, K., & Schachter, D. (2003). Remembering emotional events: A social cognitive and neuroscience apprroach. In R. J. Davidson, K. R. Scherer, & H. H. Goldsmith (Eds.), *Handbook of affective sciences* (pp. 643–660). New York, NY: Oxford University Press.

Ochsner, K. N. (2008). The social-emotional processing stream: Five core constructs and their translational potential for schizophrenia and beyond. *Biological Psychiatry, 64*, 48–61.

Ochsner, K. N., Bunge, S. A., Gross, J. J., & Gabrieli, J.D.E. (2002). Rethinking feelings: An fMRI study of the cognitive regulation of emotion. *Journal of Cognitive Neuroscience, 14*, 1215–1229.

Ochsner, K. N., & Gross, J. J. (2008). Cognitive emotion regulation: Insights from social cognitive and affective neuroscience. *Currents Directions in Psychological Science, 17*(1), 153–158.

Odgers, C. L., Moffitt, T. E., Broadbent, J. M., Dickson, N., Hancox, R. J., Harrington, H., et al. (2008). Female and male antisocial trajectories: From childhood origins to adult outcomes. *Development and Psychopathology, 20*(2), 673–716.

Oenguer, D., & Price, J. L. (2000). The organization of networks within the orbital and medial prefrontal cortex of rats, monkeys, and humans. *Cerebral Cortex, 10*(3), 206–219.

Offord, D. R., Boyle, M. H., Racine, Y. A., Fleming, J. E., Cadman, D. T., Blum, H. M., et al. (1992). Outcome, prognosis, and risk in a longitudinal follow-up study. *Journal of the American Academy of Child & Adolescent Psychiatry, 31*(5), 916–923.

Ogas, O., & Gaddam, S. (2011). *A billion wicked thoughts: What the world's largest experiment reveals about hidden desires*. New York, NY: Dutton.

Öhman, A. (1986). Face the beast and fear the face: Animal and social fears as prototypes for evolutionary analyses of emotion. *Psychophysiology, 23*, 123–145.

Öhman, A. (2000). Fear and anxiety: Evolutionary, cognitive, and clinical perspectives. In M. Lewis & J. Haviland-Jones (Eds.), *Handbook of emotions, Second Edition* (pp. 573–593). New York, NY: Guilford.

Öhman, A., & Dimberg, U. (1978). Facial expressions as conditioned stimuli for electrodermal responses: A case of "preparedness"? *Journal of Personality and Social Psychology, 36*, 1251–1258.

Öhman, A., & Mineka, S. (2001). Fears, phobias, and preparedness: Towards an evolved module of fear and fear learning. *Psychological Review, 108*(3), 483–522.

Öhman, A., & Soares, J.J.F. (1994). "Unconscious anxiety": Phobic responses to masked stimuli. *Journal of Abnormal Psychology, 103*, 231–240.

Oishi, S., Kesebir, S., & Diener, E. (2011). Income inequality and happiness. *Psychological Science, 22*, 1095–1100.

Oishi, S., Schimmack, U., & Diener, E. (2012). Progressive taxation and the subjective well-being of nations. *Psychological Science, 23*, 86–92.

Olds, D., Henderson, C. R., Cole, R., Eckenrode, J., Kitzman, H., Luckey, D., et al. (1998). Long-term effects of nurse home visitation on children's criminal and antisocial behavior. *JAMA: Journal of the American Medical Association, 280*(14), 1238.

Olds, D. L., Sadler, L., & Kitzman, H. (2007). Programs for parents of infants and toddlers: Recent evidence from randomized trials. *Journal of Child Psychology and Psychiatry, 48*(3–4), 355–391.

Olds, J., & Milner, P. (1954). Positive reinforcement produced by electrical stimulation of septal area and other regions of rat brain. *Journal of Comparative and Physiological Psychology, 47*, 419–427.

Ollendick, T. H., & King, N. J. (2004). Empirically supported treatments for children and adolescents: Advances toward Evidence-Based practice. In P. M. Barrett & T. H. Ollendick (Eds.), *Handbook of interventions that work with children and adolescents* (pp. 1–25). West Sussex, England: Wiley.

Olson, D. R. (1994). *The world on paper*. New York, NY: Cambridge University Press.

Oltmanns, T. F. (2003). *Case studies in abnormal psychology* (6th ed.). New York, NY: Wiley.

Ontai, L. L., & Thompson, R. A. (2002). Patterns of attachment and maternal discourse effects on children's emotion understanding from 3 to 5 years of age. *Social Development, 11*(4), 433–450.

Orlinsky, D. E., & Howard, K. I. (1980). Gender and psychotherapeutic outcome. In A. M. Brodsky & R. T. Hare-Martin (Eds.), *Women and psychotherapy* (pp. 3–34) New York, NY: Guilford.

Orobio de Castro, B., Veerman, J., Koops, W., Bosch, J., & Monshouwer, H. (2002). Hostile attribution of intent and aggressive behavior: A meta-analysis. *Child Development, 73*, 916–934.

Orth-Gomer, K., Wamala, S. P., Horsten, M., et al. (2000). Marital stress worsens prognosis in women with coronary heart disease: The Stockholm Female Coronary Risk Study. *Journal of the American Medical Association, 284*, 3008–3014.

Ortony, A., Clore, G., & Collins, A. (1988). *The cognitive structure of emotions*. New York, NY: Cambridge University Press.

Osgood, C. E., May, W. H., & Miron, M. S. (1975). *Cross-cultural universals of affective meaning*. Urbana: Illinois University Press.

Oskis, A., Loveday, C., Hucklebridge, F., Thorn, L., & Chow, A. (2011). Anxious attachment style and salivary cortisol dysregulation in healthy female children and adolescents. *Journal of Child Psychology and Psychiatry, 52*(2), 111–118.

Öst, L. G. (2008). Efficacy of the third wave of behavioral therapies: A systematic review and meta-analysis. *Behaviour Research and Therapy, 46*, 296–321.

Oster, H. (2005). The repertoire of infant facial expressions: An ontogenetic perspective. In J. Nadel & D. Muir (Eds.), *Emotional development: Recent research advances* (pp. 261–292). Oxford, UK: Oxford University Press.

Osumi, T., & Ohira, H. (2009). Cardiac responses predict decisions: An investigation of the relation between orienting response and decisions in the ultimatum game. *International Journal of Psychophysiology, 74*, 74–79.

Oveis, C., Cohen, A. B., Gruber, J., Shiota, M. N., Haidt, J., & Keltner, D. (2009). Resting respiratory sinus arrhythmia is associated with tonic positive emotionality. *Emotion, 9*, 265–270.

Oveis, C., Horberg, E. J., & Keltner, D. (2010). Compassion, pride, and social intuitions of self-other similarity. *Journal of Personality and Social Psychology, 98*, 618–630.

Overton, W. F. (2006). Developmental psychology: Philosophy, concepts, methodology. In R. M. Lerner, *Handbook of child psychology: Vol. 1:Theoretical models of human development* (6th ed., pp. 18–88). Hoboken, NJ: Wiley.

Owren, M. J., & Bachorowski, J. (2001). The evolution of emotional expression: A "selfish-gene" account of smiling and laughter in early hominids and humans. In T. J. Mayne & G. A. Bonanno (Eds.), *Emotions: Current issues and future directions* (pp. 152–191). New York, NY: Guilford.

Ozer, D. J., & Benet-Martínez, V. (2006). Personality and the prediction of consequential outcomes. *Annual Review of Psychology, 57*(1), 401–421.

Page, D. (1955). *Sappho and Alceus: An introduction to the study of ancient Lesbian poetry*. Oxford, UK: Oxford University Press.

Page-Gould, E., & Mendoza-Denton, R. (2011). Friendship and social interaction with outgroup members. In L. R. Tropp & R. Mallett (Eds.), *Beyond prejudice reduction: Pathways to positive intergroup relations* (pp. 139–158). Washington, DC: APA Books.

Panksepp, J. (1993). Neurochemical control of moods and emotions: Amino acids to neuropeptides. In M. Lewis & J. M. Haviland (Eds.), *Handbook of emotions* (pp. 87–107). New York, NY: Guilford.

Panksepp, J. (2001). The neuro-evolutionary cusp between emotions and cognitions: Implications for understanding consciousness and the emergence of a unified mind science. *Evolution and Cognition, 7*, 141–163.

Panksepp, J. (2005). Affective consciousness: Core emotional feelings in animals and humans. *Consciousness and Cognition, 14*, 30–80.

Panksepp, J. (2005). Beyond a joke: From animal laughter to human joy. *Science, 308*, 62–63.

Panksepp, J., Nelson, E., & Bekkedal, M. (1997). Brain systems for the mediation of social separation-distress and social-reward. Evolutionary antecedents and neuro-peptide intermediaries. In C. S. Carter, I. I. Lederhendler,

& B. Kirkpatrick (Eds.), *The integrative neurobiology of affiliation* (Vol. *807*, pp. 78–100). New York, NY: New York Academy of Sciences.

Papez, J. W. (1937). A proposed mechanism of emotion. *Archives of Neurology and Psychiatry, 38*, 725–743.

Parke, R. D. (1994). Progress, paradigms, and unresolved problems: A commentary on recent advances in our understanding of children's emotions. *Merrill-Palmer Quarterly, 40*(1), 157–69.

Parker, J. G., & Asher, S. R. (1993). Friendship and friendship quality in middle childhood: Links between peer group acceptance and feelings of loneliness and social dissatisfaction. *Developmental Psychology, 29*, 611–621.

Parkinson, B. (1996). Emotions are social. *British Journal of Psychology, 87*, 663–683.

Parkinson, B., Fischer, A. H., & Manstead, A.S.R. (2004). *Emotion in social relations: Cultural, group, and inter-personal processes*. Philadelphia, PA: Psychology Press.

Parrott, W. G., & Sabini, J. (1990). Mood and memory under natural conditions: Evidence for mood incongruent recall. *Journal of Personality and Social Psychology, 59*, 321–336.

Parrott, W. G., & Spackman, M. P. (2000). Emotion and memory. In M. Lewis & J. Haviland-Jones (Eds.), *Handbook of emotions* (2nd ed., pp. 476–490). New York, NY: Guilford.

Parrott, W. G., & Smith, S. F. (1991). Embarrassment: Actual vs. typical cases and classical vs. prototypical representations. *Cognition and Emotion, 5*, 467–488.

Parry, G., & Shapiro, D. A. (1986). Social support and life events in working-class women. *Archives of General Psychiatry, 43*, 315–323.

Paster, G. K., Rowe, K., & Floyd-Wilson, M. (Eds.). (2004). *Reading the passions: Essays on the cultural history of emotion*. Philadelphia: University of Pennsylvania Press.

Patel, V., Araya, R., De Lima, M., Ludermir, A., & Todd, C. (1999). Women, poverty and common mental disorders in four restructuring societies. *Social Science and Medicine, 49*, 1461–1471.

Patterson, G., Reid, J., & Dishion, T. (1992). *A social learning approach: Vol. 4. Antisocial boys*. Eugene, OR: Castalia.

Patterson, G. R. (1982). *Coercive family process*. Eugene, OR: Castalia.

Pauli-Pott, U., Friedel, S., Hinney, A., & Hebebrand, J. (2009). Serotonin transporter gene polymorphism (5-HTTLPR), environmental conditions, and developing negative emotionality and fear in early childhood. *Journal of Neural Transmission, 116*(6), 503–512.

Pavlov, I. P. (1927). *Conditioned reflexes* (G. V. Anrep, Trans.). New York, NY: Dover (current edition 1960).

Pecina, S., & Berridge, K. C. (2000). Opioid site in nucleus accumbens shell mediates eating and hedonic "liking" for food: Map based on microinjection Fos plumes. *Brain Research, 863*, 71–86.

Pedersen, C. (1997). Oxytocin control of maternal behavior. Regulation by sex steroids and offspring stimuli. *Annals of the New York Academy of Sciences, 807*, 126–145.

Peltola, M. J., Leppänen, J. M., Vogel-Farley, V. K., Hietanen, J. K., & Nelson, C. A. (2009). Fearful faces but not fearful eyes alone delay attention disengagement in 7-month-old infants. *Emotion, 9*(4), 560–565.

Peng, K., & Nisbett, R. (1999). Culture, dialectics, and reasoning about contradiction. *American Psychologist, 54*, 741–754.

Peng, K., Ames, D., & Knowles, E. (2001). Culture and human inference: Perspectives from three traditions. In D. Masumoto (Ed.), *Handbook of culture and psychology* (pp. 243–263). New York, NY: Oxford University Press.

Pennebaker, J. W. (1989). Confession, inhibition, and disease. In L. Berkowitz (Ed.), *Advances in experimental social psychology* (Vol. 22, pp. 211–244). San Diego, CA: Academic Press.

Pennebaker, J. W. (1997). Writing about emotional experiences as a therapeutic process. *Psychological Science, 8*, 162–166.

Pennebaker, J. W. (2002). Writing, social processes, and psychotherapy: From past to future. In S. J. Lepore & J. M. Smyth (Eds.), *The writing cure: How expressive writing promotes health and emotional well-being* (pp. 281–291). Washington, DC: American Psychological Association.

Pennebaker, J. W. (2012). Can expressive writing change emotions? An oblique answer to a misguided question. In D. Hermans, B. Rimé, & B. Mesquita (Eds.), *Changing emotions*. London, UKPsychology Press.

Pennebaker, J. W., & Chung, C. K. (2011). Expressive writing: Connections to mental and physical health. In H. S. Friedman (Ed.), *Oxford handbook of health psychology*. New York, NY: Oxford University Press.

Pennebaker, J. W., Kiecolt-Glaser, J. K., & Glaser, R. (1988). Disclosure of traumas and immune function: Health implications of psychotherapy. *Journal of Consulting and Clinical Psychology, 56*, 239–245.

Pennebaker, J. W., Mehl, M. R., & Niederhoffer, K. G. (2003). Psychological aspects of natural language use: Our words, our selves. *Annual Review of Psychology, 54*, 547–577.

Pennebaker, J. W., & Seagal, J. D. (1999). Forming a story: The health benefits of narrative. *Journal of Clinical Psychology, 55*, 1243–1254.

Pennebaker, J. W., Zech, E., & Rimé, B. (2001). Disclosing and sharing emotion: Psychological, social, and health consequences. In M. S. Stroebe, R. O. Hansson, W. Stroebe, & H. Schut (Eds.), *Handbook of bereavement research: Consequences, coping, and care* (pp. 517–543). Washington, DC: American Psychological Association.

Pennington, N., & Hastie, R. (1988). Explanation-based decision making: Effects of memory structure on judgement. *Journal of Experimental Psychology: Learning, Memory, and Cognition, 14*, 521–533.

Perälä, J., Suvisaari, J., Saarni, S. I., Kuoppasalmi, K., Isometsä, E., Pirkola, S., et al. (2007). Lifetime prevalence of psychotic and bipolar I disorders in a general population. *Archives of General Psychiatry, 64*, 19–28.

Perner, J., Ruffman, T., & Leekam, S. (1994). Theory of mind is contagious: You catch it from your sibs. *Child Development, 65*(4), 1228–1238.

Perper, T. (1985). *Sex signals: The biology of love*. Philadelphia, PA: ISI Press.

Perrow, C. (1984). *Normal accidents: Living with high-risk technologies*. New York, NY: Basic Books.

Peterson, C. (2000). Kindred spirits: Influences of siblings' perspectives on theory of mind. *Cognitive Development, 15*(4), 435–455.

Peterson, G., Mehl, L., & Leiderman, H. (1979). The role of some birth related variables in father attachment. *American Journal of Orthopsychiatry, 40*, 330–338.

Petty, R., & Cacioppo, J. (1986). The elaboration likelihood model of persuasion. In L. Berkowitz (Ed.), *Advances in experimental social psychology* (Vol. 19, pp. 124–205). New York, NY: Academic Press.

Phan, K. L., Taylor, S. F., Welsh, R. C., Ho, S.-H., Britton, J. C., & Liberzon, I. (2004). Neural correlates of individual ratings of emotional salience. *Neuroimage, 21,* 768–780.

Philippot, P., & Segal, Z. V. (2009). Mindfulness based psychological interventions: Developing emotional awareness for better being. *Journal of Consciousness Studies, 16,* 285–306.

Phillips, M. L., Young, A. W., Senior, C., et al. (1997). A specific neural substrate for perceiving facial expressions of disgust. *Nature, 389,* 495–498.

Pickles, A., & Angold, A. (2003). Natural categories or fundamental dimensions: On carving nature at the joints and the rearticulation of psychopathology. *Development and Psychopathology, 15*(3), 529–551.

Pickles, A., Rowe, R., Simonoff, E., et al. (2001). Child psychiatric symptoms and psychosocial impairment: Relationship and prognostic significance. *British Journal of Psychiatry, 179,* 230–235.

Pilowsky, I., & Katsikitis, M. (1994). The classification of facial emotions: A computer based taxonomic approach. *Journal of Affective Disorders, 30,* 61–71.

Pittam, J., & Scherer, K. R. (1993). Vocal expression and communication of emotion. In M. Lewis & J. M. Haviland (Eds.), *Handbook of emotions* (pp. 185–197) New York, NY: Guilford.

Plato. (375 BCE) *The republic.* London, UK: Penguin (current edition 1955).

Plomin, R. (1983). Developmental behavioral genetics. *Child Development, 54*(2), 253–259.

Plomin, R., & Bergeman, C. S. (1991). The nature of nurture: Genetic influence on environmental measures. *Behavioral and Brain Sciences, 14,* 373–427.

Plomin, R., Chipuer, H. M., & Loelin, J. C. (1990). Behavioral genetics and personality. In L. A. Pervin (Ed.), *Handbook of personality* (pp. 225–243). New York, NY: Guilford.

Plomin, R., & Davis, O. S. P. (2009). The future of genetics in psychology and psychiatry: Microarrays, genomewide association, and non-coding RNA. *Journal of Child Psychology and Psychiatry, 50*(12), 63–71.

Plomin, R., Haworth, C.M.A., & Davis, O.S.P. (2009). Common disorders are quantitative traits. *Nature Reviews Genetics, 10,* 872–878.

Plomin, R., Lichtenstein, P., Pedersen, N., McClearn, G. E., & Nesselroade, J. R. (1990). Genetic influences on life events during the last half of the life span. *Psychology of Aging, 5,* 25–30.

Plomin, R., & McGuffin, P. (2003). Psychopathology in the postgenomic era. *Annual Review Psychology, 54,* 205–228.

Pluess, M., Bolten, M., Pirke, K. M., & Hellhammer, D. (2010). Maternal trait anxiety, emotional distress, and salivary cortisol in pregnancy. *Biological Psychology, 83*(3), 169–175.

Plutchik, R. (1980). *Emotion: A psychobioevolutionary synthesis.* New York, NY: Harper & Row.

Polirstok, S., & Gottlieb, J. (2006). The impact of positive behavior intervention training for teachers on referral rates for misbehavior, special education evaluation and student reading achievement in the elementary grades. *International Journal of Behavioral Consultation and Therapy, 2*(3), 8.

Pollak, S. D. (2012). The emergence of human emotion: New approaches to the old nature-nurture debate. *Parenting Science and Practice, 12*(2–3), xxx.

Pollak, S. D., & Sinha, P. (2002). Effects of early experience on children's recognition of facial displays of emotion. *Developmental Psychology, 38*(5), 784–791.

Pollak, S. D., & Tolley-Schell, S.A. (2003). Selective attention to facial emotion in physically abused children. *Journal of Abnormal Psychology, 112*(3), 323–338.

Pollard, T. M. (1995). Use of cortisol as a stress marker: Practical and theoretical problems. *American Journal of Human Biology, 7*(2), 265–274.

Pollatos, O., Traut-Mattausch, E., Schroeder, H., & Schandry, R. (2007). Interoceptive awareness mediates the relationship between anxiety and the intensity of unpleasant feelings. *Journal of Anxiety Disorders, 21*(7), 931–943.

Polya, G. (1957). *How to solve it: A new aspect of mathematical method* (2nd ed.). Garden City, NY: Doubleday.

Popper, K. R. (1962a). *Conjectures and refutations.* New York, NY: Basic Books.

Popper, K. R. (1962b). *The open society and its enemies* (Vol. 2, 4th ed.). London, UK: Routledge & Kegan Paul.

Porges, S. (1998). Love: An emergent property of the mammalian autonomic nervous system. *Pychoendocrinology, 23,* 837–861.

Porges, S. W. (2003). The polyvagal theory: Phylogenetic contributions to social behavior. *Physiology & Behavior, 79*(3), 503–513.

Posner, M. I., & Rothbart, M. K. (2000). Developing mechanisms of self-regulation. *Development and Psychopathology, 12,* 427–441.

Potts, R. (1998). Variability selection in hominid evolution. *Evolutionary Anthropology, 7,* 81–96.

Power, M., & Dalgleish, T. (2008). *Cognition and emotion: From order to disorder* (2nd ed.). Hove: Psychology Press.

Power, T. G., & Hill, L. G. (2010). Individual differences in appraisal of minor, potentially stressful events: A cluster analytic approach. *Cognition and Emotion, 24,* 1081–1094.

Powers, S. I., Pietromonaco, P. R., Gunlicks, M., & Sayer, A. (2006). Dating couples' attachment styles and patterns of cortisol reactivity and recovery in response to a relationship conflict. *Journal of Personality and Social Psychology, 90*(4), 613–628.

Prinz, W. (2007). A critique of free will: Psychological remarks on a social institution. In M. Ash & T. Sturm (Eds.), *Psychology's territories: Historical and contemporary perspectives from different disciplines* (pp. 67–88). Hove: Psychology Press.

Proust, M. (1913–1927). *A la recherche du temps perdu* [Remembrance of things past] (C. K. Scott-Moncreiff, T. Kilmartin, & A. Mayor, Trans.). London, UK: Chatto & Windus (current edition 1981).

Provine, R. R. (1992). Contagious laughter: Laughter is a sufficient stimulus for laughs and smiles. *Bulletin of the Psychonomic Society, 30,* 1–4.

Provine, R. R. (1993). Laughter punctuates speech: Linguistic, social, and gender contexts of laughter. *Ethology, 95,* 291–298.

Provine, R. R., & Fischer, K. R. (1989). Laughing, smiling, and talking: Relation to sleeping and social context in humans. *Ethology, 83,* 295–305.

Prunier, G. (1995). *The Rwanda crisis: History of a genocide.* London, UK: Hurst.

Purkis, J. (1985). *A preface to George Eliot.* London, UK: Longman.

Putnam, H. (1975). The meaning of meaning. In K. Gunderson (Ed.), *Language, mind and knowledge. Minnesota studies in the philosophy of science* (Vol. *7).* Minneapolis: University of Minnesota Press.

Pynoos, R. S., & Nader, K. (1989). Children's memory and proximity to violence. *Journal of the American Academy of Child and Adolescent Psychiatry, 28,* 236–241.

Pyszczynski, T., & Greenberg, J. (1987). Self-regulatory perseveration and the depressive self-focusing style: A self-awareness theory of reactive depression. *Psychological Bulletin, 102,* 122–138.

Quigley, B., & Tedeschi, J. (1996). Mediating effects of blame attributions on feelings of anger. *Personality and Social Psychology Bulletin, 22,* 1280–1288.

Quirin, M., Pruessner, J. C., & Kuhl, J. (2008). HPA system regulation and adult attachment anxiety: Individual differences in reactive and awakening cortisol. *Psychoneuroendocrinology, 33*(5), 581–590.

Rabin, B. S. (1999). *Stress, immune function, and health: The connection.* New York, NY: Wiley.

Raine, A. (2000). Annotation: The role of prefrontal deficits, low autonomic arousal, and early health factors in the development of antisocial and aggressive behavior in children. *Journal of Child Psychology & Psychiatry, 43* (4), 417–434.

Raine, A. (2011). An amygdala structural abnormality common to two subtypes of conduct disorder: A neurodevelopmental conundrum. *American Journal of Psychiatry, 168,* 569–571.

Ramsden, S. R., & Hubbard, J. A. (2002). Family expressiveness and parental emotion coaching: Their role in children's emotion regulation and aggression. *Journal of Abnormal Child Psychology, 30*(6), 657–667.

Rasbash, J., Jenkins, J., O'Connor, T. G., Tackett, J., & Reiss, D. (2011). A social relations model of observed family negativity and positivity using a genetically informative sample. *Journal of Personality and Social Psychology, 100*(3), 474–491.

Rasbash, J. Leckie, G., Pillinger, R., & Jenkins, J. (2010). Children's educational progress: Partitioning family, school and area effects. *Journal of the Royal Statistical Society: Series A (Statistics in Society), 173*(3), 657–682.

Ready, R. E., & Robinson, M. D. (2008). Do older individuals adapt to their traits? Personality-emotion relations among younger and older adults. *Journal of Research in Personality, 42,* 1020–1030.

Reicher, S. D., & Haslam, S. A. (2011). The shock of the old. *The Psychologist, 24*, 650–652.

Reisenzein, R. (1983). The Schachter theory of emotion: Two decades later. *Psychological Bulletin, 94*, 239–264.

Reisenzein, R. (1992a). A structuralist reconstruction of Wundt's three-dimensional theory of emotion. In H. Westmeyer (Ed.), *The structuralist program in psychology: Foundations and applications* (pp. 141–189). Toronto, Canada: Hopgrefe & Huber.

Reisenzein, R. (1992b). Stumpf's cognitive-evaluative theory of emotion. *American Psychologist, 47*, 34–45.

Reisenzein, R., & Weber, H. (2009). Personality and emotion. In P. J. Corr & G. Matthews (Eds.), *The Cambridge handbook of personality psychology* (pp. 54–71). New York, NY: Cambridge University Press.

Repacholi, B. M., & Gopnik, A. (1997). Early reasoning about desires: Evidence from 14- and 18-month-olds. *Developmental Psychology, 33*(1), 12–21.

Repacholi, B. M., & Meltzoff, A. N. (2007). Emotional eavesdropping: Infants selectively respond to indirect emotional signals. *Child Development, 78*(2), 503–521.

Repetti, R. L., Taylor, S. E., & Seeman, T. E. (2002). Risky families: Family social environments and the mental and physical health of offspring. *Psychological Bulletin 128* (2), 330–366.

Richards, I. A. (1925). *Principles of literary criticism*. New York, NY: Harcourt Brace Jovanovich.

Richards, M., & Huppert, F. A. (2011). Do positive children become positive adults? Evidence from a longitudinal birth cohort study. *Journal of Positive Psychology, 6*, 75–87.

Rimé, B. (2009). Emotion elicits social sharing of emotion: Theory and empirical review. *Emotion Review, 1*, 60–85.

Rimé, B., Finkenauer, C., Luminet, O., Zech, E., & Philippot, P. (1998). Social sharing of emotion: New evidence and new questions. *European Review of Social Psychology, 9*, 145–189.

Rimé, B., Mesquita, B., Philippot, P., & Boca, S. (1991). Beyond the emotional event: Six studies on the social sharing of emotions. *Cognition and Emotion, 5*, 435–465.

Rimé, B., Philippot, P., & Cisamolo, D. (1990). Social schemata of peripheral changes in emotion. *Journal of Personality and Social Psychology, 59*, 38–49.

Rinn, W. E. (1984). The neuropsychology of facial expression: A review of the neurological and psychological mechanisms for producing facial expressions. *Psychological Bulletin, 95*, 52–77.

Roberts, B. W., & Mroczek, D. (2008). Personality trait change in adulthood. *Current Directions in Psychological Science, 17*, 31–35.

Roberts, B. W., Wood, D., & Caspi, A. (2008). The development of personality traits in adulthood. In O. P. John, R. W. Robins, & L. A. Pervin (Eds.), *Handbook of personality: Theory and research* (pp. 375–98). New York, NY: Guilford.

Roberts, T. A., & Pennebaker, J. W. (1995). Gender differences in perceiving internal state: Toward a his-and-hers model of perceptual cue use. In M. Zanna (Ed.), *Advances in experimental social psychology* (Vol. 27, pp. 143–176). New York, NY: Academic Press.

Rodrigues, S. M., LeDoux, J. E., & Sapolsky, R. M. (2009). The influence of stress hormones on fear circuitry. *Annual Review of Neuroscience, 32*, 289–313.

Rolls, E. T. (1997). Taste and olfactory processing in the brain and its relation to the control of eating. *Critical Reviews in Neurobiology, 11*(4), 263–287.

Rolls, E. T. (1999). *The brain and emotion*. New York, NY: Oxford University Press.

Rolls, E. T. (2000). The orbitofrontal cortex and reward. *Cerebral Cortex, 10*, 284–294.

Rolls, E. T., & Bayliss, L. L. (1994). Gustatory, olfactory, and visual convergence within the primate orbitofrontal cortex. *Journal of Neuroscience, 14*(9), 1532–1540.

Rolls, E. T., Hornak, J., Wade, D., & McGrath, J. (1994). Emotion related learning in patients with social and emotional changes associated with frontal lobe damage. *Journal of Neurology, Neurosurgery and Psychiatry, 57*, 1518–1524.

Romney, A. K., Moore, C. C., & Rusch, C. D. (1997). Cultural universals: Measuring the semantic structure of emotion terms in English and Japanese. *Proceedings from the National Academy of Sciences, 94*, 5489–5494.

Root, C. A., & Jenkins, J. M. (2005). Maternal appraisal styles, family risk status and anger biases of children. *Journal of Abnormal Child Psychology, 33*(2), 193–204.

Rosaldo, M. (1980). *Knowledge and passion: Ilongot notions of self and social life*. Cambridge, MA: Cambridge University Press.

Roseman, I. (1984). Cognitive determinants of emotion: A structural theory. In P. Shaver (Ed.), *Review of personality and social psychology, Vol. 5: Emotions, relationships and health* (pp. 11–36). Beverley Hills, CA: Sage.

Roseman, I. (2011). Emotional behaviors, emotivational goals, emotion strategies: Multiple levels of organization integrate variable and consistent responses. *Emotion Review, 3*, 434–443.

Roseman, I., Dhawan, N., Rettek, I., Naidu, R. K., & Thapa, K. (1995). Cultural differences and cross-cultural similarities in appraisals and emotional responses. *Journal of Cross-Cultural Psychology, 26*, 23–48.

Roseman, I., & Evdokas, A. (2004). Appraisals cause experienced emotions: Experimental evidence. *Cognition and Emotion, 18*, 1–28.

Rosen, H. J., & Levenson, R. W. (2009). The emotional brain: Combining insights from patients and basic science. *Neurocase, 15*, 173–181.

Rosenberg, D., & Bloom, H. (1990). *The book of J.* New York, NY: Grove Weidenfeld.

Rosenberg, E. L., & Ekman, P. (1994). Coherence between expressive and experiential systems in emotion. *Cognition and Emotion, 8*, 201–229.

Rosenman, R. H., Brand, R. J., Jenkins, C. D., Friedman, M., Straus, R., & Wurm, M. (1975). Coronary heart disease in the Western collaborative group study. *Journal of the American Medical Association, 233*, 872–877.

Ross, E. D. (1984). Right hemisphere's role in language, affective behavior, and emotion. *Trends in Neuroscience, 7*, 342–346.

Rothbart, M. K. (1981). Measurement of temperament in infancy. *Child Development, 52*, 569–578.

Rothbart, M. K., Derryberry, D., & Hershey, K. (2000). Stability of temperament in childhood: Laboratory infant assessment to parent report at seven years. In V. J. Molfese & D. L. Molfese (Eds.), *Temperament and personality development across the life span* (pp. 85–119). Mahwah, NJ: Lawrence Erlbaum.

Rothbart, M. K., & Rueda, M. R. (2005). The development of effortful control. *Developing individuality in the human brain: A tribute to Michael I. Posner*, 167–188.

Rothbart, M. K., Sheese, B. E., Rueda, M. R., & Posner, M. I. (2011). Developing mechanisms of self-regulation in early life. *Emotion Review, 3*(2), 207–213.

Rothbart, M. K., Ziaie, H., & O'Boyle, C. G. (1992). Self regulation and emotion in infancy. In N. Eisenberg &

R. A. Fabes (Eds.), *Emotion and its regulation in early development (New Directions in Child Development, No. 55*, pp. 7–24). San Francisco, CA: Jossey-Bass.

Rousseau, J.-J. (1755). Discourse on the origin and basis of inequality among men. In *The essential Rousseau* (pp. 125–201). New York, NY: Penguin (current edition 1975).

Rousseau, J.-J. (1762). The social contract, or principles of political right. In *The essential Rousseau* (pp. 1–124). New York, NY: Penguin.

Rozin, P., & Fallon, A. E. (1987). A perspective on disgust. *Psychological Review, 94*, 23–41.

Rozin, P., Haidt, J., & McCauley, C. R. (2008). Disgust. In M. Lewis, J. Haviland, & L. F. Barrett (Eds.), *Handbook of emotions* (3rd ed., pp. 757–776). New York, NY: Guilford.

Rozin, P., & Kalat, J. (1971). Specific hungers and poison avoidance as adaptive specialization of learning. *Psychological Review, 78*, 459–486.

Rozin, P., Lowery, L., Imada, S., & Haidt, J. (1999). The CAD triad hypothesis: A mapping between three moral emotions (contempt, anger, and disgust), and three moral codes (community, autonomy, divinity). *Journal of Personality and Social Psychology, 66*, 870–881.

Rozin, P., & Royzman, E. B. (2001). Negativity bias, negativity dominance, and contagion. *Personality and Social Psychology Review, 5*, 296–320.

Rubin, K. H., Bukowski, W., & Parker, J. (2006). Peer interactions, relationships, and groups. In N. Eisenberg (Ed.), *Handbook of child psychology: Social, emotional and personality development* (6th ed., pp. 571–645). New York, NY: Wiley.

Rubino, V., Blasi, G., Latorre, V., Fazio, L., d'Errico, I., Mazzola, V., et al. (2007). Activity in medial prefrontal cortex during cognitive evaluation of threatening stimuli as a function of personality style. *Brain Research Bulletin, 74*(4), 250–257.

Runions, K. C., & Keating, D. P. (2007). Young children's social information processing: Family antecedents and behavioral correlates. *Developmental Psychology, 43*(4), 838–849.

Rusbult, C. E. (1980). Commitment and satisfaction in romantic associations: A test of the investment model. *Journal of Experimental Social Psychology, 17*, 172–186.

Rusbult, C. E. (1983). A longitudinal test of the investment model: The development (and deterioration) of satisfaction and commitment in heterosexual involvements. *Journal of Personality and Social Psychology, 45,* 101–117.

Ruschena, E., Prior, M., Sanson, A., & Smart, D. (2005). A longitudinal study of adolescent adjustment following family transitions. *Journal of Child Psychology and Psychiatry, 46,* 353–363.

Russell, B. (1938). *Power: A new social analysis.* London; Allen & Unwin.

Russell, J. A. (1991b). In defense of a prototype approach to emotion concepts. *Journal of Personality and Social Psychology, 60,* 37–47.

Russell, J. A. (1994). Is there universal recognition of emotion from facial expression? A review of methods and studies. *Psychological Bulletin, 115,* 102–141.

Russell, J. A. (2003). Core affect and the psychological construction of emotion. *Psychological Review, 110,* 145–172.

Russell, J. A., Bachorowski, J. A., & Fernández-Dols, J. M. (2003). Facial and vocal expressions of emotion. *Annual Review of Psychology, 54*(1), 329–349.

Russell, J. A., & Fernandez-Dols, J. M. (1997). What does a facial expression mean? In J. A. Russell & J. M. Fernandez-Dols (Eds.), *The psychology of facial expression* (pp. 3–30) New York, NY: Cambridge University Press.

Rutter, M. (1979). Protective factors in children's responses to stress and disadvantage. In M. W. Kent & J. E. Rolf (Eds.), *Primary prevention in psychopathology, Vol. 3: Social competence in children* (pp. 49–74). Hanover, NH: University Press of New England.

Rutter, M. (2005). Environmentally mediated risks for psychopathology: Research strategies and findings. *Journal of the American Academy of Child and Adolescent Psychiatry, 44,* 3–18.

Rutter, M. (2009). Understanding and testing risk mechanisms for mental disorders. *Journal of Child Psychology and Psychiatry, 50*(1–2), 44–52.

Rutter, M. (2011). Research review: Child psychiatric diagnosis and classification: Concepts, findings, challenges and potential. *Journal of Child Psychology and Psychiatry, 52*(6), 647–660.

Rutter, M., Sonuga-Barke, E., & Castle, J. (2010). I. Investigating the impact of early institutional deprivation on development: Background and research strategy of the English and Romanian Adoptees (ERA) Study.

Monographs of the Society of Research and Child Development, 75(1), 1–20.

Rutter, M., & Taylor, E. A. (2002). *Child and adolescent psychiatry.* Oxford, UK: Wiley-Blackwell.

Rydell, A., Berlin, L., and Bohlin, G. (2003). Emotionality, emotion regulation, and adaptation among 5- to 8-year-old children. *Emotion, 3*(1), 30–47.

Saarni, C. (1990). Emotional competence: How emotions and relationships become integrated. In R. A. Thompson (Ed.), *Nebraska Symposium on Motivation, 1988: Socioemotional development. Current theory and research in motivation.* (Vol. 36, pp. 115–182). Lincoln: University of Nebraska Press.

Saarni, C., Campos, J. J., Camras, L. A., & Witherington, D. (2006). Emotional development: Action, communication, and understanding. In N. Eisenberg, W. Damon, & R. M. Lerner (Eds.), *Handbook of child psychology* (6th ed., Vol. 3, pp. 226–299). Hoboken, NJ: Wiley.

Saarni, C., Mumme, D., & Campos, J. J. (1998). Emotional development: Action, communication, and understanding. In N. Eisenberg (Ed.), *Handbook of child psychology, Vol. 3: Social, emotional and personality development* (5th ed., pp. 237–309). New York, NY: Wiley.

Sacks, O. (1973). *Awakenings.* London, UK: Duckworth.

Safer, M. A., Bonanno, G. A., & Field, N. P. (2001). It was never that bad: Biased recall of grief and long-term adjustment to the death of a spouse. *Memory, 9,* 195–204.

Salaman, E. (1982). A collection of moments. In U. Neisser (Ed.), *Memory observed: Remembering in natural contexts* (pp. 49–63). San Francisco, CA: Freeman.

Salem, J. E., & Kring, A. (1999). Flat affect and social skills in schizophrenia: Evidence for their independence. *Psychiatry Research, 87,* 159–167.

Sallquist, J. V., Eisenberg, N., Spinrad, T. L., Reiser, M., Hofer, C., Zhou, Q., et al. (2009). Positive and negative emotionality: Trajectories across six years and relations with social competence. *Emotion, 9*(1), 15–28.

Salovey, P. (1991). *The psychology of jealousy and envy.* New York, NY: Guilford.

Sameroff, A. (2010). A unified theory of development: A dialectic integration of nature and nurture. *Child Development, 81*(1), 6–22.

Sampson, R., Raudenbush, S., & Earls, F. (1997). Neighborhoods and violent crime: A multilevel study of collective efficacy. *Science, 277*(5328), 918–924.

Sandell, R., Blomberg, J., & Lazar, A. (2002). Time matters: On temporal interactions in long term follow-up of long term psychotherapies. *Psycho-therapy Research, 12,* 39–58.

Sander, D., & Scherer, K. R. (2009). *The Oxford companion to emotion and the affective sciences.* New York, NY: Oxford University Press.

Sanders, M. R., Ralph, A., Sofronoff, K., Gardiner, P., Thompson, R., Dwyer, S., et al. (2008). Every family: A population approach to reducing behavioral and emotional problems in children making the transition to school. *Journal of Primary Prevention, 29*(3), 197–222.

Sangsue, J., Scherer, K. R., Scherer, U., Tran, V., & Wranik, T. (2004). Emotions in everyday life: Probability of occurrence, risk factors, appraisal and reaction patterns. *Social Science Information, 43*(4), 499–570.

Sapolsky, R., Romero, M., & Munck, A. U. (2000). How do glucocorticoids influence stress responses? Integrating permissive, suppressive, stimulatory, and preparative actions. *Endocrine Reviews, 21,* 55–89.

Sarason, B. R., Shearin, E. N., Pierce, G. R., & Sarason, G. R. (1987). Interrelations of social support measures: Theoretical and practical implications. *Journal of Personality and Social Psychology, 52,* 813–832.

Sartre, J.-P. (1962). *Sketch for a theory of the emotions* (P. Mairet, Trans.). London, UK: Methuen.

Sauter, D. (2010). More than happy: The need for disentangling positive emotions. *Current Directions in Psychological Science, 19,* 36–40.

Sauter, D., Eisner, F., Ekman, P., & Scott, S. K. (2010). Cross-cultural recognition of basic emotions through nonverbal emotional vocalizations. *Proceedings of the National Academy of Sciences, 107*(6), 2408–2412.

Sauter, D., & Scott, S. K. (2007). More than one kind of happiness: Can we recognize vocal expressions of different positive states? *Motivation and Emotion, 31*(3), 192–199.

Scarr, S., & Salapatek, P. (1970). Patterns of fear development during infancy. *Merrill-Palmer Quarterly, 16,* 53–90.

Schachter, S., & Singer, J. (1962). Cognitive, social and physiological determinants of emotional state. *Psychological Review, 69,* 379–399.

Schaeffer, C. M., Petras, H., Ialongo, N., Poduska, J., & Kellam, S. (2003). Modeling growth in boys' aggressive behavior across elementary school: Links to later criminal involvement, conduct disorder, and antisocial personality disorder. *Developmental Psychology, 39*(6), 1020.

Schaffer, H. R. (1974). Cognitive components of the infant's response to strangeness. In M. Lewis & L. A. Rosenblum (Eds.), *The origins of fear* (pp. 11–25). New York, NY: Wiley.

Schank, R., & Abelson, R. (1977). *Scripts, plans, goals and understanding: An inquiry into human knowledge structures.* Hillsdale, NJ: Erlbaum.

Schechner, R. (2001). *Rasaesthetics. The Drama Review, 43,* 27–50.

Scheff, T. J. (1979). *Catharsis in healing, ritual, and drama.* Berkeley: University of California Press.

Scheff, T. J. (1997). *Emotions, the social bond, and human reality: Part/whole analysis.* New York, NY: Cambridge University Press.

Scherer, J. F., True, W. R., Xian, H., Lyons, M. J., Eisen, S. A., Goldberg, J., et al. (2000). Evidence for genetic influences common and specific to symptoms of generalized anxiety and panic. *Journal of Affective Disorders, 57,* 25–35.

Scherer, K. R. (1986). Vocal affect expression: A review and a model for future research. *Psychological Bulletin, 99,* 143–165.

Scherer, K. R. (1988). Criteria for emotion antecedent appraisal: A review. In V. Hamilton, G. H. Bower, & N. H. Frijda (Eds.), *Cognitive perspectives on emotion and motivation* (pp. 89–126). Dordrecht, The Netherlands: Kluwer.

Scherer, K. R. (1997). The role of culture in emotion antecedent appraisal. *Journal of Personality and Social Psychology, 73,* 902–922.

Scherer, K. R., Johnstone, T., & Klasmeyer, G. (2003). Vocal expression of emotion. In R. J. Davidson, K. R. Scherer, & H. H. Goldsmith (Eds.), *Handbook of affective sciences* (pp. 433–456) New York, NY: Oxford University Press.

Scherer, K. R., Zentner, M. R., & Stern, D. (2004). Beyond surprise: The puzzle of infants' expressive reactions to expectancy violation. *Emotion, 4*(4), 389–402.

Schimmack, U. (1996). Cultural influences on the recognition of emotion by facial expressions: Individualistic or Caucasian cultures? *Journal of Cross-Cultural Psychology, 27,* 37–50.

Schimmack, U., Oishi, S., & Diener, E. (2002). Cultural influences on the relation between pleasant emotions and unpleasant emotions: Asian dialectic philosophies or individualism-collectivism? *Cognition and Emotion, 16,* 705–719.

Schimmack, U., Oishi, S., & Diener, E. (2005). Individualism: A valid and important dimension of cultural differences between nations. *Personality and Social Psychology Review, 9,* 17–31.

Schnall, S. (2011). Clean, proper, and tidy are more than the absence of dirty, disgusting and wrong. *Emotion Review, 3,* 264–266.

Schore, A. N. (1999). *Affect regulation and the origin of the self: The neurobiology of emotional development.* Hillsdale, NJ: Lawrence Erlbaum Associates.

Schubert, T. W., & Koole, S. L. (2009). The embodied self: Making a fist enhances men's power-related self-conceptions. *Journal of Experimental Social Psychology, 45,* 828–834.

Schueller, S. M., & Seligman, M.E.P. (2010). Pursuit of pleasure, engagement, and meaning: Relationships to subjective and objective measures of well-being. *Journal of Positive Psychology, 5,* 253–263.

Schultz, W., Dayan, P., & Montague, P. R. (1997). A neural substrate of prediction and reward. *Science, 275,* 1593–1599.

Schwarz, N. (1990). Feelings as information: Informational and motivational functions of affective states. In E. T. Higgins & R. M. Sorrentino (Eds.), *Handbook of motivation and cognition* (Vol. 2, pp. 527–561). New York, NY: Guilford.

Schwarz, N. (2005). When thinking feels difficult: Metacognitive experiences in judgment and decision making. *Medical Decision Making, 25,* 105–112.

Schwarz, N., & Clore, G. L. (1983). Mood, misattribution, and judgments of well-being: Informative and directive functions of affective states. *Journal of Personality and Social Psychology, 45,* 513–523.

Segal, Z. V., Williams, J.M.G., & Teasdale, J. D. (2002). *Mindfulness based cognitive therapy for depression: A new approach to preventing relapse.* New York, NY: Guilford.

Segal, Z. V., Williams, J.M.G., Teasdale, J. D., & Gemar, M. (1996). A cognitive science perspective on kindling and episode sensitization in recurrent affective disorder. *Psychological Medicine, 26,* 371–380.

Selye, H. (1936). A syndrome produced by diverse nocuous agents. *Nature, 138,* 32.

Serketich, W. J., & Dumas, J. E. (1996). The effectiveness of behavioral parent training to modify antisocial behavior in children: A meta-analysis. *Behavior Therapy, 27*(2), 171–186.

Sessa, F. M., Steinberg, L., Avenevoli, S., Silk, J. S., & Morris, A. S. (2004). Neighborhood cohesion as a buffer against hostile maternal parenting. *Journal of Family Psychology, 18*(1), 135–146.

Seyfarth, R. M., & Cheney, D. L. (1992). Meaning and mind in monkeys. *Scientific American, 267,* 122–129.

Shaffer, A., Burt, K. B., Obradović, J., Herbers, J. E., & Masten, A. S. (2009). Intergenerational continuity in parenting quality: The mediating role of social competence. *Developmental Psychology, 45*(5), 1227–1240.

Shakespeare, W. (1600). *Hamlet.* London, UK: Methuen (current edition 1981).

Shakespeare, W. (1623a). As you like it. In A. Harbage (Ed.), *The complete Pelican Shakespeare: Comedies and romances* (pp. 200–229). Harmondsworth: Penguin (current edition 1969).

Shakespeare, W. (1623b). *The Norton Shakespeare* (S. Greenblatt, Ed.). New York, NY: Norton (modern edition 1997).

Sharot, T., Korn, C. W., & Dolan, R. J. (2011). How unrealistic optimism is maintained in the face of reality. *Nature Neuroscience* (Advance online).

Shaver, P., Hazan, C., & Bradshaw, D. (1988). Love as attachment: The integration of three behavioral systems. In R. J. Sternberg & M. L. Barnes (Eds.), *The psychology of love* (pp. 68–99). New Haven, CT: Yale University Press.

Shaver, P., Schwartz, J. C., Kirson, D., & O'Connor, C. (1987). Emotion knowledge: Further exploration of a prototype approach. *Journal of Personality and Social Psychology, 52,* 1061–1086.

Shaw, D. S., Gilliom, M., Ingoldsby, E. M., & Nagin, D. S. (2003). Trajectories leading to school-age conduct problems. *Developmental Psychology, 39*(2), 189.

Shaw, D. S., Lacourse, E., & Nagin, D. S. (2005). Developmental trajectories of conduct problems and hyperactivity from ages 2 to 10. *Journal of Child Psychology and Psychiatry, 46*(9), 931–942.

Shaw, P., Kabani, N. J., Lerch, J. P., Eckstrand, K., Lenroot, R., Gogtay, N., et al. (2008). Neurodevelopmental trajectories of the human cerebral cortex. *Journal of Neuroscience, 28*(14), 3586–3594.

Shay, J. (1995). *Achilles in Vietnam: Combat trauma and the undoing of character.* New York, NY: Simon & Schuster.

Shearn, D., Bergman, E., Hill, K., Abel, A., & Hinds, L. (1990). Facial coloration and temperature responses in blushing. *Psychophysiology, 27*, 687–693.

Shearn, D., Bergman, E., Hill, K., Abel, A., & Hinds, L. (1992). Blushing as a function of audience size. *Psychophysiology, 29*, 431–436.

Shelley, M. (1818). *Frankenstein, or modern Prometheus.* Harmondsworth: Penguin (current edition 1985).

Sherif, M. (1956, November). Experiments in group conflict. *Scientific American, 195*, 54–58.

Sherif, M., & Sherif, C. W. (1953). *Groups in harmony and in tension.* New York, NY: Harper & Row.

Sherman, G. D., & Haidt, J. (2011). Cuteness and disgust: The humanizing and dehumanizing effects of emotion. *Emotion Review, 3*, 245–251.

Shields, S. A. (1991). Gender in the psychology of emotion: A selective research review. In K. T. Strongman (Ed.), *International Review of Studies in Emotion* (Vol. 1, pp. 227–245). Chichester, UK: Wiley.

Shields, S. A. (2005). The politics of emotion in everyday life: "Appropriate" emotion and claims on identity. *Review of General Psychology, 9*, 3–15.

Shields, S. A. (2002). *Speaking from the heart: Gender and the social meaning of emotion.* Cambridge, MA: Cambridge University Press.

Shikibu, M. (c.1000). *The tale of Genji* (R. Tyler, Trans.). New York, NY: Viking Penguin (2001).

Shiota, M. N. Campos, B. C., Gonzaga, G.C., Keltner, D., & Peng, K (2010). I love you but . . . : Cultural differences in emotional complexity during interaction with a romantic partner. *Cognition and Emotion, 24*(5), 786–799.

Shiota, M. N., Keltner, D., & John, O. P. (2006). Positive emotion dispositions differentially associated with Big Five personality and attachment style. *Journal of Positive Psychology, 1*(2), 61–71.

Shokonoff, J. P., Boyce, W. T., & McEwen, B. S. (2009). Neuroscience, molecular biology and the childhood roots of health disparities: Building a new framework for health promotion and disease prevention. *Journal of the American Medical Association, 301*(21), 2252–2259.

Shrout, P. E., Link, B. G., Dohrenwend, B. P., Skodal, A. E., Stueve, A., & Mirtznik, J. (1989). Characterizing life events as risk factors for depression: The role of fateful loss events. *Journal of Abnormal Psychology, 98*, 460–467.

Shweder, R. (1990). In defense of moral realism: Reply to Gabannesch. *Child Development, 61*, 2060–2067.

Shweder, R. A., & Haidt, J. (2000). The cultural psychology of the emotions: Ancient and new. In M. Lewis & J. M. Haviland-Jones (Eds.), *Handbook of emotions* (2nd ed., pp. 397–414). New York, NY: Guilford.

Shweder, R. A., Much, N. C., Mahapatra, M., & Park, L. (1997). The "big three" of morality (autonomy, community, divinity), and the "big three" explanations of suffering. In A. Brandt & P. Rozin (Eds.), *Morality and health* (pp. 119–169). New York, NY: Routledge.

Sibley, C., & Ahlquist, J. E. (1984). The phylogeny of the hominid primates, as indicated by DNA–RNA hybridization. *Journal of Molecular Evolution, 20*, 2–15.

Siegle, G. J., Steinhauer, S. R., Thase, M. E., Stenger, V. A., & Carter, C. S. (2002). Can't shake that feeling: Event-related fMRI assessment of sustained amygdala activity in response to emotional information in depressed individuals. *Biological Psychiatry, 51*, 693–707.

Siegman, A. W., Townsend, S. T., Civilek, A. C., et al. (2000). Antagonistic behavior, dominance, hostility, and coronary heart disease. *Psychosomatic Medicine, 62*, 248–257.

Sijtsema, J. J., Ojanen, T., Veenstra, R., Lindenberg, S., Hawley, P. H., & Little, T. D. (2009). Forms and functions of aggression in adolescent friendship selection and influence: A longitudinal social network analysis. *Social Development, 19*, 515–34.

Silk, J. B., Alberts, S. C., & Altmann, J. (2003). Social bonds of female baboons enhance infant survival. *Science, 302*, 1231–1234.

Silk, J. S., Sessa, F. M., Morris, A. S., Steinberg, L., & Avenevoli, S. (2004). Neighborhood cohesion as a buffer against hostile maternal parenting. *Journal of Family Psychology, 18*, 120–134.

Simon, H. A. (1967). Motivational and emotional controls of cognition. *Psychological Review, 74*, 29–39.

Simon-Thomas, E., Godzik, J., Castel, E., Antonenko, O., Ponz, A., Kogan, A., & Keltner, D. (2011). An fMRI study of caring *vs* self-focus during induced compassion and pride. *Social and Cognitive Affective Neuroscience*, *7*(6), 635–648.

Simon-Thomas, E. R., Keltner, D. J., Sauter, D., Sinicropi-Yao, L., & Abramson, A. (2009). The voice conveys specific emotions: Evidence from vocal burst displays. *Emotion*, *9*, 838–846.

Simpson, J. A., & Kenrick, D. T. (1998). *Evolutionary social psychology*. Hillsdale, NJ: Lawrence Erlbaum.

Singer, J. A., & Salovey, P. (1993). *The remembered self: Emotion and memory in personality*. New York, NY: Free Press.

Singer, J. A., & Singer, J. L. (1992). Transference in psychotherapy and daily life: Implications of current memory and social cognition research. In J. W. Barron, M. N. Eagle, & D. L. Wolinsky (Eds.), *Interface of psychoanalysis and psychology* (pp. 516–538). Washington, DC: American Psychological Association.

Singer, T., Seymour, B., O'Doherty, J., Kaube, H., Dolan, R. J., & Frith, C. (2004). Empathy for pain involves the affective but not sensory components of pain. *Science*, *303*, 1157–1162.

Singh, D., Dixson, B. J., Jessop, T. S., Morgan, B., & Dixson, A. F. (2010). Cross-cultural consensus for waist-hip ratio and women's attractiveness. *Ethology and Sociobiology*, *31*, 176–181.

Singh, L., Morgan, J. L., & Best, C. T. (2002). Infants' listening preferences: Baby talk or happy talk? *Infancy*, *3*(3), 365–394.

Skarin, K. (1977). Cognitive and contextual determinants of stranger fear in six- and eleven-month-old infants. *Child Development*, *48*(2), 537–544.

Slade, A. (2005). Parental reflective functioning: An introduction. *Attachment & Human Development*, *7*(3), 269–281.

Slade, A., Grienenberger, J., Bernbach, E., Levy, D., & Locker, A. (2005). Maternal reflective functioning, attachment, and the transmission gap: A preliminary study. *Attachment & Human Development*, *7*(3), 283–298.

Slater, A., Bremner, G., Johnson, S. P., Sherwood, P., Hayes, R., & Brown, E. (2000). Newborn infants' preference for attractive faces: The role of internal and external facial features. *Infancy*, *1*(2), 265–274.

Slater, A., & Lewis, M. (2007). *Introduction to infant development* (2nd ed.). New York, NY: Oxford University Press.

Sloane, R. B., Staples, F. R., Cristol, A. H., Yorkston, N. J., & Whipple, K. (1975). *Psychotherapy versus behavior therapy*. Cambridge, MA: Harvard University Press.

Slopen, N., Fitzmaurice, G., Williams, D. R., & Gilman, S. E. (2010). Poverty, food insecurity, and the behavior for childhood internalizing and externalizing disorder. *Journal of the Academy of Child and Adolescent Psychiatry*, *49*(5), 444–452.

Smillie, L. D., Pickering, A. D., & Jackson, C. J. (2006). The new reinforcement sensitivity theory: Implications for personality measurement. *Personality and Social Psychology Review: An Official Journal of the Society for Personality and Social Psychology, Inc.*, *10*(4), 320–335.

Smit, Y., Hulbers, M.J.H., Ioannidis, J. P. A., van Dyck, R., van Tilberg, W., & Artz, A. (2012). The effectiveness of long-term psychoanalytic psychotherapy: A meta-analysis of randomized controlled trials. *Clinical Psychology Review*, *32*, 81–92.

Smith, A. (1759). *The theory of moral sentiments*. Oxford, UK: Oxford University Press (1976).

Smith, C., & Ellsworth, P. (1985). Patterns of cognitive appraisal in emotion. *Journal of Personality and Social Psychology*, *48*, 813–838.

Smith, E. R. (1993). Social identity and social emotions: Toward new conceptualizations of prejudice. In D. M. Mackie & D. L. Hamilton (Eds.), *Affect, cognition, and stereotyping* (pp. 297–315). New York, NY: Academic Press.

Smith, M. L., Glass, G. V., & Miller, T. I. (1980). *The benefits of psychotherapy*. Baltimore, MD: Johns Hopkins University Press.

Smith, J. M., Alloy, L. B., & Abramson, L. Y. (2006). Rumination, hopelessness and suicidal ideation: Multiple pathways to self-injurious thinking. *Suicide and Life-Threatening Behavior 36*(4), 443–454.

Smith, T. W., & Ruiz, J. M. (2002). Psychosocial influences on the development and course of coronary heart disease: Current status and implications for research and practice. *Journal of Consulting and Clinical Psychology*, *70*, 548–568.

Smoski, M. J., & Bachorowski, J.-A. (2003). Antiphonal laughter between friends and strangers. *Cognition and Emotion*, *17*, 327–340.

Snowdon, C. T. (2003). Expression of emotion in non-human animals. In R. Davidson, K. Scherer, & H. H. Goldsmith (Eds.), *Handbook of affective sciences* (pp. 457–480). London, UK: Oxford University Press.

Snyder, C. R., & Heinze, L. S. (2005). Forgiveness as a mediator of the relationship between PTSD and hostility in survivors of childhood abuse. *Cognition and Emotion, 19*, 413–431.

Snyder, J., Stoolmiller, M., & Wilson, M. (2003). Child anger regulation, parental responses to children's anger displays, and early child antisocial behavior. *Social Development, 12*, 335–360.

Sober, E., & Wilson, D. S. (1998). *Unto others: The evolution and psychology of unselfish behavior.* Cambridge, MA: Harvard University Press.

Sogon, S., & Masutani, M. (1989). Identification of emotion from body movements. *Psychological Reports, 65*, 35–46.

Solomon, R. C. (1977). *The passions.* New York, NY: Anchor.

Solomon, R. C. (2004). Emotions, thoughts, and feelings: Emotions as engagements with the world. In R. C. Solomon (Ed.), *Thinking about feeling: Contemporary philosophers on emotions* (pp. 76–88). New York, NY: Oxford University Press.

Solomon, R. C. (2007). *True to our feelings: What our emotions are really telling us.* New York, NY: Oxford University Press.

Solomon, Z., & Bromet, E. (1982). The role of social factors in affective disorder: An assessment of the vulnerability model of Brown and his colleagues. *Psychological Medicine, 12*, 125–130.

Sorabji, R. (2000). *Emotion and peace of mind: From Stoic agitation to Christian temptation.* Oxford, UK: Oxford University Press.

Sorce, J. F., Emde, R. N., Campos, J., & Klinnert, M. D. (1985). Maternal emotional signaling: Its effect on the visual cliff behavior of 1-year-olds. *Developmental Psychiatry, 21*(1), 195–200.

Soto, J., Perez, C. R., Kim, Y.-H., Lee, E. A., & Minnick, M. R. (2011). Is expressive suppression always associated with poorer psychological functioning? A cross-cultural comparison between European Americans and Hong Kong Chinese. *Emotion, 11*, 1450–1455.

Spangler, G., Maier, U., Geserick, B., & von Wahlert, A. (2010). The influence of attachment representation on parental perception and interpretation of infant emotions:

A multilevel approach. *Developmental Psychobiology, 52*(5), 411–423.

Spielberger, C. D. (1983). *State-Trait Anxiety Inventory for Adults.* Palo Alto, CA: Mind Garden.

Spielberger, C. D. (1996). *Manual for the State-Trait Anger Expression Inventory (STAXI).* Odessa, FL: Psychological Assessment Resources.

Spinoza, B. (1661–1675). *On the improvement of the understanding, The ethics, and Correspondence* (R.H.M. Elwes, Trans.). New York, NY: Dover (current edition 1955).

Spock, B. (1945). *The common sense book of baby and child care.* New York, NY: Dell, Sloan & Pearce.

Sroufe, A. (2009). The concept of development in developmental psychopathology. *Child Development Perspectives, 3*(3), 178–183.

Sroufe, A. (2005). Attachment and development: A prospective, longitudinal study from birth to adulthood. *Attachment & Human Development, 7*, 349–367.

Sroufe, L. A. (1997). Psychopathology as an outcome of development. *Development and Psychopathology, 9*, 251–268.

Stack, D. M. (2001). The salience of touch and physical contact during infancy: Unraveling some of the mysteries of the somesthetic sense. In G. Bremner & A. Fogel (Eds.), *Blackwell handbook of infant development* (pp. 351–378). Malden, MA: Blackwell.

Stack, E. C., Balakrishnan, R., Numan, M. J., & Numan, M. (2002). A functional neuroanatomical investigation of the role of the medial preoptic area in neural circuits regulating maternal behavior. *Behavioral Brain Research, 131*(1–2), 17–36.

Staines, J. (2004). Compassion in the public sphere of Milton and King Charles. In G. K. Paston, K. Rowe, & M. Floyd-Wilson (Eds.), *Reading the early modern passions: Essays in the cultural history of emotion* (pp. 89–110). Philadelphia: University of Pennsylvania Press.

Stanislavski, C. (1965). *An actor prepares* (E. R. Habgood, Trans.). New York, NY: Theater Arts Books.

Stanovich, K. E. (2004). *The robot's rebellion: Finding meaning in the age of Darwin.* Chicago, IL: University of Chicago Press.

Starkstein, S. E., & Robinson, R. G. (1991). The role of the frontal lobes in affective disorder following stroke. In H. S. Levin, H. M. Eisenberg, & A. L. Benton (Eds.),

Frontal lobe function and dysfunction (pp. 288–303). New York, NY: Oxford University Press.

Stearns, P. N., & Haggarty, T. (1991). The role of fear: Transitions in American emotional standards for children, 1850–1950. *The American Historical Review, 96*, 63–94.

Stein, M. B., Simmons, A. N., Feinstein, J. S., & Paulus, M. P. (2007). Increased amygdala and insula activation during emotion processing in anxiety-prone subjects. *American Journal of Psychiatry, 164*(2), 318–327.

Stein, N., Folkman, S., Trabasso, T., & Richards, T. A. (1997). Appraisal and goal processes as predictors of psychological well-being in bereaved caregivers. *Journal of Personality and Social Psychology, 72*, 872–884.

Stein, N. L., Liwag, M., & Trabasso, T. (1995). *Remembering the distant past: Understanding and remembering emotional events.* Paper presented to the Biennial Meeting of the Society for Research in Child Development. Indianapolis, March 30–April 2.

Stein, N. L., Trabasso, T., & Liwag, M. (1994). The Rashomon phenomenon: Personal frames and future-oriented appraisals in memory for emotional events. In M. M. Haith, J. B. Benson, R. J. Roberts, & B. F. Pennington (Eds.), *Future oriented processes.* Chicago, IL: University of Chicago Press.

Steiner, J. E., Glaser, D., Hawilo, M. E., & Berridge, K. C. (2001). Comparative expression of hedonic impact: Affective reactions to taste by human infants and other primates. *Neuroscience and Biobehavioral Reviews, 25* (1), 53–74.

Stemmler, G. (2003). Methodological considerations in the psychophysiological study of emotion. In R. J. Davidson, K. R. Scherer, & H. H. Goldsmith (Eds.), *Handbook of affective sciences* (pp. 225–255). New York, NY: Oxford University Press.

Stemmler, G., & Wacker, J. (2010). Personality, emotion, and individual differences in physiological responses. *Biological Psychology, 84*, 541–551.

Stenberg, C. R., Campos, J. J., & Emde, R. N. (1983). The facial expression of anger in seven-month-old infants. *Child Development, 54*(1), 178–184.

Sterba, S. K., Prinstein, M. J., & Cox, M. J. (2007). Trajectories of internalizing problems across childhood: Heterogeneity, external validity, and gender differences. *Development and Psychopathology, 19*(2), 345.

Stern, D. (1985). *The interpersonal world of the infant.* New York, NY: Basic Books.

Sternberg, R. J. (1997). Construct validation of a triangular love scale. *European Journal of Social Psychology, 27*, 313–335.

Stevenson, R. L. (1886). *Dr Jekyll and Mr Hyde.* Harmondsworth: Penguin (current edition 1979).

Stewart, R. E., & Chambless, D. L. (2009). Cognitive-behavioral therapy for adult anxiety disorders in clinical practice: A meta-analysis of effectiveness studies. *Journal of Consulting and Clinical Psychology, 77*, 595–606.

Stewart, M. E., Ebmeier, K. P., & Deary, I. J. (2005). Personality correlates of happiness and sadness: EPQ-R and TPQ compared. *Personality and Individual Differences, 38*, 1085–1096.

Stice, E. (2002). Risk and maintenance factors for eating pathology: A meta-analytic review. *Psychological Bulletin, 128*(5), 825–848.

Stice, E., Ragan, J., & Randall, P. (2004). Prospective relations between social support and depression: Differential direction of effects for parent and peer support. *Journal of Abnormal Psychology, 113*, 155–159.

Stipek, D., Recchia, S., & McClintic, S. (1992). Self-evaluation in young children. *Monographs of the Society for Research in Child Development, 57*(1), 1–84.

Storbeck, J., & Clore, G. L. (2008). Affective arousal as information: How affective arousal influences judgments, learning, and memory. *Social and Personality Psychology Compass, 2*, 1824–1843.

Strachey, J. (1934). The nature of the therapeutic action in psychoanalysis. *International Journal of Psychoanalysis, 15*, 127–159.

Strack, F., Martin, L. L., & Stepper, S. (1988). Inhibiting and facilitating conditions of the human smile: A nonobtrusive test of the facial feedback hypothesis. *Journal of Personality and Social Psychology, 54*, 768–777.

Strakowski, S. M., DelBello, M. P., Sax, K. W., Zimmerman, M. E., Shear, P. K., Hawkins, J. M., & Larson, E. R. (1999). Brain magnetic resonance imaging of structural abnormalities in bipolar disorder. *Archives of General Psychiatry, 56*, 254–260.

Stretton, M. S., & Salovey, P. (1998). Cognitive and affective components of hypochondriacal concerns. In W. F. Flack

& J. D. Laird (Eds.), *Emotions in psychopathology: Theory and research* (pp. 265–279). New York, NY: Oxford University Press.

Striano, T., Brennan, P. A., & Vanman, E. J. (2002). Maternal depressive symptoms and 6-month-old infants' sensitivity to facial expressions. *Infancy, 3*(1), 115–126.

Striano, T., Henning, A., & Stahl, D. (2005). Sensitivity to social contingencies between 1 and 3 months of age. *Developmental Science, 8*(6), 509–518.

Stringer, C., & Gamble, C. (1993). *In search of the Neanderthals.* New York, NY: Thames and Hudson.

Stroebe, W., & Stroebe, M. S. (1996). The social psychology of social support. In E. T. Higgins & A. W. Kruglanski (Eds.), *Social psychology: Handbook of basic principles* (pp. 597–521). New York, NY: Guilford.

Strohminger, N., Lewis, R. L., & Meyer, D. E. (2011). Divergent effects of different positive emotions on moral judgment. *Cognition, 119*, 295–300.

Stroop, J. R. (1935). Studies of interference in serial verbal reactions. *Journal of Experimental Psychology, 18*, 643–662.

Stroud, C. B., Davila, J., Hammen, C. L., & Vrshek-Schallhorn, S. (2011). Severe and nonsevere events in first onsets versus recurrences of depression: Evidence for stress sensitization. *Journal of Abnormal Psychology, 120*, 142–154.

Sturgeon, D., Turpin, D., Kuipers, L., Berkowitz, R., & Leff, J. (1984). Psychophysiological responses of schizophrenic patients to high and low Expressed Emotion relatives: A follow-up study. *British Journal of Psychiatry, 145*, 62–69.

Stuss, D. T., & Benson, D. F. (1984). Neuropsychological studies of the frontal lobes. *Psychological Bulletin, 95*, 3–28.

Stylianou, S. (2003). Measuring crime seriousness perceptions: What have we learned and what else do we want to know? *Journal of Criminal Justice, 31*, 37–56.

Suh, E., Diener, E., Oishi, S., & Triandis, H. C. (1998). The shifting basis of life satisfaction judgments across cultures: Emotions versus norms. *Journal of Personality and Social Psychology, 74*, 482–493.

Sullivan, H. S. (1953). *The interpersonal theory of psychiatry.* New York, NY: Norton.

Sullivan, P. F., Neale, M. C., & Kendler, K. S. (2000). The genetic epidemiology of major depression: A review and a meta-analysis. *American Journal of Psychiatry, 157*, 1552–1562.

Sulloway, F. J. (1979). *Freud, biologist of the mind: Beyond the psychoanalytic legend.* New York, NY: Basic Books.

Suls, J., & Martin, R. (2005). The daily life of the garden-variety neurotic: Reactivity, stressor exposure, mood spillover, and maladaptive coping. *Journal of Personality, 73*(6), 1485–1510.

Sutton, S. K., & Davidson, R. J. (1997). Prefrontal brain asymmetry: A biological substrate of the behavioral approach and inhibition systems. *Psychological Science, 8*, 204–210.

Svejda, M. J., Campos, J. J., & Emde, R. N. (1980). Mother–infant "bonding": Failure to generalize. *Child Development, 56*, 775–779.

Svejda, M. J., Pannabecker, B. J., & Emde, R. N. (1982). Parent-to-infant attachment: A critique of the the early "bonding" model. In R. N. Emde & R. J. Harmon (Eds.), *The development of attachment and affiliative systems* (pp. 83–93). New York, NY: Plenum.

Swain, J. E. (2010). The human parental brain: In vivo neuroimaging. Progress in Neuropsychopharmacology. *Biological Psychiatry, 35*, 1242–1254.

Szechtman, H., & Woody, E. (2004). Obsessive-compulsive disorder as a disturbance of security motivation. *Psychological Review, 111*, 111–127.

Tajfel, H. (1982). Social psychology of intergroup relations. *Annual Review of Psychology, 33*, 1–39.

Tajfel, H., & Turner, J. (1979). An integrative theory of intergroup conflict. In W. G. Austin & S. Worchel (Eds.), *The social psychology of intergroup relations.* Monterey, CA: Brooks Cole.

Tamir, M., Mitchell, C., & Gross, J. J. (2008). Hedonic and instrumental motives in anger regulation. *Psychological Science, 19*, 324–328.

Tan, E. S. (1996). *Emotion and the structure of film: Film as an emotion machine.* Mahwah, NJ: Erlbaum.

Tangney, J. P. (1990). Assessing individual differences in proneness to shame and guilt: Development of the self-conscious affect and attribution inventory. *Journal of Personality and Social Psychology, 59*, 102–111.

Tangney, J. P. (1992). Situational determinants of shame and guilt in young adulthood. *Personality and Social Psychology Bulletin, 18*, 199–206.

Tangney, J. P., Miller, R. S., Flicker, L., & Barlow, D. H. (1996). Are shame, guilt, and embarrassment distinct emotions? *Journal of Personality and Social Psychology, 70*, 1256–1264.

Tannen, D. (1991). *You just don't understand: Women and men in conversation.* New York, NY: Ballantine.

Tapias, M., Glaser, J., Vasquez, K. V., Keltner, D., & Wickens, T. (2007). Emotion and prejudice: Specific emotions toward outgroups. *Group Processes and InterGroup Relations, 10*, 27–41.

Tarrier, N., Barrowclough, C., Porceddu, K., & Watts, S. (1988). The assessment of psychophysiological reactivity to the Expressed Emotion of the relatives of schizophrenic patients. *British Journal of Psychiatry, 152*, 618–624.

Taumoepeau, M., & Ruffman, T. (2006). Mother and infant talk about mental states relates to desire language and emotion understanding. *Child Development, 77*(2), 465–481.

Taumoepeau, M., & Ruffman, T. (2008). Stepping stones to others' minds: Maternal talk relates to child mental state language and emotion understanding at 15, 24, and 33 months. *Child Development, 79*(2), 284–268.

Tay, L., & Diener, E. (2011). Needs and subjective well-being around the world. *Journal of Personality and Social Psychology, 101*, 354–365.

Taylor, G. J., Bagby, R. M., & Parker, J. D. A. (1991). The alexithymia construct: A potential program for psychosomatic medicine. *Psychosomatics, 32*, 153–164.

Taylor, G. J., Bagby, R. M., & Parker, J.D.A. (1997). *Disorders of affect regulation: Alexithymia in medical and psychiatric illness.* Cambridge, MA: Cambridge University Press.

Taylor, S. E., Burklund, L. J., Eisenberger, N. I., Lehman, B. J., Hilmert, C. J., & Lieberman, M. D. (2008). Neural bases of moderation of cortisol stress responses by psychosocial resources. *Journal of Personality and Social Psychology, 95*, 197–211.

Taylor, S. E., Klein, L. C., Lewis, B. P., Gruenewal, T. L., Gurung, R.A.R., & Updegraff, J. A. (2000). Biobehavioral responses to stress in females: Tend-and-befriend, not fight-or-flight. *Psychological Review, 107*, 411–429.

Teasdale, J. (1988). Cognitive vulnerability to persistent depression. *Cognition and Emotion, 2*, 247–274.

Thagard, P., & Nerb, J. (2002). Emotional gestalts: Appraisal, change, and the dynamics of affect. *Personality and Social Psychology Review, 6*(4), 274–282.

Thiruchselvam, R., Blechert, J., Sheppes, G., Rydstrom, A., & Gross, J. J. (2011). The temporal dynamics of emotion regulation: An EEG study of distraction and reappraisal. *Biological Psychology, 87*, 84–92.

Thirwall, K., & Creswell, C. (2010). 48. *Behaviour Research and Therapy, 48*, 1041–1046.

Thoits, P. A. (1986). Social support as coping assistance. *Journal of Consulting and Clinical Psychology, 54*, 416–423.

Thoits, P. A. (1995). Identity-relevant events and psychological symptoms: A cautionary tale. *Journal of Health and Social Behavior, 36*, 72–82.

Thomas, A., & Chess, S. (1977). *Temperament and development.* New York, NY: Brunner/Mazel.

Thomas, E. M. (1989). *The harmless people* (Rev. ed.). New York, NY: Random House.

Thompson, R. A. (1994). Emotion regulation: A theme in search of definition. *Monographs of the Society for Research in Child Development (Serial No. 240), 59*(2–3), 25–52.

Thompson, R. A. (Ed.). (2007). *Handbook of emotion regulation.* New York, NY: Guilford Press.

Thompson, R. A. (2008). Early attachment and later development: Familiar questions, new answers. In J. Cassidy & P.R. Shaver (Eds.), *Handbook of attachment* (2nd ed., pp. 348–365). New York, NY: Guilford.

Thompson, R. A., Lewis, M. D., & Calkins, S. D. (2008). Reassessing emotion regulation. *Child Development Perspectives, 2*(3), 124–131.

Tiedens, L., & Leach, C. W. (Eds.). (2004). *The social life of emotions.* New York, NY: Cambridge University Press.

Tiedens, L. Z. (2000). Powerful emotions: The vicious cycle of social status positions and emotions, *Emotions in the workplace: Research, theory, and practice* (pp 72–81). Westport, CT: Quorum Books/Greenwood.

Tiedens, L. Z. (2001). Anger and advancement versus sadness and subjugation: The effect of negative emotion expressions on social status conferral. *Journal of Personality & Social Psychology, 80*(1), 86–94.

Tiedens, L. Z., Ellsworth, P.C., & Mesquita, B. (2000). Stereotypes about sentiments and status: Emotional expectations for high- and low-status group members. *Personality and Social Psychology Bulletin, 26*(5), 560–574.

Tiedens, L. Z., & Fragale, A. R. (2003). Power moves: Complementarity in submissive and dominant nonverbal behavior. *Journal of Personality and Social Psychology, 84,* 558–568.

Tillitski, C. J. (1990). A meta-analysis of estimated effect sizes for group versus individual versus control treatments. *International Journal of Group Psychotherapy, 40,* 215–224.

Tinbergen, N. (1951). *The study of instinct.* Oxford, UK: Oxford University Press.

Tizard, B., & Hodges, J. (1978). The effect of early institutional rearing on the development of eight year old children. *Journal of Child Psychology and Psychiatry, 19*(2), 99–118.

Tomasello, M. (1999). *The cultural origins of human cognition.* Cambridge, MA: Harvard University Press.

Tomasello, M. (2008). *Origins of human communication.* Cambridge, MA: MIT Press.

Tomasello, M. (2010). Human culture in evolutionary perspective. *Advances in culture and psychology, 1*(7), 5–52.

Tomasello, M., Carpenter, M., Call, J., Behne, T., & Moll, H. (2005). Understanding and sharing intentions: The origins of cultural cognition. *Behavioral and brain sciences, 28*(5), 675–690.

Tomkins, S. S. (1962). *Affect, imagery, consciousness: Vol. 1. The positive affects.* New York, NY: Springer.

Tomkins, S. S. (1963). *Affect, imagery, consciousness: Vol. 2. The negative affects.* New York, NY: Springer.

Tomkins, S. S. (1970). Affect as the primary motivational system. In M. B. Arnold (Ed.), *Feelings and emotions: The Loyola symposium* (pp. 101–110). New York, NY: Academic Press.

Tomkins, S. S. (1978). Script theory: Differential magnification of affects. In H. E. Howe & R. A. Dienstbier (Eds.), *Nebraska Symposium on Motivation* (Vol. 26, pp. 201–236). Lincoln: University of Nebraska Press.

Tomkins, S. S. (1979). Script theory: Differential magnification of affects. In H. E. Howe & R. A. Dienstbier (Eds.), *Nebraska symposium on motivation, 1978* (pp. 201–236). Lincoln: University of Nebraska Press.

Tomkins, S. S. (1995). *Exploring affect: The selected writings of Sylvan S. Tomkins* (E. V. Demos, Ed.). New York, NY: Cambridge University Press.

Tomkins, S. S. (1984). Affect theory. In K. Scherer & P. Ekman (Eds.), *Approaches to emotion* (pp. 163–195). Hillsdale, NJ: Erlbaum.

Tong, E. M. W. (2010). Personality influences in appraisal emotion relationships: The role of neuroticism. *Journal of Personality, 78,* 393–417.

Tooby, J., & Cosmides, L. (1990). The past explains the present: Emotional adaptations and the structure of ancestral environments. *Ethology and Sociobiology, 11,* 375–424.

Tracy, J. L., & Matsumoto, D. (2008). The spontaneous display of pride and shame: Evidence for biologically innate nonverbal displays. *Proceedings of the National Academy of Sciences, 105,* 11655–11660.

Tracy, J. L., & Robins, R. W. (2004). Show your pride: Evidence for a discrete emotion expression. *Psychological Science, 15,* 94–97.

Tracy, J. L., & Robins, R. W. (2007). Emerging insights into the nature and function of pride. *Current Directions in Psychological Science, 16,* 147–150.

Tranel, D. (1994). "Acquired sociopathy?": The development of sociopathic behavior following focal brain damage. In D. Fowles (Ed.), *Progress in experimental personality and psychopathology research.* New York, NY: Springer.

Tranel, D., & Damasio, H. (1994). Neuroanatomical correlates of electrodermal skin conductance responses. *Psychophysiology, 31,* 427–438.

Triandis, H. (1972). *The analysis of subjective culture.* New York, NY: Wiley.

Triandis, H. C. (1989). The self and social behavior in differing cultural contexts. *Psychological Review, 96,* 269–289.

Triandis, H. C. (1994). *Culture and social behavior.* New York, NY: McGraw-Hill.

Triandis, H. C. (1995). *Individualism and collectivism.* Boulder, CO: Westview Press.

Trivers, R. L. (1971). The evolution of reciprocal altruism. *Quarterly Review of Biology, 46,* 35–57.

Tronick, E. Z. (1989). Emotions and emotional communications in infants. *American Psychologist, 44,* 112–119.

Tropp, M. (1976). *Mary Shelley's monster.* Boston, MA: Houghton Mifflin.

Tsai, J. L. (2007). Ideal affect: Cultural causes and behavioral consequences. *Perspectives on Psychological Science, 2,* 242–259.

Tsai, J. L., & Chentsova-Dutton, Y. (2002). Understanding depression across cultures. In I. H. Gotlib & C. L. Hammen (Eds.), *Handbook of depression* (pp. 467–491). New York, NY: Guilford.

Tsai, J. L., Chentsova-Dutton, Y., Friere-Bebeau, L. H., & Przymus, D. (2002). Emotional expression and physiology in European Americans and Hmong Americans. *Emotion*, 2, 380–397.

Tsai, J. L., Knutson, B., & Fung, H. H. (2006). Cultural variation in affect valuation. *Journal of Personality and Social Psychology*, 90, 288–307.

Tsai, J. L., & Levenson, R. W. (1997). Cultural influences on emotional responding: Chinese American and European American dating couples during interpersonal conflict. *Journal of Cross-Cultural Psychology*, 28, 600–625.

Tsai, J. L., Levenson, R. W., & Carstensen, L. L. (2000). Autonomic, expressive, and subjective responses to emotional films in older and younger Chinese American and European American adults. *Psychology and Aging*, 15, 684–693.

Tsai, J. L., Miao, F., & Seppala, E. (2007). Good feelings in Christianity and Buddhism: Religious differences in ideal affect. *Personality and Social Psychology Bulletin*, 33, 409–421.

Tsai, J. L., Simenova, D., & Watanabe, J. (2004). Somatic and social: Chinese Americans talk about emotion. *Personality and Social Psychology Bulletin*, 30, 1226–1238.

Tsang, J., McCullough, M. E., & Fincham, F. D. (2006). The longitudinal association between forgiveness and relationship closeness and commitment. *Journal of Social and Clinical Psychology*, 25, 448–472.

Tsukiura, T., & Cabeza, R. (2011). Shared brain activity for aesthetic and moral judgments: Implications for the Beauty-is-Good stereotype. *Social, Cognitive and Affective Neuroscience*, 6, 138–148.

Turner, R. A., Altemus, M., Enos, T., Cooper, B., & McGuinness, T. (1999). Preliminary research on plasma oxytocin in normal cycling women: Investigating emotion and interpersonal distress. *Psychiatry: Interpersonal & Biological Processes*, 62, 97–113.

Turner, R. A., Altemus, M., Yip, D. N., Kupferman, E., Fletcher, D., Bostrom, A., et al. (2002). Effects of emotion on oxytocin, prolactin, and ACTH in women. *Stress: The International Journal on the Biology of Stress*, 5, 269–276.

Turner, V. (1974). *Dramas, fields, and metaphors: Symbolic action in human society*. Ithaca, NY: Cornell University Press.

Uriguen, L., Arteta, D., Diez-Alarcia, R., Ferrer-Alcón, M., Diaz, A., et al. (2008). Gene expression patterns in brain cortex of three different animal models of depression. *Genes, Brain and Behavior*, 7, 649–658.

Uvnas-Moberg, K. (1994). Role of efferent and afferent vagal nerve activity during reproduction: Integrating function of oxytocin on metabolism and behaviour. *Psychoneuroendocrinology*, 19, 687–695.

Uvnas-Moberg, K. (1997). Physiological and endocrine effects of social contact. In C. S. Carter, I. I. Lederhendler, and B. Kirkpatrick (Eds.), *The integrative neurobiology of affiliation, Vol. 807* (pp. 146–163). New York, NY: New York Academy of Sciences.

Uvnas-Moberg, K. (1998). Oxytocin may mediate the benefits of positive social interaction and emotions. *Psychoneuroendocrinology*, 23(8), 819–835.

Vaccarino, F. J., Schiff, B. B., & Glickman, S. E. (1989). A biological view of reinforcement. In S. B. Klein & R. R. Mowrer (Eds.), *Contemporary learning theories*. Hillsdale, NJ: Erlbaum.

Vaish, A., Grossmann, T., & Woodward, A. (2008). Not all emotions are created equal: The negativity bias in social-emotional development. *Psychological Bulletin*, 134(3), 383–403.

Vaish, A., & Striano, T. (2004). Is visual reference necessary? Contributions of facial versus vocal cues in 12-month-olds' social referencing behavior. *Developmental Science*, 7(3), 261–269.

Vaish, A., & Warneken, F. (2011). Social cognitive contributors to young children's empathic and prosocial behavior. In J. Decety (Ed.), *Empathy from bench to bedside* (pp. 131–146). Cambridge, MA: MIT Press.

Valdesolo, P., & DeSteno, D. (2011). Synchrony and the social tuning of compassion. *Emotion*, 11, 262–266.

Van Bezooijen, R., Van Otto, S. A., & Heenan, T. A. (1983). Recognition of vocal dimensions of emotion: A three-nation study to identify universal characteristics. *Journal of Cross-Cultural Psychology*, 14, 387–406.

Van den Berghe, P. L. (1979). *Human family systems: An evolutionary view*. Amsterdam, The Netherlands: Elsevier.

van Dijk, C., de Jong, P. J., & Peters, M. L. (2009). The remedial value of blushing in the context of transgressions and mishaps. *Emotion, 9,* 287–291.

Van Egeren, L. A., Barratt, M. S., & Roach, M. A. (2001). Mother–infant responsiveness: Timing, mutual regulation, and interactional context. *Developmental Psychology, 37*(5), 684–697.

van Honk, J., Tuiten, A., de Haan, E., van, d. H., & Stam, H. (2001). Attentional biases for angry faces: Relationships to trait anger and anxiety. *Cognition & Emotion, 15*(3), 279–297.

van Ijzendoorn, M. H. (1995). Adult attachment representations, parental responsiveness, and infant attachment: A meta-analysis on the predictive validity of the Adult Attachment Interview. *Psychological Bulletin, 117,* 387–403.

van Ijzendoorn, M. H., Moran, G., Belsky, J., Pederson, D., Bakermans-Kranenburg, M., & Fisher, K. (2000). The similarity of siblings' attachments to their mother. *Child Development, 71*(4), 1086–98.

van Ijzendoorn, M., Schuengel, C., & Bakermans-Kranenburg, M. (1999). Disorganized attachment in early childhood: Meta-analysis of precursors, concomitants, and sequelae. *Development and Psychopathology, 11,* 225–249.

van Kleef, G. A., De Dreu, C.K.W., Pietroni, D., & Manstead, A.S.R. (2006). Power and emotion in negotiation: Power moderates the interpersonal effects of anger and happiness on concession making. *European Journal of Social Psychology: Special issue on social power, 36,* 557–581.

van Kleef, G. A., Homan, A. C., Beersma, B., & Van Knippenberg, D. (2010). On angry leaders and agreeable followers: How leaders' emotions and followers' personalities shape motivation and team performance. *Psychological Science, 12,* 1827–1834.

van Kleef, G. A., Oveis, C., van der Löwe, I., LuoKogan, A., Goetz, J., & Keltner, D. (2008). Power, distress, and compassion: Turning a blind eye to the suffering of others. *Psychological Science, 19,* 1315–1322.

Van Tol, M. J., Van der Wee, N.J.A., Van den Heuvel, O. A., Nielen, M.M.A., Demenscu, L. R., Aleman, A., et al. (2010). Regional brain volume in depression and anxiety disorders. *Archives of General Psychiatry, 67,* 1002–1011.

van't Wout, M., Chang, L. J., & Sanfey, A. G. (2010). The influence of emotion regulation on social-interactive decision-making. *Emotion, 10,* 815–821.

Vaughn, C. E., & Leff, J. P. (1976). The influence of family and social factors on the course of psychiatric illness: A comparison of schizophrenic and depressed patients. *British Journal of Psychiatry, 129,* 125–137.

Veblen, T. (1899). *The theory of the leisure class: An economic study of institutions.* New York, NY: Macmillan.

Vergara, C., & Roberts, J. E. (2011). Motivation and goal orientation in vulnerability to depression. *Cognition and Emotion, 25*(7), 1281–1290.

Vesga-López, O., Schneier, F., Wang, S., Heimberg, R. G., Shang-Min, L., et al. (2008). Gender differences in generalized anxiety disorder: Results from the national epidemiologic survey on alcohol and related conditions (NESARC). *Journal of Clinical Psychiatry, 69,* 1606–1616.

Visalberghi, E., & Sonetti, M. G. (1994). Lorenz's concept of aggression and recent primatological studies on aggressive and reconciliatory behaviors. *La Nuova Critica,* Nuova serie, 23–24, 57–67.

Von Uexküll, J. (1934). A stroll through the worlds of animals and men. In C. H. Schiller (Ed.), *Instinctive behavior: Development of a modern concept* (pp. 5–80). London, UK: Methuen (current edition 1957).

Vyasa. (c. 1500 BCE). *Mahabharata* (W. Buck, Trans.). Berkeley: University of California Press (current edition 1973).

Vygotsky, L. S. (1987). Emotions and their development in childhood. In R. W. Rieber & A. S. Carton (Eds.), *Collected works of L. S. Vygotsky* (Vol. 1, pp. 325–337). New York, NY: Plenum.

Wade, M., Prime, H., Browne, D., & Jenkins, J. M. (2011). A multilevel perspective on school readiness: Implications for programs and policy. In M. Boivin & K. Bierman (Eds.), *Promoting school readiness and early learning: The implications of developmental research for practice.* New York, NY: Guilford.

Wagenaar, W. A. (1986). My memory: A study of autobiographical memory over six years. *Cognitive Psychology, 18,* 225–252.

Wagner, H. L., MacDonald, C. J., & Manstead, A.S.R. (1986). Communication of individual emotions by spontaneous facial expression. *Journal of Personality and Social Psychology, 50,* 737–743.

Wakschlag, L. S., Pickett, K. E., Cook, E., et al. (2002). Maternal smoking during pregnancy and severe antisocial behavior in offspring: A review. *American Journal of Public Health*, *92*, 966–974.

Waldemann, M. R., & Dieterich, J. H. (2007). Throwing a bomb on a person versus throwing a person on a bomb. *Psychological Science*, *18*, 247–253.

Walker, S. P., Wachs, T. D., Gardner, J. M., Lozoff, B., Wasserman, G. A., Pollitt, E., Carter, J. A., & the International Child Development Steering Group (2007). Child development: Risk factors for adverse outcomes in developing countries. *The Lancet*, *369*, 145–157.

Wallbott, H. G., & Scherer, K. (1986). How universal and specific is emotional experience? Evidence from 27 countries on five continents. *Social Science Information*, *25*, 763–795.

Wallis, J. D. (2007). Orbitofrontal cortex and its contribution to decision-making. *Annual Review of Neuroscience*, *30*, 31–56.

Wang, Q. (2001). "Did you have fun?" American and Chinese mother-child conversations about shared emotional experiences. *Cognitive Development*, *16*(2), 693–715.

Wankerl, M., Wüst, S., & Otte, C. (2010). Current developments and controversies: Does the serotonin transporter gene-linked polymorphic region (5-HTTLPR) modulate the association between stress and depression? *Current Opinion in Psychiatry*, *23*, 582–587.

Warneken, F., Chen, F., & Tomasello, M. (2006). Cooperative activities in young children and chimpanzees. *Child Development*, *77*, 640–663.

Warneken, F., & Tomasello, M. (2006). Altruistic helping in human infants and young chimpanzees. *Science*, *311* (5765), 1301–1303.

Warneken, F., & Tomasello, M. (2009). The roots of human altruism. *British Journal of Psychology*, *100*, 455–471.

Washburn, S. L. (1991). Biochemical insights into our ancestry. In M. H. Robinson & L. Tiger (Eds.), *Man and beast revisited* (pp. 61–73) Washington, DC: Smithsonian Institute Press.

Waters, E., Merrick, S., Treboux, D., Crowell, J., & Albersheim, L. (2000). Attachment security in infancy and early adulthood: A twenty-year longitudinal study. *Child Development*, *71*, 684–689.

Watson, D. (1988). Intraindividual and interindividual analyses of positive and negative affect: Their relation to health complaints, perceived stress, and daily activities. *Journal of Personality and Social Psychology*, *54*(6), 1020–1030.

Watson, D., Clark, L., McIntyre, C. W., & Hamaker, S. (1992). Affect, personality, and social activity. *Journal of Personality and Social Psychology*, *63*(6), 1011–1025.

Watson, D., Clark, L. A., & Tellegen, A. (1988). Development and validation of brief measures of positive and negative affect: The PANAS scales. *Journal of Personality and Social Psychology*, *54*, 1063–1070.

Watson, J. C., Goldman, R. N., & Greenberg, L. S. (2007). *Case studies in emotion-focused treatment of depression: A comparison of good and poor outcome.* Washington, DC: American Psychological Association.

Watson J. C., Gordon, L. B., Stermac L., et al. (2003). Comparing the effectiveness of process-experiential with cognitive-behavioral psychotherapy in the treatment of depression. *Journal of Consulting and Clinical Psychology*, *71*, 773–781.

Watzke, B., Rüddel, H., Jürgenson, R., Koch, U., Kriston, L., Grothgar, B., et al. (2010). Effectiveness of systematic treatment selection for psychodynamic and cognitive–behavioural therapy: Randomised controlled trial in routine mental healthcare. *British Journal of Psychiatry*, *197*, 96–105.

Waugh, C. E., & Fredrickson, B. L. (2006). Nice to know you: Positive emotions, self-other overlap, and complex understanding in the formation of a new relationship. *Journal of Positive Psychology*, *1*, 93–106.

Weaver, I. C., Cervoni, N., Champagne, F. A., D'Alessio, A. C., Sharma, S., Seckl, J. R., et al. (2004). Epigenetic programming by maternal behavior. *Nature Neuroscience*, *7*(8), 847–854.

Weaver, I. C., Champagne, F. A., Brown, S. E., Dymov, S., Sharma, S., Meaney, M. J., et al. (2005). Reversal of maternal programming of stress responses in adult offspring through methyl supplementation: Altering epigenetic marking later in life. *The Journal of Neuroscience*, *25*(47), 11045–11054.

Weaver, I. C., D'Alessio, A. C., Brown, S. E., Hellstrom, I. C., Dymov, S., Sharma, S., et al. (2007). The transcription factor nerve growth factor-inducible protein A mediates epigenetic programming: Altering epigenetic marks by immediate-early genes. *The Journal of Neuroscience*, *27*(7), 1756–1768.

Weber, M. (1947). *The theory of social and economic organization* (A. M. Henderson & Talcott Parsons, Trans.). London, UK: Hodge.

Weber, R., Tamborini, R., Lee, H. E., & Stipp, H. (2008). Soap opera exposure and enjoyment: A longitudinal test of disposition theory. *Media Psychology, 11,* 462–487.

Webster, C. M., & Doob, A. N. (2011). Searching for Sasquatch: Deterrence of crime though sentence severity. In J. Petersilia & K. Reitz (Eds.), *Oxford handbook of sentencing and corrections.* New York, NY: Oxford University Press.

Webster-Stratton, C., & Herman, K. C. (2008). The impact of parent behavior-management training on child depressive symptoms. *Journal of Counseling Psychology, 55*(4), 473.

Webster-Stratton, C., Reid, J., & Hammond, M. (2001a). Social skills and problem-solving training for children with early-onset conduct problems: Who benefits? *Journal of Child Psychology and Psychiatry, 42*(7), 943–952.

Webster-Stratton, C., Reid, M. J., & Hammond, M. (2001b). Preventing conduct problems, promoting social competence: A parent and teacher training partnership in head start. *Journal of Clinical Child Psychology, 30*(3), 283–302.

Weiner, B. (1985). An attributional theory of achievement motivation and emotion. *Psychological Review, 92,* 548–573.

Weiner, B. (1986). *An attributional theory of motivation and emotion.* New York, NY: Springer-Verlag.

Weiner, B., & Graham, S. (1989). Understanding the motivational role of affect: Lifespan research from an attributional perspective. *Cognition and Emotion, 3,* 401–419.

Weinstein, S. M., Mermelstein, R. J., Hankin, B. L., Hedeker, D., & Flay, B. R. (2007). Longitudinal patterns of daily affect and global mood during adolescence. *Journal of Research on Adolescence, 17*(3), 587–600.

Weisfeld, G. E. (1980). Social dominance and human motivation. In D. R. Omark, E. F. Strayer, & D. G. Freedman (Eds.), *Dominance relations: An ethological view of human conflict and social interaction* (pp. 273–286). New York, NY: Garland.

Weiss, S. J., Wilson, P., Hertenstein, M. J., & Campos, R. (2000). The tactile context of a mother's caregiving: Implications for attachment of low birth weight infants. *Infant Behavior and Development, 23,* 91–111.

Weissman, M. M., Bland, R., Canino, G. J., et al. (1996). Cross-national epidemiology of major depression and bipolar disorder. *Journal of the American Medical Association, 24,* 293–299.

Wellman, H. M., Cross, D., & Watson, J. (2001). Meta-analysis of theory of mind development: The truth about false belief. *Child Development, 72*(3), 655–684.

Wellman, H. M., Harris, P. L., Banerjee, M., & Sinclair, A. (1995). Early understanding of emotion: Evidence from natural language. *Cognition & Emotion, 9*(2–3), 117–149.

Wellman, H. M., & Woolley, J. D. (1990). From simple desires to ordinary beliefs: The early development of everyday psychology. *Cognition, 35*(3), 245–275.

Weltzin, T. E., Weisensel, N., Franczyk, D., Burnett, K., Klitz, C., & Bean, P. (2005). Eating disorders in men: Update. *Journal of Men's Health and Gender, 2*(2), 186–193.

Wentzel, K. R. (2009). Peers and academic functioning at school. In K. H. Rubin, W. M. Bukowski, & B. Laursen (Eds.), *Handbook of peer interactions, relationships, and groups* (pp. 531–547). New York, NY: Guilford.

Werner, E. E. (1989, April). Children of the Garden Island. *Scientific American, 260,* 106–111.

Westen, D., Novotny, C. M., & Thompson-Bremner, H. (2004). The empirical status of empirically supported therapies: Assumptions, findings, and reporting in controlled clinical trials. *Psychological Bulletin, 130,* 631–663.

Wilkinson, R. G., & Pickett, K. (2009). *The spirit level: Why more equal societies almost always do better.* London, UK: Allen Lane.

Whalen, P. J., Rauch, S. L., Etcoff, N. L., McInerney, S. C., Lee, M. B., & Jenike, M. A. (1998). Masked presentations of emotional facial expressions modulate amygdala activity without explicit knowledge. *Journal of Neuroscience, 18,* 411–418.

Wheatley, T., & Haidt, J. (2005). Hypnotic disgust makes moral judgments more severe. *Psychological Science, 16,* 780–785.

Whipple, N., Bernier, A., & Mageau, G. A. (2011). Broadening the study of infant security of attachment: Maternal autonomy-support in the context of infant exploration. *Social Development, 20*(1), 17–32.

Whitley, B. E. (1993). Reliability and aspects of the construct validity of Sternberg's Triangular Love Scale. *Journal of Social and Personal Relationships, 10,* 475–483.

Wicker, B., Keysers, C., Plailly, J., Royet, J.-P., Gallese, V., & Rizzolatti, G. (2003). Both of us disgusted in *my* insula: The common neural basis of seeing and feeling disgust. *Neuron, 40*, 655–664.

Widen, S. C., & Russell, J. A. (2003). A closer look at preschoolers' freely produced labels for facial expressions. *Developmental Psychology, 39*(1), 114–128.

Widen, S. C., & Russell, J. A. (2008). Children acquire emotion categories gradually. *Cognitive Development, 23*(2), 291–312.

Widen, S. C., & Russell, J. A. (2010). Differentiation in preschooler's categories of emotion. *Emotion, 10*(5), 651–661.

Wierzbicka, A. (1999). *Emotions across languages and cultures: Diversity and universals.* Cambridge, MA: Cambridge University Press.

Wilkinson, R., & Pickett, K. (2009). *The spirit level: Why more equal societies almost always do better.* London, UK: Allen Lane.

Williams, J.M.G., Watts, F. N., MacLeod, C., & Mathews, A. (1997). *Cognitive psychology and emotional disorders* (2nd ed.). Chichester, UK: Wiley.

Williams, J. R., Insel, T. R., Harbaugh, C. R., & Carter, C. S. (1994). Oxytocin administered centrally facilitates formation of a partner preference in female prairie voles (*Microtus ochrogaster*). *Journal of Neuroendocrinology, 6*, 247–250.

Williams, L. A., & DeSteno, D. (2009). Pride: Adaptive social emotion or seventh sin? *Psychological Science, 20*, 284–288.

Williams, L. M., Gatt, J. M., Schofield, P. R., Olivieri, G., Peduto, A., & Gordon, E. (2009). "Negativity bias" in risk for depression and anxiety: Brain-body fear circuitry correlates, 5-HTT-LPR and early life stress. *Neuroimage, 47*(3), 804–814.

Willis, F. N., & Briggs, L. F. (1992). Relationship and touch in public settings. *Journal of Nonverbal Behavior, 16*, 55–63.

Willis, F. N., & Hamm, H. K. (1980). The use of interpersonal touch in securing compliance. *Journal of Nonverbal Behavior, 5*, 49–55.

Wilson, A. C., & Cann, R. L. (1992, April). The recent African genesis of humans. *Scientific American, 266*, 68–73.

Wilson, M. I., & Daly, M. (1996). Male sexual proprietariness and violence against wives. *Current Directions in Psychological Science, 5*, 2–7.

Winkielman, P., Zajonc, R., & Schwartz, N. (1997). Subliminal affective priming resists attributional intervention. *Cognition and Emotion, 11*, 433–465.

Winnicott, D. W. (1958). *Through paediatrics to psychoanalysis.* London, UK: Tavistock.

Witherington, D. C., & Crichton, J. A. (2007). Frameworks for understanding emotions and their development: Functionalist and dynamic systems approaches. *Emotion, 7*(3), 628–637.

Witt, D. M., Carter, C., & Walton, D. (1990). Central and peripheral effects of oxytocin administration. *Physiology and Behavior, 37*, 63–69.

Witt, D. M., Winslow, J. T., & Insel, T. (1992). Enhanced social interaction in rats following chronic, centrally infused oxytocin. *Pharmacology, Biochemistry, and Behavior, 43*, 855–861.

Witvliet, C., Ludwig, T. E., & Vander Laan, K. L. (2001). Granting forgiveness or harboring grudges: Implications for emotion, physiology, and health. *Psychological Science, 12*, 117–123.

Wong, M., Diener, M. L., & Isabella, R. (2008). Parents' emotion-related beliefs and behaviors: Associations with children's perceptions of peer competence, child grade and sex. *Journal of Applied Developmental Psychology, 29*, 175–186.

Wood, J. V., Heimpel, S. A., & Michela, J. L. (2003). Savoring versus dampening: Self-esteem differences in regulating positive affect: Self-esteem differences in regulating positive affect. *Journal of Personality and Social Psychology, 85*(3), 566–580.

Woolf, V. (1965). *Jacob's room.* Harmondsworth: Penguin.

Wordsworth, W. (1802). Preface to *Lyrical Ballads* of 1802. In S. Gill (Ed.), *William Wordsworth.* Oxford, UK: Oxford University Press (1984).

World Health Organization (1983). *Depressive disorders in different cultures.* Geneva, Switzerland: World Health Organization.

World Health, Organization (2003). *International classification of diseases* (10th Rev. ed.), Clinical Modification (ICD-10-CM), pre-release draft. Geneva: World Health

Organization (available at www.cdc.gov/nchs/about/oth-eract/icd9/icd10cm.htm).

World Health Organization (2008). ICD-10: International statistical classification of diseases and related health problems (10th Rev. ed). New York, NY: Author.

World Health Organization Consortium (2004). Prevalence, severity, and unmet need for treatment of mental disorders in the World Health Organization World Mental Health Surveys. *Journal of the American Medical Association*, *291*, 2581–2590.

Worth, L. T., & Mackie, D. M. (1987). Cognitive mediation of positive affect in persuasion. *Social Cognition*, *5*, 76–94.

Worthington, E.L.J. (1998). Empirical research in forgiveness: Looking backward, looking forward. In J. E. L. Worthington (Ed.), *Dimensions of forgiveness* (pp. 321–339). Philadelphia, PA: Templeton Foundation Press.

Wright, M. R. (1981). *Empedocles, the extant fragments.* New Haven, CT: Yale University Press.

Wright, R. (1992). *Stolen continents: The "New World" through Indian eyes.* Toronto, Canada: Penguin.

Wright, R. (2004). *A short history of progress.* Toronto, Canada: Anansi.

Wright, T. (1604). *The passions of the minde in generall* (reprint edited by T. O. Sloan). Urbana: University of Illinois Press (1971).

Xue, Y., Leventhal, T., Brooks-Gunn, J., & Earls, F. J. (2005). Neighborhood residence and mental health problems of 5- to 11-year-olds. *Archives of Genetic Psychiatry*, *62*, 554–563.

Yagoubzadeh, Z., Jenkins, J. M., & Pepler, D. (2010) Transactional models in the relationship between child behavior and maternal negativity: A 6-year longitudinal study. *International Journal of Behavioral Development*, *34*, 218–228.

Yamagata, S., Takahashi, Y., Kijima, N., Maekawa, H., Ono, Y., & Ando, J. (2005). Genetic and environmental etiology of effortful control. *Twin Research and Human Genetics*, *8*(4), 300–306.

Yang, T. T., Simmons, A. N., Matthews, S. C., Tapert, S. F., Frank, G. K., Max, J. E., et al. (2010). Adolescents with major depression demonstrate increased amygdala activation. *Journal of the American Academy of Child & Adolescent Psychiatry*, *49*, 42–51.

Yang, Y., Raine, A., Narr, K. L., Colletti, P., & Toga, A. W. (2009). Localization of deformations within the amygdala

in individuals with psychopathy. *Archives of General Psychiatry*, *66*, 986–994.

Yates, F. A. (1964). *Giordano Bruno and the Hermetic tradition.* London, UK: Routledge & Kegan Paul.

Young-Browne, G., Rosenfeld, H. M., & Horowitz, F. D. (1977). Infant discrimination of facial expressions. *Child Development*, *48*(2), 555–562.

Youngblade, L. M., & Dunn, J. (1995). Individual differences in young children's pretend play with mother and sibling: Links to relationships and understanding of other people's feelings and beliefs. *Child Development*, *66*, 1472–1492.

Yuille, J. C., & Cutshall, J. L. (1986). A case study of eyewitness testimony to a crime. *Journal of Applied Psychology*, *71*, 291–301.

Yzerbyt, V. Y., Dumont, M., Wigboldus, D., & Gordijn, E. (2003). I feel for us: The impact of categorization and identification on emotions and action tendencies. *British Journal of Social Psychology*, *42*, 533–549.

Zadeh, Z. Y., Jenkins, J., & Pepler, D. (2010). A transactional analysis of maternal negativity and child externalizing behavior. *International Journal of Behavioral Development*, *34*(3), 218–228.

Zahn-Waxler, C., & Radke-Yarrow, M. (1990). The origins of empathic concern. *Motivation and Emotion*, *14*(2), 107–130.

Zahn-Waxler, C., Radke-Yarrow, M., Wagner, E., & Chapman, M. (1992). Development of concern for others. *Developmental Psychology*, *28*, 126–136.

Zajonc, R. B. (1980). Feeling and thinking: Preferences need no inferences. *American Psychologist*, *35*, 151–175.

Zaki, J., & Ochsner, K. N. (in press). The neuroscience of empathy: Progress, pitfalls and promise. *Nature Neuroscience*.

Zald, D. (2003). The human amygdala and the emotional evaluation of sensory stimuli. *Brain Research Reviews*, *41*, 88–123.

Zald, D. H., Lee, J. T., Fluegel, K. W., & Pardo, J. V. (1998). Aversive gustatory stimulation activates limbic circuits in humans. *Brain*, *121*, 1143–1154.

Zelazo, P. D., & Müller, U. (2002). The balance beam in the balance: Reflections on rules, relational complexity, and developmental processes. *Journal of Experimental Child Psychology*, *81*(4), 458–465.

Zhou, Q., Main, A., & Wang, Y. (in press). Temperament effortful control and anger/frustration to Chinese children's academic achievement and social adjustment: A longitudinal study. *Journal of Educational Psychology.*

Zhou, Q., Sandler, I. N., Millsap, R. E., Wolchik, S. A., & Dawson-McClure, S. R. (2008). Mother–child relationship quality and effective discipline as mediators of the six-year effects of the New Beginnings Program for children from divorced families. *Journal of Consulting and Clinical Psychology, 76,* 579–594.

Zhou, Q., Wang, Y., Deng, X, Eisenberg, N., Wolchik, S., & Tein, J-Y. (2008). Relations of parenting and temperament to Chinese children's experience of negative life events, coping efficacy, and externalizing problems. *Child Development, 79,* 493–513.

Zillman, D. (1978). Attribution and misattribution of excitatory reactions. In J. H. Harvey, W. J. Ickes, & R. F. Kidd (Eds.), *New directions in attribution research* (Vol. 2, pp. 335–368). Hillsdale, NJ: Erlbaum.

Zillman, D. (1988). Cognitive excitation interdependencies in aggressive behavior. *Aggressive Behavior, 14,* 51–64.

Zillmann, D. (1989). Effects of prolonged consumption of pornography. In D. Zillman & J. Bryand (Eds.), *Pornography: Research advances and early policy considerations.* Hillsdale, NJ: Erlbaum.

Zillmann, D. (2000). Humor and comedy. In D. Zillmann & P. Vorderer (Eds.), *Media entertainment: The psychology of its appeal* (pp. 37–57). Mahwah, NJ: Erlbaum.

Zillmann, D., & Vorderer, P. (Eds.). (2000). *Media entertainment: The psychology of its appeal.* Mahwah, NJ: Erlbaum.

Zimbardo, P. G. (2007). *The Lucifer effect: Understanding how good people turn evil.* New York, NY: Random House.

Zimet, G., Dalhem, W., Zimet, S., & Farley, G. (1988). The multidimensional scale of perceived social support. *Journal of Personality Assessment, 52* (1), 30–41.

Author Index

A

Abbott, R. A., 350
Abel, A., 221
Abela, J. R. Z., 297
Abelson, R., 75
Abramson, L. Y., 297
Abu-Lughod, L., 61, 71, 73, 172
Acevedo, B. P., 216
Achenbach, T. M., 294, 295
Adam, E. K., 268
Adamec, R., 148
Adams, D., 308
Adler, N. E., 226
Agmo, A., 147
Aharon, I., 147
Aikins, J. W., 302
Ainsworth, M., 39, 266, 267, 273
Aksan, N., 193, 273, 274, 278
Alexander, R., 33
Algoe, S. B., 221
Ali, A., 341
Allen, J., 39, 75, 216
Alloy, L. B., 297
Almeida, D. M., 285
Altemus, M., 157, 158
Althoff, R. R., 294
Amaral, D. G., 144
Ambady, N., 91, 106
American Psychiatric Association, 9, 29, 294, 327, 331, 333
Ames, D., 61, 66
Anda, R. F., 309
Andersen, S. M., 370
Anderson, C., 222, 225, 226, 254
Anderson, E., 174
Andreasen, N., 327
Andrew, R. J., 34
Andrews, B., 342
Aneshensel, C. S., 315
Angell, M., 337
Angold, A., 295
Angus, L., 375, 376
Anisfeld, E., 102

App, B., 103
Applegate, B., 296
Aquan-Assee, J., 283
Arandjelovic, M., 48
Arbisi, P., 289
Arcuri, L., 355
Ariely, D., 215
Aristotle, 11
Armario, A., 283
Armstrong, K., 219
Arnold, M. B., 21, 26, 120, 163
Aron, A., 75, 147, 216, 219
Aron, A. P., 242
Aron, E. N., 75, 216, 219
Arterberry, M. E., 197
Asendorpf, J. B., 207, 286
Asher, E. R., 218
Asher, S. R., 284
Astington, J. W., 194, 283
Atkinson, L., 273
Aubé, M., 5, 214
Audrain, P. C., 243
Auerbach, S., 277
Augustine, 83
Aureli, F., 102
Austen, J., 216
Avenevoli, S., 315
Averill, J. R., 60, 73, 74, 76, 77, 108, 224
Avero, P., 247
Aviezer, H., 198
Azmitia, M., 283

B

Baars, B. J., 297
Bachorowski, J.-A., 87, 97, 105, 196, 221, 222
Backs-Dermott, B. J., 342–343
Badanes, L. S., 303
Bagby, R. M., 174
Bagot, R. C., 307, 315
Bahrick, L. E., 197, 200
Baird, B. M., 287

Bakemand, R., 195
Baker, B. L., 298
Baker, J. H., 281, 282
Bakermans-Kranenburg, M. J., 265, 267, 272, 274, 298, 304, 306, 313
Ball, S., 265
Banerjee, M., 192
Banerjee, R., 285
Banks, C., 363
Banse, R., 99
Bar-Haim, Y., 265
Bard, P., 140
Barden, J., 251
Barlow, D. H., 331
Barnett, D., 310
Baron-Cohen, S., 345, 365
Barratt, M. S., 191
Barrera, M. E., 197
Barrett, D. H., 332
Barrett, D. J., 181
Barrett, L. F., 91, 177, 181, 182
Barrett, P. H., 5, 8
Barry, R. A., 210, 273, 277
Bartlett, F. C., 247, 249, 250
Bartlett, M. Y., 220
Bartz, J. A., 159
Bates, J. E., 296, 297, 303, 309
Batson, C. D., 252
Battaglia, M., 197
Bauer, D. H., 195
Baumann, J., 246
Baumeister, R. F., 166, 254, 355, 360, 365
Baumwell, L., 274
Baxter, M. G., 144
Bayliss, L. L., 151
Bazhenova, O. V., 205
Bean, P., 296
Bearsdall, L., 280
Beauregard, M., 144, 148
Bechara, A., 133, 186
Beck, A. T., 344, 371, 372, 375
Becker, B. J., 275

Subject Index

A

Aborigines, Australian, 175
ACEs (Adverse Childhood Experiences), 312–313
Acetylcholine, 155
Achievement, failure in, 334
Acquired sociopathy, 133, 148
ACTH (adreno-corticotropic hormone), 124
Activity, 352–353
Actors, 104–105
Actor effect, 265–266
Adaptation, 33–35
Adaptations to negative environments, 298
Adjective checklists, 179–180
Adolescent limited children, 318
Adrenal glands, 124, 125, 156
Adrenaline, 118, 120, 155
Adreno-corticotropic hormone (ACTH), 124
Adult Attachment Interview, 270–272
Adverse Childhood Experiences (ACEs), 312–313
Adversities, 303
Affect-as-information perspective, 241
Affect Infusion Model, 241
Affection, 41–42. *See also* Affiliation
Affectional bonds, 39–40
Affective biases, 318
Affective bonding, 147
Affective-cognitive structures, 264
Affective forecasting, 356
Affective styles, 154
Affiliation, 41–42
  and cooperation, 47
  and friendships, 220
  and groups, 227
Agency, 170
Aggression (aggressive behavior):
  in children, 267
  in chimpanzees, 47
  in emotion-based disorders, 298, 306

between groups, 230
and limbic system, 141
psychopathy and, 345
and reaction to facial expressions, 288
and serotonin, 157
Agoraphobia, 331
Agreeableness, 157, 287–289, 340
Ainsworth, Mary, 269
Alcohol and alcohol abuse, 328
Alexithymia, 174
Alpha male, 46
Altruism, reciprocal, 252
Amae, 62, 172
Ambivalent attachment, 267
Amish, 351
Amygdala, 125, 139, 140, 143–146, 148, 150, 151, 156, 164, 200, 308, 336, 337
Anger:
  and appraisal, 171
  and bias, 265
  and core affect, 181
  and cortisol, 126
  cross-cultural comparisons of, 68
  development of, 191
  and embodiment, 132–133
  and emotional disorders, 339
  as emotion word, 174
  facial expression for, 89, 165
  in family environment, 277–278
  and frustration, 64, 65
  in infants, 188–190
  and intergroup conflict, 228–230
  and ischemic heart disease, 312
  and power, 224
  and social interaction, 104
  vocal expression for, 99
Animals, emotions as, 175
Anorexia, 347
Anterior cingulate, 139, 149, 152–153, 336–337
Anterior insula, 149
Antidepressant medications, 156, 369

Antisocial behavior, 48, 156
Antisocial motivation, 43–44
Antithesis, principle of, 87
Anxiety:
  and reaction to facial expressions, 288
  and social class, 226
  and voice, 97, 98
Anxiety disorders, 327
  cognitive biases in, 344–345
  onset of, 334–335
  prevalence of, 328–330
  types of, 331–332
Apes, human relatedness to, 49
Appraisal(s), 162–182
  automatic, 164–166
  cultural variation in, 171–172
  definition of, 162
  dimensional approaches to, 166, 169–170
  discrete approaches to, 166–168
  and emotional experience, 178–182
  and mood disorders, 334–335
  primary, 164–166, 238, 357
  secondary, 166, 170, 238–239, 357
  and two-factor theory, 120
  and verbal sharing, 172–178
Approach and withdrawal, 153–154
Aristotle, 11, 110, 163
Arnold, Magda, 21–22
Arousal response, 118, 120
Art, communication of emotions in, 107–111
Artistic approach, 15–17
Artistic expression, 107–108
Asian cultures, 61, 66–67, 70
Aspergers, 213
Assertion, 40, 46
Assessment, psychometric, 295
Attachment, 10, 38–40, 152, 266–273
  emotions and, 272–273
  failure of, 313
  genetic influences on, 269–270
  internal working models of, 270–272
  and mother-infant bond, 46